Hungary 1848: The Winter Campaign

Johann Nobili

Edited by Christopher Pringle

Helion & Company

Helion & Company Limited
Unit 8 Amherst Business Centre
Budbrooke Road
Warwick
CV34 5WE
England
Tel. 01926 499 619
Email: info@helion.co.uk
Website: www.helion.co.uk
Twitter: @helionbooks
Visit our blog at blog.helion.co.uk

Published by Helion & Company 2021
Designed and typeset by Mary Woolley (www.battlefield-design.co.uk)
Cover designed by Paul Hewitt, Battlefield Design (www.battlefield-design.co.uk)

ISBN 978-1-913118-78-5

British Library Cataloguing-in-Publication Data.
A catalogue record for this book is available from the British Library.

For details of other military history titles published by Helion & Company Limited contact the above address or visit our website: http://www.helion.co.uk.

We always welcome receiving book proposals from prospective authors.

Contents

List of Maps

Introduction

The Hungarian War of Independence was one of the largest European conflicts of the 19th century, lasting a year, encompassing a dozen major battles and many smaller actions and sieges, and seeing half a million men under arms by its end. Yet it remains strangely obscure and overlooked by the Anglophone world, perhaps because of the relative inaccessibility of Hungarian-language sources for most English readers combined with the limited number of German-language sources due to Austria's embarrassment about the whole episode.

The present work is one step towards remedying this neglect. It is a translation of *Der Winterfeldzug 1848–1849 in Ungarn unter dem Oberkommando des Feldmarschalls Alfred Fürsten zu Windisch-Grätz*. This is the closest there is to an official Austrian history of the first half of the war.

The original begins at the point where Windisch-Grätz is charged with forming an army to reimpose the Austrian *Kaiser*'s authority on Hungary and ends when he is removed from command after the failure of his campaign.[1] It was compiled by then *Generalmajor* Friedrich Jakob Heller von Hellwald from the original Austrian reports and despatches, and from captured Hungarian documents which Hungarian officers held prisoner in the fortress of Arad were made to translate. Heller had served under Windisch-Grätz in suppressing the revolt of Vienna and then as a liaison officer with the Russians. He was also editor of the Austrian army's professional journal, the *Österreichische militärische Zeitung*. After the war he commanded

1 Alfred Candid Ferdinand *Reichsfürst* Windisch-Grätz (1787-1862) is the main protagonist of the present work. He served as a cavalry officer in the Napoleonic Wars, being captured at Ulm in 1805 and chancing to meet Napoleon himself while a prisoner of the French. He subsequently fought and was wounded at Aspern in 1809. At Leipzig he led the O'Reilly Chevauxlegers in several glorious charges, earning the regiment the right to fly its colours again, which it had briefly lost to the Russians in 1812 and which the *Kaiser* had refused to return until the regiment proved it deserved them. In the next 30 years he had the usual slow peacetime succession of postings and promotions. By June 1848 he was a *Feldmarschall Lieutenant*, commandant of Prague, when an uprising broke out there. He suppressed it, but during the fighting his wife was killed by a stray bullet and his son wounded. In October 1848, when Vienna revolted again as well, Windisch-Grätz was promoted to *Feldmarschall* and put in charge of all the Austrian troops north of the Isonzo that were not already with Radetzky's army in Italy. He laid siege to the revolutionary city. In the battle of Schwechat on 30 October he fended off and defeated an invading Hungarian army that was trying to relieve the siege and link up with the insurgents. Then on 31 October he stormed the city and suppressed the revolt. Next he was charged with commanding what became the Winter Campaign, the subject of the present work. After being relieved of command in April 1849 he retired from public life. Constant von Wurzbach, *Biographisches Lexikon des Kaisertüms Österreich* (henceforth *BLKÖ*) (Vienna: K.K. Hof & Staatsdrückerei, 1856-1891), Vol.57, pp.1-39.

a brigade in Prague and was then military commandant in Klagenfurt, the duties of which presumably allowed him sufficient leisure time to write this semi-official history.[2]

Heller's first draft was deemed too critical of the Austrian army. *Generalmajor* Johann Nobili was therefore brought in to sanitize it.[3] Nobili likewise served under Windisch-Grätz as chief of his general staff and then commanded 8. Armeekorps from 1850 to 1853.[4] The result of Nobili's efforts is apparent: the work is consistently laudatory of the Austrian army's troops and commanders, with even the most egregious errors being treated with the gentlest reproach. While I have endeavoured to introduce some balance by means of annotations where appropriate, the reader should bear this bias in mind throughout.

Notwithstanding the limitations of the work's critical analysis, it excels as a detailed narrative. Being derived directly from the primary documents means it is full of fascinating episodes and invaluable factual data that have never before been available in English. These include extensive information about orders of battle, rare nuggets about uniforms, weapons and tactics, actual despatches and orders reproduced verbatim, detailed accounts of many actions from tiny skirmishes up to the major battles of Kápolna and Isaszeg, etc. It therefore provides an authoritative account in unparalleled detail.

By reproducing correspondence among the generals on both sides, it also provides fascinating insights into their personalities and how the dynamics between them influenced operations. The Austrian army is the instrument of a monarchical regime and is pervaded by the structure of its nobility, as is evident in every single report or order in which phrases such as 'His Highness desires that Your Honour should assist His Excellency …' proliferate, and every other officer seems to be *Oberst Graf* this or *Major Baron* that. Having recently also translated Clausewitz's history of the 1799 campaign in which Austria fought France in Switzerland, I found the character of the Austrian army of 1848 very reminiscent of its predecessor of 50 years before.[5] As the Austrian Archduke Charles himself said of his army in that campaign:

> [I]n the recent wars incompetent leadership generated quite opposite effects among [the Austrians] and the French; in the former it produced vacillation, in the latter, rashness. The French, inclined by the spirit of the Revolution to breach all boundaries and expecting every gamble to produce results, followed this impulse whenever they saw no other way out. [The Austrians], trained to subordinate their will, accustomed to rules and bound by responsibility, were paralysed by indecision. Hence the French superiority whenever it concerned the simultaneous action of several men left to their own devices.

2 *Österreichisches Biographisches Lexikon 1815-1950* (henceforth *ÖBL)*, Vol.2, p.262

3 According to Professor Róbert Hermann, initially Heller was commissioned to write the history of the Winter Campaign, but he was too critical of the Austrian army and pointed out Austrian mistakes. The Austrian authorities did not like this, so they 'sank' Heller's manuscript, and today it is not to be found. The work as edited by Nobili can be considered 'semi-official', as it is based on materials from the *Kriegsarchiv* and on captured Hungarian documents. (Hermann, Róbert. Personal communication, via Dr Szilárd Szilágyi, 6 March 2019.)

4 *ÖBL.*

5 Nicholas Murray and Christopher Pringle (ed. and transl.), *Carl von Clausewitz, Napoleon Absent, Coalition Ascendant: The 1799 Campaign in Switzerland, Vol.1* (Lawrence, KS: University Press of Kansas, forthcoming 2020).

Certainly, there were times when the Austrian army of 1848-1849 was as ponderous and hesitant by comparison with its agile and aggressive opponent as was its predecessor half a century earlier.

Yet, there must also have been many occasions when Windisch-Grätz found himself wishing Archduke Charles's description applied to his army more accurately and that his generals would actually do what they were told. The actions (or inactions) of his most important subordinates, Jellacic and Schlick, were frequently at odds with his orders, though in quite different ways from each other: Jellacic comes across as overly cautious, verging on panicky, and unable to see his local problems in the perspective of the bigger picture, hence at times responding slowly, partially or not at all; while Schlick breaks the stereotypical Austrian mould in not only being capable of independent action but seeming to relish and prefer it, opting to strike out in a divergent direction when Windisch-Grätz is trying to concentrate his forces. Once the army is concentrated, Jellacic and Schlick 'conspire' more than once to frustrate Windisch-Grätz's plans.

I therefore found myself coming out at the end of this book with rather more sympathy for Windisch-Grätz than I had at the beginning. The restrained diplomatic tone of his messages to his wayward subordinates displays impressive self-control, and Nobili's history is similarly kind to them. Bear in mind that Jellacic was the *Banus* of Croatia – its governor or viceroy, a vassal of the *Kaiser* and the next rank down from king – so cannot have been easy for Windisch-Grätz to order around. Apart from the personality issues, and acknowledging the original history's exculpatory slant, its presentation of the tactical and other factors affecting and justifying each of Windisch-Grätz's decisions is also helpful and by no means entirely unfair.

There is less from the 'other side of the hill', but some of the Hungarian correspondence that is included is astonishing. The disastrous Dembinski explaining how important it is that he should not let his own subordinates know what he is trying to do; Görgei's recriminations against all and sundry; Kossuth's attempts to mollify him; all of these are revealing of a fractious revolutionary regime trying to confront a monarchical monolith.

So much for the content of the original text. I have taken a number of measures to make it more accessible and useful, and added some chapters of my own for completeness. The original was organised simply as three very large chapters, essentially a stream-of-despatches compilation with minimal signposting. To help to orient the reader, I have introduced section headings which are listed in the table of contents. I have used the original German unit titles and ranks throughout, and therefore provided a brief introduction to the Austrian and Hungarian armies to help the reader to understand these and the orders of battle. (If this occasionally reads awkwardly, I hope the reader will forgive me, as it is Helion house style.)

What was then the Kingdom of Hungary now straddles Croatia, Serbia, Rumania, Ukraine, Poland, Slovakia, and the Czech Republic. Many place names that were given in German in the original text are obsolete, and even those given in Hungarian or other local languages are often misspelled or have changed. Per Helion house style, the names used by Nobili have been retained here to keep as close as possible to the original and avoid introduction of errors. However, to make it possible for the reader to follow the course of operations on a modern map, the index of place names cross-references the text version with the modern name and country, and also with the name in a third language where appropriate. In carrying out this detective work, I relied heavily on a resource which I also recommend readers use in conjunction with the text – namely the maps created for Austria's Second Military Survey (1806-69).[6]

I have also created my own set of maps, included in this volume, to help the reader to understand the operations described in the text in their full *Zusammenhang* – their context and connection. These are not based only on Nobili's text, or even mainly upon it. Instead I have drawn heavily on both text and maps by Bánlaky, Bona and Hermann (see the Bibliography for further details). Their maps are more detailed in some respects, e.g., mine are indicative of direction of operations whereas theirs give more precise routes for forces. While I have given force strengths on the maps, again these should be regarded as indicative rather than precise, partly because they fluctuate considerably during the course of operations, and partly because sources vary considerably in their estimates. On the other hand, my maps give more detail of the terrain that influenced operations. Also, as mine tend to cover shorter time periods, the resulting snapshots are clearer and, I trust, more helpful in showing how operations developed over time. This is also the case with my tactical maps for the two major battles of Kápolna and Isaszeg, for which I have provided two maps each, showing the distinct phases of the battles more comprehensibly than a single map can. Annotations on the maps talk the reader through the action so that the full set literally tells the story of the whole campaign.

House style is normally to retain the measures of distance used in the original. In this case, though, since an old Austrian mile is nearly five modern US miles (or 7.6 km), I have converted to kilometres throughout to avoid confusion.

My editorial annotations fall into several categories. I have provided brief biographical notes on the major personalities. Military matters such as weapons, tactics, conscription systems, etc., get some attention. I have put most of my effort into commenting on the battles and operations, partly to correct the bias mentioned above, partly just to offer more analysis than the narrative-focused original. My model for this has been Clausewitz's commentary on the actions of Napoleon and his adversaries, in his history of the 1796 campaign;[7] and also Captain J. Colin, the French translator of that history, who commented in turn on Clausewitz's remarks. Where I suggest alternative plans or actions, I do not claim that these are necessarily the best ones, and I certainly do not claim that I would have done a better job than the men on the spot. My aim is merely to provoke critical reflection on the part of the reader, and thereby deeper understanding of the events and course of the war.

Finally, I have filled in some major gaps in Nobili's narrative. As this begins partway through the conflict, I have provided a brief Prologue describing events leading up to the Winter Campaign. Similarly, I have added an Epilogue covering events after Windisch-Grätz's departure but that are really the culmination of his operations. Finally, since Nobili's focus on Windisch-Grätz's main army means that he touches only tangentially and very occasionally on events on the secondary fronts, I have added two Appendices summarising the concurrent operations in Transylvania and in the Bácska and the Banat. These too are accompanied by suitable maps.

6 See Europe in the XIX. Century <https://mapire.eu/en/map/europe-19century-secondsurvey/?bbox=-1106808.8710559138%2C3957699.575560347%2C5154912.486065725%2C7988682.699207402>

7 Nicholas Murray and Christopher Pringle (ed. and transl.), *Carl von Clausewitz, Napoleon's 1796 Italian Campaign* (Lawrence, KS: University Press of Kansas, 2018).

Whilst I have done my best to provide a translation that is both accurate and readable, it will almost inevitably contain some errors. If so, these are my own; I trust that they are minor, and in any case I welcome correction. Any such imperfections notwithstanding, I hope readers will enjoy learning about this fascinating conflict, its many notable events and its remarkable characters.[8]

8 Those who do may be glad to know that it is my intention in due course to complement the present work with a translation of its natural companion, *Der Feldzug in Ungarn und Siebenbürgen im Sommer des Jahres 1849* [The Campaign in Hungary and Transylvania in Summer 1849] by Wilhelm Freiherr Ramming von Riedkirchen, which chronicles the rest of the war.

Acknowledgements

I must thank a number of people who have contributed considerably, and in some cases essentially, to the creation of this work. Dr Szilárd Szilágyi provided many valuable comments and corrected some significant errors, as well as passing on some precious information from Professor Róbert Hermann. Dr Csaba Stenge enlightened me on particular historical episodes. Professor Nicholas Murray and Dr Mark Smith gave advice that helped me to improve the maps. Eszter Ballay generously chauffeured me around Hungarian battlefields and to places her car was not designed for. Once again I must express my appreciation to Hartmut 'Hardy' Steffin, who brought his native German and his linguistic talents to bear on tracking down obscure vocabulary or phrases and resolving occasional particularly challenging sections of the translation. I thank Dr Christopher Brice for his professional advice and encouragement, and all at the excellent publishing house of Helion for making this publication possible. Of course, I am hugely indebted to Glenda Pringle: despite having her patience tested to the point of exasperation at times, she has loyally supported me not only morally but also practically, with her expert copyeditor's eye and her work in creating the index. Above all, I am especially grateful to my great friend Dave Whaley, whose interest in this conflict first inspired me to study it seriously, and whose unfailing good cheer and enthusiasm sustained this project throughout.

A Note on Wargaming Hungary, 1848-49

Beyond reading the history, another route to understanding the military dimensions of a conflict is through wargaming: 'learning by doing'. At the grand tactical level, I and my comrades at Oxford Wargames Society have recreated all the major actions of the Hungarian Revolution and War of Independence. Our favoured ruleset for this is my own *Bloody Big Battles!* (BBB), published by Skirmish Campaigns at <https://skirmishcampaigns.com>. A BBB online forum currently exists on groups.io at <https://groups.io/g/bloodybigbattles>; scenarios for the Hungary 1848-49 battles are currently freely available from the group files; and a BBB campaign book geared toward wargamers is in preparation. At the operational level, this is a war that is full of wargaming potential because of its asymmetric nature, its frequent changes of fortune and the complexity of the operations. I am in discussion with Professor Nicholas Murray of the US Naval War College about creating a serious professional wargame to explore it.

Table of Place Names

Nobili refers to many places by German or Hungarian names which are now obsolete, as the places in question are now in Slovakia, Poland, Ukraine, Romania, Serbia or Croatia. This table lists all places mentioned in the text whose modern current name differs from that used by Nobili (unless the difference is a minor use of a diacritic), or whose location needs explanation to assist the reader to find it either on a modern map or on the contemporary maps cited. In cases such as 'Sz. Miklós', where the same name applies to more than one place, context should resolve any confusion. Please note that inconsistencies in the use of diacritics are a feature of the original work.

Name in text	**Modern name or location**
Abany	Abony, Hungary
Aba-Ujvárer Komitat	Abaúj-Torna County, now mostly in Slovakia
Abda	Abda, Hungary; German name Brückel
Abrány	Bükkábrány
Adlerberg	Sashegy – 'Eagle Hill', Buda, Hungary
Agram	Zagreb, Croatia
Agtelek	Aggtelek, Hungary
Agtelek-Berg	Aggtelek Mountains, Hungary
Akol-Kert	*Unknown location*
Alberti	Albertirsa, Hungary
Almás	Jabloňovce, Slovakia
Alpár	Tiszaalpár, Hungary
Alsócéce	Now a southern offshoot of Hernádcéce, Hungary
Alt-Kanisa	Magyar Kanizsa, now Kanjiža, Serbia
Alt-Ofen	Old Buda, Budapest, Hungary
Alt-Szöny	Ó-Szőny, now an eastern suburb of Komárom, Hungary
Altenburg	Bad Deutsch-Altenburg, Austria
Altsohl	Zvolen, Slovakia

Am-Berg	Berg, Austria
Apátfalva	Opatová pri Lučenci, Slovakia
Apati-Insel	A large island in the Waag just north of Komorn, now the Apálsky ostrov nature reserve, Slovakia.
Arak	Arak, Hungary (4 km southeast of Halászi, Hungary)
Arok-Szállás/Árok-Szállás	Jászárokszállás, Hungary
Assod	Aszód, Hungary
Babocza	Babócsa, Hungary
Bács	Bač, Serbia
Bácsa	Bácsa-Győr, Hungary
Bácska Komitat	Bács-Bodrog County, a former county of the Kingdom of Hungary, now mostly in Serbia
Bad Deutsch-Altenburg	Bad Deutsch-Altenburg, Austria
Bágh	Bag, Hungary
Bagyán	Bad'an, Slovakia
Bajcs	Bajč, Slovakia
Baka-Bánya	Pukanec, Slovakia
Bakonyer-Wald	Bakony Forest, Hungary
Ballassa-Gyarmath/Balassa-Gyarmath	Balassagyarmat, Hungary
Bál-Püspöky	Balpüspöki puszta, a farm north of Detk on the road from Kápolna to Markaz, Hungary
Banat	Region now straddling southern Hungary, western Romania and northern Serbia
Bánhida	Tatabánya, Hungary
Baranyer Komitat	Baranya County, Hungary
Baráthráza	Near Etyek, Hungary; unclear exactly where
Barcza	Barca, now a suburb of Košice, Slovakia
Bárok	Óbarok, Hungary
Baromház	A hamlet NW of Lébény, Hungary
Bartfeld	Bardejov, Slovakia
Báth	Bátovce, Slovakia
Bátor-Keszi/Bator-Keszi	Bátorove Kosihy, Slovakia
Batta	Százhalombatta-Óváros, Hungary
Baumern	Pama, Austria

Beje	Behynce, Slovakia
Béla-Bánya	Banská Belá, Slovakia
Benedek	Hronský Beňadik, Slovakia
Berczel	Ceglédbercel, Hungary
Beregh Komitat	Bereg County, a former county of the Kingdom of Hungary, now mostly in Ukraine
Berénke	Borsosberény, Hungary
Berthotfalva	Bertotovce, Slovakia
Besényö/Beszenyő	Besenyőtelek, Hungary
Bia	Biatorbágy, Hungary
Bethlen	Beclean, Romania
Bielitz	Bielsko-Biała, Poland
Binyocz	Bíňovce, Slovakia
Bistritz	Beszterce in Hungarian; now Bistriţa, Romania
Bixard	Buková, Slovakia
Blocksberg	Gellért Hill, Budapest, Hungary
Boczonád	Boconád, Hungary
Bod	Tarnabod, Hungary
Bohemia	Now the western half of the Czech Republic
Borgo	Prundu Bargaului, Romania
Borosjenő	Ineu, Romania
Braniszko Pass	Branyiszkó, now Pod Braniskom, Slovakia
Breznó-Bánya	Brezno, Slovakia
Briesen/Brisen	Brezno, Slovakia
Brückel	Abda, Hungary
Bucsa	Budča, Slovakia
Bucsan	Bučany, Slovakia
Buda-Keszy	Budakeszi, Hungary
Budamér	Budimír, Slovakia
Buda-Örs	Budaörs, Hungary
Budetin	Budatín, Slovakia
Bukowina	An administrative district within the Austrian Empire, now roughly covered by the Chernivtsi Oblast, Ukraine, and Suceava County, Romania
Bunia	Rumince, Slovakia

Christinen-Vorstadt	Krisztinaváros, along the southwestern side of Buda Castle
Csacza	Čadca, Slovakia
Csák-Berény	Csákberény, Hungary
Csantavér	Čantavir, Serbia
Csáth	Mezőcsát, Hungary
Csécse	Csécse, Hungary
Csécsény	Rábacsécsény, Hungary
Csege	Tiszacsege, Hungary
Csepel Island	Large island in the Danube south of Budapest
Cservenka	Crvenka, Serbia
Csocz Manor	Unknown location. Perhaps Csárda Major, now in Nagyút, Hungary.
Csucsa Pass	Ciucea, Romania
Czegléd	Cegléd, Hungary
Czibákháza	Cibakháza, Hungary
Cziffer	Cífer, Slovakia
Czinkota	Cinkota, Hungary
Czömör	Csömör, Hungary
Dalya/Dállya	Dalj, Croatia
Dargo	Dargov, Slovakia
Debreczin	Debrecen, Hungary
Deesch	Dej, Romania
Demethe	Demjata, Slovakia
Derecske	Mátraderecske, Hungary
Deth	Detk, Hungary
Deutsch-Bogya	Bodza, Slovakia
Dilin	Banská Belá, Slovakia
Döbrö	Aldebrő, Hungary
Donau	River Danube
Dotis	Tata, Hungary
Drahovcze	Drahovce, Slovakia
Drau River	Drava River
Eger-Farmos	Egerfarmos, Hungary

Eipel River	Ipoly River
Eisenburg	Vas County, Hungary
Ekecs	Okoč, Slovakia
Enyiczke	Haniska, Slovakia
Eörs	Tarnaörs, Hungary
Eperies	Eperjes, Hungary, now Prešov, Slovakia
Eperies	Jahodná, Slovakia – as distinct from the other Eperies, Prešov. They are two different places.
Erdö-Kövesd	Erdőkövesd, Hungary
Erlau	Eger, Hungary
Essegg/Eszék	Osijek, Croatia
Facset	Faget, Romania
Farmas	Farmos, Hungary
Fehértemplom	Weisskirchen in German; now Bela Crkva, Romania
Felegyháza	Kiskunfélegyháza, Hungary
Felvidék	Upper Hungary, north of the Danube and Theiss rivers, nowadays mostly in Slovakia
Fenszaru	Jászfényszaru, Hungary
Fischament	Fischamend, Austria
Földvar/Földvár	Dunaföldvár, Hungary
Franzenskanal	Great Bačka Canal, Serbia
Freistadl/Freistadel	Hlohovec, Slovakia
Freydorf	Freidorf suburb of Timisoara, Romania
Frics	Fričovce, Slovakia
Füge	Figa, Slovakia
Fülek	Fil'akovo, Slovakia
Fünfkirchen	Pécs, Hungary
Füzes-Abány	Füzesabony, Hungary
Galicia	Austrian crown land, nowadays southern Poland and western Ukraine
Gallendorf	Ganeşti, Romania
Gál-Szécs/ Gál-Szécz	Sečovce, Slovakia
Ganod	Farm north of Ipolytölgyes shown on the 2nd Military Survey map as Puszta Ganád

Generalswiese	Area abutting the NW wall of Buda Castle; now known as the Vérmező or 'Bloodfield'
Göding	Hodonín, Czech Republic
Golss	Gols, Austria
Gömörer Komitat	Gömör County, former county of the Kingdom of Hungary, now split between northern Hungary and southern Slovakia
Göncz	Gönc, Hungary
Gönyö	Gönyű, Hungary
Grabdie (Gráb)	Grab, Poland
Gran	Esztergom, Hungary
Gran (Parkány)	Štúrovo, Slovakia
Gran River	Garam River
Grasalkovich Palace/ Grassalkovich-Károlyi Kastély	Gödöllői Királyi Kastély, now the Royal Palace of Gödöllő
Gratz	Graz, Austria
Grenicz	Hranovnica, Slovakia
Grosse Schütt	Great Rye Island, a river island in Slovakia formed by the Danube, the Little Danube and the Waag. In Slovakian: Vel'ky Žitný ostrov; in German: Grosse Schütt-Insel; in Hungarian: Csallóköz.
Gross-Oroszi	Nagyoroszi, Hungary
Grosswardein	Oradea, Romania
Güns	Kőszeg, Hungary
Gutta	Kolárovo, Slovakia
Gyekes	Dekýš, Slovakia
Hadritsch	Hodruša-Hámre, Slovakia
Haimburg	Hainburg an der Donau, Austria
Halas	Kiskunhalas, Hungary
Halbthurn	Halbturn, Austria
Hámor	Dolné Hámre, Slovakia
Hámor	Košické Hámré, Slovakia
Hanselbeck	Érd, Hungary
Hanzsabék	Hansabek, roughly between Érd-Ófalu and Érd cemetery now
Harmas-Körös	River Körös

Hátszeg	Haţeg, Romania
Hatzfeld	Jimbolia, Romania
Hegyes	Mali Idoš, Serbia
Heiligenkreuz	Žiar nad Hronom, Slovakia
Hermannstadt	Sibiu, Romania; Nagyszeben in Hungarian
Hernad River	Hornád River
Hidás-Némethi/Hidas-Némethy	Hidasnémeti, Hungary
Hochstrass	Öttevény, Hungary
Horvathi	Chorvatice, Slovakia
Hrilecz	Hnilec, Slovakia
Hundsheimer Berg	Hill north of Hundsheim, Austria
Hunkovécz	Hunkovce, Slovakia
Ida	Vel'ká Ida, Slovakia
Igló	Spišská Nová Ves, Slovakia
Igmánd	Nagyigmánd, Hungary
Ipoly-Ságh	Šahy, Slovakia
Ivánka	Borsodivánka, Hungary
Jablonicz	Jablonica, Slovakia
Jablunka	Jablunkov, Czech Republic
Jákóhalma	Jászjákóhalma, Hungary
Jarendorf	Deutsch Jarndorf, Austria
Jász-Apáthi	Jászapáti, Hungary
Jász-Berény	Jászberény, Hungary
Jászkunság	Area also known as the Kunság, Hungary.
Jekelfalva	Jaklovce, Slovakia
Jökö	Dobrá Voda, Slovakia
Josafö	Jósvafő, Hungary
Kálna	Kalná nad Hronom, Slovakia
Kanyi-Folgás stream	Kánya stream
Kanisa/Kanizsa	Nagykanizsa, Hungary
Kapi	Kapušany, Slovakia
Karansebes	Caransebeş, Romania

Kardszag/Kárdszag	Karcag, Hungary
Karlburg	Rusovce, Slovakia
Karlsburg	Alba Iulia, Romania
Karva	Kravany nad Dunajom, Slovakia
Kaschau	Košice, Slovakia
Kaschauer Berg	The north-south ridge northeast of Kaschau, east of the Hornad
Käsmark	Kežmarok, Slovakia
Katalin	Katalinpuszta, Hungary
Kemend/Keménd/Kéménd	Kamenín, Slovakia
Kér	Abaújkér, Hungary
Kerecsend/Kereszend	Kerecsend, Hungary
Keresztur	Bodrogkeresztur, Hungary
Keresztur	Rákoskeresztur, now in District XVII, Budapest, Hungary
Kirchdorf (Szepes-Baralya)	Spišské Podhradie, Slovakia
Kis-Bér	Kisbér, Hungary
Kisfalu	Malá Vieska, now absorbed into Družstevná pri Hornáde, Slovakia
Kisfalud	Bodrogkisfalud
Kis-Kér	Bačko Dobro Polje, Serbia
Kis-Szeben	Sabinov, Slovakia
Kis-Tétény	Ofentétény, Hungary
Kis-Torbágy	Now merged into the eastern end of Torbágy, Hungary
Kis-Uj-Szallása	Kisújszállás, Hungary
Kis-Zombor	Kiszombor, Hungary
Klausenburg	Cluj, Romania
Klein-Kanischa	Törok-Kanisa, now Novi Kneževac, Serbia
Klein-Zell	Celldömölk, Hungary
Kluknó	Kluknava, Slovakia
Köbelkut/Köbölkút	Gbelce, Slovakia
Komját/Komjáthi	Komjatice, Slovakia
Kömlő	Perhaps the farm marked on the 2nd Military Survey map as 'Kunjhó', 5 km east of Tiszatarján
Komorn	Now Komárno, Slovakia; Hungarian name Komárom
Königgrätz	Hradec Králové, Czech Republic
Königsberg	Nová Baňa, Slovakia

Körmönd	Körmend, Hungary
Kospollag	Kóspallag, Hungary
Kovácsi	Nagykovácsi, Hungary
Krakau	Kraków, Poland
Kraszno	Krásno nad Kysucou, Slovakia
Kremnitz	Kremnica, Slovakia
Krompach	Krompachy, Slovakia
Kronstadt	Braşov, Romania
Kubin	Dolný Kubín, Slovakia
K. Ujfalu	Váckisújfalu, Hungary
K. Uj-Szallása	Kisújszállás, Hungary
Kun-Hegyes	Kunhegyes, Hungary
Kunság	Area also known as the Jászkunság, Hungary.
Kun Sz. Miklos	Kunszentmiklós, Hungary
Kurtakeszi	Krátke Kesy, Slovakia
Kurudere	Near Gyumri, Armenia
Lac	Lakszakallás, now Sokolce, Slovakia
Lemberg	Lviv, Ukraine
Lemes	Lemešany, Slovakia
Leopoldstadt	Leopoldov, Slovakia
Leutschau	Levoča, Slovakia
Léva	Levice, Slovakia
Leyden	Lébény, Hungary
Liesko	Lesko, Poland
Lipcse	Slovenská L'upča, Slovakia
Liptau Komitat	Liptó County, now around Liptov, Slovakia
Lök	Tiszalök, Hungary
Losoncz	Lučenec, Slovakia
Lovas-Berény	Lovasberény, Hungary
Lucsivna	Lučivná, Slovakia
Ludány	Ludányhalászi, Hungary
Lugos	Lugoj, Romania
Luipersdorf	Csütörtök, now Štvrtok na Ostrove, Slovakia

Máad	Mád, Hungary
Mácsa	Galgamácsa, Hungary
Madaras	Kunmadaras, Hungary
Magyaród	Mogyoród, Hungary
Malaczka	Malacky, Slovakia
March River	Morava River
Marcheck	Marchegg, Austria
Marczaltö	Marcaltő, Hungary
Margitfalva	Margecany, Slovakia
Maria-Nostra	Márianosztra, Hungary
Marienburg	Feldioara, Romania
Marienthal	Marianka, Slovakia
Maros River	Now mostly in Romania where it is the Mureş River
Marton-Vásár	Martonvásár, Hungary
Mediasch	Medgyes in Hungarian; now Mediaş, Romania
Megyer	now Vel'ký Meder, Slovakia; formerly Nagymegyer, Hungary
Melence	Melenci, Serbia
Méra	Tarnaméra, Hungary
Mező-Eörs	Mezőörs, Hungary
Mezö-Keresztes	Mezőkeresztes, Hungary
Mezö-Kövesd	Mezökővesd, Hungary
Mezö-Tárkany	Mezőtárkány, Hungary
Mezö-Tur	Mezőtúr, Hungary
Miskolcz	Miskolc, Hungary
Modern	Modra, Slovakia
Mohacz	Mohács, Hungary
Moldau	Moldava nad Bodvou, Slovakia
Moldavia	Nominally a province of the Ottoman Empire in 1848, though in practice under Russian control. Now divided among modern-day Moldova, Romania and Ukraine.
Moór	Mór, Hungary
Moravia	A crown land of the Austrian Empire in 1848. Now the eastern part of the Czech Republic.
Mosocs	Mosóc, now Mošovce, Slovakia
Mosty	Mosty u Jablunkova, Czech Republic

Mözö-Kövesd	Mezökővesd, Hungary
Munkacs	Mukachevo, Ukraine
Mur-Insel	The 'Mur island', the area between the River Mur and the River Drava
Nadas	Trstín, Slovakia
Nagy-Bálint	Törökbálint, Hungary
Nagybánya	Baia Mare, Romania
Nagy-Berczel	Bercel, Hungary
Nagy-Becskerek	Zrenjanin, Serbia
Nagy-Kikinda	Kikinda, Serbia
Nagy-Kata	Nagykáta, Hungary
Nagy-Körös	Nagykörös, Hungary
Nagy-Máros	Nagymaros, Hungary
Nagy-Sallo/Nagy-Sarló	Nagysalló, now Tekovské Lužany, Slovakia
Nagy-Tarcsa	Nagytarcsa, Hungary
Nagy-Torbágy	Biatorbágy, Hungary
Naszvad	Nesvady, Slovakia
Német-Bogsán	Bocşa, Romania
Német-Egyháza	Nagyegyháza, Hungary
Némethy/Németi	Hontianske Nemce, Slovakia
Neograd	Nógrád, Hungary
Neudorf	Sattel-Neudorf, now Nyergesújfalu in Hungary
Neuhäusel	Nové Zámky, Slovakia
Neumarkt	Marosvásárhely in Hungarian; now Târgu Mureş, Romania
Neusatz	Novi Sad, Serbia north of the Danube, Peterwardein being the part south of the river
Neusohl	Banská Bystrica, Slovakia
Neustadl	Kysucké Nové Mesto, Slovakia
Neu-Szöny	Új-Szőny, the centre of modern Komárom, Hungary
Neutra	Nitra, Slovakia
N. Ida	Vel'ká Ida, Slovakia
N. Irsza	Now merged with Alberti into Albertirsa, Hungary
N. Körös	Nagykőrös, Hungary
Nyárasd	Topol'níky, Slovakia

Ó-Arad	The old neighbourhood of Arad, Romania, on the north bank of the Maros
Ó-Becse	Bečej, Serbia
Ober-Döbrö	Feldebrő, Hungary
Ober-Galla	Alsógalla, in Tatabánya, Hungary
Ober-Gálla	Felsőgálla, Hungary
Ober Sz. János	Nagyszentjános, Hungary
Oedenburg/ Ödenburg	Sopron, Hungary
Ofen	Buda, Hungary
Ofen-Pesth	Budapest, Hungary
Ó-Kanizsa	Kanjiza, Serbia, west of the Theiss
Ó-Kér	Zmajevo, Serbia
Olmütz	Olomouc, Czech Republic
Ondód	Pusztavám, Hungary
Oravica	Oraviţa, Romania
Ördöghídja ('Devil's Bridge')	NW of Banatska Palanka, Serbia, shown on the 2nd Military Survey map as 'Teufelsbrücke'.
Orlik	Vyšný Orlík, Slovakia
Osgyan	Ožd'any, Slovakia
Osslán/Oszlan	Oslany, Slovakia
Ó-Szőny	Now an eastern suburb of Komárom, Hungary
Öttevény-Sziget	Kunsziget, Hungary
Pakfurth	Pachfurth, Austria
Palatinal Line	The western face of the Komorn fortress
Pálfalva	Zagyvapálfalva, Hungary
Pallersdorf	Bezenye, Hungary
Palota	Rákospalota, now District XV, Budapest, Hungary
Pancsova	Pančevo, Serbia
Parendorf	Parndorf, Austria
Párkány/Parkany/Parkány	Štúrovo, Slovakia
Párod	Parád, Hungary
Páta	Gyöngyöspata, Hungary
Peczel/Péczel	Pécel, Hungary
Perbete	Pribeta, Slovakia
Perk	Kremnické Bane, Slovakia

Pesth	Pest, Budapest, Hungary
Peterwardein	Petrovaradin, Serbia
Petri	Szinpetri, Hungary
Piski	Simeria, Romania
Plattensee	Lake Balaton, Hungary
Pletykafalu	Pletykafalu, Szolnok, Hungary
Pocsuvadlo	Počúvadlo, Slovakia
Polocsa	Plaveč, Slovakia
Preitzdorf	Prenčov, Slovakia
Pressburg	Bratislava, Slovakia
Prividgye	Prievidza, Slovakia
Promontorium	Budafok, Hungary
Püspöki	Tiszapüspöki, Hungary
Puszta-Harkáli	Herkálypuszta, Hungary
Puszta-Lovad	A farm that no longer exists, west of Komorn on the south bank of the Danube, due south of what is now Vel'ký Lel, Slovakia.
Puszta-Szanda	Then just a farm, now the town of Szandaszőlős, Hungary
Raab	Györ, Hungary
Raaba-Sz. Mihály	Győrszentmihály, Hungary
Raab River	Rába River
Rabnitz River	Répcze River
Rácz-Keresztúr	Ráckeresztúr, Hungary
Ragendorf	Rajka, Hungary
Rajecz	Rajec, Slovakia
Rakowa	Raková, Slovakia
Ramdorf	*Unknown location*
Raszlavicza	Raslavice, Slovakia
Rékas	Zagyvarékas, Hungary
Rima-Szecs	Rimavská Seč, Slovakia
Rima-Szombath/Rima-Sombath	Rimavská Sobota, Slovakia
Rosenau	Rožňava, Slovakia
Rosenberg	Ružomberok, Slovakia
Rothenturm Pass	Turnu Roşu, Romania
Rudno	Rudno nad Hronom, Slovakia

Ruszka	Göncruszka, Hungary
Sachsenfeld	Albertfalva, Hungary
Sachsenhausen	*See* Sachsenfeld
Saj Káll	Sajtoskál, Hungary
Salzburg	Vizakna in Hungarian; now Ocna Sibiului in Romania
S. Maria	Tarnaszentmária, Hungary
Sandberg	Now the Monostor fort in the west of Komárom, Hungary
Sár	Abasár, Hungary
Sárkany	Bakonysárkany, Hungary
Sarosser Komitat	Sáros County, former county of the Kingdom of Hungary, now in Slovakia
Sátorallya-Ujhely	Sátoraljaújhely, Hungary
Schässburg	Sighişoara, Romania
Schemnitz	Banská Štiavnica, Slovakia
Schönbrunn	Schönbrunn Palace, Vienna, Austria
Schöne Schäferin	'Fair Shepherdess', now Szépjuhászné in Budapest, Hungary
Schützen	Lövö, Hungary
Schwabenberg/Schwabenwald	The forested hills that are now the Svábhegy and Széchenyihegy districts of Budapest, Hungary
Sebes	Nižná Šebastová, now part of L'ubotice, Slovakia
Semlin	Zemun, Serbia
Sexard	Szekszárd, Hungary
Siebenbürgen	The province of Transylvania, now in Romania
Siegelberg	Siglisberg, hill north of Vindšacht, western suburb of Štiavnické Bane, Slovakia
Silein	Žilina, Slovakia
Silesia	The then Duchy of Silesia, a crown land of the Bohemian crown within the Austrian Empire, now in the Czech Republic
Skleno	Sklené, Slovakia
Slavonia	The then Kingdom of Slavonia within the Austrian Empire, now divided between Croatia and Serbia
Somos	Drienov, Slovakia
Sóvar	Now the Solivar suburb of Prešov, Slovakia

S. Peter	Petrovany, Slovakia
Stampfen	Stupava, Slovakia
Steinamanger	Szombathely, Hungary
Steinbach	Köpatak in Hungarian; nowadays at the northern end of Majere, Slovakia, where route 1579 joins route 524
Steinbrucher Vineyards	Now Óhegy, District X, Budapest, Hungary
Steinfeld	Steinfeld, Wiener Neustadt, Austria
St. Kaszimir	Albertkázmérpuszta, Hungary
St. Kiraly Farm	Now the village of Szentkirály, Hungary
St. Kiralyer-Wald	Szent Király Erdö, 'Saint King's Wood' – the Saint King being St Stephen
St. Láslo farm (on the Isaszeg battlefield)	*Unknown locatoin*
St. Lászlo	Valkószentlászló, Hungary
St. Márton-Káta	Szentmártonkáta, Hungary
Stolzenburg	Szelindek in Hungarian; now Slimnic in Romania
Strass-Sommerein	Hegyeshalom, Hungary
St. Tomas	Srbobran, Serbia
Stuhlweissenburg	Székesfehérvár, Hungary
Stureczberg	Staré Hory, Slovakia
Styria	The then Duchy of Styria within Austria; nowadays mostly in Austria, partly in Slovenia
Suly	Tápiósüly, now part of Sülysáp, Hungary
Surdok-Püspöki	Surdokpüspöki, Hungary
Swrczinowecz	Svrčinovec, Slovakia
Syrmia	The plain between the Danube and the Sava Rivers, now mostly in Serbia and partly in Croatia
Szabadhegy	Győrszabadhegy, now in the southern suburbs of Győr, Hungary
Szabadka	Subotica, Serbia
Szálád	Zala County, Hungary
Szala-Egerszeg	Zalaegerszeg, Hungary
Szalka	Salka, Slovakia
Sz. André	St Andrä am Zicksee, Austria
Sz. Antal	Svätý Anton, Slovakia
Szantó	Santovka, Slovakia

Szatmár	Satu Mare, Romania
Száss	Tiszasas, Hungary
Szecsö	Tapiószecső, Hungary
Szegedin	Szeged, Hungary
Szeghegy	Lovćenac, Serbia
Szemere	Mezőszemere, Hungary
Szén	Szin, Hungary
Sz. Endré	Szentendre, Hungary
Szenicz	Senica, Slovakia
Szent-Iván	Újszentiván, Hungary
Szentmárton	Pannonhalma, Hungary
Szerdahely	Dunajská Streda, Slovakia
Szered	Sered', Slovakia
Sziget	Szigetvár, Hungary, as distinct from Máramarossziget
Szigeth	Máramarossziget, now Sighetu Marmaţiei, Romania
Szilas	Brestovec, Slovakia
Szilas	Bódvaszilas, Hungary
Szinye	Svinica, Slovakia
Sz. István	Szentistván, Hungary
Sz. Ivánka	Borsodivánka, Hungary
Sz. Ivány	Győrszentiván, Hungary
Sz.-Jacob/Sz. Jacob	Now the northern part of Szurdokpüspöki, Hungary
Sz. Márton	Martin, Slovakia
Sz. Miklos	Liptovský Mikuláš, Slovakia
Sz. Miklos	Mosonszentmiklós, Hungary
Sz. Miklos	Rábaszentmiklós, Hungary
Sz. Miklós	Törökszentmiklós, Hungary
Szobb	Szob, Hungary
Sz. Peter	Sajószentpéter, Hungary
Sz. Petere	Komáromszentpéter, now Svätý Peter, Slovakia
Sztropko	Stropkov, Slovakia
Szvidnik	Svidník, Slovakia
Tabán	Tabán, Budapest, Hungary
Tamási	Bakonytamási, Hungary

Tapio	Felső-Tápió, Hungary
Tapio-Bicske	Tapiobicske, Hungary
Tapio-Szele	Tápiószele, Hungary
Tapolczan	Tepličany, now in Družstevná pri Hornáde, Slovakia
Tarczal/Tarczál	Tarcal, Hungary
Tehány	Ťahanovce, now a northwestern outskirt of Kaschau
Telgárth	Telgárt, Slovakia
Temesvár	Timişoara, Romania
Terenye	Bátonyterenye, Hungary
Teschen	Český Těšín, Czech Republic
Téteny	Nagytétény, Hungary
Téth	Tét, Hungary
Theiss Arm	A branch of the Tisza that has now disappeared in the reservoir that is Lake Tisza
Theiss River	Tisza River
Theresiopel	Subotica, Serbia
Thurocz	Turóc County, a county of the former Kingdom of Hungary, now in Slovakia
Thurzowka	Turzovka, Slovakia
Tisza-Bö	Tiszabő, Hungary
Tisza-Földvár	Tiszaföldvár, Hungary
Tisza-Füred	Tiszafüred, Hungary
Tiszólcz	Tisovec, Slovakia
T. Kanisa	Törökkanizsa, now Novi Kneževac, Serbia
Tokaj	Tokay, Hungary
Tölgys	Ipolytölgyes, Hungary
Tompa	Tupá, Slovakia
Torbágy	Biatorbágy, Hungary
Torna	Turňa nad Bodvou, Slovakia
Tornallya	Tornal'a, Slovakia
Törcsvár	Bran, Romania
Török-Bálint	Törökbálint, Hungary
Török-Kanisa	Novi Kneževac, Serbia
Török Sz. Miklós	Törökszentmiklós, Hungary
Toth-Almás/Tot-Almás	Tóalmás, Hungary
Tóthfalva	Tófalu, Hungary

Trentschin	Trenčin, Slovakia
Tugar river	Krivánsky river, Slovakia
Turczek Heights	Turček, Slovakia
Tyrnau/Tyrnava	Trnava, Slovakia
Ujfalu	Győrújfalu, Hungary
Ujfalu	Nádújfalu, Hungary
Ujhely	Sájtoraljaújhely, Hungary
Ujvaros	Balmazújváros, Hungary
Ungarisch-Altenburg	Now merged with Wieselburg into Mosonmagyaróvár, Hungary
Unghvár	Uzhhorod, Ukraine
Ung Komitat	Ung County in the former Kingdom of Hungary, now in Ukraine
Unt. Novaj	Now part of Novajidrány, Hungary
Ürmény	Mojmírovce, Slovakia
Vad-Kert	Érsekvadkert, Hungary
Vad-Kert	Soltvadkert, Hungary
Valk	Tiszavalk, Hungary
Valpó	Valpovo, Croatia
Vámos-Falva	Mýtna, Slovakia
Vámos-Györk	Vámosgyörk, Hungary
Varáno	Varannó, now Vranov nad Topl'ou, Slovakia
Várkony	Tiszavárkony, Hungary
Vaskapu	Vaskapu (Iron Gate), Romania
Velencze	Velence, Hungary
Verbacz	Verbász, now Vrbas, Serbia
Verebély	Mátraverebély, Hungary
Verebély	Vrablé, Slovakia
Vernárth	Vernár, Slovakia
Veröcze	Verőce, Hungary
Verpeléth	Verpelét, Hungary
Veszprim	Veszprém, Hungary
Világos	Şiria, Romania
Viscoly	Vizsoly, Hungary

Vognicza	Voznica, Slovakia
Vojvodina	The Serbian area within the Kingdom of Hungary which had declared itself independent from Hungary in May 1848
Vulka-Pordány	Wulka-Prodersdorf, Austria
Waag River	Váh or Vág River
Waitzen	Vác, Hungary
Wallachia	Nominally a province of the Ottoman Empire in 1848, though in practice under Russian control. Now part of Romania.
Wartberg	Senec, Slovakia
Warthaberg/Wartha heights	Error in the original text, presumed to mean not the Wartaberg but the Sitno Berg, the highest peak in the Schemnitz mountains [Štiavnické Vrchy, Slovakia], due east of Gyekes
Weissenburg	Fejér County, Hungary
Weisskirchen	Medveďov, Slovakia
Wien	Vienna, Austria
Wieselburg	Now merged with Ungarisch-Altenburg into Mosonmagyaróvár, Hungary
Windschacht	Vindšacht, western suburb of Štiavnické Bane, Slovakia
Zajning	Mosonszolnok, Hungary
Zamoly	Győrzámoly, Hungary
Zbóró	Zborov, Slovakia
Zeiden	Codlea, Romania
Zempliner Komitat/Zemplin	Zemplén County, former county of the Kingdom of Hungary, now divided between Hungary and Slovakia
Zenta	Senta, Serbia
Zichyfalva	Plandište, Serbia
Zips Komitate	Szepes County, former county of the Kingdom of Hungary, now mostly in Slovakia and part in Poland
Zmygrod	Stary Żmigród, Poland
Zombor	Sombor, Serbia
Zsadany	Hernádzsadány, now Ždaňa, Slovakia
Zsámbokréth	Žabokreky nad Nitrou, Slovakia

Zsarnócz	Zsarnóca, now Žarnovica, Slovakia
Zsibó	Jibou, Romania
Zsitvatö	Žitava, now part of Radvaň nad Dunajom, Slovakia
Zsolca	Felsőzsolca, Hungar
Zsomboly	Jimbolia, Romania

The Austrian and Hungarian Armies

This is not the place for an exhaustive examination of the Austrian and Hungarian armies. The purpose of this section is just to provide the reader with the essential information necessary to understand the text.

Austria

Infantry

The majority of the Austrian army was comprised of line infantry. Each infantry regiment had a number and carried the name of its *Inhaber* (honorary colonel). It had three regular battalions and an associated *Landwehr-Bataillon* – a militia battalion. (Note that '*Bataillon*' is not a spelling mistake, but the German spelling of 'battalion'.) Originally the *Landwehr* battalions were formed from trained ex-soldiers who remained in the active reserve for 8 to 13 years, depending upon which province they were in. However, this had changed in 1831: to reduce the risk of these turning into revolutionary rebel units, they lost their regional character and were instead simply made up of untrained younger men who had not been previously conscripted in the annual ballot for their class.[1] *Landwehr-Bataillons* were therefore less well trained. During the campaign, 4th and 5th *Feld-Reserve-Bataillons* were also formed by calling up more than the usual proportion of conscripts.[2] Because of the short period available to create these emergency formations they were relatively undrilled and raw, but of course the same was true for much of the Hungarian army facing them. The line infantry were predominantly armed with the M1842 Augustin musket.

An Austrian line infantry battalion had six companies, each of about 200 men. Tactically these frequently operated as a pair of companies known as a 'division'. These two-company divisions are obviously far smaller than an infantry division with its two brigades of several battalions each. It will be clear from context, which is being referred to in the text, but the reader needs to be aware of the distinction.

1 László Bencze, 'The Military System of the Habsburg Empire and the Hungarian Units of the Army on the Eve of the Revolution', in Gábor Bona (ed.), *The Hungarian Revolution and the War of Independence, 1848-1849* (New York: Columbia University Press, 1999).
2 Nigel Smith, *The Magyar War* (Pickelhaube Press, 2006).

In addition to its 18 line companies, each regiment had two grenadier companies. These were generally converged with others to form 4-company grenadier battalions, which took the name of their commander.

Alongside the line infantry were light infantry riflemen known as *jägers*. Their primary role was as skirmishers, but they were also often used as elite assault troops. *Jäger* battalions had only four companies. They were armed with the M1844 *Kammerbüchse* rifled musket.

As will be seen from the orders of battle, infantry units were typically grouped into brigades of several battalions from different regiments. Grenadier battalions tended to be grouped together into grenadier brigades. The line brigades often included some *jägers*.

A substantial proportion of the Austrian infantry, and the predominant type in Jellacic's Croatian I. Armeekorps, was the so-called '*grenzers*': border guard regiments from the Austrian formally designated and administered military border region. Like the line troops, each Grenz-Regiment had three regular battalions and an associated *Landwehr-Bataillon*. When the war started, the majority of the regular *grenzers* were in Italy, so Jellacic's force was mostly made up of poorly trained and badly organised *landwehr* without uniforms. Each *grenzer* battalion also had a small number of *seressaners* attached: paramilitary gendarmerie in distinctive red cloaks.

Cavalry

The two categories of Austrian cavalry were heavy and light. The heavies – cuirassiers and dragoons – were shock troops. The cuirassiers in particular proved how devastating they could be in this role on several occasions. The light cavalry for scouting and skirmishing and for countering the enemy's many light cavalry units came in several types: *chevauxlegers* (light horse), *uhlans* (lancers), and some hussars (though most of the army's hussars were Hungarian and had defected).

Cavalry regiments had four or six squadrons, each of about 150 men. As with the infantry, these operated in pairs known as divisions. They were designated by the rank of the officer commanding them, thus 'the Oberstlieutenant's Division', or 'the Major's 2. Squadron', etc. Squadrons comprised two wings, thus the occasional references in the text to a wing of cavalry effectively mean a half-squadron.

Cavalry operated both as separate cavalry brigades and as individual squadrons attached to infantry brigades. In the latter case they served as scouts, couriers, maintaining communications, etc., for the brigade.

Artillery

The majority of the Austrian field artillery was foot artillery batteries equipped with 6-pounder guns. These were organised in batteries of six, generally including two 7-pounder howitzers. Horse artillery batteries accompanying the cavalry brigades were similarly equipped and organised. Reserve artillery at the corps and army level included heavier batteries of 12-pounder guns.

The Austrian army, unusually for this period, made wide use of rockets. Reserve artillery also included batteries of six rocket launch stands. Their relative portability saw them often taken on cavalry raids or reconnaissances in force. They were particularly effective as incendiary weapons; the text makes several references to them setting bridges or buildings on fire.

Siege artillery in the form of heavy mortars and the like was brought up for the sieges of Leopoldstadt and Komorn.

Glossary of Ranks

Feldmarschall	Field marshal
Feldzeugmeister	General of the artillery
Feldmarschall Lieutenant	Lieutenant General
Generalmajor	Brigadier
Oberst	Colonel
Oberstlieutenant	Lieutenant Colonel
Major	Major
Hauptmann	Captain
Rittmeister	Cavalry captain
Oberlieutenant	First lieutenant
Lieutenant	Second lieutenant
Flügeladjutant	Not a rank as such but an appointment: aide-de-camp to a member of the royal household
Wachtmeister	Cavalry sergeant
Feldwebel	Sergeant
Feuerwerker	Artillery sergeant

Glossary of Noble Titles

Kaiser	Emperor
Banus	Viceroy
Erzherzog (E.H.)	Archduke
Grossherzog (G.H.)	Grand duke
Fürst	Prince
Prinz	Prince
Baron	Baron
Graf	Count
Ritter	Knight ('Sir')
Freiherr	Knight ('Sir')

Glossary of Unit Types

Chevauxlegers	Light horse, light dragoons
Dragoner	Dragoons
Fussbatterie	Foot artillery battery
Geschütz	Artillery
Grenzer	Border troops (predominantly Croatian)
Husaren	Hussars
Jäger	Riflemen (light infantry)
Kavalleriebatterie	Horse artillery battery
Kürassiere	Cuirassiers
Landsturm	Militia of the last resort, *levée-en-masse* kind
Landwehr	Militia of the organised reserve kind
Munizion	Ammunition
Raketen	Rockets
Sechspfündige	6-pounder
Uhlanen	Lancers
Zwölfpfündige	12-pounder

Hungary[3]

Unsurprisingly, the newly created Hungarian army largely followed its Austrian parent in organisation and tactics. The core of it was the former imperial regiments – some 21 line infantry battalions, one grenadier battalion, four *grenzer* battalions, and seven hussar regiments – whose Hungarian personnel opted to recognise the authority of the Hungarian government.

This was augmented first by 400,000 national guards conscripted between April and September 1848. Initially these had a police function, which turned into a counter-insurgency role because of the Serb rebellion and Croat unrest in the south of Hungary. Only one in ten of these national guards had firearms, and few had uniforms.

The Serbian insurrection in particular prompted a further step in May 1848, the creation of the *honvéd*: 10,000 volunteers formed into ten proper battalions, with cadres of former imperial officers and non-commissioned officers (NCOs). In August 1848 the Hungarian parliament passed a bill to expand the *honvéd* to 200,000 men, of which some 100,000 or so had been recruited and armed by December. In September the volunteer national guard was established (a more mobile and reliable force than the local conscript national guard), which had 12,000 men in 15 battalions; these were all incorporated into the *honvéd* between November 1848 and spring 1849.

Prologue

Events Leading Up to the Winter Campaign

Nobili's account begins on 1 November 1848. However, the conflict was already several months old by then. It is therefore important to give a brief account of the preceding events so as to set the campaign in its proper context.

It is outside the scope of this work to go into the political dimension of the conflict in any great detail, but some background is necessary. Since the 1820s, Hungarian liberals and nationalists had increasingly been seeking greater autonomy for Hungary from imperial Austria. Elections to the Hungarian Diet in 1847, a Hungarian legislative assembly with very limited powers, produced a progressive Diet committed to reforms (the so-called 'Twelve Points'). This roughly coincided with unrest and revolution breaking out in many places across Europe in early 1848, particularly in Austria's provinces in Italy and in the Austrian capital, Vienna. Thus distracted and under pressure, the Austrian *Kaiser* Ferdinand I was obliged to make concessions. He appointed *Graf* Lajos Batthyány as his first Hungarian Prime Minister and accepted all twelve demands.

However, these increased powers for the new Hungarian parliament only increased friction between Hungarians and the empire's other ethnic groups who felt lower in the pecking order: Slovaks, Romanians, Croats, and especially Serbs. The Austrians stirred these conflicts, encouraging such groups to rise against Hungary, promising them rights and autonomy in return. A Serbian nationalist movement was similarly simmering, and in April 1848 the first bloodshed occurred between Serbs and Hungarians in southern Hungary. This escalated to a Serbian insurrection, supported by the Principality of Serbia (then still nominally a vassal of the Ottoman Empire) from where thousands of volunteers arrived, more to loot than to fight, but further fuelling the conflict. The Hungarian authorities naturally tried to suppress this insurrection. By August 1848 the Serbian insurrectionists had about 30,000 men operating in Bácska and the Banat, the Hungarian authorities closer to 45,000. Hungarian successes at Versec on 11 June and Écska on 15 July were offset by defeats at the Serbian fortified camp of Szenttamás in mid-June, Neuzina on 3 August, and a serious one again at Szenttamás on 19 August. The Hungarian commander Bechtold was particularly culpable for these defeats, proving unable to prevent the establishment of fortified enemy camps or to seize these once established.[1] The extent of his failure led to suggestions that it constituted 'betrayal', though the

1 Fülöp [or Philipp] Baron Bechtold (1787-1862) was a former imperial general. In 1848 he was garrison

truth was probably simply lack of men initially and then inability to find a method to counter Serbian guerrilla warfare. Another contributory factor was the Austrian policy of sending regiments to serve in different provinces from those where they were raised; thus, the imperial forces trying to fight the Serbian insurrection were mostly not Hungarian regiments, nor especially motivated to defend Hungary.

A third attack on Szenttamás under the new Hungarian commander, Mészáros, failed again on 21 September.[2] However, on 13 October a Serb attack was defeated in turn at Ó-Beçse and Török-Becse. After that and into November, it was largely quiet on the Serbian front; by then, Jellacic had been defeated (see below), and both sides preferred to negotiate rather than fight. When the fighting resumed, it was under yet another Hungarian commander, General Antal Vetter.[3] He inflicted a major defeat at Strázsa on 9 November and another at Ördöghídja on 30 November. A Hungarian force under Ernő Kiss was thwarted at Tomasevac on 4 December but Damjanich achieved another victory at Károlyfalva on 12 December, repelling a Serbian counterattack on the 14th, finally resulting in the capture of Tomasevac on the 15th.[4] However, a Hungarian attack on another Serbian fortified camp at Pancsova was repulsed on 3 January 1849.

By this time the main Austrian army was beginning its Winter Campaign, so Hungarian forces were withdrawn from the southern front. Apart from the Hungarian-held fortress of Peterwardein, the Serbs and imperial troops were therefore left in occupation of the region south of the line Zombor-Szabadka-Szeged-River Maros.

commander in Kaschau and appointed by the Hungarian government to command its southern army against the Serbian insurrection. After the failure of his campaign he resigned on 31 August 1848 and left for Vienna on 8 September, changing sides and subsequently commanding the reserve cavalry division in Haynau's Austro-Russian army in its summer campaign against Hungary. Gábor Bona, *Tábornokok és törzstisztek az 1848/1849. évi szabadságharcban.*

2 Lázár Mészáros (1796-1858) was a former imperial colonel commanding the imperial 5. Husaren-Regiment. In April 1848 he was made Minister of Defence in Batthyány's new Hungarian government and was instrumental in extending its control over imperial troops in Hungary as well as establishing Hungary's own new forces. He alternated his ministry work with stints in the field: not only his temporary command against the Serbian insurrection in September 1848, but also commanding the corps on the upper Tisza that was defeated by Schlick in January 1849. On 29 July he resigned from the ministry and became Dembinski's chief of staff, escaping with him to Ottoman territory at the end of the war. Sentenced to death *in absentia*, he ended his days in exile in England. Bona, *Tábornokok.*

3 Antal Vetter (1803-82). In June 1848 he was a lieutenant colonel commanding the 37. Infanterie-Regiment in Arad. After promotion to division command in November he joined the ministry of defence in December. In March 1849 he was given command of the Upper Danubian Army but soon fell ill and handed it over to Görgei. Fit again at the end of June he took over command of the southern army but found himself increasingly subordinated to Dembinski; they fell out and he resigned on 7 August. At the end of the war he hid and then escaped abroad in May 1850, being condemned to death *in absentia*. He was involved in the failed Milan uprising (1852-1853), then helped to organise the Hungarian Legion fighting against Austria in Italy in 1859, and Prussia's Hungarian Legion in 1866. He returned to Hungary after the Compromise of 1867 and helped to establish the Royal Hungarian Army. Bona, *Tábornokok.*

4 Ernő Kiss (1799-1849) was a colonel commanding 2. Husaren-Regiment when the Serbian insurrection broke out and served on the southern front until January 1849. From February onward he saw no further field service but served in a series of administrative roles. He surrendered with Görgei at Világos at the end of the war and was executed at Arad. Bona, *Tábornokok.*

Meanwhile even greater danger to Hungary had emerged from Croatia. In March 1848, Josip Jellacic had been appointed as the new *Ban* of Croatia. Politically he steered a clever course, managing at the same time to satisfy Croatia's own national autonomy movement and to display staunch loyalty to the *Kaiser* by severing the administrative and political ties between Croatia and Hungary in April. Tension rose, with troops mobilised on both sides of the border. In August, with the secret connivance and encouragement of the *Kaiser* who was now regretting his concessions to the Hungarians, Jellacic prepared to invade Hungary and march on Ofen-Pesth.

On 11 September Jellacic crossed the Drau with over 50,000 men, supposedly to restore order in Hungary which he declared had no legitimate government, but without any formal authority from Vienna to do so. There were very few Hungarian forces in the area initially, and the Hungarian government was trying to resolve matters by negotiation rather than fighting. However, negotiations failed, and the Croat army's looting and depredations along its march had antagonised the Hungarian population, so matters came to a head at the battle of Pákozd on 29 September. Despite the Croats' superior numbers, Jellacic was defeated; rather than return through hostile territory to Croatia, he zagged off to the northwest to join the imperial forces besieging revolutionary Vienna. A 9,000-strong Croat division under *Generalmajor* Roth was cut off, surrounded, and forced to surrender at Ozora in October.

Also, in October, *Kaiser* Ferdinand made a proclamation to the imperial troops stationed in Hungary and Transylvania effectively demanding that they disobey the orders of the Hungarian government. As a result, *Feldmarschall Lieutenant* Puchner commanding the forces in Transylvania declared against Hungary, as did the important fortresses of Arad and Temesvár.

Meantime, the growing Hungarian army led by Móga pursued Jellacic but paused at the River Leitha, the boundary between Hungary and Austria.[5] This was Hungary's Rubicon: crossing it would be a serious step and would change its posture from one of self-defence and lawful quest for autonomy to one of outright disobedience. Vienna had revolted on 6 October and the Hungarians awaited a Viennese invitation to cross the Leitha, but this did not come. There was much debate in the Hungarian camp: Kossuth arrived in person, demanding that the army cross unless its commanders could convince him it would bring disaster, and offering command to whoever would lead the army into Austria. Görgei spoke in favour of invasion, saying there was more to lose by not doing so, and this decided the matter. After some tentative trespasses earlier in the month, the portentous step was finally taken on 28 October.

Invading Austria proved unwise: at the battle of Schwechat outside Vienna on 30 October, Móga's largely raw and untrained force was soundly beaten by superior numbers of seasoned imperial troops under Windisch-Grätz. The Hungarian army retreated to Hungary to lick its wounds, while Windisch-Grätz crushed the Vienna revolution. The stage was set for the Winter Campaign.

5 János Móga (1785-1861) served in the Napoleonic Wars and was seriously wounded at Wagram in 1809. In May 1848 when he declared his loyalty to the Batthyány government he was commanding an imperial brigade in Kaschau. Promoted to lieutenant general in June, he assumed command of the Upper Danubian Army in September. He defeated Jellacic in the first significant battle of the war at Pákozd, but then his army was routed at Schwechat outside the walls of Vienna. After that defeat he resigned and retired from the army. He was sentenced to five years in prison after the war. Bona, *Tábornokok*.

Preface by *Feldmarschall Fürst* Windisch-Grätz

I address these words to the army to which I dedicated almost 50 years of my life, whose history was my destiny, whose members are my friends, and whose future was tied to me by a bloody cord during the events of recent years, in the days of Prague, Vienna, Kápolna and Isaszeg.[1]

Because the winter campaign in Hungary belongs to such a recent era, it was my intention to leave this account for later. However, the countless biased commentaries with their inaccurate accounts of the facts have compelled my decision to present the public with a truthful and accurate depiction of it, to secure for the army which accomplished so much under my command the recognition it is due for all time to come.

I dedicate the following pages to the army as a memento of the travails we endured, and of the deeds that we performed in an arduous winter campaign against superior numbers of the enemy, as an ingredient for the advancement of military science, to which accurate knowledge of such an unusual campaign may contribute something.

Those mistakes by individuals that are criticised herein cannot diminish your glory; such things happen in every campaign throughout history and are outweighed many times by glorious feats of arms and by displays of rare courage and endurance.

The time for war may come again, but so long as the army's spirit and its institutions remain unchanged, so long shall our most gracious monarch's cause and that of social order rest on unshakeable pillars.

Liesko [Lesko, Poland], September 1851
Alfred *Fürst* Windisch-Grätz,
Feldmarschall

1 Thus, the suppression of the revolts in the two cities, and then the two major battles of the Winter Campaign.

Foreword by *Feldmarschall-Lieutenant* Johann Nobili

In the following depiction of the Winter Campaign of 1848-1849 in Hungary, we have chronicled the events of the war as far as possible in the order in which they came to the knowledge of the *Feldmarschall*; likewise the incoming news and reconnaissance reports, as well as the orders resulting from them, are mostly presented verbatim, so as on the one hand to put the reader in the position the *Feldmarschall* was in at the moment when he was making his dispositions, and on the other to avoid any arbitrary later explanation or interpretation of these orders and reports.

We have also felt obliged to refrain from any polemics or embellishment of the events, because such retrospective rationalisation and adornment is unsuitable for giving a true picture of the actual situation.[1]

This manner of presentation – which we have chosen quite deliberately – is certainly not particularly attractive or lively, leading as it does to frequent repetition, exhaustive detail, and the like; but it seems to us the most suitable for putting the reader in a position to make an unbiased, independent judgement on the particular and unusual circumstances of that period. It should therefore be interesting and instructive for thinking soldiers, particularly for those who took part in this remarkable campaign.

The sources at our disposal were: an already completed official account of the campaign,[2] and partly the actual records from the operations, though we found the latter to be not so complete as we might have wished – and it could hardly have been otherwise, given the repeated changes in the high command and in the personnel employed in the headquarters; this is particularly true of the strength reports, casualty returns and after-action reports. If as a result some gaps or errors should occur, or individual feats of arms be touched on only superficially, or the names of some who distinguished themselves or who fell on the battlefield not be mentioned, we wish to ascribe this to the circumstance noted above.

Data concerning the operations of the Hungarian army are understandably even less complete. We only find a few interesting details about these coming up from the end of March 1849, while nothing reliable is available for the earlier period.

The actions of the formations employed in remote parts of the extensive theatre of operations, such as those in Transylvania or on the lower Theiss, etc., can only be touched on superficially here, since we lack official documentation of these. The same is true of the glorious defence of

1 'We' here being Johann Nobili; perhaps his line about refraining from polemics and retrospective rationalising is pointedly directed at Heller von Hellwald, whose original manuscript was rejected as being too critical of the Austrian army.

2 Presumably Heller von Hellwald's original manuscript, since lost.

the fortresses of Temesvár [Timişoara, Romania], Arad and Karlsburg [Alba Iulia, Romania], and of the attacks on Essegg [Osijek, Croatia], Peterwardein [Petrovaradin, Serbia, that part of Novi Sad south of the Danube], and Komorn [Komárno, Slovakia]; a dedicated account of these notable events must be saved for some other time.

Finally, as far as the political and administrative developments of this period are concerned, they have not been mentioned here – even though they exerted a decisive influence on the course of operations – since our mission is exclusively to present the military events. Let us just say here that the criticism that 'people were busying themselves with the pacification and administration of the country before the enemy army had even been beaten' is unfair. The *Feldmarschall* had to take care of rations and supplies for his army. For all the wealth of foodstuffs of every kind that Hungary possesses, these are not concentrated in particular transport nodes, trading centres, large cities and the like, as they are in other countries that are densely populated and endowed with good road networks. They are much more spread out across the whole country and must first be got to where they are needed from a long distance away. From this it follows that it is necessary constantly to remain master of an extensive stretch of territory, which was only possible by installing administrative authorities under military protection, unless one wanted to see oneself robbed of all resources from the outset and the whole country abandoned without impediment to the tireless and all too successful agitation of the agents, emissaries and partisans of the revolution. It cannot be denied that this led to some detachments that weakened the field army, but this is one of those evils that is easier to criticise after the event than to avoid at the time.

1

The army's deployment. Events from the start of operations until the imperial troops' entry into Ofen-Pesth [Budapest]. The period from 1 November 1848 to 5 January 1849

The Situation at the Start of the Campaign, 1 November 1848

After Wien [Vienna] had been suppressed, and the offensive undertaken by the Hungarian rebel army to support the rebellious imperial capital had been simultaneously repelled at Schwechat, there was no longer any doubt that the only way the legitimate order could be restored in Hungary was by force of arms. Consequently, the first question to consider was whether this should be done immediately, while it was still winter, or could be postponed until later.

An immediate intervention at least had the advantage that it could put a stop to the way that the revolutionary party was spreading every day and was arming itself militarily with exceptional energy. Beside this, the view was held that for the time being all there was to deal with in Hungary was just a faction, albeit a strong one; that the core of the people was still sound and ill-disposed toward the agitation of the revolutionaries; and that as soon as the imperial army appeared, that well-intentioned part of the populace that was oppressed through terror would rise up powerfully and cooperate with the suppression of the rebellion throughout the country. Finally, it could be hoped that the Hungarian imperial regiments that had been led astray could still be made to realise the true situation and thereby returned to doing their duty.

On the other hand, it was undeniable that the revolutionary party had very significant means of defence at its disposal, while the numbers of [imperial] troops available when operations began were very small by proportion, and were not at all equipped for a campaign, or at least only very incompletely so. Since the summer, out of the Hungarian and Transylvanian regiments belonging to the imperial army in Hungary, 26 infantry battalions and 59 hussar squadrons, or 41,769 men and 9,198 horses altogether, had gone over entirely to the side of the rebellion. On 11 July the Hungarian parliament had decreed the mobilisation of 200,000 men and had provisionally made 42 million forint[1] available to the so-called 'National Defence

1 Forint being the Hungarian 'florins' currency.

Committee' headed by Kossuth.[2] The levying of these men was driven with extraordinary energy by the many agents of the revolutionary party who spread out across the whole country. The organisation of the *honvéd* battalions likewise made rapid progress, since their cadres were formed largely from oath-breaking officers and veteran former NCOs and soldiers present in the country.[3] The hussar regiments were gradually increased to 18 regiments of eight squadrons each by establishing new regiments: Lehel, Bocskay, Karoly, Kossuth, etc. The rebels had no lack of artillery, since all the guns present in the country at the outbreak of the revolution – a total of 2,402 pieces, of which 672 were field guns – fell into their hands. They were drawn by excellent horses, handed over by the nobility either voluntarily or compulsorily, and crewed partly by the personnel of the fortress artillery and of the 5. Artillerie-Regiment that was stationed in Pesth, partly by students, technicians and foreigners who had served in the artillery somewhere before. With the exceptions of Temesvár, Arad and Karlsburg Castle in Transylvania, all the country's fortresses were in the power of the rebels together with their immeasurable *matériel* of guns and ammunition. The defection of a number of artillery and engineer officers from the imperial army also put them in a position to form technical units, and generally gave a significant boost to the process of armament. They sought to remedy their lack of commanders with war experience by summoning foreigners such as the Polish generals Bem,[4] Dembiński,[5] Wysocki[6] and Poninski,[7] among others. Finally, they formed Polish, German and Italian legions, whose ranks were also joined by adventurers from many countries.

While the measures for armament and defence presented here had indeed not yet fully come into being by the month of November, still much had been done, and what was lacking was being worked on with a tireless energy worthy of a better cause. The one thing the rebels felt a palpable lack of initially was firearms. Kossuth had already placed an order with the Pesth engineering works toward the end of April 1848 to deliver 100,000 muskets, ostensibly to arm

2 Kossuth, Lajos (1802-1894) had served as minister of finance under Batthyány. He subsequently became president of Hungary and then escaped into exile after the war. Bona, *Hungarian Revolution*, p. 506.

3 *Honvéd* is a word for a Hungarian soldier (lit. 'homeland defender'). In this context it refers to the revolutionary army created by Hungary in 1848 or to the new units of that army.

4 Bem, Józef (1794-1850) fought the Russians in Poland's November Uprising of 1830-31 and was then exiled to Paris. He commanded rebel forces in the Vienna Revolution of 1848. After that was suppressed, he offered his services to Kossuth. After the war he escaped to Turkey and served the Sultan until his death. Bona, *Hungarian Revolution*, p. 495.

5 Dembińsky [Dembinski or Dembinsky], Henryk Count (1791-1864). Like Bem, Dembińsky was a general in the Polish November Uprising of 1830-31; also like Bem, he was then exiled to France and briefly served the Sultan after Hungary's defeat, before returning to France. Bona, *Hungarian Revolution*, p. 498.

6 Wysocky, Józef (1809-73), a lieutenant in the November Uprising of 1830-1831, was a national guard officer in Krakau in 1848. He commanded the Polish Legion fighting for Hungary and served as a *honvéd* general and brigade, division and corps commander. He emigrated after the war. Bona, *Hungarian Revolution*, p. 520.

7 Poniński, Władisław (1823-1901) was a lieutenant in Dragoner-Regiment Nr. 1 in 1848. Only ever a junior commander in the Hungarian War of Independence, he reached the rank of lieutenant colonel in command of the Polish Legion's cavalry in July 1849. At the end of the war he escaped through Serbia. During the Crimean War he commanded a Polish lancer regiment in Turkish service. In 1859 he joined the Piedmontese army to serve in Italy against Austria, eventually becoming an Italian lieutenant general in 1871 before retirement in 1881. Bona, *Tábornokok*.

the national guard, and had placed very substantial orders in England and Belgium besides. But the supply of weapons could not keep pace with the need and with the levying of recruits, all the less so as several consignments of the weapons ordered from abroad were stopped at the border and impounded. On the other hand, the numerous iron foundries and powder mills in Upper Hungary delivered sufficient munitions that were then prepared in the great artillery establishments in Pesth, Grosswardein [Oradea, Romania] and Nagybánya [Baia Mare, Romania] for use in fortresses and in the field.[8]

Feldmarschall Fürst Windisch-Grätz, to whom His Majesty the *Kaiser* entrusted the difficult task of bringing the turmoil in Hungary to an end in a manner befitting the welfare of the grand monarchy and to the dignity of the throne, was under no illusion as to the difficulties that had to be overcome and the magnitude of the responsibility he was taking on. For the mood at that moment was still very agitated, not just in Wien but in most of the provinces. The efforts of the revolutionary party had to be suppressed everywhere by deploying military force; but this would become absent or inadequate if even halfway sufficient combat forces were used for the operations against Hungary, under which circumstances the flanks and rear of the army, as well as its supplies of replacements, rations, munitions and the like, would also be threatened and insecure. It is therefore easy to see the risky nature of this operation, particularly in a winter campaign. In spite of this, the *Feldmarschall* decided on an immediate intervention, since postponing the operation would have put in question the few favourable opportunities mentioned at the start, and the benefit that would have been gained by waiting in terms of reinforcing the army would have been outweighed many times by the progress that the rebels could have made meanwhile in arming for war, since they displayed such energy in this and generally brought such means and powers into play as can only be summoned during revolutions, not in conventional states.

Forces Available, December 1848

The *Feldmarschall*'s first concern was to decide on and organise those combat forces that were to be used for the offensive operations against Hungary. After deducting 16 battalions, ten squadrons and 36 guns that had to remain behind to garrison Wien, three army corps were formed from the troops concentrated outside Wien, whose order of battle was as follows:

I. Armeekorps

Corps commander: *Feldmarschall Lieutenant* and *Banus Baron* Jellacic[9]

8 Upper Hungary or 'Felvidék' generally means that part of the Kingdom of Hungary north of the Danube and Theiss rivers, nowadays mostly Slovakia.

9 Jellacic [Jellačić], Josip (1801-59). A regimental colonel for seven years, in March 1848 he was appointed *Banus* (ban, i.e., viceroy) of Croatia and promoted to *Feldmarschall Lieutenant.* He struck a middle course politically, tempering Croat nationalism and resistance to Croatia's subordination to Hungary with loyalty to the *Kaiser.* Thus, on 4 September 1848 he declared war on Ferdinand V, King of Hungary, in the name of Ferdinand V, King of Croatia. The Croat invasion of Hungary was defeated at Pákozd but Jellačić and his Croats then supported the subsequent imperial invasion. Brian G. Smith, 'Ban Josip Jellacic', in James Chastain (ed.), *Encyclopedia of 1848 Revolutions*

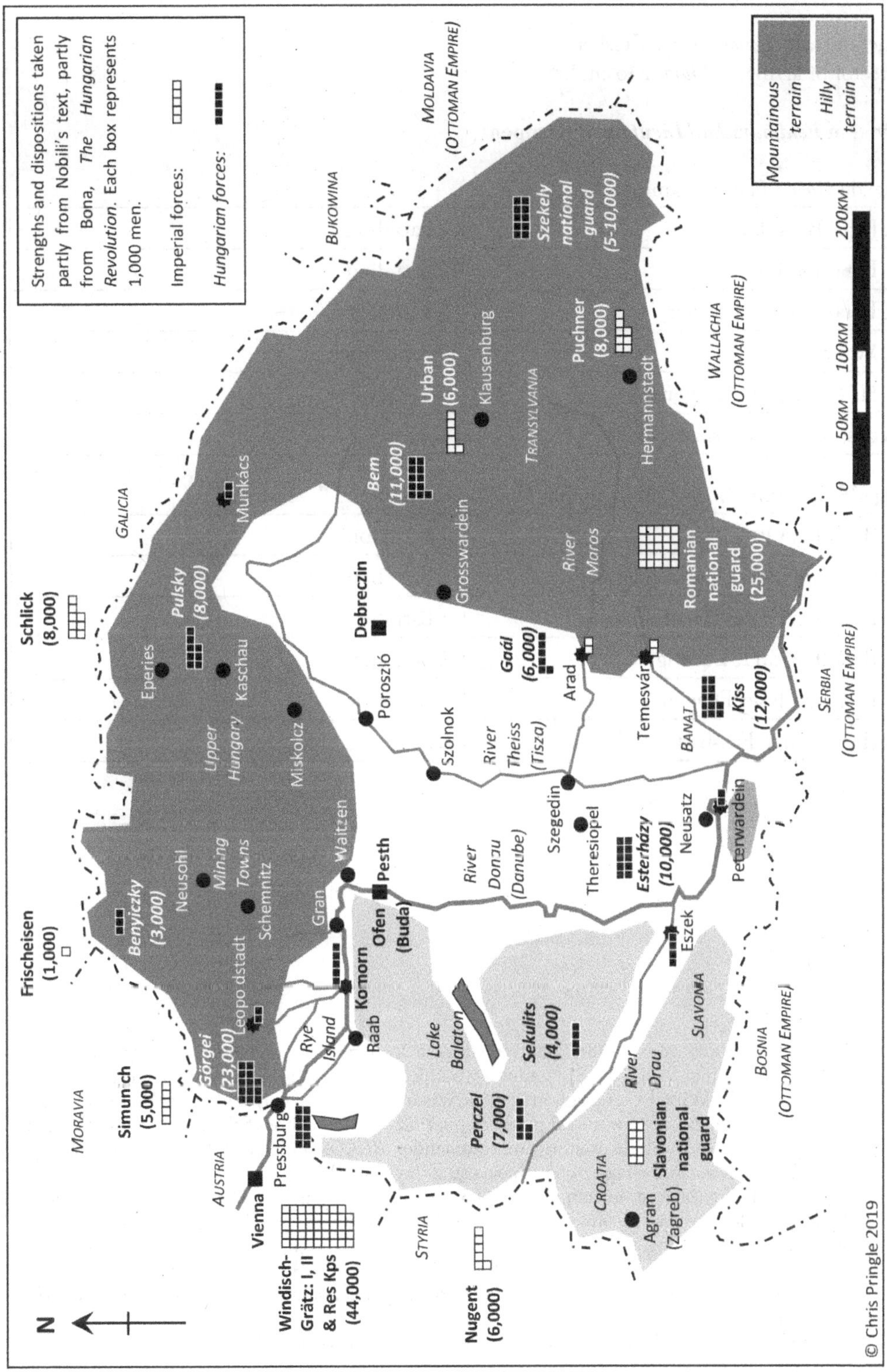

Map 1: The situation at the start of the Winter Campaign, 1 December 1849

Chief of staff: *Generalmajor* Zeisberg[10]
Director of artillery: *Major* Mosmüller

Division *Feldmarschall Lieutenant* Kempen[11]

Brigade *Oberst Baron* Grammont[12]

5. Jäger-Bataillon	1 battalion
3. Bataillon Liccaner	1 battalion
2. Bataillon Gradiscaner	1 battalion
2. Wallachen	2 companies
E.H. Franz Josef Dragoner	2 squadrons
Sechspfündige Fussbatterie Nr. 2	6 guns

Brigade *Generalmajor Baron* Neustädter[13]

1. Bataillon Ottochaner	1 battalion
3. Compon. Bat. Ogulin-Szluiner	1 battalion
3. Bataillon Erstes Banal	1 battalion
3. Bataillon E.H. Ludwig	1 battalion
E.H. Franz Josef Dragoner	2 squadrons
Sechspfündige Fussbatterie Nr. 1	6 guns

10 Zeisberg, Karl *Ritter* von (1788-1863) served as a lieutenant in the Austrian corps supporting Napoleon's invasion of Russia in 1812 and was wounded at Leipzig in 1813. While serving as Jellacic's chief of staff in the Winter Campaign in 1849 he was more or less openly critical of Windisch-Grätz's hesitant command. Zeisberg was held partly responsible for the failure of the campaign and in April 1849 was transferred to Styria as a brigade commander. *BLKÖ*, Vol.59, p.289; Róbert Hermann, *Az 1848–1849-es szabadságharc nagy csatái* (Budapest: Zrínyi, 2004).

11 Kempen von Fichtenstamm, Johann (1793-1863) fought in the battle of Dresden in 1813. Evidently a thinking soldier, he was involved in various technical branches and developments: mapping and surveying, pioneer training, the introduction of percussion-cap muskets, and training his regiment in tactics to the point where it was used as a model demonstration unit. A favourite of Haynau's, in 1849 he was appointed General Inspector of the Gendarmerie and then also military governor of Vienna. *ÖBL*.

12 Franz Adam Grammont von Linthal.

13 Joseph von Neustädter (1796-1866). Bona, *Hungarian Revolution*, p.512.

Division *Feldmarschall Lieutenant* Ritter von Hartlieb[14]

Brigade *Generalmajor* von Karger[15]

3. Bataillon Zweites Banal	1 battalion
2. Bataillon Brooder	1 battalion
2. Bataillon Latour	1 battalion
3. Bataillon E.H. Carl	1 battalion
E.H. Franz Joseph Dragoner	2 squadrons
Sechspfündige Fussbatterie Nr. 5	6 guns

Brigade *Generalmajor* von Kriegern

3. Bataillon Warasdiner-Kreuzer_1 battalion	
3. Bataillon Warasdiner St. Georger	1 battalion
3. Bataillon Ottochaner	1 battalion
Wiener Freiwillige[16]	2 companies
Turopolier[17] (did not go on campaign)	1 company
König von Sachsen Kürassiere	2 squadrons
Sechspfündige Fussbatterie Nr. 3	6 guns

Brigade *Generalmajor* Ottinger[18]

Wallmoden Kürassiere	6 squadrons
Heinrich Hardegg Kürassiere	6 squadrons
Sechspfündige Kavalleriebatterie Nr. 1	6 guns

14 Karl Hartlieb von Wallthor (1785 1862) served in the Austrian corps in Napoleon's invasion of Russia in 1812, and then fought at Dresden in 1813 and other actions. He distinguished himself in the suppression of the revolt in Vienna in 1848. At the end of the war he retired from the army in 1849 after 45 years' service. *BLKÖ*, Vol.7, p.408.

15 Titus *Freiherr* von Karger (1808-1860) had the distinction of tracking down the Hungarian crown in 1853 which had been taken and hidden by Kossuth during the war. *BLKÖ*, Vol.10, p. 476.

16 Viennese volunteers.

17 There is no Grenz-Regiment with this title. However, these are presumably Croat troops from Turopolje, the area between Zagreb, Sisak and Karlovac.

18 Franz Ottinger (1793-1869) was a brave cavalry leader who had been wounded in the Napoleonic Wars and led from the front in the 1848-1849 war. *BLKÖ*, Vol.21, p. 132.

Korps-Reserveartillerie

Sechspfündige Fussbatterie Nr. 4 and 6	12 guns
Zwölfpfündige Fussbatterie Nr. 1 and 2	12 guns
Unterstützungs-Munizions-Reserve	

Note: Banderial-Husaren and Seressaners[19] were at the disposal of the corps's command.

Strength of I. Armeekorps:
14 battalions, five individual companies, 20 squadrons, 54 guns, one pioneer company and one bridging train.

II. Armeekorps

Corps Commander: *Feldmarschall Lieutenant Graf* Wrbna[20]
Chief of staff: *Oberst* von Pott
Director of artillery: *Major* Scherpon

Division *Feldmarschall Lieutenant Baron* Csorich[21]

Brigade *Generalmajor* von Wyss

2. Jäger-Bataillon	1 battalion
1. Bataillon Schönhals	1 battalion
3. Bataillon Fürstenwärther	1 battalion
1. Landwehr-Bataillon Reisinger	1 battalion
Sappers	1 company
E.H. Karl Chevauxlegers	2 squadrons
Civallart Uhlanen	2 squadrons
Sechspfündige Kavalleriebatterie Nr. 2	6 guns
Raketenbatterie Nr. 14	6 launch stands

19 *Seressaners* were Croatian paramilitary gendarmerie.

20 Ladislaus *Graf* Wrbna-Freudenthal (1795-1849), while showing promise as a young officer, was apparently soured over the years by garrison life. He became a difficult character, harsh on his subordinates and widely disliked, which cannot have helped the efficient operation of his corps. After the battle of Kápolna he was recalled from the front because of his poor performance and given a garrison command in Verona. Here he shot himself, allegedly depressed at his recall. *BLKÖ*, Vol.18, pp.188-190.

21 Anton *Freiherr* von Csorich de Monte Creto (1795-1864) fought in the campaigns of 1813-1815. He performed creditably during the suppression of the revolt in Vienna and then during the 1848-1849 war. *BLKÖ*, Vol.3, pp.69-71.

Brigade *Oberst Fürst* Jablonowsky[22]

1. Bataillon Nassau	1 battalion
2. Bataillon Nassau	1 battalion
1. Landwehr-Bataillon Nassau	1 battalion
2. Bataillon Ceccopieri	1 battalion
Kress Chevauxlegers	1 squadron
Sechspfündige Fussbatterie Nr. 7	6 guns

Division *Feldmarschall Lieutenant* von Ramberg[23]

Brigade *Generalmajor Fürst* Colloredo[24]

12. Jäger-Bataillon	1 battalion
1. Bataillon E.H. Stefan	1 battalion
2. Bataillon E.H. Stefan	1 battalion
1. Landwehr-Bataillon Baumgarten [sic]	1 battalion
Kress Chevauxlegers	1 squadron
Sechspfündige Fussbatterie Nr. 8	6 guns

Brigade *Generalmajor Baron* Karl Lederer[25]

1. Bataillon Khevenhüller	1 battalion
2. Bataillon Khevenhüller	1 battalion
3. Bataillon Hess	1 battalion
1. Landwehr-Bataillon Hess	2 companies
Kress Chevauxlegers	1 squadron
Sechspfündige Fussbatterie Nr. 9	6 guns

22 Felix *Fürst* Jabłonowski (1808-1857). *BLKÖ*, Vol.10, pp.1-2.

23 Georg Heinrich *Freiherr* von Ramberg (1786-1855) served in the Napoleonic Wars from 1805 to 1815, fighting at Aspern, Wagram, Dresden and Leipzig, among others. He fought throughout the 1848-1849 war except for a period of illness in April-July 1849. *BLKÖ*, Vol.24, pp.307-310.

24 Franz de Paula Gundaccar II. *Fürst* Colloredo-Mansfeld (1802-52) was a popular and effective commander. *BLKÖ*, Vol.2, pp.422-424.

25 Karl Joseph *Freiherr* von Lederer (1800-?). Lederer's listing in Bona, *Hungarian Revolution*, as 'Lederer, Ignaz von Baron, (1769-1849)' would appear to be incorrect. *BLKÖ*, Vol.14, p.297.

Korps-Reserveartillerie

Sechspfündige Fussbatterie Nr. 10 and 11	12 guns
Zwölfpfündige Fussbatterie Nr. 3 and 4	12 guns
Unterstützungs-Munizions-Reserve	

Strength of II. Armeekorps:
15 battalions, three individual companies, seven squadrons, 54 artillery pieces, one pioneer company and one bridging train.

Armee-Reservekorps

Corps commander: *Feldmarschall Lieutenant Duca* Serbelloni[26]
Chief of staff: *Oberstlieutenant* Herdy
Director of the Artillerie-Hauptreserve: *Oberstlieutenant* Handl
Director of the Divisions-Reserveartillerie: *Major* Schmidt

Division *Feldmarschall Lieutenant Fürst* Edmund Schwarzenberg[27]

Brigade *Generalmajor* von Schütte

Grenadier-Bataillon Rattay	1 battalion
Grenadier-Bataillon Chmielnizky	1 battalion
Grenadier-Bataillon Ferrari	1 battalion
6. Jäger-Bataillon	1 battalion
Sechspfündige Fussbatterie Nr. 12	6 guns

Brigade *Generalmajor* von Liebler

Grenadier-Bataillon Strastil	1 battalion
Grenadier-Bataillon Martini	1 battalion
Grenadier-Bataillon Richter	1 battalion
1. Bataillon Ceccopieri	1 battalion
Sechspfündige Fussbatterie Nr. 13	6 guns

26 Ferdinand Serbelloni *Duca* von St. Gabrio (1788-1858) was nominally appointed commander of the reserve corps, but his name is not mentioned again in this account. He formally retired from the army on 1 April 1849. It is possible that he left the field earlier in the campaign and therefore played no active part in it. *BLKÖ*, Vol.34, p.135.

27 Edmund *Fürst* Schwarzenberg (1803-1873) commanded a brigade with distinction in Radetzky's campaign in Italy in 1848 and was promoted to *Feldmarschall Lieutenant* and given a division in the Armee-Reservekorps. In the reorganisation after the battle of Kápolna, he was to take over command of III. Armeekorps, but had to leave the campaign because of illness. He served again in the Italian War of 1859. *BLKÖ*, Vol.33, pp.36-39.

Divisions-Reserveartillerie

Raketenbatterie Nr. 23	6 launch stands
Zwölfpfündige Fussbatterie Nr. 5	6 guns

Division *Generalmajor Fürst* Franz Liechtenstein[28]

Brigade *Generalmajor* von Parrot

Civallart Uhlanen	4 squadrons
Kress Chevauxlegers	5 squadrons
Ficquelmont Dragoner	4 squadrons
Sechspfündige Kavalleriebatterie Nr. 3	6 guns

Brigade *Generalmajor Graf* Bellegarde

Karl Auersperg Kürassiere	6 squadrons
Max Auersperg Kürassiere	6 squadrons
Sechspfündige Kavalleriebatterie Nr. 4	6 guns

Divisions-Reserveartillerie

Raketenbatterie Nr. 13	6 launch stands
Unterstützungs-Munizions-Reserve	

Artillerie-Hauptreserve

Zwölfpfündige Fussbatterie Nr. 6, 7 and 8	18 guns
Sechspfündige Kavalleriebatterie Nr. 5, 6, 7 and 8	24 guns
Raketenbatterie Nr. 15, 16, 17 and 18	24 launch stands
Munizions-Hauptreserve	
Sappers	1 company
Pioneers	4 companies

Strength of the Armee-Reservekorps:
Eight battalions, one sapper company, four pioneer companies, 25 squadrons, 108 artillery pieces and eight bridging trains.

28 Franz de Paula Joachim *Fürst* Liechtenstein (1802-87) served as a brigade commander in the campaign in Italy in 1848. Promoted to *Feldmarschall Lieutenant* for the Winter Campaign, he successively commanded a cavalry division, an infantry division and then IV. Armeekorps. Evidently an effective commander, he played a particularly decisive role in the last major battle at Temesvár, marching his troops rapidly enough to arrive at the crucial moment. *BLKÖ*, Vol.15, pp. 143-146.

Summary

	Battalions	Companies	Squadrons	Artillery pieces	Bridging trains
I Armeekorps:	14	6	20	54	1
II Armeekorps:	15	4	7	54	1
Reserve-Armeekorps:	8	5	25	108	8
Total:	37	15	52	216	10

The number of men fit for duty is given in the strength and duty tables for December 1848 as 36,911 infantry and 6,202 cavalry, plus another 802 men in the corps of sappers and pioneers. However, this was soon significantly reduced by the severe sickness rate, establishment of field hospitals, medical detachments, courier detachments, etc.
In addition, the following troops were available for the offensive operations:

1. The units deployed at Göding [Hodonín, Czech republic] on the River March [Morava] since the beginning of November under the orders of *Feldmarschall Lieutenant* Simunich:[29] five infantry battalions, two cavalry squadrons and 12 guns, whose combat strength came to 4,273 infantry and 223 cavalry.

2. Those under *Oberstlieutenant* Frischeisen at Teschen [Český Těšín, Czech Republic]: four infantry companies, a half-squadron and half a rocket battery, or about 800 infantry and 60 horse altogether. Finally,

3. *Feldmarschall Lieutenant Graf* Schlick's division that was concentrating around Dukla in Galicia, comprising eight infantry battalions, six squadrons and 27 guns, whose combat strength was given as 7,134 infantry and 751 cavalry.[30]

The total strength of the combat forces available at the start of offensive operations accordingly came to 49,118 infantry, 7,236 cavalry and 258 guns, of which the main body of 43,915 men was at Wien under direct command of *Feldmarschall Lieutenant Fürst* Windisch-Grätz, as stated,

29 Balthasar *Freiherr* Simunich (1785-1861) served in many campaigns and actions during the Napoleonic Wars. He fought through the Winter Campaign of 1848-49 but was unexpectedly relieved of command in May 1849 and sent back to Vienna. He subsequently wrote a memoir critical of *Feldzeugmeister* Welden. In November 1849 he was appointed fortress commander in Komorn where he apparently rendered good and humane service to the city's unfortunate inhabitants. *BLKÖ*, Vol.34, pp.346-350.

30 Franz Heinrich (II) *Graf* Schlik (1789-1862) served in the Napoleonic Wars but resigned from the army during the period when Austria was a French ally, rejoining to fight at Dresden and Leipzig, where he lost his right eye to a Russian Cossack's carelessness. A charismatic commander, he fought all through the 1848-1849 war, making particularly important contributions at Kápolna and at the first battle of Komorn in April 1849. *BLKÖ*, Vol.30, pp.116-124.

with two secondary columns each about 5,000-6,000 strong at Göding and Dukla, and a weak detachment of 800-900 men at Teschen.

In addition, the 5,442 infantry and 973 cavalry under *Feldzeugmeister Graf* Nugent[31] deployed in the Mur-Insel [the 'Mur island', the area between the River Mur and the River Drava] to cover the Croatian and Styrian borders could also be counted on to come into action quickly, insofar as the larger rebel detachments facing those troops would be threatened and forced to retreat the moment the Army of the Danube first advanced; Nugent could thereby gain a degree of freedom for his own manoeuvres.

The remaining troops spread around the provinces could not be relied on to participate directly and effectively, or at most only in a very limited way. Their presence was of use only insofar as the enemy might find himself obliged to leave equivalent forces deployed against them. So, for example, the 7,000-8,000 men under *Feldmarschall Lieutenant Baron* Puchner in Siebenbürgen [the province of Transylvania, then part of the Austrian Empire, now in Romania] had quite enough to do just suppressing the revolutionary party in their own area.[32]

While the units in the Banat, Slavonia and Croatia certainly looked numerous enough from their strength and ration returns, they consisted for the most part of completely raw recruits – not fully armed or equipped – who were scarcely fit to guard the frontier against the Magyars' incursions, and would not be ready to go on campaign until all their many deficiencies had been made good in a few months' time. Apart from a couple of battalions, every battle-ready unit in these territories had already been sent to Italy, while the *Banus* had taken any others that were half-serviceable with him on his march on Ofen.

After deducting the combat forces assigned to *Feldmarschall Lieutenant Graf* Schlick, *Feldmarschall Lieutenant Baron* Hammerstein's dispersed forces in Galicia were scarcely sufficient to keep the major cities of Lemberg [Lviv, Ukraine] and Krakau [Kraków, Poland] under control, to maintain order in the province, and to dispatch small mobile columns to the Bukowina and to the Transylvanian border.

After the occupation of Wien, the state of the units designated for the offensive operations against Hungary was anything but ready for action. On the contrary, they were lacking in almost everything, and the *Feldmarschall* first had to fashion them into his army, so to speak. First and foremost, the *Banus*'s corps demanded the most urgent attention. Anyone who saw his troops arrive outside Wien on 10 October had to admit that they lacked everything save loyalty and devotion to the throne and Fatherland. The units led from Bohemia to Wien by the *Feldmarschall* himself, who had had to set off from their garrisons 24 hours after receiving their marching orders, could not be regarded as equipped for campaigning either. Even the barely

31 Laval *Graf* Nugent-Westmeath (1777-1862). The Irish-born son of *Graf* Michael Anton, Nugent joined the army in 1793, serving and fighting mostly in Italy and Croatia. A dedicated soldier who 'tested his courage on more than a hundred battlefields', during the 1848-49 war he operated mostly on the southern front but toward the end of the war took over the siege corps outside Komorn. He subsequently attended the 1859 campaign in Italy as a volunteer. *BLKÖ*, Vol.20, pp.430-434.

32 Anton *Freiherr* von Puchner (1779-1852) served in the Napoleonic Wars. Subsequently, as commander of the Austrian forces in the Papal States in Bologna, he displayed diplomatic talents which later proved very valuable when he was posted as governor of Transylvania, with its Romanian, Magyar, and German populations. After his defeat by Bem in the difficult Transylvanian campaign of 1848-1849 he was made governor of Venice. *BLKÖ*, Vol.24, pp.49-52.

5,000-strong former garrison of Wien had lost almost all of their campaign equipment during the October uprising.

A thorough and organised mobilisation of the army could not be embarked upon until toward mid-November when the *Feldmarschall* had staffed his headquarters and surrounded himself with all the necessary agencies to have his intentions implemented swiftly without disruption. Every effort was made to establish field hospitals, herds for slaughter, and provisions of bread and forage. Because of the desperate need to clothe the 10,000-12,000 *grenzers* belonging to the *Banus*'s corps, the German infantry regiments had to give up their spare uniforms, while greatcoats and boots were sought from elsewhere. The best 12,000 of the muskets rounded up during the disarmament of Wien were picked out and used to arm the *grenzers*.

The *Banus*'s artillery that mostly consisted of 3-pounders with meagre ammunition supplies and drawn by weak farm horses underwent a total reorganisation from the ground up. The small-calibre weapons were exchanged for 6-pounders, and a proportionate number of foot and horse artillery batteries were established. In general, equipping the artillery with horses, crews and ammunition was what demanded the most attention. So far as possible, the deficiency in gunners was sought to be made good with suitable men from the infantry who had previously received the necessary practical instruction in serving the guns and were now practised further. Over 6,000 horses were required to complete the limber teams alone and had to be hastily purchased. The driver teams were also made up of recruits, so the training of both men and horses to serve the guns had to go on at the same time. Provision of campaign scales of artillery ammunition and cartridges was extraordinarily time-consuming, because after the immense ammunition expenditure outside Wien and some at Schwechat, almost the entire requirement had to be manufactured anew.

But it was not only the Army of the Danube's requirements that had to be considered, since the units in Croatia, Slavonia, the Banat and Transylvania also turned to the *Feldmarschall* with no less urgent requests for everything necessary for their mobilisation. Weapons and every item of equipment in general had to be found to establish a Slovakian *Freikorps*[33] under commanders such as Hurban, Stur and Janitschek among others, which was to be attached to *Feldmarschall Lieutenant* Simunich's force for the invasion of Hungary.[34]

Given that the army had such extensive needs for equipment to be fit to campaign, it is easy to understand that innumerable problems and delays arose. Everything at all that could be mustered in the way of replacements, reinforcements and war materiel of every kind had already been sent to Italy during the course of the summer, shortly before the October revolution, so as to provide the maximum possible support to our forces that were fighting there for Austria's rights and for the glory of our army. However, this considerably increased the military high command's difficulties, even though all its establishments were activated.

33 A *Freikorps* ('Free Corps') being an irregular volunteer formation.

34 Jozef Miloslav Hurban (1817-88) and L'udovit Štúr (1815-56) were anti-Magyar Slovak nationalists who advocated the separation of Slovak lands from the Kingdom of Hungary; B. Janeček was a Czech they brought in as a military commander. See Daniel Rapant, 'Slovak Politics in 1848-1849', *Slavonic and East European Review*, Vol.27, No.68 (1948), pp.67-90; Daniel Rapant, 'Slovak Politics in 1848: Part II', *Slavonic and East European Review*, Vol.27, No.69 (1949), pp.381-403; and Albert Pražák, 'Czechs and Slovaks in the Revolution of 1848', *Slavonic Review*, Vol.5, No.15 (1927), pp.565-579.

Preliminary Moves, 10 November to Early December1848

Whilst the most strenuous possible efforts were being made to get the army ready to campaign, part of I. Armeekorps and Kavallerie-Division Liechtenstein were pushed forward to the Leitha to guard the Hungarian border, and two brigades of II. Armeekorps, namely Wyss's and Jablonowsky's, were deployed at the most important crossings of the March [Morava river] – the former at Angern an der March, the latter at Schlosshof and Marcheck [Marchegg, Austria]. *Oberst Baron* Horvath was likewise detached with eight companies and two squadrons to protect the artillery depot at the Steinfeld in Wiener Neustadt, and he pushed his outposts forward as far as the Oedenburger Strasse and the Leitha that constituted the border there. In the course of November numerous skirmishes had taken place between all these troops spread along the frontier and the rebel outposts facing them.

At the *Feldmarschall*'s request, on 10 November *Feldmarschall Lieutenant* Simunich had moved from Göding to Szenicz [Senica, Slovakia] and Jablonicz [Jablonica, Slovakia] again, at the foot of the White Carpathians, and numerous small actions likewise arose against the rebel outposts entrenched in their position on the mountain ridge.

Throughout the whole of November the rebels displayed great energy in amassing war *matériel* and expanding their so-called 'Upper Danubian Army' at Pressburg [Bratislava, Slovakia]. Every preparation had been made for stubborn resistance at Pressburg, the nearby heights crowned with redoubts, abattis felled,[35] the bridgehead enlarged, a steamboat armed and held ready to command the Danube, etc.[36] Likewise at Raab [Györ, Hungary] and Ofen-Pesth extensive earthworks had been under construction for months, and an entrenched camp had been prepared at Komorn [Komárno, Slovakia and Komárom, Hungary].[37]

35 Abattis are a type of improvised fortification 'made with middling sized trees, or with heavy limbs full of branches, having all the slender boughs cut off, and the branches sharpened. The trees or limbs thus prepared, are laid side by side with their boughs and branches interwoven, and their sharpened points towards the enemy. To render the whole more solid and prevent the enemy from removing them, the trunks of the trees and limbs are pinned to the earth by crochet pickets driven very deep. To attack such abattis, is a difficult operation, requiring cannon to ruin and cut openings through them.' Simon François Baron Gay de Vernon, *A Treatise on the Science of War and Fortification* (New York: J. Seymour, 1817), p.292.

36 This was the *Mészáros*, which was subsequently captured by the Austrians and renamed the *Schlick*. Originally launched in 1841 as the *Franz I*, it was bought from the Danube Steamship Company by the Hungarian government in 1848, converted into a warship, and armed with eight 6-pounder guns, two 12-pounder guns and two 7-pounder howitzers. In addition to the ship's crew of 26, there were 34 gunners and 44 marines aboard. 'A Franz I: a császári-királyi szabadalmazott első dunagőzhajózási társaság első hajója', *SRY Modell* (2004).

37 Komorn was an important fortress at the junction of the Danube and the Waag, northwest of Budapest, and played a vital role in the war. After finding refuge from Napoleon there in 1809, *Kaiser* Franz I had decided to build Komorn up into the largest and strongest fortress in Europe. This work was not yet complete when the 1848 war broke out. The main fortification was a walled city in the angle of the two rivers (modern-day Komárno in Slovakia). It had a small bridgehead across the Waag to the east, and a larger one south of the Danube protected by a substantial partially built star fort, which the Hungarians reinforced with a chain of ten earthworks to create their entrenched camp around what is now Komárom in Hungary. Three major battles would be fought in front of the entrenched camp during the Summer Campaign in April and July 1849. *Monostori Erőd Komárom: az erődrendszer története [Monostor Fort, Komárom: The History of the Fortification System.*

Anyone who tried to transport foodstuffs out of Hungary to Austria was threatened with summary punishment, while all supplies near the border were taken away to the interior of the country and largely used to provision the fortresses. The border was finally completely closed on 24 November. There was no longer any traffic between Hungary and Austria. This closing of the border seriously impeded the obtaining of reliable intelligence. Given the general agitated mood in Hungary and the open aversion to anything German, and the regime of terror generated there by the agents of the revolutionary government, it was doubly difficult to find suitable people to provide basic information. It therefore also followed that information about the strength and distribution of the rebel forces, about the mood of the former imperial regiments, and about the defensive measures being taken was generally very incomplete and mostly contradictory, even though no expense or effort was spared to discover reliable information about these.

Already on 17 October the *Feldmarschall* had issued a call to *Feldmarschall Lieutenant* Moga, who commanded the rebel forces concentrated at Pressburg since the battle of Schwechat, as well as to all the former imperial generals, staff and field officers in Hungary, in which he ordered them to place themselves and their troops under his command without delay. This call was repeated on 12 November, and the period for their voluntary return to the imperial colours was extended to 26 November. After the expiry of this deadline, any such would be regarded as traitors and rebels and treated according to the full rigor of military law.

This summons did not have the hoped-for effect, any more than did the proclamations issued by His Majesty the *Kaiser* from Olmütz [Olomouc, Czech Republic]; for the leaders of the revolution, particularly Kossuth who at that very time was right with the Upper Danubian Army at Pressburg, made every effort by falsely representing the situation with misleading lessons and conclusions to reinforce the troops' illusions that they were on a legitimate course, and that they were bound by their oaths, honour and duty to defend the threatened Hungarian constitution. Where this heresy met with little approval, either terror or money, prospects of promotion, and suchlike methods of seduction were used to influence them.

In the first third of December 1848, scarcely six weeks after the revolt of Wien was quelled, the equipping of the army for campaign had at least reached the point where the *Feldmarschall* could issue orders to prepare to march and could set the date on which offensive operations against Hungary were to begin. There were still a few things, though not many, that were necessary for the complete mobilisation of the army and for its satisfactory supply and that despite every effort could still not be obtained and had to be sent on to the troops afterwards. For example, the army was endowed with a support ammunition reserve, but not with an actual main ammunition reserve;[38] the regimental transport only had some of its horse teams in harness, the bridging trains none at all; most of the units required draft horses to move their cooking utensils; the transport detachments so necessary for securing and organising rations had still not yet been set up, etc.

38 Munizions-Unterstützungs-Reserve: a quarter to a third of the reserve ammunition wagons. Munizions-Haupt-Reserve: two thirds to three quarters of the reserve ammunition wagons. Joseph *Freiherr* von Smola, *Handbuch für k.k. österreichische Artillerie-Offiziere* (Vienna: Fr. Beck'schen Universitäts-Buchhandlung, 1839), pp.219-221. Thus, the assertion here is that the army lacked two thirds of its reserve ammunition wagons. We shall see problems of ammunition replenishment causing delays on 1 March 1849 during the pursuit after Kápolna.

Regardless, the *Feldmarschall* decided not to delay the start of the operation a moment longer; for each day it was deferred just brought the rebels' defensive measures closer to completion, which they were driving forward with unprecedented energy and activity, and would have made this task even more difficult to resolve when it was already difficult enough, being undertaken with insufficient forces.[39]

The Plan of Operations

The plan of operations the *Feldmarschall* envisaged was briefly as follows. The decisive action of the campaign must necessarily be carried out by the army concentrated at Wien; this must consequently stay united as long as possible.

For now, there could be little expectation of any significant contribution from the weak detached flanking contingents forcing their way into Hungary from more or less distant points; at least, not until these had managed to combine into larger formations. Besides, these flanking contingents' offensive manoeuvres absolutely had to set out from wherever they found themselves concentrated at the start of operations, unless one was willing to dispense with any help from them entirely. For example, the troops concentrated at Dukla under *Feldmarschall Lieutenant Graf* Schlick could only advance along the Kaschau [Košice, Slovakia] highway, because they thereby covered the approach route from Hungary to Galicia, so that this stretch of territory that was seriously threatened and yet totally denuded of troops when they marched away would benefit indirectly. Likewise, to avoid exposing the Styrian and Croatian borders, *Feldzeugmeister Graf* Nugent's advance could only happen from the Mur-Insel.

The extensive defensive measures that the rebels had taken at Pressburg, Raab, Komorn and Ofen-Pesth justified the assumption that, before the army entered the Hungarian capital, there would have to be a battle at one of these places that would decide the fate of the country. Such a collision was very much to be desired. The enemy's numerical superiority was outweighed many times over by the splendid spirit of the imperial army,[40] and given the lack of discipline that prevailed in the rebel ranks, they could hardly be expected to hold together and fight on after losing a battle.

The offensive operations of the army concentrated at Wien were to start with an attack on the entrenched position outside Pressburg, but after that was taken, all the troops were to move across to the right bank of the Danube, so as to continue their advance upon Raab and Ofen united on that side of the river. So long as the army was obliged to advance along a single road, as for example between Pressburg and Raab, the corps were to follow one another echeloned

39 It is hard to disagree with this assessment. Any delay would not only give the revolutionary cause time to strengthen itself militarily, it would also let it entrench its political control, perhaps even obtain recognition from other Great Powers. The situation is analogous in that respect to the secession of the Confederacy from the United States of America. Had that rebellion not been opposed militarily immediately, the economic interests of other powers might eventually have led to the breach becoming permanent. The analogy continues to hold militarily to some degree as well, Windisch-Grätz playing the part of McClellan in terms of excessive ponderous caution, facing an army imbued with zeal and mercurial leadership that inflicted some surprising reverses on its opponent and his successors, but was ultimately crushed by superior numbers and industrial power.

40 A proud assertion which Nobili himself frequently contradicts later on in this work, when Hungarian superior numbers are offered as a reason for caution or failure.

at intervals of a day's march at most. Separation by greater intervals, or having individual detachments rush on ahead, was absolutely to be avoided, for that would have exposed them to the risk of being attacked and defeated in detail. However, in view of the supply difficulties and the late season of the year, meaning the troops could not be bivouacked without suffering badly, remaining together in anything larger than corps formation was unfeasible.

From Raab, which constituted the next operational objective after Pressburg and where stubborn resistance had to be expected given the rebels' large-scale prepared defences, the army was to advance toward Ofen by the most direct route, the so-called 'Fleischhacker-Strasse',[41] rather than along the usual post road. Whether a detachment was to operate on the right along the Stuhlweissenburg [Székesfehérvár, Hungary] road was left to be decided according to the situation, but thought was already given to this in establishing the order of battle; for I. Armeekorps, which would be given this task if it arose and which in any case would always form the right wing of the army, was allocated 20 cavalry squadrons, while II. Armeekorps, which was designated constantly to operate together with the Reservekorps and its numerous cavalry, only had seven. Komorn was to be summoned to surrender, and if the summons was rejected, it was to be lightly cordoned off. Halting before Komorn was only to be contemplated if the rebels had occupied the entrenched camp there with their whole force.

Simunich's division that was in the immediate strategic vicinity of the army at Jablonicz was to advance over the White Carpathians, thereby outflanking the enemy position at Pressburg, then move to the Waag [Váh or Vág] river, aiming primarily to hold that line and to take the small fortress of Leopoldstadt [Leopoldov, Slovakia], which it was hoped could be achieved within a few days by means of field artillery. This division's subsequent mission, and that of the small column under *Oberstlieutenant* Frischeisen advancing from Teschen via Jablunka [Jablunkov, Czech Republic] and Silein [Žilina, Slovakia], as well as liberating the Slovak population from Magyar pressure and demands that they revolt, was to advance through the Bergstädte [the so-called 'Mining Towns'] into Upper Hungary and establish communications with *Feldmarschall Lieutenant Graf* Schlick's division invading from Dukla through Kaschau.[42] With these two divisions, the latter of which was supposed to number 14,000-15,000 men but was reduced to half that size at the last minute, it was hoped that Upper Hungary could be conquered. This was the foremost objective to aim for after the occupation of Ofen-Pesth and seemed all the more achievable as the rebels had only deployed small forces in that extensive stretch of territory, and the better-disposed, mostly Slovak populace could easily be brought under control and indeed induced to rise up against the Magyar subversion.[43]

Feldmarschall Lieutenant Graf Schlick's division was above all to try to reach Kaschau as soon as was feasible, since possession of this town was of great importance for the subjugation

41 Literally 'Butcher's Road', the road from Raab to Ofen via Nagyigmánd and Bicske.

42 A *Bergstadt* is a mountain town with special mining privileges. There were two major clusters of these in Upper Hungary (now in Slovakia). The oldest group is further east in Zips County. The western group is centred on Schemnitz [Banská Štiavnica, Slovakia] and includes Kremnitz [Kremnica, Slovakia], Neusohl [Banská Bystrica, Slovakia], Dilin [Banská Belá, Slovakia], Königsberg [Nová Baňa, Slovakia] and Altsohl [Zvolen, Slovakia], among others. Gold, silver, and copper were their most important products.

43 The original text says *Schilderhebung* ('raising up [on] a shield'), a term originally used in the sense of coronation to refer to the elevation of the kings of the Goths and the Merovingians. In the 19th century it also came to mean an uprising.

of Upper Hungary as well as to protect Galicia.[44] Nobody was under any illusions about the practicality of trying to direct this division with detailed orders, for it was clear that even after the army's entry into Ofen, any orders sent to Schlick could only be transmitted via Wien, Olmütz, Dukla, etc., a detour of over 800 km, so they could not conceivably arrive in good time. Besides, it could not be foreseen what obstacles the division might encounter. Its advance could easily be held up not only by the enemy combat forces opposing it, but also by impassable roads; a factor which at that late season of the year, particularly in a mountainous region, could not be left out of consideration.

Consequently the instructions given to Schlick were limited to designating the road through Losoncz [Lučenec, Slovakia] to Waitzen [Vác, Hungary] as the most suitable one for continuing his advance after the occupation of Kaschau, because it led through territory inhabited by Slovaks, and it was the fastest route by which a junction could be effected with the detachments advancing from Hungary's western border toward Neutra [Nitra, Slovakia] and the Mining Towns. It was suggested to him that in the event that this mountain route should be made impracticable by snow, particularly the passage over the Agtelek [Aggtelek, Hungary], he should take the better road through Miskolcz [Miskolc, Hungary] to Pesth that was usable at any time of year.

Notification concerning the imminent opening of offensive operations was sent to the commanders of the forces in the other provinces bordering Hungary, as well as to the general in command in Transylvania, *Feldmarschall Lieutenant Baron* Puchner. The latter was in the Klausenburg [Cluj, Romania] area at the time, and in the event that the rebels should concentrate all their forces to oppose the progress of the Army of the Danube, he could advance on Grosswardein. However, given the bad popular mood that prevailed in Transylvania and that could only be suppressed by military force, this was hardly to be counted on; still less any decisive concerted intervention by him in the course of operations, since all the orders, instructions etc., to this remote formation could only reach their destination via Wien, Gratz [Graz, Austria], Agram [Zagreb, Croatia], Semlin [Zemun, Serbia], thus by a detour of more than 1,100 km. The same was also true of the weak detachments in the Banat, Slavonia, and Croatia, which for the time being had enough to do just guarding the border and their own homes.

Feldzeugmeister Graf Nugent, who had 5,000-6,000 men in the Mur-Insel, was likewise notified of the Army of the Danube's advance, and was asked to indicate in due course whether he was going to advance on the northern or southern shore of the Plattensee [Lake Balaton, Hungary], since this depended on the direction of retreat of the enemy detachments opposing him, the mood of the local people, the state of the roads and other factors that could not be anticipated.

Finally, all the commanders were instructed that as they advanced into Hungary, they should dismiss the officials installed by the revolutionary party, replace them with loyally minded men who enjoyed the confidence of the public, explain the true state of affairs to the people by distributing proclamations, and assure them of protection and safety for persons and property; in short, to effect the pacification and reorganisation of the country in every way; for the security

44 As we shall see later on, Windisch-Grätz and his subordinates may actually have attached too much importance to Kaschau, at the expense of concentrating maximum strength to destroy the enemy's field forces. While Kaschau was one of the two major population centres and crossroads in eastern Slovakia (the other being Eperies), its value in military terms was negligible.

of the army's rear communications, as well as its ability to feed itself, primarily depended on this.

This was essentially the plan the *Feldmarschall* established at the start of the campaign; and which, despite some expectations and assumptions not being met, and some intentions being thwarted by chance events or unexpected enemy moves, he consistently followed. For the time being no decision was made as to what should be done after the army had entered the Hungarian capital, since this depended on too many unforeseeable factors, and moreover the fairly general opinion was that at that point the campaign would be over.[45]

A particular factor that essentially hindered any exhaustive operational design was the fact that, as stated above, no information was available about the strength and dispositions of the rebel forces, or at least none that was very reliable. In any war with a foreign foe one has a certain degree of knowledge about his army's structure and distribution, the names of his generals and regiments, where his magazines are stored, etc., and can therefore reach conclusions with reasonable certainty about his strength, positions, organisation into corps, divisions and brigades, etc. But here such reference points were entirely lacking. It was known that the whole country constituted one great field camp, so to speak, in which on all sides recruits were being conscripted, battalions established, horses requisitioned, and items of equipment manufactured; but nothing was known about where these scattered combat forces were concentrating, who would command them, or how far they had got with arming themselves in general; for long before the October days[46] the Hungarian war ministry had made itself so independent that it took charge over the troops that were in the country quite without constraint, and later on it was extremely difficult to learn any details about them. So for example the first credible data about the strength and composition of the rebel combat forces at Pressburg, that is in the immediate vicinity [of the imperial army], were obtained from *Oberlieutenant* Orosz of the Alexander Hussars, who found a way to get from Pressburg to Wien by a roundabout route and reported to *Feldmarschall Fürst* Windisch-Grätz on 3 December, shortly before operations began.

According to this officer's testimony, *Feldmarschall Lieutenant* Moga had become unfit for duty after falling from his horse during the battle of Schwechat, and command of the Upper Danubian Army had passed to Artúr Görgei.[47] This force allegedly comprised eight brigades at the time, of which one was deployed at Nadas [Trstín, Slovakia] facing *Feldmarschall Lieutenant* Simunich, two brigades were in Pressburg, and the other five on the right bank of the Danube between Kittsee and Lake Neusiedl. The strength of these brigades reportedly averaged

45 The plan consists essentially of a march on Budapest while expecting and hoping for a 'collision' before reaching the capital. As the *Feldmarschall* subsequently realised, the enemy army made a better objective for his manoeuvres than the mere occupation of cities. Had he known that from the start, he might have operated differently against Görgei's Upper Danubian Army in the opening phases of the campaign. However, in such a war the political effects of symbolic actions such as capturing capital cities are imponderable, so Windisch-Grätz and his master might be forgiven for miscalculating in this case.

46 i.e., the time when open conflict began.

47 Artúr Görgei (alt. sp. Görgey) (1818-1916). A former lieutenant in the imperial army, during the 1848-49 war he progressed from *honvéd* captain to general, commander-in-chief, minister of war and ultimately, on 11 August 1849, dictator. Two days later he agreed to the final unconditional surrender at Világos [Şiria, Romania]. After the war he was interned in Klagenfurt, returning to Hungary in 1867. He remains a controversial figure. See Bona, *Tábornokok.*

3,000-4,000 men, their total strength being 28,000 men with 70-80 guns. Apart from these there were significant formations in Raab, Komorn and Ofen.

The dispositions for the attack on Pressburg were based on the data above, and 16 December was set as the date for the advance. The guiding idea was the following:

Simunich's division was to go over on the offensive, reinforced by:

2. Bataillon Ceccopieri-Infanterie
2. Companie, 12. Jäger-Bataillon
Two companies Landwehr Hess Infanterie
Two squadrons Kress Chevauxlegers
One rocket battery.

On the 14th, two days ahead of the attack on Pressburg, this division was to drive the enemy facing it out of their position, cross the White Carpathians, advance on Nadas and then seek to establish communications via Modern [Modra, Slovakia] with II. Armeekorps advancing meanwhile from Angern toward Pressburg. This diversion directly preceding the army's advance was intended to attract the enemy's attention away from Pressburg and to encourage him to detach forces against it.

Out of the army under the *Feldmarschall*'s direct command outside Wien, three brigades (13,000 men) from II. Armeekorps were to move along the left bank of the Danube as far as the March, to take position at Angern and Marcheck, to act purely defensively on the 16th or at most to push a detachment forward to Malaczka [Malacky, Slovakia], but to go over onto the attack on the 17th, possibly after receiving reinforcement.

However, the remaining ten brigades of the army (31,000 men) were to advance on the 16th through Prellenkirchen and Bruck an der Leitha on a reconnaissance along the right bank of the Danube, and possibly to convert that into an actual attack to break through the centre of the enemy's extended position, which reportedly stretched from Kittsee to Lake Neusiedl, and then to pursue the enemy vigorously.

Because of the defensive posture already noted of the weaker formation deployed on the left bank of the Danube while the main body launched its powerful offensive on the right bank, in the event that the enemy had suddenly changed his position and moved his main body to the left bank to defend Pressburg, the imperial army would be in a position to appear there as well on the next day in superior force; for a pontoon bridge thrown across the Danube at Bad Deutsch-Altenburg provided the means to project the necessary reinforcements quickly across to the far bank.[48]

48 The *Feldmarschall* had learned that the enemy army at Pressburg was 28,000 strong. He had over 40,000, not including Simunich's division, and Nobili has told us that the imperial army's splendid spirit made it worth far more than equivalent numbers of rebels. Given these factors, and what Nobili has said about the need to have a winter campaign in the first place so as to quell the revolution before it gets any stronger, the *Feldmarschall*'s plan seems tentative. Speed rather than subtlety was of the essence, so it might be suggested that a two-day delay for a diversionary attack by Simunich was an unnecessary luxury; that, instead, the *Feldmarschall* should have committed right away to smashing through the enemy line between Kittsee and Lake Neusiedl; and also, that the force from II. Armeekorps at Angern was too far from the action and covering against an imaginary threat.

Finally, the detachment under *Oberst* Horvath in Wiener Neustadt was to advance toward Oedėnburg [Sopron, Hungary] on the 15th, and from there to patrol along Lake Neusiedl toward Golss [Gols, Austria] according to the situation, to re-establish communications with the column advancing through Bruck on the 16th.

The Advance on Pressburg, 16-23 December 1848

On 15 December the units of the Army of the Danube were distributed as follows:

On the left bank of the Danube, under *Feldmarschall Lieutenant Graf* Wrbna:
Division Csorich (Brigades Wyss and Jablonowsky) at Angern;
Brigade Colloredo at Marcheck.

On the right bank of the Danube:

Brigade Lederer by the pontoon bridge at Deutsch-Altenburg;
Brigade Neustädter at Haimburg [Hainburg an der Donau, Austria] and Wolfsthal;
Brigades Ottinger and Gramont at Prellenkirchen;
Division Hartlieb (Brigades Kriegern and Karger) at Bruck an der Leitha;
Franz Liechtenstein's Kavallerie-Reserve-Division (Brigades Bellegarde and Parrot) with two horse artillery batteries from the Artillerie-Hauptreserve behind Bruck an der Leitha;
Edmund Schwarzenberg's Infanterie Reserve-Division (Brigades Schütte and Liebler) with the Artillerie-Hauptreserve behind Prellenkirchen.

Four 12-pounders were brought up to a suitable position to cover the pontoon bridge.

The *Feldmarschall* had transferred his headquarters from Schönbrunn to Fischament [Fischamend, Austria] on the 14th, and to Petronell on the 15th, on which day he undertook a reconnaissance forward of Prellenkirchen.[49]

Feldmarschall Lieutenant Graf Wrbna commanding the three brigades on the left bank had already asked for reinforcements on the 15th, as he felt his force was too weak for the mission he had been given. However, in view of the orders already issued and the resulting troop distributions, this petition was without result.[50]

According to these orders, the troops concentrated on the right bank were to be set in motion at 08:00 a.m. on the 16th in three columns.

49 Fischament is 25 km from Prellenkirchen or Marcheck, which is rather too far away to command effectively during an advance. Petronell is more sensible, but Prellenkirchen itself might be even better, especially if the *Feldmarschall* was indeed anticipating having to decide whether to convert a reconnaissance in force into an outright attack.

50 This is an early intimation of Wrbna's timidity. It may be that he was justified on this occasion, but later on at Poroszló we will see him seriously culpable of exaggerating the strength of an enemy position and therefore refusing to attack it.

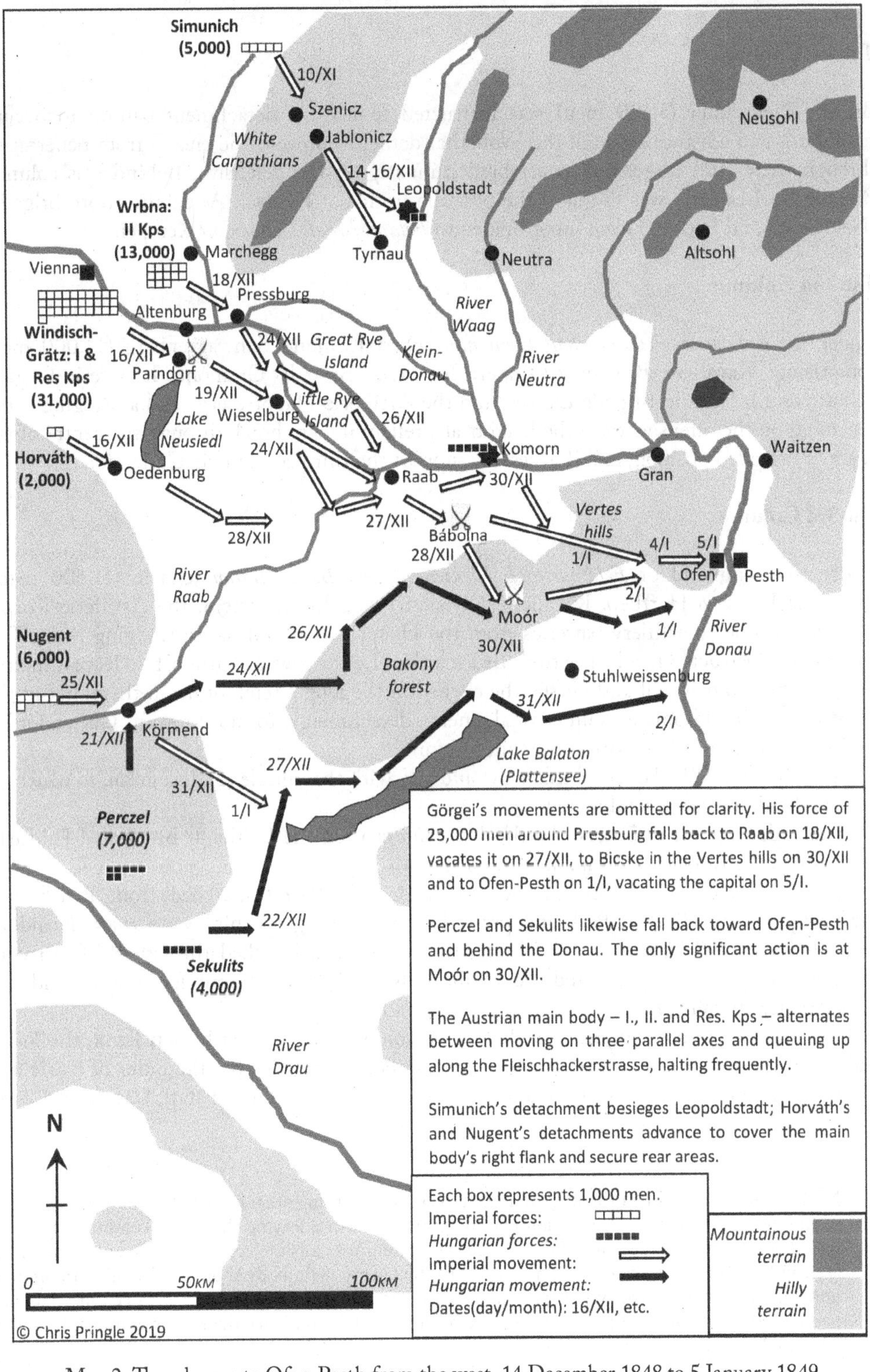

Map 2: The advance to Ofen-Pesth from the west, 14 December 1848 to 5 January 1849

The 1st Column

Brigade Neustädter (5,500 men) was instructed to leave a detachment behind to occupy Haimburg and advance through the Wolfsthal defile, to prevent the enemy from penetrating through there, and in general to act predominantly on the defensive. Behind this column, Brigade Karl Lederer was to guard the pontoon bridge at Deutsch-Altenburg. Both brigades (Neustädter and Lederer) were subordinated to *Feldmarschall Lieutenant* Kempen.

The 2nd Column

Under the orders of *Feldmarschall Lieutenant Fürst* Edmund Schwarzenberg (14,000 men) comprising: Kavallerie-Brigade Ottinger; Infanterie-Brigade Gramont, Infanterie-Brigade Schütte and Infanterie-Brigade Liebler; and the Artillerie-Hauptreserve and a bridging train, was to go on the offensive from the heights at Prellenkirchen, break through the centre of the enemy's extended position, and if necessary support the third column via Gattendorf.

The 3rd Column

Under the command of *Feldmarschall Lieutenant and Banus Baron* Jellacic (11,500 men): Infanterie-Division Hartlieb, Kavallerie-Division Franz Liechtenstein, the Artillerie-Korps-Reserve, two horse artillery batteries from the Hauptreserve and half a bridging train. This column was instructed to advance from Bruck an der Leitha toward Parndorf, to leave it mainly to the cavalry to drive off and pursue the enemy on the long stretch of heath there, but in the event that it should only encounter weak enemy detachments, to move toward Gattendorf to establish communications with the second column.[51]

The *Feldmarschall* had decided that he would stay with the middle (2nd) column, to which all reports should therefore be directed.

In accordance with its orders, the third column crossed the Leitha at Bruck and Pakfurth [Pachfurth, Austria] at 8:00 a.m. in the morning.

Infanterie-Division Hartlieb and Kavallerie-Brigade Parrot marched from Bruck over the bridge in the Harrach Park and pressed forward along the highway toward Parndorf, while *Feldmarschall Lieutenant Fürst* Franz Liechtenstein debouched through Pakfurth with Kavallerie-Brigade Bellegarde and the Artillerie-Reserve (two 12-pounder batteries and two horse artillery batteries).

To maintain communications with the second column and to cover his left flank, the *Banus* had taken the squadrons attached to his corps's infantry brigades per the order of battle and formed them into a separate brigade under the command of his chief of staff, *General* Zeisberg.

51 Notice that this column is evidently not meant to take on anything other than weak enemy detachments, while the 1st column is to act predominantly on the defensive, leaving the centre column as the only one allowed to do any serious fighting. There is no attempt at a Napoleonic-style advance on multiple axes with each corps tasked with grappling with the enemy main body should it find him, to pin him until the other columns arrive to crush him. It has more in common with the 18th century Austrian habit of advancing in multiple columns more for logistical convenience than for operational flexibility and rapid effect.

Crossing the Leitha and re-ordering the troops took some time, so it was not until 11:00 a.m. that the columns reached the gently rising high ground at Parndorf, on which the enemy had taken position.

The enemy detachments posted here (Brigades Karger,[52] Szegedy[53] and Zichy[54]) belonged to Division Schweidel.[55] Parndorf was held by one battalion of Infanterieregiment Nr. 60, two *honvéd* battalions and 12 guns, some of the latter being in a redoubt.

Under the cover of a lively artillery bombardment, Division Hartlieb was just on the point of attacking from Parndorf when the enemy began retreating in two columns through Zurndorf toward Nickelsdorf and Neusiedl. They must have feared being outflanked and cut off from their line of retreat by the rapid advance of Kavallerie-Division Franz Liechtenstein that had meanwhile recombined. Twenty dead were found in Parndorf and as many wounded, and an officer and 25 men who had been too slow to retreat from the village were taken prisoner.

During this time *Generalmajor* Zeisberg's cavalry had outflanked Neudorf on the right and advanced swiftly between there and Parndorf.

The enemy columns were now seen to be retreating at all points, yet the pursuit could not happen quickly enough because delays were caused by deep ditches that had first to be filled with fascines to enable the artillery to cross.[56]

Toward 4:00 p.m. in the afternoon *Generalmajor* Zeisberg and his cavalry reached the area of Wittmannshof and St Kaszimir [Albertkázmérpuszta, Hungary], where he encountered strong enemy columns that occupied the said villages as soon as he appeared. He could not assault the villages for lack of infantry, so he was limited to bombarding them. Besides, darkness had fallen meanwhile, preventing any further pursuit, and the enemy detachments that had deployed at St. Kaszimir, worried about being forced away from the direct road to Wieselburg [now merged with Ungarisch-Altenburg into Mosonmagyaróvár, Hungary], used the night to withdraw along a side road through Frauenkirchen and Sz. André [St. Andrä am Zicksee, Austria].

The *Banus* had meanwhile moved up to Halbthurn [Halbturn, Austria] and Nickelsdorf, where his troops spent the night. The Hungarian division commander Schweidel was facing him in Strass-Sommerein [Hegyeshalom, Hungary] with Brigade Szegedy, but withdrew early on the morning of the 17th to Ungarisch-Altenburg [now merged with Wieselburg into Mosonmagyaróvár, Hungary].

52 Ferdinand Karger (1803-?). A major in the 4th Hussars at the outbreak of war, on 30 December 1848 he reported sick and returned to his family in Grosswardein. After the war he was stripped of his rank and sentenced to three years in prison but was released by Haynau. Bona, *Tábornokok*.

53 Imre Szegedy (1812-78) was a captain in the 9th Hussars at the outbreak of war. On 24 January 1849 he left the Hungarian army and rejoined the imperials. Bona, *Tábornokok*.

54 *Gróf* Lipót Zichy (1805-69). A major in the 10th Hussars in 1848, he fought at Schwechat and then in the actions of December 1848. He distinguished himself at Parndorf, and again in the cavalry action at Tétény on 3 January 1849 but left the army the next day when the imperial army was about to enter Pesth. After the war he was stripped of his rank but later rehabilitated. Bona, *Tábornokok*.

55 József Schweidel (1796-1849) was a major in the 4th Hussars in 1848 and fought at Pákozd and Schwechat. On 19 December 1848 he went on extended sick leave, returning to duty in July as commander of the fortress of Arad. After surrendering at the end of the war he was one of the thirteen 'Martyrs of Arad' executed by order of the Austrian commander-in-chief, *Feldzeugmeister* Julius Haynau. Bona, *Tábornokok*.

56 A 'fascine' being a bundle of brushwood or similar material, useful for filling in ditches so they can be crossed during an assault.

A captured message from Schweidel to Brigades Karger and Zichy, written in Strass-Sommerein at 18:45 in the evening, shows that he had heard nothing from them. He designated Altenburg as the direction in which they should retreat, and complained about not having received any reports all day about the course of the action.

Amongst those who particularly distinguished themselves during the advance on Parndorf, the *Banus* named *Oberst Baron* Simschen of the Ficquelmont dragoons; *Major Graf* Mensdorf, *Flügeladjutant* [aide-de-camp] to His Majesty the *Kaiser*; *Hauptmann* Drechsler of the general staff; and battery commander *Oberlieutenant* Haug.

The 2nd Column moved off at almost the same time as the action around Parndorf began, from the Prellenkirchen heights toward the plain spreading out beyond. Brigade Ottinger chased the advanced hussar pickets back behind Baumern [Pama, Austria]. Since Brigade Gramont faced no strong enemy detachments, it headed straight for Potzneusiedl and from there toward Neudorf. After a brief action there against 800 enemy infantry, 400 cavalry and 12 guns, it drove them out and established communications with the *Banus*'s column. Meanwhile Brigade Schütte had moved up together with Brigade Gramont and occupied Gattendorf, which the enemy had already vacated, while Brigade Liebler remained in reserve on the heights behind.

In the attack on Neudorf, 5. Jäger-Bataillon from Brigade Gramont particularly distinguished itself, as did *Oberstlieutenant Graf* Sternberg's division of the Wallmoden cuirassiers.

The 1st Column (Brigade Neustädter) led by *Feldmarschall Lieutenant* Kempen, who sent two companies of Brigade Lederer to occupy Haimburg, had carried out its advance through the Wolfsthal unhindered, and suitably occupied the heights by the border village of Am-Berg [Berg, Austria]. According to its orders, this column was just to prevent the enemy from advancing through the Wolfsthal defile and attaining the eastern slopes of the Hundsheimer Berg [the hill north of Hundsheim, Austria]. But when the enemy soon abandoned Kittsee, threatened by the 2nd Column's advance through Baumern, and the bridgehead garrison also withdrew to the left bank of the Danube, Brigade Neustädter occupied both these places that same evening.

An attempt to destroy the floating bridge at Pressburg using boats filled with stones and left to drift with the current, and thereby to interrupt communications between the two banks, was a failure, for the boats got stuck on the bank before reaching the bridge. However, soon after vacating the bridgehead the enemy dismantled the floating bridge himself and let its component parts float away.

The Reserve-Brigade Lederer did not come into action, it just moved some distance away from the pontoon bridge at Deutsch-Altenburg (that was completely set up by 1:00 p.m.) to be closer to the Prellenkirchen plateau, so as to be available to be used there if necessary.

So as to reorganise the columns that had got somewhat disjointed during the course of the action and that were also separated by the Leitha, and to make them ready for battle for the next day, as dusk fell the *Feldmarschall* found himself obliged to direct the units to specific muster points for the night. Thus, the villages of Nickelsdorf, St. Kaszimir, Halbthurn and Frauenkirchen were designated as the forward line for the *Banus*'s columns. Brigade Ottinger was pushed forward to Jarendorf [Deutsch Jarndorf, Austria] and Karlburg [Rusovce, Slovakia]. Edmund Schwarzenberg's Infanterie-Reserve-Division occupied Jarendorf and Gattendorf, while Brigade Liebler and the Artillerie-Hauptreserve remained in Prellenkirchen. Brigade

Neustädter spent the night in Kittsee and the Pressburg bridgehead, Brigade Lederer at Deutsch-Altenburg.[57]

Late in the evening the *Feldmarschall* returned to his headquarters in Petronell,[58] from where he issued the order to Brigade Lederer to march across the bridge at Deutsch-Altenburg early next morning (the 17th) to Schlosshof, to relieve the detachments of Brigade Colloredo there, and then to rejoin II. Armeekorps to which it belonged.

The after-action reports coming in revealed that our losses on the 16th were insignificant. The enemy, however, had suffered a fair amount of damage, particularly from artillery fire.

Seven men of 5. Artillerie-Regiment who had been forcibly detained by the enemy until now reported to Brigade Gramont. They vouched that many of their comrades would do the same at the first favourable opportunity. Also, two officers of the two battalions of Infanterie-Regiment Nr. 2 stationed in Pressburg came to Petronell that evening and reported that another 25 officers of that regiment had stayed behind to await our entry into the city.

The advance of II. Armeekorps along the left bank of the Danube from the river March ensued at 4:30 a.m. next morning, the 17th, as planned. Brigade Wyss had already been pushed forward from Angern to Malaczka on the 16th and advanced to Stampfen [Stupava, Slovakia] on the 17th, to where it was closely followed by Brigade Jablonowsky and where both these two brigades of Division Csorich took position. While Brigade Jablonowsky was crossing the March at Angern, Brigade Colloredo had crossed it on a pontoon bridge constructed at Marcheck, and joined Csorich's division at Stampfen. Brigade Karl Lederer however remained halted at Schlosshof on this day to guard the crossings of the lower March. The 700-800 strong enemy detachment that had been deployed in Stampfen had already retreated to Pressburg early that morning, so there was no fighting there.

On the 18th II. Armeekorps continued its march toward Pressburg. *General* Wyss was detached to the left through Marienthal [Marianka, Slovakia] with the *jägers* and a rocket battery to occupy the forested heights that dominate the road leading to Pressburg. But the enemy had already retreated everywhere, even evacuating the city, which was therefore occupied by our troops without resistance at 3:00 p.m.

The *Feldmarschall*, who had hastened from Petronell to the left bank of the Danube via the bridge at Deutsch-Altenburg early in the morning, crossed the March on the railway bridge, followed by Brigade Lederer, and arrived in time to enter Pressburg at the head of his troops. His first concern was now to restore communications as soon as possible between the two banks of the Danube, which had been interrupted by the destruction of the bridge. To this end, *Pionnier-Oberst* Schön was ordered to dismantle the pontoon bridge at Altenburg as quickly as possible and transfer it to Pressburg next day (the 19th). *Feld-Artilleriedirektor* (Director of Field Artillery) *Generalmajor* Dietrich and *Feld-Geniedirektor* (Director of Field Engineering)

57 From Haimburg to Karlburg, from Prellenkirchen to Jarendorf, and from Bruck to Frauenkirchen etc., the imperials had advanced some 20-25 km on this day. Even allowing for the presence of the enemy and obstacles such as ditches, and for the short winter day, this is still a little on the slow side.

58 The imperial army was encamped on a 30 km front. Had the *Feldmarschall* established his headquarters at, say, Zurndorf, close to the centre of the front line, he would have been 15 km from each of his furthest wings. Petronell is twice that distance, 30 km, from Frauenkirchen. That 15 km difference is the best part of an hour added to the time taken for a mounted courier to reach the wing, slowing down the process of issuing orders and receiving reports. This is an early sign of the *Feldmarschall*'s tendency to lead from the rear.

Oberst von Trattnern were instructed to submit a report on fortifying the castle hill in Pressburg. After issuing these orders, and after receiving the city authorities and a number of officers who had remained in Pressburg – some retired, others active-duty, the latter including those of Infanterie-Regiment Nr. 2 mentioned above – the *Feldmarschall* crossed the Danube on a hastily prepared ferry and betook himself to Karlburg, to where his headquarters was also transferred.

While II. Armeekorps was advancing along the left bank of the Danube and taking possession of Pressburg, at 9 a.m. on the 18th the *Banus* carried out a reconnaissance toward Ungarisch-Altenburg and Wieselburg with six squadrons and 12 horse artillery pieces. Since both towns were still strongly held by the enemy, he bypassed them on the right. The rebels now set light to the bridge over the Leitha and two large granaries and retreated along the road toward Raab. They deployed again 2 km beyond Wieselburg with two line infantry battalions, ten hussar squadrons, two 12-pounder guns and two 6-pounder batteries in the first line. Meanwhile *Feldmarschall Lieutenant Fürst* Franz Liechtenstein had approached from Nickelsdorf with two squadrons and a horse artillery battery, whereupon after a fairly lively cannonade the enemy broke off the fight, set alight several haystacks on either side of the road, and continued his retreat toward Raab.

Our losses in this action were two men wounded and seven horses killed.

Feldmarschall Lieutenant Fürst Franz Liechtenstein praised the conduct of *Rittmeister* Göttmann of the Ficquelmont dragoons who had immediately occupied Ungarisch-Altenburg without being ordered to do so. In the evening two battalions arrived there and two squadrons were pushed forward toward Wieselburg.

On the 19th Division Hartlieb advanced to Ungarisch-Altenburg and Wieselburg together with nine squadrons and 36 guns, and the *Banus* set up his headquarters in the former place. Although the *Banus* would gladly have advanced further toward Raab from Wieselburg and asked repeatedly for permission to do so, the *Feldmarschall* held firm by his original intention not to begin advancing any further until the army was united again on the right bank of the Danube; for while it could clearly be concluded from the action at Parendorf that we were numerically superior to the enemy, he could however have been considerably reinforced in Raab and even drawn troops from nearby Komorn, and be preparing for serious resistance in the naturally favourable position at Raab which was known to have been strengthened with fieldworks.

In the situation at that time it would therefore not have been advisable to advance against the entrenched position at Raab with 18 battalions – for that is all that were available on the right bank of the Danube at the moment of the advance – for it could be hoped that within a couple of days, after the arrival of II. Armeekorps, 33 battalions could advance to the attack, and then be able to advance as far as Ofen without any further pause. The *Feldmarschall* therefore ordered the *Banus* not to advance any further for the time being and, given the winter season, to get his troops under shelter as far as possible.[59]

59 On this occasion, the *Banus* may have been right, rather than the *Feldmarschall*, as a bold advance immediately might have yielded better results than a cautious one later in greater force. As acknowledged in the modern UK principles of war, momentum matters: 'Offensive action is the practical way in which a commander seeks to gain advantage, sustain momentum and seize the initiative.' UK Ministry of Defence, *Joint Doctrine Publication 0-01: UK Defence Doctrine, 5th Edition* (London: Ministry of Defence, 2014), p.50. Giving the enemy breathing space during a pursuit is therefore to be avoided.

The short period that the *Feldmarschall* had to wait in Karlburg until completion of the bridge construction at Pressburg that was necessary before continuing the advance was used for making arrangements of many kinds. *Feldmarschall Lieutenant* Kempen was designated civil and military commandant of Pressburg. One battalion of Szluiner *grenzers* from Brigade Neustädter arrived to garrison the city, as did a battalion from the Wien garrison which *Feldmarschall Lieutenant Baron* Welden had been asked to provide until two battalions expected from Galicia via Wien could arrive. The necessary fortress artillery, ammunition, and crews to fortify the Pressburg Castle hill were requested from the Ordnance Bureau in Wien. *Major* Wurmb of the engineer corps was assigned a sapper company and tasked with overhauling the castle hill fortifications.

Since it was difficult to tell our troops apart from those regular troops fighting in the rebel ranks by their uniforms, it was ordered that the troops should provide themselves with insignia consisting of a broad wide ribbon on the shako running from each end of the peak to the cockade. Similar emblems were fastened to the grenadiers' caps and *jägers'* hats.

New, legitimate officials loyal to the throne were installed in the counties that had already been occupied, which was the only possible way to maintain order in the rear areas with relatively small forces while continuing the advance. All the towns were also ordered to disarm their inhabitants, dissolve the national guard, and the like.

Between the 19th and the 23rd the *Feldmarschall* sent reports on the progress of operations to His Majesty the *Kaiser*. In these he did not conceal the fact that appointing right-minded, influential and energetic officials was very difficult and was somewhat hindering the rapidity of operations, because avoiding dissipation of force had to remain a basic principle – yet he was firmly determined to continue the offensive as soon as a degree of order had been restored to political affairs in the occupied counties.

Simunich takes Tyrnau, 14-22 December 1848

The first news of the operations that had meanwhile been carried out by *Feldmarschall Lieutenant* Simunich's column was received from *Rittmeister Graf* Alberti of the Kress Chevauxlegers who had sped from Tyrnau [Trnava, Slovakia] via Pressburg to the headquarters at Karlburg. In accordance with the general plan, Simunich had advanced to attack the enemy position in front of him on the 14th. After reinforcements had reached him, he had divided his troops into two brigades.

Brigade Lobkowitz

1. Bataillon Hartmann
1. Landwehr Bataillon Nugent
3. Bataillon Haynau
Two companies of 12. Jäger-Bataillon
Two squadrons of Kress Chevauxlegers (2. Major's Division)
Two squadrons of E.H. Karl Chevauxlegers (1. Major's Division)

If Görgei had turned on the *Banus*, or made a serious stand around Raab, well, then the *Feldmarschall* might have got the 'collision' he sought, especially if his other corps had been equally boldly handled.

Fussbatterie Nr. 15
Raketenbatterie Nr. 14
Altogether: three and a third battalions, four squadrons, 12 artillery pieces.

Brigade Sossay

1. Landwehr Bataillon E.H. Wilhelm
3. Bataillon Hohenegg
2. Bataillon Ceccopieri
2 companies of Landwehr, Hess
Fussbatterie Nr. 16
Altogether, three and a third battalions, six guns.

In total these came to six and two thirds battalions, four squadrons and 18 artillery pieces.

Not counting the national guard or militia, the enemy combat forces facing him at the time came to not many more than 3,000 men with eight to 12 guns, namely:

One battalion of Infanterie-Regiment Nr. 34
One battalion of Infanterie-Regiment Nr. 48
1. Honvéd-Bataillon
2. Pesth Bataillon
3. Pesth Bataillon
One division of Husaren-Regiment Nr. 6.

The advance ensued at 7 a.m. on the 14th in three columns, of which the central one advanced on the highway leading from Jablonicz to Nadas, the right-wing column through Bixard [Buková, Slovakia] toward the enemy position in the White Carpathians, and the left-wing column left of the road. After brief resistance the rebels retreated to Nadas and from there further toward Tyrnau, during which they were able to avoid any rapid pursuit by creating all kinds of obstacle.

Feldmarschall Lieutenant Simunich's troops had only lost a few men lightly wounded and two horses killed in this action. His force went into camp that evening beyond Nadas and between there and Binyocz [Bíňovce, Slovakia].

The troops had a rest day on the 15th during which they repaired the damaged road, sorted out rations and reconnoitered toward Jökö [Dobrá Voda, Slovakia]. Meanwhile the rebels continued their retreat through Tyrnava to Szered [Sered', Slovakia] on the Waag. But when reinforcements reached them from Pressburg, during the night of 15/16 they returned to Tyrnau again, led by Guyon, and occupied the town with 8,000-9,000 men.[60]

60 Richard Debaufre Guyon (1813-56) was an Englishman who had served as an officer in the Austrian army. He joined the *honvéd* when war broke out in 1848 and reached the rank of general. Serving under Görgei, Guyon learned how to execute bold and rapid manoeuvres. After the war he escaped to Turkey and served the sultan. The *Encyclopaedia Britannica* says he 'served with distinction'. However, during the Crimean War, as chief of staff to Mustafa Zarif Pasha, he was responsible for the Ottoman plan of attack that ended in the destruction of their field army in the Caucasus. Guyon devised a bold plan for a pincer movement by two columns conducting a night march to trap and destroy the Russian

On the 16th *Feldmarschall Lieutenant* Simunich continued his march toward Tyrnau and arrived outside the city in thick fog between 3:00 and 4:00 p.m. The cavalry and the rocket battery formed the vanguard. They were followed by Brigade Sossay and then by Brigade Lobkowitz. After some exchange of cannon fire in the vicinity of the enemy position, the units of Brigade Sossay formed up into assault columns, while Brigade Lobkowitz followed immediately behind in reserve. The Hohenegg battalion pushed forward along the road with the E.H. Wilhelm battalion on its right and the two Hess companies on the left. It was 4:30 p.m., so darkness was about to fall when the attack began. In next to no time, they had taken three cannon. The Hartmann battalion and a platoon of *jägers* pressed in along Tyrnau's main street, followed by the E.H. William and Hohenegg battalions. *Unterlieutenant* Franz Prysak of 12. Jäger-Bataillon and *Hauptmann* De Kin of the Hartmann infantry with his division at the head of the battalion were the first to storm the barricade across the entrance and took 30 prisoners. Another two cannon were taken here, the ring and the church square completely cleared of rebels, 133 rebels taken prisoner and 14 horses captured.[61]

Gradually every unit came into action apart from the Haynau and Nugent battalions, which stayed in reserve.

After saying a few inspiring words, *Generalmajor* Sossay sent 2. Bataillon Ceccopieri to assault the railway station, which was strongly held. Under intense musket fire this battalion advanced with the bayonet, forced its way into the station and took many *honvéd*s prisoner, as well as a troop of hussars.

Toward 6:30 in the evening the town was completely under our control, and the enemy was fleeing in disorder toward Szered and Cziffer [Cífer, Slovakia] under cover of darkness. The troops bivouacked for the night in the town's streets and squares, after pushing outposts and patrols forward along the roads to Szered and Pressburg.

Feldmarschall Lieutenant Simunich praised the bold conduct of his troops in general, as well as of his two brigadiers and of *Hauptmann* Gastgeb of the quartermaster-general's staff,[62] who was wounded. In this action we took five guns and the flag of the oath-breaking battalion of Infanterie-Regiment Nr. 48. Eight field officers and 790 NCOs and men, five cartloads of ammunition, 43 horses and many weapons, etc., fell into our hands. The captured guns were formed into a battery under *Lieutenant* Hussarek. Our losses on this day consisted of one dead and 38 wounded. Among the latter were *Oberlieutenant Baron* Fahnenberg of the E.H. Karl

force at Kurudere. This manoeuvre could no doubt have been performed with ease by the Upper Danubian Army but was too ambitious for the Ottoman force, one column arriving late, resulting in being defeated in detail. The defeat at Kurudere was decisive for the course of events on the Caucasus front. Arthur Kinglake, *The Patriot and the Hero: General Guyon on the Battle fields of Hungary and Asia* (London: Hamilton, Adams & Co., 1856); *Encyclopaedia Britannica, 1911 Edition*; William Allen and Paul Muratoff, *Caucasian Battlefields: A History of the Wars on the Turco-Caucasian Border, 1828-1921* (Cambridge: Cambridge University Press, 2011).

61 I have been unable to ascertain what this 'ring' was.

62 The Austrian general staff grew out of the quartermaster's branch. These roots in the logistics branch perhaps help to explain why the Austrian army of the Napoleonic Wars and here in the Hungarian War of Independence was often so ponderous and slow: manoeuvre being dictated by logistical and geometrical considerations, rather than focusing on destruction of the enemy. Certainly, here in the Winter Campaign we see Windisch-Grätz's concern about supplies and lines of communication regularly holding him back from seeking out and destroying the enemy. Hubert Zeinar, *Geschichte des österreichischen Generalstabes* (Vienna: Böhlau Verlag, 2006).

Chevauxlegers and *Unterlieutenant* Mück of the E.H. Wilhelm infantry. The enemy's losses were far more considerable. After reaching Szered, he crossed the Waag and burned the bridge behind him.

On the 17th *Feldmarschall Lieutenant* Simunich summoned the fortress of Leopoldstadt to surrender, but in vain. It was hoped that the place could be taken just with high-angled field artillery,[63] since it had been very neglected for years and had no casemates; an expectation which however was not fulfilled.

During the night of the 16/17, an enemy courier was captured not far from Tyrnau carrying an order from Görgei written in Pressburg on 15 December (the day before the attack on Parendorf), in which the commander of the first brigade was ordered: 'Occupy Neuhäusel [Nové Zámky, Slovakia] immediately upon receipt of this order, and hold this position at all costs until the main body of the army arrives.' The brigadier was held personally responsible for carrying this out. It therefore seems that on the 15th Görgei was still willing to retreat along the left bank of the Danube to behind the Waag, which he may have been prevented from doing by the unexpected attack that followed on the 16th. There is no doubt that the rebels were surprised by this attack, for some of their detachments were parading for inspection even as the advance was happening.[64]

Rittmeister Alberti returned to Tyrnau with instructions for *Feldmarschall Lieutenant* Simunich 'to limit his further operations for the time being to securing the line of the Waag, treating Tyrnau as the central point and Szered and Freistadl [Hlohovec, Slovakia] as advanced posts'.[65] He was also ordered to take the fortress of Leopoldstadt as soon as possible, and to establish communications with *Oberstlieutenant* Frischeisen in the upper valley of the Waag, as well as via Wartberg [Senec, Slovakia] and Luipersdorf [Štvrtok na Ostrove, Slovakia] with the Grosse Schütt [the Great Rye Island, a river island in Slovakia formed by the Danube, the Little Danube and the Waag; Hungarian name, Csallóköz; now in Slovakia, Vel'ky Žitný ostrov] to where Brigade Neustädter was intended to be pushed forward. Finally, two bridging trains were assigned to him, which arrived in Tyrnau on the 22nd.

The Advance on Raab, 23-28 December 1848

Returning to operations of the Army of the Danube, before anything else we must mention that in accordance with the *Feldmarschall*'s orders, on the 19th *Oberst* Schön of the pioneer corps had dismantled the pontoon bridge that had been set up at Deutsch-Altenburg, transported it to Pressburg, and driven its construction there with such zeal that it was almost complete on the evening of the 20th when suddenly, because of the very cold spell of the previous two days (10-15°) heavy drift ice appeared on the Danube![66] The bridge could no longer be maintained

63 i.e., field howitzers and mortars rather than large-calibre siege guns.

64 All the more reason to have pressed the advance more vigorously if it surprised Görgei by both its timing and its direction.

65 'Limiting operations' is a recurring theme. Windisch-Grätz is always wary of taking any risk at all, careful to guard against every conceivable threat, advancing by measured steps. While it is impossible to know how other courses of action might have turned out, the opportunities lost through this caution may well have been greater than the risks averted.

66 It is unclear whether this means degrees Fahrenheit, a scale in common use at the time, or degrees Réaumur, a scale which gets mentioned specifically elsewhere in the text; the former makes more sense

without risk and without exposing the pontoons to being totally destroyed. It had to be quickly dismantled during the night of 20/21, which was done, but not without being damaged anyway and even losing some of its components. This unexpected event was all the more unfortunate as it meant that II. Armeekorps, which was supposed to cross immediately as soon as the bridge was completed, was held up yet again.

Every effort was now made to repair Pressburg city's floating bridge as quickly as possible, whose fabric was better able to withstand the ice floes. As already mentioned, before the rebels left they had dismantled it and let most of its parts float off downriver; but these had mostly got stuck along the bank or on the islands close by, so they could be collected together again and used to rebuild the bridge, albeit with considerable effort. This was pushed forward by the pioneer personnel, Pressburg's river boatmen and the municipal authorities, as directed by *Feldmarschall Lieutenant* Count Wrbna, with such commendable energy that the bridge was completed before dawn on the 22nd, and II. Armeekorps was able to start crossing immediately. But at 4:00 p.m. the drift ice grew so strong that the bridge broke, leaving 2. Bataillon E.H. Stefan, three companies of the Khevenhüller regiment and a half-battery behind on the left bank, which could only finally be brought across by boat on the 23rd.

To make the necessary space for II. Armeekorps's arrival on the right bank of the Danube, the Reservekorps and part of I. Armeekorps had already been pushed further forward on the 21st, so that on the 22nd the army was echeloned along the Raab road as follows:

I. Armeekorps and the Reserve-Kavallerie

In Ungarisch-Altenburg, Wieselburg, Zajning [Mosonszolnok, Hungary], Strass-Sommerein, Nickelsdorf.

The Reserve-Infanterie-Division and the Artillerie-Hauptreserve

In Ragendorf [Rajka, Hungary], Pallersdorf [Bezenye, Hungary], Karlburg, etc.

II. Armeekorps

In the cantonments vacated by the Infanterie-Reserve-Division at Gattendorf, Baumern, Jarendorf, etc.

Lastly, Brigade Neustädter of I. Armeekorps, which was still in the bridgehead in front of Pressburg, was instructed to leave one battalion of Szluiner *grenzers* behind to garrison Pressburg and to advance across the Great Rye Island toward Komorn keeping roughly level with the army, but first just moving to Luipersdorf and Sommerein to disarm the surrounding villages and establish communications with *Feldmarschall Lieutenant* Simunich via Wartberg.

Since the last action at Wieselburg the enemy had kept completely quiet. He had retreated to Hochstrass [Öttevény, Hungary] and Raab. Baromház [a hamlet northwest of Lébény, Hungary], Leyden [Lébény, Hungary] and Sz. Miklos [Mosonszentmiklós, Hungary], where there were large grain stores, were unoccupied. An enemy detachment with four cannon had

unless a minus sign was accidentally omitted.

been posted at the crossing of the Rabnitz river [Répcze river, Hungary] at Abda ('Brückel' in German).

The *Feldmarschall* ordered the *Banus* and his corps to advance on the 23rd to Leyden, Baromház and Sz. Miklos, and even to Hochstrass if circumstances allowed; for on that day (the 23rd) II. Armeekorps had finished crossing, so the moment had arrived when the whole army could resume the offensive united and with complete security. II. Armeekorps had already been instructed to move by forced march past the Reservekorps and into the cantonment at Altenburg and Wieselburg to be vacated by I. Armeekorps, whereby the corps would be placed in the most suitable position with respect to the attack on Raab.

The *Feldmarschall* had decided on the following concept for attacking the entrenched position at Raab. It was very difficult to attack this position frontally. The bridges across the Rabnitz had been burned, as we have seen, and it would have to be crossed in the face of the enemy, the earthworks to the front would have to be taken, and then finally streetfighting could develop in Raab itself. Outflanking it on the right, that is to say round the enemy's left wing, entailed crossing three watercourses: the Rabnitz, the Raab [Rába river, Hungary] and the Marcal, which could easily cause hold-ups and loss of time, and in any case would very quickly be detected by the enemy. In the best case, if the enemy did accept battle, this outflanking would push the enemy toward Komorn, thus leading to exactly what had to be prevented; for pushing the enemy's combat forces together in this great armed camp astride the Danube would have pinned our army there, hindered continuing the offensive toward Ofen, and even exposed the detachments operating on the left bank of the Danube, because the enemy in Komorn could move from one bank to the other, which our own army was not in a position to do except at Wien or Ofen since the bridge at Pressburg had been broken by the drift ice. Finally, the enemy could be pursued effectively in any other direction, but not through Komorn.

Because of this the *Feldmarschall* decided to engage the enemy frontally and pin him with I. Armeekorps and the Reservekorps, while II. Armeekorps and Franz Liechtenstein's Reserve-Kavallerie-Division advanced on the Little Rye Island to outflank him, to cross the Little Danube at least 7-10 km beyond Raab, take the enemy position in the rear, and drive the enemy completely away from Komorn.[67]

The essential conditions for this outflanking to succeed were:

1. That the enemy's forward elements should already have been cleared from the Little Rye Island and driven back into the Raab position, to conceal from him the massing of larger bodies of troops on the Rye Island;

67 It could be argued that the *Feldmarschall* did not need to wait for II. Armeekorps on the 21st after the bridge was broken by ice. Continuing the march regardless could have given a head start to I. Armeekorps outflanking on the right, while if II. Armeekorps had simply marched down the left bank of the Danube instead of waiting to cross and then re-crossing, the outflanking on the left could have happened simultaneously. Yes, this double envelopment astride the Danube could have exposed Windisch-Grätz to defeat in detail, but the enemy had shown no sign as yet of wishing even to stand and fight, let alone to attack. In fact, as it transpired, a double envelopment did actually come about – but contrary to his orders, not because of them – and therefore not in a sufficiently swift and organised manner; and no defeat in detail ensued, merely another enemy retreat to dodge the ponderous blow.

2. That II. Armeekorps should reach the designated crossing point on the Little Danube unnoticed as far as possible, thus by a night march, so as to be able to begin bridge construction at daybreak; and finally,

3. That the enemy should not be alerted prematurely by I. Armeekorps and the Reservekorps's movements and made aware of the impending attack.

Since II. Armeekorps's crossing point was just about 10 km in the rear of the enemy position, so could be reached in a single night march undetected, or in any case before the enemy could prepare any serious resistance there, this operation had every chance of success; indeed this necessarily increased in proportion to how serious the enemy was about holding Raab and concentrating his combat forces and all of his attention there.

Nothing definite was known about the enemy's strength. In any case, it could be assumed that the five brigades that had been between Parendorf and Kittsee on the 16th had concentrated at Raab, and in addition, that the enemy had been joined by reinforcements there and probably moved troops up from nearby Komorn as well, so his combat forces could be estimated at 20,000-25,000 men.

The army resumed its advance on the 24th following the general plan of attack above. On this day, Division Ramberg of II. Armeekorps was pushed forward to Arak [4 km southeast of Halászi, Hungary] and Hédervár to clear the Little Rye Island of any parties of enemy and drove before it the enemy outposts and patrols posted there. On the 25th its advance guard clashed with three troops of hussars at Zamoly [Győrzámoly, Hungary], who were quickly attacked and beaten by a detachment of Kress Chevauxlegers under *Rittmeister* Kukstatscher, in which one seriously wounded officer, nine men and four horses were captured.

The rest of II. Armeekorps, namely Division Csorich and the Artillerie-Korpsreserve, suffered some delay in following on behind, in that they had to march to the Little Rye Island over two small temporary bridges across the Little Danube; but by 4:00 p.m. on the 26th they had already reached Dunaszeg, the place from which the outflanking of Raab was to start on the following day.

On the 26th, Division Ramberg's advance guard had already advanced to Ujfalu [Győrújfalu, Hungary], and had driven all enemy detachments off the Little Rye Island back into Raab. As for the Reservekorps, on the 26th the Infanterie-Division was in Hochstrass and Leyden, the Kavallerie-Division in Leyden, Baromház, Mecsér, etc. The Artillerie-Hauptreserve was in Hochstrass and Öttevény-Sziget [Kunsziget, Hungary].

Brigade Neustädter on the Great Rye Island was ordered to conform with the army's advance and move further toward Komorn, to occupy the towns of Nyárasd [Topol'níky, Slovakia] and Deutsch-Bogya [Bodza, Slovakia] beyond Megyer [Veľký Meder, Slovakia], to patrol toward Komorn, to keep an eye out for any offensive manoeuvres by the garrison, and to inform *Feldmarschall Lieutenant* Simunich and *Feldmarschall Lieutenant* Kempen as quickly as possible of any such intention on the part of the enemy.

The *Feldmarschall* had transferred his headquarters from Karlburg to Altenburg on the 24th, and to Sz. Miklos on the 26th. From the latter place he issued the detailed orders for the attack on Raab which was set for the 27th.

To establish more direct communications between II. Armeekorps advancing on the Little Rye Island and the rest of the army a bridge was ordered to be built across the Little Danube at Zamoly, which was completed by the evening of the 26th.

The *Feldmarschall* had summoned the corps commanders and their chiefs of staff to Sz. Miklos for the 26th to discuss the orders for the attack with them in detail. The *Banus* and his chief of staff were prevented from joining this briefing as they were making preparations for the next day.[68] According to the detailed dispositions as issued, part of I. Armeekorps was to secure the crossing over the Rabnitz at or near to Börcs on the 26th, while the corps's main body was to follow it just before daybreak on the 27th, to cross the Rabnitz and then move downstream toward the Pressburg- Raab highway, to enable the Reservekorps that had to advance along this road to build a bridge at Abda, where the bridge had been burned by the enemy.

I. Armeekorps deviated from this plan. Part of it had already crossed the Rabnitz on the 25th, the corps itself spent the night of 26/27 close to the Raab at Csécsény [Rábacsécsény, Hungary], and before setting off it had pulled in all its outposts from in front of Hochstrass on the Raab highway.[69]

At 7:00 a.m. on the 27th, Schwarzenberg's Infanterie-Reserve-Division (from which one battalion and a half-battery had been detached to guard the bridge at Zamoly) and the Artillerie-Hauptreserve had begun to move along the highway toward Raab, while II. Armeekorps and the Reserve-Kavallerie under *Feldmarschall Lieutenant Fürst* Franz Liechtenstein, who were supposed to carry out the outflanking across the Little Rye Island, had already set off during the night at 1:00 a.m.

The *Feldmarschall* betook himself to *Feldmarschall Lieutenant Fürst* Edmund Schwarzenberg's column, joining the head of it just at the moment when it arrived at Abda on the Rabnitz. No enemy were visible on the far bank, which had a fair amount of cover. The bridge had been burned. To repair it would have taken too much time. Instead, it was decided to build a trestle bridge upstream of it, for which however the frozen surface of the river had first to be cleared of ice in the relevant places. While this was being done, the *jägers* went across the ice one by one to the far bank. The first ones to cross spurred imitation. Reeds and straw were brought from the houses nearby and laid on the ice. Now whole companies and battalions of Brigade Schütte crossed over. Finally, they were followed by 6-pounder guns. Even a 12-pounder was carefully got across. Meanwhile the trestle bridge had been completed and the cavalry and the rest of the troops and artillery crossed the Rabnitz on it. Far away, from beyond Raab in the direction of the Little Rye Island, a few cannon shots were heard. This was II. Armeekorps.

Oberstlieutenant Baron Langenau, the *Feldmarschall*'s aide-de-camp, who had been first to cross the icy surface with his horse was charged with finding I. Armeekorps, which according

68 This is an ominous early sign of what was to plague Windisch-Grätz throughout the campaign – namely his subordinates' frequent non-compliance with his orders. In this instance, we must ask why Jellacic did not attend the *Feldmarschall*'s briefing and leave his chief of staff Zeisberg to make whatever preparations these were that detained them both (Csécsény is 15 km from Sz. Miklos). The result of their non-attendance is visible immediately when I. Armeekorps deviates from the plan. We must also wonder what response Jellacic's absence generated from the *Feldmarschall*; subsequent form suggests it was a diplomatic and restrained one, and not the kind of warning shot that might have prevented further bad behavior by Jellacic.

69 Csécsény is nearly 15 km from Abda, the destination the *Feldmarschall* intended for I. Armeekorps.

to the plan should have arrived there already, but he was unable to do so because it had taken a different direction of march from that which had been ordered.

While *Generalmajor* Schütte's brigade and the Artillerie-Hauptreserve were crossing the Rabnitz partly on the ice and partly over the trestle bridge, *Feldmarschall Lieutenant Fürst* Edmund Schwarzenberg advanced with Brigade Liebler on the left of the road into the sharp angle that the Rabnitz makes with the Little Danube, pushed into the suburb of Sziget, crossed the Rabnitz there over a bridge that was partly still standing and was quickly repaired, and entered Raab which had already been completely evacuated by the enemy. In fact, Görgei and his last brigade had left the city at 9:00 a.m.

When the *Feldmarschall* and Brigade Schütte advanced from the Abda bridge closer to Raab, they discovered the very extensive earthworks straddling the highway outside the city that had been abandoned by the enemy, in front of which it was later found there were also fougasses, one even still loaded.[70] All the trees along the road had been felled [for abattis], and in general all preparations made for a stubborn defence.

An officer coming from Raab gave the *Feldmarschall* the news that the city was already occupied by our troops. Soon after that a delegation from the Raab municipal authorities met the *Feldmarschall* with the keys to the city, which were sent with *Major Graf* Moriz Palffy to His Majesty the *Kaiser* at Olmütz. In the evening the city was lit up with festive illuminations. The inhabitants seemed partly amazed by the rapid turnaround in fortunes, partly delighted by the victory of the legitimate cause.[71] The *Feldmarschall* moved his headquarters to Raab.

It still remains to describe what had transpired meanwhile with I. and II. Armeekorps, and about which news was not received until after our entry into Raab. The latter corps had set off at 1:00 a.m. During its night march in an unfamiliar area all kinds of obstructions and traffic jams arose, so that instead of reaching the point where it was supposed to build its bridge over the Little Danube before daybreak as ordered, the column did not arrive there until 8:00 a.m.

The artillery that was tasked with defending the bridge construction if necessary was too far away from the head of the column. One battery was not brought up until after a passing enemy battery had fired a few very effective shots that killed five men and some horses, had also hit three pontoon wagons, and had then continued its retreat. The ice would have allowed infantry and rockets at least to be got across to the far bank, and indeed many *jägers* from 2. Bataillon actually did rush across to snipe at the passing enemy, but they were called back again. The bridge building was started too late and besides proceeded very slowly, since the ice surface had to be hacked away before the trestles could be erected, which took a lot of time. In short, the enemy was able to complete his retreat undisturbed. The bridge was finally ready toward 3:30 p.m., whereupon II. Armeekorps and Franz Liechtenstein's Kavallerie-Division marched across to the far bank at Sz. Ivány [Győrszentiván, Hungary].

Feldmarschall Lieutenant Ramberg had stayed at Bácsa on the Little Rye Island with Brigade Karl Lederer to cover II. Armeekorps's advance; but when he found no enemy in front of him,

70 A 'fougasse' is essentially a type of landmine. Perhaps these were shell fougasses: 'Shells may be buried singly, or in small heaps, and be made to burst either under the ground, or on its surface.' Dennis Hart Mahan, *An Elementary Course of Military Engineering, Part I: Comprising Field Fortification, Military Mining and Siege Operations* (New York: John Wiley & Son, 1867).

71 As a large proportion of the population in western Hungary was German-speaking, particularly in the towns, it is quite possible that they did indeed celebrate the arrival of the imperial army in Raab.

he advanced to Raab and arrived at almost the same time as *Feldmarschall Lieutenant Fürst* Edmund Schwarzenberg did with Brigade Liebler. Meanwhile, I. Armeekorps had set off from the vicinity of Csécsény at 3:00 a.m. on the 27th, had crossed the Raab at Raaba-Sz. Mihály [Győrszentmihály, Hungary], then also crossed the Marcal, and arrived via Koroncó at Szabadhegy [Győrszabadhegy, now a suburb of Győr, Hungary] behind Raab toward midday, without encountering the enemy. The laborious crossing of the Raab and the Marcal during the night had created gaps, so that the brigades only sorted themselves out again at daybreak and arrived at Raab in a fairly exhausted state. Thus a double envelopment of both wings of the enemy position had occurred – an operation that was not really intended and for which the army was certainly not strong enough.

The *Feldmarschall* had decided to outflank the right wing because this was the strategically correct and most effective option. But meanwhile adequate combat forces had to remain deployed in front of Raab to be able to cross swords with any enemy offensive manoeuvre, which was only possible if the Reservekorps and I. Armeekorps stayed together. The result of I. Armeekorps's deviation from the orders issued was that instead of 18 battalions, 21 squadrons and 144 guns facing the actual enemy position there were only eight battalions, one squadron and 96 guns, which was obviously too few to handle any enemy breakout from Raab.[72]

The fact that it really was II. Armeekorps's outflanking manoeuvre that led to the evacuation of the position at Raab emerges undeniably from Görgei's proclamation 'To the Upper Danubian Army', discovered after the rebels' retreat from Pesth, in which it says verbatim:

> After the army corps on the Upper Danube had protected the frontier for a month and a half with rare self-denial during the most arduous outpost duty as ordered by the National Defence Committee, after it victoriously drove back (?) [*sic*][73] the significantly stronger enemy in the action at Wieselburg, after it held the hopeless position at Raab courageously until the moment when it had already been outflanked on its right by the numerically superior enemy, and its necessary retreat to protect the capital cities was only made possible by hard fighting with the outflanking enemy column [etc.]

On the evening of the 27th, the army was deployed at Raab as follows. I. Armeekorps was deployed between Szabadhegy and the Pápa road, in which direction it was diligently patrolling because the enemy corps under Perczel was suspected to be in that area.[74] II. Armeekorps had Brigades Wyss, Jablonowsky and Colloredo in Sz. Iván, and Brigade Lederer in Raab. The

72 Except that, as we have seen, no enemy offensive manoeuvre materialised. Had I. Armeekorps begun its march on the 20th or 21st rather than the 22nd, it could have arrived at Raab in better time and in better shape and perhaps produced a more significant result.

73 The question mark in parentheses is Nobili's, presumably because he is puzzled about what 'driving back' Görgei is referring to. Bánlaky notes an incident on 18 December during I. Armeekorps's approach toward Wieselburg when Görgei's cavalry won a skirmish against the *Banus*'s cavalry. This may be what Görgei means. József Bánlaky, '*A parendorfi ütközet (1848. december 16-án)*', in *A magyar nemzet hadtörténelme* (Budapest: Grill Károly, 1928-42).

74 Mór Perczel (1811-99) was serving in the Hungarian government in 1848. He raised the Zrínyi volunteer force to fight Jellacic's invasion. Promoted to colonel in October and general in November, he led forces fighting on several fronts to the end of the war. He escaped to Turkey and then emigrated to Jersey in 1851, returning to Hungary in 1867. Bona, *Tábornokok.*

Reserve-Kavallerie-Division was likewise in Sz. Ivány. This place was therefore so overflowing that the troops could not all be found shelter. Some had to bivouac in the severe cold. A division of Ficquelmont dragoons was pushed forward to Gönyű and a division of Civallart *uhlans* to Ober Sz. János [Nagyszentjános, Hungary] as outposts. The Paumgarten battalion remained behind at the pontoon bridge. The Infanterie-Reserve-Division and the Artillerie-Hauptreserve were in Raab. Many supplies were found in Raab that the rebels had not had time to remove. Several boats laden with grain had been sunk before they left, but most of their cargo was able to be salvaged.

Nothing definite could be discovered about the enemy's strength or direction of retreat. Görgei and the main body had reportedly moved to Bábolna, a flanking column to Komorn, and a weak detachment to Moór [Mór, Hungary]. It was said that Perczel had turned away from Pápa toward Stuhlweissenburg, about which definite information was also expected very soon from *Oberst* Horváth, who must be at Egyed and Téth [Tét, Hungary].

After entering Raab the *Feldmarschall* wasted no time in taking measures to cause as much damage to the enemy as possible. The *Banus* was instructed to have Kavallerie-Brigade Ottinger set off in such a way as to arrive at Bábolna at 2:00 a.m. on the 28th and surprise the enemy encamped there. Kavallerie-Brigade Bellegarde at Sz. Ivány was given the same mission and in the same direction; but *Feldmarschall Lieutenant Graf* Wrbna, to whose command this brigade belonged, felt that its horses were too fatigued, so the required expedition was carried out by Brigade Ottinger alone.[75] This brigade had already had to make strenuous efforts the day before, and the night march to Bábolna was at least 20 km long, during which two divisions of Hardegg cuirassiers got delayed. For these reasons the brigade, to which a division of Civallart *uhlans* had also been attached, did not reach Bábolna until 5:30 a.m. It therefore only found the enemy rear guard there – that is, one battalion of Infanterie-Regiment Nr. 34, four *honvéd* battalions and a battery. These were just preparing to depart, while their main body had already left earlier.

Generalmajor Ottinger immediately attacked the rebels. The aforementioned renegade battalion, about 600 strong, quickly formed battalion mass[76] and fired a volley at 20 paces against the two divisions of Wallmoden cuirassiers and one of Civallart *uhlans* that were charging it, but despite that was broken in a flash.[77] The rebels' defeat was now complete. As well as the infantry battalion, the cuirassiers and *uhlans* took many hussars and *honvéd*s prisoner, captured a flag and an ammunition cart, and sent seven officers and 700 men, including 200 wounded, to Raab as prisoners. The hussars and artillery had run away in time.

Generalmajor Ottinger praised the distinguished and determined conduct of *Oberstlieutenant Graf* Nostiz, *Rittmeister Graf* Wallis and *Lieutenant Baron* Dankelmann of the Civallart *uhlans* on this occasion.

75 As we shall see, this will not be the only time in the Winter Campaign that Wrbna finds a reason to decline to press an advantage and attack a retreating enemy.

76 In battalion mass, all six companies form up one behind the other, each company in a line three ranks deep, so the formation is 18 ranks deep with (in this case) about 30 men in each rank. Tamás Csikány, *A Szabadságharc Hadművészete 1848-1849* (Budapest: Zrínyi, 2015).

77 This shows the shock value of the Austrian cuirassiers, which we will see demonstrated again later in the campaign. Admittedly three divisions of cavalry must have somewhat outnumbered the Hungarian infantry. Even so, these were not newly raised *honvéds* but regular troops, in a dense mass formation, with the opportunity to fire a volley at the charging cavalry, yet they still broke.

The brigade remained at Bábolna on this day, but on the next joined up with I. Armeekorps which had meanwhile marched away from Raab to Mező-Eörs [Mezőörs, Hungary].

Before their retreat from Bábolna the rebels had taken away 103 of the finest thoroughbred horses and 138 draught oxen from the military stud farm there.

On the same day (the 28th) on which Brigade Ottinger performed the glorious feat of arms described above, Kavallerie-Brigade Parrot had advanced to Ács and Kavallerie-Brigade Bellegarde to Gönyö [Gönyű, Hungary]. All the other units stayed in their positions in front of Raab, since they were extremely fatigued from their night marches and needed to sort out their rations. Their herds for slaughter and their camp kettles, particularly those of II. Armeekorps, had been left far behind during the outflanking march across the Little Rye Island. There was nothing to be found in Sz. Ivány, where the corps arrived late in the evening; so the troops had no meat at all on the 27th and it was not until the 28th that they could get some and cook it.

Despite this the army resumed its advance toward Ofen-Pesth on the 29th and continued without a pause until it got there.

The Plan for the Advance on Ofen-Pesth

The *Feldmarschall* had come up with the following plan for this.

Three roads lead from Raab to Ofen-Pesth:

1. The post road through Gönyö, past the Komorn bridgehead, to Almás [Almásfüzitő, Hungary], Dorog, etc.

2. The so-called 'Fleischhackerstrasse' through Bábolna, Kocs, Bicske, etc.

3. Lastly, the road through Moór, Stuhlweissenburg, etc. or, avoiding the latter place, on a transverse road from Moór through Lovas-Berény [Lovasberény, Hungary], which route however could not be assumed to be entirely usable at this late season of the year.

The *Feldmarschall* decided to advance along the most direct line with the main body of the army – that is with II. Armeekorps, the Reservekorps and the Artillerie-Hauptreserve along the Fleischhackerstrasse; to direct I. Armeekorps through Moór to cover his right flank against the suspected presence of Perczel's corps in that direction; while ignoring the post road running along his left flank apart from summoning Komorn to surrender, and in the event that this should be rejected, leaving one strong brigade to besiege the bridgehead there.[78]

The precise details of the march necessarily had to be arranged so that the columns would arrive outside Ofen at the same time, and that the army would be united again there. Since I. Armeekorps had to cover seven or eight days' march to get to Ofen on its designated line of

78 These three routes diverge so that at their widest point the two flanking routes are about 30 km from the central one; in the case of the southern route, 40 km unless Stuhlweissenburg is bypassed via Lovas-Berény. Lateral communications between them existed but were limited by the rugged country north and south of Tatabánya and by the poor state of the roads at this time of year. Mutual support between the corps advancing on these three axes was therefore limited as it could well take more than one day to arrive. This would have contributed to the *Banus*'s caution.

march through Moór, while the main body only had to do six, I. Armeekorps had to be given a head start of at least one day's march. This interval was used to push II. Armeekorps forward along the Komorn post road initially, rather than straight up the Fleischhackerstrasse, and it was only to turn off to join its actual line of march at Kocs after issuing the summons to Komorn to surrender; in this way the appropriate march relationship between the two columns would be restored, and also the enemy would be deceived for a while as to the intended direction of march. Besides, the appearance of a whole army corps outside Komorn could have an intimidating effect on its garrison, which was known to consist mostly of raw recruits; and could make it easier for the fortress commander at the time, Maitheny – a former hussar *rittmeister* in the imperial army and not one of the Ultra-Magyars – to follow what could be assumed to be his personal inclination at the time, given his history, and to surrender the fortress.[79]

Accordingly, the following provisional plan for the march to be carried out was issued to the corps commanders on the 28th:

> I. Armeekorps was to march to Mező-Eörs on 29 December 1848, to Kis-Bér [Kisbér, Hungary] on the 30th, Moór on the 31st, Lovas-Berény on 1 January 1849, Marton-Vásár [Martonvásár, Hungary] on the 2nd, and Tétény [Nagytétény, Hungary] on the 3rd, 15 km from Ofen.
>
> II. Armeekorps and the Kavallerie-Reserve-Division were to march to Ács on 29 December 1848, to outside Komorn on the 30th, to Kocs on the 31st, to Ober-Galla [Alsógalla, in Tatabánya, Hungary] on 1 January 1849, to Bicske on the 2nd, to Bia [Biatorbágy, Hungary] on the 3rd, and to Buda-Örs [Budaörs, Hungary] on the 4th, 8 km outside Ofen.
>
> The Infanterie Reserve-Division, Artillerie-Hauptreserve and Headquarters were to march to Bána and Bábolna on 31 December 1848, to Kocs on 1 January 1849, to Ober-Galla on the 2nd, to Bicske on the 3rd, to Bia on the 4th, and to Buda-Örs on the 5th.
>
> In the event that the road from Moór to Lovas-Berény and Marton-Vásár should not be usable, I. Armeekorps was instructed to march from Moór via Stuhlweissenburg, Velencze [Velence, Hungary] and Marton-Vásár, to arrive in Tétény on 4 January instead of on the 3rd.

Since the designated waypoint villages were much too small to provide the necessary room to accommodate such large bodies of troops but the men could not camp out in the cold

79 Major General Baron István Majthényi (1788-1868). In September 1848, as a lieutenant colonel in the national guard, he was instrumental in retaining control of the fortress of Komorn for the Hungarian government. He was later promoted to major general. However, rather than fight against the imperial army, he resigned on 9 January 1849. He offended officers of the garrison by continuing to wear his uniform and was therefore expelled from the fortress. After the war he was stripped of his rank and briefly imprisoned but soon pardoned. Bona, *Tábornokok*.

weather that had set in (10-20°),[80] it was anticipated that all the villages in the vicinity of the waypoints would have to be used for billeting, as a result of which the march interval between II. Armeekorps and the Reservekorps would disappear naturally.

The Flanking Detachments' Actions during December 1848

Before we follow the army's manoeuvres toward Ofen, we must mention what had transpired meanwhile with the detachments operating on the army's flanks and rear under *Oberstlieutenant* Frischeisen, *Feldmarschall Lieutenant* Simunich, *Oberst* Horváth, etc., as well as what else the *Feldmarschall* had decreed in Raab.

Oberst Graf Appony was appointed city commandant of Raab, and the city was prepared for defence against any *coup de main*. *Sappeur-Hauptmann Baron* Rüstel and his company were tasked with constructing the works for that purpose. The Reisinger battalion of Brigade Wyss and half a 6-pounder battery remained behind as garrison in Raab for the time being. The country folk thereabout were ordered to be disarmed.

Oberstlieutenant Frischeisen's column (four Palombini companies, a half-squadron of E.H. Karl Chevauxlegers and half a rocket battery) had made little progress. From its muster point in Teschen it had moved toward the Hungarian border and crossed the Jablunka Pass on 4 December 1848, after one company and a dozen *chevauxlegers* under *Hauptmann Baron* Lewartowsky, who had been attached to the said *Oberstlieutenant* as a general staff officer, had occupied the pass the day before and had cleared the barricade that had been piled up there.

A few thousand rebels, mostly national guard and militia, who had mustered in Csacza [Čadca, Slovakia] under Kossuth's notorious commissar Ballogh and had also occupied the very defensible inn at Swrczinowecz [Svrčinovec, Slovakia] with 120 *honvéd*s, retreated hurriedly to Neustadl when our troops appeared.[81] Csacza was occupied and many weapons that the rebels had left there were captured, and even a flag. A significant cargo of boots that had come from Prussia and was destined for the rebels also fell into our troops' hands. *Oberstlieutenant* Frischeisen halted in Csacza. But when the enemy had evacuated Neustadl and withdrawn into the advantageous position at Budetin [Budatín, Slovakia], he occupied the former town, and finally advanced against the aforementioned position on the 11th in very thick fog.

The enemy may have numbered about 3,000 men with six guns. The position was difficult to attack frontally, so it was outflanked on its right by two companies and 220 Slovak volunteers led by Blaudek[82] and Zach,[83] whereupon the enemy soon retreated behind the Waag and demolished

80 Again, presumably this is degrees Fahrenheit.

81 János Balogh (1796-1872), a member of the Hungarian parliament, served as a battalion and then brigade commander in 1848-49. At the end of the war he escaped to Turkey, was sentenced to death *in absentia*, and only returned to Hungary after a long exile. Bona, *Tábornokok*.

82 Bedřich Bloudek (1815-75). A former imperial officer, he took part in the failed uprising in Prague in early 1848, and then the abortive declaration of Slovakia's independence from Hungary in September 1848. In November 1848 the imperial government commissioned him to organise and command a Slovak volunteer corps to fight the Hungarians. After the 1848-49 war he rejoined the imperial army until his death. Dusan Skvarna, 'Bedich Bloudek', in *Encyclopedia of 1848 Revolutions*.

83 I assume this is František Zach (1807-92), a Czech-born pan-Slavist. He fought in the Polish uprising of 1830-1831 and was an active participant in the Slav Congress in Prague in 1848. In 1849 he went to Serbia where he served in the Serbian army, founding the Belgrade artillery academy, becoming a

the bridge. Firing went on until late in the evening between our troops and the enemy posted on the far side of the river. It was especially heavy near the Budetin castle belonging to *Graf* Czaky, in whose windows some rocket launch stands had been set up. When night fell and the firing ceased, *Oberstlieutenant* Frischeisen received a message that the militia were assembling in his rear, the bridges had been broken, and that the enemy was making preparations to cross the Waag in his flank and go onto the offensive. This caused Frischeisen to begin his retreat during the night. On the 12th he was back at Jablunka again.

This retreat aroused concern in the provinces of Silesia and Moravia. The interim commander there, *Feldmarschall Lieutenant Baron* Böhm therefore immediately sent a Deutschmeister battalion and a division of the Schönhals regiment to Teschen together with half a horse artillery battery to serve as immediate support if necessary, and also sent mobile columns along the border and took other security measures to which the military commandant in Krakau, *Feldmarschall Lieutenant* Legedics, lent a helping hand.

When the *Feldmarschall* received word of this, the order was sent to the two H.v. Nassau and Bianchi battalions expected from Galicia that instead of marching from Bielitz [Bielsko-Biała, Poland] to Wien they should march straight to Jablunka and join *Oberstlieutenant* Frischeisen's troops. A 6-pounder battery destined for Galicia was also directed there instead. Command of these troops was now given to *Generalmajor* Götz, who had just returned from Italy, with the instruction to resume the offensive after he had finished fully concentrating this force; which he indeed achieved on 31 December, as will be seen in what follows below.

With the arrival of these reinforcements, the troops placed at *Generalmajor* Götz's disposal came to three battalions, half a squadron, 12 guns and a quickly improvised bridging train. In detail:

3. Bataillon H.v. Nassau
3. Bataillon Bianchi
1. Bataillon Palombini
Half a squadron of E.H. Karl Chevauxlegers
Half a horse artillery battery
Half a rocket battery
One 6-pounder battery

The Mining Towns were designated as the appropriate direction for his advance.

On 20 December *Feldmarschall Lieutenant* Simunich had sent a patrol force of one E.H. Wilhelm battalion, one *jäger* company, a half squadron of *chevauxlegers*, a half-battery and two rocket launch stands under *Major Graf* Ervin Neipperg from Tyrnau into the upper valley of the Waag, to clear the valley and to try to establish communications with *Oberstlieutenant* Frischeisen. Neipperg returned on the 23rd with the message that he had not encountered any enemy but had learned that Frischeisen had retreated to Jablunka and did not propose to advance again until after receiving reinforcements. Meanwhile the crossings of the Waag at Freistadel

general and losing a leg while commanding an army against the Ottomans in 1876. Curiously, the *BLKÖ* makes no mention of him fighting in Hungary in 1848, but this is the only Zach listed in the *BLKÖ* that could plausibly be him. *BLKÖ*, Vol.59, pp.72-73.

and Szered had been garrisoned, and the small fortress of Leopoldstadt,[84] which had a garrison of more than 1,000 men under Ordody,[85] had been summoned to surrender but in vain.

On the 20th the investment of Leopoldstadt progressed to a full-blown siege, and the necessary preparations were made for bombarding it. The means available for this comprised: four 30-pounder long-range mortars, one 12-pounder heavy rocket battery, two iron 12-pounder siege guns and numerous field guns. *Major* Wurmb of the engineer corps and *Hauptmann* Ambrosi of the artillery were charged with directing the attack. Since the ground was frozen solid, the battery positions mostly had to be built from sandbags and woolsacks; but these were pushed forward with such energy that on the evening of the 29th five batteries were completely constructed and armed, so the bombardment could begin next day. Unfortunately, on the afternoon of the 29th the artillery ammunition works at Drahovcze [Drahovce, Slovakia] blew up, together with the ammunition it had been manufacturing, and *Bombardier Oberlieutenant* Lechner and four men lost their lives. Only 200 shells had been delivered, with which the bombardment of Leopoldstadt was begun but without result, after once again vainly summoning it to surrender. By 4:00 p.m. the small amount of ammunition that was still usable had been completely expended, so during the night the guns were withdrawn from the batteries. We had suffered some losses of men and horses. There could be no thought of renewing the attack until more ammunition had been brought from Wien. *Feldmarschall Lieutenant* Simunich therefore sought meanwhile to get his troops under shelter, so far as was compatible with maintaining the siege, which had become extremely necessary because of the bitter cold that had set in.

As we will see later, this delay in the fall of Leopoldstadt caused by the accident that had just occurred exerted an extremely negative influence on the course of operations. This fortress's location in the vicinity of the crossing over the Waag at Freistadl is certainly only of secondary strategic importance. But in the circumstances at the time it could not be ignored, since it constituted a place for the militia organising themselves in the upper valley of the Waag to assemble and find support, it dominated Tyrnau and the Waag crossings, and was generally a base from which the whole region could be kept in a state of unrest and the rear of the army, denuded of troops, could be constantly harassed. The prolonged defence of Leopoldstadt had the consequence that *Feldmarschall Lieutenant* Simunich was pinned there for an excessively long time and could not participate in the operations in Upper Hungary as had been intended, and finally the possibility of any operation against Komorn had to be put off until February.[86]

In Raab the *Feldmarschall* received more detailed news about the movements of *Oberst* Horváth's patrol force from *Rittmeister* Escherich. Horváth had advanced from Wiener Neustadt and the border villages toward Oedenburg on 13 December as ordered. To support this manoeuvre, on his own initiative *Feldmarschall Lieutenant Baron* Welden had formed a flanking column of three Oguliner *grenzer* companies and a division of Wrbna *chevauxlegers* from the Wien garrison

84 Leopoldstadt [Leopoldov, Slovakia] is a classic small 17th century fortress: just over 600 m across, perfectly symmetrical, with six bastions.

85 Kálmán Ordódy (1815-1871) was a former imperial officer who was appointed a *honvéd* captain in June 1848. He fought at Pákozd, then against Simunich until he surrendered at Leopoldstadt. At the end of the war he was sentenced to three years' imprisonment but pardoned in 1851. See Bona, *Tábornokok*.

86 Note, though, that Simunich had 4,500 men with which to besiege a garrison of 1,000 or so. Even allowing for the threat of militia gathering, he could probably have besieged it with just 2,500, say, and sent the other 2,000 to join Windisch-Grätz or carry out some other more active mission.

under *Major Graf* Schaffgotsche, which pushed forward from Ebenfurth and Grosshöflein to cover the left flank of *Oberst* Horváth's column as it advanced along the highway. After carrying out a night march on 15/16 the two columns were outside Oedenburg at 11:00 a.m. During the advance, *Major Graf* Schaffgotsche had taken prisoner two officers and 26 hussars in Vulka-Pordány [Wulka-Prodersdorf, Austria] at daybreak, and defeated another hussar detachment in a later clash in which there were quite a lot of dead and wounded on both sides. An Oguliner company under *Hauptmann* Kossanovich and a detachment of Wrbna *chevauxlegers* under *Oberlieutenant* Moldovany had distinguished themselves in this. The rebels who numbered not more than 400 men, including 80 men of the so-called German 'Legion of Death'[87] had fled Oedenburg in great haste toward Kapuvár after stealing 53,000 forint from the county treasury, destroying the Oedenburg-Neustadt railway, and demolishing all the bridges behind them.

The imperial troops entered Oedenburg surrounded by cheering townsfolk.[88] *Oberst* Horváth was detained a few days in Oedenburg while he made the necessary preparations to appoint capable officials who were completely loyal to the legitimate government, as well as to repair the damaged road network. On the 17th the *Feldmarschall* sent him a written order from Petronell telling him to remain in Oedenburg for now anyway, to clear the enemy entirely from the area between the Leitha mountains and Lake Neusiedl, to disarm the national guard in all the towns, and then to advance at the same time as the army through Kapuvár toward Raab; this was confirmed by a written order from Karlburg on the 21st. Horváth had pushed his advance guard forward to Kapuvár on the 24th (one wing of Kress *chevauxlegers*, two companies of Viennese volunteers and two companies of Romanen *grenzers*), but he and the rest of his force did not reach Sz. Miklos [Rábaszentmiklós, Hungary] until the 25th.

In an order from the *Feldmarschall* on the 25th which asssumed he had advanced further than he had, he was instructed to enter Egyed on the 26th – that being the day before the attack on Raab – and then to push on toward Téth and Szentmárton [Pannonhalma, Hungary] on the 27th, an order which however he could not fulfil as he did not reach Egyed until the 28th and Téth on the 29th. While the advance continued toward Ofen, *Oberst* Horváth was now tasked with scouting on the right flank of the *Banus*'s column in the direction of Veszprim [Veszprém, Hungary] and Stuhlweissenburg.

Rittmeister Escherich, who galloped back to *Oberst* Horváth with this order, had brought the first credible information about the movements of the rebel corps under Moritz Perczel.

87 Presumably, this was the first company of the German Legion raised by Peter Giron in Oedenburg. This unit sported a death's head emblem on its hats, hence the nickname. The initial core of the Legion was formed from members of the Wiener Akademische Legion who had escaped from Vienna when the revolution was suppressed. Maximilian Bach, *Geschichte der Wiener Revolution im Jahre 1848* (Vienna: Ignaz Brand, 1898), p.919. Giron claimed to have been a Prussian officer, but in 1848 he was a labourer in Vienna. He fought in the Vienna revolutions, then fled to Hungary where Kossuth commissioned him to form a legion from other Austrian and German fugitives, which joined Görgei's army for the Winter Campaign. He himself was wounded in the action at Bábolna, and from January 1849 was raising and organising the 2nd and 3rd battalions of the German Legion. He went absent in June and was charged by Görgei; he then resigned in July, while the Legion was dissolved for disciplinary reasons and converted into the 126th *honvéd* battalion. He was executed by the imperial authorities at the end of the war. Bona, *Tábornokok*.

88 The majority of Oedenburg's population was German-speaking rather than Hungarian at that time. This is no longer the case today.

This reportedly numbered about 15,000 men when it abandoned its position on the river Mur and moved north toward Güns [Kőszeg, Hungary], followed by *Feldzeugmeister Graf* Nugent. Its advance guard, reportedly 5,000-6,000 men with 18 guns, entered Körmend on the 21st and had announced that it would arrive in Güns on the 22nd. But the news that Görgei had meanwhile retreated to Raab had made Perczel change his direction of march and turn quickly toward Raab, leaving 9,000-10,000 men facing Nugent. Accordingly, he marched to Rum on the 23rd and Jánosháza on the 24th, from where he still had 70 km to go to get to Raab. There he received the order to march immediately to Pápa to cover the exposed left wing of the main army that was at Raab. He therefore moved to Devecsér on the 25th and reached Pápa on the 26th. From there it was still three posts (45 km) to Raab.[89] It was therefore impossible for him to reach Raab in time on the 27th, the day it was attacked.

From the above it emerges that Görgei certainly intended to hold the Raab position and may have counted on Perczel's assistance but began his retreat when he saw his right wing being outflanked and had to give up on the hope that Perczel would arrive in time. On hearing that Raab had been evacuated, Perczel marched to Tamási [Bakonytamási, Hungary] on the 27th and to Kis-Bér on the 28th, where he incorporated a detachment Görgei had sent along this road: a Pesth battalion, two squadrons of Husaren-Regiment Nr. 9 and a horse artillery battery. There he received the order to cover the army's left wing from now on, to occupy the very advantageous position behind Kis-Bér at Sárkany [Bakonysárkany, Hungary] on the 30th, and to accept battle there; for Görgei had been instructed to hold the line of Neszmély, Dotis [Tata, Hungary], Bánhida [Tatabánya, Hungary] and Kömlőd with the main army. In the event of further retreat he was instructed to use the route through Lovas-Berény toward Márton-Vásár, and to occupy a position on the heights behind Baracska.

Understandably, none of these details were known until later. The fact that Perczel was in Pápa on the 26th and had moved from there into the hills toward the Stuhlweissenburg road was only learned in Raab from *Oberst* Horváth on the 28th, immediately before the army resumed its advance toward Ofen. Nothing definite was known about Perczel's strength, and even less about where he had been roaming around before he arrived in Pápa; for until then he had been assumed to be still facing *Feldzeugmeister Graf* Nugent in the area of Körmend, Sárvár or Jánosháza. But in any case, it could be expected that any move of his toward Raab would be discovered soon enough by Horváth.

Feldmarschall Lieutenant Baron Welden had generally shown himself to be remarkably active and effective and had been granted extended authority by the *Feldmarschall* to act on his own initiative. So as to re-occupy the stretch of territory that had been exposed by *Oberst* Horváth's continued advance toward Raab, to guard the area of Oedenburg, Güns and Steinamanger [Szombathely, Hungary] against attempts at sedition, to cover the borders of Austria and Styria, to disarm the country, and to maintain communications with the army and with *Feldzeugmeister Graf* Nugent's force, he had pushed forward a force under *Oberst* Klehe of the Wrbna Chevauxlegers:

89 Presumably 'posts' means posthouses at which mail couriers would obtain fresh horses at intervals of about 15 km, roughly an hour's ride.

One battalion of Szluiner *grenzer*
One battalion of Oguliner *grenzer*
One division of the Wocher regiment
Four squadrons of Wrbna *chevauxlegers*
Two rocket launch stands.

Some of these were sent to Wiener Neustadt on the 19th, and some to the border villages nearby. They then patrolled in mobile columns throughout the area of Oedenburg, Eisenstadt, Güns and Körmend. A battalion of Liccaner *grenzer* that belonged to the Wien garrison but had been detached to Graz was also detailed for this purpose, but meanwhile had been summoned by *Feldzeugmeister Graf* Nugent and otherwise employed.

A further reinforcement of two battalions, a squadron of Wrbna *chevauxlegers* and a battery was sent to Oedenburg on the 25th, and after *Oberst* Klehe was recalled, command of the whole force was transferred to *Oberstlieutenant Graf* Althan of the Wrbna Chevauxlegers, to whom *Major* Jungbauer of the general staff was attached.

Güns had already been garrisoned by a division of Wocher *landwehr* and a division of Wrbna *chevauxlegers* on the 25th. On the 27th *Oberstlieutenant* Althan arrived there as well with four Oguliner companes, two squadrons of Wrbna *chevauxlegers* and two rocket launch stands, and moved to Steinamanger on the 28th, establishing communications with *Feldzeugmeister Graf* Nugent who was in Körmend. A contribution of 100,000 forint was levied from Güns as reparation for the shameful murder of 50 Croats there in the previous autumn.[90] When the perpetrators were subsequently handed over, *Feldmarschall Lieutenant Baron* Welden reduced this sum by half, which was duly collected and in March 1849 on the order of the *Feldmarschall* was given to the *Banus* to be distributed to the families of those who had been murdered.

While the advance continued toward Güns and Steinamanger, Oedenburg remained garrisoned and communications were maintained continuously with *Oberst* Horváth's column via Sz. Miklós and Kapuvár. Since *Feldmarschall Lieutenant Baron* Welden assumed that *Feldzeugmeister Graf* Nugent would push forward to Steinamanger, he had ordered *Oberstlieutenant* Althan in that case to return to Oedenburg but to keep a garrison in Güns. When this did not happen, he instructed Althan to send a patrol force of four Liccaner companies and a division of Wrbna *chevauxlegers* under *Major* Krapf by forced march through Sárvár and Klein-Zell [Celldömölk, Hungary] to Marczaltö [Marcaltő, Hungary] on the 29th, from where the Liccaners were to advance to Raab and form the garrison there, while *Major* Krapf was to patrol toward Pápa and remain in communications with *Oberst* Horváth for as long as possible.

90 Bánlaky says that on 12 October 1848, as the beaten Croat army was heading toward Austria for refuge, Todorovic's contingent of about 10,000 Croats was confronted by Karger with 2,000 national guards who were then joined by three more battalions from Kanizsa; and that Todorovic was then forced to march via Güns. He quotes an official report to the Hungarian war ministry that mentions the capture of 37 Croats and says the 'barbaric enemy' had committed such acts of rape and pillage that the people could hardly be restrained from taking bloody vengeance on unarmed prisoners. Bánlaky, *A magyar nemzet*. There was also precedent from the battle of Pákozd, when outraged Hungarian locals set upon a Croat military wagon train and beat the Croats to death. Robert Hermann, 'A pákozdi csata, 1848. szeptember 29', *Hadtörténelmi közlemények*, Vol.127, No.2 (2014), pp.353-394.

After leaving a small garrison in Steinamanger and Güns, *Oberstlieutenant* Althan returned to Oedenburg, making a small detour through Saj Káll [Sajtoskál, Hungary] and Schützen [Lövö, Hungary].

Feldmarschall Lieutenant Baron Welden had retained control of these small detachments belonging to the Wien garrison. Given that the army was now advancing further, the *Feldmarschall* asked him likewise to take responsibility for direction and support of the forces under *Generals* Götz and Simunich, for reports from those formations could only reach the army high command with considerable delay via Wien; an arrangement which while in and of itself appropriate, had however sometimes caused plans to diverge from one another.

The Action at Moór, 30 December 1848

Returning now once more to the offensive operations of the army outside Raab, before anything else we should describe I. Armeekorps's detached advance along the Moór road. This corps had arrived in Mező-Eörs on the 29th. Since this place did not provide enough accommodation and the troops could not camp out in the severe cold, Brigade Gramont and the Kaiser Franz Josef dragoons and the Banderial hussars were pushed forward to Kis-Bér, to where the *Banus* also transferred his corps headquarters.

Despite having just fought its glorious action at Bábolna on the 28th, Kavallerie-Brigade Ottinger joined I. Armeekorps on the 29th and was billeted in the villages between Mező-Eörs and Kis-Bér.

The *Banus* had originally intended to grant his men a rest day on the 30th; but when he arrived in Kis-Bér he learned that Perczel had marched from there that very morning toward Moór, reportedly with 8,000 infantry, 600-800 cavalry and 24 guns.[91] The *Banus* therefore decided to set off toward Moór with all his combat forces before dawn on the 30th. The troops were ordered to be on the march at 5:00 a.m.

The Banderial-Husaren regiment formed the advance guard, followed by Brigade Gramont. Kavallerie-Brigade Ottinger followed approximately 7 km behind, with Division Hartlieb and the Artillerie-Korpsreserve another 7 km behind that. The march therefore began with the units in the same order and at the same intervals as for their billeting. The Kaiser dragoon regiment that was over on the other side of the highway had also been assigned to the advance guard, but the order went astray and was not received in time, so the dragoons only followed on later.

The leading corps elements moved out beyond Sárkány, with woods lining the road on either side, when its foremost vanguard encountered the enemy and pushed back his advance outposts to his position 2 km this side of Moór.

In the enemy centre there were a couple of batteries on a gentle rise from which the very long narrow strips of woods in which our troops were advancing alongside the highway were completely enfiladed. The enemy right wing extended along heights covered with vineyards, his left was covered by a fairly deep watercourse and was right in front of the edge of the woods from which our troops had to debouch.

In this situation, where the enemy had only been contacted by the leading elements of I. Armeekorps comprising the Banderial-Husaren and the three battalions of Brigade Gramont,

91 Against which the *Banus* with his 14 battalions and 20 squadrons had about twice as many men and guns.

with a 7 km gap between it and Brigade Ottinger in the second echelon, and the third echelon (Division Hartlieb and the Artillerie-Korpsreserve) being 15 km away, the *Banus* found himself obliged to occupy as covered a position a possible for the time being, and sent orders to *Generalmajor* Ottinger and *Feldmarschall Lieutenant* Hartlieb to move up with the utmost haste. Once the corps was united, the infantry were to advance against the enemy's right flank and if possible drive him away from his line of retreat, while the cavalry attacked his left wing. Until then the enemy was just to be engaged frontally and pinned.

The rebels meanwhile had opened up and maintained an ineffective long-range fire against the head of the column. *Generalmajor* Ottinger and his cuirassier brigade arrived on the battlefield at 10:00 a.m. Now the 3. Bataillon Liccaner was sent to the edge of the wood on the left of the road to watch out for any enemy moves on that side. The 5. Jäger-Bataillon and 2. Bataillon Gradiscaner were pushed into the wood on the right. Meanwhile the horse artillery batteries had come up and opened fire on the centre of the enemy position, in which they were however very much at a disadvantage in their lower position completely in the open.

Under cover of the artillery fire, *Generalmajor* Ottinger and the Wallmoden Kűrassiere Regiment advanced on the right of the highway while the Hardegg Kűrassiere Regiment moved up in reserve on the left. These preparatory manoeuvres must have made the enemy worry that a serious attack was coming, as he prepared to retreat. There was therefore no time to wait any longer for the troops in the rear who were still a long way away, so Ottinger advanced to the attack.

The Oberstlieutenant's Division of the Wallmoden cuirassiers charged the nearest enemy battery, obtaining the significant trophy of an ammunition caisson, and at the same time being attacked by a division of hussars that had been deployed to protect the artillery. But although *Rittmeister Graf* Schaffgotsche was killed, *Rittmeister Baron* Laferté and *Hauptmann Graf* Pimodan of the quartermaster-general's staff seriously wounded and a fair number of men and horses lost, the battery was taken, the hussars beaten, a nearby battalion routed, and the centre of the enemy position smashed.[92]

From now on the enemy did not make any further stand anywhere. He fled in all directions: the cavalry and 15 or 16 guns mostly along the road to Stuhlweissenburg, some of the infantry through the nearby vineyards into the hills, others toward Lovas-Berény, taking two guns with them. Those who could not get away quickly enough sought refuge in Moór, firing at the pursuing cavalry in the streets and from windows. This factor, together with the cavalry's understandable fatigue after the arduous marches, the surprise attack at Bábolna, and their rush to the battlefield made it impossible to pursue the fleeing enemy any further. Nor was it advisable to press into Moór immediately with the few battalions available when it was still strongly held by the enemy; this could not be done until Division Hartlieb finally arrived, whereupon the battle ended.

Apart from the very significant number of enemy dead left on the battlefield, nearly 2,200 prisoners were taken in the course of this day and the next, including 23 officers. Our losses were insignificant. *Rittmeister Graf* Schaffgotsche was killed, as we have said, at the head of his squadron, covered in countless sabre cuts. As well as the officers named earlier, *Oberst* Feyerváry of the Wallmoden cuirassiers was also lightly wounded.

92 We noted the impact of the Austrian cuirassiers at Bábolna two days earlier. Here again we see a destructive cuirassier charge routing an enemy battalion and deciding the action.

The decisive outcome and the laurels of the day were due to Brigade Ottinger, which had been allowed to prove its courage in the most glorious way on two different battlefields 40 km apart within 24 hours of each other. The *Banus* particularly praised *Generals* Ottinger, Zeisberg and Gramont. The troops had fought with courage and endurance throughout. *Oberstlieutenant Graf* Sternberg and *Hauptmann Grad* Pimodan took the first enemy cannon at the head of a division of Wallmoden cuirassiers. The other five guns fell into our hands later. A detachment of 5. Jäger-Bataillon also captured an enemy howitzer.

After news arrived that the rebel *Oberst* Sekulich[93] was reportedly coming to join Perczel in Stuhlweissenburg with 5,000-6,000 men, the *Banus* felt that he should not continue his march any further but should stay as concentrated as possible in and around Moór.[94] Division Hartlieb and the Artillerie-Korpsreserve therefore spent the 30th and 31st in Moór. Brigade Ottinger was pushed forward to Csák-Berény [Csákberény, Hungary], and Brigade Gramont to Bodajk and Söréd together with the Banderial hussars and four squadrons of Kaiser dragoons.

Meanwhile the *Banus* had asked the *Feldmarschall* to assign the Reserve-Kavallerie-Division Franz Liechtenstein 'to rapid pursuit of the enemy', and on that condition offered to march quickly via Lovas-Berény to Márton-Vásár. The *Feldmarschall* could not accede to this request. Apart from the Banderial-Husaren Regiment, there were another 20 squadrons with I. Armeekorps already. If the Reserve-Kavallerie-Division had now been added to these, then this flank column – which was moving through the Bakony Forest and mostly broken terrain anyway – would have had 45 squadrons with it in addition to the oft-mentioned Banderial hussars, while the main body of the army that was advancing through much more open country would have had just seven squadrons left. The *Banus* was therefore told to continue his march according to the orders that had been issued.

As was only learned from Hungarian official documents after the end of the war, Perczel's force in the action at Moór consisted of just five and a half infantry battalions, six and a half hussar squadrons and 24 guns, or 5,620 infantry and 730 cavalry altogether.

In detail:

1. Pesther Bataillon
35. Honvéd-Bataillon
47. Honvéd-Bataillon
48. Honvéd-Bataillon
50. Honvéd-Bataillon
One company of pioneers
Two squadrons of 1. Husaren-Regiment
One squadron of 4. Husaren-Regiment

93 István Szekulics (1810-85) was a former imperial lieutenant who joined the new *honvéd* in May 1848. He held field commands until July 1849 when he was assigned to the war ministry, surrendering at Világos at the end of the war. He was sentenced to 18 years in prison but pardoned in 1850. Bona, *Tábornokok.*

94 The (exaggerated) reported strength of Perczel and Sekulich combined would still have been somewhat less than the *Banus*'s, and Perczel's force had just been routed and split up. In the circumstances, the *Banus* would have done better to continue his advance and carry out rapid pursuit himself, rather than asking that Liechtenstein's division should do it. Evidently the *Feldmarschall* thought so too.

A half-squadron of 5. Husaren-Regiment as headquarters escort
Three squadrons of 9. Husaren-Regiment
Half a 6-pounder battery (4 guns)
One 6-pounder battery (8 guns)
One horse artillery battery (8 guns)
A third of a 1-pounder battery (2 guns)
A third of a 10-pounder battery (2 guns).

As previously mentioned, Perczel had arrived in Kis-Bér on the 28th and had been instructed by Görgei to occupy and hold the extremely advantageous position at Sárkány, between Kis-Bér and Moór. He set off to march toward Moór early in the morning on the 29th. However, instead of halting as ordered and deploying at Sárkány, he carried on marching to Moór and quartered his troops there, which he may well have been caused to do by the bitter cold that had set in.

The area around Moór does not provide any advantageous position. The town is enclosed by the surrounding heights, can easily be outflanked, and has an extensive forest about 1,000 paces in front of it that would conceal an attacker's movements.

Perczel, who had given up the position at Sárkány, soon convinced himself that Moór could not be held, and supposedly had already taken the decision to continue to retreat when a despatch from the government ordered him to accept battle there; which, as we have seen, turned out disastrously for him. Since there had been no pursuit, he was able to rally the remnants of his shattered corps again on the 31st, and also brought up a detachment of approximately 1,000 men under *Oberst* Sekulich through Stuhlweissenburg.[95] He continued his retreat through Márton-Vásár toward Ofen.

The *Banus*'s decision to set off immediately upon receiving the news of Perczel's presence in Moór, without regard for the march plan that had been issued, deserves the highest praise.[96] The result of the battle would have been more significant if the attack could have been carried out with his force united, for which however a march plan that took into account the extended dispersal of the troops necessitated by the bitter weather would have been necessary.

The Investment of Komorn, 29-31 December 1848

We now return to the manoeuvres that II. Armeekorps and the Reserve-Kavallerie-Division had carried out in the meantime.

II. Armeekorps had likewise set off from its position at Sz. Ivány on the 29th. Division Csorich and Brigade Colloredo had reached Ács toward 3:00 p.m., while Brigade Lederer that had started from Raab took position at the confluence of the Concó and the Danube to secure the left flank. Kavallerie-Division Liechtenstein was at Puszta-Harkáli [Herkálypuszta,

95 Sekulich's force turns out to be rather smaller than the 5,000-6,000 men whose alleged approach halted the *Banus* on the 30th and 31st.

96 Nobili praises the *Banus*'s aggressive action on the 29th but refrains from balancing it with criticism of his caution on the 30th and 31st. Presumably the *Banus* liked the prospect of two-to-one odds, which in reality was closer to three-to-one, better than facing Sekulich and Perczel combined on the 30th on (as he thought) closer to even terms – though in fact he would again surely have had double the enemy strength.

Hungary], Mocsa and Alt-Szöny [Ó-Szőny, now an eastern suburb of Komárom, Hungary], patrolling toward the Komorn bridgehead.

The ten redoubts that the enemy had spent months building at great cost in money and effort, which enclosed the Sandberg [now the Monostor fort in the west of Komárom] and the village of Neu- Szöny [Új-Szőny, the centre of modern Komárom, Hungary] and formed an extended entrenched camp in front of the bridgehead, had been abandoned. Part of the breastworks remained unfinished. The tricolour still waved above one of the redoubts.

What could be learned of the situation in Komorn at the time, and indeed subsequently proved to be correct, was essentially as follows:

The garrison numbered 9,000-10,000 men, of whom very many were new recruits. There were 35 field guns with limbers and teams. The garrison was therefore barely sufficient to occupy the extensive fortifications of the fortress itself and the bridgehead on the right bank of the Danube. There could be no thought of it holding the works around the entrenched camp as well.[97] The director of engineering was a former *Oberstlieutenant* in the engineer corps, Török;[98] the fortress commander, as mentioned already, the former hussar *Rittmeister* Majtheny. What was not known at the time, and what significantly undermined the hope cherished until then that the fortress would voluntarily surrender, is that at his side was one Meszleny, a former imperial officer and Kossuth's brother-in-law, who was among the most exalted of the revolutionaries and had been assigned to be *Platz-Major* [deputy commandant] of the fortress and keep an eye on Majtheny.[99]

Feldmarschall Lieutenant Wrbna and his force advanced toward the Komorn bridgehead on the 30th. According to the instructions he had been given, he was supposed to deploy just outside artillery range of the bridgehead so that the garrison could see how very considerable the forces at his command were, because the intended intimidation of the garrison relied on this. However, Wrbna deployed too far away to suit this purpose.

Major Bach of the quartermaster-general's staff was now sent with verbal orders as a negotiator to the Komorn fortress commandant, with a written demand for his unconditional surrender and the capitulation of the fortress.

Majtheny, who had served as a *Rittmeister* in the same regiment of which that Wrbna who now stood before Komorn had been colonel – another factor which could be expected to facilitate the negotiation – seemed initially irresolute and visibly diffident but was soon persuaded by Meszleny and his crowd to make a written declaration that he would defend the fortress to the death.

97 The main fortress was 2.5 km across with 4 km of wall frontage on its western (landward) side, about 5 km fronting onto the rivers Danube and Waag, and 2.5 km of walls defending the Waag bridgehead. The entrenched camp south of the Danube had a 5 km frontage, so might indeed have stretched the garrison too far. The fortress also had some 200 defensive guns in the fortifications in addition to the field artillery. Bona, *Hungarian Revolution*, p.382.

98 Bona lists four Hungarian officers by the name of Török; however, none of them fits this description and none is listed as having participated in the defence of Komorn.

99 Jenő Meszlényi (1814-1900) was indeed Kossuth's brother-in-law. He was also a former imperial officer who joined the *honvéd* in September 1848. He took part in the defence of Komorn from January to April 1849 but in May 1849 transferred to the national high command, where he served until the surrender at Világos. He was sentenced to death, commuted to 18 years' imprisonment, and released in 1850. Bona, *Tábornokok*.

Upon this declaration, as night fell *Feldmarschall Lieutenant Graf* Wrbna shifted some of his troops into the abandoned quarters, and some into villages closer to the Fleischhackerstrasse along which he was supposed to move next day. However, *Feldmarschall Lieutenant* Ramberg was ordered to stay and besiege the bridgehead with Brigade Lederer, the Ficquelmont dragoon regiment, one 12-pounder battery and one horse artillery battery from the artillery reserve: a total of three battalions, five squadrons and 18 guns. He was to establish communications as soon as possible with *Generalmajor* Neustädter, who was deployed on the Great Rye Island on the left bank of the Danube for the same purpose.

The *Feldmarschall* ordered up *Feld-Genie-Direktor Oberst* von Trattern and *Major Baron* Smola of the artillery from Raab to Komorn, so as to provide a suitable report as soon as possible on the state of the fortress, especially of the bridgehead. This report stated that it was particularly necessary to demolish part of the entrenched camp's earthworks on the Sandberg, and to occupy and fortify Alt-Szöny, where some artillery should also be deployed. *Ingenieur Hauptmann* Kochmeister was put at *Feldmarschall Lieutenant* Ramberg's disposal with a company of sappers and tasked with carrying out these works.

Feldmarschall Lieutenant Graf Wrbna entered Kocs on the 31st with II. Armeekorps and Reserve-Kavallerie-Division Liechtenstein, thus getting into the right position for continuing the army's coordinated march toward Ofen. On this day the Reserve-Infanterie-Division and the Artillerie-Hauptreserve were at Bána and Igmánd [Nagyigmánd, Hungary], the *Feldmarschall*'s headquarters was in Bábolna, and I. Armeekorps was still at Moór.[100]

Upon the news of Perczel's defeat, Görgei had abandoned his plan to hold the Bánhida position and retreated through Ober-Gálla toward Bicske.

The last day of the year had brought the first snow, and with it, cold reaching 20 degrees on the Réaumur scale.[101]

The March to Ofen, 1-4 January 1849

On 1 January 1849, I. Armeekorps was in Lovas-Berény, II. Armeekorps in Ober-Gálla from where the last hussars had fallen back shortly before our vanguard arrived, the Reserve-Kavallerie in Bánhida, the Reserve-Infanterie-Division Edmund Schwarzenberg and the Artillerie-Hauptreserve partly in Kocs and partly in Dotis, and the headquarters in Kocs. *Feldmarschall Lieutenant Graf* Wrbna was charged with directing his attention primarily toward the area on his left flank, in particular the roads from Zsámbék, Páty, etc., toward Ofen, and was to patrol in that direction. Similar instructions were also issued to the Reservekorps.

On 2 January, I. Armeekorps reached Márton-Vásár unopposed. II. Armeekorps advanced to Bicske, from which the last hussars were chased out by a detachment of Civallart *uhlans*.

The Reserve-Kavallerie-Division was at Német-Egyháza [Nagyegyháza, Hungary], Bárok [Óbarok, Hungary], etc., and patrolled right toward the Stuhlweissenburg road and left toward Zsámbék and Tinnye. The reserve infantry and artillery were in Ober-Gálla and thereabouts, the headquarters in Ober-Gálla. Here it was reported that Görgei had moved from Bicske toward

100 This puts the headquarters between the two reserve formations, but over 15 km behind Wrbna's force at Kocs. It should surely have been further forward.

101 As the Réaumur scale defines the freezing and boiling points of water as 0 and 80 degrees respectively, presumably here Nobili means –20 Ré, which is –25°C.

Márton-Vásár the day before. It is certain that he halted in Bicske all day on 31 December and took a look around the area accompanied by one *Graf* Kasimir Bathiany's forest wardens.

I. Armeekorps began its march toward Tétény at 8:00 a.m. on 3 January in extremely severe, bitter cold. Brigade Gramont formed the advance guard together with the Kaiser dragoons and the Banderial hussars and was supposed to move through Tétény to Promontorium [Budafok, Hungary] if possible and take position there. Kavallerie-Brigade Ottinger that was deployed to the right of Márton-Vásár in Rácz-Keresztúr [Ráckeresztúr, Hungary] was ordered to march by the most direct route to Batta [Százhalombatta-Óváros, Hungary] and Hanzsabék [Hansabek, roughly between Érd-Ófalu and Érd cemetery now]. Division Hartlieb and the Artillerie-Korpsreserve were to move along the highway from Márton-Vásár to Tétény, and to leave the Artilleriereserve in Hanzsabék. The corps had already moved through the latter place and Brigade Gramont as advance guard was just in the process of crossing the last hill 2 km this side of Tétény when it ran into enemy hussars on the far slope, who, however, quickly retreated. A cuirassier detachment chased after them, but soon had to turn back again when it met larger enemy forces.

Six squadrons of hussars with 16 guns were now discovered in the open ground this side of Tétény, between the road and the vineyards to the north of it. The vineyards were held by infantry. There were strong hussar detachments between Tétény and the Danube. These were Perczel's troops, but they had been significantly reinforced by Görgei.

Feldmarschall Lieutenant Schulzig, who had only just joined the army in Hungary and had come to I. Armeekorps to replace *Feldmarschall Lieutenant* Kempen who had remained behind in Pressburg, now quickly sent a couple of divisions of cavalry with two batteries to the left of the road, while the *Banus* directed Kürassier-Brigade Ottinger from Hanzsabék across the snow-covered fields against the hussar detachments deployed between Tétény and the Danube, which entailed considerable difficulty because of the state of the ground.

The Kaiser Franz Josef dragoons marched left of the highway by divisions, coming under very heavy fire from the enemy batteries facing them, but without losing their customary composure and order in the slightest. In general, the enemy artillery was served with unusual accuracy on this day, while by contrast the batteries we deployed to take on the enemy were very much at a disadvantage because of the nature of the terrain.

Infanterie-Brigade Gramont pushed 5. Jäger-Bataillon and a battalion of *grenzers* under *Generalmajor* Zeisberg to the left into the vineyards, with Division Hartlieb supporting this manoeuvre.

Worried about his right flank, the enemy now retreated in good order into the very advantageous position at Promontorium behind Tétény, whose left wing rested on the Danube, its front being covered by a deep ravine, while the right wing rested on extensive vineyards.

The action was broken off by this retrograde manoeuvre of the enemy's into a stronger position. Later he retreated completely to Ofen, which may have been caused by the sudden appearance of *Feldmarschall Lieutenant Fürst* Franz Liechtenstein, who having been alerted by the heavy cannon fire moved swiftly from Etyek, where he had just arrived, toward Tétény with four squadrons of Max Auersperg cuirassiers and a rocket battery, thereby threatening the flank and rear of the enemy position.

As darkness was falling, Brigade Gramont and the four squadrons of Kaiser dragoons moved to Kis-Tétény [Ofentétény, Hungary], Division Hartlieb and the Artillerie-Korpsreserve to Tétény, and Kürassier-Brigade Ottinger stayed further back in Érd for the sake of finding shelter. This whole deployment was covered by outposts and strong quick reaction forces and was also in communications with II. Armeekorps on its left.

On this day the latter corps had arrived in Bia at 1:30 p.m. and pushed a battalion forward to Kis-Torbágy [now merged into the eastern end of Torbágy, Hungary]. Outside Bia the advance guard ran into a division of hussars with two cannon who quickly retreated toward Buda-Örs after a few long-range shots. It is not unlikely that these cannon shots signalled II. Armeekorps's advance to the enemy standing at Tétény, and were intended to make him aware that his line of retreat was already threatened.

Brigade Parrot of the Reserve-Kavallerie-Division was in Kis-Torbágy, and had detached a division to the left to Páty that later patrolled as far as Tinnye and Kovácsi [Nagykovácsi, Hungary] again.

Brigade Bellegarde was to the right of the road in Etyek, Baráthāza [it is unclear where this is], etc. When this brigade arrived in Etyek, *Feldmarschall Lieutenant Fürst* Franz Liechtenstein who was with it was informed that 50 or 60 hussars had moved from Etyek to Sóskút shortly before, and that that village was also held by infantry. To make sure of this, he immediately hurried there with four squadrons of Max Auersperg cuirassiers and a rocket battery, but found the village empty; however, as mentioned above, he did hear the piercing thunder of cannon from the direction of Tétény, so quickly set off and arrived in good time to threaten the right wing of the enemy position. After the enemy had retreated, the cuirassiers also returned to Etyek apart from one division that remained in Sóskút to maintain communications with I. Armeekorps.

On the 3rd the *Feldmarschall* had just arrived in Bicske with Reserve-Infanterie-Division Edmund Schwarzenberg and the Artillerie-Hauptreserve when very lively cannon fire was heard from the direction of I. Armeekorps.[102] He did not hesitate for a moment in ordering *Feldmarshall Lieutenant Graf* Wrbna, who was 15 km ahead in Bia, to advance without delay with a suitable force to support I. Armeekorps. In addition he sent his son and aide-de-camp, *Major Fürst* Alfred Windisch-Grätz, with twelve *uhlans* directly toward the gunfire, to obtain definite information as soon as possible.

Feldmarshall Lieutenant Graf Wrbna was just in the process of sending a brigade from Bia toward Tétény to carry out the mission he had been given when the thunder of the guns suddenly fell silent. He therefore restricted himself to sending one squadron of Kress *chevauxlegers* under *Rittmeister* Friederici to Török-Bálint [Törökbálint, Hungary] to seek to establish communications with the *Banus* from there. However, this squadron got no further than the vicinity of Kis-Torbágy, where it was prevented from continuing its march any further by abattis, and by the road being dug up in multiple places and the like and was obliged to turn back. The day before, Görgei had had hundreds of peasants render this road completely unusable as it was the one that led directly from Bia to support the *Banus*.[103]

Completely unexpectedly, a delegation sent to the *Feldmarschall* by the illegally perpetuated Hungarian parliament arrived in Bicske, comprising the ex-Prime Minister *Graf* Lajos

102 Bicske does not seem a sensible location for Windisch-Grätz's headquarters. In effect, his three formations were now echeloned almost directly behind one another: I. Armeekorps at the front in contact with the enemy at Tétény, II. Armeekorps 15 km behind it at Bia, and the *Feldmarschall* 15 km further back again with the rearmost formation, the Reserve-Infanterie-Division at Bicske. He should surely have been in a more central position with II. Armeekorps. This is not the first time we have seen him 'leading from behind'.

103 Good anticipation and energetic action by Görgei – and effective.

Batthyány,[104] the former minister Ferenc Deák,[105] Bishop Lonovics of Erlau [Eger, Hungary], *Graf* Anton Mailáth and Georg von Mailáth, *judex curiae*,[106] who had come to propose a ceasefire and recognition of the concessions that had recently been made.[107] In the event that the *Feldmarschall* should not feel he had the authority to negotiate them, they wished to present themselves to His Majesty the *Kaiser* in Olmütz.

When the presence of these magnates was announced, the *Feldmarschall* had it conveyed to them that he absolutely could not receive them as an official delegation [from what he regarded as an illegal parliament], but that it was open to them as it was to anyone to present themselves to him as private individuals, with the exception of *Graf* Lajos Batthyány, whom he could not receive as a private citizen. When they then presented themselves to the *Feldmarschall*, he explained to them that the only way to put an end to further bloodshed was by unconditional surrender. They were not permitted to continue their journey to Olmütz. Furthermore, since these magnates' proposals seemed designed to stall for time, and since during their stay at headquarters they could also have observed a few things, caution dictated that they be detained for a few days at least. They were therefore kept in Bicske and only escorted to Ofen by a troop of *uhlans* once the army had entered there, where they were all set free, though *Graf* Lajos Batthyány was then taken into captivity again that same evening.[108]

The further advance toward Ofen that was set for the next day absolutely had to be carried out with the utmost coordination among the individual corps advancing on separate roads; all the more so as the closer they got to the Danube, the more hilly, broken, rough and forested the terrain became, thus favouring surprise attacks and ambushes, which could be very handy for the rebels who were thoroughly familiar with the area and had the full support of the locals.

After it became possible for I. Armeekorps to advance on the shorter connection through Lovas-Berény instead of through Stuhlweissenburg, it had already reached Tétény on the 3rd and was therefore relatively further forward than II. Armeekorps which was in Bia on that day. Consequently, the instruction was issued to the *Banus* not to advance any further on the 4th, to reconnoitre the enemy position, and to take and hold Promontorium if it was not strongly occupied; however, this should not be done until II. Armeekorps had arrived in Buda-Örs and communications had been established with it via Török-Bálint and Nagy-Torbágy [Biatorbágy, Hungary], where Brigade Ottinger was.

II. Armeekorps accomplished its advance to Buda-Örs on the 4th, arriving there at 12:30 p.m.

104 Lajos Batthyány (1807-49) was prime minister of the first Hungarian government to answer to the Hungarian parliament. He was executed in Pesth on 6 October 1849. Bona, *Hungarian Revolution*, p.495.

105 Ferenc Deák (1803-76) was minister of justice in the Batthyány government. Bona, *Hungarian Revolution*, p.498.

106 Judge of the Country, the second-highest judge in Hungary.

107 Presumably, the concessions referred to are the 'Twelve Points' or 'March Laws' which gave Hungary a considerable degree of autonomy from Austria. These had been approved by *Kaiser* Ferdinand I in March 1848 when he had bigger problems than Hungary to worry about, but he then thought better of it and sought to recant.

108 And then held until the end of the war, when he was executed in Pesth on the same day as the 13 Martyrs of Arad.

Brigade Parrot of the Reserve-Kavallerie-Division was at the head of the column, while Brigade Bellegarde brought up the tail.

The division of Civallart *uhlans* detached to Páty under *Oberst* Almasy moved to Buda-Keszy [Budakeszi, Hungary], arriving there at midday. Halfway between the two towns they found an abatti that had to be cleared away. *Major* Kossuth and a good few hundred Hungarian troops had departed from Buda-Keszy shortly before the *uhlans* arrived there.

Part of Brigade Parrot occupied Török-Bálint, while Brigade Bellegarde and a battalion of infantry moved to Buda-Keszy.

Feldmarschall Lieutenant Graf Wrbna had been told not to make any isolated move beyond Buda-Örs, but just to reconnoitre the area ahead and the enemy position, and to maintain communications with I. Armeekorps.[109]

The Reserve-Infanterie-Division and the Geschütz-Hauptreserve occupied Páty, Torbágy, Etyek and Bia on the 4th, the headquarters also being in Bia. The bridging trains and all the baggage stayed behind in Bicske with suitable escort.

Among the escort units was a squadron of Civallart *uhlans*, of which one troop was to bring an 18-pounder field battery to the army immediately next day (the 5th). This had arrived in Bicske and was intended to be used in the attack on Ofen.

On the 4th the *Feldmarschall* had united his army in the small area around Promontorium, Tétény, Buda-Örs and Török-Bálint, barely 10 km from Ofen, and could proceed to attack the entrenched position on the following day.

When we take into account that the resumption of the offensive could not begin until 23 December, the day when II. Armeekorps was fully transferred to the right bank of the Danube next to Pressburg; that this corps needed four days' march to reach Raab; and that I. Armeekorps needed at least seven days' march or the next stage of the advance from Raab to Ofen, so there were 11 days' march to be covered altogether, but this whole stretch of march was covered by the army in just 13 days from 23 December 1848 to 4 January 1849; then this advance can only be described as swift and strenuous.[110] This is all the more so as this period included the manoeuvres to attack Raab and the actions at Bábolna, Moór and Tétény, the weather was extremely harsh, the winter days were short, and it was often necessary to spread the troops out for miles either side of the line of march.

The Occupation of Ofen-Pesth, 5 January 1849

Nothing was known exactly about the situation in Ofen, and there was still the constant expectation of encountering resistance. The fact that the enemy had abandoned the favourable defensive position at Bánhida and Ober-Gálla without a single blow being struck could be explained by Perczel's defeat at Moór; for by enabling I. Armeekorps to continue to advance through Márton-Vásár, this threatened the rear of that position. The great extent of the entrenched position outside Ofen was no reason to assume that the enemy felt too weak to

109 Caution and coordination being the *Feldmarschall*'s watchwords – but especially caution.

110 Except that, as noted above, it is debatable whether II. Armeekorps needed to cross the Danube, and if it did, whether the rest of the army needed to wait two days for it to do so; and the *Banus* halted unnecessarily for two days on the way from Raab to Ofen, wary of a force significantly smaller than his own.

defend it; for it was actually only the relatively short stretch from the 'Schöne Schäferin'[111] to the Blocksberg [Gellért Hill in Buda, Hungary] that was vulnerable to an attack, while the eastern and northern sectors of the entrenched line were not exposed at all, so only needed to be observed; lastly the line of retreat across the Chain Bridge could easily be protected by Buda Castle and the suburbs. The fact that moreover the enemy was undecided right to the last moment as to whether or not he should accept battle at Ofen is amply demonstrated by the proclamations that were found there, in which the inhabitants were exhorted to uprising and desperate resistance, and among which an appeal from the former *Artillerie-Feuerwerker* Mack stood out in particular for its impudent boasting.

On the afternoon of the 4th *Feldmarschall Lieutenant Graf* Wrbna reported that a patrol commander had crawled forward very close to the enemy position and thought he had detected that the suburbs of Ofen were no longer occupied, or at most only weakly held. The order was therefore issued that the troops at Buda-Örs and Nagy-Bálint [Törökbálint, Hungary] should advance along the road toward Ofen at dawn on the 5th; should deploy between the Blocksberg and the Adlerberg [Sashegy – 'Eagle Hill', Buda, Hungary]; and from there should push forward reconnaissance detachments toward the suburbs and Buda Castle. During this advance a *jäger* battalion should move to the left through the Schwabenwald [the forested hills that are now the Svábhegy and Széchenyihegy districts of Budapest, Hungary] to confirm that this was no longer occupied by the enemy.

That part of Division Liechtenstein that was in Buda-Keszy and the battalion that was there with it were ordered to join Brigade Schütte on its way through and to advance via the 'Schöne Schäferin' toward Ofen.

Kavallerie-Brigade Ottinger and the rest of Infanterie-Reserve-Division Schwarzenberg, as well as the Reservekorps's artillery reserve and the Artillerie-Hauptreserve were to follow II. Armeekorps, and to that end were to arrive on the plateau forward of Buda-Örs at 10:00 a.m., while the three infantry brigades of I. Armeekorps and the Korps-Artillerie-Reserve were to be deployed at Sachsenfeld [Albertfalva, Hungary] by the same time.

Oberst Schön of the Pionnierkorps was sent to Promontorium to investigate whether it might not be possible to cross the Danube there, partly on the ice where the surface was frozen, partly by bridging across the gaps where it was not; in which case it was intended to move troops across to the far bank, especially cavalry, to get onto the road from Pesth to Szolnok ahead of the retreating enemy formations. However, this planned crossing of the Danube proved to be completely unfeasible.

Between 5:00 and 7:00 a.m. in the morning on the 5th, *Feldmarschall Lieutenant Graf* Wrbna carried out the advance toward Ofen as planned. He had received word from his outposts that for a while they had been hearing a clatter like wagons and artillery on the move. Two peasants who had provided draft horses to the rebels and were returning from Ofen stated that the enemy had moved across the Chain Bridge during the night and was in full retreat on the left bank of the Danube.

111 The 'Fair Shepherdess', now Szépjuhászné in Ofenpest, Hungary. Supposedly the place where King Matthias Corvinus met a beautiful girl in the 15th century; in 1848 it was a restaurant that had been established in the 18th century.

A detachment of *uhlans* from Wrbna's advance guard now dashed forward onto the saddle of the Adlerberg lying directly in front of Ofen and found an abandoned redoubt there with three spiked 18-pounders.

As the advance continued toward the suburb of Christinen-Vorstadt [Krisztinaváros, along the southwestern side of Buda Castle] a few shots fell among the advance guard, but it soon became clear that the enemy had evacuated Ofen and even the castle, for thousands of curious spectators could be seen along its walls waiting for the entry of the imperial forces.

While *Feldmarschall Lieutenant Graf* Wrbna moved through Christinen-Vorstadt into Ofen undisturbed, Brigades Schütte and Bellegarde under *Feldmarschall Lieutenant Fürst* Edmund Schwarzenberg bypassed the Schwabenberg [the forested hills that are now the Svábhegy and Széchenyihegy districts of Budapest, Hungary], advanced past the 'Schöne Schäferin' and moved directly through the Vienna Gate into the castle, with Wrbna entering through the Stuhlweissenburg Gate immediately afterward.

When the *Feldmarschall* received word of the successful occupation of Ofen soon after his arrival in Buda-Örs, he betook himself to I. Armeekorps which had advanced meanwhile from Sachsenhausen [presumably Sachsenfeld] to the foot of the Blocksberg. On the way there he met a delegation from the municipal authorities of Ofen and Pesth, who declared that the sister cities submitted to him and pleaded to him to protect them. When he arrived at the point where the head of I. Armeekorps had halted, the *Feldmarschall* was received by the *Banus* while the troops cheered 'Hurrah!' at him from a thousand throats. Every soldier's eye shone with the knowledge that great things were being striven for and an important moment had arrived.

The *Feldmarschall* placed himself at the head of I. Armeekorps with the *Banus* at his side. The entry into Ofen ensued toward 1:00 p.m. through the suburb of Tabán, among thousands of onlookers on the streets, at the windows and on the slopes of the Blocksberg, who all behaved peacefully but who also brought no enthusiasm to the show, with few exceptions.

Afterthe troops of I. Armeekorps had paraded past the *Feldmarschall* at the foot of the Buda Castle rock, and he had made the necessary arrangements for pursuit of the enemy and for his troop dispositions, be betook himself to the royal castle where he set up his headquarters.

The Reserve-Infanterie Division occupied the fortress and the Ofen suburbs. The artillery park was driven onto the Generalswiese.[112]

I. and II. Armeekorps and the Kavallerie-Reserve-Division were transferred to Pesth in such a way that the units of I. Armeekorps were divided from those of II. Armeekorps by the Hatvan road, the former having to find accommodation to the right of this line and the latter to its left. Responsibility for security measures was divided between the two corps in the same way, and they were tasked with obtaining information about the direction of the enemy's retreat.

The imperial troops immediately took possession of all public buildings, military establishments and magazines, and of the steamboats as well. The gunboat *Meszáros* was later renamed the *Feldmarschall Lieutenant Graf Schlick* in recognition of his victory over the insurgent *General* Meszáros at Kaschau. All the artillery, ammunition supplies and the like that were found in the entrenchments constructed outside Ofen and then hastily abandoned by the enemy were brought into the fortress.

112 An area next to the northwestern wall of Buda Castle; the 'General's Meadow' as it was known around 1849, but before then and since as the Vérmező or 'Bloodfield' because of political executions that took place there. Gárdonyi, Albert, *A Krisztinaváros településtörténete.*

For the immediate pursuit of the enemy, *Generalmajor* Wyss advanced with one cavalry regiment and a battery along the Waitzen road and other detachments moved down the roads toward Gyöngyös and Czegléd [Cegléd, Hungary], which gradually brought in 670 prisoners. About 70 officers and 400 men had voluntarily turned themselves in. In Gödöllő, the stallions that had been taken away from the Bábolna stud farm were overtaken and brought in on the 6th by a cavalry detachment that had been sent there, as was the squadron of Husaren-Regiment Nr. 4 that had been escorting them and that immediately opted to change sides as well.

The *Feldmarschall* sent the following report to His Majesty the *Kaiser* on the 5th:

> In deepest reverence I report to Your Majesty that at midday today I took possession of Ofen and Pesth without striking a blow. Yesterday the advance guard of II. Armeekorps still had the enemy rear guard constantly in sight, so I thought that I could expect the rebel army to accept battle in its position outside Ofen that was favoured by nature and had been crafted to be still more defensible; and that I would be able to defeat it. But after the reverses he suffered at Bábolna and Moór the enemy seems to have completely lost what remained of his composure and self-confidence and this past night, after still behaving very boastfully the day before, he abandoned both cities and retreated toward Szolnok on the Theiss. His actual strength now consists only of the regular cavalry and artillery, since the remaining number of regular infantry present is only small, and even these are very demoralised. It is likely that most of the *honvéd* battalions and volunteers will gradually disperse during their retreat.[113] Before I entered Ofen I was received by delegations from the two cities declaring their submission to Your Majesty's Supreme Will, about which the official documents will arrive tomorrow. I found six spiked 12-pounder guns in the entrenchments outside Ofen, on the Stuhlweissenburg road and on the Blocksberg. As for what other supplies and war *matériel* may yet be discovered in the two cities, I shall wait to inform Your Majesty most humbly in a future report. According to all the signs and various assurances I have received in these first hours of my presence here, the arrival of our troops was yearned for by the great majority of the people of Ofen and Pesth, and all rejoice that they will partake again of the blessings of a speedy peace and an orderly government under which the country can recover again from the wounds inflicted on it by anarchy.[114]

This report, based on the statements taken from the senior officers and city officials who had detached themselves from the rebel cause at the first moment we entered the city, was taken by *Major und Flügeladjutant Fürst* Alfred Windisch-Grätz and carried together with the keys to the city to His Majesty the *Kaiser* in Olmütz.

Detailed information about the enemy's strength and direction of retreat was not obtained until the following day, and likewise it was only by staying in the country's capital for a while

113 The *Feldmarschall* was to be disappointed on this point, as the *honvéds* proved more resilient than he expected. Had his advances been bolder and his pursuits more vigorous in general, rather than regularly giving the enemy respite, this might have been otherwise.

114 This is clearly at odds with Nobili's comment above that the inhabitants watching the imperial army enter the capital 'brought no enthusiasm to the show'; but of course, the *Feldmarschall* is telling his *Kaiser* what he wants to hear.

that one was in a position to obtain more precise data about what state it was actually in and about the hopes and intentions of the revolutionary party.

Schlick's Corps Musters in Galicia, 5 November to 1 December 1848

While the army under the direct leadership of the *Feldmarschall* had advanced from the Hungarian border into the heart of the country in the space of barely three weeks, driving back or dispersing the enemy wherever he sought to resist, conquering the counties of Pressburg, Oedenburg, Wieselburg, Raab, Veszprém, Eisenburg [Vas County, Hungary], Szálád [Zala County, Hungary], and part of Komorn and Weissenburg [Fejér County, Hungary], occupying the capital, restoring order everywhere, and reinstating the lawful authorities, fortune had also favoured imperial arms in the other parts of the extensive theatre of operations, particularly *Feldmarschall Lieutenant Graf* Schlick's corps pushing in over the Carpathians into Upper Hungary.

However, before we turn to the operations themselves, brief mention should be made of the negotiations that had gone on with the commandant of Galicia, *Feldmarschall Lieutenant Baron* Hammerstein, concerning the mobilisation and deployment of the units of this corps.[115] Between 5 and 7 November the *Feldmarschall* had asked him to state what combat forces he could commit to support operations against Hungary from there. *Feldmarschall Lieutenant Baron* Hammerstein replied on the 11th offering to assign 14 battalions, 12 squadrons and 18 guns for this purpose (14,000-15,000 men), to command this corps in person, and to push into Hungary through Bartfeld [Bardejov, Slovakia], Eperies [Eperjes, Hungary, now Prešov, Slovakia] and Kaschau in concert with the main army's movements.

Given the situation in Galicia at the time, it did not seem advisable that *Feldmarschall Lieutenant Baron* Hammerstein should be away from his important post even just for a short time, since in Bochnia and Wieliczka we were already on the trail of the subversive activities of Kossuth's agents, who were making every effort to incite the workers in the salt mines to rebel. After the departure of four Palombini companies and a half-squadron of E.H. Karl *chevauxlegers*, the garrison of Krakau had dwindled to 2,196 men – many Poles had already gone across to Hungary, which demanded a close watch be kept on the border – and lastly the situation in neighbouring Prussia likewise aroused serious concern.

In weighing up these factors the *Feldmarschall* felt himself obliged to transfer command of the corps destined for Hungary to *Feldmarschall Lieutenant Graf* Schlick who had been posted to Krakau as military commandant, and to replace him there with *Feldmarschall Lieutenant* Legedics, who was as sensible as he was energetic. Legedics took over command in Krakau on 28 November 1848, while Schlick proceeded directly to Dukla where the corps was to concentrate. But on 17 November *Feldmarschall Lieutenant Baron* Hammerstein declared that

115 Wilhelm *Freiherr* von Hammerstein-Ecquord (1785-1861). A cadet in the King of Hannover's guard at the age of 14, he fought against Napoleon at Jena, and then for him in the service of the King of Westphalia until 1814 when he joined the Austrian army. During the unrest in Lemberg [Lviv, Ukraine] in November 1848 he was responsible for bombarding the city, destroying its university, its town hall, and its library of 60,000 volumes. He then maintained a state of emergency in Galicia and the Bukowina to suppress any further unrest. In 1849 he was retired from the army on grounds of deafness. He certainly seemed deaf to the *Feldmarschall*'s pleas for support. *BLKÖ*, Vol.7, pp.291-293.

after examining all factors more closely he would only be able to let six battalions, six squadrons and 15 guns leave for Hungary. After a great deal of bother he was persuaded to concede one more battalion and a half-battery, so that the corps's strength was brought up to seven battalions, six squadrons and 18 guns (18,000 men), organised as follows:

Brigade *Generalmajor* Fiedler

3. Bataillon E.H. Wilhelm
3. Bataillon Nugent (four companies)
2. Bataillon Hartmann
One division of the Kaiser Chevauxlegers
Sechspfündige Batterie Nr. 36

Brigade *Generalmajor Graf* Pergen
(This general only arrived later on, in Kaschau. In the interim the brigade was commanded by *Major* Podhayski of the Koudelka infantry.)

3. Bataillon Koudelka
3. Bataillon Mazzuchelli
One Landwehr-Bataillon Parma
One division of the Kaiser Chevauxlegers
Raketen-Batterie Nr. 11

Reserve-Brigade *Generalmajor Graf* Deym

1. Bataillon E.H. Wilhelm
One division of Sunstenau Kürassiere
Zwölfpfündige Batterie Nr. 11

Which were to be followed later by Sechspfündige Batterie Nr. 34 and half of Raketen-Batterie Nr. 12.

The deployment of these troops had generated multiple negotiations between the *Feldmarschall* and *Feldmarschall Lieutenant Baron* Hammerstein. On 23 November the former asked in vain that at least ten battalions, 12 squadrons and four and a half batteries should be sent. Hammerstein replied on the 27th that he could do no more.

On 5 December the *Feldmarschall* requested another two battalions from Galicia for Wien. The commandant in Lemberg only agreed reluctantly, since he seemed extremely disturbed by the continuous weakening of the troop strength in Galicia and declared that 'he could not let one more man go without incurring blame for it'. When the *Feldmarschall* specifically ordered him on 12 December to provide garrisons for Bartfeld and Eperies from Galicia, which only involved some eight to ten companies, and requested that he send a reinforcement of two battalions to Schlick to cover Eperies and Kaschau, Hammerstein asked to be excused from doing this and attached this handwritten letter to his report of the 16th from Lemberg:

> Without any troops in the country my power would be gone, and all that would be left for me to do would be running the administration, which cannot possibly satisfy my ethos as an old soldier; since boyhood I have only ever been happy at the head of my troops, and ever ready to shed my last drop of blood there; so before I see myself deprived of all my combat forces, I must respectfully ask Your Highness to seek another mission for me from His Majesty the *Kaiser.*

Although the *Feldmarschall* was absolutely entitled to order more troops to move to Hungary from Galicia without getting involved in any discussion about it, he still took Hammerstein's objections into consideration, since it was a well-known fact that only military force could keep the peace in Galicia and could counter the efforts of Hungarian subversives, Polish democrats and revolutionaries.

The instances of individual customs posts on the Galicia-Hungary border being surprised and disarmed by rebels, treasuries robbed and property endangered, had been increasing every day since the end of November, so that peasants were already being used for watch duty and patrols along the border.

Kossuth and his crew were counting on the certainty of an uprising in Galicia and tried to bring it about particularly by sending messengers to the few Hungarian battalions and hussar detachments in Lemberg.

On 20 November the then Hungarian War Minister Mészáros sent an impudent letter to *Feldmarschall Lieutenant Baron* Hammerstein demanding that he immediately release all the officers and men of the Hungarian regiments in Galicia who were in prison charged with disloyalty, or else reprisals would be carried out.

November was spent mobilising and concentrating the units destined to move into Hungary.

The *Feldmarschall* had expressed the basic principle to *Feldmarschall Lieutenant Graf* Schlick: 'The faster we unite our forces and defeat the Hungarian uprising, the better', and pushed forward the concentration of the units at Dukla as much as was feasible.

Schlick had arrived there on 1 December, and before his departure from Krakau had assured the *Feldmarschall* in simple words that: 'It will be my most eager endeavour to use my best efforts to justify the flattering confidence that it has pleased the *Feldmarschall* to place in me and honour me with.'[116]

On 1 December Brigade Fiedler was in Zmygrod [Stary Żmigród, Poland], Brigade Pergen in Dukla and Brigade Deym in Krosno.

To remedy the lack of pioneers, two companies were established, each of nine NCOs and 108 men, under *Oberlieutenant* Frölich of the Deutschmeister regiment and *Lieutenant* Schmidt of E.H. Wilhelm. For his general staff, *Feldmarschall Lieutenant Graf* Schlick received *Hauptmann* Scudier as its chief and *Oberlieutenant* Kerner.

Schlick Crosses the Carpathians and Occupies Kaschau, 5-11 December 1848

On the 5th the troops moved somewhat closer to the border; then at midday on the 6th Brigade Fiedler crossed the Hungarian border at Grabdie (Gráb) [Grab, Poland] and occupied Zbóró

116 Simpler words might have been 'I'll do my best, sir, I won't let you down'; but this is the Austrian army.

[Zborov, Slovakia] unopposed, while Brigade Pergen marched by the direct route from Dukla to Szvidnik [Svidník, Slovakia] and had to clear away more than 30 barricades along the way in the narrow Hunkovécz [Hunkovce, Slovakia] valley. Two Mazzuchelli companies and a half-squadron of *chevauxlegers* were detached to Sztropko [Stropkov, Slovakia] to cover the left flank. Brigade Deym reached Barwinek. Schlick and his headquarters were with Brigade Pergen. No resistance was encountered anywhere, and our troops were greeted in the most friendly way by cheering locals.

The next objective to be reached as soon as possible was the strategic crossroads of Eperies. On the 7th Brigade Fiedler therefore moved to Bartfeld, Brigade Pergen to Zbóró and Brigade Deym to Orlik [Vyšný Orlík, Slovakia]. On the 8th, Brigade Fiedler left the Nugent battalion in Bartfeld and moved to Raszlavicza [Raslavice, Slovakia] with its advance guard at Demethe [Demjata, Slovakia]. Brigade Pergen arrived in Bartfeld, Brigade Deym in Zbóró.

The rebels who had been spread around that area hurried back through Kapi [Kapušany, Slovakia] to Eperies.

At 6:00 p.m. in the evening of the 9th, Brigade Fiedler occupied Eperies amid the cheers of its inhabitants. The rebels had continued their retreat to Kaschau just a few hours earlier. Outposts were pushed forward beyond Sóvar [now the Solivar suburb of Prešov, Slovakia]. Brigade Pergen marched to Kapi, Brigade Deym to Demethe.

According to the information received in Eperies, Kaschau had been fortified and was reportedly defended by 20 guns, and there were supposedly entrenchments on the Kaschauer Berg as well. Furthermore, from captured letters it had been learned that the rebels were expecting reinforcements from Miskolcz.

Although *Feldmarschall Lieutenant Graf* Schlick had left four companies in Bartfeld and had also had to leave another two with the baggage in Eperies, he took the bold decision to advance against Kaschau without delay with his relatively small number of remaining troops (six battalions, six squadrons, 18 guns), which he may also have been encouraged to do by the *Feldmarschall*'s instruction 'to advance as swiftly as possible and give the enemy no time to muster new forces'.

On the 10th Brigades Fiedler and Pergen were concentrated in Eperies, and Brigade Deym moved to Sebes [Nižná Šebastová, now part of L'ubotice, Slovakia] close by.

It must have been Schlick's intention to surprise the enemy in Kaschau and force him to fight before he had received the expected reinforcements. Accordingly, the troops were set on the march from Eperies during the night of 10/11 in total silence, so as to arrive as early as possible in front of the position at Budamér that the enemy had occupied to cover Kaschau. The aftermath showed how important this early start was; for if Schlick had set off at 8:00 a.m. instead of 1:00 a.m., he would not have reached Kaschau that day, and on the next he would have found the enemy reinforced.

Brigade Fiedler set off as advance guard toward Kaschau at 1:00 a.m. in the morning of the 11th, after swapping its 6-pounder battery for a rocket battery. *Oberlieutenant* Fröhlich's pioneer company was also with this brigade; the other company had been disbanded again. After Brigade Fiedler came Brigade Pergen, followed by Brigade Deym. It was rainy, chilly and damp when they reached Somos [Drienov, Slovakia] early in the morning. The enemy had set fire to the truss bridge over the Tarcza there. Constructing a temporary bridge caused some delay; but the valiant *Oberlieutenant* Fröhlich soon had it fit for infantry to use, while the cavalry and artillery waded through the water after the steep bank had been dug away.

After the troops had crossed successfully, *General* Fiedler received the order 'to take the road to the right from Lemes [Lemešany, Slovakia] through Kisfalu [Malá Vieska, now absorbed into Družstevná pri Hornáde], Tapolczan [Tepličany, also now in Družstevná pri Hornáde, Slovakia] and Tehány [Ťahanovce, now a north-western outskirt of Kaschau] into the valley of the Hernad [Hornád], so as to take both the enemy position behind Budamér and that on the Kaschauer Berg [the north-south ridge, northeast of Kaschau, east of the Hornad] in rear'. This road was very bad, so the rocket battery's ammunition carts had to stay behind; indeed, the brigade did not reach Tapolczan until 10:00 a.m., from where it still had another two hours' march to go along the road to Kaschau.

Brigades Pergen and Deym had meanwhile advanced along the highway. Around 11:00 a.m. they contacted the enemy who had taken position a couple of miles behind Budamér, reportedly with 12,000-15,000 men including the Polish Legion. This corps was commanded by the rebel leader *Oberst* Pulsky, not to be confused with the diplomatic intriguer of the same name.[117]

The position at Budamér had a fairly good field of fire but no support to rest its flanks on; also the line of retreat from it over the bridge across the Hernad to Kaschau was extremely awkward, although the Kaschauer Berg provided an intermediate position. Its front was covered by a fire trench, the wood on its left flank lightly protected by abattis.

The Poles were deployed in the first line as skirmishers along the highway as far as the inn, and to the right as far as the wood that they also occupied. Twenty-four guns had been brought up to the front, and two were pushed forward under suitable escort to within cannon-shot of Budamér, but soon retreated to the main position after a few shots. The infantry, being some *honvéds* and some militia, were some distance behind the batteries. The enemy immediately opened up a well-directed artillery fire on our troops as they approached.

Sechspfündige Fussbatterie Nr. 36 commanded by *Oberlieutenant* Bartelmus now moved to the right of the road. The 12-pounder battery had initially moved to the right wing, but soon returned to the road because of the soft ground. Covered by the fire of these batteries, Brigade Pergen deployed to the right of the road and Brigade Deym to the left, both in two lines; the first line being deployed into line, the second in column of divisions. Now *Feldmarschall Lieutenant Graf* Schlick had the troops advance under heavy artillery fire. Two divisions of H.v. Parma-Landwehr under *Major* Singer were directed to the right against the extensive enemy-held wood, while the 3. Division of this battalion under *Oberlieutenant* Calvas advanced between that wood and Brigade Pergen's position, under the most intense artillery fire. The wood was attacked with great determination, taken and cleared of the enemy. Scarcely had the rebels become aware of this than they began to abandon their position, which they may also have been caused to do by the well-aimed fire of our batteries and of the infantry advancing on the road.

Schlick now sought to outflank the enemy's right with the whole of his cavalry under *Generalmajor Graf* Deym, and thereby to drive them all the more certainly toward Brigade Fiedler; but the broken ground thwarted this plan.

Brigade Fiedler had meanwhile debouched from the wood north of Tehány toward the highway, and protected its right flank with strong swarms of skirmishers against the enemy

117 Sándor Pulszky (1804-49). A former imperial officer who transferred to the *honvéd* in June 1848, after the operations against Schlick around Kaschau he was made military commander of Debreczin in March 1849. He then took command of the new reserve corps at Tokaj in May. He died of cholera in August 1849. Bona, *Tábornokok.*

occupying Tehány, which greatly delayed its march. The cavalry was also held back in reserve. Because of this, and also because of the extremely bad state of the roads, the brigade did not reach the heights to the east of the highway until 2:00 p.m.; so it was no longer possible to reach the bridge over the Hernad before the enemy to cut him off from Kaschau completely, which was actually its original mission.

The units that had advanced along the highway linked up with those of Brigade Fiedler near the Hernad bridge. But the enemy had already retreated entirely across it to Kaschau, and even his artillery had escaped, with the exception of one dismounted gun which was left lying by the farm at the foot of the Kaschauer Berg. The militia had mostly run away at the start of the fight anyway. The enemy left a strong detachment with several guns at the Hernad bridge as a rear guard.

Feldmarschall Lieutenant Graf Schlick had been given an inaccurate message that this bridge had been destroyed, so he could have no thought of forcing this well guarded crossing point. *Hauptmann* Scudier, formerly of the quartermaster-general's staff but meanwhile promoted to *Major* and corps aide-de-camp, now volunteered to cross the Hernad upstream of the bridge with the Major's Division of the Kaiser Chevauxlegers, to be followed by the 3. Bataillon Mazzuchelli as rear support, which seemed the only possible way to force the enemy rear guard deployed at the bridge to retreat, and so to reach Kaschau before nightfall. A ford was soon located, and within a few minutes the *chevauxlegers* were on the far bank of the Hernad and trotting swiftly forward.

Meanwhile on his own initiative *Oberlieutenant* Bartelmus and his battery had also driven up onto a hilltop to the left of the highway and opened up such effective fire against the defenders at the bridge and even against those that were still in front of the city that they retreated behind Kaschau all the more hastily when *Major* Scudier's cavalry approached.

A marshy ditch running square across the Hernad valley caused the *chevauxlegers* some delay; yet as soon as the leading half-squadron was across, it began the pursuit of the enemy toward Kaschau anew without waiting for the other six troops.

At the outskirts of Kaschau it was learned that the enemy had continued his retreat in three directions, namely: the Leutschau contingent toward Leutschau, the main body toward Torna [Turňa nad Bodvou, Slovakia], and the artillery and some infantry – mostly Polish troops – toward Miskolcz.

Full of courage and enthusiasm, *Major* Scudier and the half-squadron he had with him quickly chose the latter direction in the hope of taking a few more guns from the enemy. Just outside the city they took 100 prisoners and captured a wagon laden with weapons and powder barrels.

About 200 paces this side of the village of Barcza [Bárca, now a suburb of Košice, Slovakia], the half-squadron suddenly ran into an enemy detachment 80-100 strong. These were the Polish infantry who formed the artillery park's rear guard. They held their fire until the charging *chevauxlegers* were just 20 paces away. *Major* Concorreggio and *Major* Scudier, riding at the head of the half-squadron, were hit; the former by several balls, the latter taking a graze to the head, his horse shot from under him, and he himself taken prisoner. *Oberlieutenant* Begg met a similar fate, lying lightly wounded under his horse that had been shot dead, but managed to escape being captured. By the time reinforcements came up from the rear, the enemy had continued his retreat again and also darkness had fallen, so nothing more could be done to rescue the captured *Major* Scudier.

At 5:00 p.m. in the evening *Feldmarschall Lieutenant Graf* Schlick and all his troops entered Kaschau, which was already waving the white flag. The people stayed silent, for here too Kossuthian terror had the upper hand. The rebels had lost many dead and wounded, as well as 250 prisoners. Many weapons, supplies of cloth and provisions of all kinds were found in Kaschau. Our losses came to only a few dead and wounded.

All units had fought with courage and endurance. In his subsequent after-action report of 26 December to the army high command, *Feldmarschall Lieutenant Graf* Schlick especially commended the following officers of his entourage: corps aide-de-camp *Major* Scudier, *Oberstlieutenant Fürst* Franz Lobkowitz, *Rittmeister Graf* Starczinsky, *Oberlieutenants Baron* Wocher of the Savoyen Dragoner, Geusau of the E.H. Karl Chevauxlegers, *Graf* Bawarowsky of the Würtemberg Husaren, *Baron* Riesenfels of the Deutschmeister infantry and Würth of the Hohenegg infantry; also, from the units, *Major* Singer of the H.v. Parma infantry who led the fight in the wood on the right flank with both skill and courage, *Oberlieutenant* Calvas of H.v. Parma who also took part in it, *Hauptmann* Schuster commanding the Koudelka battalion, *Major* Podhayski also of the Koudelka who on this day commanded Brigade Pergen and displayed particular cool-headedness, *Oberlieutenants* Frölich of the Deutschmeister, Kollenstein of the Kaiser Chevauxlegers, and Kerner of the general staff, *Lieutenant* Schwarz of the Mazzuchelli infantry, and finally the two excellent battery commanders: *Oberlieutenants* Bartelmus and Hödl.

The after-action report of 11 January from *Obersts* Pulsky and Tokay to the Hungarian war ministry, found later in the Hungarian files, essentially says:

> The action at Kaschau is sufficient demonstration that the units under command of the corps are completely unfit to cross swords in earnest with the enemy. A few enemy cannon shots sufficed to panic all the columns deployed by the centre and left wing and part of the advance guard and cause them to scatter, so that scarcely a third of the infantry has rallied so far and stragglers are still constantly turning up in Miskolcz or Tokay, mostly unarmed. This reverse is mostly to be ascribed simply to the inexperience of the troops, who are no more than recruits stuck in uniforms. From this it can be seen that for the time being at least, it would be impossible to take on the enemy with these troops, even defending the best of positions.

The occupation of Kaschau accomplished the first and most pressing mission for the units that had advanced over the Carpathians from Galicia into Hungary. However, *Feldmarschall Lieutenant Graf* Schlick thought he was too weak to pursue the enemy any further. He also wanted to wait for the Danube Army to advance, which at that time had not yet crossed the border, and not to move too far from the Galician border until then.[118] He therefore halted in Kaschau for the time being and requested instructions and reinforcements. Brigades Fiedler, Pergen and Deym occupied Kaschau.

118 Simunich's division began its diversionary advance toward Pressburg on 14 December, and the main body began to move on 16 December.

From the Occupation of Kaschau to the Battle of Kaschau, 11 December 1848 to 7 January 1849

On 20 December two Nugent companies that had stayed behind in Galicia arrived in Eperies along with the reserve ammunition train, Sechspfündige Batterie Nr. 34 and half of Raketenbatterie Nr. 12. Four of these guns were moved to Kaschau, so the garrison of Eperies comprised one Nugent battalion, two Koudelka companies, two guns and half a rocket battery. The artillery that had followed on from Galicia as noted above brought the total number of artillery pieces up from 18 to 27.

As replacement for *Major* Scudier who had been taken prisoner outside Kaschau, *Major* Roesgen was sent from Lemberg, but the army high command sent *Major Baron* Gablenz from the headquarters in Karlburg. Gablenz arrived in Kaschau on 25 December and officially took charge of *Feldmarschall Lieutenant Graf* Schlick's general staff on 2 January, while Roesgen returned to Lemberg again.

Schlick had used his stay in Kaschau since 12 December to install officials loyal to the throne, to disarm the population and the national guard, etc. The whole stretch of territory from the Carpathians to Kaschau seemed pacified at this time, with the exception of the Zips and Zempliner Komitates [Szepes and Zemplén counties, now in Slovakia] where a predominantly rebellious spirit still reigned; order had been restored in the cities where it had been disturbed, some of those who had been led astray had been brought back onto the path of duty, and the well-intentioned had been encouraged.

Among the latter, above all we must mention *Graf* Stephan Szirmay, one of the most respected and influential men of Sarosser Komitat [Sáros County, now in Slovakia].[119] Spirited and full of love and self-sacrifice for his King's just and holy cause,[120] he volunteered to raise a *Freikorps* of men from Sarosser and Aba-Ujvárer [Abaúj-Torna County, now mostly in Slovakia] Komitates. This offer was readily accepted and deserves all the more recognition as many of Szirmay's estates were still in rebel hands, so were exposed to destruction; and anyway, at this grave moment he was the only one who demonstrated his loyalty by actions rather than merely by words. If more had followed his example, then many an evil could have been prevented and much bloodshed avoided.

The *Freikorps* was soon brought up to a strength of four companies of 120 men each, armed with the weapons captured from the rebels, and approved by His Majesty the *Kaiser* at the request of the *Feldmarschall*. *Graf* Szirmay was appointed as its commander and made a *Major* in the army, and later decorated with the Knight's Cross of the Hungarian Order of St. Stephen.[121]

119 Stephan Thomas *Graf* (István) Szirmay (1794-1857). When *Kaiser* Franz Joseph visited Miskolc in 1857, Szirmay paid homage to his emperor but then fell from his horse; he had suffered a stroke from which he did not recover. *BLKÖ*, Vol.42, pp. 207-208.

120 The *Kaiser* of Austria being also the King of Hungary.

121 Pražák refers derisively to how 'the Hungarian nobles [...] had supplied Szirmay with volunteers to fight against Kossuth. Even if he were worsted, they trusted in that way to ensure that Hungary would be governed by Hungarians. And in fact Vienna soon joined Hungary against the Slovaks.' Pražák, 'Czechs and Slovaks'.

The rebels who had been beaten in the action at Budamér and completely dispersed used the lull that had occurred to gradually rally and reorganise themselves to some degree in the vicinity of Tokay and Miskolcz.

Major Baron Gablenz of the general staff, who as noted had been sent by the *Feldmarschall* as a courier to *Feldmarschall Lieutenant Graf* Schlick right after the occupation of Pressburg to take charge of Schlick's general staff, arrived in Kaschau on 25 December. Before his departure he was made aware of the instruction that had already been issued to Schlick on 12 December by courier concerning the direction of march he was to take after occupying Kaschau. This written order said:

> From the latter place (Kaschau) there are two roads available to you for advancing toward Pesth: the highway through Erlau, and the cart track leading through Rosenau [Rožňava, Slovakia] and Losoncz to Waitzen. The former is certainly the better, but it has the disadvantage that it runs through an entirely Magyar area, while the latter is less good but runs along a stretch of country inhabited by Slovaks. This factor, and the consideration that by choosing this latter route (namely through Losoncz to Waitzen) you would move closer to the detachments advancing toward Neutra and the Mining Towns from hereabouts later, speak for using this route.

Major Baron Gablenz, who had previously been stationed in Upper Hungary and knew the area well, expressed his concern as to whether the road from Kaschau through Losoncz to Waitzen would be usable at this late season of the year, and regarded the highway through Miskolcz as more reliable. Consequently, it could not absolutely be insisted upon that *Feldmarshall Lieutenant Graf* Schlick should keep to the former as his line of march, and the choice of one or the other was left to his judgement depending on circumstances; but in any case, seeking to establish communications with the Danube Army advancing toward Ofen and with the detachments advancing north of it was strongly recommended.

At the time when *Major Baron* Gablenz arrived in Kaschau, the road from there through Losoncz to Waitzen was completely open and usable, whereas all reports indicated that there was no way through on the highway through Miskolcz, for the enemy was there in substantial force. *Feldmarshall Lieutenant Graf* Schlick nevertheless felt that he should carry out a reconnaissance in force in the latter direction, which may have been prompted by concern about being harassed from the flank while marching to Losoncz, as well as worrying about exposing Galicia. With this reconnaissance he also intended to drive out the rebel administration of Abaujvarer Komitat that had been transferred to Szikszó, and while returning to Kaschau, to have a column patrol through Zempliner Komitat and disarm it.

Accordingly, on 26 December four battalions, four squadrons and 18 guns advanced from Kaschau along the Miskolcz road, thus: *Generalmajor Graf* Pergen to Hidás-Némethi with three battalions, two squadrons, one 6-pounder battery and a rocket battery, as well as a pioneer detachment; *Generalmajor Graf* Deym to Enyiczke [Haniska, Slovakia] with one battalion, two squadrons, a 12-pounder battery and a pioneer detachment. *Generalmajor* Fiedler remained in Kaschau with two battalions, two squadrons and four 6-pounder guns; *Major* Kiesewetter stayed in Eperies with his Nugent battalion, two Koudelka companies, two 6-pounder guns and half a rocket battery.

Brigade Pergen's outposts at Hidás-Némethi were attacked by a small detachment of enemy hussars, who however quickly retreated.

On the 27th, Brigade Pergen marched to Forró and Brigade Deym to Unt. Novaj [now part of Novajidrány, Hungary] and Bicsoly. During the march a couple of demolished bridges had to be repaired by *Oberlieutenant* Frölich's pioneer detachment. The enemy had deployed in front of the village of Forró, and the village itself was held by Rembowsky's Polish Legion and a couple of guns. However, when our troops approached the enemy withdrew without a fight. *Feldmarschall Lieutenant Graf* Schlick had hurried after the troops from Kaschau on the 27th and was with Brigade Pergen. In Forró he received more definite information that the enemy had taken position at Szikszó 20,000 strong, and also that *General* Mészáros, commander of the Upper Hungarian army, had arrived in Miskolcz.

The continued advance on the 28th was prepared in such a way that Brigade Pergen was to outflank the enemy's position at Szikszó and threaten his left flank and rear, while Brigade Deym attacked him frontally. This operation was successful. Brigade Pergen, led by *Major Baron* Gablenz of the general staff who knew the area, bypassed the enemy left flank and took a half-company of *honvéds* prisoner (76 men). Another *honvéd* detachment was overtaken by the *chevauxlegers* of the advance guard and likewise captured. When *Feldmarschall Lieutenant Graf* Schlick reached Szikszó with Brigade Deym, the place was already occupied by Brigade Pergen.

Upon receiving the message that the enemy had taken position on the heights south of Szikszó, Schlick hurried forward to reconnoitre with the division of Kaiser Chevauxlegers and the 6-pounder foot artillery battery and had the division of Sunstenau cuirassiers and the 12-pounder battery follow, as well as the infantry *en échelon*. Because of the misty weather the enemy position could not be made out until within artillery range. The left wing was on a fairly steep hillside bordering the Hernad valley below Szikszó and was pushed forward somewhat toward that place, but the right wing was refused at the foot of the heights running south next to the Miskolcz road. The whole open plain of the Hernad valley was effectively dominated by this position.

Having arrived in artillery range, Schlick had the 6-pounder battery draw up partly on the highway and partly to the left of it and open fire against the right wing of the enemy position, supported later by the 12-pounder battery deploying to the right of the highway. The enemy replied with a lively but ineffective artillery fire from one battery at the foot of the hill next to the road and another on the heights further north and had about three divisions of hussars on the right wing form up on the plain for a charge. Schlick now ordered the division of Sunstenau cuirassiers under *Major Baron* Corizzutti that was in reserve behind the division of Kaiser Chevauxlegers to counter-charge; but a few well-aimed shells soon threw the hussars into disorder and caused them to retreat. Meanwhile Brigade Pergen's infantry had followed up from Szikszó. Despite the late hour of the day and the troops' fatigue, Schlick decided nevertheless to drive the enemy back toward Miskolcz. *Generalmajor Graf* Pergen now advanced with the 3. Bataillon Hartmann, a division of E.H. Wilhelm and the rocket battery toward the enemy left wing deployed on the edge of the heights. The rocket battery took an advantageous position from which it bombarded the enemy units obliquely, forcing them to retreat, and after gaining the abandoned hillside sent a few more well-aimed shots after them. The arrival of dusk meanwhile, and the exhaustion of the troops, prevented any further pursuit of the enemy, who was thereby preserved from total annihilation.[122]

Feldmarschall Lieutenant Graf Schlick now decided to withdraw his troops to Szikszó because camping on the heights abandoned by the enemy in the face of superior numbers of enemy seemed risky, plus they could easily be outflanked there, and finally the main aim of the reconnaissance had been achieved and the offensive was not intended to be continued any further. As night fell the 3. Bataillon Koudelka (four companies) and a half-squadron of Kaiser Chevauxlegers occupied the outposts outside Szikszó.

Our losses in the action at Szikszó consisted of five wounded and three missing from the Hartmann infantry. Those of the enemy could not be established but must certainly have been significant, because his retreat from a good position cannot be explained otherwise.

On the 29th the troops stayed in Szikszó until nightfall, whereupon the retreat to Forró began, 'after sufficient knowledge about the superior enemy force concentrated at Miskolcz had been obtained, and also an offensive manoeuvre on the enemy's part during the course of the day had been awaited in vain, so it was now hoped to induce one by retreating'.

On the 30th, after a cooked breakfast, *Generalmajor Graf* Pergen set off with two battalions, two squadrons of Kaiser Chevauxlegers, the 6-pounder battery and the rocket battery along the left bank of the Hernad and marched through Bicsoly [Vizsoly, Hungary] to Ruszka [Göncruszka, Hungary], while *Generalmajor Graf* Deym marched to Hidás-Némethi with two battalions, two squadrons of cuirassiers and the 12-pounder battery. The corps headquarters was in Göncz [Gönc, Hungary] with a cavalry detachment. *Feldmarschall Lieutenant Graf* Schlick hurried on to Kaschau on this day. There he learned that the rebels supposedly intended to attack from the Zips and Zempliner Komitats while Mészáros advanced from Miskolcz toward Kaschau. This caused Schlick to call off his plan to send Brigade Pergen into Zempliner Komitat, and to concentrate his troops in Kaschau instead.

Accordingly, the troops remained in their quarters on the 31st, and entered Kaschau on 1 January 1849, thereby concentrating Brigades Deym and Pergen with Brigade Fiedler.

Major Kiesewetter of the Nugent infantry in Eperies had likewise been instructed on the 31st to send some of his troops to Kaschau; but news of enemy detachments (militia and the like) approaching from Zips and Zempliner Komitats caused him not to comply with this, but to confront them on 1 January 1849 with five companies, three rocket launch stands and two 6-pounders.

After the enemy had been repulsed there, another enemy detachment showed up on the Bartfeld road. *Major* Kiesewetter quickly turned on this, put it to flight and pursued it beyond Kapi. In this action he lost one dead and two wounded. *Oberlieutenant* Schäfer, attached to the general staff, ventured too far ahead to reconnoitre and was captured. The enemy losses are unknown but 25 prisoners were taken and an ammunition wagon and many weapons fell into our hands.

On 2 January *Feldmarschall Lieutenant Graf* Schlick sent *Major* Kiesewetter to Margitfalva [Margecany, Slovakia] with five companies and a rocket launch stand, and *Major* Singer of the H.v. Parma infantry there too from Kaschau with three companies, one wing of cavalry and two cannon, to disperse the militia reported to be mustering there. The latter detachment had a rest

122 This seems a strong claim, given how little actual fighting there had been during this action.

day in Margitfalva on the 3rd and returned to Kaschau again on the 4th, while the former was already back in Eperies on the 3rd.

The division of H.v. Parma under *Hauptmann* Matischek that was deployed together with a troop of cavalry out to one side of Kaschau to guard the Dargo [Dargov, Slovakia] Pass leading to the Zempliner Komitat was attacked on the 2nd by about 1,000 men (militia, Tokay national guard and Polish Legionaries) under Torniczky, as well as 50 hussars with four guns under *Rittmeister* Bellany, and driven back through Szinye [Svinica, Slovakia]. On the morning of the 3rd, almost immediately upon receiving word of this, Schlick sent two E.H. Wilhelm companies, a troop of cavalry and two guns under *Hauptmann* Sternegg with orders to retake the Dargo Pass. This detachment together with the division of H.v. Parma that was already there surprised the enemy in Szinye during the night, put him to flight and took 20 prisoners. On the 4th a further reinforcement of two E.H. Wilhelm companies, a troop of *chevauxlegers* and a rocket launch stand was sent there under *Major* Rapaic. But the enemy had already retreated through the Dargo Pass to Gál-Szécs [Sečovce, Slovakia], and the pass had been completely occupied and barricaded by our troops; so in the evening *Major* Rapaic's detachment returned to Kaschau again.

Toward midday on the 4th, *Feldmarschall Lieutenant Graf* Schlick received the first indication from his outposts that enemy columns were approaching Kaschau on the roads from Miskolcz, Ida and Moldau. This was Mészáros, to whom the National Defence Committee had given the mission of retaking Kaschau, the key to Upper Hungary. His strength combined with Szemere's was reported by Schlick as 18 battalions of *honvéds* and national guard, 900-1,000 hussars and 34 guns.[123]

As soon as he heard word of the enemy's approach, Schlick immediately deployed outside Kaschau. He was only just in time, for the outposts reinforced by their relief that had just arrived were already heavily engaged. On the left, between the Miskolcz highway and the Hernad mill stream, *Generalmajor Graf* Deym deployed two companies of 3. Bataillon E.H. Wilhelm in the first line, and four companies of the 1. Bataillon of the same regiment further back in reserve together with a division of Sunstenau cuirassiers. Two guns from Zwölfpfündige Batterie Nr. 11 were on the road, the other four to the right of it. Further to the right, a division of 1. Bataillon E.H. Wilhelm was deployed on a steep hill with a rocket battery nearby. From there to the Moldau road were two Hartmann companies, three troops of *chevauxlegers* and four guns.

Major Baron Gablenz with four Hartmann companies and two guns had the special mission of outflanking the left of any enemy advancing on the Moldau road through the bridge defile, seizing the bridge, and thereby cutting the enemy off from his line of retreat and preventing him from getting his artillery to safety. *Generalmajor Graf* Pergen stood on the calvary hill with one Koudelka battalion and one squadron of Kaiser *chevauxlegers* ready to support Gablenz if necessary, or to fall on the flank of the enemy if he should make headway along the Miskolcz road. Finally, *Generalmajor* Fiedler stayed back in reserve on the Miskolcz road with the few Mazzuchelli companies that could still be spared and the outposts that had been relieved.

123 Bertalan Szemere (1812-69). Primarily a politician, in December 1848 he was made the minister responsible for Upper Hungary, so found himself involved in organising the forces opposing Schlick's advance.

Lively skirmishing soon broke out along the whole front line and then turned into an artillery duel. The enemy artillery shot poorly while receiving very effective fire from ours, and indeed an enemy howitzer was soon dismounted.

Meanwhile *Major Baron* Gablenz had advanced with his four Hartmann companies and two guns and had soon reached the bridge on the Moldau road. An enemy horse artillery battery whose retreat had been cut off by this tried to escape across the steep bank of the stream but got stuck. Under fire from Gablenz's cannon, its crew left their guns, limbers and horses behind and fled for their lives. The units nearest to them did the same. While this was happening on the right wing, the artillery battle on the Miskolcz road continued without interruption. The fire of our guns was so effective that the enemy facing them, about three battalions and 600-700 hussars, soon retreated to Barcza. Now the rocket battery and the four E.H. Wilhelm companies from the left wing's reserve moved up against the hill in front, during which the battery ventured so far forward to bombard the enemy infantry formations that it came under swift and unexpected attack and would soon have fallen into enemy hands, had it not received timely support from its infantry escort. From this moment on, the retreat that had begun on the enemy's left wing degenerated into the whole enemy line fleeing in disorder, throwing away weapons, knapsacks and any other encumbrances.

A rapid pursuit would have led to the total destruction of the enemy, but this did not happen for lack of cavalry and because night was falling. Nonetheless, 20 officers and 500 men were taken prisoner, and ten guns, six ammunition caissons, a flag and many weapons captured. *Feldmarschall Lieutenant Graf* Schlick established a new battery with the captured guns, forming its crews partly from the personnel of the other batteries, partly from infantrymen.

A *chevauxleger* detachment that did pursue the enemy brought back six small mortars as well as two ammunition caissons and many muskets. Likewise the H.v. Parma battalion that had fought with exceptional bravery against the Polish Legion captured a chest of documents belonging to *General* Mészáros, including some important ones about the subversion in Poland in particular.

Our losses amounted to no more than three dead, 13 wounded and nine missing.

In his after-action report, *Feldmarschall Lieutenant Graf* Schlick praised the troops' outstanding courage, and commended the following officers in particular: *Major Baron* Gablenz of the general staff, *Generalmajor Graf* Deym, *Generalmajor Graf* Pergen, *Generalmajor* Fiedler, *Oberstlieutenant Fürst* Franz Lobkowitz, *Major Prinz* Moriz Nassau (who had met Schlick at Szikszó before the action and served as his *Flügeladjutant* during it), *Hauptmann Graf* Erbach, *Oberlieutenants Baron* Wocher, Miltitz, Podlewsky, Würth. *Major* Piattoli and *Hauptmann* Sterner, both being battalion commanders, *Lieutenant* Seiler commanding the 12-pounder battery, *Oberlieutenant* Chasteler of the Sunstenau cuirassiers, Boldrini of the E.H. Wilhelm infantry. *Hauptmanns* Lanko and Jamzolet, *Oberlieutenant* Pokorny and *Lieutenants* Gügenmós and Wassinger, all of the Hartmann battalion, *Oberlieutenant* Czihal of the battery driver teams, *Hauptmann* Liebler, *Oberlieutenants* Weiss and Bartels of the Mazzuchelli infantry.

After the action at Kaschau, the Hungarian newspapers boasted that: 'Schlick has been completely wiped out by Mészáros.' At the same time, Kossuth also spread the rumor that 12,000 Galicians were poised to revolt in Schlick's rear.

Feldmarschall Lieutenant Graf Schlick remained at Kaschau after the battle. His first intention was to pursue the enemy with his entire force, by doing which in all likelihood he would have entered Miskolcz unopposed. 'However, I thought that the agitated mood in the Zempliner

Komitat and in the Lutheran county of Zips required my full attention, and I just had two small columns pursue the rebels.'

The rout of Mészáros's corps had also been extremely effective in cowing the populace, as well as greatly reducing the hopes and subversive activities of the revolutionary party for the time being. This much is certain, that the rebel band that had gathered in Gál-Szécz at the foot of the Dargo Pass in the Zempliner Komitat instantly scattered when they heard of the outcome of the action at Kaschau, abandoning baggage, horses, weapons, everything in fact, and only 140 Poles and 200 Hungarians made it to Sátorallya-Ujhely [Sátoraljaújhely, Hungary] (near the Theiss [Tisza], 50 km from Kaschau) on the afternoon of the 6th.

The commander of these Poles – Tornicky[124] – was so flabbergasted by the outcome of the action at Kaschau that he wrote to Mészáros on the 6th: 'Could you advise me as to what we unfortunate Poles are supposed to do in the event that Pesth should be occupied by the Austrians, as it is said to be?' He goes on, 'for we know what fate awaits us if we fall into the enemy's hands. In my view the best thing for us would be if we could move away from Schlick toward Moldavia and Wallachia.'

On 7 January the 3. Bataillon E.H. Stefan sent from Galicia to reinforce Schlick's corps arrived in Eperies, whereupon the units were organised as follows:

Brigade *Generalmajor* Fiedler

2. Bataillon Hartmann
3. Bataillon E.H. Wilhelm
3. Bataillon E.H. Stefan (in Eperies)
1. Majors-Division, Kaiser Chevauxlegers (one wing of these in Eperies)
Sechspfündige Fussbatterie Nr. 36

Brigade *Generalmajor Graf* Pergen

3. Bataillon Mazzuchelli
3. Bataillon Koudelka (two companies in Eperies)
1. Landwehr-Bataillon H.v. Parma
Oberstlieutenant-Division, Kaiser Chevauxlegers
Sechspfündige Fussbatterie Nr. 34 (two guns in Eperies)

Brigade *Generalmajor Graf* Deym

1. Bataillon E.H. Wilhelm
3. Bataillon Nugent (in Eperies)
Oberstlieutenant-Division, Sunstenau Kürassiere
Zwölfpfündige Batterie Nr. 11

124 Władisław Tchórznicki (1793-1862) had been a Polish lancer captain in Napoleon's army and was said to have taken part in the Polish uprising in 1830-1831 as well as the smaller one in Krakau in 1846. He joined the Hungarian army in November 1848 and served throughout the war, escaping through Turkey to exile in England, France and Bavaria before returning to Galicia in 1861. Bona, *Tábornokok.*

Raketen-Batterie Nr. 11
Half of Raketen-Batterie Nr. 12 (in Eperies)
One pioneer detachment

Altogether eight battalions, six squadrons and 27 artillery, to which number the newly established battery with eight captured cannon was also added, bringing the artillery up to 35 pieces.

Before we follow *Feldmarschall Lieutenant Graf* Schlick's operations any further, it is necessary to return to the main army's operations during the second segment of the campaign.

2

Events from the occupation of Ofen-Pesth until after the battle of Kápolna. The period from 6 January to the beginning of March 1849

The Situation after the Occupation of Ofen-Pesth, 6 January 1849

After the occupation of Ofen-Pesth the conduct of the war entered a new and much more difficult period. Some of the hopes and expectations cherished at the start of the campaign had not been fulfilled; for example, that a battle to decide the fate of the country would come about before reaching the Hungarian capital; that the small fortress of Leopoldstadt would be taken in a few days, so that *Feldmarschall Lieutenant* Simunich could advance toward the Mining Towns without delay and link up from there with *Feldmarschall Lieutenant Graf* Schlick, who for his part had been instructed to approach the army from Kaschau via Losoncz if possible; furthermore, that the Hungarian former imperial regiments would return to doing their duty, that the well-disposed populace would rise up and cooperate in suppressing the revolutionary party, etc. – none of this came to fulfilment! On the other hand the army was unavoidably made weaker than its original order of battle suggests through leaving the two Brigades Neustädter and Lederer in front of Komorn, garrisoning Pressburg and Raab, and then sending nine and a half battalions, nine squadrons and 30 guns to reinforce *Feldmarschall Lieutenant* Simunich right at the start of operations. Thus altogether no more than 28 battalions (of which six were grenadier battalions with their smaller establishment), 43 squadrons, 186 guns and the technical troops entered Ofen-Pesth. Their combat strength had also been significantly reduced by sickness, losses from enemy action, etc.

To reinforce the army as much as possible, on 4 January the *Feldmarschall* had already urged the war ministry to draft recruits for replacements for the army and asked it to assign them by the start of February without delay. To this request that was extremely urgent given its content, the war ministry retorted: 'A lot of time is required for the preliminaries, since the next ballot which is being implemented at the moment will not come into effect until the end of February, so the drafted recruits cannot be assigned until the beginning of March.'[1] Since at that time even some of those battalions of the first reserve that were still in the country had not yet been

1 As each year-group became eligible for conscription, not every eligible man was drafted. Instead, recruits were chosen by ballot.

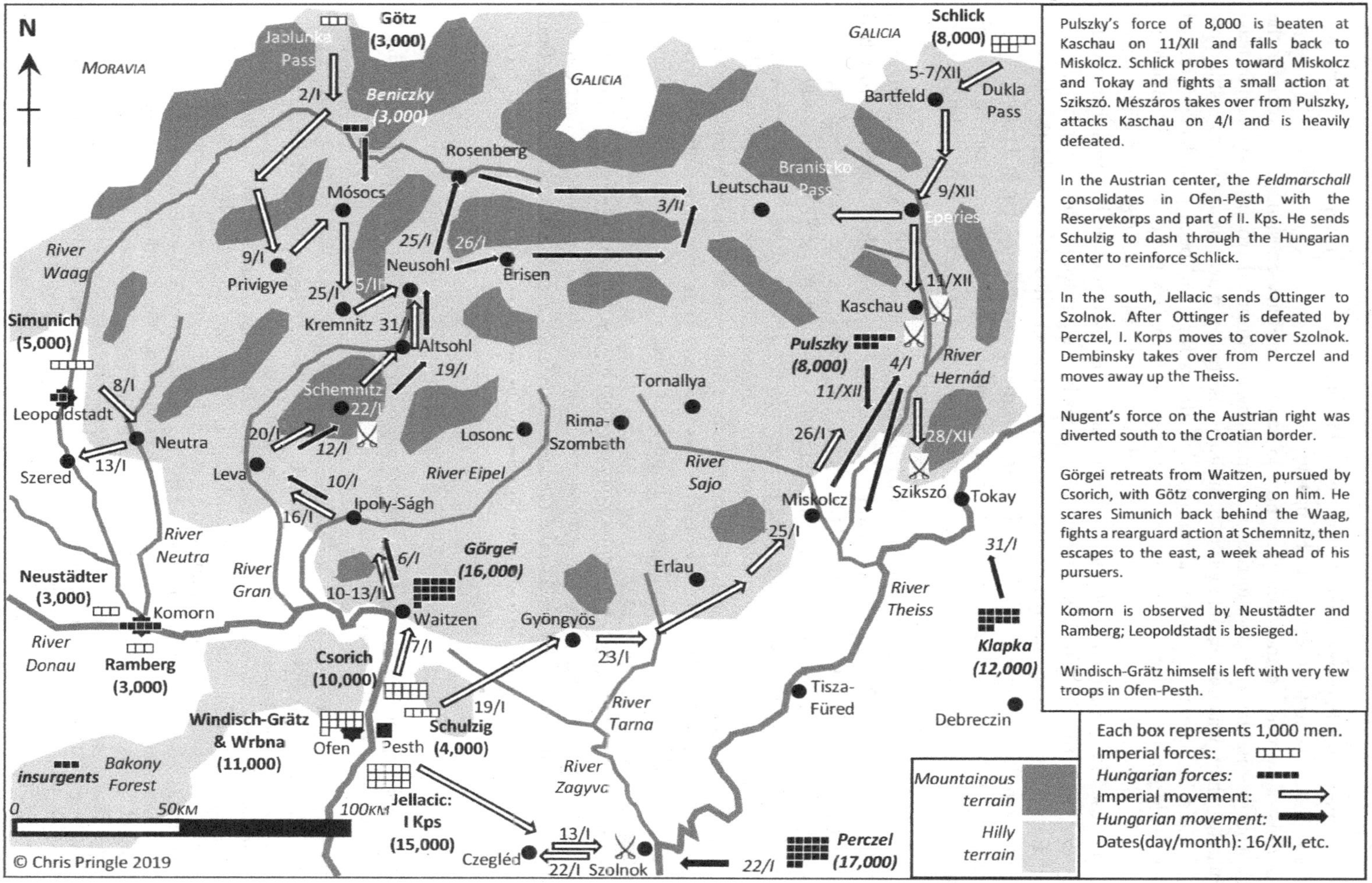

Map 3a: Hunting Görgei, hunting Schlick, December 1848 to late January 1849

fully equipped, what hope was there for the second reserve battalions from which a reserve was supposed to be created for the army in Hungary?

Administrative worries and difficulties now joined the military ones, since in order for the civil authorities in the extensive territory occupied by the imperial troops to operate at least adequately, which was not feasible without military assistance, it was necessary to install new officials, and in general to put the administrative affairs that had been completely wrecked by the revolution on a footing that would to some degree pacify the country and enable its administration. Lack of money was soon added to this, so the *Feldmarschall* found himself obliged to use Hungarian banknotes found in the municipal treasuries or delivered there by the salt offices to pay the civil officials, however pernicious he recognised this measure to be.[2]

Detailed reports of the enemy's movements were not received until the 6th, the day after entering Ofen. In the night between 4-5 January a signal gun fired in Ofen at 11:30 p.m. had summoned all the rebels to the left bank of the Danube. Görgei had then moved through Dunakeszi to Waitzen with the majority, the actual core of the Hungarian army, while Perczel took the road to Szolnok with the rest; thus they carried out a divergent retreat.

The last rebel detachments left Pesth at 7:00 a.m. on the morning of the 5th. The parliament, the National Defence Committee, the banknote printing press and the weapons factory had already been rushed off to Debreczin [Debrecen, Hungary] via the Szolnok railway on 1 January. During their retreat the rebels destroyed both the Waitzen and Szolnok railways, after first taking the operating equipment [i.e., presumably the rolling stock] to the two termini and partially destroying it there.[3] Their troops were depicted as being totally demoralised and completely exhausted, so the general view was that their units would completely dissolve during their retreat and disperse into the country. It was also said that they were suffering from a serious lack of percussion caps and fuzes.[4] Reports of their strength varied greatly. Görgei's corps was estimated at 10,000-15,000 men at most, Perczel's at 8,000-10,000.[5] The latter had incorporated some of Görgei's battalions in Pesth. Sixty guns were carried away from Pesth on the Szolnok railway. Since the 5th supposedly 10,000-15,000 Cumans under a certain Sz. Kiraly had arrived on Csepel Island in the Danube just below Pesth to prevent our troops from

2 The Habsburg monarchy operated an important monopoly over salt. The salt offices administering it were significant institutions.

3 Starting in 1841, the empire had constructed a strategic rail network. In Hungary it comprised the Pressburg-Tyrnau, Wiener Neustadt-Oedenburg, Pesth-Waitzen and Pesth-Szolnok lines. László Bencze, 'The Military System of the Habsburg Empire and the Hungarian Units of the Army on the Eve of the Revolution', in Bona, Hungarian Revolution, p.19.

4 'Manufacturing percussion-caps caused special problems and finally it took place on machines imported from England and installed in a converted chemical factory.' But although 'plagued by raw material shortages and frequent moves and not working at their full capacity, [the new ammunition factory and ammunition assembling shops] still produced the necessary quantity. And so the reason why troops did not have ammunition in quantities they needed was due to problems with distribution and delivery.' Tamás Csikány, 'Logistics of the Honvéd Army', in Bona, *Hungarian Revolution*, pp.118, 121.

5 These figures seem not too far out. Bánlaky gives the combat strength of Görgei's force at this time, now designated VII. Corps, as 16,000 men after incorporating 4,000 who were at Vác, while Perczel's force was brought up to 17,000 men on 14 January after receiving reinforcements. Bánlaky, *A magyar nemzet*, Chapters 14 and 16.

any attempt at crossing in the Földvar [Dunaföldvár, Hungary] area, etc.[6] The *Feldmarschall* had to base all his subsequent dispositions on these more or less credible accounts.

There was no way Görgei's move could be ignored. Given the fact that he commanded the largest and most organised part of the Hungarian rebel army, the direction of march he had chosen was a very good one for attracting our full attention. From Waitzen he could move along the left bank of the Danube to Komorn and ensconce himself in this fortress in the rear of the imperial army that was only weakly besieged, or march to Upper Hungary against *Feldmarschall Lieutenant Graf* Schlick, or finally wend his way through Ipoly-Ságh [Šahy, Slovakia], Léva [Levice, Slovakia] and Neutra toward Leopoldstadt, drive away Simunich's weak division that was deployed there, and then continue his operations toward Pressburg or even Wien, without encountering serious resistance anywhere.

In the circumstances at the time, the impression that could have been created and the incalculable consequences that could have followed from simply threatening the Austrian border need hardly be described.

Wrbna Takes Waitzen, 7 January 1849

In view of this situation, the *Feldmarschall* decided to send *Feldmarschall Lieutenant Graf* Wrbna to Waitzen next day (7 January) with ten battalions, ten squadrons and 48 guns – namely Brigades Wyss, Jablonowsky and Colloredo plus four squadrons of Max Auersperg cuirassiers and Kavallerie-Batteries Nr. 3 and Nr. 4 from the Reservekorps. In addition, to support this expedition, nine troops of Civallart *uhlans* and a rocket battery were detached along the right bank of the Danube through Sz. Endré [Szentendre, Hungary] to opposite Waitzen, to foil any enemy attempt to escape across the frozen surface of the Danube. In the event that the enemy should move from Waitzen directly to Upper Hungary or spread out in the mountains, so that there was no longer any risk to Division Simunich and the Austrian border, it was the *Feldmarschall*'s intention to send Division Csorich quickly to reinforce *Feldmarschall Lieutenant Graf* Schlick, who was notified of this on the 8th.

Feldmarschall Lieutenant Graf Wrbna began his march at 8:00 a.m. on the 7th in extremely inclement weather, deep snow and bitter cold, and reached Fót and Dunakeszi after a very arduous

6 The Cumans, or Kuns, were a nomadic Turkic tribe that settled in Hungary in the 13th century in the area known as the Kunság. This area to the south and southeast of Budapest was a formal political entity within Hungary until the early 18th century. Its self-rule was reinstated as Jászkunság in 1745. The Jászkunság is close to Csepel Island. However, this supposed force of 10,000 Cumans on Csepel Island seems to have been no more than a rumor; Perczel's force had retreated behind the Tisza, so it is unlikely that anything more than small groups of militia remained in this area. 'Szent Kiraly' is presumably Móric Szentkirályi (1807-1882), a very successful reform politician from Pozsony who left the Hungarian Diet in 1848 after falling out with Kossuth. He then became Jászkun Grand Captain (főkapitány), a title of the political and military leader of the Jászság and Kunság region, a relic of their old distinct ethnic autonomy. This may explain the reference to Cumans. He served in the summer of 1848 against the Serbians but was found 'not suitable' for this mission and fell out with Mór Perczel as well. At the end of 1848 he became totally inactive politically and militarily, and there is certainly no evidence of him leading these supposed 10,000-15,000 Cumans on Csepel Island. He was captured by the Austrians in the spring of 1849, imprisoned in Buda, but then released. He subsequently became the last mayor of the city of Pest before it was united with Buda and Óbuda. József Szinnyei, *Magyar írók élete és munkái* (Budapest: Hornyánszky, 1891-1914).

march. There he received news that at 10:00 a.m. the day before, the rebels had retreated from Waitzen to Veröcze [Verőce, Hungary] and Katalin [Katalinpuszta, Hungary]. Accordingly at 1:00 a.m. on the 8th he sent *Feldmarschall Lieutenant Fürst* Franz Liechtenstein, who had attached himself to the cuirassiers from the Reservekorps, to Waitzen with six squadrons, a Kavallerie-Batterie and 2. Jäger-Bataillon, then followed with the rest of his corps at 5:00 a.m. By this time Liechtenstein had already reached Waitzen, where his *jägers* exchanged just a few shots with enemy stragglers.

Feldmarschall Lieutenant Graf Wrbna sent a report to the *Feldmarschall* on the 8th concerning the successful occupation of Waitzen, as well as the information he had obtained there about the enemy's strength and intentions. This report said:

> According to corroborating statements from several credible individuals, the insurgents who withdrew from Waitzen comprised nine infantry battalions (six *honvéd*, one grenadier[7] and two line battalions), two divisions of Husaren-Regiment Nr. 4, a detachment each from Husaren-Regiments Nr. 1 and Nr. 10, and several squadrons of the newly raised Hunyady hussars. The line and *honvéd* battalions were each 700-800 strong, while the cavalry may have numbered 2,000 horse in total. The insurgents took 60 guns with them, mostly drawn by only two horses each. In addition the insurgents were followed by 3,000 militia armed variously with pikes, scythes and the like. These are the troops that moved through the city here. If we also reckon in some detachments on the flank, together with the baggage train and militia about which several details have reached me here from a credible source, the insurgents' total strength may have come to 15,000 men. The majority of these have retreated along the road through Katalin, Rétság and Vad-Kert [Érsekvadkert, Hungary], and their rear guard is supposed to have arrived in the latter place, 30 km from here today. A second column including artillery and the two wings of Husaren-Regiment Nr. 9 retreated through Veröczö and Nagy-Máros [Nagymaros, Hungary], which their rear guard left early today. Part of this column is supposed to have moved toward Ipoly-Ságh, part toward Komorn. The insurgent leaders are: Görgei as commander-in-chief; Karger,[8] Szegedy,[9]

7 This was presumably the Weissl grenadier battalion, which was the only regular imperial grenadier battalion to accept the authority of the Hungarian government in October 1848. Bona, *Hungarian Revolution*, pp. 93, 110.

8 Ferdinand Karger (1803-?). A major in Husaren-Regiment Nr. 4 when it accepted the Hungarian government's authority in October 1848, he therefore fought against Jellacic and then against the imperials at the start of the Winter Campaign. However, on 30 December he reported sick and went home; thus, Wrbna's information is a few days out of date on this point. After the war he was stripped of his rank and sentenced to three years' imprisonment but released in March 1850. Bona, *Tábornokok*.

9 Imre Szegedy (1812-78) was a former imperial officer who was assigned to the Hungarian ministry of defence in the summer of 1848. After taking part in the fighting against Jellacic and the initial phase of the Winter Campaign, on 24 January he left the army and turned himself in to the imperials. After the war he was stripped of his rank in 1850. Bona, *Tábornokok*.

> Szabo[10] and Gáspár[11] as his brigadiers. The men of the line regiments as well as the *honvéds* are supposed to have been very fanatically inspired earlier by the word 'Freedom', but that has largely diminished since. Infanterie-Regiment Nr. 2 and many of the hussars are talking about defecting to us. Great confusion and dejection reign among the officers. As for the insurgents' intentions, it is said they plan to retreat behind the Eipel (Ipoly) and from there to turn toward either the Mining Towns or Rima-Szombath [Rimavská Sobota, Slovakia].

This report also stated:

> [T]hat as the enemy has already gained a significant head start, and my troops' footwear is very worn out with a considerable number unfit with foot problems and taking into consideration that on every march the draft animals have to be whipped hard since the guns and wagons can only be got forward with the utmost effort, which will be even more the case in the mountainous terrain ahead, I (*Feldmarschall Lieutenant Graf* Wrbna) intend to leave 1. Landwehr-Bataillon Paumgarten and a squadron of Kress *chevauxlegers* to garrison Waitzen, and to return to Pesth with the rest of my corps in a single day's march on the 9th.

This was understandably not approved by the *Feldmarschall*, who was necessarily anxious to obtain reliable information about the enemy's strength and true direction of retreat.[12] Consequently, at 10:00 p.m. in the evening on the 8th this order was issued to *Feldmarschall Lieutenant Graf* Wrbna: after leaving behind whichever brigade was most in need of rest, he was to send the other two brigades under *Feldmarschall Lieutenant Baron* Csorich to continue to pursue the enemy, about which it noted 'that this pursuit should be all the more effective given that the enemy guns are reported to be drawn by just two horses, so getting them away through that mountainous region should be very difficult'. Furthermore, it recommended that more precise information about the enemy's strength should be obtained, since the previous report appeared to be exaggerated.

Feldmarschall Lieutenant Graf Wrbna himself was summoned back to Ofen to take over the military district command there, as was *Feldmarschall Lieutenant Graf Fürst* Franz Liechtenstein with the four squadrons of Max Auersperg cuirassiers and the two horse artillery batteries from the Reservekorps, while the nine troops of Civallart *uhlans* at Szentendre were ordered to go to Waitzen in their stead.

10 Zsigmond Szabó (1798-1882) organised and commanded the 6th *honvéd* Battalion in June 1848 and fought Serbian insurgents in the south before becoming a brigade commander in Görgei's corps. He later took over command of the fortress of Komorn from April 1849 until its capitulation. Bona, *Tábornokok*.

11 András Gáspár (1804-84). A captain in the 9th Hussars at the outbreak of the war, he performed well in early battles against the Croats in September/October 1848, at Mór in December, and against Schlick at Hatvan. However, his passivity at the battle of Isaszeg cost the chance of a decisive victory. He resigned shortly afterwards in protest at Hungary's declaration of independence. After the war he was imprisoned until 1850. Bona, *Tábornokok*.

12 This was one of many instances of the *Feldmarschall*'s orders not being implemented or of attempts to avoid implementing them.

The instruction to have whichever brigade was most in need of rest remain in Waitzen was based on the report received from *Feldmarschall Lieutenant Baron* Csorich concerning the exhaustion of his troops who were approaching the point of being unfit to march.

Ottinger Takes Szolnok, 13 January 1849

Before we follow *Feldmarschall Lieutenant Baron* Csorich's subsequent operations, we must mention what other arrangements the *Feldmarschall* made, as well as what had transpired meanwhile with the detached forces in the rear of the army.

After *Feldmarschall Lieutenant Graf* Wrbna had been sent to Waitzen, the combat forces left in Ofen-Pesth came to no more than 18 battalions, 31 squadrons and 126 guns. When we take into account that although the people of Pest were apparently keeping quiet they were far from dependable, that Buda Castle had not yet been put in a defensible state, that the internal and external security of the two cities demanded a strong garrison, that the Chain Bridge between Ofen and Pesth constituted the only crossing point over the Danube and was all the more important as throwing a bridge across anywhere else was quite unfeasible because of the drifting ice, that the rear of the army and communications with the provinces behind it seemed vulnerable to the fortress of Komorn – which could barely be considered cordoned off – and to the dubious attitude of the populace, it must be acknowledged that adequate forces were lacking for continuing the offensive toward the Theiss or indeed beyond it to Debreczin, the current heart of the revolution – an operation that if undertaken with 25 or 30 battalions could certainly have had a decisive result at that time.[13] Added to this was the fact that the army lacked the Munizions-Reserve (the ammunition trains)[14] that was indispensable for any operation far afield, as well as its transport divisions, which were only set in march from Wien toward Ofen on 11, 13 and 16 January, so could not arrive in Ofen before the end of the month!

In order to gain more accurate knowledge at least about the strength and movements of the rebel column under Perczel that had fallen back from Pesth to Szolnok on the Theiss, this order was issued to the *Banus* on the 8th: to push Kavallerie-Brigade Ottinger with a horse artillery battery and a rocket battery forward to Szolnok.[15] This brigade was tasked with repairing the railway and the telegraph line as well. It was also known that in their stampede to evacuate Pesth, the rebels had removed war materiel of all kinds to Szolnok in great quantities, including the remaining railway rolling stock. It was therefore to be expected that much of this was still to be found in Szolnok, the terminus of the railway, as it could not all have been taken any further from there by conventional means of transport. It had also been learned that significant stores of salt, copper and all kinds of grain were to be found piled up in Szolnok. *General* Ottinger was therefore to attempt to seize these supplies, as well as taking care of repairing and guarding the bridge over the Theiss. 'To this end,' it says in this edict to the *Banus*, 'later on,

13 Or could it? Later on, we will see Nobili asserting the opposite, that capturing Debreczin would achieve nothing, and that only destruction of the enemy combat forces could bring victory. Perhaps he imagines that a swift march to Debreczin might have had more impact at this early stage than later on.

14 The term in the original is '*Kondukteurschaften*', meaning transport columns formed according to standard organisation. Smola, *Handbuch*.

15 Note the implied high mobility of a rocket battery: it could keep up with a formation of cavalry and horse artillery.

once communications along the railway have been established, a suitable contingent of infantry is to be detached to Szolnok.'

In the event that it should no longer be possible to get hold of these supplies, '*General* Ottinger shall restrict himself to guarding the Theiss crossings, sending out patrols to obtain information about the enemy's positions, and finally to disarming the villages in his vicinity.'

Detaching a brigade like this behind an enemy who was in full retreat could be done without any concerns anyway, since a cavalry brigade armed with two batteries is independent enough to be able to manoeuvre on its own without any other support on an open, unobstructed plain 90 km across like that between the Danube and the Theiss, for that is the distance between Pesth and Szolnok; whereas dispatching an infantry detachment necessarily had to be deferred for the time being until the railway was repaired, which would then offer the possibility of withdrawing them quickly from any danger in the event of being attacked in superior numbers.[16]

Generalmajor Ottinger and his brigade began their march on the 9th, arrived in Alberti [Albertirsa, Hungary] on the 10th, and reported from there to his commander the *Banus* that he had learned from travellers that 'Czegléd is only weakly held by the enemy, who will probably retreat to Szolnok today or tomorrow'. He also gave some indications as to the state of the railway and the measures necessary for its repair and concluded his report by mentioning 'that since reports from the inhabitants of Alberti suggest that the enemy may be concentrating in Szolnok, it is my considered opinion that it would be desirable if some infantry or cavalry could be sent to join me'.

The *Banus* forwarded this report to the field marshal's attention and was sent this reply on the 12th: that for his part *Oberst* Schön of the Pionnier-Korps had been instructed to press on with repairing the Szolnok railway as quickly as possible, and that 'as soon as this has been done, a suitable infantry detachment can be pushed forward to Szolnok, but that cannot happen right now without risk, because of the great distance to this place and its exposed position'.

General Ottinger reached Szolnok on the 13th without encountering any enemy, since these had already retreated completely behind the Theiss to Török Sz. Miklós [Törökszentmiklós, Hungary]. Substantial supplies were found in Szolnok and immediately impounded, namely: 3 cwt of gunpowder, 25 cwt of saltpetre, 350 cwt of copper, 40,000 cwt of salt, 88,496 pots[17] of grain and 560 pots of maize on barges; in the town itself, another 800 pots of grain, 80 cwt of hay, 100 cavalry sabres and 5,000 scythes and pikes. These supplies were partly removed to Pesth after the railway was repaired. The mood of the inhabitants of Czegléd, Abany [Abony, Hungary] and Szolnok was described as good, likewise that of the inhabitants of N. Körös [Nagykőrös, Hungary] and Kecskemét. Thus within a few days *General* Ottinger had fulfilled the first part of his mission – namely repairing the railway and seizing the supplies stored in Szolnok.

16 Windisch-Grätz may have been mindful of the precedent set at Ozora on 7 October 1848, when after Jellacic's main body was defeated at the battle of Pákozd on 29 September, a detached Croat division of 9,000 men under Generals Roth and Philippovich was cut off by Hungarian national guards and militia and forced to surrender. Hence the *Feldmarschall*'s wariness of exposing an infantry force to a similar fate was not without foundation.

17 This is the archaic Austrian measure, *Metzen*. One 'pot' is 61.5 liters.

Meanwhile in Ofen every measure had been taken to arm and provision the fortress, as well as for the overhaul and security of the Chain Bridge.[18] For the latter purpose construction of blockhouses at both ends of the bridge had begun, while the large artillery barracks in Pesth (the Neugebäude [New Building]) had been securely connected with one of the Chain Bridge blockhouses and thereby with Buda Castle by means of a barricade. All the considerable artillery stores found in the Pesth Neugebäude, among them a very large number of siege guns and iron shot which the rebels had not had time to remove to Komorn or behind the Theiss, were partly moved into the Buda Castle arsenal, partly used to arm the fortress itself, and two companies quickly formed from the personnel of 5. Artillerie-Regiment who were still there, since the fortress particularly relied on artillery crews. The armed steamer *Schlick* (formerly *Mészáros*) and all the steamboats and tugs found in the Alt-Ofen [Old Buda] boatyard were assigned to the pioneer command, and the former was crewed by pioneers and a garrison company. The redoubts thrown up by the rebels outside Ofen were filled back in, the disarming of Pesth and the surrounding area was begun, and many supplies of food and kit collected and stored securely.

The *Feldmarschall* had entrusted the task of bringing Buda Castle into a suitable condition to *General* Hentzi, along with *General* Dietrich of the artillery and *Oberst* von Trattern of the engineer corps. This was carried out by Hentzi with his characteristic energy, as was the leadership of the city command that was likewise transferred to him.

Feldmarschall Lieutenant Grueber, who had formerly been in charge of the army high command's administrative office, was designated commandant of Buda Castle in place of its previous commandant, *Feldmarschall Lieutenant Baron* Kress.

Rear Security and the Mining Towns, 30 December 1848 to 10 January 1849

Disturbing news soon arrived from the territory in the army's rear. The Bakonyer-Wald [Bakony Forest], the Fleischhackerstrasse and the area of Dotis [Tata, Hungary] and Gran [Esztergom, Hungary] had been rendered unsafe by rebel gangs – in particular that led by a certain Mednyansky[19] – which included officials and clerics in their ranks. Couriers, working parties, cattle herding parties, and even small-formed units had been attacked; so it was urgently

18 Perhaps not 'all measures'. See this criticism by Szilágyi of Hentzi's inadequate preparations: 'Hentzi prepared a plan for the defence of the capitals, and after this was criticised because it did not include Buda Castle, he quickly made another one. But this plan was also criticised by Colonel Trattnern, the director of imperial military engineering, criticisms which were later proved to be justified. Hentzi thought that the cannon in the 1st to 4th rondellas (the circular bastions) needed almost no protective entrenchments; that the gates were well protected by the artillery which could easily prevent enemy artillery positioning itself before them; that the curtain wall of the castle was so strong that 12-pounder cannon could not damage it, so it was unnecessary to make earth revetments around it; that an enemy attack on the Chain Bridge could easily be stopped with gunfire; that there was no need for shell-proof shelters because the Hungarians had no mortars; that Svábhegy was too far from the castle to be dangerous, contrary to the side of the Royal Palace, which is close to the Little Gellért Hill.' This is my version of Szilágyi's text, which I edited for him and he approved. Szilárd Szilágyi, 'Re: Siege of Buda', Email correspondence, 18 December 2018.

19 Sándor Mednyánszky (1816-75), a former officer in Infanterie-Regiment Nr. 34, organised a guerrilla detachment in December 1848 that operated in the rear of the imperial army as noted here by Nobili. In March 1849 he was promoted to captain and made adjutant of II. Corps, being in Komorn when the war ended. He emigrated to England and then served in the Hungarian Legion fighting against

necessary to sweep this area, even if only so much as was required to secure the line of operations. To this end *Major* Kronenberg was detached with 6. Jäger-Bataillon and a squadron of Civallart *uhlans* toward Moór and Kis-Bér on 8 January, to patrol from there into the Bakonyer-Wald as well as toward Stuhlweissenburg, Pápa and Raab. To guard the Fleischhackerstrasse, the 1. Landwehr-Bataillon Reisinger – which had been left behind to garrison Raab but had become superfluous there because of the arrival of the Liccaner battalion sent by *Feldmarschall Lieutenant Baron* Welden – was echeloned along it by companies in Bána [Bana, Hungary], Kocs, Ober-Gálla [Felsőgálla, Hungary] and Bicske, and a troop of Ficquelmont dragoons was attached to each company. On the 8th an instruction was issued to *Oberst Baron* Horváth, whose patrol force had remained behind as a garrison in Stuhlweissenburg since the army's entry into Ofen-Pesth, likewise to patrol into the Bakonyer-Wald and to disperse any scattered rabble who might be trying to gang up.

Oberst Graf Almasy was sent with a division of Civallart *uhlans* to Sz. Endré, scarcely 20 km above Ofen, where the militia was in the process of mustering, but he did not think he could carry out his mission with such a small force and requested some infantry.

Oberstlieutenant Schiffmann was ordered to occupy and disarm the important and very ill-disposed nearby city of Gran with four Ceccopieri companies, two companies of Grenadier-Bataillon Richter, one wing of the Kress Chevauxlegers and half a rocket battery. The disarming encountered such universal open hostility and lack of cooperation that *Oberstlieutenant* Schiffmann felt obliged to ask for a battalion of reinforcements, all the more so as 400 hussars were supposed to have shown up in the area of Bator-Keszi [Bátorove Kosihy, Slovakia] on the left bank of the Danube. The army was not strong enough to meet all these requests for reinforcements. Each company to be sent off had to be weighed against the small combat forces available, so the commanders of the detached formations were mostly told to make do with the troops they had been given.

From Körmönd [Körmend, Hungary], *Feldzeugmeister Graf* Nugent had turned through Szala-Egerszeg [Zalaegerszeg, Hungary] toward Kanisa [Nagykanizsa, Hungary], since 5,000 rebels led by *Graf* Nitzky[20] and *Graf* Festetics[21] had gathered in that area and were threatening the Croatian border. Upon the *Feldzeugmeister*'s approach these bands retreated toward Kaposvár, so Kanisa was occupied unopposed on the 10th. Garrisons remained behind in Körmönd and Szala-Egerszeg, on the one hand maintaining communications with *Oberstlieutenant* Althan's patrol force that had advanced to Pápa, and on the other pushing forward as far as Keszthely on Lake Balaton. The Feldzeugmeister's indefatigable activity soon enabled him to bring his corps up to 9,000 men after incorporating the troops under *Feldmarschall Lieutenant* Dahlen, without exposing inner Austria and Croatia at all, which cannot be applauded highly enough.

Austria in Italy in 1859, and in Prussia's Hungarian Legion in 1866. Despite this he returned to Hungary in 1869. Bona, *Tábornokok*.

20 György Niczky (1809-?) served as an officer in the Somogy county national guard on the southern front, then with a Bács county battalion in IV. Corps. After the war he served briefly in an imperial *uhlan* regiment. Bona, *Tábornokok*.

21 Miklós Festetich (1794-1857), a former officer in the 5th Hussars and 7th Chevauxlegers, he was a major in the mounted national guard in June 1848. The following December he was tasked by Kossuth with organising a raiding force. He duly reported that he had raised 1,000 infantry and 200 cavalry under Major Bódog Nemegyei in Somogy County. When the county was occupied by the imperials, he remained there. He received an amnesty after the war. Bona, *Tábornokok*.

Since the bombardment of Leopoldstadt, which had been interrupted by the ammunition works blowing up, nothing significant had happened with *Feldmarschall Lieutenant* Simunich's division. The ammunition lost in the aforementioned accident was replaced from Wien, as well as another two 60-pounder and two 30-pounder mortars being sent to Tyrnau to add weight to the bombardment. *Artillerie-Hauptmann* Navarra now took over command of the artillery and together with *Ingenieur-Major* Wurmb undertook all the preparations to commence bombardment of the fortress in accordance with the *Feldmarschall*'s order of the 8th. When the news of the successful occupation of Ofen-Pesth arrived, *Feldmarschall Lieutenant* Simunich once again summoned the fortress commander Ordody to surrender, but without success. Meanwhile the bridge over the Waag at Freistadel [Hlohovec, Slovakia] that the rebels had destroyed during their retreat had been repaired, whereupon Simunich pushed forward to Neutra.

Part of the force of three battalions, a quarter-squadron and 12 guns concentrated at Jablunka, where *Generalmajor* Götz had taken over command from *Oberstlieutenant* Frischeisen, had already crossed the Hungarian border again on 30 December 1848 and arrived in Csacza [Čadca, Slovakia] on the 3rd, where one Palombini division and two rocket launch stands under *Hauptmann* Schewitz were directed to cover the right flank from Mosty [Mosty u Jablunkova, Czech Republic] toward Rakowa [Raková, Slovakia] and Thurzowka [Turzovka, Slovakia] as the centre of all the revolutionary agitation in that area.

Generalmajor Götz's communications with the province behind him were maintained by units that were not part of his column. Thus, two companies of the 4. Bataillon Deutschmeister were in Jablunka, and another company of the same battalion plus one each from the Fürstenwärther and H.v.Parma regiments in Csacza under the command of *Major* Trenk, where they were to remain while Götz continued his advance. On 1 January Götz moved to Neustadl [Kysucké Nové Mesto, Slovakia], while the flanking column under *Hauptmann* Schewitz again covered his right flank. The advance continued on the 2nd. The enemy was first encountered at the Brodnó [Brodno, Slovakia] defile,[22] where an abatti and a couple of *flèches*[23] had been prepared but was soon driven back into the position at Budetin. Here there were three *honvéd* battalions, some *honvéd* cavalry, several thousand national guard and the like, and eight guns.[24] Six more guns were posted further back at the bridge across the Waag at Silein that was similarly defended. *Generalmajor* Götz outflanked this position and drove the enemy back across the Waag after a fairly lively action lasting more than an hour. The bridge that had been partly destroyed by the enemy was quickly repaired, whereupon Götz advanced to the attack again, dismounting three rebel guns and scattering the rebels partly toward Rajecz [Rajec, Slovakia], partly into the Waag valley. The pursuit could not be carried out quickly enough for lack of cavalry, so only a few

22 A 'defile' meaning a very narrow gap between two mountains or other obstacles.

23 'A FLECHE is a small work consisting of two faces only' – a V-shaped earthwork. Sir Charles Pasley, *A Course of Elementary Fortification*, 2nd edn (London: John Murray, 1822), p.432.

24 While Hungary was still trying to pursue a lawful course and seek devolution rather than rebel, it was not allowed to establish its own army but was permitted to raise national guards. In the summer of 1848, 200,000 were conscripted, but their training and weapons were rudimentary: only 40,000 had firearms, most carrying scythes or pitchforks, etc. Gábor Bona, 'Armed Forces of the Hungarian War of Independence', in Bona, *Hungarian Revolution*, pp.79-80.

prisoners were taken. Our losses were just two wounded, while those of the enemy must have been much more considerable since their artillery shot poorly and ours very well.[25]

One company was brought forward from Csacza to Neustadl, another to Kraszno [Krásno nad Kysucou, Slovakia], while *Generalmajor* Götz concentrated his force at the important crossroads of Silein. Patrols were sent into the Waag valley toward Trentschin [Trenčin, Slovakia] to establish communications with *Feldmarschall Lieutenant* Simunich.

As mentioned above, *Generalmajor* Götz had been instructed by the *Feldmarschall* to advance toward the Mining Towns. In the same spirit, on the 4th *Feldmarschall Lieutenant Baron* Welden asked him to continue to move in that direction, but at the same time to send detachments toward Kubin [Dolný Kubín, Slovakia] and Rosenberg [Ružomberok, Slovakia].

The road from Silein to the Mining Towns leads through Sz. Márton [Martin, Slovakia], the main town in the rebel stronghold of Thurocz [Turóc County]. The rebels had a very strong position there, held by a substantial force with 14 guns. There could be no thought of carrying this. *Generalmajor* Götz therefore decided to get to Kremnitz [Kremnica, Slovakia] through Rajecz, Bacskó [sic – Nobili must mean Fačkov, Slovakia, not Bačkov, which is at the other end of Slovakia] and Prividgye [Prievidza, Slovakia], whereby he hoped to link up with *Feldmarschall Lieutenant* Simunich's force via Zsámbokréth [Žabokreky nad Nitrou, Slovakia] in the Neutra valley.

Meanwhile, to prevent any enemy offensive move against Silein, *Major* Trenk and three companies were moved from Csacza to Budetin, with instructions to block the exit from the road defile there toward Silein. Despite the foul weather that had set in and the deep snow, the column began its march on the 8th, reaching Rajecz at 2:00 p.m. without any enemy interference, then occupied Prividgye on the 9th.

Nothing significant had occurred with the besieging force outside Komorn. *Generalmajor* Neustädter was on the Great Rye Island, had occupied Nyárasd and Megyer [Vel'ky Meder, Slovakia; Nagymegyer in Hungarian] and had pushed observation posts toward the Palatinal Line [the western face of the Komorn fortress]. *Feldmarschall Lieutenant* Ramberg was facing the Komorn bridgehead, had distributed his troops in Ács, Mócsa and Ó-Szőny, and maintained communications through Raab and Weisskirchen [Medved'ov, Slovakia] with *Generalmajor* Neustädter's troops on the Rye Island. On 1 January he issued a summons to the fortress commandant, Majtheny, to surrender, but without success.

Csorich Hunts Görgei in Vain, 10-15 January 1849

We now return to *Feldmarschall Lieutenant Baron* Csorich's troops of II. Armeekorps in Waitzen and their movements since the 8th and 9th. In accordance with the *Feldmarschall*'s order of 10:00 p.m. on the 8th, Csorich had left Brigade Colloredo and the two 12-pounder batteries from the Korps-Artillerie-Reserve in Waitzen and pushed Brigades Wyss and Jablonowsky forward through Rétság on the 10th. The first of these two had been reinforced with a 6-pounder battery from the Korps-Artillerie-Reserve, the second with Colloredo's 6-pounder battery and half a 6-pounder battery from the Reserve.

25 The low casualties suggest this action was just an artillery duel and an outflanking manoeuvre, in which the two sides' infantry and cavalry did not actually come to blows.

The road forks in Rétság. One road leads through Vad-Kert to Ballassa-Gyarmath [Balassagyarmat, Hungary], the other to Ipoly-Ságh. Only a small detachment of about 500 men had retreated along the former, while the enemy's main body took the road to Ipoly-Ságh, along which the brigades noted above followed it and reached Gross-Oroszi [Nagyoroszi, Hungary] and Berénke [Borsosberény, Hungary] at 6:00 p.m. in the evening. There the enemy strength was said by some to be 16,000 and by others 30,000. *Feldmarschall Lieutenant Baron* Csorich, who had personally remained in Waitzen, now saw fit to send two battalions of Brigade Colloredo and the 12-pounder batteries from the troops that had stayed in Waitzen to join the brigades that had pushed ahead, and to continue pursuing the enemy with nine battalions, eight squadrons and 36 guns.

The *Feldmarschall* endorsed this on the 11th, instructing *Feldmarschall Lieutenant Baron* Csorich that if the enemy should make a stand at Ipoly-Ságh he should be attacked, which was all the more likely to produce a good result as the rebels must be very fatigued and demoralised by marching, lack of discipline and their continuous retreat from Parendorf, so any numerical superiority they might have could be disregarded. But if the enemy were to continue his retreat beyond Ipoly-Ságh, it was all the more necessary to pursue him, as he might turn against *Feldmarschall Lieutenant* Simunich.

Given that the enemy's direction of march was now clearly revealed and was threatening Simunich, it was necessary to inform him quickly of this and of Csorich's march, which was done by means of the following message sent by courier on the 11th:

> I hereby inform Your Honour that a strong column of the Hungarian army driven out of Ofen-Pesth, said by spies to be 10,000-12,000 strong and with artillery, has retreated through Waitzen and taken the road from there through Gross-Oroszi and Ipoly-Ságh. Nine battalions, eight squadrons and 36 guns under command of *Feldmarschall Lieutenant Baron* Csorich have been sent after this column, but these have only reached Gross-Oroszi today, while the enemy must already have reached Ipoly-Ságh. If the enemy should make a stand there, *Feldmarschall Lieutenant Baron* Csorich is under orders to attack him, or alternatively to pursue him if he retreats further. At the moment the direction of his continued retreat cannot be predicted. He could move to the Mining Towns or he may follow the road to Neutra. The *Herr Feldmarschall Lieutenant* is therefore requested for your part to obtain news of the enemy column's direction of retreat, to concentrate your force as much as possible, and generally to be prepared to oppose the enemy forcefully should he approach your position. In this you may always count on *Feldmarschall Lieutenant Baron* Csorich's column to pursue the enemy and support you, and you should act in harmony with it so far as possible. The enemy force is said to be commanded by Görgei and Guyon, and to be very fatigued and demoralised, so can hardly be in a state to resist a serious attack.

On the 13th the *Feldmarschall* wrote to *Feldmarschall Lieutenant Graf* Schlick, partly in response to his report of the 5th concerning the action at Kaschau, that he approved of his decision to pursue the enemy with appropriate detachments; but that the reinforcements promised to him on the 8th would not arrive so soon as had been intended because Division Csorich had been given another mission in the meantime; but that this did not matter right now anyway as he had victoriously beaten back the enemy forces facing him.

For all that the *Feldmarschall* had planned that *Feldmarschall Lieutenant Graf* Schlick should turn through Losoncz toward Waitzen soon after occupying Kaschau, so as to link up there with the other army formations, it no longer seemed acceptable to move him there at the present moment. This would have given up again every advantage that had been gained in Upper Hungary, and the whole stretch of territory where order was in the process of being restored would have been exposed and sacrificed to the revolutionary party again, which would necessarily have made an extremely unfavourable impression on the well-disposed portion of the population and alienated what little sympathy we had found in the country; quite apart from the danger that vacating Kaschau might create for Galicia.

Consequently, as far as his future operations were concerned, it was indicated to *Feldmarschall Lieutenant Graf* Schlick that for the time being Miskolcz should be the furthest point that he should try to reach, from where Debreczin would constitute his next operational objective after reinforcements had arrived. Finally, at the end of this message it said verbatim: 'As for exactly when the reinforcements will reach you and how the operations generally outlined here should be executed, I will inform you of the details in due course.' Thus, the *Feldmarschall* cherished the hope that at the time was still well-founded that *Feldmarschall Lieutenant Baron* Csorich in cooperation with *Feldmarschall Lieutenant* Simunich would manage to wipe out or disperse Görgei's force, in which case continuing operations up to and beyond the Theiss would have been possible, and indeed extremely necessary to support hard-pressed Transylvania.

On the 12th *Feldmarschall Lieutenant Baron* Csorich followed on from Waitzen to Rétság with the two E.H. Stefan battalions from Brigade Colloredo and the two 12-pounder batteries, while *Generalmajor Fürst* Colloredo remained behind in Waitzen with the Landwehrbataillon Paumgarten, two squadrons of Civallart *uhlans* and the Munizions-Reserve. When he informed the *Feldmarschall* of this, he expressed the view that this reinforcement was all the more necessary as it seemed increasingly clear from all Görgei's manoeuvres that he intended to divert us from his main direction by splitting into several columns, and then to fall on *Feldmarschall Lieutenant* Simunich with his forces combined. This perfectly correct view was founded on a report from *Generalmajor* Wyss, who with his brigade and *Generalmajor Fürst* Jablonowsky's had encountered an enemy rear guard reportedly of three battalions, two divisions of cavalry and 21 guns at Ipoly-Ságh at around 11:00 a.m. on the 11th. He had driven these back and after occupying Ipoly-Ságh had had them pursued by two cavalry divisions and a horse artillery battery to Tompa [Tupá, Slovakia] on the road to Leva, to where the enemy's main body had headed the day before and so now did his rear guard. This obviously indicated that he intended an operation against Neutra and from there against *Feldmarschall Lieutenant* Simunich's position; for the road to the Mining Towns already turns north at Horvathi [Chorvatice, Slovakia], near to Ipoly-Ságh, but this had only been taken by a flanking column.

Some horses were captured from the enemy and 20 prisoners taken. Our own losses in this rearguard action came to two wounded E.H. Karl *chevauxlegers* and three horses.

At the end of his report *General* Wyss complained that none of the urgently needed items of uniform and kit had reached him, but that these were absolutely essential to keep the troops in a fit state to march and fight; a couple of rest days were also unavoidably necessary for the horses to be roughshod, since they could no longer make progress across the slippery frozen ground.[26]

26 'Roughshod' meaning the horses were given shoes with projecting nails for more grip.

The *Feldmarschall* responded to *Feldmarschall Lieutenant Baron* Csorich's report on the same day (the 12th), imparting his view 'that the majority of the enemy combat forces are now turning against *Feldmarschall Lieutenant* Simunich's position', and concluded by adding: '[I]t is accordingly of particular importance that the enemy should be pursued without let-up, so that if he clashes with *Feldmarschall Lieutenant* Simunich he shall be caught between two fires and unable to make his numerical superiority count against the latter.'

Generalmajor Wyss had halted at Ipoly-Ságh on the 12th and 13th and restricted himself to pushing forward strong patrols toward Németi [Hontianske Nemce, Slovakia] and Szantó [Santovka, Slovakia]. In the former place these ran into an enemy detachment, while the latter was found to be unoccupied. On the 13th *Feldmarschall Lieutenant Baron* Csorich arrived in Ipoly-Ságh with the two battalions of Brigade Colloredo and the two 12-pounder batteries, so all the troops under his command were united there. On the 14th he stopped for a rest day and to bring up the Munizions-Unterstützungs-Reserve from Waitzen, with only Brigade Wyss advancing to Szantó and sending a patrol from there through Léva to obtain information about the enemy.

These moves did not seem swift enough to the *Feldmarschall*, since the troops had covered no more than two days' march between the 9th and the 14th. Since he was also worried about *Feldmarschall Lieutenant* Simunich's situation, on the 14th he sent *Oberst* Pott of the general staff and his aide-de-camp *Major Baron* Langenau to speed up the march. *Oberst* Pott was to remain with *Feldmarschall Lieutenant Baron* Csorich, while *Major Baron* Langenau was to return with explanations and information. The two arrived in Ipoly-Ságh on the 15th, where Csorich still was with most of his troops, but leaving one H.v. Nassau battalion, a half-squadron of Kress *chevauxlegers* and a half-battery in Ipoly-Ságh, after breakfast he advanced to Szantó, while simultaneously Brigade Wyss was pushed forward from there to Léva to establish communications with Simunich.

Concern for Simunich and Neustädter, 13-14 January 1849

The *Feldmarschall*'s concerns were increased to the maximum by a message from the city command in Raab. This said that while the courier sent to *Feldmarschall Lieutenant* Simunich on the 11th was in Raab, he had lost the dispatch by which the said *Feldmarschall Lieutenant* was to be informed of Görgei's movements and *Feldmarschall Lieutenant Baron* Csorich's pursuit, so that Simunich had still not heard anything about them!

The latter had meanwhile obtained reports from spies and prisoners of the approach of significant enemy combat forces through Léva, and he had also been told that troops and militia numbering 14,000 men were mustering at Nagy-Sarló [Nagysalló, now Tekovské Lužany, Slovakia] under a certain Ballogh with the intention of moving on Neutra. However, understandably, he knew nothing of *Feldmarschall Lieutenant Baron* Csorich being sent to pursue the enemy. In his plight, *Feldmarschall Lieutenant* Simunich now requested that Brigade Neustädter deployed on the Rye Island to besiege Komorn should force march through Szered [Sered', Slovakia] to join him. All the preparations for the bombardment of Leopoldstadt were called off for the moment and the guns moved to safety. The majority of the siege artillery and the bridging trains were taken by rail to Pressburg.

Already on the 13th *Feldmarschall Lieutenant* Kempen had pushed forward two battalions and a battery from Pressburg to Wartberg [Senec, Slovakia] and from there to Szered to support

Feldmarschall Lieutenant Simunich, after *Feldmarschall Lieutenant Baron* Welden had sent Landwehr-Bataillon Khevenhüller and a battery from Wien to Pressburg the day before to serve as garrison there for the time being.

Major Ervin *Graf* Neipperg, who had been sent to Neutra with a patrol force by *Feldmarschall Lieutenant* Simunich, retreated to Freistadel on the 11th. Nonetheless Simunich had 17 companies, three squadrons and 18 guns advance to Neutra again on the 12th while four companies remained in Szered, 13 companies with two squadrons and five guns outside Leopoldstadt, and one company in Tyrnau. But when word arrived that evening that Görgei's advance guard was reportedly already in Ürmény [Mojmírovce, Slovakia] and Komját [Komjatice, Slovakia] and that a brigade (Gáspár's) had entered Verebély [Vrablé, Slovakia], Simunich decided to vacate Neutra and withdraw his troops to Szered, where they arrived on the 13th without having encountered the enemy.

At the same time he had issued the order to the force besieging Leopoldstadt to raise the blockade entirely and part of it to move to Bucsan [Bučany, Slovakia], the rest to Tyrnau where the whole division was to concentrate, when finally the field marshal's message of the 11th which had gone astray in Raab arrived, having been found on the 13th by *Gemeiner* [Private] Benesch of 1. Landwehr-Bataillon Reisinger and immediately sent on to its destination by the Raab city command.[27]

Generalmajor Neustädter had received *Feldmarschall Lieutenant* Simunich's request to hurry to Szered to support him but was uncertain whether he should abandon the blockade of Komorn on the Rye Island entirely. He therefore consulted *Feldmarschall Lieutenant* Ramberg, who given the apparent urgency of Simunich's request told him to act on it.

On the 13th, *Generalmajor* Neustädter was just in the process of leaving his position at Nyarasd for Szerdahely [Dunajská Streda, Slovakia] when he himself was attacked by an enemy column, reportedly of six battalions, two squadrons and three batteries. Initially he could only oppose it with eight companies, one squadron of Banderial hussars and a 6 pounder battery; for his other ten companies were about 12 km away to the side, in Szilas [Brestovec, Slovakia], Lac [Lakszakallás, now Sokolce, Slovakia] and Ekecs [Okoč, Slovakia]. The enemy's superior numbers forced Neustädter to retreat toward Szerdahely, where he arrived that evening without having been pursued any further, and the detached companies also joined him there. His losses in this action came to two dead, two wounded and 18 missing (the latter from the Banderial hussars). Among the former was the brave *Oberstlieutenant Baron* Geramb, who died a hero's death at the head of his battalion.

Hauptmann Kappler of the general staff was mentioned in despatches for his good judgement, energy and courageous determination; likewise *k.k. Kadet* Zwiedinek commanding the brigade battery, which fought back very bravely against the enemy's 18 guns and drew all their fire upon itself during the retreat.

On the 14th *Generalmajor* Neustädter continued his march to Luipersdorf [Csütörtök, now Štvrtok na Ostrove, Slovakia], so as to move to Wartberg next day.

On hearing that *Feldmarschall Lieutenant* Simunich had arrived in Szered and had not been attacked, *Feldmarschall Lieutenant* Kempen had called back the reinforcements he had sent him,

27 This is a curious little episode. Of course, it is impossible to know exactly what happened. I like to imagine the courier enjoying a drink in a Raab tavern and having his purse lifted by a sly *landwehr* private, who then turns it in when it is safe for him to do so.

but when the request was renewed, on the 14th he again sent one battalion with a battery through Wartberg to Szered. But when he learned of *Generalmajor* Neustädter's retreat from the Rye Island, he asked Simunich to deploy at least one battalion and some guns on the Rye Island so as to protect Pressburg which was now under threat, this being all the more important as the magazines, paychest, political prisoners, etc., and the siege artillery and bridging trains sent back from Leopoldstadt were all there. In addition he appealed to the *Feldmarschall* to order Brigade Neustädter back to the Rye Island again soonest. He also emphasised the need to take Leopoldstadt as soon as possible, since despite the small size of its garrison, this fortress exerted a very evil influence over the mood of the whole area.

The *Feldmarschall* Orchestrates Simunich, Neustädter and Csorich, and Reinforces Schlick, 16-21 January 1849

The reports about all these events reached the headquarters in Ofen between the 16th and 18th. On the 16th the *Feldmarschall* now issued detailed instructions to *Feldmarschall Lieutenant* Simunich as well as to *Generalmajor* Neustädter in which he remarked to the former that the most effective way of covering the siege of Leopoldstadt as well as securing the crossing of the Waag at Szered on his right flank would be to move swiftly with all his force to Neutra, whose local terrain would enable a very sustained defence. This would put him in a position to hold up the enemy and beat him, in combination with *Feldmarschall Lieutenant Baron* Csorich's pursuing column. Neustädter was instructed by the *Feldmarschall* to return to his previous position. Support was only to be provided for Simunich in the most absolutely urgent case, for Neustädter's departure from the Rye Island left Komorn unobserved and the whole stretch between that fortress and Pressburg exposed. Pursuit of the enemy toward the Mining Towns was entrusted to Csorich. Simunich was therefore to press on with reducing Leopoldstadt above all else.[28]

In his dispatch to *Generalmajor* Neustädter the *Feldmarschall* accepted that he had been responding to urgent requests from *Feldmarschall Lieutenant* Simunich, but nevertheless explained that he did not agree with him completely abandoning the Rye Island from the moment when he himself was threatened by a strong enemy column. He was therefore ordered to resume his previous mission on the Rye Island.

Meantime, a report from *Feldmarschall Lieutenant* Simunich dated the 16th arrived, in which he indicated that he had already informed *Generalmajor* Neustädter that he no longer needed his support; on the contrary, he was now ready to aid Neustädter; furthermore that he had tasked *Generalmajor Fürst* Lobkowitz with sending strong patrols toward Komjáthi, Ürmény and Neutra to obtain information. In response to this report, on the 19th he was instructed to concentrate his force, to hold the important town of Neutra, to press on energetically with the reduction of Leopoldstadt, and to avoid detaching individual companies and squadrons in

28 Neutra does indeed seem an obvious position at which to cover Leopoldstadt. Again, though, one might ask whether the *Feldmarschall* could have been bolder. Perhaps he could have charged Simunich with using part of his force more aggressively, in coordination with Csorich, to trap Görgei. A column directed on Neusohl via Prividgye would have had a good road for most of the way, its flanks protected by mountains if attacked, would have linked up with Götz's force in Mosocs, and could have covered Leopoldstadt against an enemy advance from Schemnitz by threatening the enemy flank.

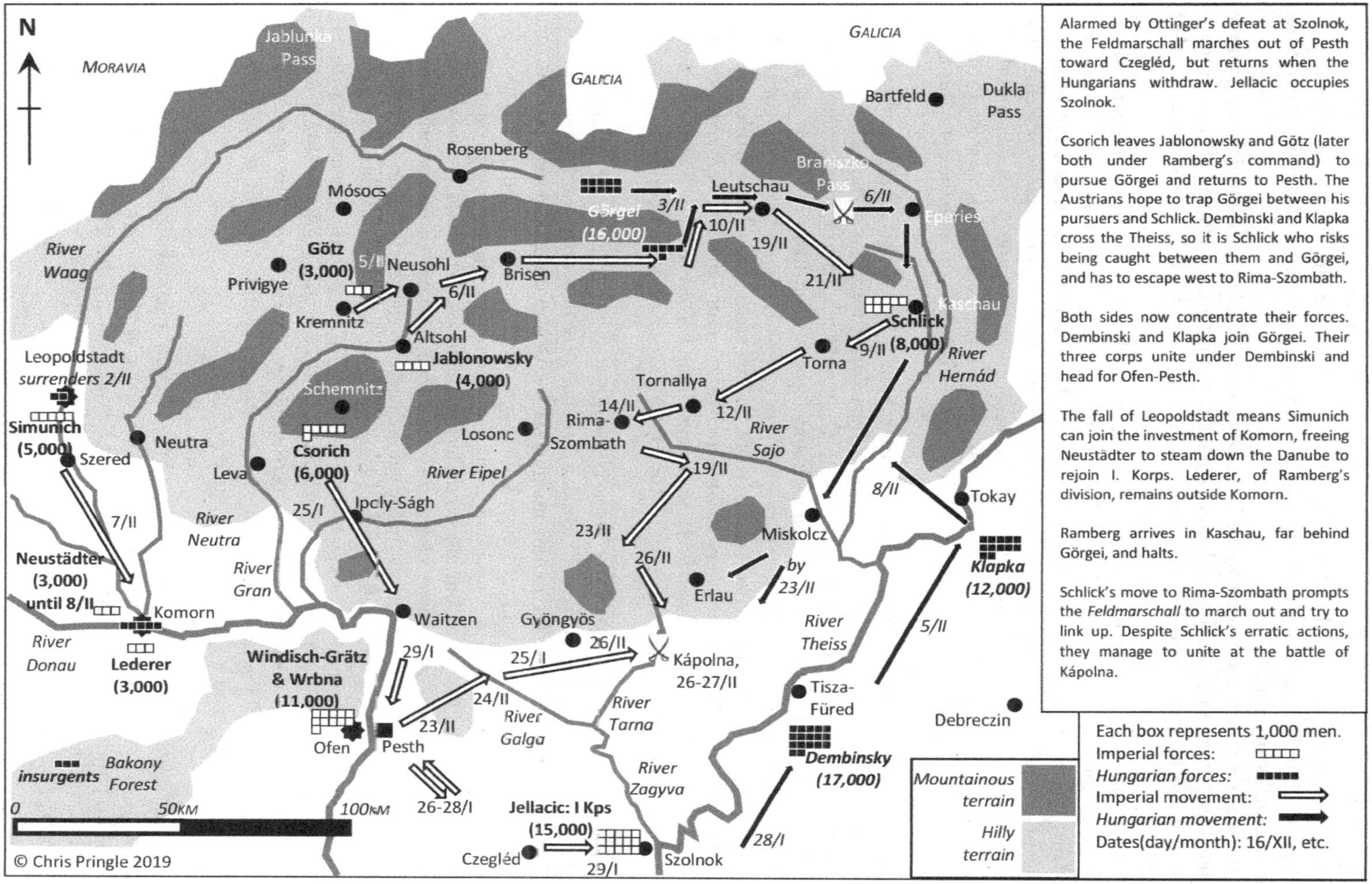

Map 3b: Converging on Kápolna, February 1849

response to mere rumours of the enemy's approach, since on the one hand these detachments were too weak to hold up the enemy, but on the other they were too strong to be regarded as mere reconnaissance patrols.

After receiving the order written on the 16th, *Feldmarschall Lieutenant* Simunich immediately arranged for Neutra to be garrisoned by four companies of infantry, a platoon of *jägers*, a troop of cavalry and half a battery, betaking himself there personally so as to coordinate further operations with *Feldmarschall Lieutenant Baron* Csorich.

Generalmajor Götz, who was in Mosocs [Mosóc, now Mošovce, Slovakia] and with whom communications had been established via Zsámbokréth and Prividgye, was notified of the state of affairs. On the 15th word was sent to *Feldmarschall Lieutenant Baron* Csorich of what had meanwhile been learned from *Feldmarschall Lieutenant* Simunich and *Generalmajor* Neustädter, as well as respectfully requesting that he should prosecute the pursuit of the enemy with the utmost energy. *Generalmajor Fürst* Colloredo was charged with leaving just two companies of infantry and one squadron in Waitzen, and following on to Ipoly-Ságh with the rest of his force, there to await orders from Csorich.

The latter had arrived in Léva on the 16th with the main body of his division and reported from there that the enemy had already abandoned Léva during the night of the 12th and moved toward Schemnitz [Banská Štiavnica, Slovakia]. Only a detachment of a few thousand men had marched toward Verebély but on the 13th and 14th this had likewise turned off toward the Mining Towns, as reported by *Generalmajor* Wyss who had advanced to Verebély with four companies of 2. Jäger-Bataillon, two squadrons of Civallart *uhlans* and a horse artillery battery. From Verebély Wyss had sent a very reliable and resourceful officer, *Oberlieutenant Baron* Bujanovich of the E.H. Karl *chevauxlegers*, to Neutra to find *Feldmarschall Lieutenant* Simunich. At the end of the aforementioned report, *Feldmarschall Lieutenant Baron* Csorich said:

> From all this it can be seen that there was nothing more to fear for *Feldmarschall Lieutenant* Simunich after the 12th, the day the rebel corps fell back toward Schemnitz, and also that probably nothing more stood in the way of him linking up with me, if he had been aware of my advance through Ipoly-Ságh. Since my arrival in Ipoly-Ságh on the 15th I have made every conceivable effort to obtain news from him and to establish communications with him, but in vain up to this point. Abandoning Léva now with my main body in order to move closer to *Feldmarschall Lieutenant* Simunich would be a retrograde movement for me and sufficient invitation to the rebels to hurl themselves upon my line of communications before I can catch up with them. I therefore have no option but to remain in Léva tomorrow (the 17th) so as to communicate with *Feldmarschall Lieutenant* Simunich if possible. If I do not manage to do this, I will pursue the enemy alone; in the event that the enemy should already have abandoned Schemnitz, which I hope to discover tomorrow from my confidants, I will follow in his path through Losoncz so as to smash him if possible.

The *Feldmarschall* replied to this letter on the 18th that, desirable and successful though a joint action with *Feldmarschall Lieutenant* Simunich would have been so long as the enemy was still between his position and *Feldmarschall Lieutenant Baron* Csorich's, this was less important right now when the enemy had extracted himself from their joint operation by his flank march to Schemnitz; all the more so as Simunich had been instructed to reduce Leopoldstadt, secure the line of the Waag, etc., so could not move into the Mining Towns; on the other hand the participation of *Generalmajor* Götz could perhaps be counted on, who had already arrived in Mosocs on the 12th and was now advancing toward the Mining Towns. Concerning the proposed outflanking through Losoncz, the *Feldmarschall* replied that he did not consider this advisable, since the enemy, not being constrained either by adhering to one line of operations or by protecting a base, could quickly fling himself first in one direction, then in the other, avoiding any decisive blow; so the surest way was still to follow in his footsteps. It would take at least five or six days' march to move on Losoncz, which would run the risk of the enemy suddenly turning back from Schemnitz and hurling himself upon Simunich and Leopoldstadt, where it would then be quite impossible to do anything to support him.[29]

On the same day as this letter went off to *Feldmarschall Lieutenant Baron* Csorich (the 18th), news was received from *Feldmarschall Lieutenant Graf* Schlick via the direct route through Miskolcz and Gyöngyös for the first time. Dressed as a student, the very skilful and enterprising *Lieutenant* Tomasini of the Mazzuchelli infantry had managed to get right through the enemy lines into the *Feldmarschall*'s headquarters in Ofen. Since his victorious action at Kaschau, Schlick had attempted to pacify and establish administrative control over the adjacent counties by sending out mobile columns. These columns went to Varáno [Varannó, now Vranov nad Topl'ou, Slovakia] in the Zempliner Komitat, and to Käsmark [Kežmarok, Slovakia] and Leutschau in Zips. *Major* Kiesewetter remained behind in the latter place with four Nugent companies and two companies of the Koudelka regiment, a troop of *chevauxlegers* and half a rocket battery as a garrison.

Through these detachments and the garrisons needed for Bartfeld [Bardejov, Slovakia], Eperies [Prešov, Slovakia], Kaschau, etc., *Feldmarschall Lieutenant Graf* Schlick's available combat forces had dwindled away to a very small number of troops (six battalions, five squadrons, 26 guns). Conversely, the rebels dispersed at Kaschau had recovered from their initial shock, rallied behind the Theiss and the Bodrog, and also garrisoned Miskolcz suitably again. Command of these forces had been transferred from Mészáros to the insurgent leader Klapka.[30] In these circumstances Schlick found himself obliged to ask the *Feldmarschall* for the immediate dispatch of reinforcements with the utmost urgency, to which end, as already noted, he had sent *Lieutenant* Tomasini with verbal instructions to the headquarters in Ofen.

29 This situation can be viewed in either of two ways. At Schemnitz, Görgei was facing Simunich to the west, Götz to the north and Csorich to the southwest. Csorich's proposed move via Losoncz would have shifted him more to the east and offered the prospect of Csorich and Götz converging on Görgei from north and south, cutting off his rear if he advanced west, or catching him if he retreated to the east. However, the cautious *Feldmarschall* saw only the threat to Simunich. I believe Csorich was right, and that in turning down his proposal the *Feldmarschall* reduced the chance of inflicting a serious defeat on Görgei.

30 György Klapka (1820-92), one of the youngest generals in the war, was a former imperial officer who became a captain in the *honvéd* in June 1848. In between his succession of increasingly senior field commands, he was involved in work for the war ministry and in staff work, planning operations. In July 1849 he was commander of II. Corps, which remained in Komorn when the rest of Görgei's army marched away. He negotiated the agreement for the capitulation of Komorn on 29 September, including amnesty for its garrison. After the war he emigrated to Switzerland, was involved in raising a 3,500-man Hungarian Legion to fight against Austria in the 1859 war in Italy, and again in raising a Hungarian Legion for Prussia in 1866. He returned to Hungary in 1868.

The only choice left was either to call *Feldmarschall Lieutenant Graf* Schlick in to join the main army, which would necessarily have entailed evacuating the whole extensive stretch of territory where lawful order had only just been restored; or else immediately to use the reinforcements that had long been intended for him but that had been delayed by *Feldmarschall Lieutenant Baron* Csorich's mission having changed meanwhile. The *Feldmarschall* opted for the latter measure, all the more so as voluntarily abandoning Kaschau and the whole area could not have been justified, would have made the worst possible impression, and would also have exposed the Galician border; as against which, appropriate reinforcement of Schlick's corps could put him in a position to be equal to any eventuality that could be expected in that theatre of operations.

Feldmarschall Lieutenant Schulzig was accordingly given the mission of setting off from Pesth on the 19th with the troops listed below taken from the Reserve-Korps, and joining *Feldmarschall Lieutenant Graf* Schlick without delay via Gyöngyös, Mezö-Kövesd [Mezőkővesd, Hungary] and Miskolcz:

Brigade *Generalmajor* Kriegern

2. Bataillon Latour
3. Bataillon Ottochaner
3. Bataillon Warasdiner Kreutzer
3. Bataillon Warasdiner St. Georger
One 6-pounder battery

Brigade *Generalmajor* Parrot

Six squadrons of the Prinz von Preussen Kürassiere
Two squadrons of the Max Auersperg Kürassiere
One horse artillery battery
One 12-pounder battery

Altogether four battalions, eight squadrons and 18 guns.

This brought *Feldmarschall Lieutenant Graf* Schlick's corps up to 12 battalions, 14 squadrons and 53 guns.

Lieutenant Tomasini returned to *Feldmarschall Lieutenant Graf* Schlick without delay with the news that this reinforcement was coming and managed to reach him by the same road he had arrived along. In order to fill the gap to some degree that this detachment left in the ranks of the troops concentrated in Ofen-Pesth, on the 21st the *Feldmarschall* wrote to *Feldzeugmeister Graf* Nugent that he should send four battalions of his corps forward to Stuhlweissenburg, which should remain available there as a reserve until it should be possible for a detachment sent to pursue the enemy to return there, which should be the case shortly.

Görgei Eludes Csorich, 17-22 January 1849

Let us return now to *Feldmarschall Lieutenant Baron* Csorich's operations.

On the 17th communications were established with *FeldmarschallLieutenant* Simunich's troops deployed at Neutra. It was also learned that the enemy brigade under Aulich that had advanced to Verbély on the 13th had now retreated through Benedek [Hronský Beňadik, Slovakia] toward Heiligenkreuz [Žiar nad Hronom, Slovakia] on the road to Kremnitz, and had burned the bridge over the River Gran [Hungarian name: Garam] behind it. It was further reported that the enemy had taken position on the mountain plateau before Schemnitz and held the difficult approach through the Báth [Bátovce, Slovakia] defile with artillery. In order to confirm this, on the 18th *Feldmarschall Lieutenant Baron* Csorich sent *Oberst* Collery of 12. Jäger-Bataillon with two companies of *jägers*, two E.H. Stefan companies and a troop of cavalry into the Gran valley to Benedek, and *Major* Salis of the E.H. Stefan with two companies of his battalion, two companies of *jägers*, a half-squadron of cavalry and two rocket launch stands toward Báth. At the same time he sent *Hauptmann* Kalik of the general staff to ask *Feldmarschall Lieutenant* Simunich to support his planned advance toward Schemnitz by sending a column into the Neutra valley through Osslán [Oslany, Slovakia] and Prividgye.

Feldmarschall Lieutenant Simunich, who had been informed by an allegedly very well-disposed official that the enemy intended to move into the Neutra valley through Zsámbokréth to relieve Leopoldstadt, had already detached *Major Graf* Neipperg to that area on the 16th with six infantry companies, a half-squadron of cavalry and half a rocket battery. He now also ordered *Generalmajor* Sossay there as well with a further four Haynau companies, a platoon of *jägers* and a battery, with orders to advance as swiftly as possible through Zsámbokréth, Osslán, Prividgye and Handlová, to support *Feldmarschall Lieutenant Baron* Csorich's march on Schemnitz which was expected to take place on the 21st; and from there also to communicate with *Generalmajor* Götz, who was simultaneously to advance from Mósocs on Kremnitz and operate against the enemy's line of retreat. However, after this expedition Sossay was to return immediately.

On the 19th *Feldmarschall Lieutenant Baron* Csorich had pushed forward 3. Bataillon Fürstenwärther and half a 6-pounder battery through Báth toward Steinbach [Köpatak in Hungarian; nowadays located at the northern end of Majere, Slovakia, where route 1579 joins route 524] to support *Major Baron* Salis's little column, while the main body still remained in Léva. While informing the *Feldmarschall* of this, he also shared with him the intelligence reports that he had obtained meanwhile concerning the enemy's strength, positions and movements. The strength of the rebels under Görgei was estimated at 17,000-20,000 men with 50 or 60 guns![31] On the 12th Görgei had marched with the two or three brigades of his main body from Léva via Báth to Schemnitz, while a fourth brigade under one Pongratz had moved along a side road to Németi.[32] On the 13th Aulich was supposed to have retreated with four brigades from Verebély through Benedek to Heiligenkreuz, and to have burned all the bridges across the Gran behind him and the like.[33] However, this report had come in from *Major Baron* Salis who had been detached toward Schemnitz: 'Görgei is still in Schemnitz with a few battalions, Husaren-Regiment Nr. 4, one or two divisions of Husaren-Regiment Nr. 9 and about 30 guns,

31 As noted earlier, Bánlaky gives the combat strength of Görgei's force around this time as 16,000 men with 72 guns; but, as we shall see later, whether because of detaching forces or other reasons, by the 21st he seems to have had only at most 10,000 men and 24 guns.

32 István Pongrácz [Pongratz] (1821-1900).

33 Lajos Aulich (1793-49). A career officer who had served in the Napoleonic Wars, Aulich and his regiment were allocated to the Hungarian war ministry in May 1848. He held field commands until May 1849 when he went on sick leave. In July he became minister of war and surrendered at Világos in August. He was sentenced to death at Arad and executed on 5 October 1849. Bona, *Tábornokok*.

some of which are posted on the mountain plateau; all the rest of his troops have marched away through Altsohl [Zvolen, Slovakia] to join Mészáros.' Csorich went on to express his view that by occupying the Mining Towns that were very favourable for defence, 'even with just one or two brigades, [the enemy] could find the opportunity to move the majority of his troops away in successive echelons through Altsohl into Gömörer Komitat [Gömör County] to join Mészáros, and then combine to crush *Feldmarschall Lieutenant Graf* Schlick'. As far as his future operations were concerned, he said:

> If the enemy is holding Schemnitz, even if with just one or two battalions, about which I await *Major* Salis's report, then I will either attack him in his position there – even though this can be held by a small force against greatly superior numbers because of the difficult approaches to it – or else, if the bridges in the Gran valley can be repaired swiftly (about which I likewise await reports) I will outflank Schemnitz through the Gran valley toward Altsohl, while driving out the enemy that is said to be in Heiligenkreuz. Unfortunately, the enemy main body that has already marched away through Altsohl will have gained such a head start that it will be able to join Mészáros unhindered and attack Schlick. *Generalmajor Fürst* Colloredo, who has arrived in Ipoly-Ságh with four Paumgarten companies and a squadron of *uhlans*, has been charged with supporting my attack by advancing to demonstrate through Némethy and Preitzdorf [Prenčov, Slovakia] toward Schemnitz with the 10 companies, half-squadron and half-battery under his command.

This message dated the 19th had still not been sent off when Csorich received the report from *Major Baron* Salis on the morning of the 20th which caused him to set off that very day via Báth toward Schemnitz.

For during his reconnaissance toward Schemnitz, *Major Baron* Salis ran into the enemy's forward elements 5 km this side of Windschacht [Vindšacht, western suburb of Štiavnické Bane, Slovakia]. He had just driven these back into that place and occupied the first few houses there when the enemy received reinforcements from elsewhere in the village, perhaps from Schemnitz itself. *Major Baron* Salis felt he was too weak to hold the position he had taken with his four companies and half a rocket battery; he therefore gradually broke off the action and withdrew to Steinbach in good order, only pursued by a hussar detachment with two guns, which in any case did not venture more than a couple of kilometres out of Windschacht. In this action, which would probably have resulted in the occupation of Schemnitz if undertaken with sufficient forces, *Major Baron* Salis had one killed and four wounded, as against 13 enemy left dead on the battlefield and 18 taken prisoner. *Major Baron* Salis remarked:

> From my clash with the enemy today, I believe I may conclude that Schemnitz is not so strong as we thought by a long way, but is just held by a few thousand men, and that the enemy will hardly make a stand against an attack undertaken in appropriate strength. He supposedly has 600 hussars and 23 guns in Schemnitz; what he brought into action against me was approximately 2,000 infantry with five guns and about a squadron of hussars. These seem to have been well armed, at least their musketry had a very

> long effective range.[34] Guyon commanded in Windschacht. Görgei is not thought to be there anymore. According to corroborating reports, a grenadier battalion marched away this morning (the 19th).[35] The guns are supposed to have been distributed around the entrances to the town and are mostly on the side toward Kremnitz.

As well as the brave conduct of his troops, *Major Baron* Salis praised the service performed by *Akademiker* [Lecturer] Weiglein from the Bergschule whose local knowledge was very helpful.[36]

In reply to this report the *Feldmarschall* sent a letter to *Feldmarschall Lieutenant Baron* Csorich on the 21st in which he expressed the view that all there was in Schemnitz was a strong enemy rear guard, a tactic which the enemy usually used to gain a significant head start. The *Feldmarschall Lieutenant* was therefore to concentrate his forces as much as possible and then quickly get stuck into the enemy, all the more so as after his failed attack on *Feldmarschall Lieutenant* Simunich the enemy would probably turn against *Feldmarschall Lieutenant Graf* Schlick. The latter had already been informed of this by the *Feldmarschall* and had been told that he could rely on Csorich's cooperation with his own operations up to a certain point; and *Feldmarschall Lieutenant* Schulzig had also been sent via Gyöngyös to support Schlick. From now on Csorich was to operate independently in the spirit of the general instructions he had received, for given the great distance from headquarters, it was no longer realistic to expect to receive detailed orders about how to act; nonetheless the *Feldmarschall* was to be kept informed of how manoeuvres were progressing as often as feasible. A captured order of battle provided evidence that Görgei did not have 20,000 men and 60 guns but was at most 10,000 strong with 24 guns.

This whole expedition had not lived up to the *Feldmarschall*'s expectations. True, Görgei had been driven away from *Feldmarschall Lieutenant* Simunich's position, the fortress of Leopoldstadt, and the Austrian/Moravian border. But because of the obstacles encountered, the enemy had not been pursued swiftly enough, and Simunich, who had learned of the true situation 48 hours too late because of the lost dispatch, had withdrawn his force from the Neutra to behind the Waag.

Görgei, worried by the clash between his rear guard and Brigade Wyss, and on the other hand afraid of being delayed on the Neutra or the Waag, had turned rapidly from Léva and Verbély toward the Mining Towns as we have seen, a manoeuvre that of course he was only able to execute because the main body of the forces pursuing him was still so far behind that he could hope to complete his march in the defiles and along the poor roads of the Mining Towns totally unmolested; which indeed he entirely managed to do, despite the many wagons he had with him. There could really no longer be any thought of catching up with him, for the bulk of his corps had already left Léva on the 12th, while *Feldmarschall Lieutenant Baron* Csorich did not follow on after him from there until the 20th. Thus, even taking into account manifold obstacles his march might have encountered on the way, he could have gained a head start of at least four to five days' march. Besides, the roads were getting worse and worse, the enemy

34 A rather strong assertion to make after suffering only five casualties.

35 Presumably the Weissl grenadier battalion.

36 The *Bergschule* was the School of Mining and Metallurgy in Schemnitz. Weiglein is described as an *Akademiker*, which here presumably means he was a teacher rather than a student, especially as the students joined the Hungarian army. *History of the University of Miskolc.*

could create multiple delays in this mountainous country crisscrossed by many watercourses by demolishing the bridges, blocking the roads and the like, so the gap would get larger every day rather than smaller. At that moment it was therefore a matter of deciding whether or not one was prepared to have three brigades dragged along four or five days' march behind the enemy, perhaps for several weeks, simply on the off chance. The army was not strong enough for that. After sending reinforcements to *Feldmarschall Lieutenant Graf* Schlick, 6. Jäger-Bataillon to clear the Bakonyer-Wald, and the Ceccopieri battalion to garrison Gran, the number of combat forces concentrated in Ofen-Pesth came to no more than 12 battalions, 14 squadrons and 105 guns!

Taking these circumstances into account, and in case it should be confirmed that the enemy's main body really had gained a head start of several days' march, which *Feldmarschall Lieutenant Baron* Csorich had to establish in the next few days, the *Feldmarschall* decided to summon him back with two brigades. The pursuit was to be continued by the third brigade, since it would not do to let the enemy out of one's sight entirely when the direction of his retreat was still not clear, and besides, this would oblige him constantly to leave a strong rear guard behind, which would benefit *Feldmarschall Lieutenant Graf* Schlick in the event that the enemy should turn against him. Consequently the following message was sent to Csorich on the 22nd:

> I believe I may assume that at the moment when this order reaches you, you will not only be in possession of Schemnitz but will also have confirmed the enemy's direction of retreat. If he has taken the road through Losoncz as suspected, and his main body has already gained a head start of a couple of days' march, it can no longer be possible anyway for you to overtake him in good time, namely before a clash with *Feldmarschall Lieutenant Graf* Schlick's force. Because of this, as well as the fact that reinforcements have reached the said *Feldmarschall Lieutenant* directly from here, I consider it superfluous for you to pursue the enemy with all of the troops under your command. I therefore wish you to pursue him only with Brigade Jablonowsky, and to return to here with the rest without the slightest delay.[37]

Finally, at the end of this order it says:

> The instructions hereby imparted to Your Honour are based on the assumption, as stated at the beginning, that the enemy main body has taken the road through Losoncz and gained a significant head start, and they are perhaps to be interpreted in that spirit.

37 The clash the *Feldmarschall* anticipated between Görgei and Schlick did not turn out as he hoped; in the event, it was Schlick who risked being caught between the two fires of Görgei and Dembinski and had to dash to the west to escape. Jablonowsky's pursuing force was unable to coordinate with Schlick and never caught up with Görgei. A full pursuit with all of Csorich's corps would presumably have done no better and simply punched thin air harder, so the *Feldmarschall* is right to call it superfluous. One might ask though whether the pursuit was conducted with too large a force rather than too little. If Götz had been left to pursue alone, and Jablonowsky's force had been with the main army at the battle of Kápolna a month later, instead of sitting passively in Kaschau, that victory could have been more decisive.

Events in the Rear and on the Theiss, 13 January to 1 February 1849

Before we follow *Feldmarschall Lieutenant Baron* Csorich's operations any further from the point where he set off from Léva toward Schemnitz, we must take a look at what had happened meanwhile in the rear of the army and on the Theiss.

Oberstlieutenant Graf Althan, who had *Major* Jungbauer of the general staff assigned to him, was operating with his patrol force in the area of Ödenburg, Güns, Steinamanger, Csorna, Szány [Szany, Hungary] and Marczaltö. On the evening of the 13th he had assembled five companies, three squadrons and two rocket launch stands in Pápa,[38] with the intention of dispersing a rebel band concentrated in the Bakonyer-Wald and at Bakonybél led by Bihár, Andor and Medniansky. In a surprise night attack and ensuing two-hour battle he succeeded in this completely.[39] In this action *Hauptmann* Roknich, *Lieutenant* Kottas (who was lightly wounded) and *Lieutenant* Orlich of the Oguliner regiment particularly distinguished themselves.

On the 16th five companies, half a squadron of *chevauxlegers* and three guns from *Oberst Baron* Horváth's patrol force were sent from Stuhlweissenburg to Veszprim under the command of *Rittmeister* Escherich, to restore law and order and patrol into the Bakonyer-Wald. *Major* Kronenerg of 6. Jäger-Bataillon, detached to sweep the Bakonyer-Wald, had patrolled throughout the area between Kis-Bér, Pápa and Veszprim and disarmed the villages. He described the mood of the local inhabitants as generally very hostile.

Feldmarschall Lieutenant Ramberg was informed by the *Feldmarschall* about everything that had occurred on the left bank of the Danube and was told to redouble his watch on the bridgehead at Komorn, as well as to look out for any opportunity for an operation that promised any kind of success.

Generalmajor Neustädter had not been able to comply with the order given him that he should reoccupy his previous position on the Rye Island, for the Little Danube had overflowed its banks so much that any attempt to cross it proved unfeasible. This flooding also greatly helped the siege of Komorn, as almost the whole of the left bank of the Danube was underwater, which hindered any operation by the garrison.

Concerning events on the Theiss, on the 18th the *Banus* reported that the enemy had hastily retreated on the 14th from Török Sz. Miklós through K. Uj-Szallása [Kisújszállás, Hungary], and that *Generalmajor* Ottinger had requested a small infantry detachment to run a hospital and guard the enemy deserters that were constantly coming in. Ottinger also described the need to deploy infantry detachments in Czegléd, Abony and Tapio-Szele, to clamp down on the courier communications the rebels were receiving from these places.

However, on the 22nd the following report from the Ban arrived that was bound to attract the *Feldmarschall*'s full attention to *Generalmajor* Ottinger's position:

> According to a report sent with yesterday's date, because of information received, to avoid a surprise attack *Generalmajor* Ottinger felt himself obliged to vacate Szolnok in the middle of the night of the 20th/21st and to keep his whole brigade mounted and

38 Again, note the use of rockets and their valuable mobility in such raiding operations, which is why British forces made extensive use of rockets in colonial expeditions in the latter half of the century.

39 Note there is no mention of rebel casualties. Rather than being an Austrian success in scattering a rebel band, perhaps this was a rebel success in escaping from the Austrian attack without serious damage.

> in readiness until morning. The enemy is said to have reconnoitred on the 19th with 1,000 hussars, and to intend crossing the Theiss at Czibákháza [Cibakháza, Hungary] to advance toward Abony, so Abony has been occupied with one division and half a rocket battery. The *General* describes the mood of the country people as fairly good, but there are said to be many agitators among the officials and the nobility.

This report continued:

> The rumour is spreading here that Görgei and his men have turned east from Léva, marched across behind Schlick's corps and managed to link up with the insurgents' main body under Kossuth at Debreczin. *General* Ottinger therefore certainly could appear to be in a somewhat dangerous position.

As it was known for certain that Görgei was still in Léva on the 12th, he could not possibly have marched past behind Schlick's position and joined up with the force at Debreczin by the 22nd, so this concern for *Generalmajor* Ottinger's position on the basis of Görgei's movements did not seem justified. Still the *Feldmarschall* felt he had to comment on more detailed dispositions concerning the position and security of Brigade Ottinger, since that general's repeated requests for infantry support had produced no result, regardless of the fact that the *Feldmarschall*'s written orders of 8 and 12 January had stipulated that this should happen as soon as the railway was repaired (which had been the case since the 17th).[40] Furthermore, it did not seem appropriate to the *Feldmarschall* that this cavalry brigade should be deployed with instructions to watch the Theiss crossing but not to hold it. Therefore, immediately after receiving the above report he ordered that it be ascertained whether the terrain by the bridge was such that it could be successfully defended by an infantry detachment, as already indicated in his order of 12 January, while still being able to retreat quickly by rail if necessary; and further, whether it might not be more appropriate just to keep an advanced post in Szolnok, but to withdraw the main body of the brigade to Abány, so as not to immediately be threatened from the rear by any enemy attempt to cross the Tisza above or below Szolnok.

It was too late! For on the very day on which the *Feldmarschall* was going into these details, *General* Ottinger was attacked by very superior enemy forces and forced to evacuate Szolnok. The *Feldmarschall* received a verbal report on this on the 23rd from *Oberlieutenant* Sastavnikovic, who was under Ottinger's command but attached to the quartermaster-general's staff. According to this officer's statement, at 9:00 a.m. on the 22nd Ottinger had sent a patrol toward Török Sz. Miklós to obtain information about the enemy. Halfway there the patrol had run into enemy

40 Another instance of the *Feldmarschall* pressing the buttons but nothing happening! His army was not a very reliably responsive machine. The contrast with the dynamic and effective Haynau who commanded in the latter part of the war is notable. The difference was presumably due to their different personalities and leadership styles. Haynau is described as 'a born leader, free from pedantry, inexhaustibly active, modest in his own needs, ruthlessly energetic, he pursued his goals with a determination that occasionally bordered on obstinacy'. *ÖBL*, Vol.2, p.228. Windisch-Grätz also gets praised, but not with quite the same qualities of leadership or ruthlessness attributed to Haynau: '[He] gave the impression of an imposing personality. Measured, taciturn but dignified to the core. … Set against the indecision, even cowardice of the government officials, he provided a cool head, energy and indomitable willpower.' *BLKÖ*, Vol.57, p.28.

hussars, and despite the thick fog blanketing the whole area, detected strong columns following them. Upon this news Ottinger had quickly deployed two guns on the Szolnok bridge, while the brigade mustered in its stand-to positions. But the enemy, who had crossed the frozen Theiss above Szolnok, was already threatening the brigade's line of retreat; so Ottinger, who understandably could not hold Szolnok with his cavalry, deployed about 1,000 paces behind the town. A division of Hardegg cuirassiers under *Major* Algyay that was somewhat forward of the left wing attacked a carelessly advancing division of hussars so decisively in flank and rear that the latter were driven back with the loss of several dead and wounded, and a *Rittmeister* and 18 hussars were taken prisoner. But the enemy soon deployed such superior force, particularly in artillery which he quickly brought forward over the bridge, that Ottinger could have no thought of resisting there any longer; he therefore began his retreat to Abony and suffered considerable losses from enemy artillery fire while doing so. The enemy strength was given as 20,000 men and 40 guns, which was probably an exaggeration.

This was an alarming moment! With five days' march the enemy could be outside Pesth, whose garrison numbered no more than 12 battalions! 5. Jäger-Bataillon, two battalions of *grenzers* and three batteries were immediately sent off to support *General* Ottinger – some via the railway, others by road – to Czegléd, to where the said general had retreated during the night of the 22nd/23rd and sent a written report on the events that were already partly known from *Oberlieutenant* Sastavnikovic's verbal message. At the end of this report it says:

> 5. Jäger-Bataillon has just arrived here. I request another horse artillery battery and just a little cavalry support, which could put me in a position to sweep this side of the Theiss clean of the enemy, unless he plans to advance here from Debreczin with his entire army. I request your noble instruction as to whether I may act on the offensive at my own discretion.

General Zeisberg, I. Armeekorps chief of staff, was sent to Czegléd to report on the situation on the spot.

Although *Generalmajor* Ottinger's last report had sounded less disturbing, as he was not attacked again on the 24th either, the *Feldmarschall* neglected nothing in preparing for all eventualities; particularly if it should be established that the enemy really was as strong as initially reported, and was continuing his advance on Pesth, in which case given the enemy's local numerical superiority the outcome of a clash would always have been very much in doubt. Accordingly, the following instructions were issued without delay. On the 23rd the order was sent to *Feldmarschall Lieutenant Baron* Csorich that it was now imperative that he should return to Pesth by forced march. He could arrive there in four days' march, thus still in good time to support the *Feldmarschall* or add to his strength. At the same time on the 23rd a message was sent to *Feldmarschall Lieutenant* Schulzig, who at that time had reached Kápolna with his column:

> It is important to me that the enemy at Szolnok should be made to worry about his line of retreat by way of a diversion via Poroszló and Tisza-Füred [Tiszafüred, Hungary] toward Debreczin. To that end the *Herr Feldmarschall Lieutenant* is desired to detach a squadron toward Poroszló with the mission of spreading the rumour in that area of the approach of a force of 10,000 men with 30 guns, but after achieving the intended

> aim it should return to its column again. Since the success of this detachment will depend on how subtly the officer entrusted with this task carries it out, it is important to choose a suitable man for the job. The *Herr Feldmarschall Lieutenant* is also desired to continue his march with the utmost speed, so as to effect his junction with *Feldmarschall Lieutenant Graf* Schlick's corps as soon as possible.

Generalmajor Neustädter was still in Wartberg but was quite useless there as he could not move back to the Rye Island because of the high water. He was therefore instructed to march to Neuhäusel immediately, to establish communications between Neutra and Gran (Parkány) [Štúrovo, Slovakia], and also to occupy Sz. Petere [Hungarian name Komáromszentpéter, now Svätý Peter, Slovakia] so as to observe Komorn from that direction.

But when the *Feldmarschall* heard the news on the evening of the 25th that *Generalmajor* Ottinger had been attacked again in Czegléd, and in spite of the reinforcements he had received had been obliged to retreat to Alberti, he immediately decided to leave just two battalions in Ofen-Pesth and to move against the enemy with all the troops at his disposal, or ten battalions, 24 squadrons and 72 guns altogether including those with *General* Ottinger. These troops were immediately set in march from Pesth toward Alberti, some by rail, the rest by road.[41]

All the measures necessary at this critical moment had already been taken on the 23rd by means of the orders sent out to *Feldmarschall Lieutenant Baron* Csorich, *Feldmarschall Lieutenant* Schulzig and *Generalmajor* Neustädter; for in the worst case one could retreat to Waitzen to link up with Division Csorich and Brigade Neustädter there and, thus reinforced, resume the offensive. Pesth would certainly be abandoned temporarily, but Ofen had to be held.

To reinforce the Ofen garrison that had shrunk to just two battalions, as noted, the battalion of the G.H. Baden regiment in Stuhlweissenburg and that of the Ceccopieri regiment in Gran were summoned to arrive in Ofen on the 27th; 6. Jäger-Bataillon patrolling the Bakonyer-Wald was also ordered to move to Ofen. Beside these, the four battalions already requested from *Feldzeugmeister Graf* Nugent on the 21st could be expected to arrive soon; all the more so as he had reported on the 23rd that these battalions, to which he had also attached one squadron and a half-battery on his own initiative, would arrive toward the end of the month under command of *Generalmajor* Dietrich:

> 4. Bataillon, 2. Banal-Regiment
> 4. Bataillon Kreutzer
> Komponirtes Bataillon Eckert (two Hess companies, two Prohaska companies)
> Bataillon Mundsingen (four Hohenlohe companies)
> One squadron of E.H. Johann Dragoner
> One foot artillery battery

Altogether this was 3,000 infantry and 120 cavalry.

The attitude of the population of Pesth was far from inspiring confidence; rather, their mood was strikingly agitated. As our troops marched out there were grim, defiant faces on all sides, and characters now emerged and were seen on the streets who had seemed to be missing

41 This deserves to be noted as a rare decisive and aggressive response by the *Feldmarschall.*

without trace since our entry into Ofen-Pesth. In such circumstances, it could have proved very awkward if it became necessary to retreat through Pesth. Consequently *Oberst* Schön of the Pionnier-Korps was given the order to throw a bridge across the Danube outside the city of Pesth immediately, and also to identify and clear convoy routes from the Üllő/Szolnok highway, so as to be able to reach the road to Waitzen by going round Pesth if necessary and thereby come into direct communication with Csorich's approaching division. But so as not to be unprepared in the event that it should not be possible for *Feldmarschall Lieutenant Baron* Csorich to comply immediately with the order to move to Waitzen, or that the *Feldmarschall* should be somehow obliged to retreat to Pesth, the said *Feldmarschall Lieutenant* was sent the following instruction on the 26th:

> After leaving two battalions to garrison Buda Castle and the Chain Bridge, all available troops are moving against the enemy, who is approaching from Szolnok but whose strength is not yet accurately established. Circumstances may arise which impede the troops under Your Honour's command from linking up via Waitzen and Pesth with those here. Accordingly you are hereby instructed to obtain accurate information about the situation when you arrive in Waitzen, and in the event that a junction with me on the left bank of the Danube should prove to be unfeasible, you should move by the most direct route to Párkány (across the river from Gran) to make the necessary preparations for transferring your force across the Danube there, and then to seek to link up with me on the right bank of the Danube in Ofen. These instructions are imparted to Your Honour merely as a precaution – by no means because of the present state of affairs – and are therefore to be interpreted in that spirit.

The *Feldmarschall* left *Feldmarschall Lieutenant Graf* Wrbna in Ofen with orders to ensure that the pontoon bridge at Gran be built without delay. The bridge construction ordered to take place outside Pesth could not do so because the Danube suddenly overflowed its banks, so this had to be done near the Salt Office in Pesth.

In the afternoon of the 26th the *Feldmarschall* hurried on after the troops that had already moved along the railway during the night and early that morning, and it was already getting dark when he arrived in Üllő, where he spent the night. During the course of the night a report arrived that the enemy had not advanced any further forward from Czegléd but had begun retreating toward Abany, in which direction Brigades Ottinger and Gramont were going to pursue him. Upon this news the *Feldmarschall* had two grenadier battalions march back to Pesth on the 27th. These could immediately be brought forward again by rail if needed, while their presence in Pesth could be urgently necessary to suppress the evil-minded. However, early in the morning the *Feldmarschall* travelled in person to Czegléd by rail, so as acquaint himself with events on the spot. When he arrived there, the troops had already largely moved off to Abany in pursuit of the enemy, but he did learn more precise details of the actions that had been fought. Brigade Ottinger had suffered considerable losses from the fire of the superior enemy artillery: altogether six dead, 15 wounded, 22 missing. Of the artillery teams and cavalry horses, there were 53 dead, six wounded and 18 missing.[42]

42 The *Feldmarschall* does not seem to make a habit of leading from the front. (The foray toward Hatvan

As well as the glorious charge by the division of Hardegg cuirassiers under *Major* Algyay that has already been mentioned, all the units of this brave cuirassier brigade had proved their rare boldness and endurance. The artillery deployed to Czegléd to reinforce *Generalmajor* Ottinger had operated splendidly, among which the crews of Kavallerie-Batterie Nr. 5 in particular had performed very bravely, and *Oberlieutenant* Loschan and *Lieutenant* Gugg of the artillery had especially distinguished themselves. At the start of the action at Czegléd on the 25th, *Fahrkanonier* [Artillery Driver] Ferdinand Scheder was lead rider when his right thigh was shattered by a cannonball, yet he possessed such willpower that he remained in the saddle right until the end of the fight.

Oberstlieutenant Staufer of the Hardegg cuirassiers and *Oberlieutenant* Sastavnikovic, attached to the quartermaster-general's staff, were also named among those who particularly distinguished themselves.

Given the haste with which the enemy had begun his retreat toward Szolnok on the 26th for no real reason, it could be foreseen that he intended to retreat completely behind the Theiss again. The *Feldmarschall* therefore handed over further pursuit to the commander of I. Armeekorps and returned to Ofen again on the evening of the 27th.

The garrison of Ofen-Pesth had been brought up to a halfway adequate strength of seven battalions again by the two grenadier battalions sent back to Pesth from Üllő, the G.H. Baden battalion coming from Stuhlweissenburg, that of the Ceccopieri regiment from Gran, and finally 6. Jäger-Bataillon, though this last did not arrive in Ofen until the 30th. However, the reinforcements requested from *Feldzeugmeister Graf* Nugent on the 21st and already promised had not yet arrived, because meanwhile he had received news that the resistance groups in and around Fünfkirchen [Pécs, Hungary] had been significantly reinforced by troops from the camp at Verbacz [Verbász, now Vrbas, Serbia] and Eszék [Osijek, Croatia], and had reached a worrying level. The brigade under *Generalmajor* Dietrich that was already on the march to Stuhlweissenburg had therefore been directed to Kaposvár.

It was also reported that Damjanich had invaded Baranyer Komitat [Baranya County] with 6,000 men and 19 guns and could try to use the haven offered to him by Eszek to organise the rebellion, indeed even to strike a blow against the weak besieging force under General Trebersburg deployed in Valpó [Valpovo, Croatia], so as to invade Slavonia and Croatia from there. *Feldzeugmeister Graf* Nugent had therefore advanced quickly to Fünfkirchen with 6,000 infantry, 800 cavalry and 21 guns altogether: Brigade Dietrich moving there from Kaposvár, and the troops in Kanisa marching through Babocza [Babócsa, Hungary].

The *Feldmarschall* replied to this information from the *Feldzeugmeister* on the 28th as follows: that at the present moment the support he had requested no longer seemed so necessary as possibly might have been the case. The *Feldzeugmeister* was to finish his expedition that was already in progress against Fünfkirchen as quickly as possible, and in any case to keep his troops together and ready to respond immediately to the first call to use them for a different mission. Regarding the enemy forces at Verbacz, there was reliable information that these had moved not toward Fünfkirchen but to Szegedin [Szeged, Hungary]. This latter had been told to the

on 4 April 1849 was a rare exception.) His action here is quite a rapid response in terms of decisively setting troops in motion on the evening of the 25th. However, he himself only manages to travel 15 km from Ofen to Üllő next day, rather than the whole 30 km to Czegléd, which he leaves until the 27th. Again, note the contrast between him and his successor Haynau.

Feldmarschall by some officers of Husaren-Regiment Nr. 2 who had found a way to escape to Ofen; these also assured him that the majority of the regular troops at Verbacz, who had only been fighting the Serbs until now, might be inclined to return to their duty upon the appearance of even a small detachment of imperial troops.

The *Feldmarschall* received a report from the *Banus* that on the 28th the enemy had completely vacated the right bank of the Theiss, burning four spans of the Szolnok bridge behind him, which the townsfolk were immediately ordered to repair by *Feldmarschall Lieutenant* Hartlieb who had arrived there with three battalions, nine squadrons and two batteries. It was also mentioned that the river was already flowing over the top of its covering of ice at Szolnok, so a surprise attack there was no longer so easy to carry out.

Upon receiving this report, on the 29th the *Feldmarschall* ordered that except for what was needed by the troops there, the state-owned supplies found in Szolnok should be taken to Ofen-Pesth; that information about the enemy's line of retreat should be provided as soon as possible; and that a cavalry detachment should be sent to Kecskemét and maintain an intermediary post in Örkény. Two squadrons were to be sent toward Poroszló to observe the Theiss crossing at Tisza-Füred, for the *Feldmarschall* had heard reports that hussars were patrolling toward Mezö-Kövesd, which could threaten communications with *Feldmarschall Lieutenant Graf* Schlick. Finally, the *Banus* was instructed to secure the Szolnok bridge against all eventualities by constructing fieldworks.

However, on 1 February the *Banus* reported that significant enemy combat forces were concentrating in Török Sz. Miklós, and that he was not unconcerned for his troops deployed right on the Theiss in Szolnok. The *Feldmarschall* replied to this report the same day that it could be more appropriate to deploy his main body in and around Czegléd, leaving Szolnok held by the minimum necessary, but to have the nearby crossings over the Theiss observed by suitable detachments. In the event of an attack in superior force, this should be reported to him forthwith. The infantry should retreat along the highway, while the cavalry should take position on the flank. Finally, it was recommended that particular attention should be given to fortifying the crossing point at Szolnok.

We now wish to briefly cite what has become known from Hungarian sources since the end of the campaign about the enemy's strength on the Theiss, as well as at the action at Szolnok.

The total strength of the so-called 'Army of the Tisza' under Perczel's command came to 15,310 infantry, 1,470 cavalry and 34 guns, which were formed into two divisions and a reserve:

Division Hertelendy:[43] Brigade Mihály,[44] Brigade Mandy;[45]

43 Miklós Hertelendy (1813-77) was a captain in the 6th Hussars in 1848. He led his regiment home from Galicia to fight against Jellacic's invasion. He served in Perczel's force, then in II. Corps until the capture of Ofen. He was amnestied when Komorn surrendered.

44 Károly Mihály (1810-?) was a lieutenant in Infanterie-Regiment Nr. 34 who joined the new *honvéd* and fought Serbian insurgents in July 1848. Made brigade commander at the start of January 1849, he went on sick leave in June 1849 after the battle of Pered. He emigrated to France, and then England after the war, returning in 1859 when he was briefly detained.

45 Ignác Mándy (1814-83) was a captain in the 6th Hussars. Like Hertelendy, he fought Jellacic, then served in Perczel's force and in II. Corps. He commanded the cavalry in Komorn from July until the fall of the fortress.

Division Sekulich: Brigade Venturini, Brigade Buttler;[46]
Reserve: Brigade Kazinczky, Brigade Nikolaus Perczel.

At the start of January this corps had continued its retreat from Pesth through Szolnok toward Debreczin, and had already reached Kardszag [Karcag, Hungary] on the 19th when the government politely ordered it to turn around immediately and retake Szolnok at any cost. Consequently, Perczel moved back through Kis-Uj-Szallása to Török Sz. Miklós, where he arrived with his main body on the 21st. However, Kazinczky and his troops were ordered to go straight to Tisza-Bö [Tiszabő, Hungary] where he crossed the Theiss during the night of the 21st/22nd and was to cross the Zagyva next day (22nd) and thus penetrate behind Szolnok, while Division Hertelendy was tasked with advancing directly on Szolnok to attract the enemy's full attention.

In accordance with these orders, Hertelendy arrived in the vicinity of the Szolnok bridge at 1:00 p.m. on the 22nd and fired two cannon shots as the agreed sign for Kazinczky's outflanking column to attack. As soon as *Generalmajor* Ottinger vacated Szolnok, Hertelendy and his regiment crossed the bridge that had been left intact and soon brought the whole of his artillery across it as well. After taking Szolnok, Perczel's main body halted and took a rest day there on the 23rd. On that day *General* Dembinsky arrived in Szolnok, charged by the government with acting as advisor to Perczel. He was welcomed, and Dembinsky and Perczel conducted the affair at Czegléd on the 25th together. After the action at Czegléd, Perczel intended to leave a garrison in Szolnok and march with the majority of his force through Jász-Apáthi [Jászapáti, Hungary] and Heves to the upper Theiss to link up with Klapka there. He was all the more inclined to do this because the rebel general Vécsey was moving up the Theiss from Szeged to Czibakháza, while Damjanich and the army in the Banat moved to Szentes. However, a dispatch from the government arrived in Czegléd and scotched this plan. A report had been received in Debreczin that imperial troops were approaching from Poroszló via Tisza-Füred. In this plight, Perczel's corps was swiftly called back across the Theiss; it immediately began its retreat, as we have seen, and on the 28th had vacated Szolnok again. However, when word arrived that the government had established that this was a false report, and that the outpost commander in question had been replaced and another sent forward again with his troops to Tisza-Füred, Perczel wanted to debouch through Szolnok once more and resume his earlier operation anew. Dembinsky then produced an order from the government appointing him commander-in-chief of all the troops on the upper Theiss, and authorising him to select 4,000 men from Perczel's corps and march off with them toward Tokay [Tokaj, Hungary]. Aggrieved by this, after a storming row with Dembinsky, Perczel formally resigned and handed over command of the entire corps to him.[47] Not until mid-March did he hold a command with the Army of the South again. Dembinsky now immediately marched the corps up the Theiss to Tisza-Füred, to act as a reserve for the Army of the North. Only a few detachments remained behind in Török-Sz.-Miklós, which

46 Alexander Buttler (1818-90), a former lieutenant in the Bavarian army, commanded a group of volunteer national guards in Ung County in September 1848. He served in various capacities until retiring because of ill-health in June 1849. After the war he was released to Bavaria but expelled from the Hapsburg Empire.

47 Another example of the personality clashes that seem to have plagued the Hungarian side.

sought to alarm the troops on the other side by spreading false information and making preparations to create ice-crossings over the Theiss.

Csorich Takes Schemnitz and Returns to Pesth, 20-29 January 1849

Let us now return to *Feldmarschall Lieutenant Baron* Csorich's operations directed toward the Mining Towns, and in particular to the one he carried out in the short period between the 22nd – the day on which the *Feldmarschall* ordered his recall – and the 24th, the day on which that order arrived.

As stated above, recognising the difficulty of outflanking through the Gran valley, and reassured by *Major Baron* Salis's report about the feasibility of a direct advance on Schemnitz through Báth, *Feldmarschall Lieutenant Baron* Csorich had set off from Léva with Brigade Wyss around midday on the 20th and marched to Baka-Bánya [Pukanec, Slovakia], while Brigade Jablonowsky and the artillery reserve moved to Báth. The 1. Bataillon E.H. Stefan was detached to Almás [Jablonovce, Slovakia] to cover the right flank. The advance and frontal attack by the main body were to take place on the 21st along the road itself, which was the only one between Steinbach and Schemnitz that was usable by artillery and therefore constituted one long defile there. To facilitate the advance, the following arrangements were made:

Hauptmann Marochini of 12. Jäger-Bataillon, with two companies of that battalion and one from E.H. Stefan and with *Bergakademiker* Weiglein as a guide, moved right from Steinbach through Gyekes [Dekýš, Slovakia] and along poor forest tracks running parallel with the road in the valley toward the Warthaberg.[48] This column was to move in coordination with the one sent even further to the right under *Oberst* Pott of the general staff, who was to take two companies of 2. Jäger-Bataillon, 1. Bataillon E.H. Stefan and three rocket launch stands through Almás, Bagyán [Bad'an, Slovakia] and Pocsuvadlo [Počúvadlo, Slovakia] to turn the Wartha heights and the position at Windschacht completely.[49] *Generalmajor Fürst* Colloredo was instructed to advance against Schemnitz from Ipoly-Ságh and Nemethi through Preitzdorf with four H.v. Nassau companies, three Paumgarten companies, a squadron of Civallart *uhlans* and half a 6-pounder battery, and to support the direct attack. To cover the right flank, *Oberst* Collery's column (two companies of 12. Jäger-Bataillon, two from E.H. Stefan, three platoons of pioneers and a troop of E.H. Karl *chevauxlegers*) was to advance from Benedek through Zsarnócz [Zsarnóca, now Žarnovica, Slovakia], Vognicza [Voznica, Slovakia] and Hámor [Dolné Hámre, Slovakia], and to demonstrate against the right flank and rear of the enemy position. Finally, as agreed in the verbal discussion with *Hauptmann* Kallik of the general staff in Neutra as mentioned above, on the 21st *Feldmarschall Lieutenant* Simunich was to push forward *Generalmajor* Sossay with ten companies, one squadron and nine guns through Oszlan [Oslany, Slovakia], Prividgye and Handlova toward Kremnitz and to establish communications with *Generalmajor* Götz advancing from Mosócs.

48 This confusing reference to the Warthaberg, and to the Wartha heights further down the page, appears to be an error by Nobili or his source document. The 2nd Military Survey map shows the Wartaberg to be a relatively small hill just east of Almás. Nobili must surely mean the Sitno Berg, the highest peak in the Schemnitz mountains [Štiavnické Vrchy, Slovakia] which is due east of Gyekes.

49 Note again the relative mobility of rockets being exploited in difficult terrain.

After an extremely arduous five-hour march between 7:00 a.m. and midday, at 12:30 p.m. *Feldmarschall Lieutenant Baron* Csorich entered the Steinbach defile with Brigade Wyss in the van. The enemy had taken position forward of Windschacht and posted his guns appropriately. Because of the very limited visibility offered by the broken forested terrain, neither the enemy's strength nor his position could be fully ascertained. So far as could be established afterwards, the enemy troops posted there were commanded by Guyon; whether Görgei was still present remains in doubt, but most likely he had already left on the 19th. Apart from these, the rebel *Oberstlieutenant* Aulich reportedly had two brigades in Kremnitz, and *Oberstlieutenant* Pustelnik four companies, one squadron, six guns and a *Freikorps* in Heiligenkreuz. The strength of the enemy detachments spread about in these various places was given in Csorich's after-action report as 20,000 men with 60 guns.

Brigade Wyss, reinforced with Zwölfpfündige Batterie Nr. 3 and Sechspfündige Batterie Nr. 11, now advanced to the attack, while the rest of the artillery reserve remained behind at the entrance to the Steinbach defile, as did the cavalry apart from one squadron of Civallart *uhlans*. At 3:00 p.m. the advance guard ran into the first enemy barricade on the 'Pfarrwiese',[50] which the sappers cleared within three quarters of an hour while the *jägers* drove off the enemy pickets with a few shots. In spite of the fairly lively fire of two enemy guns, two *jäger* companies scaled the Wartha heights up a gorge without firing a shot and drove the Hungarian forward troops back toward their main position,[51] while two 7-pounder howitzers and the rocket launchers set up in an open area left of the road and returned fire effectively. The 1. Bataillon Schönhals advanced swiftly along the road keeping level with the *jägers* and soon reached the saddle of the Wartha heights, from which the enemy driven off by the *jägers* had retreated to Windschacht. The partly forested approaches to this place had been occupied by the rebel *Oberstlieutenant* Schrötter with the 12., 23. and 33. Honved-Battalions, a squadron of hussars and a battery, while *Major* Görgei (the corps commander's brother) and his troops were to one side on the Siegelberg [Siglisberg, the hill north of Vindšacht], and the reserve was on the bare ridge behind Windschacht.

Feldmarschall Lieutenant Baron Csorich now ordered *Generalmajor* Wyss to attack this position, to which end a column was sent along the heights west of Windschacht, while Wyss moved against the front with the rest of the brigade. This attack was as carefully prepared as it was energetically carried out. While Zwölfpfündige Batterie Nr. 3 silenced the enemy gun posted at the entrance to the village, *Major* Brzezina advanced on the heights with four Fürstenwärther companies on one side and two Schönhals companies on the other and drove the enemy off them with the bayonet. Now *Major* Dürfeld and four companies of 2. Jäger-Bataillon bayonet-charged into the village, followed by a Schönhals division, and took it after a tough fight lasting almost an hour and a half in which an enemy horse artillery piece was taken.

In this assault, beside *Major* Dürfeld, *Hauptmann* Weckbecker and *Hauptmann* Dietl especially distinguished themselves.

50 This does not appear on any of the maps I have consulted. It means roughly 'parish common'. Given that this action occurs about two and a half hours after Brigade Wyss enters the defile, I think it is about 5 km from Steinbach, at the north-eastern edge of the large open area above Gyekes. An abatti at the edge of the woods there, where the road enters them and starts to wind up the Sitno heights, would make sense.

51 Here again Nobili must mean the Sitno Berg.

Oberst Pott and his column had meanwhile advanced as far as the heights not far from the Siegelberg after a very arduous march lasting more than six hours. Darkness was already falling when the attack began here. While *Hauptmann* Schreiber with one division of 2. Jäger-Bataillon took the steep and strongly defended heights with the bayonet, *Hauptmann* Schwarz and his detachment penetrated into the enemy's flank. Now *Hauptmann* Radanovich with a division of E.H. Stefan attacked the 'Fuchsloch' ('Foxhole') and the lower part of Windschacht. Toward 10:00 p.m. all these points had been taken and communications established with Brigade Wyss.

Feldmarschall Lieutenant Baron Csorich and his troops spent the night of the 21st/22nd in the Windschacht position, only lightly pursuing the enemy toward Schemnitz, since the terrain provided so much cover that it meant this had to be done extremely cautiously. There were frequent patrols all night both in front of the position and to the flanks. Brigade Jablonowsky which had remained behind as reserve was brought up to the Wartha heights, as were the artillery reserve and the cavalry as well.

After midnight word arrived that *Generalmajor Fürst* Colloredo had reached Nemethi. He was ordered to move to Schemnitz on the 22nd.

On the morning of the 22nd *Feldmarschall Lieutenant Baron* Csorich had Brigade Wyss advance toward Schemnitz. Thick fog covered the whole area, and black ice made the march extremely difficult. The flanking columns had already gained a significant head start, during which *Hauptmann* Dietl and his company of 2. Jäger-Bataillon were able to seize a horse artillery piece from an enemy detachment by means of a determined bayonet charge. Toward 9:00 a.m. the rebel rear guard had retreated entirely behind Schemnitz. After successfully occupying the town, the advance guard was pushed forward to Béla-Bánya [Banská Belá, Slovakia].

Toward 11:00 a.m. word arrived in Schemnitz from *Oberst* Collery that he had actually advanced out of the Gran valley through Hámor on the 21st, but that he had been prevented from debouching through the Hadritsch [Hodruša-Hámre, Slovakia] defile onto the Schemnitz plateau by a much larger enemy detachment with six guns. *Feldmarschall Lieutenant Baron* Csorich therefore immediately detached 2. Bataillon H.v. Nassau in that direction, so as to support *Oberst* Collery if necessary. However, he had meanwhile been attacked from behind on the 22nd by an enemy column approaching from Heiligenkreuz comprising three companies of Infanterie-Regiment Nr. 2, one battalion of Nógrád volunteers, a squadron of Husaren-Regiment Nr. 9 and a 3-pounder battery including two 7-pounder howitzers, led by the rebel *Oberstlieutenant* Pustelnik, Görgei's chief of staff. This called for a quick decision! *Oberst* Collery swiftly fell upon the enemy appearing in his rear with two companies of *jägers*, the three pioneer platoons and the troop of cavalry, while he had two E.H. Stefan companies keep in check the enemy detachments posted on his front toward Schemnitz. The brave *jägers* shot down the gunners as they were preparing to open fire, and seized the guns in a trice. Then, with as much speed as audacity, they pressed on against the three companies of Infanterie-Regiment Nr. 2, who scattered and fled back toward Zsarnócz in wild rout carrying the Nógrád volunteers with them. The four 3-pounder guns and the two 7-pounder howitzers remained in the *jägers*' hands. Pustelnik was seriously wounded and taken prisoner and died in Schemnitz soon after. The enemy artillery commander lay dead. In addition, 31 men and 28 horses were captured.[52]

52 This is one of the occasions where the Austrian *jägers* seem to have lived up to their high reputation.

Oberst Collery had not yet heard that Schemnitz had been taken and returned to Rudno [Rudno nad Hronom, Slovakia] in the Gran valley on the 22nd. However, when he learned of the victory at Schemnitz, he marched to Hadritsch on the 23rd and entered Schemnitz on the 24th. *Generalmajor Fürst* Colloredo had also arrived in Schemnitz from Sz. Antal [Svätý Anton, Slovakia] on the afternoon of the 22nd.

In his after-action report *Feldmarschall Lieutenant Baron* Csorich praises the iron endurance and absolute devotion to duty of the troops under his command who took part in the action (2. and 12. Jäger-Bataillons; 2. Bataillon E.H. Stefan; 3. Bataillon Fürstenwärther; Zwölfpfündige Batterie Nr. 3; Raketenbatterie Nr. 15) and who, after a seven-hour march along rough, snow-covered, partly barricaded mountain trails, hurled themselves upon the enemy wherever he made a stand. *Generalmajor* Wyss, *Hauptmann* Kalik of the general staff and *Oberlieutenant* Ludwig Windischgrätz were especially commended.

Our troops took two horse artillery guns, four 3-pounder cannon and two 7-pounder howitzers, thus eight guns in all. Eighteen mortars were also found in Schemnitz. In addition two swivel guns,[53] 271 muskets, 219 scythes and many ammunition wagons were captured, and nine officers and 500 men taken prisoner, among them one officer and 145 men from Infanterie-Regiment Nr. 2. The 33. Honved-Bataillon was completely destroyed. The enemy left 60 dead and 120 wounded behind.

Our own troops' losses were quite insignificant by comparison.[54] The dead were *Hauptmann* Marochini of 12. Jäger-Bataillon, *Oberlieutenant Graf* Berthold of the Civallart *uhlans* – a very brave and skillful officer – and three men of *Feldwebel*'s rank and below. Sixteen men were wounded, among them *Oberlieutenant* Finkenberg of 2. Jäger-Bataillon and *Oberlieutenant* Menapace of 12. Jäger-Bataillon.

The success of the action at Windschacht could have been far more complete if Brigade Sossay had advanced from Rudno (in the Waag valley) through Skleno [Sklené, Slovakia] and Perk [Kremnické Bane, Slovakia] toward Kremnitz on the 21st, as agreed with *Feldmarschall Lieutenant* Simunich, whereby it would also have become possible for *Generalmajor* Götz to advance on the offensive in this direction from Mosócs. But Simunich, who had heard an entirely false rumour that 8,000 insurgents were mustering in Neuhäusel, suddenly called Sossay back to Neutra again. He justified this later by citing an instruction from the *Feldmarschall* that reached him on the 12th and 19th to leave it to *Feldmarschall Lieutenant Baron* Csorich to pursue the enemy into the Mining Towns, since he was tasked with securing the line of the Waag and reducing Leopoldstadt. But this did not take into account, the fact that on the 12th and the 19th the *Feldmarschall* in Ofen could not foresee what would need to be done at Schemnitz on the 21st.[55]

Generalmajor Götz's advance was likewise thwarted by the subsequent recall of *Generalmajor* Sossay, in conjunction with whom he was supposed to operate toward Kremnitz as agreed. The

53 The text says '*Doppelhaken*', which Müller translates into French as '*amusette*'. Karl Christian Müller, *Allgemeines Verteutschungswörterbuch der Kriegssprache* (Leipzig: Bruder und Hofmann, 1814).

54 These good results reflect what appears to have been a thoroughly well organised and executed operation, exhibiting good use of local intelligence, effective coordination with flanking columns, preparatory fire, determined assaults and decisive action throughout, notably Collery's reaction on the 22nd.

55 This rejection of Simunich's justification could be regarded as a disingenuous attempt to deflect blame from the *Feldmarschall* onto his subordinate.

former had already driven the enemy off the Turczek [Turček, Slovakia] heights on the 15th, taking a howitzer off him on this occasion. On the 16th there was another action there in which the enemy was repulsed with the loss of 54 dead and 60 wounded, including four officers, and 117 taken prisoner. In this action *Major* von Pichel of the H.v. Nassau *Lieutenant Baron* Baum of the Bianchi infantry were lured across, ventured too far forward, and were taken prisoner by officers and soldiers of the Hungarian Infanterie-Regiment Nr. 60 who pretended they wanted to change sides. In addition, we lost 40 men killed or wounded.

Toward evening *Generalmajor* Götz returned to Mosócs again since the detachments pushed into the Neutra valley by *Feldmarschall Lieutenant* Simunich were still too far away to be able rely on support from them. But on the 19th he received word from that general that *Generalmajor* Sossay had been ordered to advance through Prividgye, and Götz had therefore made preparations for their joint operation, when on the 21st he learned of the said general's sudden recall. Götz felt it inadvisable to advance on Kremnitz without any other support; he therefore abandoned the planned offensive and stayed in Mosócs during the action at Schemnitz. Another embarrassing event was that a courier sent by Simunich to Götz, carrying precise written details of *Feldmarschall Lieutenant Baron* Csorich's strength and of the agreed plan of attack on Schemnitz, was captured by the rebels.

Meanwhile the action at Windschacht and the occupation of Schemnitz had caused the enemy to vacate Kremnitz and begin to retreat to Neusohl [Banská Bystrica, Slovakia]. When *Generalmajor* Götz learned of this and entered Kremnitz on the 25th, the retreat degenerated into a mad rout in which six cannon and a lot of ammunition were captured as the enemy was not able to get them away quickly enough along the bad mountain roads. The rebels had taken 63,000 forint with them from Kremnitz, partly in gold and silver coins, partly in bullion. In accordance with the orders he had received, *Generalmajor* Götz now prepared to occupy the Mining Towns but was instead told to start pursuing Görgei right away together with Brigade Jablonowsky, while *Feldmarschall Lieutenant* Simunich was tasked with occupying Kremnitz and Schemnitz.

After the victory at Windschacht on the 21st, *Feldmarschall Lieutenant Baron* Csorich had stayed in Schemnitz on the 22nd, 23rd and 24th. On the latter date he was deployed as follows: the advance guard under *Oberst* Sartorius of E.H. Stefan in Bela-Bánya (Düllen) [Banská Belá, Slovakia], about 5 km beyond Schemnitz; the main body in Schemnitz; *Generalmajor Fürst* Colloredo in Sz. Antal (5 km to the rear of Schemnitz) with four infantry companies, one and a half batteries, and one and a half squadrons; *Oberstlieutenant* Braun had been sent back to Németi on the 23rd with four infantry companies and a half-squadron, to receive a convoy expected from Ipoly-Ságh carrying boots, coats and recovered convalescents, and to protect it against rebel bands roaming the area.

On the 24th *Feldmarschall Lieutenant Baron* Csorich reported that the snow that had begun falling on the 23rd had made moving the guns up almost impossible, but that since midday it had started to thaw. He commented that prisoners had been taken from Infanterie-Regiment Nr. 48, a grenadier battalion, and some *honvéd* battalions, none of which were listed in the captured order of battle that had been sent to him, so Görgei could be stronger than had been assumed and could have 16,000-18,000 men. As for the rebels' plans and intentions, he had learned from a fairly reliable source that they had decided not by any means to give up the Mining Towns, but to keep them as important bases for their operations. A large hospital had been established in Neusohl as their main depot. On the 23rd Görgei had sent artillery and troops, especially cavalry, from Neusohl toward Altsohl to occupy Bucsa [Budča, Slovakia]; all the bridges across the Gran had been demolished;[56] nothing more had been heard about the previously suspected march through Losoncz; according to eyewitnesses, the enemy detachments beaten at Schemnitz had arrived in Altsohl on the 22nd in a state of complete disarray, etc.

Feldmarschall Lieutenant Baron Csorich was now planning to establish communications with *Generalmajor* Götz, from whom he still had not had any word by the 24th, when the *Feldmarschall*'s order of the 22nd arrived concerning his possible recall, and that of the 23rd making it definite. Accordingly, he added these words at the end of his report mentioned above:

> I shall leave behind *General Fürst* Jablonowsky with three H.v. Nassau battalions, 12. Jäger-Bataillon, the Oberstlieutenant-Division of the E.H. Karl Chevauxlegers, a 6-pounder battery with two captured howitzers added, a rocket battery and half a company of pioneers. I shall begin my return march with all the rest of my troops tomorrow (25th) and arrive in Pesth on the 30th at the latest.

When we take into account how much of a head start the enemy must in all likelihood already have gained on the 24th, and how many obstacles could have been put in the path of the pursuers – quite apart from the natural obstacles associated with that bitter time of year – and finally the urgency of the circumstances in which *Feldmarschall Lieutenant Baron* Csorich was recalled, we may acknowledge that this seems more than justified, even if some have maintained that 'his action was called off right at its finest hour'.[57] As we have seen, because of all manner of chance events and obstacles that turned out to affect the march, this hour had already passed. Csorich would most likely not have caught up with Görgei's corps any more than the other troops sent after him were able to and would have been somewhere around Kaschau right on the day of the battle of Kápolna.

On the 29th *Feldmarschall Lieutenant Baron* Csorich arrived in Pesth with his troops badly in need of rest. He brought the captured guns and *honvéd* prisoners with him so his entry into Pesth was like a victory parade, which had the effect of quelling its inhabitants who had been getting insolent again since the events at Szolnok. The *Feldmarschall*'s first concern now was to provide these troops with what they needed most, for which all available supplies of clothing material and every tradesman had to be used.

Miscellaneous Troop Movements, 25-30 January 1849

Feldmarschall Lieutenant Schulzig had completed his march through Gyöngyös unimpeded with the reinforcements destined for *Feldmarschall Lieutenant Graf* Schlick, arriving in Miskolcz on the 25th and establishing communications with Schlick's outposts in Forró on the 26th. Notwithstanding that Schulzig and especially *Major Graf* Palfy who was with him made every effort to obtain information about the enemy, they could not discover anything reliable. So for example it was said that Görgei's outposts were in Losoncz. *Oberst Graf* Montecuccoli of the Prinz von Preussen Kürassiere, who had been left behind on his own in Gyöngyös because

56 We have to admire Görgei's decisiveness and the energy and agility of his manoeuvres, as well as his thorough attention to detail.

57 Perhaps the critic referred to here is Heller von Hellwald, but this is mere surmise on my part.

of illness, was seized a few days later by six armed men who arrived on a wagon and took him across the Theiss into captivity. In accordance with the *Feldmarschall*'s order of the 23rd, Schulzig had sent a squadron of the Prinz von Preussen Kürassiere under *Rittmeister Baron* Henniger out from Kápolna to Poroszló – as already mentioned – to say they needed to arrange billeting for a corps of 10,000 men with 30 guns. Sufficient evidence that this ruse had the desired result emerges from the following order found in the Hungarian records and dated 25 January from War Minister Mészáros in Debreczin to the corps commander at Tokay, *Oberst* Klapka, which says:

> The enemy is advancing on Poroszló in force. Tisza-Füred must therefore be supported until Dembinsky's corps reaches it. The *Herr Oberst* is therefore given the express order to send a well-armed battalion without delay on wagons through Lök [Tiszalök, Hungary], Polgár and Csege to Tisza-Füred, and also to have one of the hussar detachments that are separated from their regiments follow on by forced marches, assuming that the preceding order 171/13 of the 23rd inst concerning the departure of a half-battery and a hussar detachment has already been followed, which said order remains fully in force. The infantry shall travel day and night, and the garrison of Tisza-Füred is subordinated to *Generallieutenant* Dembinsky. Should the enemy have seized Tisza-Füred in the meantime, this force shall move from Csege to Ujvaros [Balmazújváros, Hungary] and place itself under the command of the Reservekorps. In general the march should be carried out with due precaution.
>
> Debreczin, 25 January 1849.
> Mészáros m.p.[58]

The fact that the corps that had already advanced to Czegléd had been ordered to be recalled emerges from the reference to Dembinsky in the order above. As we have seen, on the 25th he was in front of Czegléd, but on the 26th he began his otherwise quite unprovoked hasty retreat behind the Theiss with the corps he had taken over from Perczel.

If we take into account the fact that according to the order of battle found in the Hungarian files the enemy combat forces concentrated at Czegléd came to 15,310 infantry, 1,470 cavalry and 34 guns, against which not more than ten weak battalions could be deployed while behind them was the ungarrisoned city of Pesth with its 80,000 mostly ill-disposed inhabitants, it must be acknowledged that the demonstration ordered toward Poroszló was a timely and decisive one.[59]

After carrying out his mission with great discretion and to best effect, as we have seen, *Rittmeister Baron* Henniger returned from Poroszló to *Feldmarschall Lieutenant* Schulzig's column, to which end he marched to Szihalom on the 25th, arriving in Miskolcz on the 26th without being disturbed in the least on the way, since all he ran into in Poroszló was just a few hussar vedettes.

The following had transpired in the army's rear, in brief:

58 'M.p.', *manu propria* ('signed by his own hand').
59 It does indeed seem to have been an ingeniously simple but effective ruse.

Feldmarschall Lieutenant Simunich had Neuhäusel occupied on the 26th by the 1. Landwehr-Bataillon E.H. Wilhelm, a squadron of *chevauxlegers* and half of Fussbatterie Nr. 15, under the command of *Major Baron* Vorberg, without encountering any resistance. The necessary guns and ammunition for the bombardment of Leopoldstadt arrived from Pressburg and Tyrnau on the 27th, 28th and 29th, so it could be hoped that the bombardment would begin imminently. *Hauptmann* Neperzeny of the Bombardier-Korps arrived in place of *Artillerie-Hauptmann* Navarra, who had fallen ill. The besieging troops who were meanwhile under the command of *Generalmajor Fürst* Lobkowitz repelled the garrison's feeble sorties. Neutra and Freistadel were suitably garrisoned, the bridge over the Waag at the latter place partly destroyed by the drift ice. *Generalmajor* Sossay whose expedition to the Mining Towns had been recalled was back in Neutra on the 26th.

Generalmajor Neustädter and his brigade had already returned to the Rye Island from Wartberg when the *Feldmarschall*'s order of the 24th to march to Neuhäusel reached him. Although hindered by the high waters of the Little Danube, he arrived in Szered on the 30th, where *Feldmarschall Lieutenant* Simunich summoned him to a meeting in Tyrnau at which arrangements for crossing the Waag were agreed. The crossing of the Little Danube at Eperies on the Rye Island nevertheless remained occupied by a division of 3. Bataillon, 1. Banal-Regiment. On this side of Komorn there was nothing to worry about, since the whole area on the left bank of the Danube was under water which only began to drain away on 5/6 February. Likewise nothing serious had transpired on the right bank of the Danube outside Komorn, although the Danube had only overflowed its banks in a few places; on the other hand communications between the fortress and its bridgehead had been interrupted by the drift ice, which circumstance *Feldmarschall Lieutenant* Ramberg exploited to summon the garrison of the bridgehead to surrender, but without success. In addition, the thaw that had set in was used to set to work demolishing the fortifications of the entrenched camp. As for the request sent to Ramberg on the 19th concerning presenting a plan for a closer siege of Komorn, on the 26th he replied that another two brigades of three or four battalions each would be needed for that.

Feldzeugmeister Graf Nugent entered Fünfkirchen unhindered on the 30th, and took the necessary measures for a close siege of Eszek.

Finally, out of *Oberst* Horvath's force only two companies of Viennese volunteers, the division of Romanen *grenzers* and a half-division of Kress Chevauxlegers remained in Stuhlweissenburg and its environs, since the G.H. Baden battalion had been taken to Ofen as mentioned above. This battalion was attached to Brigade Wyss to replace the Reisinger battalion that was still echeloned along the Fleischhacker-Strasse, while 6. Jäger-Bataillon joined Brigade Colloredo of the Reserve-Infanterie-Division in place of 12. Jäger-Bataillon that had been given to Brigade Jablonowsky, whereby Division Csorich was brought back up to its complement of eight battalions. After this division arrived in Pesth the strength of the troops echeloned along the line from Szolnok to Ofen-Pesth came to 19 battalions, 34 squadrons, 150 guns; beside these, Gran and Waitzen were suitably garrisoned.

The General Situation at the End of January 1849

Before we follow the course of operations any further, it is necessary to take a look at the general situation at this time.

Görgei, or rather his advance guard, was in Neu- and Altsohl. It was not known whether he would linger in that area or continue his retreat through Losoncz or through Brisen [Brusno, Slovakia] into Zips. The latter was more likely, because there in his native county he could find support and followers, beside which it could have been convenient for joining up with the formations behind the Theiss. On the other hand, it could be called into question because of his proclamation 'To the Upper Danubian Army' and the disagreements with the revolutionary regime that he expressed in it.

We offer some excerpts from this proclamation here. After stating the reasons for the document's publication in its introduction, Görgei starts by, as he says, confessing his own mistakes as corps commander. As the first of these he names the extended border defence he conducted by order of the National Defence Committee, which was mainly responsible for the reverses suffered by his corps; and then the retreat of the corps to the first line in front of Ofen that was influenced in the same way. As the reason for these operations which he criticises yet he himself carried out, he cites the order he had received from the Committee chosen by the nation itself and also recognised by the Hungarian war minister Mészáros. Now he observes:

> On 1 January 1849 – when despite being urged to retreat, the Upper Danubian army corps stood ready for battle on the first Ofen line at Hanselbeck [Érd, Hungary], Tárnok, Sóskút, Bia etc. – instead of justifying the confidence that we always place in its loyalty by heroically holding firm in the presence of danger, the National Defence Committee suddenly incomprehensibly abandoned the capital. It thereby put us in a helpless and hopeless, indeed equivocal position; even more so by sending a deputation without our foreknowledge or consent to the enemy commander-in-chief. That must have aroused the suspicion in some of us that instead of the lofty heights we deserved as the defenders of Hungary's constitutional liberty, we had been disparaged as using vulgar means to pursue our own selfish ends. Without questioning the loyalty of the National Defence Committee, however much it shattered our confidence in it by its sudden disappearance from the capital, I nevertheless consider it my duty to ask the corps – so that it may be protected from the most wretched of fates, from total collapse – either to adopt the following declaration, which is designed to protect us from any insults that abuse our honourable position, or else to state openly its divergent view.

Görgei goes on to mention that 'the hearts and minds of the Hungarian army corps on the upper Danube once belonged to the soldiers of the united Austrian army' before the Hungarian regiments were placed solely under the Hungarian ministry, and he invokes the oath they swore on the Hungarian constitution. He accordingly wants it known that he and the corps under his command protest against the insult:

> [T]hat we serve the personal interests of any one party in Hungary, and we declare all such rumours to be vile slander. But exactly this irrefutable fact of the unshakeable loyalty with which the army corps on the upper Danube has complied untiringly with all of the National Defence Committee's orders in the struggle to uphold the Hungarian constitution, despite the most unspeakable privations and discouragements, justifies the corps in its modest expectation that the National Defence Committee will at least conscientiously avoid one thing, namely putting the corps in any invidious position.

> After the corps on the upper Danube had protected the border as ordered by the National Defence Committee for a month and a half with rare self-denial on the most demanding outpost service; after it victoriously drove back the significantly stronger enemy in the action at Wieselburg; after it held the hopeless position at Raab courageously right up to the moment when it had already been outflanked on its right by superior numbers of the enemy, and its necessary retreat to protect the capital was only made possible by a tough fight with the enemy's outflanking column; after it had held out skilfully partly in front of and partly behind the said town – without having found the support they had dreamed of among the people of the district across the Danube, and without the slightest preparation on the part of the National Defence Committee to hinder the superior enemy force's advance on the highways and side roads of the Dotis, Bánhida, Neszmély, Csákvár, Zámoly, Ondód [Pusztavám, Hungary] and Sárkány road network – until the victorious advance of the enemy's right wing through Moór caused us for our part to attack through Martonvásar, only for us to have to give up this offensive and defend Ofen on the express orders of the National Defence Committee; our beleaguered corps was left with only one prospect to console it – that of a decisive battle directly in front of and inside Hungary's capitals. The previous decisive tone of the National Defence Committee's orders, and its proclamations to the people, justified the expectation that now this long yearned-for decisive moment had finally arrived it would inspire us all with its energy.

He then observes:

> Instead of everything that could and should have happened, on 1 January 1849 the following arrived at the headquarters in Promontorium:
> 1. The report that the National Defence Committee had abandoned the capital;
> 2. An order from it that a decisive battle should be fought on the so-called first line in front of Ofen, on the heights at Teteny, Bia etc., but without sacrificing the corps or exposing the capitals to bombardment. That is to say that – should the battle be lost – despite there being only one secure crossing and despite enemy pursuit, the corps should escape to the left bank of the Danube without defending the city;
> 3. 3. The instruction to let a deputation be sent to the commander-in-chief of the enemy army.

As a conclusion to the proclamation, these three points are followed by Görgei's explanation that:

> 1. The corps on the upper Danube will remain true to its oath;
> 2. It will decisively oppose all republican subversion;
> 3. It will follow orders solely and only from the Hungarian War Minister responsible, or from the representatives appointed by him; and,

4. The result of any agreement reached with the enemy will only be recognised if it guarantees the constitution and the military honour of the corps.[60]

In the event that Görgei should continue his march in an eastward direction, it could be hoped that by a vigorous joint pursuit on the one side by Brigades Jablonowsky and Götz (seven battalions, three squadrons, 26 guns), and on the other by being confronted by *Feldmarschall Lieutenant Graf* Schlick, whose combat forces with the reinforcements sent to him came to 12 battalions, 14 squadrons and 53 guns, it would be possible to destroy Görgei; for what had opposed Schlick directly until now was not to be rated highly.[61] Indeed, Schlick had dispersed the enemy at Kaschau, who were assumed to be strong, with no more than 16 companies and later driven them completely behind the Theiss.

The troops echeloned along the line between Szolnok and Pesth were sufficient if necessary to fend off any fresh direct blow from Szolnok. However, they were inadequate for any operation elsewhere unless Pesth were to be completely exposed. This absolutely had to be avoided; for quite apart from its political significance and the fact that it contained the one crossing over the Danube that was immune to all the vagaries of the weather, namely the Chain Bridge, all the military establishments, magazines, hospitals, barracks etc., in short everything that is indispensable for maintaining a large army, was in Pesth.

A new offensive manoeuvre in that direction from Szolnok was still within the realms of possibility. The retreat that had taken place had been caused simply by the false rumour of an intended advance on our part through Poroszló, and the burning of four spans of the Szolnok bridge was not of great import, for the enemy could find a much more convenient and secure crossing over the Theiss 20 km below Szolnok at Czíbakháza. Besides, it was known that reinforcements were approaching from the region downstream, and all reports arriving from Szolnok spoke of significant bodies of enemy troops collecting in Török Sz. Miklós, of impending danger, and the like.

Nothing definite could be discovered about the former; as far as the latter was concerned, there was no doubt that the situation of the forward units in Szolnok was a very exposed one, demanding considerable precaution and more than usual alertness. But Szolnok could not and must not be abandoned. The evacuation of Szolnok would have been just as significant as that of Pesth, for any position adopted for Pesth's protection on the boundless plain between the Theiss and the Danube would have been far more untenable and dangerous than that at Szolnok. After the evacuation of Szolnok the enemy would certainly have instantly thrown his light troops onto the right bank of the Theiss, and constantly swarmed round and harassed any position hanging in the air, so to speak, on this endless plain, and our troops being obliged to do outpost service

60 This is truly a remarkable proclamation, and Hungarian historians have been debating it for over 150 years. For a general to express such criticisms of his government so openly can only have exacerbated the concerns he claims to be dismissing, about his possible political ambitions. Kossuth's correspondence hints at these concerns. However, Bona notes that it was intended at least in part to stem a flood of officer resignations – approximately 100 had left the army because of tensions between radical republicans and the more conservative constitutional-minded – and in this it was successful. Bona, *Hungarian Revolution*, pp.301-303.

61 Of course it did not turn out like that; it was Schlick who ended up having to escape from being caught between Görgei and Dembinsky.

stretched in all directions would have been wiped out in short order without a battle.[62] The same was true of any position adopted in the immediate vicinity of Pesth. Szolnok at least offered the advantage of being protected by the Theiss, which since its ice cover had broken could only be crossed at a few known places, or else only after time-consuming preparations. This meant security measures could be focused in a particular direction as well as essentially making them easier.

It was likewise unfeasible to hope to cover the line from Szolnok to Pesth with a strategic flank position, namely by concentrating forces to one side, for example along the Gyöngyös road so as to stand closer to *Feldmarschall Lieutenant Graf* Schlick. Anyone who has set foot on the moorland across which the side roads run between the Gyöngyös and Szolnok highways will concede that no operations relying on rapid execution could be based on such transverse communications.[63]

These are essentially the reasons that obliged the *Feldmarschall* to insist on continuing to hold Szolnok.[64]

As already noted, the construction of a simple bridgehead to secure the bridge had been ordered. This was more an offensive measure than a defensive one; for the idea of seizing the offensive, should any favourable opportunity arise following the arrival of reinforcements, had by no means been abandoned. For this purpose, Szolnok and Tokay stood out as the only suitable places for a crossing from the right bank of the Theiss to the left, for a crossing cannot be forced at Poroszló if the exit from the 5 km-long bridge and causeway defile on the far (left) bank of the Theiss is even lightly held. Besides, an advance against Debreczin through Szolnok would also cover Pesth, just as one through Tokay would cover Kaschau and upper Hungary, which would not be the case if any other crossing point were chosen.

As has been said, these were only ideas, whose execution depended on circumstances; for in this distinctive type of warfare where the enemy fell back from any decisive battles so as to appear again somewhere else – where he was not tied to protecting any particular place or stretch of territory, where he found support and military supplies of all kinds wherever he went – there was no other target, no other object of operations, than the enemy army. So long as things could not be brought to the point where this was forced to stand and fight, nothing had been won. A march to Debreczin and the occupation of that city would have been equally as inconclusive as occupying the capital had been. The parliament and the banknote printing press would have abandoned Debreczin and moved to Grosswardein or Szegedin, while the enemy army would have avoided any clash and crossed the Theiss at some unguarded point, harassed our rear, completely interrupted our line of communications; in short, would have achieved more

62 The *Feldmarschall* was particularly concerned about the Hungarian superiority in light cavalry, which would have been very telling on the open plain. We will see later that his concern on this point led him to request the transfer of light cavalry from Italy to Hungary.

63 The *Feldmarschall* is contradicting himself to some extent. The same moorland which hampers transverse communications – being cut up by ditches and streams and marshy areas – also mitigates the threat, as it makes positions on the 'endless plain' much more defensible and harder to outflank and surround. He can't have it both ways. But of course, we regularly see him exaggerating the enemy threat and underestimating the enemy's own problems (as many commanders do).

64 Although the *Feldmarschall* may have overestimated the enemy threat, I agree with his basic rationale for holding Szolnok.

in any case than we would have by temporarily occupying an open city with 50,000 ill-disposed inhabitants, whose occupation would have been less an asset than a liability.[65]

Above all else, the *Feldmarschall* needed to try to reinforce his army. This was easier said than done. Nothing at all had happened yet to create the reserve of 35 battalions envisaged at the start of the campaign; on the contrary, this had been postponed yet again. On 23 February the war ministry reported:

> The necessary preparations have been made so that this year's recruiting can be carried out as scheduled on 1 March of this year, insofar as this is up to the military authorities; but the General Command in Bohemia has complained that, after multiple objections from the district governors that the preparatory work for the recruiting cannot be completed within the short period allocated for it, the Ministry of the Interior has been obliged to extend the deadline for the ballot until 5 March, and to order that the ballot lists for the purpose of distributing the contingents of recruits should be sent to the Gubernium [Austrian provincial government] by 8 March.
>
> Because of this deadline extension which is unavoidable in the circumstances prevailing and taking into account the time required for distribution of the contingents, informing the district offices and officials and the transport of those called up for military service, this year's recruiting cannot begin before 22 March. Since this is then interrupted once again by the onset of Holy Week and Easter when no assignments take place, bringing the 4. Feld-Bataillons and other units up to establishment and establishing the Reserve-Bataillons will be delayed by almost a month, but then hopefully brought to a swift conclusion without difficulty.

Not a single man more could be taken from the provinces for the army without exposing them completely. The *Feldmarschall* therefore had to reach for anything at all that could be spared from the rear of the army. Accordingly, as we shall see later on, Brigade Neustädter was taken from Neuhäusel, and Brigade Dietrich from *Feldzeugmeister Graf* Nugent's corps at Fünfkirchen.

Schlick's Operation against Tokay, 19 January to 1 February 1849

Generalmajor Fürst Jablonowsky, whom *Feldmarschall Lieutenant Baron* Csorich had left behind in Schemnitz for rapid pursuit of Görgei, was still there on the 28th. He had first had to call in a detached battalion of his brigade from Németi; all the bridges across the Gran had been destroyed, the roads blocked, and the like. On the 28th he also reported that he was short of rifle ammunition, his troops' footwear was in a very bad state, etc. As for the enemy's movements,

65 The parallels between the Hungarian Revolution and the American one are many and striking, and merit fuller exploration than is possible here. The one to mention at this point is the British occupation of Philadelphia (the rebel capital), which was described by Benjamin Franklin as not so much a general capturing a city, as the city capturing the general. Craig L. Symonds, *A Battlefield Atlas of the American Revolution* (El Dorado Hills, CA: Savas Beattie, 2018), p.59. Its futility was echoed by the Austrian occupation of Ofen-Pesth; here the *Feldmarschall* recognises that merely occupying Debreczin would have been equally futile.

he had learned that they had moved away from Neusohl on the 25th and 26th, some taking the road through Brisen, others the one to Rosenberg.

On the 30th *Generalmajor Fürst* Jablonowsky's advance guard marched to Bucsá, the brigade itself advancing to Heiligenkreuz and then to Neusohl on the 31st, from where a detachment sent to Altsohl managed to seize 1,140 cwt of silver-bearing lead ore reportedly worth a million and took it to Schemnitz.

Also on the 30th, the *Feldmarschall* wrote to the said general that what mattered above all was that he should pursue Görgei's corps relentlessly so that if the latter should turn against *Feldmarschall Lieutenant Graf* Count Schlick, then taken between two fires, he could no longer escape being defeated. So as to be more certain of achieving this aim, *Generalmajor* Götz would also be ordered to pursue the enemy, so *Generalmajor Fürst* Jablonowsky should link up with him as soon as possible. Jablonowsky was also charged with operating independently according to the situation and the aim stated above, since it was impossible to direct his operations there from the headquarters; all the more so as constant movement remained the major condition for success, particularly in a mountainous region. The same instructions were issued to Götz on the 30th, while *Feldmarschall Lieutenant* Simunich was ordered to take over the occupation of the Mining Towns from Götz. Finally, since it was thought not entirely impossible, in view of his falling out with the National Defence Committee, that Görgei might be inclined to enter negotiations, Jablonowsky was empowered to conduct these, and to this end he was sent the outline of a letter which he should address to Görgei, should the opportunity present itself. However, this was not done due to the circumstance that Görgei had already gained a significant head start, and also that nobody consented to give an authoritative order for the letter.

On the 28th a report was received from *Feldmarschall Lieutenant Graf* Schlick, brought via the direct route by *Hauptmann Graf* Erbach of the G.H. Rainer infantry serving as a courier. This report was dated 25 January from Boldogkő, and its content was essentially as follows: after Zips and Zemplin counties had been patrolled through by mobile columns, Schlick set off toward Tokay with Brigades Fiedler and Pergen (six battalions, five squadrons, 26 guns) on the 19th; thus on the very day when the *Feldmarschall* directed Division Schulzig to Miskolcz to reinforce him. This move toward Tokay was explained by Schlick as follows:

> By this operation I intend on the one hand to pin the enemy in Tokay and Tarczal [Tarcal, Hungary] if he should be too strong (which will also bring me closer to the line of communications to Pesth), and to engage him so as to keep him from sending detachments to the parts of the country that have already been pacified; on the other hand, if he should not be too superior in numbers, to drive him across the Theiss at Tokay and to seize the Theiss crossing. Once the present weather improves and I have a bridging train with my corps, this will be of decisive importance for the future offensive operations to be carried out toward Debreczin.

On the 19th the advance guard under *Major* Piattoli had driven the enemy out of Szantó. Brigades Pergen and Fiedler followed him there on the 20th, and then had a rest day there on the 21st, while the advance guard went on ahead to Tallyá [Tállya, Hungary]. *Major* Herzmanowsky advanced through Ujhely [Sájtoraljaújhely, Hungary] with his own E.H. Stefan battalion, one squadron and four guns to cover the left flank, while at the same time the right flank was secured by *Major* Zimburg of the Mazzuchelli infantry with five Mazzuchelli companies, one squadron and two guns advancing through Szikszó.

According to the reports coming in, the enemy had occupied an advantageous position at Keresztur [Bodrogkeresztur, Hungary], Tarczal and Tokay, and reinforced himself with those detachments that had been driven out of Ujhely and Szikszó by the flanking columns. *Feldmarschall Lieutenant Graf* Schlick decided to attack the enemy on the 22nd, to which end he advanced with the main body through Tallyá and Máad [Mád, Hungary] toward Tarczal, while the flanking column under *Major* Herzmanowsky was directed against Keresztur.

The enemy had occupied a very advantageous position on the heights at Tarczal, whose front was covered by a thick cloud of skirmishers. A dense fog lay over the whole area so that it was difficult to gauge the enemy's strength and positions accurately. Our infantry were at a visible disadvantage in the skirmish action that soon developed, since the enemy skirmishers were mostly armed with rifles.[66] To put an end to this unequal struggle, 3. Bataillon E.H. Wilhelm was ordered to storm one of the heights to the left of the road, while a detachment of *chevauxlegers* charged the enemy skirmishers as they were retreating across the plain. The hill was quickly taken, but soon had to be relinquished again because of a counterattack in superior force, while the *chevauxlegers* were likewise driven back by an unexpected cavalry charge in which *Rittmeister Baron* Böhm died a hero's death. After rallying 3. Bataillon E.H. Wilhelm, *Feldmarschall Lieutenant Graf* Schlick had it assault the hill once again. When it reached the top, the enemy made as if to defect; that is to say, the rebels cried 'Long live the *Kaiser*!' and mingled with the ranks of the unsuspecting battalion, so its officers made every effort to make it cease fire while the brigadier *Generalmajor* Fiedler called on the rebels to lay down their arms. But the enemy used this moment – under cover of the fog – to bring up reinforcements. The battalion suddenly found itself greeted by salvoes of musketry, and those rebels who had already laid down their arms picked up their weapons again or sought to disarm our soldiers.[67]

It is understandable that in the temporary confusion that arose from the rebels' treacherous behaviour, the hill had to be abandoned for the second time, and with not insignificant losses. Since everything depended on holding it, *Feldmarschall Lieutenant Graf* Schlick decided on a third assault on it. However, this time he used the Oberst 1. Eskadron of the Sunstenau Kürassiere, followed by four companies of 1. Bataillon E.H. Wilhelm in support. Intelligently led by *Major Baron* Corizzutti, the brave cuirassiers hurled themselves impetuously upon the enemy's flank, broke two infantry formations, purged the whole hill of its defenders in a few minutes, and gloriously completed their difficult mission with the loss of no more than three men dead and five wounded, along with six horses dead and ten wounded. The rebels would have been even more thoroughly defeated if they had not found shelter from pursuit in the vineyards nearby.

66 The text refers to '*Kammerbüchsen*', so presumably this was the Augustin M-1844 Kammerbüchse tubelock rifle. Unlike most regular Austrian brigades, Schlick's forces had no *Jägers* attached, which may indeed have put them at a disadvantage if the Hungarians had specialist skirmishers armed with rifles.

67 There had been a similar episode at the battle of Pákozd in September of the previous year. On that occasion it was the Hungarians on the receiving end, as the Croats they were attacking feigned surrender only to then pick up their weapons again and shoot down the Hungarians. Hermann, 'A pákozdi csata'.

After this decisive assault the enemy did not try to retake the hill again. As it was late in the day and the fog persisted, *Feldmarschall Lieutenant Graf* Schlick abandoned the pursuit entirely, returning to Máad after dusk where the troops went into quarters.

As mentioned above, *Major* Herzmanowsky was supposed to advance on Keresztur with his column. *Feldmarschall Lieutenant Graf* Schlick's report of the 22nd to the *Feldmarschall* explicitly states that he did not receive this order because it had been intercepted by the rebels. He therefore got no further than Kisfalud [Bodrogkisfalud] on this day.

Feldmarschall Lieutenant Graf Schlick remained in Máad on the 23rd because the thick fog covering the area made any manoeuvre difficult and rendered the artillery useless. However, a reconnaissance detachment was sent toward Keresztur to deliver the order to *Major* Herzmanowsky to retreat to Máad with his column. In addition, one battalion, two guns and some cavalry were also later detached in his direction. But *Major* Herzmanowsky, who had been attacked by six times as many enemy at dawn on the 23rd, had nonetheless driven them back to Keresztur and repelled all the enemy's attacks, when *Hauptmann Graf* Erbach brought him Schlick's order to fall back to Máad. In this action against a far more numerous enemy *Major* Herzmanowsky and his E.H. Stefan battalion had fought with rare courage and endurance, receiving first class support from battery commander *Oberlieutenant* Bartelmus and from *Rittmeister* Limpens of the Kaiser Chevauxlegers. The rebels had tried to use the same shameful ruse here as at Tarczal, declaring that they wanted to defect to our side. *Hauptmann* Müralt of E.H. Stefan ceased fire so as to parley with the enemy commander. Meanwhile the two E.H. Stefan companies had been approached by a division each of Infanterie-Regiments Nr. 34 and 39, a *honvéd* battalion and a detachment of Husaren-Regiment Nr. 10. The commander of the *honvéd* battalion, Kalnoky, called out to our officers: 'Now it is up to you to lay down your arms; for you are surrounded on all sides.' At these words *Hauptmann* Dreskovich of the E.H. Stefan dealt him a couple of blows with his sabre and led his company forward with bayonets levelled. The other companies quickly followed and a very bloody melee developed in which five enemy officers and over 100 men were slain and the rest routed. In addition, three enemy officers and 165 men were captured during this action, and one standard was taken. *Major* Herzmanowsky began his retreat to Máad as ordered without being pursued by the enemy, met the battalion sent to receive him along the way, and arrived in Máad at 2:00 p.m.

Among those who particularly distinguished themselves in the actions of the 22nd and 23rd, the after-action report names: *Generalmajor* Fiedler, *Oberstlieutenant* Franz *Fürst* Lobkowitz, *Major Prinz* Nassau, *Rittmeister Graf* Török, *Lieutenant Brigade-Adjutant* Mattausch, *Major Baron* Corizzutti and *Rittmeister Baron* Hornstein of the Sunstenau Kürassiere, *Oberlieutenant* Angerer of the rocket battery, *Oberlieutenant* Csihal of the corps of drivers, *Lieutenant* Hahn of the Hartmann infantry, *Major* Herzmanowsky, *Hauptmann* Oreskovich, *Hauptmann* Peskier and *Lieutenant* Zellinger of the E.H. Stefan infantry, *Oberlieutenant* Bartelmus of the artillery, *Rittmeister Baron* Geusau of the E.H. Karl Chevauxlegers and *Rittmeister* Limpens of the Kaiser Chevauxlegers.

The combined losses in the actions at Tarczal and Keresztur were: *Rittmeister Baron* Böhm of the Kaiser Chevauxlegers, *Oberlieutenant* Herbing of the E.H. Stefan infantry, and 25 men of *Feldwebel* rank and below killed; Hauptmann Gilberti of the Hartmann infantry, *Oberlieutenant* Hoffman of the Kaiser Chevauxlegers, *Oberlieutenant* Fischer of the H.v. Parma infantry, *Oberlieutenant* Grubishich and *Lieutenant* Hillich of the E.H. Stefan infantry, and 63 men of *Feldwebel* and *Wachtmeister* rank and below wounded; *Hauptmann* Pabst of the König Wilhelm der Niederlande infantry, *Hauptmann* Müralt of the E.H. Stefan infantry (who was wounded and taken prisoner), and 51 men missing. Three officers' horses and 17 other horses were killed and nine wounded.

At 2:00 p.m. on the 23rd the enemy appeared in front of *Feldmarschall Lieutenant Graf* Schlick's position but did not go over to the attack. As for what Schlick planned to do next, let us follow the relevant sections of his report of the 25th here:

> Abandoning Keresztur made my position at Máad a very dangerous one, for it could be outflanked on its left, and after receiving the happy news that reinforcements would soon arrive, I decided to retreat to the much better position at Szantó and thereabouts that could not be outflanked. From there, if the enemy followed me as I hoped, I would have conducted a fighting withdrawal to Németi, where I would have adopted a suitable position and tried to engage the enemy until the reinforcements so graciously sent to me by Your Highness took him in flank and rear, perhaps leading to his destruction.
>
> Probably being just as well informed as I was about the reinforcements on the way, he has remained halted in Tokaj, Tarczal and Keresztur. I myself have adopted concentrated dispositions that are therefore good for the troops, in which I am using this quiet period until the reinforcements arrive for rest, to repair any damage, and for the units to be assembled in full force once more and ready for action again, so far as this is possible.
>
> Thus united, I will attack Tokay once more and hurl the enemy back across the Theiss, opening direct communications with the Danube Army that will then bring me further orders from Your Highness. However, in view of the fact that being close by I have the opportunity to find out how things stand, permit me respectfully to remark that the enemy cannot hold Debreczin, and that realising this, he will not try to. Two possible options are that he will either move from there toward Grosswardein, or else to Unghvár [Uzhhorod, Ukraine], Munkacs [Mukachevo, Ukraine] and Szigeth [Máramarossziget, now Sighetu Marmaţiei, Romania] to break through to Galicia. The latter is very probable in that, as is apparent from a report from the General Command in Galicia, there are Poles organising themselves in Munkacs and Szigeth, and considering the people's sympathies in Galicia, a breakthrough there is by no means unlikely; for the more they are driven away from Debreczin and Grosswardein, the more they will seek refuge in Transylvania. If the enemy should be driven back across the Theiss, I think it would be very beneficial to seek to establish a line of communications with *Feldmarschall Lieutenant* Malkowsky, especially as this would significantly ease Transylvania's situation.[68] Finally, in this eventuality Munkacs could also be taken again, which admittedly is only a small fortress, but nevertheless one that is still a dangerous place in the hands of the insurgents.

68 Ignaz Malkowsky Edler von Dammwalden (1784-1854) served as a field officer in many campaigns during the Napoleonic Wars, fighting at Aspern and Dresden, among other actions, and being wounded on more than one occasion. He was already 64 years old when the 1849 campaign brought him back into action. BLKÖ.

In any case, while awaiting Your Highness's noble orders, which can now reach me directly in an unbelievably short time, if I can dislodge the enemy from Tokay I will do so and strive to secure the crossing.

Feldmarschall Lieutenant Graf Schlick's advance on Tokay just at that moment came as a complete surprise to the *Feldmarschall*, since Miskolcz – which was where the reinforcements were marching to right then – had been designated for Schlick as the southernmost place he should actually seek to take. Nor did the *Feldmarschall* agree with the proposed operation toward Munkacs, since he recognised the need to finish off Görgei before anything else, so he sent the following letter to Schlick on the 29th:

In noting Your Honour's report of the 25th concerning the hard-fought action of the 22nd at Tarczal which your troops came through with courage and endurance, I can but completely approve of Your Honour's decision not to engage in any serious operation until you are joined by the reinforcements on their way to you.

Before I go on to indicate the operations which Your Honour will now be in a position to execute once you have linked up with *Feldmarschall Lieutenant* Schulzig, I consider it necessary to explain the general situation to you briefly.

As you know, the enemy corps under Görgei has been pursued from Waitzen through Léva by *Feldmarschall Lieutenant Baron* Csorich, who finally caught up with it at Schemnitz on the 21st and 22nd and made it give way after a fairly tough fight. It is not entirely clear whether this action was just against a strong enemy rear guard or against Görgei's whole corps, but the first assumption is the more likely.

It is also unclear whether the enemy has retreated through Losoncz or northward toward Zips. As soon as I receive more definite reports about this, I will apprise Your Honour of this without delay, and I likewise request that for your part you should obtain as much information about this as possible from spies.

As far as the strength of Görgei's corps is concerned, this is given variously and probably exaggeratedly as 10,000-12,000 men. It is being pursued by Brigade Jablonowsky with four battalions, two squadrons and two batteries. Jablonowsky has been instructed to follow hard on the heels of the enemy, and if the latter should move into the same area as Your Honour's troops, he is to link up with them. I have ordered the rest of the units under *Feldmarschall Lieutenant Baron* Csorich's command to return here, which was all the more necessary as meanwhile a strong enemy detachment under Perczel had advanced through Abany and Czegléd after pushing back the advanced cavalry brigade in Szolnok. This obliged me to move against Perczel with all available combat forces, leaving only a weak garrison in Ofen-Pesth. However, Perczel hastily retreated back across the Theiss again simply upon hearing of my approach, so some of the troops deployed against him were able to be ordered back to Pesth the next day. Perczel, whose strength is given as four brigades and 36 guns, must have reached Szolnok again on the 27th. At this time I have had no report as yet of his further line of retreat or intentions. As soon as I receive reliable information about these, I will share this with Your Honour without delay.

As far as Your Honour's future operations are concerned, I think that for the time being what is most important is to obtain definite information about Görgei's

> corps's movements so as not to expose the counties in the rear that have only just been reorganised to any danger, as well as on the other hand obtaining reliable information about the strength of the enemy detachments between Tokay and Debreczin.
>
> Only then will it be possible to decide on the timing and direction of our offensive manoeuvres. Without therefore wishing to express any definite view about this now, I think that a move through Unghvár toward Munkács could not be made without endangering Kaschau and the whole area above it, which the enemy could reach in a few days' march from Tokay, even if only with weak combat forces. It could be more appropriate to advance from Tokay toward Nyiregyháza, which would secure Tokay and cover Unghvár and Beregh Komitats [Ung and Bereg counties] on the one hand while threatening Debreczin on the other. Perhaps after the arrival of reinforcements, which has already been initiated, I could also be in a position for my part to support an offensive move against Debreczin by advancing from Szolnok, which however at this moment is still not feasible.
>
> I therefore request Your Honour, after the usual review of the situation in your theatre of operations, to inform me frankly of your views as to those future operations that seem expedient to you. I will not take any further decision until then.[69]

This letter, to which a second was attached in unofficial form giving instructions about the need to concentrate the troops more in the upper region and about the possible importance of the Braniszko [Branyiszkó, now Pod Braniskom, Slovakia] Pass, etc., was given to *Hauptmann Graf* Erbach to present to *Feldmarschall Lieutenant Graf* Schlick forthwith.

As Erbach was about to report to the *Feldmarschall* before leaving, the latter received a report from a stagecoach driver who had just arrived from Kaschau via Miskolcz, saying that hussars were patrolling in the Mezö-Kövesd area which was therefore unsafe. In the circumstances it did not seem advisable for *Hauptmann Graf* Erbach to travel as a courier, particularly with such important orders. He was therefore held back for the time being, and not sent off until 3 February with the instruction to attach himself to a patrol comprising a division of Auersperg cuirassiers under *Oberst* Kisslinger, which had been sent off earlier through Hatvan, Gyöngyös and Kápolna toward Poroszló to obtain information about the enemy and to scout the line of communications with *Feldmarschall Lieutenant Graf* Schlick. A second patrol was sent from Waitzen through Balassa-Gyarmath toward Losoncz with the same mission. Erbach was only to leave *Oberst* Kisslinger's patrol and continue his journey alone if the area was completely clear and safe. Before he left, the *Feldmarschall* also gave him verbal orders which we give the essence of here, quoting said captain:

> His Highness expressed himself disparagingly about the fact that many generals sent reports saying that the enemy was holding here or marching or there, or was of such and such strength, without these gentlemen actually having seen the enemy or obtained enough certainty about these things themselves, but he mentioned however that *Graf*

69 This is a major instance of Schlick being a loose cannon and not only failing to obey the *Feldmarschall*'s order but doing the opposite and dislocating his plans. The very moderate tone of the *Feldmarschall*'s reply is therefore impressive for its restraint; but we cannot help wondering whether a more intemperate and furious response such as Haynau would have written might not have produced better results.

> Schlick was a laudable exception.[70] The *Feldmarschall* quite specifically said to order *Graf* Schlick verbally that he should search ceaselessly for Görgei and his corps, about whom we had no definite information at that time, and as soon as he learned anything about him, he should report it.
>
> The *Feldmarschall* repeated this several times with emphasis, while pointing out on the map where Görgei could turn up. He said furthermore that I should tell *Graf* Schlick to establish communications with *Generals* Götz and Jablonowsky as quickly as possible and gave me some explanation of this on the map.

If these instructions had reached *Feldmarschall Lieutenant Graf* Schlick, he would quite certainly have called off his expedition against Tokay and directed all his attention to Görgei's movements, quite apart from the fact that his troops under *Major* Kiesewetter that were pushed forward as far as Leutschau in Zips County were in a much better position to learn directly and reliably about Görgei's approach than the *Feldmarschall* was, who only received vague and delayed reports about this. But this mishap was made complete when *Hauptmann Graf* Erbach, having left *Oberst* Kisslinger's patrol in Átány to try to get through alone, was stopped in Mezö-Kövesd by a hussar patrol led by the rebel commissar Töltényi and taken prisoner.[71]

Hauptmann Graf Erbach wanted to hasten to *Feldmarschall Lieutenant Graf* Schlick from Beszenyő [Besenyőtelek, Hungary], and therefore asked *Oberst* Kisslinger for an escort troop. However, the latter did not feel he had the authority to grant this request, which was all the more regrettable since it emerges from data obtained later that at this time the line of communications was not so dangerous that a troop of cavalry could not have got through.

Feldmarschall Lieutenant Graf Schlick and his troops, who as we have seen had taken position at Máad after the action of the 23rd at Tarczal, were deployed as follows on the 24th: one battalion, one troop of cavalry and two guns in Szantó; five companies and a troop of cavalry in Forró; two companies in Gibárt to maintain communications between the detachments in Forró and Szantó; two battalions, three troops of cavalry and 12 guns in Kér [Abaújkér, Hungary]; five companies, a squadron and six guns in Boldogkő, which was also where the headquarters was;[72] one battalion, a squadron and six guns in Vicsoly [Vizsoly, Hungary]; one squadron in Alsó-Czécze [now a southern offshoot of Hernádcéce, Hungary].

On the 26th communications were established with Division Schulzig that had been sent to reinforce Schlick, by means of Brigade Parrot pushing forward from Miskolcz toward Szikszó and Forró.

70 While the *Feldmarschall* exercised the utmost restraint in his written communications, he evidently occasionally allowed himself to vent his frustrations verbally.

71 Remember that circa the 18th 'the courier sent by Simunich to Götz, carrying precise written details of *Feldmarschall Lieutenant Baron* Csorich's strength and of the agreed plan of attack on Schemnitz, was captured by the rebels'; and also the daring lengths to which individual officers had to go to carry messages between Schlick and Windisch-Grätz (see the exploits of Zsedeny and Nassau later). The rebels operated under no such handicap, their orders and reports travelled swiftly and reliably and were supplemented by plentiful intelligence from sympathetic locals. This contrast helps to explain why Windisch-Grätz's manoeuvres were often tentative and hesitant compared to those of his adversaries.

72 This dramatic castle on a crag with a commanding view of the Hornád valley is an excellent position for a headquarters.

On the 27th *Feldmarschall Lieutenant Graf* Schlick detached Brigade Pergen from Vicsoly toward Ujhely, since it was reported that an enemy column was planning to advance from there toward Kaschau. However, this later proved to be unfounded; instead, on learning that reinforcements had arrived in Miskolcz, the enemy had retired behind the Theiss.[73]

Upon the news that Ujhely had already been occupied by our troops and that no attack need be expected from there, the units sent to cover the road from Ujhely to Kaschau were ordered to halt, whereupon they went into cantonments again on the 29th. On this day the dispositions of *Feldmarschall Lieutenant Graf* Schlick's corps were as follows:

Brigade *Generalmajor* Fiedler (three battalions, two and a half squadrons, 14 guns) in Mád; Brigade *Generalmajor Graf* Pergen (ten companies, one and a half squadrons, 12 guns) in Ujhely; two companies in Kér; one battalion, one squadron and the headquarters in Boldogkő.

Division *Feldmarschall Lieutenant* Schulzig: Brigade *Generalmajor* Parrot: two companies in Gibárt; four companies, six squadrons and six guns in Szantó and Kér; Brigade *Generalmajor* Kriegern: two and four sixths battalions, a half-squadron and 12 guns in Forró; two companies and a half-squadron at the bridge over the Sajó river at Zsolca [Felsőzsolca, Hungary], in Miskolc; one squadron, with *Oberlieutenant* Tomasini attached, reconnoitring toward Putnok to find Görgei, who however was in Zips County at this time.

Brigade *Generalmajor Graf* Deym (detached): one battalion, a half-squadron and four guns in Kaschau; two companies, two guns, plus Szirmay's *Freikorps* that was still in the process of formation, in Eperies; four companies, a half-squadron and three guns under *Major* Kiesewetter in Leutschau.

The troops remained in the above positions on the 30th, with the exception of Brigade Pergen which advanced from Ujhely to Olaszliszka. On the 31st *Feldmarschall Lieutenant Graf* Schlick resumed his operation toward Tokay. Brigade Pergen moved through Keresztur and Brigade Fiedler through Tarczal to Tokay, while Brigade Parrot followed in reserve. When our troops approached, the enemy withdrew completely across the ice to the left bank of the Theiss; for he had already burned down the fine bridge at Tokay a couple of days earlier. On the far bank of the Theiss he deployed behind thick treelines but was soon driven off from these by a few rockets, whereupon he retreated to a wood further back.

To reconnoitre the enemy position better, *Feldmarschall Lieutenant Graf* Schlick had four companies of 3. Bataillon E.H. Stefan cross the frozen Theiss. However, since this crossing seemed too difficult for larger detachments equipped with artillery to use, those companies were called back to the near bank again, which the enemy exploited by advancing to the bank of the Theiss in several columns. A heavy exchange of musketry and artillery fire then arose between the two sides separated by the river. A couple of houses on the riverbank in which the enemy had ensconced himself were set on fire by rockets,[74] so he then shelled the town of Tokay starting fires in four places. So as to spare the town from which not a single shot had been fired at the

73 Following on from the note above about couriers, here is an instance of the imperials without the Hungarians' advantage of good local intelligence having to respond to misleading rumours, with resultant expense of time and energy and dissipation of effort.

74 Note the effectiveness of rockets as incendiaries. We shall see this demonstrated again on 4 February when they set light to the bridge at Czibakháza; and then during the Summer Campaign, most notably at the battle of Pered.

enemy anyway, and since darkness had already fallen, the troops were withdrawn to Keresztur, Tarczal, Máad, Szerencs, etc.

Our losses in this action came to three dead and 11 wounded, among the latter being *Major Baron* Gablenz of the general staff, *Major* Herzmanowsky of the E.H. Stefan, and *Feldmarschall Lieutenant Graf* Schlick's *Inhaber-Adjutant* [senior aide-de-camp], *Oberlieutenant Baron* Wocher, who was, however, only slightly injured. Apart from those named above as wounded, *Oberstlieutenant Fürst* Lobkowitz and the commander of the rocket battery, *Oberlieutenant* Angerer, were praised in the after-action report.

Feldmarschall Lieutenant Graf Schlick learned from deserters that the enemy facing him at Tokay consisted of three regular battalions, a couple of *honvéd* battalions, a few squadrons of hussars and nine guns, including two 12-pounders. The rest of the enemy corps that had been at Keresztur and Tarczal on the 22nd and 23rd had retreated to Debreczin. The account of the action at Tokay was enclosed with a later letter sent to the *Feldmarschall* by Schlick on 1 February from Máad in which he reported at length about the progress of operations since his previous report of 28 January, as well as about what he intended to do next.

In particular, this report of 1 February indicated that Brigade Pergen had marched to Keresztur, Brigade Fiedler to Máad, and Brigade Parrot to Szantó, while *Feldmarschall Lieutenant* Schulzig with one Ottochaner battalion, one Latour battalion, two guns and four squadrons of cuirassiers had marched to Kaschau to calm down the agitated mood in that city. The Ottochaner battalion and two guns were to move from Kaschau to Leutschau to relieve the Nugent battalion that was there, which was to patrol in two mobile columns toward Sz. Miklos [Liptovský Mikuláš, Slovakia] and Breznó-Bánya [Brezno, Slovakia], disarm the inhabitants of the mountain valleys there, destroy the cannon foundry in Telgárth [Telgárt, Slovakia], and then return to Kaschau.

Concerning the enemy's movements, *Feldmarschall Lieutenant Graf* Schlick stated:

> A large part of Görgei's corps, which according to reports received from several quarters is scattered, is supposed to have turned through Erlau and Mezö-Kövesd toward Heves; this includes in particular the hussars who are making communications between Your Highness and my corps very insecure, if not indeed blocking them completely.
>
> I therefore find myself obliged to send this report via Dukla and Krakau, while nonetheless at the same time taking measures to re-establish direct communications by means of patrols from Miskolcz toward Mezö-Kövesd.
>
> Additional information about the enemy is that the Polish Legion,[75] which constitutes a small part of the corps facing me, has moved to Munkács to join its compatriots there. Another part is supposed to have retreated to Debreczin, while

75 In fact, there were two Polish Legions fighting for Hungary. These were formed from Polish volunteers, mostly fleeing Galicia from November 1848. The Legion with the Upper Hungarian Army eventually reached a size of three battalions, four lancer squadrons and two half-batteries, but at this point was only about battalion strength. It was commanded by Jerzy Bułharyn (see next footnote). The other Polish Legion was in Transylvania and had two battalions and a few lancer squadrons. Bona, 'Armed Forces', p.103.

8,000–10,000 men including many cavalry as well as heavy artillery are facing me[76] across the river. While crossing the ice is possible for individuals on foot and perhaps even for individual riders, it is not at all practical for the artillery, but in particular, the black soil softened by the last thaw has so ruined the roads leading to the Theiss crossings that it is not possible to move the artillery there at the present time. Two situations may therefore arise: if it thaws completely and frees the Theiss, then an operation from here directly toward Debreczin is impossible for the immediate future, and an operation via Unghvár toward Munkács and then beyond toward Szigeth would probably be the most appropriate; for it would be decidedly useful to draw the rebels away from the Galician border and out of the mountains down to the plain. The other possibility is a hard frost that firms up the roads and the ice on the Theiss again so that an advance on Debreczin becomes feasible. While awaiting Your Highness's further instructions, I shall meanwhile muster every effort to consolidate the order that has been restored in the region hereabouts.

This report, which did not reach the *Feldmarschall* until 8 February since it was despatched via Krakau as has been said, was unlikely to reassure him about the situation there. *Feldmarschall Lieutenant Graf* Schlick was talking about an operation against Szigeth (200 km east of Tokay) at a time when Görgei's corps was in his rear just a couple of days' march from Leutschau,

76 This extensive footnote appears in the original: '*The following has since been learned concerning the strength of the enemy combat forces deployed behind the line of the Theiss at that time: Klapka's corps posted opposite Tokay in Rakamaz comprised Bułharin's, Zako's, Dessewffy's, Sulc's and Gedeon's brigades, altogether 7,920 infantry, 695 cavalry, half a 12-pounder battery, one and a half 6-pounder and two and a half 3-pounder batteries and two 2-pounder guns. The regular troops among them were one battalion of the Infanterie-Regiment Nr. 39 and a company of Infanterie-Regiment Nr. 34; the corps also included 350 Poles, and the 17., 19., 20., 26., 34., 42., 43. and 52. Honved-Bataillons. The rest of them were *Freikorps*. In Tisza-Füred, about 80 km below Tokay, were 1,500 men of Dembinsky's corps, which being combined with Perczel's had a strength of 15,310 infantry, 1,470 cavalry and 34 guns, and was marching up the Theiss after the retreat from Szolnok. Other troops were in Debreczin, and Vécsey's and Damjanich's corps were in the process of approaching Czibakháza and Török Sz. Miklós from the region downstream.'

Jerzy Bułharyn (1798-1885) was a Polish noble who served in the Polish uprising in 1830-1831 and was then exiled to France. In September 1848 he proposed to Kossuth that he should raise a Polish Legion and was appointed commander of Polish troops in the Hungarian army. After serving with I. Corps in January 1849 he spent March organising the Polish Legion's 2nd and 3rd battalions and 1st and 2nd lancer regiments in Debreczin, before serving in command roles. At the end of the war he escaped via Serbia to exile in England. Bona, *Tábornokok*.

István Zakó (1810-60) was a member of parliament in June 1848. In October he became a major commanding the 34. Honved-Bataillon. He fought until April 1849 when he transferred to the war ministry. At the war's end he surrendered with Görgei's army at Világos. Charges against him were dropped. Bona, *Tábornokok*.

Arisztid Dessewffy [Aristid Dessöffy] (1802-49) was a former captain with service in the artillery, engineers, and cavalry. In September 1848 he became a major in the national guard. He fought all through the war holding various commands. At the end, rather than emigrate, he decided to surrender to his former comrade, Liechtenstein, whose intercession did not save him from execution but only changed the sentence from hanging to firing squad. Bona, *Tábornokok*.

'Sulc' is Bódog Bátori-Schulcz (1804-85), author of *Emlékiratai 1848/9-ki szabadságharczból* (Pest: Vódiáner, 1870).

where *Major* Kiesewetter had just four companies, a half-squadron and three rocket launch stands.[77] However, the hope was still cherished that Schlick would meanwhile have received the dispatch of the 29th carried by *Hauptmann Graf* Erbach, and would have made his dispositions accordingly; for it was not until the 9th or 10th that headquarters learned that the said captain had been captured. However, it remains inexplicable that, as seems to emerge from his report of 1 February, Schlick still had no idea that Görgei was approaching through Zips County. Something must surely have been known about this matter and reported from Leutschau on the 29th or 30th. However, the justifiable hope was clung to that perhaps on the very day that he sent his report to the *Feldmarschall*, Schlick would have had a message from Leutschau and after leaving a rear guard on the Theiss, which at that time (1 February) was still not crossable by large bodies of troops, would immediately have moved upstream by forced marches so as to fall on Görgei with concentrated force, in which case the outcome could hardly have been in doubt. Finally, on the 28th Schlick managed to send a note written in code carried directly to the *Feldmarschall* by a reliable stagecoach driver, in which he said: 'My main aim is to cover Kaschau, which is why Görgei has not been strongly pursued. My hands are tied until Görgei is destroyed; then I can do anything.' It therefore seemed that he understood his situation perfectly well, so reassurance was found in this that he would act appropriately at the present decisive moment.

Before we follow how events developed in that theatre of operations, we must mention what had transpired meanwhile with the other army formations.

Events around Leopoldstadt, Komorn and rear areas, 31 January to 9 February 1849

On 31 January *Feldmarschall Lieutenant* Simunich reported that he was making preparations to enable Brigade Neustädter to cross the Waag at Szered. It was also said that the enemy had invaded the Rye Island with 4,000 men from Komorn and advanced as far as Nyarasd.

To occupy the Mining Towns, on the 2nd the *Feldmarschall Lieutenant* sent one Nugent division to Kremnitz and a Hartmann division to Schemnitz to relieve *Generalmajor* Götz's men there. On that same day the fortress of Leopoldstadt finally surrendered after a bombardment of barely an hour. The garrison comprised *Major* Ordody as fortress commander, *Major* Zinner, *Major* Mednyansky, 38 field officers, and 1,272 men of *Feldwebel* rank and below. Thirty-eight artillery pieces were taken, as well as enough supplies of food and ammunition for a fairly long defence. The surrender was unconditional and read: 'The garrison surrenders and entrusts itself to His Majesty's mercy.' *Feldmarschall Lieutenant* Simunich was now ordered to place Leopoldstadt in a state of defence again, to leave two companies to garrison it, and to march to Neuhäusel with the rest of his force and undertake the closer siege of the fortress of Komorn together with Brigade Lederer on the right bank. This seemed all the more necessary as the Danube flooding was beginning to recede, so the Komorn garrison could move more freely, and *Generalmajor* Neustädter had already vacated the Rye Island. The latter was now instructed to move with the greatest possible haste through Neuhäusel and Párkány to join the army in Ofen-Pesth.

77 Schlick in loose cannon mode again.

Feldmarschall Lieutenant Ramberg, who until now had been charged with observing Komorn, was now ordered immediately to hurry after Brigades Götz and Jablonowsky, to take over command of these, and to drive the pursuit of Görgei with maximum energy.

Some of the units under *Feldmarschall Lieutenant* Simunich's command entered Neuhäusel on the 7th, while Brigade Neustädter had already arrived on the 6th, since *Pionnier-Lieutenant* Fiedler's inexhaustible activity had managed to repair the crossing of the Waag at Szered on the 5th. At 4:00 a.m. on the 8th this brigade was just in the process of forming up to depart for Párkány when a strong enemy column under *Major Graf* Paul Esterhazy sortied from Komorn, crossed the Neutra at Naszvad [Nesvady, Slovakia] and advanced to attack Neuhäusel. This column had driven back the outposts of the E.H. Wilhelm regiment and was already pushing into the town in several places. *Generalmajor* Neustädter immediately threw three companies of the composite Oguliner-Szluiner battalion against the rebels and drove them back, while the Major's 2. Eskadron of the Banderial-Husaren advanced upon the town square and attacked the enemy detachments that had already reached there with such vigour that the square was cleared in an instant. The actual Neuhäusel garrison – a battalion of E.H. Wilhelm, a troop of Kress Chevauxlegers, and a 6-pounder battery – now took over and drove the enemy completely out of the last houses in the town. Meanwhile, the three other Oguliner-Szluiner companies and the Banderial hussars moved to the Neutra bridge where the road from Bajcs [Bajč, Slovakia] comes in and left some of their men there in ambush. When an enemy column advancing from Bajcs arrived there, it was received with a volley of musketry which killed the column commander, whereupon his men hastily fled back to Bajcs. Dawn had not yet broken, which hindered the pursuit.

Generalmajor Neustädter now began his march through Köbölkút [Gbelce, Slovakia] to Párkány, arriving there on the 9th, and was carried from there by steamers down the Danube to Pesth, from where he rejoined I. Armeekorps.

The division of 1. Banal Regiment that he had left behind to guard the crossing of the Little Danube at Eperies [Jahodná, Slovakia – as distinct from the other Eperies, Prešov. They are two different places] on the Rye Island, which had not yet been relieved by *Feldmarschall Lieutenant* Simunich, was taken completely by surprise at midday on the 7th by an enemy detachment that had advanced from Komorn through Gutta [Kolárovo, Slovakia], and was taken prisoner. Only one officer and 40 men managed to escape.

Oberst Baron Horváth, who had been sent to Gran by the *Feldmarschall* to restore lawful order there and to expedite the construction of the pontoon bridge over the Danube as much as possible, had learned that a revolutionary society had formed in Bátor-Keszi whose chief, Palkovics, was staying in Karva [Kravany nad Dunajom, Slovakia] and was in constant communication with the Komorn garrison. To arrest this dangerous party leader, on the 4th Horváth sent the steamer *Hermine* carrying a company of grenadiers under *Hauptmann Baron* Prohaska to Karva. However, when the boat came level with Neudorf [Sattel-Neudorf, now Nyergesújfalu in Hungary], it was fired on by artillery from the left bank of the Danube and two men were wounded. One ball struck the engine without rendering it unusable; but the boat was forced to turn about and retire quickly.

On the morning of the 5th, four *honvéd* companies, a half-squadron of hussars and four guns advanced from Komorn to the immediate vicinity of the bridge being built across the Danube at Gran and drove off the civilian laborers with a few cannon shots before retreating again. This incident, and the Komorn garrison's repeated sorties on the Rye Island and toward Neuhäusel, etc., obliged the *Feldmarschall* to order *Feldmarschall* Simunich on the 6th and again on the

10th to organise the siege of Komorn in such a way that sorties of the kind that had taken place recently could no longer occur, since these were agitating the population of the whole area and even causing concern in Raab. The positions for the besieging units were also to be chosen with a view to enabling successful bombardment of the fortress, which was to proceed as soon as the artillery arrived. Finally, he was instructed about the need to throw bridges across the Danube as well as the Waag and the Neutra, to establish secure communications between the separated parts of the siege corps.[78]

Hauptmann Drechsler of the general staff was sent to *Feldmarschall Lieutenant* Simunich in place of the wounded *Hauptmann* Gastgeb, while *Hauptmann* Kochmeister of the corps of engineers took care of matters in the engineering domain.

In Raab it had been reported that the Komorn garrison was planning a *coup de main* against the city by outflanking the besieging units via the Rye Island. On the 8th the *Feldmarschall* therefore felt obliged to order *General Baron* Lederer that he was immediately to detach two squadrons and a half-battery to the Little Rye Island to observe the Danube crossings, particularly that at Weisskirchen. Likewise on 8 February, *General Baron* Lederer himself reported that a militia was actively being organised on the left bank of the Danube. Every man there was supposed to arm himself with a scythe, axe or the like, so as to be ready to strike as soon as they were called. Similar rumours had also reached *Feldmarschall Lieutenant* Kempen, who thereupon sent small mobile columns from the weak garrison of Pressburg to patrol the Rye Island, and who requested that a cavalry detachment be assigned to him to help to carry out this mission as it was a difficult one for infantry.

The royal commissioners the *Feldmarschall* had installed in the counties to the rear were also constantly asking for military assistance, without which they could not carry out their duties. Understandably, these requests could only be met in very urgent cases if we were not to get involved in endless detachments. On the 8th *Hauptmann* Paumgarten of the general staff, who had remained in Stuhlweissenburg when *Oberst* Horváth was sent to Gran, and who was occupying that town and Veszprim with four companies and two squadrons, requested the urgent return of the G.H. Baden battalion since the need had arisen to send out mobile columns down the Danube – a request which likewise could not be granted.

Information reached the executive committee of the Moravian district administration that 30,000-40,000 insurgents were planning to invade Moravia, and then to move from there to Wien where an uprising was supposed to break out at the same time. The *Feldmarschall* was

78 Such things as security against sorties, preparation for bombardment, and ensuring communications between sections of siege lines are surely basic elements of conducting a siege and should not have needed Windisch-Grätz's intervention to make them happen; perhaps Simunich was indeed trying to do these things anyway, so far as forces available and circumstances allowed. Perhaps, rather than this being another instance of Windisch-Grätz's subordinates letting him down and frustrating him, he was just supervising excessively, interfering too much in detail and imposing too little of his will on the major outlines of operations. Two paragraphs later we see him ordering the detachment of two squadrons and a half-battery. A *Feldmarschall* should not be giving instructions down to that level at all. This is reminiscent of the French marshal, Bazaine: suddenly put in command of the French army outside Metz in a dire situation in 1870, he was too overwhelmed to make the decisive command decisions the situation demanded and retreated into his comfort zone of ordering low-level tactical actions, siting individual batteries, and even getting involved in a cavalry skirmish. David Ascoli, *A Day of Battle* (Edinburgh: Birlinn, 2001), pp.144, 153.

informed of this on the 6th by the governor of Moravia, though the governor did not attach any particular worth to the credibility of this information.

Events in the South, 30 January to 20 February 1849

The news from the region downriver was more encouraging. On the 5th *Feldzeugmeister Graf* Nugent reported that on the night of 30/31 January, after a fairly lively action, *Generalmajor* Trebersburg had seized the suburbs of Eszek and was still holding them. The commanders of the assault columns were *Oberst* Van der Nüll of the Gradiskaner regiment, *Oberst* Hallawanya of the Brooder, *Major* Dragich of the Peterwardeiner, *Hauptmann* Tarbuk of the St. Georger and *Hauptmann* Barisich of the E.H. Leopold infantry. Our losses came to 15 dead and 30 wounded.

Feldzeugmeister Graf Nugent indicated that a close siege of Eszek was necessary, and that *Generalmajor* Trebersburg should be sent more artillery, some cavalry and also regular infantry; this last seemed particularly important as it was reported that a not insignificant faction inside the fortress was inclined to surrender if they could conclude the capitulation with the imperial military, which they did not consider Trebersburg's *grenzer* battalions to be, clad as they were simply in peasant clothing.[79] Finally, Nugent gave assurance that, quite independent of the fall of Eszek which might happen anyway, within four or five days Brigade Dietrich would be available for some other mission. On the 6th he reported that the rebel commissar, *Graf* Kasimir Bathiany, had fled Eszek with his family and had crossed the Danube at Batina on the evening of the 4th to seek refuge in Bácska County.

A message arrived from *Generalmajor* Todorovich, who commanded the composite corps of 10,000-12,000 Serbs and *grenzers* in the area of Hatzfeld [Jimbolia, Romania] and Kikinda, that he had sent six *grenzer* battalions, the Nazional-Uhlanen[80] and 400 Serbian cavalry toward Arad, so as to link up with a detachment under *Feldmarschall Lieutenant* Gläser sent out from the fortress of Temesvár and drive the enemy off the right bank of the Maros, and if circumstances allowed, even to open communications with Transylvania. However, this expedition limited itself to foraging for provisions for the fortress of Arad and reinforcing the garrison with one company of the Romanen Banater-Grenz-Regiment. *Generalmajor* Todorovich had already previously indicated the need to establish communications with the main army, and indeed reported that he would adopt such a position as to effect a junction with I. Armeekorps, which according to His Excellency the *Banus*'s promise was approaching from Pesth via Theresiopel [Subotica, Serbia] or Szegedin.

To give the operations in that region more definite direction, to get the units deployed there organised more quickly, and finally also to sort out to some degree the very complicated political relations among the various nationalities in that stretch of territory – and to obtain reliable

79 The Hungarians had already experienced atrocities at the hands of Croat troops: see the footnote above about outraged Hungarian civilians taking revenge on Croat prisoners at Güns. The garrison and inhabitants of Eszek undoubtedly feared pillage and massacre at the irregulars' hands, hence their insistence on only surrendering to regular troops. Bona notes that on 1 February 1849, Serbian irregulars massacred 2,000 Hungarian civilians at Zenta. Bona, *Hungarian Revolution*, p.313.

80 *National-Truppen* are native troops (Müller, *Allgemeines Verteutschungswörterbuch*, pp.197, 337). It can mean local forces from the individual provinces of the Austrian Empire. Presumably these Nazional-Uhlanen are therefore Croatian mounted militia.

information about all this – on the 8th the *Feldmarschall* sent *Oberstlieutenant* Herdy of the general staff to *Generalmajor* Todorovich with suitable instructions.

At the present moment, when the enemy's main body was clearly concentrated on the Theiss from Szolnok up to Tokay, it was quite unfeasible for I. Armeekorps to undertake an operation toward Theresiopel or Szegedin as implied above. Nevertheless, the *Feldmarschall* did not wish to neglect establishing communications with the units in that area, and if possible seizing the important town of Szegedin which at that time was only weakly held by the enemy; but that could only be done by a combined operation supported from the right bank of the Theiss. *Feldzeugmeister Graf* Nugent's cooperation was enlisted for this. On the 5th he had already been asked to transfer Brigade Dietrich across to the left bank of the Danube at Tolna, and to have it move from there upriver through Hajós toward Felegyháza [Kiskunfélegyháza, Hungary], with the aim of better securing the right flank of the troops on the Szolnok line and generally standing ready to be able to cooperate with any offensive operation on the Theiss. However, on the 9th this brigade was tasked with establishing communications with *Generalmajor* Todorovich's corps and possibly cooperating with an expedition against Szegedin, which *Oberstlieutenant* Herdy was supposed to discuss in more detail with the unit commanders concerned.

Since Brigade Dietrich could not arrive in Szekszárd before the 16th and the 20th, by when matters would surely have been decided in the northern theatre of operations, the position still remained such that the above plan might have to be abandoned and this brigade be moved up the Danube to Pesth, which as we shall see later on became urgently necessary and did indeed happen.

Feldzeugmeister Graf Nugent had as always complied most readily with the *Feldmarschall*'s requests[81] and had taken measures so that on the 16th, 19th and 20th *Generalmajor* Dietrich stood ready at the *Feldmarschall*'s disposal in Szekszárd with:

Two Wimpffen battalions
Bataillon Eckert (composite battalion of two Hess companies and two Prohaska companies)
4. Bataillon, 2. Banal-Regiment
4. Bataillon, Warasdiner Kreutzer-Regiment
Three squadrons of E.H. Johann Dragoner
Half a horse artillery battery
Half a foot artillery battery

or 3,000 infantry and 400 cavalry altogether. In his report regarding this, *Feldzeugmeister Graf* Nugent mentioned it would have been quite impossible for him to detach this strong force if he had not secured his line of communications by occupying the strongpoints of Sziget [Szigetvár, Hungary, as distinct from Máramarossziget] and Siklós and by repairing several crossings over the Drau [Drava].

At this time the rest of his corps was distributed as follows: 1,600 infantry and 120 cavalry in Körmend, Szala-Egerszeg, Veszprim and Kanisa to maintain order and to secure the line of communications with the provinces to the rear; 2,200 infantry and 320 cavalry outside Eszek;

81 Hurrah – a subordinate who does what he is told!

1,200 infantry and 240 cavalry garrisoning Fünfkirchen and guarding the Danube crossings. He had already made all the preparations for a determined assault on Eszek, and expected the necessary high-angle siege artillery for this within a few days. *Oberst* Mamula took over direction of the siege works for the assault.

Events on the Middle Theiss, 1-12 February 1849

On 1 February the *Banus* reported that the enemy was occupying Török Sz. Miklós in force, had brought up troops from the rear, and was planning to prepare or execute crossings over the frozen Theiss in several places. According to patrol reports, the bridge at Czibakháza was guarded by the enemy, admittedly with its central span removed, but still easily repairable. In the circumstances he had found himself obliged to push forward the Brooder battalion together with the Artillerie-Korps-Reserve from Berczel [Ceglédbercel, Hungary] to Czegléd, while leaving the E.H. Karl battalion and the two batteries of the Artillerie-Hauptreserve in Alberti for the time being; however, he had authorised *Feldmarschall Lieutenant* Hartlieb to call on these troops as well should he need to do so.

On 4 February, *Generalmajor* Ottinger moved against Czibakháza with two divisions of Hardegg cuirassiers, one division of 2. Banal-Regiment, Kavallerie-Batterie Nr. 5 and Raketen-Batterie Nr. 17 to destroy the bridge there, in which he succeeded completely. After the launch of the fourth rocket the bridge caught fire and the *honvéd* battalion posted on the far bank to defend it scattered.[82] Meanwhile the horse artillery had silenced two enemy guns and set light to a house beyond the bridge with shellfire. This expedition cost only one man wounded and six horses killed.

Generalmajor Ottinger commended the commander of Kavallerie-Batterie Nr. 5, *Oberlieutenant* Loschau, and *Lieutenant* Kollmann of the rocket battery for their distinguished conduct.

On the 4th and 5th the patrol force of Civallart *uhlans* under *Rittmeister* Ivichich that had been sent toward Losoncz in the Ipoly valley reported that it had scouted beyond Balassa-Gyarmath and found no enemy in that area; on the other hand it was said that Görgei was at Leutschau, while some of his force had moved to Rosenau and Telgárth to advance from there toward Kaschau.

The patrol force under *Oberst* Kisslinger that had been sent toward Poroszló entered Gyöngyös on the 4th. There Kisslinger learned of the abduction of *Oberst* Montecuccoli of the Preussen cuirassiers by a *feldwebel*, a *korporal* and six *honvéds* that had taken place on the 1st, in which obviously treachery on the part of the inhabitants of Gyöngyös had played a part. The Hungarian tricolour also still waved above the town hall.

Travellers coming from Kaschau and Debreczin said that there were neither imperial military nor rebels between Miskolcz and Gyöngyös; that Poroszló was held by the enemy, and the bridge over the Theiss had been prepared for demolition.

To punish the town of Gyöngyös for its treachery, *Major Baron* Schneider was sent there on the 8th with the 1. Bataillon Schönhals as a punitive detachment.[83]

82 Note the incendiary effect of the rockets, as commented on above.

83 The original says '*Exekuzions-Kommando*' but this means levying a fine rather than executions as such. We may surmise that Haynau, the 'Hyena of Brescia', might have reacted more forcefully and ordered actual executions. Of course, we cannot know whether this would have been more effective in cowing

Oberst Kisslinger had meanwhile moved to Poroszló and found it occupied by the enemy. He was therefore in the process of returning to Pesth when he received the order to send the division of Max Auersperg cuirassiers that was with him under *Major* Coudenhove to join *Major* Schneider's punitive detachment in Gyöngyös, but to return to Pesth himself.

A contribution was levied from the town of Gyöngyös. After exacting this, *Major* Schneider began his retreat to Pesth on the 11th, while the division of Max Auersperg cuirassiers was pushed forward through Gyöngyös once more. The general outline of the mission given to this cuirassier division by *Major* Schneider in a special order on the 12th was that it should immediately move from Gyöngyös through Kápolna into a position at Füzes-Abány [Füzesabony, Hungary], from where it was to observe both Poroszló and the Theiss crossing at Tisza-Füred as well as the area up- and downriver, and to keep an eye on the crossings near Csáth,[84] Ároktő and Kömlő[85]. Reports of any important enemy movement were to be sent to the *Feldmarschall* by courier without delay.

Sending out such wide-ranging patrol detachments was the only means of obtaining information about the enemy, and of being made aware of any enemy advance in good time; for anything learned from spies was just contradictory, false or exaggerated, leaving aside the fact that such messages also usually arrived too late. Besides, this way the seditious business of the revolutionary agents who roamed the country finding protection and safe houses everywhere could be impeded to some degree, and also the small enemy patrols that were gallivanting about on all sides could be neutralised. Thus, for example, on the 12th, the very day after the departure of the punitive detachment from Gyöngyös, nine hussars of Husaren-Regiment Nr. 9 appeared there and got up to all manner of mischief, raising the tricolour over the town hall again, etc. When *Major* Coudenhove sent a detachment there to apprehend them, they had already headed for the hills again without running any risk of being betrayed or discovered in their hideouts.[86]

Upper Hungary: Görgei Escapes the Trap; Schlick Eludes Görgei, 29 January to 29 February 1849

Generalmajor Fürst Jablonowsky, who as already mentioned had arrived in Neusohl on 31 January, reported from there on 2 February that the day before he had pushed *Oberst* Collery forward to Lipcse [Slovenská L'upča, Slovakia] with five companies, a half-squadron, two howitzers and a half-company of pioneers, to repair the bridges over the Gran below Medzibrod that had

the locals, or counter-productive in provoking even more determined Hungarian resistance. As it was, given that much of this war was a counter-insurgency operation, the imperial regular forces seem to have shown commendable restraint and not to have treated the Hungarian civilian population unduly harshly, but more like errant children requiring moderate chastisement rather than hostile enemies to be harmed. Sadly the same cannot be said of the irregular forces, especially Romanian and Serbian, who committed serious large-scale atrocities against Hungarian civilians, which were in part reciprocated: Bona mentions how several thousand Hungarians were killed in the 'disarmament period' after 18 October 1848, while the Hungarian national guard burned Romanian villages in revenge. Bona, *Hungarian Revolution*, p.283.

84 Presumably Mezőcsát, therefore meaning the nearby crossing at Tiszakeszi.

85 Perhaps the farm marked on the 2nd Military Survey map as 'Kunjhó', 5 km east of Tiszatarján.

86 This impudent episode is a nice illustration of the ease and impunity with which the Hungarians could roam the country in small parties while the imperials had to operate in force.

been destroyed by the enemy. Another detachment of four companies, a troop of *chevauxlegers*, a pioneer platoon and two rocket launch stands under *Hauptmann* Abele was sent through Stureczberg [Staré Hory, Slovakia] toward Rosenberg to clear the abattis as well as to obtain information about the enemy and was supposed to return to Neusohl next day (the 3rd). At that time *Generalmajor* Jablonowsky thought that because of the many obstacles that had confronted his march, Görgei must have gained a head start of four or five days' march, so he could hardly hope to catch up with him along the direct route. Therefore, instead of advancing through Zips County, he planned to use the parallel road through Briesen and Tiszolcz [Tisovec, Slovakia] toward Kaschau. To this end the advance guard under *Oberst* Collery was to enter Briesen next day, on the 3rd, but the main body of the brigade would not arrive there before the 4th. He had already reached agreement about this with *General* Götz, who was still in Kremnitz on the 4th, thinking he ought to wait for *Feldmarschall Lieutenant* Simunich's detachment that had been ordered to go there. But since the latter had still not arrived, he concentrated his brigade on the 5th and moved to Briesen on the 6th, where he linked up with *Generalmajor Fürst* Jablonowsky's force.

The *Feldmarschall* wrote this to the latter on the 4th:

> I note your report of 2 February, and the view expressed in it that you could reach Kaschau before the enemy does, or at least catch up with him there, by means of a rapid advance through Briesen seems to me to be entirely appropriate. Now, when Görgei's corps is apparently continuing to move into the upper valley of the Waag and can no longer head in a different direction so easily and is rendering the roads and bridges behind him unusable, exploiting a parallel road to pursue him is advisable, during which however one eye must constantly be kept on the possibility of a sudden about-turn by Görgei's column. I desire that you, *Herr Generalmajor*, should also inform *Generalmajor* Götz about this, who must be close to you by now, but in any case you should continue your march without the slightest delay.

If the plan proposed by *Generalmajor Fürst* Jablonowsky and, as can be seen from the above letter, approved by the *Feldmarschall* – namely that the enemy should be pursued by a parallel route rather than directly – had been followed, then as we shall see later, the junction of Brigades Götz and Jablonowsky with *Feldmarschall Lieutenant Graf* Schlick's corps in Torna via Rosenau on the 10th would have come about naturally without difficulty. But instead of this, these brigades under *Generalmajor* Götz moved to Polomka on the 7th, to Telgárth on the 8th and from there through Vernárth [Vernár, Slovakia] into Zips County, arriving in Leutschau on the 10th which had already been vacated by Schlick's troops a week earlier.[87]

Although *Generalmajor* Götz and *Feldmarschall Lieutenant Graf* Schlick had both been instructed to do their best to establish communications and to exchange reports with one another, which seemed feasible at least by means of trusted individuals via Gömör and Torna

87 Yet again the imperial military machine malfunctions. The pincer movement of Jablonowsky and Schlick against Görgei fails because one of the pincers goes astray. Götz did not do as Jablonowsky had proposed and as the *Feldmarschall* had approved. Nobili's account does not tell us why; perhaps the poor condition of the secondary roads on the Briesen route was responsible. (After all, Görgei could likewise have cut the corner by that route but did not do so.)

counties as these were not occupied by the enemy, they did not manage to reach a mutual understanding that would have brought some harmony to their operations. On the 10th an officer from Schlick's corps reached Götz in Leutschau, but he had come via Krakau, so was very delayed, and had not brought anything in writing with him and could only give a very superficial indication of Schlick's situation there.

From the 8th, the day on which *Feldmarschall Lieutenant Graf* Schlick's letter of 1 February from Máad reached the *Feldmarschall*, the headquarters had been left without any news from that theatre of operations. Since the direct line of communications was interrupted by bands of rebels, attempts were made to send reports to Schlick by means of short cipher notes written in invisible ink and given to trusted individuals to deliver, but this was only partly successful. Late in the evening of 12 February the first verbal report from Schlick was finally received, brought by *Rittmeister* Zsedeny, and on the 16th once again, this time by *Major Prinz* Moriz Nassau. Both had dashed through Losoncz and Waitzen to Ofen, the former in civilian clothes and not without risk of being apprehended along the way by the evil-minded; but the latter had met a squadron of Civallart *uhlans* in Losoncz who had been pushed forward along the road from Waitzen as soon as word came of Schlick's approach, to establish communications. In general, all *Rittmeister* Zsedeny had to say was that *Feldmarschall Lieutenant Graf* Schlick's troops, being spread out from Leutschau to outside Tokay, had been under pressure from Görgei on one side and from Dembinsky's and Klapka's troops advancing through Miskolcz on the other, had concentrated at Kaschau, but so as not to be caught between two fires, from there they had turned through Moldau [Moldava nad Bodvou, Slovakia] toward Torna on the 9th, from where they would continue their march toward Rima-Szombath. Whether the enemy had followed Schlick in that direction the *Rittmeister* did not know, as he had left from Moldau, nor did he know anything about the enemy's strength. Many of the inhabitants of Kaschau and Eperies had tagged on to our forces to escape the rebels' revenge,[88] so the baggage train had grown to no fewer than 1,000 wagons, which moved with Brigade Parrot at the head of the column. How these would cross the Agtelek-Berg [Aggtelek Mountains, Hungary] remained to be seen, since the road was extremely steep and slick with ice.

After the enemy's combination of manoeuvres obliged *Feldmarschall Lieutenant Graf* Schlick to abandon Kaschau and with it Upper Hungary, the direction he chose for his retreat to Rima-Szombath was the strategically correct one, for it made it possible for him to link up with the main army. This linking up was also the goal that the *Feldmarschall* set himself immediately after learning of the evacuation of Kaschau and that, as we shall see later – despite the concerns raised against it in some quarters and the obstacles that arose – he was able to achieve in a timely way at the decisive moment.[89] Whether this junction was to happen at Losoncz or on the

88 This is an interesting comment. Although the Hungarian policy of Magyarisation since the 1830s had alienated the Slovaks and contributed to Slovak nationalists fighting on the imperial side, and although there must surely have been friction between supporters of the revolution and imperial sympathisers, I am not aware of any instances of this resulting in serious violence against the latter or of ethnic conflict between Slovaks and Hungarians. Leaving aside the ethnic conflict and atrocities in the Serbian and Romanian border areas, this was a relatively civil civil war. It is unclear whether these refugees were Slovaks or ethnic Germans (or, indeed, pro-imperial Hungarians).

89 After over a month of frantically sending forces hither and thither to stamp out fires and chase phantoms, at last the *Feldmarschall* is seeking concentration of force – one of the foremost principles of

Gyöngyös road was not yet decided, since that depended on whether the enemy's main body would move after *Feldmarschall Lieutenant Graf* Schlick or hurl itself through Miskolcz at Pesth.

So as to obtain information about this in good time, Brigade Colloredo was set on the march toward Gyöngyös on the 13th, from where it was to send out patrols along the Miskolcz road while also trying to establish communications with *Feldmarschall Lieutenant Graf* Schlick's corps via Pétervására. *Generalmajor* Wyss and his brigade (four battalions, four squadrons, nine guns) were directed through Waitzen toward Losoncz to serve as initial support for Schlick if necessary, but on the 16th were ordered to remain in Waitzen and just maintain communications with him by means of cavalry detachments; for it had been learned from *Major Prinz* Moriz Nassau that Schlick had reached Rima-Szombath without being pressed by the enemy, so had no need of support. So long as the enemy's direction of march was not definitely confirmed, detaching troops in any direction that might turn out to be the wrong one was generally to be avoided; all the more so as there was every chance that the enemy would seek to strike a decisive blow after successfully concentrating his combat forces.

To reinforce himself as much as possible against this eventuality, on the 14th the *Feldmarschall* issued the order to *Generalmajor* Dietrich that the four battalions, two squadrons and two half-batteries of his brigade which were supposed to arrive in Tolna on the 17th were then to move up the Danube to Pesth without delay, for which purpose the necessary steamers would be made available. The one battalion and one squadron that would not arrive in Szekszárd until the 19th and 20th were to march to Tolna on the 21st and await further orders there. Nothing more could be done for the time being. Any future plans had to be postponed until more detailed information about the enemy's strength and intentions had been obtained.

The following had been learned from *Major Prinz* Moriz Nassau as well as from later reports about what had transpired with *Feldmarschall Lieutenant Graf* Schlick's corps since 1 February. His troops were spread out between Tokay and Leutschau, as already mentioned. On the 29th *Major* Kiesewetter reported from the latter place that, 'according to a message from the county commissioner in Lucsivna [Lučivná, Slovakia] (on the border between Liptau [Liptó County, now around Liptov, Slovakia] and Zips Komitats) Görgei's corps was already in Rosenberg and Sz. Miklos (Liptau Komitat) on the 28th, and he is going to invade Zips County on the 30th with 10,000 men'. The above information was essentially repeated in two more reports, one after the other on 30 January, and finally on the 31st Kiesewetter reported that, 'the sentry posts at Hrilecz [Hnilec, Slovakia], Ramdorf[90] and Grenicz [Hranovnica, Slovakia] were attacked by the insurgents' advance guard between 3:00 and 4:00 a.m. in the morning and some of the sentries were captured'. At the end of this report it says, 'the garrison of Leutschau is expecting an attack by the enemy approaching in this direction'.

Feldmarschall Lieutenant Graf Schlick may have regarded these reports as exaggerated and therefore not paid any particular attention to them. However, on the 2nd *Generalmajor Graf* Deym was ordered to march from Kaschau to Margitfalva with a battalion of H.v. Parma infantry, three Ottochaner companies, a half-squadron of Kaiser Chevauxlegers and four guns, from where he was to move to Leutschau and link up with the four companies there. At the same time three Ottochaner companies and two guns were deployed to Eperies, where there were

war. *UK Defence Doctrine*, p.50. He has already recognised the futility of simply occupying major cities and realised he must aim at the destruction of the enemy's main combat forces, if he can only find them.

90 I have been unable to establish where this is.

Szirmay's not yet fully equipped *Freikorps*, two Nugent companies and two guns. The Nugent companies and the guns moved off to guard the Braniszko Pass. The Mazzuchelli battalion and Batterie Nr. 34 were brought up from Máad to replace the troops sent out from Kaschau.

Meanwhile *Major* Kiesewetter had deployed his four companies, half-squadron and half a rocket battery forward of Leutschau. When he learned that the enemy had already occupied Igló [Spišská Nová Ves, Slovakia], threatening his left flank, he decided to carry out a surprise attack during the night of 2/3 February. This was so successful at first that his troops advanced as far as Igló's market square and took seven guns. But the enemy soon brought such superior numbers into action that *Major* Kiesewetter not only had to relinquish all but one of the cannon he had taken, but also had to begin his retreat to Kirchdorf (Szepes-Baralya) [Spišské Podhradie, Slovakia] with the loss of two boxes of rocket ammunition, three carts and a launch tripod. He arrived in Kirchdorf at 9:00 a.m. on the 3rd without having been pursued by the enemy. But when strong enemy columns approached, he continued his retreat to the Braniszko Pass, where he met up with the two companies of his battalion that had been sent there from Eperies.

Generalmajor Graf Deym had arrived in Krompach [Krompachy, Slovakia] with his nine companies, half-squadron and four guns on the 3rd. He brought the above-mentioned episode to the attention of *Feldmarschall Lieutenant* Schulzig, asked him for a battalion of reinforcements, and stated that he would join up with *Major* Kiesewetter that day and then perhaps advance toward Leutschau again tomorrow. Schulzig decided not to act on this request yet but rather to wait for another report from Deym. On the 4th he informed *Feldmarschall Lieutenant Graf* Schlick about this, who was still in Máad, and concluded his report with the words, 'I await a second, clearer and more detailed report from *General Graf* Deym before I can commit to sending him any more troops, and I await further noble orders about this from Your Honour!'

Our troops' losses during the surprise attack at Igló came to four dead and more than twenty wounded, with *Lieutenant* Kalik being among the former, and the latter including *Hauptmann* Wereszczynski and *Oberlieutenant* Wurzinger of the Nugent infantry. The cavalry lost ten horses, the artillery eleven.

Army *Hauptmann Baron* Ripperda and *Oberlieutenant* Müller of the Kaiser Chevauxlegers displayed particular courage during the attack on Igló.

When *Feldmarschall Lieutenant Graf* Schlick learned of the events at Leutschau, he hurried from Máad to Kaschau during the night of 4/5. On the way there he ordered Brigade Parrot to march to Kaschau. This set off from its cantonments toward midday on the 5th, leaving the 12-pounder battery behind in Máad, and spent the night in Vicsoly and Boldogkő.

Brigades Pergen and Fiedler were likewise ordered to move to Kaschau. The former arrived in Kér on the 5th and then reached Kaschau late on the evening of the 6th after a forced march. Early the next day *Feldmarschall Lieutenant Graf* Schlick sent every available infantry unit from Kaschau toward Eperies, mostly on wagons, together with six squadrons and two batteries.[91] *Feldmarschall Lieutenant* Schulzig had already betaken himself there the day before. Brigade Fiedler was in Szantó on the 5th and arrived in Hidas-Némethi on the 6th.

Oberstlieutenant Baron Lauingen had left Miskolcz during the night of 5/6 and marched back to Forró.

91 The unusual expedient of transporting his infantry on wagons so that they can continue to move after a forced march illustrates Schlick's dynamism and singlemindedness in pursuit of a goal.

All these march plans designed to concentrate the corps in the upper region came too late! For as we shall see, Görgei had already forced the Braniszko Pass on the 5th, driven back the weak detachments deployed there, and occupied Eperies unopposed on the 6th. After leaving the three Ottochaner companies to occupy the Kluknó [Kluknava, Slovakia] Pass on the 4th, *Generalmajor Graf* Deym had successfully accomplished his junction with *Major* Kiesewetter at the Braniszko Pass, uniting 1,800 men altogether: two infantry battalions (the H.v. Parma-Landwehr and the Nugent), a half-squadron of Kaiser Chevauxlegers and six guns.

At 9:00 a.m. on the 5th, the enemy advanced to the attack 6,000-7,000 strong, led by Guyon who commanded Görgei's advance guard division. Our troops had deployed on the zigzag winding road. The enemy initially limited himself to a firefight along the front, while sending a strong column to outflank the left wing. *Generalmajor Graf* Deym detached a Nugent company under *Hauptmann* Adler and two H.v. Parma companies to the heights to the left of his position to oppose this turning movement. But despite their brave resistance, this detachment was driven back toward the pass itself by the tenfold more numerous enemy's ever more sweeping outflanking manoeuvre, which seriously threatened the position and the line of retreat of the troops posted there.

Although all the enemy's attempts at frontal assault had been repelled, *Generalmajor Graf* Deym recognised the absolute impossibility of holding out with his small number of troops against so many more enemy and decided to retreat, all the more so as the road he had to march back on was already under effective fire from the enemy who had advanced to the forested heights running along either side of the road. The division of H.v. Parma acting as rear guard had to endure murderous fire from the enemy pressing after it. Both its company commanders were wounded and 15 men killed. Once out of the pass and the forested area around it, *Rittmeister* Hain and three troops of Kaiser Chevauxlegers took over the rear guard and tried to hold off the pursuing hussars by charging them repeatedly. At 1:30 a.m. during the night of 5/6, after a march of almost 13 hours, the brigade reached Eperies in a very exhausted state, where it met up with the units under *Feldmarschall Lieutenant* Schulzig that had been rushed up from Kaschau. Meanwhile the three Ottochaner companies had repelled all the enemy's attacks on the Kluknó Pass and were later reinforced by a division of the Latour regiment, until they were likewise obliged to retreat because of the evacuation of the Braniszko Pass.

In the bloody battle at the Braniszko Pass, *Generalmajor Graf* Deym's force suffered very significant losses.[92] All his units had given the most glorious proof of their courage and devotion. In the H.v. Parma battalion alone, seven officers were killed or seriously wounded, in particular *Hauptmann* Schulcz and *Hauptmann Baron* Fürth, *Oberlieutenant* Calvas and *Lieutenants* Grimm and Novak.

The official report cites the especially distinguished conduct of the following: *Major* Kiesewetter and *Hauptmann* Adler of the Nugent infantry; *Major* Singer and *Oberlieutenant* Calvas of H.v. Parma; and *Lieutenant* Koupelka, *Brigade-Adjutant*, of the E.H. Wilhelm infantry. *Oberlieutenant* de Grazia, attached to the general staff, also merited mention. One company of *grenzers* and a troop of cavalry that *Feldmarschall Lieutenant* Schulzig had detached from Eperies to Kis-Szeben [Sabinov, Slovakia] on the 5th to observe the road from Käsmark through Lubló [Stará L'ubovňa,

92 'Very significant losses', yet Nobili does not report the actual numbers. This suggests a case of editorial sanitising by Nobili.

Slovakia] were completely cut off and were only able to escape across the Carpathians into Galicia, suffering unspeakable hardships in this bitter season of the year.

After *Generalmajor Graf* Deym's troops had successfully joined those already in Eperies, *Feldmarschall Lieutenant* Schulzig took over command there himself. Although the enemy had not made any moves toward the town during the course of the night, Schulzig thought that with such a small and totally exhausted force he could not hold Eperies against an attack by Görgei. He therefore vacated the town between 7:00 and 8:00 a.m. on the 6th and retreated to S. Peter [Petrovany, Slovakia], where he ran into the detachments pushed forward from Kaschau. He also met *Feldmarschall Lieutenant Graf* Schlick there, who had rushed up from Kaschau, and who now deployed all the troops in an advantageous position further back at Lemes [Lemešany, Slovakia], hoping to stop any further enemy advance toward Kaschau there. The enemy had occupied Eperies at 4:00 p.m. and only pushed a weak advance guard forward along the Kaschau road.

On the 7th the outposts of the units deployed at Lemes were only lightly harassed. On the 8th the troops were concentrated further back into the more advantageous position at Budamér [Budimír, Slovakia]. On this day *Oberstlieutenant Baron* Lauingen's detachment that had been in Miskolcz arrived in Kaschau.

Brigade Fiedler was in Enyiczke but was holding the crossings over the Hernad [Hornád] river at Hidas-Némethi and Zsadany [Hernádzsadány, now Ždaňa, Slovakia], the former with the Hartmann battalion, a half-squadron and two guns, the latter with a division of infantry. This was all the more necessary as after evacuating the right bank of the Theiss, the enemy corps under Klapka and Dembinsky had crossed the Theiss again further upriver and had already advanced to Forró, Novaj, Kér, Boldogkő, Vicsoly, etc., on the 8th. On the evening of the 8th the enemy drove the Hartmann battalion out of Hidas-Némethi and seized this important crossing over the Hernad.

Feldmarschall Lieutenant Graf Schlick's situation was now an extremely dangerous one, critical even! On one side (to the north) Görgei's forward troops were within gunshot of Budamér, barely 10 km from Kaschau; on the other (southern) side the combined enemy corps under Klapka and Dembinsky was holding Hidas-Némethi and the crossing over the Hernad there, just 15 km from Kaschau. Görgei, Klapka and Dembinsky were now so close to one another that the chance of attacking one of them in full force without running the risk of being seriously bothered from the rear by the others had already passed. In this difficult situation Schlick called a council of war at 9:00 p.m. on the evening of the 8th to discuss at length and assess what could and should be done. Three options were considered, namely: (1) whether to break out with the whole force through Eperies to Galicia, or (2) to hold out in Kaschau, or lastly (3) to retreat through Moldau and Torna to Tornallya [Tornal'a, Slovakia] and Rima-Szombath without waiting for a decisive attack, to seek to establish communications with the *Feldmarschall* and so strive to regain the advantages that had been given up. This last proposal was decided on unanimously as the most natural and the one most appropriate in the circumstances, but it was agreed that one last attempt should be made to provoke a battle with the advancing enemy to the south [i.e., Klapka and Dembinsky].[93] If we were to win this battle then Kaschau should not by

93 One suspects the aggressive Schlick found it hard to resist having one more go at the enemy. (Though as we see a paragraph later, he finally thought better of it.)

any means be abandoned, but in the converse case it was to be vacated during the night and the retreat to Moldau and Torna should be carried out under cover of darkness.

Meanwhile Brigade Parrot was directed to go immediately from Kaschau to Torna together with the baggage, the sick and wounded and the refugee families. *Feldmarschall Lieutenant* Schulzig stayed in Kaschau, but *Feldmarschall Lieutenant Graf* Schlick moved along the Miskolcz road at 11:00 p.m. to join Brigade Fiedler at Enyiczke with six squadrons and 12 guns. Having arrived there, upon more mature reflection Schlick aborted his planned attack on the enemy in Hidas-Némethi, so the march to Moldau was begun immediately via N. Ida [Vel'ká Ida, Slovakia].

Feldmarschall Lieutenant Schulzig, who had still not received any further orders by 10:00 a.m. on the 9th, but who had been informed of the approach of an enemy column by a cavalry orderly dispatched to Schlick at Hidas-Némethi who ran into enemy hussars, evacuated Kaschau and arrived in Moldau at midnight, where the troops posted on the Kaschauer Berg had also arrived after burning the bridge over the Hernad. Thus, with the sole exception of Brigade Parrot, which had already pushed on to Torna, the whole corps now stood united in and around Moldau. From there, as already noted, *Rittmeister* Zedeny was sent to Ofen with a verbal message for the *Feldmarschall.*

On the 10th Brigade Parrot moved to Szén [Szin, Hungary] while the other units of the corps had a rest day. On the 11th, *Generalmajor* Parrot reached Tornallya after a 13-hour march, in which however barely a third of the transport wagons could be got across the Agtelek mountains. The rest had to be brought forward along this steep and extremely difficult mountain road partly during the course of the following night, and some not until the next day, which was successfully accomplished thanks to the tireless activity and energy of *Generalmajor* Parrot. Brigade Fiedler marched to Josafö [Jósvafő, Hungary], Brigades Pergen and Kriegern to Petri [Szinpetri, Hungary] and Szén, and Brigade Deym to Szilas [Bódvaszilas, Hungary] as the rear guard.

On the 12th Brigade Parrot got to Batka [Bátka, Slovakia], Fiedler to Bunia [Rumince, Slovakia], and Pergen and Kriegern to Beje [Behynce, Slovakia] and Tornallya. Bringing up the rear, Brigade Deym occupied Agtelek but had left some detachments of infantry, a division of Sunstenau cuirassiers and half a horse artillery battery behind in Szén. These were surprised and attacked on the morning of the 13th, in which the cuirassiers suffered some losses, but then joined the rest of Brigade Deym at Petri.

Other units of the corps had a rest day on the 13th.

On the 14th Brigade Parrot moved to Keresztur, Brigade Fiedler to Rima-Szombath, and Pergen to Batka. Brigade Deym, which had handed over the role of rear guard to Brigade Kriegern, was to march to Füge [Figa, Slovakia] but turned about again since meanwhile Brigade Kriegern had come under attack from the enemy at Tornallya. This was a column under Dembinsky, reportedly of six battalions, eight squadrons and 20 guns, which had advanced through Putnok.

Feldmarschall Lieutenant Graf Schlick, who soon joined Brigade Kriegern when this happened and had also brought up Brigade Deym, immediately made appropriate dispositions. After a short skirmish action, nine horse artillery pieces were brought into action, soon followed by a 12-pounder battery and a rocket battery, which fired on the enemy to such effect that he hastily retreated, pursued by two divisions of cuirassiers. Our losses in this action comprised one dead and a few wounded. One gun was dismounted but made serviceable again after minor repair.

Major Wimmer of the Ottochaner battalion and *Oberlieutenant* Haug commanding the horse artillery battery particularly distinguished themselves.

In the evening Brigade Deym continued its march that had been interrupted by the action at Tornallya, while Brigade Kriegern spent the night in its position. On the 15th *Generalmajor* Parrot arrived in Losoncz. The rest of the corps camped echeloned along the road between there and Rima-Szombath, from where a detachment was pushed forward to observe the road coming from Miskolcz through Putnok to Pálfalva [Zagyvapálfalva, Hungary]. Communications with the main army had already been established by the squadron of Civallart *uhlans* sent from Waitzen through Balassa-Gyarmath toward Losoncz.

Thus, *Feldmarschall Lieutenant Graf* Schlick's corps reached safety. By occupying Rima-Szombath and Losoncz it had gained two places of great strategic importance, and its junction with the other parts of the army should be considered as having been secured as much by the awareness and energy of its leader as by the courage and endurance of its troops.[94]

From Rima-Szombath *Major Prinz* Moriz Nassau was sent to Ofen with verbal reports for the *Feldmarschall*, as mentioned earlier.

As already noted, Brigades Götz and Jablonowsky were in Leutschau on the 10th, scarcely two days' march from Schlick's corps encamped in Torna and thereabouts on that day. Nothing stood in the way of them linking up as these brigades had been instructed to do from the outset. It therefore seems that they learned too late about the true state of affairs and what had transpired around Kaschau, otherwise they certainly would not have continued their now completely isolated operation against Eperies and Kaschau.

In ignorance of the situation, as *Feldmarschall Graf* Schlick apparently had not asked them to link up with his corps via Rosenau, these brigades moved to Kirchdorf [Spišské Podhradie, Slovakia] on the 11th. From there they continued their march through the Braniszko Pass and reached Frics [Fričovce, Slovakia] and Berthotfalva [Bertotovce, Slovakia] on the 13th, while *Oberst* Pott of the general staff was detached toward Margitfalva with a flanking column. This ran into the enemy there, but drove him out of his position with significant loss after several hours' fighting. However, *Generalmajor* Götz was worried that the enemy would advance into the Hernad valley with reinforcements from Kaschau and threaten his line of retreat. He therefore retreated back through the Braniszko Pass to Kirchdorf during the night of 13/14 January. He still had not been able to learn anything about the location of Schlick's corps. In Kirchdorf *Feldmarschall Lieutenant* Ramberg arrived (together with the squadron of Kress Chevauxlegers that he had brought with him as his escort from the corps besieging Komorn) and took over command of both brigades. In the report he then sent to the *Feldmarschall*, he mentioned that *Feldmarschall Lieutenant* Vogel was on his way from Galicia via Bartfeld with 19 companies, two squadrons and a half-battery, and that he intended to have Vogel join him while he advanced further toward Eperies via Polocsa [Plaveč, Slovakia]. Ramberg stayed in Kirchdorf from the 14th to the 19th, since he had received information that Eperies and Kaschau were held by 45,000 men with 130 guns, of which 6,000-7,000 men and 20 guns were holding the impregnable mountain pass at Margitfalva, etc. On the 19th, the following letter from the *Feldmarschall* written in code and dated the 15th was delivered to him, which imparted

94 I endorse this verdict.

to him what had been learned from *Rittmeister* Zsedeny about the situation in Upper Hungary at that time:

> Schlick has vacated Eperies and Kaschau and concentrated at Torna on the 10th without having fought an action. He is facing superior enemy combat forces under Klapka and Dembinsky, possibly also some detachments of Görgei's. Schlick intends to retreat toward Rima-Szombath if necessary. No more detailed information is available. It is incomprehensible that neither you nor Schlick have managed to obtain information about each other's positions! As far as what you should do now is concerned, it absolutely cannot be decided from here. Perhaps you could still link up with Schlick, perhaps you could begin to retreat through Zips County, or lastly, perhaps you could base your retreat upon Galicia if forced to do so, which however would be most unfortunate.[95]

Since those in Ofen still did not know whether *Feldmarschall Lieutenant* Ramberg had joined his new division, this letter was addressed to *Generalmajor* Götz, but he handed it over on the 19th to the aforesaid *Feldmarschall Lieutenant* who had turned up in the meantime. When *Generalmajor* Götz informed the *Feldmarschall* of this, he wrote 'that it had not been my intention to move to Kaschau, since this could no longer be of any advantage to *Feldmarschall Lieutenant Graf* Schlick. Rather, I had intended to operate toward Schlick via Rosenau on the 14th without delay. However, *Feldmarschall Lieutenant* Ramberg has taken over command and has found occupying Kaschau to be more appropriate in the circumstances.'

Feldmarschall Lieutenant Ramberg, who learned at 1:00 p.m. on the 19th that the Margitfalva Pass was no longer held by the enemy, moved to Margitfalva, Jekelfalva [Jaklovce, Slovakia] and Hámor [Košické Hámré, Slovakia] on the 20th, and to Kaschau on the 21st, which had already been vacated by the enemy main body some days earlier anyway.

In his report about the occupation of Kaschau *Feldmarschall Lieutenant* Ramberg sought to demonstrate the need to reinforce him with a few batteries, squadrons and guns. With his seven battalions, three and a half squadrons and 21 guns he felt he was too weak to pursue the enemy who was now concentrating at Miskolcz, all the more so as he could not count on *Feldmarschall Lieutenant Graf* Schlick's cooperation. He had had to leave the Slovakian *Freikorps*, which had grown to 19 companies of 90 men each under its capable and intelligent leaders Stur and Blaudek, in Zips County to maintain security in that territory and ensure food supplies got through. He asked that the *Feldmarschall* should order *Feldmarschall Lieutenant* Vogel and his 19 companies, two squadrons and three guns to join him. But Vogel had been instructed by *Feldmarschall Lieutenant Baron* Hammerstein to act to protect the Galician border rather than in any active combined operation.

Even in the best possible case, *Feldmarschall Lieutenant* Ramberg's desire to bring *Feldmarschall Lieutenant* Vogel into play could not be realised for 14 days, since it would take almost that long for his request to reach the *Feldmarschall* in Ofen and for the appropriate orders to be issued from there to Galicia. This assistance was therefore not to be relied upon.

We now leave *Feldmarschall Lieutenant* Ramberg in Kaschau, where he remained until the 29th, and return again to the main army's operations.

95 A rare case of the *Feldmarschall* letting some of his frustration leak out into his written correspondence.

The Lead-up to Kápolna: Coordinating with Schlick, 15-24 February 1849

Generalmajor Fürst Colloredo and his brigade had arrived on Gyöngyös on the 15th and immediately established communications with *Feldmarschall Lieutenant Graf* Schlick via Pétervására, patrolled toward Kápolna and Poroszló, and generally been very active, particularly in obtaining information.

On the 16th the important news that the fortress of Eszek had fallen on the 13th arrived from *Feldzeugmeister Graf* Nugent. As a result of the surrender agreement, the 4,500 men of the garrison laid down their arms on the glacis at 9:00 a.m. on the 14th. Nugent gave the main credit for the fall of Eszek to *Generalmajor* Trebersburg, commander of the besieging force. While Nugent may indeed have deviated from the principle of 'no negotiation with rebels', yet the advantages gained from possession of the fortress of Eszek were so significant and lasting that his action seemed not only fully justified but deserving of the highest praise.

On the 18th a letter dated the 16th arrived from *Feldmarschall Lieutenant Graf* Schlick in Rima-Szombath, in which he indicated that he would send the Kaschau refugees, the sick and Szirmay's *Freikorps* to Waitzen, and use this rest period to arrange supplies and overhaul equipment. He also offered to transfer a 6-pounder battery to Brigade Colloredo, since it seemed to him that Colloredo had too little artillery. At the end of this report he says:

> Reconnaissance reports have just brought me provisional information that Dembinsky is on the march back to Miskolcz with two brigades and 20 guns, along with numerous swarms of hussars, and will arrive there this evening. Even though Klapka is there too and the junction of these two rebel leaders will mean Miskolcz is strongly held, and endowed with more numerous artillery in particular, still a combined attack by my corps and Brigade Colloredo on a specified day, myself from Sz. Peter [Sajószentpéter, Hungary] and Brigade Colloredo from Harsány (thus from Gyöngyös via Kápolna, Mezö-Kövesd, etc.), could not fail to produce a favourable result. I am in a position to be standing in front of Miskolcz with two brigades ready to attack at 10:00 a.m. on the fourth day from the moment when I receive the order to do so. In accordance with this, *General Fürst* Colloredo could receive an order from Your Highness to carry out a simultaneous attack at the designated hour on perhaps the 22nd or 23rd. In any case, I will remain halted awaiting your further noble orders until then.

Feldmarschall Lieutenant Graf Schlick had quite appropriately detached Brigade Parrot to Petervásara, thereby completely securing communications with the Gyöngyös road. In the expectation that the *Feldmarschall* would approve the proposed expedition against Miskolcz, he also informed the above-mentioned general about it, and discussed with him the possibility of a combined attack on Kaschau.

The *Feldmarschall* had taken the decision now to concentrate the army at the decisive point, as already mentioned. Also, given his recent experiences he was very disinclined to let detached forces carry out extended, isolated, independent operations. He therefore did not agree with this plan. Besides, he had received information from Schlick and from Colloredo that Miskolcz, Mezö-Kövesd and even Erlau were held by strong enemy detachments, so an advance by the combined enemy combat forces along the Gyöngyös road toward Pesth was highly likely. Accordingly he sent the following letter to Schlick on the 18th:

> Given the way the enemy keeps manoeuvring around erratically, as well as the fact that he quickly learns about our every move from his countless spies, I regard any operation combining several marches starting from different places as fruitless, as has been sufficiently demonstrated in the 14 days just gone. For this reason I feel I cannot agree to Your Honour's proposal to advance via Sz. Petri against Miskolcz so as to bring Klapka's corps that is supposed to be in the vicinity of Erlau between your column and Brigade Colloredo's position; all the less so as the enemy would remain free to gain the left bank of the Theiss via Poroszló and thus evade any clash with superior combat forces. Since my intention now is to concentrate my forces as much as possible so as to strike a decisive blow with my force united, Your Honour is hereby instructed to leave a rear guard to screen and protect your march and to move immediately and with the utmost haste via Petervásara to Gyöngyös.[96]

Brigade Colloredo, whose position in Gyöngyös seemed too exposed, was ordered to march back to Hatvan on the 18th. Likewise the division of Max Auersperg cuirassiers under *Major Graf* Coudenhove that had been pushed out on patrol was to retreat from Kápolna to Gyöngyös, for given the recently received messages about significant enemy detachments gathering in the area of Erlau, it was considered to be too far forward and at risk. This concern was only too well founded, for at 5:30 a.m. on the 18th this division was surprised by 11 troops of hussars, an infantry detachment that came up on wagons and three guns, led by the rebel *Oberst* Aristid Dessöffy [Arisztid Dessewffy]. The division was billeted in the great Carolian manor house [the Grassalkovich-Károlyi Kastély] in Kompólt. The horses stayed saddled up all night. A half-squadron manned the pickets. The surprise attack was favoured by treachery and a very stormy wind that made it almost impossible to hear in the darkness. The wing deployed as pickets fought as bravely as lions with total self-sacrifice, gaining time for the division to bridle the horses and lead some of them out of the lower stalls, during which some confusion understandably arose. Nevertheless, the officers, especially the brave *Rittmeister Baron* Scheibler, managed by their inspirational example not only to make a fight of it, but actually to go on the attack themselves. By this determined action the two *Rittmeisters* Fluk and *Baron* Reitzenstein, who were both already wounded and surrounded and about to be taken prisoner, were freed again, and time was gained for others to mount up. The wing on picket duty certainly suffered significant losses, since apart from *Rittmeister* Fluk who was seriously wounded by several blows to the head, *Oberlieutenant* Leidesdorf, three corporals and 16 men were killed or seriously wounded. But the devoted death-defying urge to protect their comrades until they had gained time to prepare for battle did not waver for a moment in the breasts of these brave men. It was thanks only to this that the division was able to muster and form up. The cuirassiers now charged at the enemy with the utmost determination and laid into him heartily. Many hussars were cut down, and one man and nine saddled horses captured. The cuirassier division finally managed to disengage entirely and moved at a walk without enemy pursuit as far as the bridge at Bál-Püspöky [Balpüspöki puszta, a farm north of Detk on the road from Kápolna to Markaz, Hungary], from where

96 Here we see Schlick's 'target fixation', his urge to attack the enemy in front of him regardless of the bigger picture, competing with Windisch-Grätz's efforts to impose coherence at the operational level. As we shall see below, Schlick could not resist charging off in his own chosen direction, contrary to the *Feldmarschall*'s wishes.

they sent a message about what had happened and stayed there until the order arrived to retreat through Gyöngyös to Hatvan. Their total losses in dead, wounded and prisoners were: one *Rittmeister*, one *Oberlieutenant*, one *Oberarzt*, one *Wachtmeister*, six *Korporals*, 25 *Kürassiers*, 17 horses. *Oberlieutenant* Leidesdorf was left for dead, fell into captivity, but escaped with his life, although he lost his sight to a sabre cut.

Since detachments had frequently been surprised by the enemy lately – in particular a picket of an officer and 26 men of the Kaiser dragoons near Szolnok on 9 February, and a patrol of 12 cuirassiers near Czibakháza on the 14th, etc. – the *Feldmarschall* found himself obliged to issue specific instructions to the troops and their generals about this, and about the course of the war in general, on the 18th.

On the 19th *Generalmajor Fürst* Colloredo reported from Hatvan that according to reports just received, very strong bodies of troops were concentrating at Kápolna and Kompólt which might perhaps yet march to Arok-Szállás that day, and that some might already be there. He said he was sending a strong patrol in the latter direction to obtain more definite information. If this should be confirmed, then he would retreat to Bágh [Bag, Hungary] so as to be closer to the support of the troops deployed behind him.

It was hard to assess how accurate this news was, but this much seemed certain, that the enemy was concentrating on the Gyöngyös road and was planning something there. The *Feldmarschall* therefore did not delay for a moment in echeloning all the available troops along the road between Hatvan and Pesth. Accordingly, Brigade Colloredo was authorised to retreat to the more advantageous position at Bágh, while on the other hand Brigade Wyss was pushed forward to Gödöllő, and Brigade Dietrich – which had just arrived up the Danube in Pesth as ordered with only three and a half battalions, one squadron and two half-batteries – moved forward to Kerepes, as did the Korps-Artillerie-Reserve. *Feldmarschall Lieutenant Baron* Csorich took over command of these units for the time being. If the enemy were to advance any further, Csorich was to take position at Gödöllő, so the terrain there was to be reconnoitred carefully and all baggage trains left behind.

The following edict was issued to *Feldmarschall Graf* Schlick on the 19th:

> According to reports just received, fairly substantial enemy combat forces are on the march toward Gyöngyös. Today Brigade Colloredo has retreated to Hatvan without being pressed by the enemy. It is under orders to fall back on Gödöllő if attacked by superior numbers of enemy, to where at the same time I have deployed the necessary troops to receive it. In these circumstances Your Honour will appreciate how important it is that you should execute your march to Gyöngyös with the utmost possible speed, since you may thereby be able to threaten the rear of any enemy advancing toward Gödöllő. I am therefore relying on Your Honour to continue your march without pause in the direction already mentioned in my orders yesterday. It also goes without saying that upon your arrival in Gyöngyös you will choose the direction of march that leads you directly to the enemy.

However, that same day a letter sent by *Feldmarschall Lieutenant Graf* Schlick from Putnok at 8:00 p.m. on the 19th arrived in which he indicated that he had resumed the offensive once more with Brigades Deym, Kriegern and Pergen and advanced to Putnok. He had also established communications with *Generalmajor Fürst* Colloredo who, reinforced by Brigade Parrot at

Petervásara, would number seven battalions, seven squadrons and 15 guns, and would therefore be in a position to cross swords even with a significantly more numerous enemy. Concerning the offensive operations planned and already begun, he stated:

> Although I have already detached one brigade from my corps and sent it to support *General Fürst* Colloredo as required by the general aim, I have actually decided not to limit myself to that but intend to strike a decisive blow if possible. Part of the enemy main body is in Kaschau, Eperies and Zips County under Görgei, part of it toward Mezö-Kövezd. There are therefore only two possible options: either to stay here quietly until Colloredo has beaten the enemy or driven him back toward Miskolcz, so as then to attack together, in which case I would be superfluous in that the enemy Colloredo had beaten alone could also be pursued by him alone; or else I push forward to Miskolcz with my four brigades compactly together, don't worry about Görgei for the moment, and take the enemy in rear, who could then no longer evade and thus a decisive battle would be brought about. Since I regard the latter option as the best one, I will set off from here the day after tomorrow, abandoning my base of operations and my line of communications for the moment, and march after the enemy via Miskolcz. At the same time *General Fürst* Colloredo will be made aware of my plan and advised to avoid a decisive battle until I arrive in the enemy's rear. While I am convinced that the Mining Towns are not threatened by the enemy for now anyway, they would be completely protected if Your Highness were to order *Generalmajor* Wyss to advance to Rima-Szombath and either take position there or perhaps advance as far as Rosenau, where he could easily establish communications with *Generalmajors* Jablonowsky or Götz, who could then continue toward Ofen again.

The *Feldmarschall*'s two edicts of the 18th and 19th, which ordered *Feldmarschall Lieutenant Graf* Schlick to march rapidly to Gyöngyös, had still not been received by Schlick when he began his march to Putnok. But this advance was not at all consistent with his previous letter of the 18th, which closed by saying: 'In any case, I will remain halted awaiting your further noble orders until then.' At the very least the march to Putnok delayed the intended junction with his corps, as well as the new direct line of march to Petervásara being terribly tiring for the troops because of the extremely bad mountain roads. However, some reassurance was to be found in that Schlick mentioned that he 'intended to halt in Putnok until the day after tomorrow (the 21st)', hence the order to march to Gyöngyös would surely reach him there.[97]

Generalmajor Fürst Colloredo, informed of Schlick's plan, did not want to agree to advance on Mezö-Kövesd before being authorised to do so by the *Feldmarschall*. The latter had apprised him of the true state of affairs on the 20th by the following order:

> In reply to Your Highness's report today, you should remain in your present position until further notice, since I absolutely do not intend an offensive manoeuvre toward Gyöngyös for the moment. *Feldmarschall Graf* Schlick is already aware of your change

97 Here, Schlick's unreliability – not doing what he was told, nor even what he himself said he would do – obviously makes it difficult for the *Feldmarschall* to implement his own plans.

of position and has been instructed to refrain from any independent, isolated operation. He has been sent an order to advance toward Gyöngyös immediately via Petervásara. He may already be on the march to there now. I await details of his plans for the march, and I will inform Your Highness as soon as I know what day he will arrive.

In any case he has been told to carry out his march with the utmost speed. In the circumstances you will appreciate that it is all the more important to me not to deter the enemy from any advance he may intend against Gyöngyös, since this will expose his flank and rear all the more to Schlick's column.

Feldmarschall Graf Schlick had received the *Feldmarschall*'s order of the 18th in Putnok on the 20th. He reported that although this order contradicted the plan he had submitted the previous evening he would begin the march to Petervásara immediately, his advance guard would arrive there on the 23rd, he would definitely be concentrated at Erlau on the 26th, and would be available for any mission on the 27th. Schlick also seems not to have been entirely in agreement with the *Feldmarschall*'s efforts to unite the army on the Gyöngyös road, at least as indicated by the following excerpt from his report:

In conclusion, I cannot restrain myself from respectfully expressing my view. This is that as soon as the enemy, who knows everything and hears everything, learns of my move toward Petervásara and thus that the whole area between Miskolcz and Waitzen up as far as the Mining Towns and Rosenau is denuded of imperial troops, he will exploit this by leaping into the mountains he likes so well. He will thereby escape from the noose once more to threaten the Mining Towns, take *Generals* Götz and Jablonowsky in the rear, support Görgei's operations, and create renewed unrest in the territory that has already been subjugated and pacified.

Now that the *Feldmarschall* thought he could definitely rely on linking up soon with Schlick's corps, he did not delay a moment longer to make the necessary dispositions for advancing on the offensive.

Generalmajor Fürst Colloredo reported that it was not confirmed whether the enemy held Árok-Szállás [Jászárokszállás, Hungary] or Gyöngyös. Instead, all reports agreed that the enemy was concentrated in Mezö-Kövesd, with Erlau and Kápolna being only weakly held. His total strength at the time was wrongly given as no more than 10,000-12,000 men, since Görgei was thought to still be at Kaschau.

On the basis of this information, during the night of the 21st the order was issued to *Feldmarschall Graf* Schlick to effect a junction with the corps moving out from Pesth, Gödöllő, etc., by the best and most direct route from Petervásara via Erlau and Kápolna. This order stated:

As the enemy main body is at Mezö-Kövesd, rather than advancing on the road through Gyöngyös as I had thought and as I indicated in my message of the 18th, it is entirely appropriate that Your Honour should direct your march from Petervásara through Erlau. If you wish to call in Brigade Parrot to you at Petervásara you are free to do so, since the column moving out from this side is strong enough not to need his support. Upon your arrival in Erlau you should attempt to establish communications with the column from here toward Kápolna, which I will also try to do from this side. Perhaps

> we will be able work out along the way how to execute our subsequent advance to the attack on the 27th. If the enemy accepts battle at Mezö-Kövesd, I intend to attack him decisively with all my might. He may retreat toward either Poroszló or Miskolcz. In the former case it will be up to me to drive him away from his line of retreat; in the latter, it will fall to Your Honour to do so. Should the enemy avoid a fight by retreating early, then according to circumstances I will either use the opportunity to destroy the bridge at Poroszló, or cross there myself, or lastly choose some other course appropriate to the situation. From the plans for the march Your Honour will see where my headquarters will be each day, and thus send your reports to me there. Should Your Honour learn in Petervásara that the enemy has definitely advanced from Mezö-Kövesd toward Pesth meanwhile, you will continue your march through Gyöngyös.

On the 22nd the *Feldmarschall* received a letter from Schlick dated the 21st from Rima-Szecs [Rimavská Seč, Slovakia], whose content was of great interest, and partly modified the above dispositions. Specifically, *Feldmarschall Lieutenant Graf* Schlick reported that he would arrive in Petervásara on the 23rd; and furthermore that according to the information he had received, the enemy intended to strike a decisive blow with his combat forces united, to which end Görgey's corps was to move to Forró on the 20th and Miskolcz on the 21st. From this it was clear that there were no longer just 10,000-12,000 enemy at Mezö-Kövesd to deal with, as originally thought; rather, it was likely that the advance would run into the enemy's combined forces likewise advancing on the offensive. Consequently, the *Feldmarschall* could no longer seek to link up with Schlick via the more distant point of Erlau; instead, it had to happen by the most direct route – namely via Gyöngyös. The *Feldmarschall* ordered Schlick to do this, adding a note that, if the news of Görgey's march should be confirmed, he [Görgey] could arrive in Gyöngyös on the 25th, thus on the same day as the corps moving out from Pesth. This letter was sent to *Generalmajor Fürst* Colloredo to ensure it was presented to Schlick.

The dispositions and unit organisations issued for the march were as follows: after leaving a rear guard in Rima-Szombath that would be supported or relieved by two Paumgarten companies and a squadron of Civallart *uhlans* setting off at the same time from Waitzen via Losoncz, Schlick's corps was to arrive in Gyöngyös on the 26th at the latest. This seemed easily achievable given that Schlick would reach Petervásara on the 23rd.

II. Armeekorps under *Feldmarschall Lieutenant Graf* Wrbna moving out from Pesth and its environs comprised the following units:

Division *Feldmarschall Lieutenant Baron* Csorich

Brigade *Generalmajor* Wyss
2. Jäger-Bataillon
1. Bataillon Schönhals
3. Bataillon Fürstenwärther
1. Landwehr-Bataillon E.H. Baden
One squadron of Kress-Chevauxlegers (Oberst 2.)
Kavallerie-Batterie Nr. 2
Half of Raketen-Batterie Nr. 15

Brigade *Generalmajor Fürst* Colloredo
6. Jäger-Bataillon (four companies)
1. and 2. Bataillon E.H. Stefan
1. Landwehr-Bataillon Paumgarten (four companies)
One squadron of Kress-Chevauxlegers (Oberstlieutenant 2.)
Sechspfündige Batterie Nr. 8
Half of Raketen-Batterie Nr. 15

Divisions-Artillerie-Reserve
Zwölfpfündige Batterie Nr. 3
Sechspfündige Batterie Nr. 10
Sechspfündige Batterie Nr. 11

Division *Feldmarschall Lieutenant Fürst* Edmund Schwarzenberg

Brigade *Generalmajor* Dietrich
2. Bataillon Wimpfen (four companies)
One composite Bataillon Eckert (two Hess companies, two Prohaska companies)
4. Bataillon Warasdiner-Kreutzer Grenzer (four companies)
4. Bataillon, 2. Banal (three companies)
One and a half batteries

Brigade *Generalmajor* Schütte
Grenadier-Bataillon Rattay
Grenadier-Bataillon Richter
One battery

Kavallerie-Brigade *Generalmajor Graf* Bellegarde
Four squadrons of Max Auersperg Kürassiere
Five squadrons of Civallart-Uhlanen
Two squadrons of E.H. Johann Dragoner
Kavallerie-Batterie Nr. 4
(Out of these, the 1. Majors-Division of the Civallart-Uhlanen was attached to Brigade Wyss, and the dragoons to headquarters.)

Divisions-Artillerie-Reserve
One and a half batteries

Artillerie-Haupt-Reserve

Six batteries

Altogether 13 and a half battalions, 13 squadrons, 102 artillery pieces.

The march out from the units' various cantonments was to begin on the 23rd and to be executed so that II. Korps arrived echeloned in Kerepes, Gödöllő and Bágh that day, then in Hatvan and Hort on the 24th. On the 25th Division Csorich, Grenadier-Brigade Schütte and the artillery reserves were to move to Gyöngyös and then to Kápolna on the 26th, while in parallel *Feldmarschall Lieutenant Fürst* Edmund Schwarzenberg was to move with Brigades Dietrich and Bellegarde along the road to Arok-Szállás on the 25th and to Kál on the 26th. Thus, on that day the corps would be concentrated again in an area scarcely 3 km across.

The Munizions-Reserve was ordered to follow at an interval of one day's march, and the bridging trains two days behind.

The *Feldmarschall* and his headquarters were to attach themselves to Division Csorich.

General Liebler remained in Ofen-Pesth with a garrison of Grenadier-Bataillon Martini, Grenadier-Bataillon Schneider, 1. Bataillon Ceccopieri and one battery, which were to be joined by 1. Bataillon Wimpffen and a squadron of E.H. Johann dragoons from Brigade Dietrich that had stayed behind in Tólna. Meanwhile *Generalmajor* Hentzi took over the district command from *Feldmarschall Lieutenant Graf* Wrbna. Gran was held by Grenadier-Bataillon Strastil, two companies of which were however taken to reinforce the Ofen garrison. Szirmay's *Freikorps* stayed garrisoning Waitzen.

Appropriate orders for all these arrangements were issued on the 22nd, as well as informing the detached army formations. In particular, *Generalmajor* Todorovich was made aware of Brigade Dietrich's change of mission, and of the temporary abandonment of the expedition to Szegedin. *Feldmarschall Lieutenant* Ramberg was likewise informed of the impending offensive operation and instructed to advance toward Miskolcz, the documents concerning this being couriered by *Oberlieutenant* Usz of the Palatinal hussars on the 23rd.

The necessary notification was also sent to *Feldzeugmeister Graf* Nugent. On the 20th he had been requested to send 3,000-4,000 men to tighten the siege of Komorn. Now on the 23rd and 25th he was asked to hold these troops ready in Batina from where they were to be moved to Pesth by water, so they could join the army in the field if needed. But meanwhile word was received that the boats sent downstream had been fired on by artillery in the area of Kalocsa. Accordingly, *Oberst* Zülich, who had been left in Tólna with one Wimpffen battalion, was sent the order to cross to Kalocsa, punish the village, capture the guns and enable safe transport by water again; but he felt he was too weak to do this. However, on the 24th he reported that the enemy had already left Kalocsa and retreated to Szegedin.

The Lead-up to Kápolna: Covering the Right Flank, 15-24 February 1849

A cavalry force was detached through Mende and Jasz-Berény to cover the right flank of the army advancing along the Gyöngyös road. Also, a brigade formed out of 12 companies, four squadrons and two batteries from I. Armeekorps and placed under command of the *Banus*'s chief of staff, *Generalmajor* Zeisberg, was to move out of its cantonments around Czegléd via Tapio-Szele [Tápiószele, Hungary] and Jasz-Berény with the same mission. Grenadier-Bataillon Bitermann was assigned to the *Banus* to replace these troops taken from I. Armeekorps.

The *Banus*'s mission was still to guard the Theiss crossings around Szolnok. The units under his command were now Infanterie-Brigades Gramont, Karger and Rastic (formerly Neustädter, who had meanwhile been given another assignment in Croatia) and finally Kavallerie-Brigade

Ottinger. Altogether this was nine battalions, 16 squadrons of heavy cavalry, six squadrons of Banderial hussars and 48 artillery pieces.

The *Feldmarschall*'s written orders, by means of which he informed the *Banus* of all the arrangements being made as well as of the need for some of his own troops deployed on the Szolnok line to cooperate with the advance on Gyöngyös, said: 'Much as I recognise the importance of Szolnok and of the Theiss crossings there in general, at the present time when such a paramount decisive moment is imminent elsewhere I regard them as secondary.' As the *Banus* was further required to guard the Theiss crossings with redoubled vigilance during the impending advance, the *Feldmarschall* also gave him command over Brigade Palffy with its four battalions, two squadrons and one and a half batteries, which was about to arrive up the Danube in Pesth from *Feldzeugmeister Graf* Nugent's corps.[98] Finally he stated, 'unfortunately the state of affairs obliges me to give Your Excellency a very important but nevertheless defensive sphere of operations for the moment. However, I do anticipate putting Your Excellency in a position to be able to operate forcefully on the offensive, which hopefully will happen soon.'

Many reports had been coming in from the Szolnok area lately about enemy combat forces mustering in that region, as well as of danger threatening and the like. On the 15th *Oberstlieutenant* Stauffer of the Hardegg cuirassiers, detached in Kecskemét, reported that an enemy corps of 6,000 men with 24 guns under *General* Vecsey had crossed to the right bank of the Theiss at Csongrád and pushed its outposts a couple of kilometres toward Kecskemét. He suspected that the enemy would turn toward Szegedin to the aid of the weak garrison there that was under pressure from *Generalmajor* Todorovich. *Oberlieutenant Graf* Hompesch who had been sent out with a patrol reported that he had met enemy hussars and guns outside Alpár [Tiszaalpár, Hungary].

Upon this news the *Banus* brought Brigade Rastic forward from Pesth to Czegléd, and asked the *Feldmarschall* to consider whether it might not be advisable to call back Brigade Wyss from Waitzen to Pesth. On the 19th the *Banus* highlighted a report from *Generalmajor* Gramont at Szolnok in which he stated that on the 18th the enemy had moved with two battalions, two hussar divisions and a battery against the Szolnok bridgehead, which had only just been completed on the 17th, but that he was soon forced to retreat again by the well-aimed fire directed against him. According to some travellers' statements the garrison of Szegedin had been reinforced with two battalions of Infanterie-Regiment Nr. 39 and a division of Husaren-Regiment Nr. 3. It had not been possible to establish how strong the enemy was in Csongrád and Alpár. Quarters for large bodies of troops had been arranged in Felegyháza. The mood in Kecskemét and N. Körös was described as very hostile. Finally, heavy artillery was requested to arm the Szolnok bridgehead.

On the 21st and 22nd *Generalmajor* Gramont reported that according to reliable information, the enemy would carry out an attack on Szolnok that day from three sides: from Csibakháza; directly against the bridgehead; and lastly through Püspöki [Tiszapüspöki, Hungary] and Szajol, to where 30 wagons carrying bridging material had already moved. The enemy was said to have 28 guns. When Gramont brought this to the *Banus*'s attention, he requested support urgently. On the other hand, it was reported that the villages of Szentes and Száss [presumably

98 Footnote in the original: '*2. Ottochaner Feld-Bataillon, Szluiner komponirtes Bataillon Mirkovic (four companies), four Hohenlohe companies, 1. Bataillon Wimpffen (four companies), Fussbatterie Nr. 1, two rocket launch stands, two squadrons E.H. Johann dragoons.'

Tiszasas, Hungary] were strongly held by the enemy who had 16 cannon there, and that *General* Vecsey and his troops had moved up to Sz. Miklós [presumably Törökszentmiklós, Hungary], etc. Finally on the 23rd the *Banus* wrote that according to unanimous statements from all informants, the enemy facing our right wing was being significantly reinforced.

> It is after all very possible that the enemy, who always quickly gets accurate information about everything, may exploit the fact that all our available combat forces are advancing along the Kaschau (Gyöngyös) road, and that consequently he may burst forth against our right flank. I therefore feel I must submit it to the discretion of Your Highness's noble judgement as to whether these considerations might not seem to dictate pushing forward one brigade to Alberti as a reserve against any vicissitude.[99]

The *Feldmarschall*, whose accurate military insight had recognised that a battle was going to happen in the Gyöngyös area that could perhaps decide the fate of the campaign, did not let these concerns divert him from the decision he had already taken to concentrate the army in that area. Far from wanting to take a brigade from the already meagre combat forces designated for the offensive and echeloning it on the Szolnok line, as we have seen, he had actually taken a brigade from the Szolnok line under *Generalmajor* Zeisberg to secure his right flank.[100] He had judged the situation correctly, and in particular was right to attribute only secondary significance to Szolnok for the moment, as will soon become clear.

Nevertheless, in order to make the *Banus*'s position as secure as possible, he told him it was necessary to destroy the enemy-held bridge at Czibakháza, since the main threat to Szolnok was from there. This operation was to take place on the 25th or 26th, because this would create a diversion to the benefit of the army in the process of advancing through Gyöngyös at that time.

From an order of battle dated 23rd February from Török-Sz. Miklós and discovered after the end of the campaign, the strength of the enemy forces deployed opposite Szolnok and Czibakháza under Vecsey,[101] Repásy,[102] Lenkey,[103]

99 The *Banus* seems to have consistently exaggerated enemy threats. Perhaps he cried wolf too often, causing Windisch-Grätz to discount the threat he reported after the action at Tapio-Bicske leading up to the battle of Isaszeg. His alarmism and constant requests for more troops provide a nice counterpoint to Schlick's excessively confident boldness.

100 The *Feldmarschall*'s decision here is commendable. Unfortunately, Zeisberg rather let him down at Kápolna.

101 Károly Vécsey (1803-49), a major in Husaren-Regiment Nr. 2, fought against Serbian insurgents in 1848. In January 1849 he took over command of the Bácska corps from Esterházy when the latter refused to fight against imperial troops. He fell out with General Damjanich at the battle of Szolnok in March 1849; besieged Arad and Temesvár; and surrendered to the Russians at Borosjenő in August 1849. He was sentenced to death and executed at Arad. Bona, *Tābornokok.*

102 Mihály Répásy (1800-49) was a major in Husaren-Regiment Nr. 6 who fought at Pákozd and Schwechat in 1848. Then as Chief Inspector of Cavalry he was responsible for refitting the existing hussar regiments and establishing the new ones (13th to 18th). He formed a new corps in Budapest and served as corps and army commander. In March he handed over his field command to serve in the war ministry. He died of cholera in Szeged on 29 July 1849. Bona, *Tābornokok.*

103 Károly Lenkey (1803-74) was a former captain in Husaren-Regiment Nr. 2. In June 1848 he was a major in the national guard and fought in the south. In December he was put in command of the 'mounted national guard regiment'. In January 1849 he resigned from the army, but rejoined in April as

Kaszonyi,[104] Knezic[105] and Buttler came to 8,144 infantry, 1,332 cavalry and 30 guns, though some of these were detached under Repásy. From a letter similarly discovered later and dated 23 February from *General* Dembinsky at Tisza-Füred to *General* Repásy we learn the following:

> How operations are to be carried out is quite simply always my secret as the general in command. Nevertheless on this occasion, so as to limit your doubts in future, I will explain to you, *Herr General*, the reason for my changed orders. I had been informed that *Feldmarschall Lieutenant* Schlick had been reinforced and was advancing toward Miskolcz, and indeed had already reached Putnok. To be ready for all eventualities I had to call Görgei's corps to me (which – and I write this for your eyes only – is extremely weak and therefore by my reckoning is not sufficiently battle-worthy). But so as to effect these manoeuvres as quickly as was required, I had to write directly to Görgei's individual divisions. This was not received by *General* Görgei with the moderation that should have been expected from an intelligent soldier, yet it was unavoidably necessary,[106] since it was evident that an hour's delay in the arrival at Sz. Peter [presumably Sajósszentpéter, Hungary] of the units I was concentrating there would have risked Görgei's corps being completely fragmented, as well as Miskolcz falling into enemy hands. But now that I had forced the enemy to retreat like this, Erlau could be the place to which he retreated. This prompted the manoeuvre I ordered *Oberst* Klapka to carry out, as well as my order to you, *Herr General*, to transfer your cavalry to Madaras [presumably Kunmadaras, Hungary]. These manoeuvres are consistent with my overall plan of operations, as will become clear to you in good time. It is not my intention either to break up the existing corps or to encroach on their commanders' prerogatives; nonetheless the common good must not suffer from the unnecessarily dangerous loss of time that would be the principal result if my despatches first had to make long detours to get to the corps commanders before reaching the division commanders under them. I hope that this has given you, *Herr General*, a fairly comprehensive explanation of my military views. But I cannot neglect to say that this must be the first and last time, since as I have already remarked, secrecy of operations is half the victory, and you – as an officer of long and meritorious service whom I esteem so very highly among all others, and whose praiseworthy qualities I fully acknowledge – you yourself will realise and agree with me that if subordinates always had to be

colonel of the 10th Vilmos Hussars and fought in the summer campaign. He was initially sentenced to death in 1850, but this was commuted to 11 years in prison and he was freed in 1853. Bona, *Tábornokok*.

104 József Kászonyi (1810-88) was a major in Husaren-Regiment Nr. 1 in July 1848. He fought on the southern front, then in the main theatre of operations from January 1849, ending up in Komorn. At the end of the war he emigrated and lived in London, Paris and Brussels, returning to Hungary in 1856. Bona, *Tábornokok*.

105 Károly Knezich (1808-49), a captain in Infanterie-Regiment 34 in 1848, fought in the south and was then made brigadier in December 1848 and corps commander in March 1849. He was sacked by Görgei after failing to support Asbóth's corps in the battle of Pered in June. He took over a smaller command in July and surrendered with the Upper Danubian Army at Világos. He was sentenced to death and hanged at Arad. Bona, *Tábornokok*.

106 Not observing the chain of command is a good way to ruffle feathers, especially when dealing with such a sensitive character as Görgei.

told everything, this could only be very harmful. I regard war as a game of chess and I keep my moves hidden. The outcome will show you, *Herr General*, that I always have the common good in mind and will act accordingly. I would therefore ask you in future to put my orders into effect as quickly as possible without hesitation, which will always be the best way to contribute to our overall success. I note your dispatch Nr. 50 of the 22nd, which I have just received, and would have you know that *Oberst* Klapka is in Erlau, with one division of his corps in Miskolcz. You yourself will act entirely according to my orders of the 19th, but do not bring all your infantry with you, since the enemy at Szolnok could well make a feint manoeuvre to draw our attention away from here; on the contrary, it could be good to use some of your infantry to screen our combined manoeuvres according to the situation, which I leave to your military judgement. Görgei's corps will arrive in the Mezö-Keresztes [Mezőkeresztes, Hungary] area today (the 23rd), so that soon all our combat forces will be concentrated here. Inform *General* Vecsey of your movements, and at the same time let him know that, should he perhaps come under pressure from stronger enemy forces he should retreat in good order, nevertheless keeping his main focus on covering the road to Debreczin. By this I mean to the extent that an eye should always be kept on the Debreczin road and the Tisza-Füred road; therefore Vecsey should cover the one to Debreczin, and you, *Herr General*, should cover the one to here, which would best be done if we combine our forces to exploit the terrain offered in the fork between the two roads. I also hope that *General* Damianich has already moved forward toward Török-Sz. Miklós. The pioneer detachment in Kun-Hegyes [Kunhegyes, Hungary] is greatly needed here since the entrenchments have to be changed completely. Therefore order it to move here, *Herr General*, and to bring any tools, picks and shovels, etc., with it. This place (Tisza-Füred) remains our constant main point of support, from which one can also continuously observe the crossing point at Tokay and can oppose any possible attempted crossing.[107]

Final Prelude to Kápolna, 25 February 1849

That same day when Dembinsky wrote this, as we have seen, the *Feldmarschall* had set his troops on the march to begin the offensive operation connected with concentrating his army. On the 24th the *Feldmarschall* and his headquarters had hastened after Division Csorich to Hatvan. There he received word from *Generalmajor Fürst* Colloredo that the officer whom he had sent from Bágh to Petervásara escorted by a few *uhlans* to relay the *Feldmarschall*'s letter of the 22nd to *Feldmarschall Lieutenant Graf* Schlick had not been able to carry out his mission, since he had run into strong hussar detachments in the vicinity of Parád. He had also heard the thunder of guns from Petervásara. Soon after that *Major Prinz* Nassau arrived at headquarters from *Feldmarschall Lieutenant Graf* Schlick. He too had heard cannon fire on his way there about an hour after leaving Petervásara. One was therefore not unconcerned about what might have happened there. Anyway, it remained highly regrettable that Schlick had not received the letter

107 This is an astonishing letter. It 'could only be very harmful' if a general tells his subordinates what he is trying to do? This looks like Dembinsky blustering to disguise the fact that he himself does not really know what he is doing.

of the 22nd instructing him to march directly to Gyöngyös, all the more so as that of the 21st still talked about him possibly advancing through Erlau and Kápolna. From *Major Prinz* Nassau it was learned that Brigade Parrot was in Verebély [Mátraverebély, Hungary] close to Pásztó, that *Feldmarschall Lieutenant* Schulzig was in Petervásara with Brigades Kriegern and Deym, and Brigades Fiedler and Pergen quite nearby in Ujfalu [Nádújfalu, Hungary] and Erdö-Kövesd [Erdőkövesd, Hungary]. The roads had been very bad and the troops were suffering from lack of bread and salt. In his letter of the 24th brought by the *Major*, Schlick reported that he had not left any rear guard in Rima-Szombath, and that if this really was still necessary, it would only be possible via Fülek [Fil'akovo, Slovakia] and Osgyan [Ožd'any, Slovakia] because of the bad roads and would take three days' march. He said he would remain in his present position on the 24th and 25th, but then on the 26th in accordance with the order he had received he would attack Erlau, which was fairly strongly held and whose approaches were protected by abattis and entrenchments.

The *Feldmarschall* did not waste a moment but sent Schlick the order to march immediately to Gyöngyös via Pásztó and Páta [Gyöngyöspata, Hungary]; for the direct route via Parád was quite unusable at this time of year, and finally in the event that the enemy should have advanced in the meantime, it would still be possible to link up with Schlick along the designated road via Szantó and Hatvan. This order which was expedited by the utterly reliable postmaster at Hatvan at 6:00 p.m. on the 24th and went directly to Schlick during the course of the night said the following:

> Given the difficulty your troops face in obtaining supplies in the area they currently occupy and given the impossibility of providing them from here in good time, and finally given the fact that the march from Petervásara to Erlau could be at the mercy of considerable difficulties and delays caused by the barricades and abattis reported to be on this route, I find myself moved to summon Your Honour's corps through Pásztó to Gyöngyös. Accordingly, it should be possible to push forward Brigades Parrot and Fiedler to Páta tomorrow (the 25th), while the rest of the corps could perhaps follow as far as Pásztó or its vicinity. On the day after tomorrow, the 26th, Brigades Parrot and Fiedler should continue their march to Gyöngyös, the rest of the corps to Páta (10 km from Gyöngyös).
>
> Considering the reasons put forward by Your Honour, we must give up on the idea of leaving a brigade in Rima-Szombath.[108]
>
> Should Your Honour find it possible to arrive in Gyöngyös in person tomorrow to confer with me there, I would desire that greatly. *Feldmarschall Lieutenant Graf* Wrbna's corps will be concentrated in Gyöngyös and Árok-Szállás tomorrow.
>
> No detailed information about the enemy position has reached me. *Major Prinz* Nassau said he heard fairly heavy cannon fire from the area of Petervásara on his way here. To what extent he is right in this, and whether anything has happened that could influence the dispositions transmitted to you herein, cannot be gauged from here, so I leave it to you to judge.

108 A curious idea anyway, at odds with the guiding concept of concentrating the army. A brigade at Rima-Szombath would have been 75 km from Kápolna and effectively taken out of the fight that would ensue there on the 26th and 27th, for no obvious purpose.

The *Feldmarschall* issued an order directly to *Generalmajor* Parrot to be sure to march with his brigade and *Generalmajor* Fiedler's to Páta on the 25th. During the night of 24/25 a message was received from *Feldmarschall Lieutenant Graf* Schlick about the surprise attack on Division Schulzig in Petervásara that had taken place on the morning of the 24th. This was the cannon fire that *Major Prinz* Nassau had heard on his journey to Hatvan. In his report on this occasion, Schlick wrote:

> The fact that the surprise attack had no unfortunate consequences for us is due solely and entirely to the cool-headed indomitable courage of our artillery and to the good conduct of the Ottochaner Grenz-Bataillon. The rockets proved particularly successful, having such a demoralising effect on the enemy that although he had already occupied the outskirts of the town, he soon began a retreat that then degenerated into a frantic rout.[109] Our losses in dead and wounded are not yet confirmed but the enemy took no prisoners, whereas we took some from Infanterie-Regiment Nr. 34, while others including officers were immediately massacred by the *grenzers*.[110]
>
> After the attempted surprise attack from the direction of Derecske [Mátraderecske, Hungary] had been repulsed, a fairly substantial enemy force deployed from the direction of Erlau, but when we advanced it retreated in good order without giving battle. The prisoners state that Görgei has arrived in Erlau and has occupied the town in force, with the rest of his corps being at Maklár and Kerecsend. Mezö-Kövesd is only weakly held, mostly by hussars. The enemy force under Klapka that fought in today's action consisted of four *honvéd* battalions, three companies of Infanterie-Regiment Nr. 34, a corps of *jägers* formed mostly from Viennese students, one division of Husaren-Regiment Nr. 1, one division from another hussar regiment, and 12 guns.

Among those who especially distinguished themselves in fending off the surprise attack were *Hauptmann* Kantar and *Lieutenant* Mikschic of 3. Ottochaner Bataillon, as well as *Oberlieutenants* Hauck, Hödl and Angerer, and *Unterlieutenants* Haas and Pollet, all from the artillery.

Whilst the above report provided some degree of reassurance about the events at Petervásara, on the other hand, one could not help reflecting most sombrely on what could have happened if the surprise attack had been completely successful.

On the 26th II. Armeekorps under *Feldmarschall Lieutenant Grad* Wrbna reached Gyöngyös and Árok-Szállás in accordance with the march plans as issued.

The *Feldmarschall* had likewise betaken himself from Hatvan to Gyöngyös early that morning, and made his dispositions for the following day there, assuming that Brigades Parrot and Fiedler of Schlick's corps would arrive in Gyöngyös and the rest of his corps in Páta as ordered. Based on this assumption, the units concentrated in Gyöngyös were given provisional orders for an advance to Kápolna next day, to where Brigades Parrot and Fiedler of Schlick's corps were expected to follow on, while the column under *Feldmarschall Lieutenant Fürst* Edmund Schwarzenberg was to move from Árok-Szállás to Kál. The rest of Schlick's corps was to move up to Gyöngyös meanwhile, to be deployed from there according to circumstances either to

109 Interesting to note the rockets' effect on morale, to add to their incendiary effect already noted.

110 Here is an instance of the savage behaviour of the Croat *grenzers* that the Hungarian defenders of Eszek feared, attested to by the imperials' own commander.

Kápolna, or else toward Heves if the information received from spies about an enemy column marching in that direction should be confirmed.

Generalmajor Zeisberg, who had arrived in Eörs [Tarnaörs, Hungary] with his brigade and who as mentioned was tasked with scouting and covering the right flank of the army during its advance, was ordered 'to march to Heves and to report immediately to the *Feldmarschall* in Gyöngyös, and in especially urgent cases also directly to *Feldmarschall Lieutenant Graf* Wrbna in Kápolna, whatever he may learn of enemy movements in the area beyond Heves'.

Concerning enemy strength and positions, it was generally reported that he had about 40,000 men at Mezö-Kövesd, Maklár and Erlau, had a suitable force holding Poroszló, and as mentioned, had pushed forward a column in the direction of Heves. The relevant unit commanders were informed of all of this, especially *Generalmajor* Zeisberg.

The outposts deployed about 5 km forward of Gyöngyös had not detected any enemy, but nor were any countryfolk or travellers coming from the direction of Kápolna, which led to the conclusion that enemy detachments were present in that area. A message was received from the *Banus* about the failed expedition to destroy the bridge at Czibakháza. On 24 February he had ordered *Generalmajor* Ottinger to undertake this operation with 3. Bataillon of 2. Banal-Regiment, 3. Bataillon E.H. Karl Infanterie, six cuirassier squadrons (Wallmoden and Hardegg), Kavallerie-Batterie Nr. 5, Zwölfpfündige-Batterie Nr. 1 and Raketen-Batterie Nr. 17. Ottinger had set off with these troops from Abany and after a seven-hour march arrived in the loop of the river this side of the bridge toward 5:00 a.m., hoping to surprise the enemy. But the rebels had already been informed of our troops' approach by their excellent spy network. The enemy was therefore suitably prepared, and there could be no more thought of achieving the surprise attack that had been the point of the exercise. Warning beacons had also been spotted in various places during the advance. Czibakháza and the bridge were held by two *honvéd* battalions, one battalion of Infanterie-Regiment Nr. 19, one division of Infanterie-Regiment Nr. 52, one division of Husaren-Regiment Nr. 6 and one and a half batteries. Toward 8:00 a.m. both sides' guns opened up, in which even though the enemy artillery was lighter, it was at a conspicuous advantage being in fortifications and on higher ground.

Generalmajor Ottinger personally led his two battalions to the bridge under intense fire. But the bridge deck had been removed for a width of several metres. There could therefore be no thought of forcing a crossing, and besides the enemy cannister fire against the troops halted in the open was so murderous that the attack had to be abandoned completely. Our troops' losses came to ten dead and eleven wounded.[111] *Hauptmann* Georg Hammer and *Lieutenants* Strasser and Kobusil of the E.H. Karl battalion were wounded, while in the Banal battalion *Hauptmann* Jovanovic was killed and *Lieutenant* Lasic seriously wounded. Having voluntarily attached himself to the assault column, bold *Oberliutenant* Digby of the Wallmoden cuirassiers fell on the bridge, shot through by a cannister ball.

Soon after this message was received, *Feldmarschall Lieutenant Graf* Schlick arrived in Gyöngyös from Petervásara accompanied by his chief of staff, *Major Baron* Gablenz, and *Rittmeister Graf* Török. This was the first time since the start of the campaign that this brave general favoured by fortune had been seen in the *Feldmarschall*'s headquarters; thus, his reception was extremely

111 A total of 21 casualties for the whole action hardly seems enough to justify the description of 'murderous fire', especially as Ottinger's force must have been about 2,000 strong. This rather smacks of an attempt to excuse a half-hearted and poorly planned effort.

cordial and sympathetic. From him it was learned that, with the exception of Brigade Parrot which the *Feldmarschall* had ordered directly to march to Páta, all the other units had stayed in the cantonments they had occupied since the 23rd in and around Petervásara – so the order of the 24th instructing them to march through Pásztó to Gyöngyös had not been carried out, which was ascribed to the poor state of the roads, the troops' fatigue, supply problems and the like![112]

Feldmarschall Lieutenant Graf Schlick's corps had already been delayed from linking up once by its march from Rima-Szombath through Putnok to Sz. Peter.[113] This latest delay frustrating the whole march calculation once again could only have the most disruptive effect on the course of an operation which relied on speed and if possible, on surprising the enemy before he could concentrate his forces completely.

Given the enemy's proximity and numerical superiority and the possibility of perhaps being attacked in detail by superior forces next morning, staying in the current march deployment – namely with Division Csorich in Gyöngyös and Division Edmund Schwarzenberg 15 km away in Árok-Szállás – until Schlick's corps could arrive in Gyöngyös via Pásztó was unthinkable! The *Feldmarschall* therefore stood by his earlier decision to continue the march to Kápolna and Kál next day (the 26th) anyway, so as at least to have II. Armeekorps united, and at 11:00 p.m. he repeated the order to that effect already issued early that morning.

Feldmarschall Lieutenant Graf Schlick for his part now proposed that instead of marching through Páta to Gyöngyös, he should use the better road through Sirok to Verpeléth [Verpelét, Hungary], which he could definitely reach next day (the 26th) and which would make up the time lost by lingering so long in Petervásara. There were some reservations about this proposal. The debouchement from the narrow mountain defile at Sirok could be obstructed, while on the other hand, the column could be seriously harassed on its left flank, even actually in danger from the enemy known to be in Erlau! However, there was no option but to agree to this proposal, since this was the only way in which the now urgently needed junction with *Feldmarschall Lieutenant Graf* Schlick's corps could be achieved, and it could not be postponed any longer. Besides, the enemy was not thought to be so near as he actually was. Neither the outposts nor the patrols that had been sent out had discovered any enemy in the course of the day, which justified the assumption that the following day would also pass without any clash.

It must have been 8:00 p.m. when the necessary agreement was reached with *Feldmarschall Lieutenant Graf* Schlick, and also Brigade Parrot's march to Gyöngyös next day was confirmed unchanged. Schlick returned to Petervásara before daybreak on the 26th to set his corps on the march to Verpeléth as agreed.

On the 26th, after a cooked breakfast, those units of II. Armeekorps in Gyöngyös and Árok-Szállás were set in motion toward Kápolna and Kál. The Geschütz-Hauptreserve moved out from Gyöngyös an hour later escorted by Grenadier-Brigade Schütte, and the other units followed on the Kápolna road. For the moment, all that was left in Gyöngyös to protect the headquarters, the baggage trains that were left behind there, the hospitals, magazines, ammunition reserves and the like, was one division of grenadiers and a squadron of E.H. Johann dragoons. However, toward midday these were joined by the three battalions, four squadrons and one battery of

112 Yet again, one of Windisch-Grätz's orders is not carried out.
113 Thus, 60 km to the east, away from the *Feldmarschall*'s main body.

Brigade Parrot, which had marched from Páta to Gyöngyös as ordered. This brigade took over the job of security and sent patrols toward Pärod [Parád, Hungary] as well as in the direction of Verpeléth, for one was not unconcerned about the situation in the nearby Matra Mountains.

To portray the views about the general situation that were held at that moment as accurately as possible, let us follow the report the *Feldmarschall* submitted to His Majesty the *Kaiser* from Gyöngyös on the 26th:

> With regard to my most humble report of the 24th, I should not neglect to indicate to Your Majesty in deepest reverence that yesterday, the 25th, I pushed all my troops further forward and transferred my headquarters to here in Gyöngyös. According to reports coming in, after abandoning Eperies and Kaschau the enemy has united all his troops between Erlau and Mezö-Kövesd, so that his army consisting of Görgey's, Dembinsky's and Klapka's corps has reached a strength of 40,000-45,000 men. He now seems willing to accept a decisive battle in this position and with these numbers. After linking up with *Graf* Schlick, I can oppose him with barely half that many: I have had to leave a garrison of at least three battalions in Wien, as many again in Pressburg and Raab, the siege of Komorn is taking 8,000 of my men, and those elements of the *Banus*'s I. Armeekorps deployed between Pesth and Szolnok cannot be regarded as available since I have to use them to keep my right flank and Pesth covered. While the reports of the strength of the enemy combat forces are indeed not always entirely reliable, still the total figure mentioned largely tallies with what I have been able to learn so far about the strengths of the individual corps. It is therefore quite certain in any case that I have to deal with a far more numerous enemy and must rely simply on the moral value of my troops. This is certainly very great in that they are burning with the desire to pit themselves against the foe and to prove once more their loyalty and devotion to their *Kaiser*.
>
> Your Majesty will nevertheless most graciously not overlook the fact that my position is an extremely difficult one: in the middle of a country in revolt, to rely simply on the courage of a smaller force to decide a battle against a numerically superior enemy, when as experience teaches, often small incidents can put the outcome in doubt even when a force is of equal strength and has equally brave troops. Nevertheless, I will probably attack the enemy in his position tomorrow if I finish linking up with *Graf* Schlick today.

We shall see that just a few hours after the *Feldmarschall* had sent this most humble report to His Majesty, II. Armeekorps was already in action, while the expected junction with Schlick's corps had still not happened on this day.

The Battle of Kápolna: The First Day, 26 February 1849

The column under *Feldmarschall Lieutenant Graf* Wrbna that had marched out from Gyöngyös – namely Division Csorich (Brigades Wyss and Colloredo) with Brigade Wyss at its head, and Brigade Schütte with the Artillerie-Reserve following on behind, making ten battalions, four squadrons and 78 guns altogether – was no more than an hour's march away from Kápolna at around 2:00 p.m. when a few cannon shots were heard from the right flank, in the direction of Division Schwarzenberg's route of march. Soon after that the enemy was detected deployed for battle on the heights this side of Kápolna, with his right wing extended in the direction of the village of Döbrö [Aldebrő, Hungary] and his left in front of Kál. In front of this extended line were detachments of hussars, and numerous batteries were deployed at favourable points.[114]

Feldmarschall Lieutenant Graf Wrbna now immediately ordered an attack on this advantageous position held by far superior numbers of enemy.[115] Covered by the 1. Major's Division of Civallart Uhlanen attached to Brigade Wyss, and by three troops of Kress *chevauxlegers* and Kavallerie-Batterie Nr. 2, Brigade Wyss shook out to the right of the road and Brigade Colloredo to the left. However, the latter brigade soon had to stretch further left to present a proportionate front to the enemy's very extended position. *Feldmarschall Lieutenant Baron* Csorich ordered one company of 6. Jäger-Bataillon to occupy an open wood on the left flank. In addition, two companies of 6. Jäger-Bataillon under *Hauptmann* Brandenstein and a division of E.H. Stefan had been detached and sent from Gyöngyös through Sár [Abasár, Hungary] and Domoszló toward Verpeléth to cover the corps's march. Their mission was to stay in Verpeléth until the head of *Feldmarschall Lieutenant Graf* Schlick's corps arrived there, and then rejoin the brigade at Kápolna.

Brigade Colloredo was facing strong enemy detachments, on dominant high ground, whose batteries were deployed out in front protected by three divisions of hussars. The enemy seems not to have recognised the importance of the wood on the left flank of Brigade Colloredo until our troops moved to occupy it, because it was only then that he sent strong infantry detachments toward it, accompanied by artillery. When *Generalmajor Fürst* Colloredo became aware of this, he immediately ordered *Major* Kronenberg of 6. Jäger-Bataillon to go there with the remaining company of his battalion and a division of Paumgarten infantry under *Hauptmann Fürst* Ruspoli to reinforce the *jägers* who had already been sent into the wood, whereupon a very lively skirmish action developed there. However, under *Major* Kronenberg's sound leadership the *jägers* managed not only to clear the wood completely of the enemy that had already penetrated into it, but also to hold it against three successive attacks by 1., 14. and 31. Honved-Bataillons.

Correctly judging how important this point was, *Feldmarschall Lieutenant Baron* Csorich now sent *Major Baron* Salis there with four companies of 2. Bataillon E.H. Stefan and a reserve battery, which arrived just as the third enemy assault was beaten back. During their advance these troops were exposed to exceptionally murderous cannister and shellfire, in which brave *Major Baron* Salis received a dangerous wound in the eye from a shell splinter and *Hauptmann* Oppenauer of the same battalion was also wounded. Meanwhile Reserve-Brigade Schütte had arrived on the battlefield with its ten companies of grenadiers and the Artillerie-Hauptreserve. Now, taking a proper overview, just at the right time *Feldmarschall Lieutenant Graf* Wrbna had six batteries with only a small escort deploy into the substantial completely open area separating

114 The Hungarian forces were actually quite divided. Only seven of their 23 brigades were deployed on the line of the Tarna initially, on the lower (east) bank; the rest were scattered in Maklár, Mező-Kövesd and Bükkábrány, between 15 and 35 km to the rear. When the Austrian advance was reported, two Hungarian divisions deployed forward across the river to its higher western bank, but the third was slow to conform and neglected the vital wood subsequently occupied by Colloredo. Consequently, the Hungarian line at the start of the battle was understrength and dislocated, which contributed to the Austrians being able to push the Hungarians back into Kápolna. Hermann, *Az 1848-1849-es*; Bánlaky, *A magyar nemzet*.

115 In fact, the Hungarian forces actually engaged were similar in number and had far fewer guns.

Brigade Colloredo from Brigade Wyss and open up such an effective fire that all the enemy's efforts to gain ground there remained fruitless. But the enemy did not give up on his aim of taking possession of the wood on our left flank. As night was falling, he undertook a fourth and final assault against it with five battalions. Three battalions supported by a battery advanced to carry out the actual assault, while the other two followed in reserve to the right rear. *Major* Kronenberg did not let himself be caught unprepared. Without hesitation he bayonet-charged the enemy with five companies, while at the same time *Hauptmann Baron* Feldegg bayonet-charged them in the right flank with 2. Jäger-Kompanie and 6. Division, E.H. Stefan. Right at the perfect moment, *Hauptmann* Brandenstein arrived with his command (3. Division of 6. Jäger-Bataillon and a division of E.H. Stefan). This officer, who as we said had been sent from Gyöngyös toward Verpeléth to establish communications there with *Feldmarschall Lieutenant Graf* Schlick's troops, had found the place strongly held by the enemy instead. There was neither sight nor sound of the approach of Schlick's corps, but *Hauptmann* Brandenstein did hear cannon fire on his right flank. Without a moment's hesitation, he swiftly headed in that direction and arrived just at the right time to play an honourable part in deciding the action in the wood, and with it the outcome of the day, in that he and his four companies joined in with *Hauptmann Baron* Feldegg's flank attack and made a vital contribution to its success.

Now the enemy could stand no longer and fell into a mad rout, leaving behind many dead and wounded as well as 41 prisoners, and completely abandoning the wood into our hands, where it remained from then on. As soon as *Generalmajor Fürst* Colloredo saw the enemy wavering, he went over to a determined general attack with the rest of his troops outside the wood. This was prepared frontally by Batteries Nr. 8 and 10, and by Battery Nr. 11 under *Oberlieutenant* Alten moving further to the left. The enemy now gave way here too, and soon after that his last battery at this point fell silent.

The brigade's losses were not insignificant. The brave 6. Jäger-Bataillon alone had lost 19 dead and wounded in the bloody forest fighting, including four NCOs. *Major* Kronenberg, *Hauptmann Baron* Feldegg, *Hauptmann* Brandenstein and *Oberlieutenants* Klein and Stenglin were mentioned in particular in the after-action report.

While this was happening on the extreme left wing and the artillery duel in the centre of the battle line was continuing without pause, Brigade Wyss forming the right wing had got involved in a no less hard-fought action. This brigade had marched up on the right of the road, as mentioned above, in two lines by columns of divisions. In the first line were the Fürstenwärther and Schönhals battalions, in the second the G.H. Baden battalion and 2. Jäger-Bataillon. The latter was echeloned somewhat toward the right rear. Kavallerie-Batterie Nr. 2 that had been sent forward with the cavalry suffered serious losses from the fire of the three enemy batteries facing it, during which *Hauptmann* Dobner of the general staff had his horse shot from under him and suffered a badly bruised foot. *Feldmarschall Lieutenant Graf* Wrbna now sent forward Zwölfpfündige Batterie Nr. 3 and Sechspfündige Reserve-Batterie Nr. 10, followed later by three more batteries. By committing these against the enemy artillery that had also been increased to five batteries, the very protracted artillery duel was initially maintained, and then decided in our favour. But suddenly one of those critical moments came that occur so frequently in war, and that can only be defused by sound judgement and decisive action on the part of the commander. Division Edmund Schwarzenberg, likewise, engaged in serious fighting, was a long way to the right of Brigade Wyss and separated from it by an extensive wood. This fact must have invited the enemy to penetrate between the two under cover of the wood. Soon an enemy column actually revealed itself at the edge of the wood with a strength of about three battalions, five divisions of hussars and two batteries. This advanced in a determined manner into the empty gap, and even managed to come level with Brigade Wyss's second line. A quick decision had to be made. *Generalmajor* Wyss immediately ordered *Major Baron* Baselli to charge the enemy's front with his division of Civallart *uhlans*, while he himself attacked the enemy's right flank with three troops of Kress *chevauxlegers* as well as Kavallerie-Batterie Nr. 2 under brave *Oberlieutenant* Seidl and half of Raketen-Batterie Nr. 15 commanded by *Oberfeuerwerker* Neubauer.

Major Baron Baselli led his division with determination and inspiring courage to charge by squadrons while under intense enemy artillery fire. In an instant an enemy square was broken, with *Korporal* Schöntag being first to get inside it, followed by *Uhlans* Wissniuk, Kantorek and Ballczak.[116] The hussar divisions thrown against the *uhlans* one after the other were likewise driven back, during which understandably the two sides' cavalry got so intermingled that our artillery could not get a clear shot, and things certainly did not play out without significant losses to both friend and foe. The *uhlans* fought with their customary bravery. *Rittmeister* Hoffman and *Oberlieutenant Graf* Zedwitz conducted themselves with rare courage. But the enemy kept bringing up fresh hussar detachments against the *uhlan* division that was now exhausted from fighting and already fairly depleted. *Major Baron* Baselli and the two *Rittmeisters Graf* Messey and Du Mesnil did their utmost to make a stand, but one feared the worst for the outcome of the fight. At this critical moment, *Oberst Graf* Montenuovo smashed into the enemy's flank with three troops of Kress Chevauxlegers. This beautifully executed flank attack on a whole hussar division was performed with the kind of precision that is usually only found on the parade ground, and not only *Oberst Graf* Montenuovo but also *Major Graf* Alberti and *Rittmeister* Fischer deserve particular credit for it.

The result was glorious and decisive. The *uhlans* were disengaged; the hussars were defeated and could not rally again until they reached their supports, which had however visibly gained ground. Now *Oberlieutenant* Seidl advanced swiftly with his Kavallerie-Batterie and the half of Raketen-Batterie Nr. 15, quite unperturbed by the heavy enemy artillery fire, and opened up such effective fire on the enemy's flank that he hastily fell back to the heights in front of Kompolt, pursued by the *chevauxlegers* and the batteries noted above, joined also by Raketen-Batterie Nr. 17. With that the fighting ended here too.

Major Baron Baselli's *uhlan* division lost seven dead and 35 wounded. Among the former was *Lieutenant* Franul von Weissenthurm, one of the most highly esteemed and best loved officers in the regiment. Fifty-three enemy lay dead or wounded on the field.

All the troops spent a bitterly cold night sleeping on wet ground without campfires, in the immediate proximity of the enemy, astride the road. Only those units of Brigade Colloredo that had fought in the wood stayed there.

The column under *Feldmarschall Lieutenant Fürst* Edmund Schwarzenberg had begun its march from Árok-Szállás toward Kál at 9:00 a.m. It comprised:

116 During the Napoleonic Wars, for an infantry square to be broken by cavalry was an uncommon and notable event. The 1848 war was fought with essentially the same weapons, so for the Austrian cavalry to break a Hungarian square could be regarded as a signal success. However, Bánlaky notes that it was only a company in square, not a whole battalion. Thus, this was not quite so dramatic an achievement as might be thought. Bánlaky, *A magyar nemzet*.

Brigade *Generalmajor* Dietrich

2. Bataillon Wimpffen (four companies)
Composite Bataillon Ecker (four companies)
4. Bataillon Warasdiner-Kreutzer (four companies)
4. Bataillon, 2. Banal-Grenz-Regiment (three companies)
One and a half batteries

Brigade *Generalmajor Graf* Bellegarde

Four squadrons of Max Auersperg Kürassiere
Three squadrons of Civallart-Uhlanen
One Kavallerie-Batterie

Divisions-Artillerie-Reserve

One Zwölfpfündige Batterie
Half a Raketen-Batterie

Altogether 15 companies (2,562 men), seven squadrons and 24 artillery pieces.

About 10 km this side of the village of Kál, the advance guard of Civallart *uhlans* led by *Oberstlieutenant Graf* Nostiz ran into enemy cavalry detachments which however were soon hurled back toward Kál, with many hussars being cut down and 14 taken prisoner. When the column approached the Csocz manor the enemy position was discerned more clearly.[117] The infantry were deployed in several lines in front of Kál. The wood that projected a long way forward between this place and Kápolna was occupied by the enemy, and also their artillery that was far more numerous than ours was drawn up on advantageous points. About 1,200 paces in front of this position was a wide canal crossed by a stone bridge. *Feldmarschall Lieutenant Fürst* Edmund Schwarzenberg had Brigade Dietrich march up to this side of the canal with the Wimpffen battalion and the Warasdiner-Kreutzer in the first line, Bataillon Eckert and the Banal-Grenz-Bataillon in the second. The half-batteries deployed on each wing of the brigade completely commanded the ground in front and the bridge over the canal, while Zwölfpfündige Batterie Nr. 4 remained hidden behind the centre for the time being. The cavalry under *Generalmajor Graf* Bellegarde had meanwhile carried out several successful charges, in which they found themselves excellently supported by Kavallerie-Batterie Nr. 4 commanded by *Oberstlieutenant* Hirschmann. To maintain communications with Division Csorich, particularly with Brigade Wyss, a division of Max Auersperg cuirassiers was sent to the left with a half-battery. Their appearance also had a favourable effect on the outcome of *Major Baron* Baselli's cavalry action described above. On the other side, *Oberstlieutenant Baron* Minutillo was detached to the right flank of Brigade Dietrich with one squadron and a half-battery.

117 I have been unable to identify Csocz manor on any map. Perhaps it is Csárda Major, from the 2nd Military Survey map, now in Nagyút, Hungary.

Now the enemy's more numerous guns opened up a very lively artillery fire, in response to which the division gradually brought all its batteries into action. Fortunately, the ground was quite sodden, making a lot of the cannon fire ineffective, but our artillery still suffered some losses. *Lieutenant* Morovitzer, commanding the half Kavallerie-Batterie detached to the right flank with *Oberstlieutenant Baron* Minutillo, had his head smashed by a cannonball, whereupon *Artillerie-Korporal* Stuhlpfarrer took command and bravely fought on with the half-battery, which had also had one cannon put out of action and several men wounded. The 12-pounder battery also suffered some losses.

Feldmarschall Lieutenant Fürst Edmund Schwarzenberg could see very well that he could not advance with his small combat forces before the enemy-held wood on his left flank was cleared, so he ordered 4. Bataillon Warasdiner-Kreutzer under *Major* Regelsberg to storm it. As darkness was falling, the battalion charged into the wood with the bayonet and drove out all the enemy deployed in there. This decisive assault caused the enemy to abandon his position and retreat to Kompolt. With that, and since night had now fallen, the fighting at this point ended as well.

The troops spent the night partly in their position, partly in the nearby wood, with only a few campfires and keeping a sharp eye on the enemy camped in the immediate vicinity.

The *Feldmarschall,* who had not reckoned on any clash with the enemy on this day, had stayed behind in Gyöngyös to deal with all the urgent correspondence arriving in large part from Ofen but some also from Olmütz.[118] It was not until toward evening that he received word from *Feldmarschall Lieutenant Graf* Wrbna about the action that had taken place, for the thunder of the guns had not been heard at all in Gyöngyös because of the large distance from the battlefield and the prevailing west wind.

The report on this occasion was very calm and composed and was sent even before the fighting was completely over. It talked about the enemy's significant numerical superiority,[119] but did not express any concern at all about the outcome of the fighting that had been endured by our troops with exemplary courage. On the other hand, the non-arrival of *Feldmarschall Lieutenant Graf* Schlick's corps was mentioned, and it was also noted that according to prisoners' statements, Görgei's corps had not yet arrived but was expected to join the line of battle next day. Consequently, one was reassured about today, but not at all so for what the next day might hold; for leaving aside the fact that linking up with Schlick's corps now seemed in doubt again, next morning Görgei's corps could join the superior enemy combat forces already concentrated at Kápolna and Kál and produce a numerical preponderance that we would not be able to resist without some other support.

Nothing had been heard from *Feldmarschall Lieutenant Graf* Schlick, which gave rise to the fear that on his way back from Gyöngyös to Petervásara he might have been caught by one of the enemy bands roaming the mountains there, leaving his corps without orders, so it might not even have moved! Therefore during the night a courier was sent to Petervásara with appropriate orders for this eventuality. Thus, the night of 26/27 passed not without concerned contemplation of the prospects that might possibly be in store. On the other flank, a message had come in from

118 Again we find the *Feldmarschall* over 20 km behind his army (though it appears to have managed without him on this occasion).

119 As noted above, Hermann indicates that Hungarian numerical superiority was not as significant as both the *Feldmarschall* and Nobili suggest. Hermann, *Az 1848–1849-es.*

Generalmajor Zeisberg that on this day he had not marched as far as Heves, but only to Méra [Tarnaméra, Hungary] and Boczonád [Boconád, Hungary] – scarcely covering 15 km – so that in relation to II. Armeekorps standing in front of Kápolna and Kál, his position seemed much too refused if he was to fulfil his mission of 'covering and scouting on the army's right flank'.[120]

When battle was joined by Division Schwarzenberg, Zeisberg's brigade had advanced as far as Nagyút led by *Oberst* Liubimiresko, since *Generalmajor* Zeisberg had betaken himself to Gyöngyös, but when Zeisberg returned that evening it was called back to Méra and Boczonád.

The Battle of Kápolna: The Second Day, 27 February 1849

Early on the 27th, the *Feldmarschall* hurried to join the troops deployed for battle in front of Kápolna. Before his departure from Gyöngyös he ordered *Generalmajor* Parrot to march the two squadrons of Max Auersperg Kürassiere and two squadrons of Kaiser Chevauxlegers that were attached to his brigade toward Kápolna immediately, to take position in front of Gyöngyös with the rest of his troops – three infantry battalions, one battery and a squadron of E.H. Johann dragoons assigned to him – and to garrison the town itself appropriately to protect the magazines, hospitals, ammunition depots and the like there, while also sending patrols toward Parád, Verpeléth and Heves.

As soon as the *Feldmarschall* arrived before Kápolna, he personally reconnoitred the enemy position. This revealed that its front was protected by the Tarna stream that ran through a mostly marshy depression criss-crossed by ditches and canals, which could only be crossed by means of the bridges in the villages of Kápolna and Kál. Any frontal offensive manoeuvre therefore had to start by taking possession of one of these places that were strongly held by the enemy, which seemed all the more difficult since the heights on the far side were crowned with numerous troops and guns. On the other hand, the slope of the valley on this side of the Tarna was fairly high, especially near Kápolna, and was favourable for bombarding this village that lay right down in the dip, affording the attack some advantage. The *Feldmarschall* therefore decided to launch the attack at this point as soon as the moment for advancing on the offensive should definitely have arrived.

During this reconnaissance, all eyes were on the high ground around Verpeléth, which was clearly visible and from where the approach of *Feldmarschall Lieutenant Graf* Schlick's corps was eagerly awaited. Toward 8:00 a.m., the first plumes of smoke were finally spotted in that direction and the first cannon shots were heard. The inexpressible feeling of joy that filled each man's breast at that moment can only be understood by those who have found themselves in a similar situation!

Athough *Feldmarschall Lieutenant Graf* Schlick's corps was still 10 km away from the position on this side, it could now be regarded as certain to link up, and indeed in a tactically favourable situation since from Verpeléth Schlick was pushing down the enemy-held far side of the Tarna

120 Zeisberg's dilatory and tentative actions meant his force made no contribution to the battle of Kápolna. Had he been bolder and more energetic, he could have arrived on the Hungarian left flank while Schlick descended on the right, perhaps producing a more decisive outcome for Windisch-Grätz. Incidentally, as Jellacic's chief of staff, it was Zeisberg who commanded initially at Pákozd, the first significant battle of the war, until Jellacic arrived on the battlefield. The Croat force was soundly defeated at Pákozd. Hermann, 'A pákozdi csata'.

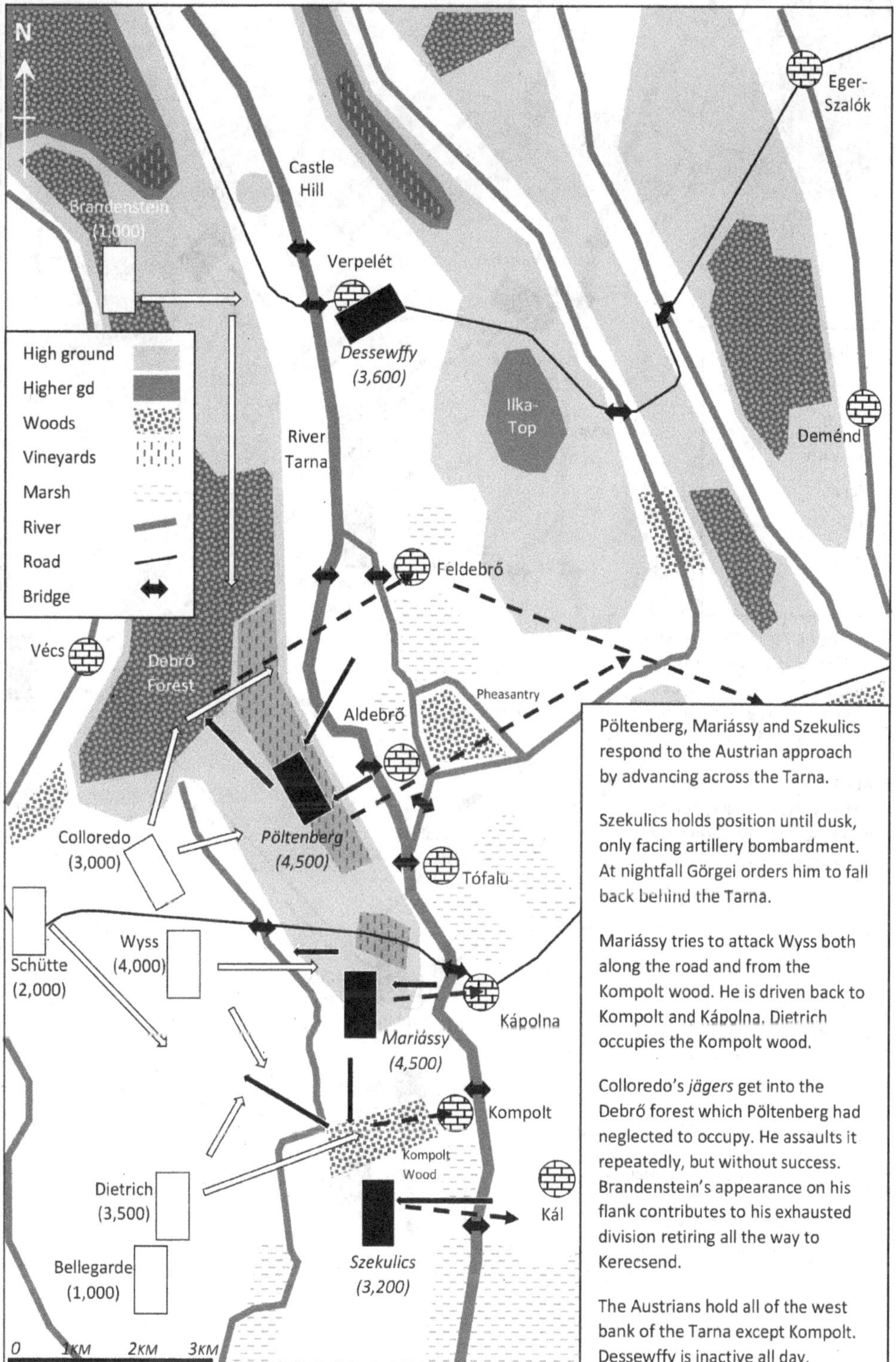

Map 4a: The battle of Kápolna, Day 1: 26 February 1849

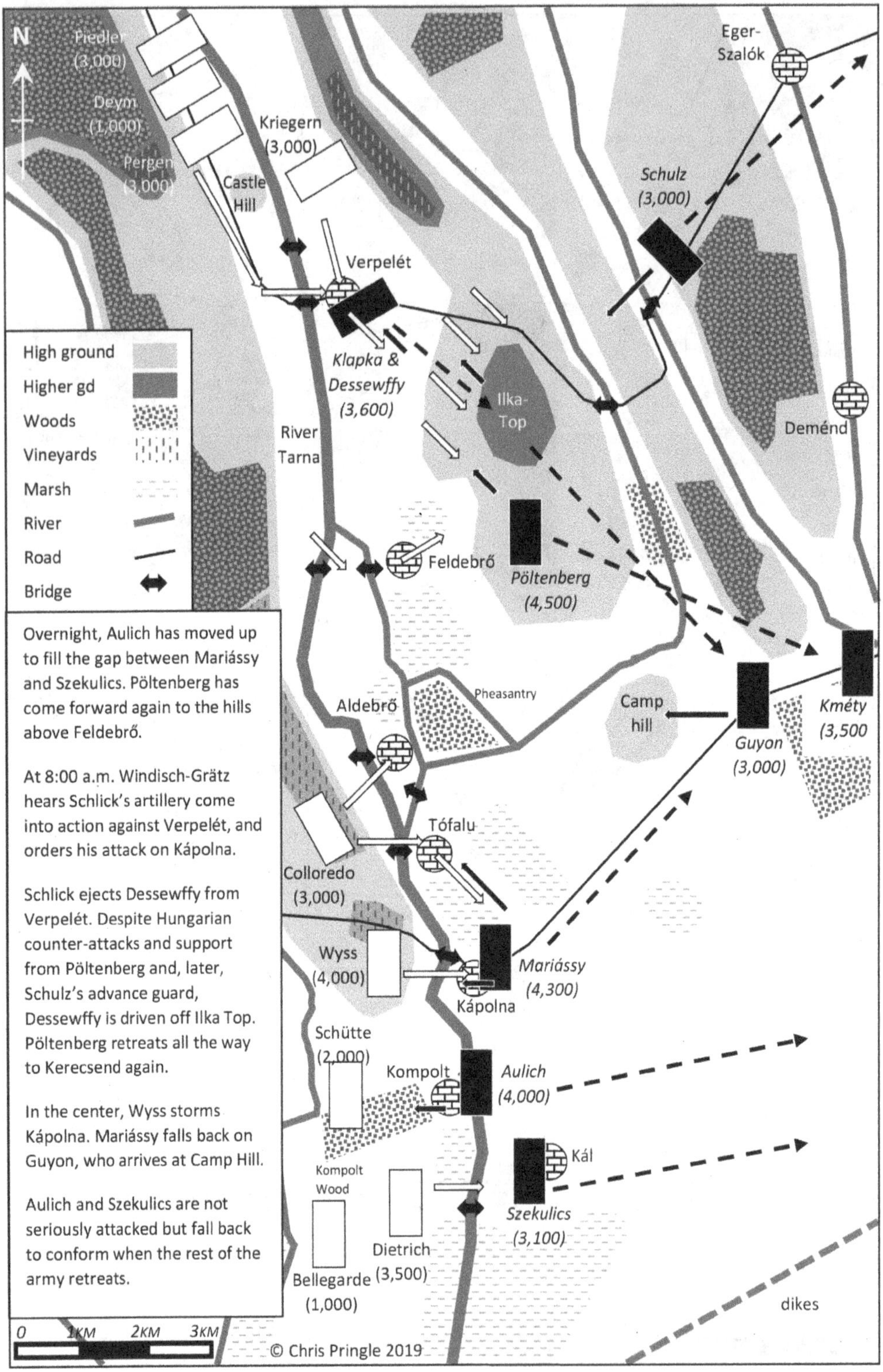

Map 4b: The battle of Kápolna, Day 2: 27 February 1849

stream, mostly had the advantage of the higher ground, and was moving straight into the right flank of the enemy position.

Now the *Feldmarschall* did not hesitate for a moment but gave the order for the attack on Kápolna. Soon after that, *Rittmeister Graf* Török rode up to the *Feldmarschall*, sent by *Feldmarschall Lieutenant Graf* Schlick to report on what had happened since the day before yesterday and to obtain further orders. From the said *Rittmeister* it was learned that Schlick had arrived in Petervásara toward midday the day before (the 26th). By the time the troops had been issued bread and were ready to march it was 1:00 p.m. The march to Verpeléth would take at least six hours and would have needed an early start, so there could be no thought of arriving in good time that day. This was all the more the case as at this time of year the days were very short and the roads very bad. The corps therefore actually moved no further than Sirok (10 km from Petervásara), where the village was found to be occupied by the enemy, and the corps proceeded to attack it as darkness was already falling. To that end Schlick sent the Ottochaner battalion and the Warasdiner-St. Georger battalion against the right flank of the enemy position, followed by the Landwehr-Bataillon H.v. Parma as rear support. This sufficed to clear Sirok and indeed the whole mountain defile, without our troops having suffered the slightest loss in doing so. Meanwhile night had fallen, so the corps had to camp in the narrow pass, and besides the last detachments only arrived later. Only the Warasdiner-Kreutzer battalion and the Landwehr-Bataillon H.v. Parma were pushed forward to S. Maria [Tarnaszentmária, Hungary] as the foremost vanguard. Thus, the corps had not arrived at the point designated for it on this day, so had taken no part in the action that *Feldmarschall Lieutenant Graf* Wrbna had begun so triumphantly.

At 4:00 a.m. the next day (the 27th) the troops set out on the march again, reached the exit from the pass unchallenged, and did not run into the enemy until this side of Verpeléth. They were about to advance to attack the enemy when *Rittmeister Graf* Török was sent off to the *Feldmarschall* on a long and daring ride that he completed swiftly and successfully. He was now sent back to *Feldmarschall Lieutenant Graf* Schlick with suitable instructions. These were very simple. Schlick's corps was right on the enemy's flank and had only to advance straight through Verpeléth into the sector between the Tarna and the Laskó [the stream that runs due south into Kerecsend] in order to link up with II. Armeekorps and at the same time threaten the enemy's line of retreat from Kápolna and Kál. This order was issued and indeed acted upon.

Meanwhile Brigade Wyss had been preparing to attack Kápolna. The 2. Jäger-Bataillon was occupying the vineyard along the fairly steep valley slope on both sides of the road leading to Kápolna. The Fürstenwärther battalion was deployed to the left of the road in support of the *jägers*. Now Zwölfpfündige Batterie Nr. 3 and the two Kavallerie-Batteries Nr. 8 and 10, led forward by *Artillerie-Direktor Generalmajor* Dietrich himself, opened up a lively and very effective fire on the village of Kápolna that was strongly held by the enemy. The enemy guns posted at the entrance to the village were soon silenced and the infantry next to them shaken, as *Generalmajor* Wyss brought up 2. Jäger-Bataillon, and the E.H. Baden battalion that he had moved up earlier and deployed under cover level with the *jägers*, to storm Kápolna. Under intense fire from the enemy batteries deployed on the heights beyond the village, these brave troops pressed into the village. The enemy quickly fell back from its front edge but without yet totally abandoning the fairly extensive village.

Generalmajor Wyss's cavalry were deployed outside the village in the direction of the Kompolt manor house under the command of *Oberst Graf* Montenuovo, together with half a rocket battery and Kavallerie-Batterie Nr. 2, to maintain communications with Division Schwarzenberg that was likewise in action in front of Kál. Perhaps thinking the capture of the village was now certain, Wyss hurried off toward them. While he was doing that, the enemy had thrown fresh troops into that part of Kápolna he still held and pushed forward there in such superior force that our troops were soon driven back in some places. A manor house had just been abandoned by a *jäger* detachment when *Oberlieutenant* Heissler with two platoons of E.H. Baden infantry, together with *Oberlieutenant* Peduzzi commanding a detachment of 2. Jäger-Bataillon, pressed forward with rare determination and threw the enemy out again. Likewise, *Oberlieutenant Fürst* Ludwig Windisch-Grätz acted with particular merit 'at the moment when the enemy pushed into Kápolna once more, by the energy with which he rallied the troops who were wavering under an intense hail of bullets and led them forward again', as *Generalmajor* Wyss stated in his after-action report.

The two battalions fighting in the village could hardly have held out any longer if they had not quickly been supported. At this decisive moment *Generalmajor* Wyss came straight back to Kápolna. He quickly flung *Oberstlieutenant* Schneider's Schönhals battalion into the village. This bold battalion and its dynamic commander charged forward, driving all before them, and soon restored the situation. One division had already taken position by the church while the two others moved off to occupy the exits from the sides of the village, when a battalion of Infanterie-Regiment Nr. 16[121] under Major Venturini pressed toward the church followed by some detachments of *honvéd* infantry. *Oberstlieutenant* Schneider made a quick decision and led his division that was standing there in a bayonet charge against the enemy, while the two others that had been detached toward the exits from the village also quickly turned around and threw themselves on the enemy's flank and rear. Hemmed in on all sides, after brief resistance the enemy battalion laid down its arms. A flag, one staff officer, 27 field officers and 963 men fell into our hands. Soon after that the village was completely cleared of enemy, and even the manor house just outside the village next to the inn was taken and occupied by the *jägers* and the E.H. Baden battalion.

For a while the enemy limited himself to showering the village with a hail of projectiles from four batteries, to which our brave troops paid no heed and held firm at every point. Suddenly, a senior enemy commander appeared accompanied by a large retinue, who it seems was giving orders to retake the village, for soon after his arrival several columns advanced to the assault.[122] This was his last desperate attempt to recapture Kápolna, but it shattered on the bravery of the defenders and the well-aimed fire of our artillery and ended in the hasty retreat of the assault columns after suffering significant losses.

However, the capture of Kápolna had not gained us much, as debouching from the village was extremely difficult because of the heights directly in front of it that were strongly held by the enemy. The *Feldmarschall* therefore decided to drive the enemy out of his advantageous position by means of an outflanking manoeuvre. To this end *Generalmajor Fürst* Colloredo was ordered to cross the Tarna stream about 2 km above Kápolna at the village of Tóthfalva [Tófalu, Hungary] that had already been abandoned by the enemy, and to move against the

121 The Zanini regiment, a former imperial unit of Italians now fighting on the Hungarian side.
122 One of these assaults was famously accompanied by the Upper Danubian Army's senior chaplain, Cézár Mednyánszky, in full ecclesiastical dress, waving his cross, as immortalised in the painting by Mór Than. Bánlaky, *A magyar nemzet*.

flank of the enemy position from there. At the same time *Major* Augustinec of the Paumgarten infantry was ordered to cross the Tarna still further upstream at Döbrö with 6. Jäger-Bataillon, one Paumgarten division and three E.H. Stefan divisions, to establish communications with *Feldmarschall Lieutenant Graf* Schlick's columns advancing through Verpeléth.

Generalmajor Fürst Colloredo carried out his mission with both prudence and determination. After successfully passing through the Tóthfalva defile, by skilful use of the ground he was able to conceal his relatively small number of troops from the enemy and deployed his batteries (Sechspfündige Nr. 8 and 10, soon joined by Zwölfpfündige Batterie Nr. 5 from the reserve led by *Oberstlieutenant* Lang of the general staff) so advantageously on the flank of the enemy deployed in front of Kápolna that they wavered and were soon obliged to retreat.

Major Augustinec for his part, after successfully repairing the destroyed bridge across the Tarna, had occupied the village of Ober-Döbrö [Feldebrő, Hungary] and paved the way for linking up with *Feldmarschall Lieutenant Graf* Schlick's troops.

While the battle was raging with all its might at Kápolna and generally along the whole of the extended front from Tóthfalva to Kál, most of *Feldmarschall Lieutenant Graf* Schlick's corps had moved out from the mountain pass at Sirok and S. Maria covered by its advance guard and deployed behind the hills facing Verpeléth, as concealed as possible. The enemy, fully recognising the importance of Verpeléth as the key to Schlick linking up with the *Feldmarschall*'s force, had concentrated his forces there to make a stand, and occupied both the village and the neighbouring hills with troops and numerous guns. Schlick now brought up Zwölfpfündige Batterie Nr. 11, *Oberlieutenant* Angerer's rocket battery and nine horse artillery pieces, as well as the batteries attached to the leading brigades, and opened up such heavy fire on Verpeléth that in less than 20 minutes the enemy guns posted there were either silenced or badly shaken.

Now Brigade Kriegern advanced to attack the village. The 3. Bataillon Ottochaner and 3. Bataillon Mazzuchelli formed up in assault columns, while the Landwehr-Bataillon H.v. Parma followed on behind in reserve. Brigade Pergen debouched later across the stone bridge over the Tarna. After fairly protracted street fighting, in which the Ottochaner battalion particularly distinguished itself and the enemy had still resisted stubbornly right to the last houses of the village, Verpeléth was in our troops' hands. The rebels fled in disorder to the hills nearby, where they rallied again, covered by their cavalry and artillery.[123] Then *Feldmarschall Lieutenant Graf* Schlick brought the Kürassier-Regiment Prinz von Preussen forward through Verpeléth. The cuirassiers hurled themselves upon the enemy with outstanding bravery and inflicted very severe losses on him. Also, under *Generalmajor Graf* Deym they had already taken four guns, but these could not be got away because of the sandy soil and lack of horse teams, not to mention the fact that the cuirassiers were taking heavy fire from a *honvéd* battalion deployed on their flank.

In this glorious charge the Kürassier-Regiment Prinz von Preussen suffered significant losses, namely four officers and 55 cuirassiers dead and wounded. Among the former was *Rittmeister Baron* Zülow; among the latter, *Rittmeister Baron* Uichtritz (who later died of his wounds), *Oberlieutenant Baron* Rolshausen and *Lieutenant* Urbani.

123 According to Görgei, these included 'those troops of the seventh army corps that could least be depended upon, namely, the Tyrol chasseurs. These, together with the Pöltenberg division, had been ordered early in the morning to Verpelét, but had taken flight from thence by themselves'. Arthur Görgey, *My Life and Acts in Hungary in the Years 1848 and 1849* (New York: Harper & Brothers, 1852), p.201.

Meanwhile on the left flank *Major Baron* Gablenz of the general staff had advanced into the vineyard with four H.v. Parma companies, one squadron and a half-battery, creating ever more of a threat to the enemy's right wing. When Brigades Deym and Kriegern had debouched from Verpeléth, they linked up with *Major* Augustinec's men of 6. Jäger-Bataillon from Brigade Colloredo.

Feldmarschall Lieutenant Graf Schlick now had to wait for Brigades Pergen and Fiedler to follow on, since what mattered now was to take the steep hills in front that were strongly held by the enemy. After these two brigades had got close enough, *Feldmarschall Lieutenant* Schulzig advanced to attack the well-defended heights with Brigades Kriegern and Deym. Meanwhile Schlick turned left with Brigade Pergen and the cavalry toward the road from Erlau, as he was worried about being attacked in his left flank from there. Some detachments of the Polish Legion deployed there had given rise to this concern, which later proved to be unfounded.

Feldmarschall Lieutenant Schulzig had the H.v. Parma battalion advance to storm the heights. After this first attack had been repulsed, a second attempt was made with the Latour, Hartmann and Ottochaner battalions. After a tough fight in which in particular the Latour battalion led by brave *Major Graf* Künigl suffered significant losses, *Hauptmann* Sauer lying dead and *Lieutenant* Hostosch wounded, it succeeded in taking and holding the heights. The Poles who had appeared on the left flank were also put to flight. The enemy formed up again on a second range of wooded hills, from which he was driven off by Brigades Pergen and Fiedler and thrown back all the way to Kerecsend.

During this fighting on the left wing of the battle line, *Major* Augustinec, who had received three squadrons of reinforcements, had also gained ground on the far bank of the Tarna. He had debouched from Döbrö with two divisions of 6. Jäger-Bataillon and two E.H. Stefan divisions. Followed by a division of *jägers* and a Paumgarten division in support, he had advanced to attack a hill held by two battalions, a hussar division and two batteries. Under heavy fire the brave troops crossed a six- or seven-foot wide ditch, then a second one, and climbed the steep hill. Arriving at its crest they came under such murderous fire that they wavered for a moment. At this instant another *honvéd* battalion and a hussar detachment attacked the flank of the assault column. But just at the critical moment the division of E.H. Johann dragoons advanced determinedly, while on the other side *Hauptmann Baron* Feldegg, who had already distinguished himself the previous day, threatened the flank of an enemy battery at the head of his division, silencing it, and the enemy was forced into a general retreat.

Major Kronenberg, *Hauptmann* Fritsch, *Oberlieutenants* Stenglin, Henninger and Kirchsberg, the latter being from E.H. Stefan, who were able to keep their units in good order while under intense fire, and finally *Lieutenant* Petrides commanding Sechspfündige Batterie Nr. 12 had especially distinguished themselves.

When the enemy rallied again and was about to advance to attack anew, *Generalmajor Fürst* Colloredo appeared. He had rushed up with two batteries far ahead of the rest of his troops just at the right time to finally decide the action at this point in our favour. After earlier causing the enemy deployed behind Kápolna to fall back by harassing his right flank, Colloredo himself had swiftly advanced and linked up more closely with *Major* Augustinec's column advancing from Döbrö, which as we have seen, he supported in a timely manner.

The enemy now no longer tried to make a stand anywhere. What mattered to him was to reach the Kerecsend defile behind him and get through it before *Feldmarschall Lieutenant Graf* Schlick's troops arrived there.

On the hills this side of Kerecsend, Brigade Colloredo linked up directly with Division Schulzig from *Feldmarschall Lieutenant Graf* Schlick's corps that had moved up meanwhile. But by this point the last enemy infantry detachments were already crossing the bridge at Kerecsend, and besides, darkness was falling; so the troops gave up any further pursuit and had to spend the night in the advantageous position they held.

Brigade Wyss was so exhausted from several hours of intense street fighting that it was incapable of following the enemy as he fell back the 10 km from Kápolna to Kerecsend, which would have led to linking up with Brigade Colloredo and would certainly have had most favourable results. For that it would have been necessary to have a reserve of fresh, well-rested troops to send after the enemy falling back from Kápolna and to reap the fruits of this bloody victory at the Kerecsend defile. But it was impossible to do this. The forces used in this two-day battle directly before Kápolna, the centre of the enemy position, had a strength of no more than ten weak battalions, all of which had to remain in action continuously because of the great extent of the battle line and the enemy's numerical superiority. Ten grenadier companies under *Generalmajor* Schütte and six cavalry squadrons under *Oberst Graf* Montenuovo of the Kress Chevauxlegers were all that deserved to be called a reserve.

The *Feldmarschall* did not waste a moment before at least sending *Oberst Graf* Montenuovo after the enemy with his six squadrons (two of Civallart *uhlans*, two of Kress *chevauxlegers*, two of Max Auersperg cuirassiers) and two Kavallerie-Batteries, Nr. 2 and 8. The units in question were between Kápolna and Kompolt. Initially they tried head directly across the Tarna, but this proved unfeasible because of the many ditches and marshy areas, so finally they had to use the Kápolna bridge. Thus, by the time they had crossed the stream the enemy had already got a fair head start. Also, the terrain in the direction of Kerecsend was very uneven, and near the village it was forested. Once he was beyond Kápolna, *Oberst Graf* Montenuovo therefore moved somewhat to the right, and ran into the enemy columns that were retreating from Kál toward Füzes-Abány [Füzesabony, Hungary] under pressure from Division Schwarzenberg. He immediately brought up his batteries and opened up a very effective fire on the enemy rushing back in disorder. This was repeated twice more during the advance until after suffering significant losses the enemy finally reached Füzes-Abány, where he could not be attacked for lack of infantry so the pursuit had to be suspended.

It now just remains to describe the honourable part that Division Schwarzenberg played in the outcome of the battle of Kápolna. While Brigade Wyss was executing its attack on Kápolna, *Feldmarschall Lieutenant Fürst* Schwarzenberg had advanced against Kompolt and Kál. The enemy was still present in fairly strong numbers on this side of Kál, which was strongly held, as were the heights behind it on the left bank of the Tarna. Schwarzenberg's first concern had to be to drive the enemy back entirely behind the Tarna. To that end *Oberstlieutenant Baron* Minutillo was detached against the enemy's left flank with a division of Max Auersperg cuirassiers and Kavallerie-Battery Nr. 4, while at the same time all the artillery was brought into action against the front of the enemy position. This soon forced the enemy detachments deployed in front of Kál to withdraw to the position proper behind the Tarna, whereupon the advance continued against Kál and the Kompolt manor house. The 4. Bataillon Warasdiner-Kreutzer was detached against the latter, followed by the Banal battalion in support; but they found the manor already abandoned by the enemy, who had meanwhile concentrated all his combat forces at Kál. To attack this latter place and the heights behind it with the small force available was extremely difficult. Schwarzenberg therefore limited himself to bombarding the village with his attached artillery for a while. But when the progress that our other units had made at Kápolna in the meantime obliged the enemy to send detachments in that direction, at the right moment Schwarzenberg took the decision to go on the offensive himself and ordered *Generalmajor* Dietrich to attack Kál immediately. Dietrich carried out his mission with great skill and determination. The village was divided into two almost equal parts by a broad street, and after a short but intense bombardment the Warasdiner-Kreutzer battalion moved against one half, while the Banal battalion turned against the other. At the same time *Oberstlieutenant Graf* Nostiz with three squadrons of Civallart *uhlans* was ordered to drive back the hussar detachments deployed downstream of Kál. The enemy opened up a lively skirmish fire from the approaches to the village and the gardens around it, though this did not prevent the two battalions from storming into the village and driving the enemy out of it completely. During the initial approach to envelop the village *Generalmajor* Dietrich had suffered a seriously bruised leg, but this did not stop him from staying with his troops during the fight. The two battalions formed up again about 1,200 paces beyond Kál, while the Wimpffen and Eckert battalions that had followed on meanwhile, together with the artillery, crowned the heights directly in front of the village and so secured possession of it. After vacating the village the enemy had retreated toward Füzes-Abány, where as we have seen, he was overtaken by the cavalry brigade under *Oberst Graf* Montenuovo that the *Feldmarschall* had sent in that direction and that inflicted serious damage on him.

Brigade Dietrich had just nine men wounded. *Major* Regelsberg, *Hauptmann* Perakovic, *Oberlieutenant* Riedl and *Lieutenant* Sossky of the Warasdiner-Kreutzers, *Major* Petrovic and *Lieutenant* Hofmann of 2. Banal-Regiment, and finally *Brigade-Adjutant Oberlieutenant* Jakshin were named among those who had distinguished themselves.

Like all the other units spread out along the extended battle line, Division Schwarzenberg spent the night in the position in which nightfall caught it.

Our troops' total losses in the battle of Kápolna came to, dead: *Rittmeister Baron* Zülow of the Prinz von Preussen Kürassiere, *Hauptmann* Sauer of the Latour infantry, *Unterlieutenant* Franul von Weissenthurm of the Civallart-Uhlanen, *Lieutenant* Morvitzer of the artillery, and 56 men of *Feldwebel* and *Wachtmeister* rank and below; wounded: *Major Baron* Salis, *Hauptmann* Oppenauer and *Unterlieutenant* Briglewitz of the E.H. Stefan infantry; *Rittmeister Baron* Uichtritz (who later died of his wounds) and *Unterlieutenant* Urbani of the Prinz von Preussen Kürassiere; *Hauptmann* Liebler and *Oberlieutenant* Weiss of the Mazzuchelli infantry, *Hauptmann* Wekbecker and *Lieutenant* Schulz of 2. Jäger-Bataillon, *Unterlieutenant* Hostosch of the Latour infantry; *Unterlieutenant* Knesevich of the Ottochaner Grenz-Regiment; and 248 men of *Feldwebel* and *Wachtmeister* rank and below; missing: *Oberlieutenant Baron* Rolshausen (wounded) of the Prinz von Preussen Kürassiere, and 31 men of *Feldwebel* and *Wachtmeister* rank and below. Thus our losses came to 16 officers, 335 men and 152 horses altogether. Of these, nine officers, 166 men and 60 horses were lost by *Feldmarschall Lieutenant Graf* Schlick's corps.

If we take into account that the total number of units used in the battle of Kápolna only came to 22 and a half battalions, 25 squadrons and 147 guns (namely *Feldmarschall Lieutenant Graf* Wrbna's corps with 13 and a half battalions, 13 squadrons, 102 guns; and *Feldmarschall Lieutenant Graf* Schlick's corps, less Brigade Parrot detached to Gyöngyös, with nine battalions, 12 squadrons and 45 guns) and that the combat strength of these units came to no more than 18,696 infantry and 2,974 cavalry, and that this small force had to fight a two-day battle against

35,000-40,000 enemy troops, thus almost twice its strength,[124] then the losses suffered seem very small in proportion,[125] while the endurance, courage and unshakeable devotion of our troops are beyond all praise.

In his report sent most humbly to His Majesty the *Kaiser* on the very evening of the battle (the 27th), the *Feldmarschall* says: 'In this two-day battle we had to contend with significantly superior numbers of the enemy on all sides, but the superb spirit and courage of the troops, the purposeful leadership of the *Herr Generals* and the effective fire of our brave artillery were able to overcome this numerical superiority at every point.'

In the official account the following generals, staff and field officers were especially praised and some recommended for decoration. For the Order of the Iron Crown, 2nd Class: *Generalmajor Fürst* Colloredo. For the Knight's Cross of the Order of Leopold: *Oberst Graf* Montenuovo of the Kress Chevauxlegers, *Major* Kronenberg of 6. Jäger-Bataillon and *Major Baron* Baselli of the Civallart-Uhlanen. For the Order of the Iron Crown, 3rd Class: *Oberstlieutenant Baron* Minutillo of the Auersperg Kürassiere, *Major* Wimmer of the Ottochaner-Regiment, *Major* Künigl of the Latour-Infanterie, *Hauptmann* Hubatschek of the Hartmann-Infanterie, *Hauptmann* Liebler of Mazzuchelli, *Rittmeister* Fischer of the Kress-Chevauxlegers, *Hauptmann Baron* Feldegg of 6. Jäger-Bataillon, *Oberlieutenant Fürst* Ludwig Windisch-Grätz of the Prohaska-Infanterie, *Oberlieutenants* Seidl and Hirschmann of the artillery, *Lieutenant* Haas of the Feuerwerks-Korps [rocketeers], *Lieutenant* Guggenoss of the Hartmann-Infanterie and *Hauptmann* Kantar of the Ottochaners, who distinguished himself in the surprise attack at Pétervására.

In addition, the following were especially praised: the two corps commanders *Feldmarschall Lieutenant Graf* Schlick and *Feldmarschall Lieutenant Graf* Wrbna, *Feldmarschall Lieutenant*

124 Hermann provides figures that suggest the disparity was not quite as extreme as Nobili claims. He says that on the first day of the battle, 22,000 Hungarians with 63 guns were present – of whom only 14,000 and 48 guns were engaged along the Tarna, the rest merely holding Verpeléth – with 6,500 more men and 17 more guns arriving that evening to join in on the second day; a further 9,000 (Kmety and Guyon) with 44 guns only turned up in time to cover the retreat after the battle was over. Against these, Hermann says Wrbna's II. Armeekorps had 15,000 men and 102 guns, while Schlick had 13,000 and 51. The total forces engaged were therefore of similar strength, with Hungarian superiority in manpower compensated for by superior numbers and weight of Austrian guns. Hermann, *Az 1848-1849-es.*

125 At about 1.5% of the forces engaged, these casualties are indeed low, but this seems to have been the case generally in this war. For all the main battles of the Hungarian War of Independence, my estimate of average casualties – dead and wounded only, not including captured and missing – is that they tended to be around 2% (lower for the victor, higher for the defeated side). This contrasts with casualty rates of sometimes 20% or more for the Napoleonic Wars fought with basically the same weaponry a few decades earlier. I surmise that the reason for the relatively low casualty ratios may be to do with relatively low troop density and with the relatively open terrain of Hungary, with the resulting effect that commanders with few reserves behind them tended to be wary of threats to their flanks in open country, and to fall back sooner than they would have if better supported and in more secure positions. Some data to support this surmise: the battles of Kápolna and Isaszeg in 1849 were both fought by about 25,000-30,000 men a side, on battlefields 15 km across, producing a troop density of about 2,000 men per km and casualties of 1.5-2.5%. A similar sized Napoleonic battle from the Peninsular War, Albuera, involved 25,000-35,000 men on a 7-8 km front, 4,000-5,000 per km, and 20-25% casualties. A larger more open battle, Salamanca, had more men: 50,000 a side, about 5,000-6,000 per km, 5% casualties for the victor, and 10% for the loser. Climactic battles such as Waterloo and Borodino reached troop densities of 10,000-20,000 per km and casualty rates around 20 percent.

Baron Csorich, *Feldmarschall Lieutenant Fürst* Edmund Schwarzenberg, *Generalmajor und Brigadier* Wyss, *Generalmajor und Brigadier* Dietrich, *Oberstlieutenant* Dürfeld of 6. Jäger-Bataillon, *Oberstlieutenant Graf* Nostiz of Civallart-Uhlanen, *Major* Augustinec of Paumgarten Infanterie; *Major Graf* Alberti of Kress-Chevauxlegers, *Major Baron* Gablenz of the general staff, *Major* Regelsberg of the Warasdiner-Kreutzer, *Major Baron* Salis of E.H. Stefan Infanterie, *Major* Karajan of E.H. Ferdinand Husaren, *Major* Bach of the general staff, *Major* Scherpon of the artillery, *Major* Zailler (*Korps-Adjutant* of II. Armee-Korps), *Major* Bogdanovics of the Warasdiner-S. Georger, *Major* Piatolli of Hartmann Infanterie; *Hauptmanns* Dobner, Kalik and Krzisch of the general staff; *Hauptmanns* Brandenstein and Fritsch of 6. Jäger-Bataillon; *Hauptmanns* Wiedenmann, *Don* S. Agnese, Kögler and Krump of Schönhals Infanterie; *Rittmeister* Ziegler of Kress-Chevauxlegers; *Rittmeisters Graf* Méssey, Du Mesnil and Hussey of Civallart-Uhlanen; *Rittmeister* Greipl of Reuss-Husaren; *Rittmeisters* Liebler and Klement of Kaiser Husaren; *Rittmeisters Graf* Königsegg and De Best of Kaiser Ferdinand Kürassiere; *Rittmeister* Levritz of Kaiser Nikolaus-Husaren; *Rittmeister Fürst* Hugo Windisch-Grätz of Palatinal-Husaren; *Rittmeister Graf* Török; *Hauptmann* Egkh of Konstantin-Infanterie; *Hauptmann* Brandenstein of Geppert-Infanterie, attached to the general staff; *Hauptmann* Hasslinger of Prinz Emil Infanterie; *Hauptmanns* Sauer, Horaczek and Fialka of Latour-Infanterie; *Oberlieutenant* Bujanovic of E.H. Karl Chevauxlegers; *Oberlieutenant Fürst* Ludwig Windisch-Grätz of Prohaska-Infanterie; *Oberlieutenant* Weiss of Mazzuchelli-Infanterie; *Oberlieutenants* Miskosch and Alten of the artillery; *Oberlieutenant* Friedberg of Latour-Infanterie; *Oberlieutenants* Dworaczek and Angerer of the Feuerwerks-Korps; *Oberlieutenant Baron* Henniger attached to the general staff; *Oberlieutenant* Heyssler of E.H. Baden Infanterie; *Oberlieutenants* Heinold, Fastenberger and Kneiper of Schönhals Infanterie; *Oberlieutenants* Klein and Stenglin of 6. Jäger-Bataillon; *Oberlieutenants* Peduzzi, Schulz and Czizek of 2. Jäger-Bataillon; *Oberlieutenant Baron* Scholley of Kaiser Nikolaus-Husaren; *Unterlieutenant* Hausner of the transport corps; *Unterlieutenant* Grigar of Hartmann-Infanterie; *Unterlieutenants* Henerici and Fiala of Latour-Infanterie;[126] *Unterlieutenants* Lendvich and Kirchsberg of E.H. Stefan; *Unterlieutenant* Gastheimb of König von Preussen Husaren; *Unterlieutenants* Petrides and Csap of the artillery.

Aftermath of Kápolna: Pursuit to Mezö-Kövesd, 28 February to 1 March 1849

The *Feldmarschall* had advanced with Kavallerie-Brigade Montenuovo for a while when he sent it to pursue the enemy but returned to Kápolna as darkness was falling to make the necessary dispositions for the following day. He issued the order to both corps to march at 7:00 a.m. in pursuit of the enemy. *Feldmarschall Lieutenant Graf* Schlick's corps and Division Csorich of II. Armee-korps were to advance through Kerecsend, Division Schwarzenberg through Füzes-Abány. *Generalmajor* Zeisberg had moved his brigade forward to Bod [Tarnabod, Hungary]

126 In this particular list of those who distinguished themselves, the Latour regiment is listed throughout as 'vac. Latour'. I believe 'vac.' means 'vacant', the late *Oberstinhaber* (regimental colonel) of Infanterie-Regiment Nr. 28 being Theodor *Graf* Baillet von Latour (1780-1848), the imperial minister of war who had been murdered by the mob during the revolution in Vienna on 6 October 1848. *BLKÖ*, Vol.1, p.125. Baillet (Latour) was succeeded as *Oberstinhaber* by then *Generalmajor* Ludwig *Ritter* von Benedek in July 1849.

while Division Schwarzenberg was fighting at Kál and then, without having taken part in the battle, had marched to Erdőtelek that evening. At 10:30 p.m. that night (the 27th) he was sent the following order:

> At 7:00 a.m. tomorrow, *Feldmarschall Lieutenant Graf* Schlick's corps and that of *Feldmarschall Lieutenant Graf* Wrbna will advance on Kerecsend and Füzes-Abány. Roads divide off from there to Erlau, Mezö-Kövesd and Poroszló, so it is not until there that we will be able to tell in which direction the enemy must be pursued. Your Honour's mission remains to ensure the security of my right flank toward Heves and Poroszló. According to unconfirmed reports, an enemy column is supposed to have headed toward Heves. I imagine that this would not have escaped Your Honour's notice.

Before 7:00 a.m. on the 28th, *Feldmarschall Lieutenant Graf* Schlick sent *Major Prinz* Moriz Nassau to report to the *Feldmarschall* that the position at Kerecsend was strongly held by the enemy, and that he thought attacking it would be very difficult.

While the units of II. Armeekorps set off from Kápolna and Kál at 7:00 a.m. in accordance with the orders received, the *Feldmarschall* hurried ahead to reconnoitre the Kerecsend position for himself. On arriving there he found that the position was indeed strong, but had been abandoned apart from a weak enemy rear guard that retreated soon after; yet Schlick's men were still busy cooking breakfast, so they could not be ready to march for a couple of hours.[127] It was therefore decided that II. Armeekorps at least should carry on marching without pause to Maklár and Füzes-Abány, but should then wait there for Schlick's corps. However, the cavalry were to carry on pursuing the enemy anyway.

Brigade Pergen, on the left wing of *Feldmarschall Lieutenant Graf* Schlick's camp, received the order to stay there until it had been established for certain that Erlau was no longer held by the enemy, and then to move to rejoin the corps at Maklár.

Finally, the order was issued to Brigade Parrot to leave a garrison in Gyöngyös and follow the army as far as Kápolna, to where the Munizions-Reserve was also to be sent.

II. Armeekorps reached Maklár and Füzes-Abány around midday without having encountered the enemy. *Feldmarschall Lieutenant Graf* Schlick's corps did not reach the camp at Maklár until the afternoon. But Kavallerie-Brigade Deym had arrived there with *Major Baron* Gablenz of the general staff a couple of hours earlier and advanced from there in the direction of Mezö-Kövesd, to where Kavallerie-Brigade Montenuovo of II. Armeekorps had also set off together with *Major* Bach of the general staff. Brigade Deym (two Sunstenau squadrons, five squadrons of Prinz von Preussen cuirassiers and nine horse artillery pieces) ran into much stronger detachments of enemy cavalry about 4 km this side of Mezö-Kövesd. Paying more heed to lust for battle than to reason, this brigade got involved in a very unequal fight which turned out badly for it, as was to be expected. Attacked in front and flank by hussar detachments of more than twice their number, the cuirassiers were driven back with the loss of nine dead and 49 wounded. Three horse artillery pieces that could not get away quickly enough across a ditch also fell into the enemy's hands. Among the wounded were *Major Prinz* Holstein who

127 This is uncharacteristic of the aggressive Schlick. Unfortunately for Windisch-Grätz, not only does Schlick's hesitation cause a delay by requiring a reconnaissance, Schlick then compounds the delay by letting his men cook so that they are not ready to attack when the reconnaissance is completed.

had volunteered to join the charge, *Rittmeister* Wenzelides, *Lieutenants* Daniek and Reyl of the Prinz von Preussen cuirassiers, and *Lieutenant* Melcher of the Sunstenau cuirassiers.

Kavallerie-Brigade Montenuovo (2. Majors-Division of Civallart-Uhlanen, Majors-Division of Max Auersperg Kürassiere, two squadrons of Kress-Chevauxlegers and Kavallerie-Batterie Nr. 2), which had diverged somewhat to the left of the road to Mezö-Kövesd, was just approaching that town when Brigade Deym was driven back by the enemy. A marshy ditch prevented it from charging the enemy's flank, but *Major* Bach of the general staff managed to find a place where at least a battery could be got across to a point from which the enemy cavalry could be fired on effectively. This indeed produced the most favourable result. Scarcely had the first shots landed when the hussars gave up the pursuit and now, worried about their own flank, retreated to their earlier position in front of Mezö-Kövesd. There the enemy army was formed up ready for battle and apparently awaiting a serious attack. Our cavalry gradually withdrew to the area of Maklár and Szihalom, where outposts were established as darkness fell. Among the guns that were lost were two pieces that had been taken from the enemy at Kaschau.

The *Feldmarschall,* who had set up his headquarters in Maklár, was understandably displeased by the outcome of this pointless cavalry action. Furthermore, as a consequence of his exertions over the last few days he was feeling seriously unwell and was finding it an effort to stay in the saddle. Upon receiving the news around 3:30 p.m. that the enemy army had taken position at Mezö-Kövesd and might stay there to await an attack, he wasted no time in making arrangements to advance next day.

The terrain that had to be crossed in advancing from Maklár to Mezö-Kövesd was quite open and flat, with barely noticeable undulations in only a few places. This therefore called mainly for cavalry and artillery action. In any case, on this quite open ground lacking any points of support, the deepest possible battle formation had to be adopted as the most suitable method for keeping units in hand to be used as necessary and for security against being outflanked. Accordingly the following battle formation was established for the advance and issued to the corps commanders with the instruction that the troops should be deployed as follows at 8:00 a.m. the next morning (1 March):

> Brigades Kriegern, Fiedler and Colloredo (10 battalions) in the centre
> Brigade Wyss (four battalions) on the right wing, Brigade Pergen (three battalions) on the left, both wings being refused in echelon
> The brigade batteries with their assigned brigades
> The corps artillery reserves behind the two wings of the centre
> Infanterie-Division Edmund Schwarzenberg with Kavallerie-Brigades Deym and Bellegarde (5 and a third battalions, 24 squadrons) in reserve behind the centre
> The Artillerie-Hauptreserve behind Division Schwarzenberg
> *Oberst Graf* Montenuovo's cavalry to form the advance guard.

From the above battle formation, by taking one or other of the brigades echeloned behind the wings, once could either extend the front line or, by having them move forward beyond it, easily shift into an oblique line. The cavalry and artillery were kept as massed as possible to be able to be used according to the situation.[128]

Brigade Pergen arrived in the camp at Maklár that evening, as Erlau had been found to have been abandoned by the enemy so there was no need to worry about the army's left flank. As far as the security of the right flank was concerned, whatever would be, would be. This was Brigade Zeisberg's sole mission, and there was all the less concern about what could have happened there meanwhile, particularly at Poroszló, since the said general had reported from Erdőtelek at 3:30 a.m. on the morning of the 28th that, 'in accordance with your noble orders, today (the 28th) I will operate through Besenyö toward Poroszló'. Besides, at that time it was not thought that the enemy would retreat from Mezö-Kövesd to Poroszló. If that had been his intention, then after the battle of Kápolna he could have headed directly there from Kerecsend via Mezö-Tárkany [Mezőtárkány, Hungary]. Thus while one did want to be sure that particular attention was always being paid to Poroszló, this was more because of the concern that an enemy column might debouch from there.

Toward 8:00 p.m. that evening the two corps commanders, *Feldmarschall Lieutenants Graf* Schlick and *Graf* Wrbna came to the *Feldmarschall* and stated that the advance ordered for the next day could not take place. They said that their troops were very fatigued, and also that they were short of artillery ammunition. *Feldartilleriedirektor Generalmajor* Dietrich was immediately summoned to explain this last point. He stated 'that on the two previous days of battle certainly a quite disproportionately large quantity of artillery ammunition had been expended (over 6,000 rounds), and also the units had neglected to attend to replacing it in good time. However, this could still be done overnight, as the Munizions-Reserve was in Kápolna.' The *Feldmarschall* therefore felt himself obliged – albeit with visible reluctance – to ordain that the troops should deploy for battle at 8:00 a.m. as ordered, but that the planned further advance should then only take place if the enemy himself were advancing to attack.[129]

The next day (1 March) therefore had to be seen as yet another one lost to inaction, which at that particular moment could only be regarded as seriously detrimental. This misfortune was finally rendered complete when word came in from *Generalmajor* Zeisberg that he had marched back to Erdőtelek again, since his artillery could not move down the chosen road to Besenyö. He was now going to move along the road through Tenk and Átány.[130]

128 This is reminiscent of colonial expeditionary forces like the British in the Sudan in the 1890s, or the French in Algeria in the 1830s and 1840s, advancing against a mobile and irregular enemy in hostile territory, and doing so by moving in large hollow squares ready to face a threat from any direction.

129 This is one of several occasions where the *Feldmarschall*'s plans are stymied by his subordinates' objections or non-compliance. A more forceful personality than Windisch-Grätz might have overridden these objections this time and said, 'press on now, exploit our success, accept that we may lose stragglers temporarily from fatigue, take the risk of the batteries falling silent, but we must push home our advantage now'; and this would probably have been the right thing to do. But Windisch-Grätz gave in again.

130 Zeisberg lets the *Feldmarschall* down again. He could surely have pressed down the direct route with most of his force, and just sent his artillery on the detour with suitable escort. Having said that, the instruction given to him as noted above was: 'Your Honour's mission remains to ensure the security of my right flank toward Heves and Poroszló.' Perhaps this was not clear enough about the specific importance of Poroszló.

The repeated non-occurrence of the march to observe Poroszló was extremely unfortunate, all the more so as it was now too late to remedy this mishap in some other way. Thus at 9:00 p.m. a letter was sent to *Generalmajor* Zeisberg informing him of the army's position as well as the dispositions for the next day, and along with that it was intimated, 'that your present position at Erdőtelek is too far refused. You should therefore move to Besenyö as early as possible tomorrow (1 March). You will thereby come into closer communications with the army, and will be able to observe the road leading to Poroszló effectively, as well as generally covering the army's right flank.'

At 8:00 a.m. on 1 March the army stood formed up for battle on the road leading to Mezö-Kövesd, about 5 km in front of Maklár, in accordance with the dispositions as issued. Led by *Feldmarschall Lieutenant Fürst* Franz Liechtenstein, who did not actually have an assignment among the units concentrated here but had been placed at the *Feldmarschall*'s disposal, cavalry detachments were pushed forward toward Mezö-Kövesd to reconnoitre the enemy position, but could scarcely see 100 paces ahead initially because of a snowstorm. Toward midday the weather cleared up somewhat, and it now became possible to get a better view of the area. Liechtenstein then realised that the enemy had already abandoned Mezö-Kövesd, and at the same time detected the rear guard of an endless column that was moving in great haste through Sz. István [Szentistván, Hungary] to Ivánka [Borsodivánka, Hungary], a village on the road from Mezö-Kövesd to Poroszló. It was now clear that the enemy was in full retreat to Poroszló and must already have begun to retreat during the night. Thus, one had learned of this manoeuvre at least eight hours too late, despite the fact that the strategic importance of Poroszló had never been overlooked, and that all the necessary dispositions had been made to obtain news in good time of anything noteworthy that might occur there.

The Hungarian Army Escapes through Poroszló, 1-2 March 1849

When *Feldmarschall Lieutenant Fürst* Liechtenstein gave the *Feldmarschall* the message about the discovery of the enemy's direction of retreat, he expressed the view that, even if there was now no hope of reaching Poroszló ahead of the enemy, his rear guard could still be overtaken and be done some serious damage.

The *Feldmarschall* ordered *Feldmarschall Lieutenant Graf* Wrbna to march on Poroszló immediately via Szihalom and Eger-Farmos [Egerfarmos, Hungary] with Division Csorich and the assembled Kavallerie-Brigade Montenuovo. Brigades Dietrich and Zeisberg were directed there too, the former from Füzes-Abány via Mezö-Tárkany. The relevant order for the latter was passed to *Feldmarschall Lieutenant Fürst* Schwarzenberg for urgent delivery to Zeisberg, since it was not actually known exactly where his brigade was.

The number of units put at *Feldmarschall Lieutenant Graf* Wrbna's disposal for the pursuit of the enemy thus came to 13 and a half battalions, ten squadrons and 63 guns, namely:

Division Csorich: eight battalions, 18 guns, Artillerie-Reserve 18 guns
Kavallerie-Brigade Montenuovo: six squadrons, six guns
Brigade Dietrich: three and a half battalions, nine guns
Brigade Zeisberg: two battalions, four squadrons, 12 guns.

The *Feldmarschall* accompanied Division Csorich until it was beyond Szihalom, then returned to Maklár where *Feldmarschall Lieutenant Graf* Schlick's corps had occupied Csorich's former camp, while the cavalry under *Generalmajor Graf* Deym was pushed forward through Mezö-Kövesd so as overtake individual enemy detachments from that side as well if possible. Scarcely had he arrived in Maklár, which must have been about 3:00 p.m., when heavy artillery fire was heard from the direction of Poroszló. There was now no longer any doubt that *Feldmarschall Lieutenant Graf* Wrbna had run into the retreating enemy, and one could now quite justifiably cherish the hope that Wrbna would press the enemy hard and pursue him. To make this even more certain, the *Feldmarschall* sent his son and aide-de-camp, *Major Fürst* Alfred Windisch-Grätz, as quickly as possible to Wrbna with the verbal order, 'to continue the pursuit vigorously and to do as much damage to the enemy as possible'.

A second officer was likewise sent to find *Generalmajor* Zeisberg and indicate to him that the *Feldmarschall* hoped, 'that when he heard the artillery fire while in the Eger-Farmos area, he had immediately hurried toward Poroszló'. At the same time he was to be given the necessary information concerning the lines of march of Division Csorich and Brigades Montenuovo and Dietrich and advised that 'he should also make every effort to overtake the enemy before he has completed his crossing, and to inflict as much damage on him as possible'.

A very dark night had already fallen when *Major Fürst* Alfred Windisch-Grätz arrived in Eger-Farmos, where he found *Feldmarschall Lieutenant Graf* Wrbna. During his march from Szihalom through Szemere [Mezőszemere, Hungary], Wrbna had run into a substantial enemy force at Eger-Farmos, obviously a strong rear guard which the enemy had deployed to protect his retreat through the long defile at Poroszló. Wrbna had Brigade Wyss advance with Kavallerie-Batteries Nr. 2 and 8, Zwölfpfündige Batterie Nr. 3 and half of Raketen-Batterie Nr. 15, keeping Brigade Colloredo in reserve. A heavy artillery duel arose immediately, as the enemy had brought three batteries into action. After a while 2. Jäger-Bataillon advanced against the village of Eger-Farmos that was only weakly held by the enemy, while Kavallerie-Brigade Montenuovo advanced swiftly to the side of it in echelon, during which *Lieutenant* Sternberger of the Civallart *uhlans* had his right foot torn off by a cannonball. The *jägers* pressed determinedly into the village and drove the enemy rear guard out of it entirely. About 1,600 paces beyond Eger-Farmos the enemy formed up once again but it was not possible to press the advantage gained any further as night had fallen in the meantime and the ground was very sodden, marshy and generally extremely difficult going. The troops therefore spent the night in Eger-Farmos where, as we have seen, *Major Fürst* Alfred Windisch-Grätz found *Feldmarschall Lieutenant Graf* Wrbna.

The troops formed up to march off early on 2 March. After conducting a reconnaissance, *Feldmarschall Lieutenant Graf* Wrbna decided to move across to the road leading to Poroszló from Füzes-Abány via Mezö-Tárkany since this was a better road and also the bridges on it were still standing, while the enemy had demolished those on the other routes. In Mezö-Tárkany he met up with Brigades Dietrich and Zeisberg. The latter had come there from Besenyö. Wrbna now disposed Brigade Zeisberg to the right onto the road that joins the Besenyö road from the Theiss, while he took the direct route to Poroszló with the main column. The two columns came into close communication again about 2,000 paces this side of Poroszló.

The ground around Poroszló is broken up by marshy depressions crossed by tongues of dry ground often only 100-200 paces wide, which greatly hindered the approach to the village and generally meant it was only possible in a few places. The enemy rear guard had deployed behind these defiles and commanded the approaches with some batteries.

After *Feldmarschall Lieutenant Graf* Wrbna had reconnoitred the terrain and the enemy rear guard's position, he stated that: 'I see the only possible way to attack as being that *Generalmajor* Zeisberg should advance with his own brigade and Brigade Dietrich against the enemy's left flank where the village of Poroszló extends furthest toward the defiles, should set light to the village and then advance swiftly. This is the only way to make it possible to debouch against the front without significant losses.' When Wrbna discussed this with Zeisberg, the latter remarked that 'in carrying out this plan, two thirds of the troops would be left behind, which would be irresponsible given the chronic weakness of the army as a whole'.

The corps commander now asked *Major Fürst* Windisch-Grätz to ride back to the *Feldmarschall* and report back to him, adding: '[Y]ou have seen that I wanted to attack. However, I cannot take it upon myself to take this chance. I will summon my generals to a council of war at which you will be present so as then to report to the *Feldmarschall* about it.' Calling a council of war at a moment when any general should have been able to make an independent decision was a mistake. Generally such conferences rarely produce anything useful, least of all when there is a need to act quickly, and the responsibility rests solely with the commander. When the generals had gathered and Wrbna had told them his original plan and the reason for his hesitation, *Generalmajor* Zeisberg spoke up:

> I cannot change my mind. It is possible that the whole enemy army is waiting there for us. The position cannot be attacked frontally; but it is already too late to unite all the troops on the two flanks, where we do not know the state of the ground in this variable terrain [Nobili notes that it must already have been between 2:00 and 3:00 p.m.]. Besides, we would do less harm to the enemy than we would suffer ourselves. Perhaps the *Feldmarschall* could bring his whole army here to attack the enemy position successfully.

The other generals endorsed Zeisberg's view. *Major Fürst* Windisch-Grätz permitted himself to remark:

> I will happily explain to headquarters about the difficulties that attacking the enemy position would present. However, it cannot possibly turn out that the whole enemy army is at Poroszló, since it cannot be thought that the enemy who was unable to hold the advantageous position at Kápolna, and who later would not accept battle on the plain at Mezö-Kövesd despite his cavalry superiority, would now be willing to make a stand at Poroszló with a 5 km defile behind him.

Wrbna now raised the question, 'where should we spend the night?' The corps's position in front of Poroszló was felt to be too dangerous, since there was concern about it being outflanked during the night. There was also a shortage of provisions. With the exception of *Generalmajor* Wyss, who spoke in favour of staying in the present position and for close and continuous observation of the enemy, it was agreed that the corps should withdraw. Wrbna now dispatched *Major Fürst* Windisch-Grätz to give the *Feldmarschall* a verbal report about the state of affairs.[131]

The troops were pulled back to Mezö-Tárkany (15 km from Poroszló). The enemy was able to continue his retreat all night and the next day as well without being disturbed in the least. With that the last hope of causing him any serious loss disappeared.

The Imperial Army Shifts Back to the Middle Theiss, 3-7 March 1849

If we summarise the events of the previous days in a few words, it turned out that:

1. With the exception of Division Ramberg, which had sat inactive in Kaschau since 22 February, all available combat forces had been united at the decisive point of Kápolna. Any not fighting at Kápolna were indispensable wherever they were, namely: the siege corps outside Komorn (nine and four-sixths battalions, nine squadrons, 36 guns); the garrison of Ofen-Pesth (three battalions); and finally nine battalions, 22 squadrons and 48 guns observing the middle Theiss and covering Pesth, from whence all the field army's requirements for ammunition and provisions had to be supplied.[132]
2. The army could have been united a couple of days earlier if the *Feldmarschall*'s plans had not been frustrated, whereby it might have been possible to attack the enemy before he had finished concentrating his forces.[133] At all events, it would have given more coordination and impact to the offensive manoeuvre than was actually possible in the battle of Kápolna, where on the first day (the 26th) formations ran into the enemy unexpectedly while still separated, and on the second day (the 27th) were fighting on such an excessively extended line from Verpeléth to Kál (a 15 km stretch) that it was impossible to get an overview of the battle and to conduct it with any certainty.

131 In its small way, this is a classic episode illustrative of the defective instrument that was Windisch-Grätz's army. His generals are excessively cautious and unwilling to take responsibility; they seek safety in numbers by holding a council of war, and perhaps by now they know they are unlikely to receive more than a mild reproof from the *Feldmarschall.* They ignore the common sense spoken by *Major* Windisch-Grätz, and the verbal order he brought 'to continue the pursuit vigorously and to do as much damage to the enemy as possible', and thus miss an opportunity to exploit the victory at Kápolna. We must also give some credit to the Hungarian commander, Dembinsky, for successfully executing this risky withdrawal across the enemy's front and through the Poroszló defile.

132 Ramberg's inaction was not Windisch-Grätz's fault but due to Ramberg's own excessive caution and to a delay in orders reaching him. Komorn did need to be masked, as its garrison had already shown energy and activity in sorties, and it could threaten Windisch-Grätz's supply lines. Garrisoning Ofen-Pesth was likewise important for supplies. Screening Pesth on the middle Theiss is given the same justification; we might argue that this force could have been given a more active mission, but perhaps the advantage gained would not have been worth the risk.

133 Notwithstanding his problems in putting his plans into effect, by the measure of who best concentrated his force and who best used it for offensive action, Windisch-Grätz at least proved himself superior to his adversary Dembinsky.

3. On the 28th the pursuit was delayed by the erroneous message that the enemy seemed to be intending to make a stand in the Kerecsend position, and then by the troops not being kept in readiness to march.
4. On 1 March the advance was suspended as a consequence of the *Feldmarschall* being informed too late about the lack of ammunition.
5. The enemy's retreat toward Poroszló was not discovered early enough, even though no effort was neglected to obtain information in good time concerning anything significant that might be occurring on the army's right flank; and finally,
6. The pursuit toward Poroszló was not carried out with the necessary energy and self-sacrifice that such situations demand.[134]

However, despite the fact that the enemy had not suffered a complete defeat of the kind to exert a decisive influence on the course of the campaign, the result of the battle of Kápolna remained a very important one; for it had succeeded in stopping an opponent almost twice as numerous from advancing on Pesth as he intended, and in beating him and throwing him back across the Theiss. This success consisted mainly in not being beaten ourselves, something which had after all been a possibility given the enemy's numerical superiority.[135]

We do not know the reasons that motivated the enemy to choose to retreat from Mezö-Kövesd through Poroszló, but they soon become clear when we take into account that, from the moment when he found himself forced to seek shelter behind the Theiss, his only options were to cross there or at Tokay. Continuing his retreat to Tokay would have been risky, for Division Ramberg could have moved out of Kaschau at last and threatened his line of retreat, whereas Poroszló could be reached in a single day's march. Mind you, this march was a flank march that had to be carried out partly in sight of his adversary, but anyone who knows the area between Mezö-Kövesd and Poroszló will concede that this manoeuvre was not so risky as one might think from a glance at the map; for the road running through Sz. István and Ivánka is protected throughout by the Kanyi-Folgás stream [the Kánya], the Erlau river and extensive marshlands, so that flank attacks against a column following this road are quite unfeasible.

Now that the enemy army's retreat behind the Theiss was to be regarded as complete, there could not be much doubt about what to do next. Pursuing the enemy across the Theiss was unfeasible because of the nature of the local terrain around the crossing point. The only approach from Poroszló to the great bridge over the Theiss more than 6 km away from the town leads along a narrow causeway that runs through marshy ground and has many wooden culvert bridges. At the end of this causeway directly in front of the Theiss bridge, as well as on the far (left) bank, the enemy had constructed entrenchments enfilading the bridge lengthwise and the causeway as well, so that approaching the bridge would have been extremely difficult and forcing a crossing absolutely impossible.[136] On the other hand, within four or five days the enemy army

134 Items 2-6 are all problems caused by the unreliability of Windisch-Grätz's subordinates. Schlick, Zeisberg and Wrbna are all culpable – but the common factor is Windisch-Grätz failing to impose his will on them.

135 While it is true that this was a successful defence of Pesth, given the multiple avoidable mishaps that Nobili has just listed it could also be seen as a missed opportunity to destroy the enemy's main body.

136 Footnote in the original text states: 'These details about the local terrain around the Poroszló crossing had come partly from spies, partly from *Lieutenants* Starich, Zuna and Gruber of Infanterie-Regiment

could have marched along the left bank of the Theiss from Tisza-Füred to Czibakháza in perfect safety, crossed the Theiss there, and pounced on and smashed the weak I. Armeekorps deployed between Szolnok and Pesth; then, substantially reinforced by Vecsey's and Damjanich's corps that had stayed at Török-S. Miklos and Czibakháza, it could have resumed the offensive against Pesth or Waitzen again with the prospect of success.

There was therefore no option but to deploy the army as quickly as possible between Szolnok and Pesth[137] – namely facing the middle Theiss – so that whether the enemy were to turn toward the upper Theiss again, or to debouch from Czibakháza, or lastly to cross the Theiss further down at Csongrád where he likewise held a crossing, our army could be concentrated in whichever direction was threatened within one or two days' march. This could only be achieved by transferring its formations to Jász-Berény [Jászberény, Hungary], Tapio-Szele, Czegléd, Nagy-Körös [Nagykörös, Hungary] and Kecskemét – in short, onto the route running through those towns parallel with the Theiss.

Although Brigades Kriegern and Fiedler had now also been put at the disposal of *Feldmarschall Lieutenant Graf* Wrbna, on the 3rd he reported that regardless, he still did not see any promise of success from attacking Poroszló. Instead he pointed to the danger that could arise from staying in front of Poroszló for any period of time. The *Feldmarschall* therefore had to abandon any hope of swift and energetic action in this area, and unless he wanted to waste yet more time in inaction, had to execute his decision to set the army on the march to the south without hesitating any longer.[138]

Dispositions for the march were issued accordingly to all units on the 3rd. I. Armeekorps was provisionally directed into cantonments around Kecskemét, II. Armeekorps to Czegléd, and *Feldmarschall Lieutenant Graf* Schlick's corps to Jász-Berény. I. Armeekorps was not to leave its present positions between Szolnok and Pesth until II. Armeekorps had arrived there.

Feldmarschall Lieutenant Schulzig was left at Mezö-Tárkany to observe Poroszló for the time being with Brigades Fiedler and Kriegern and Kavallerie-Brigade Montenuovo, or nine battalions, six squadrons and 24 guns altogether. After Schulzig was taken ill on the 4th, the *Feldmarschall* assigned *Feldmarschall Lieutenant Fürst* Franz Liechtenstein to take over command of the units left in front of Poroszló. Liechtenstein arrived on the 5th and decided to advance to attack Poroszló the very next day (the 6th), for he wanted to be certain at any cost of the strength of the enemy force posted there, about which we were still completely in the dark up to that point. The advance ensued on the 6th after cooking breakfast, and followed the road leading from Besenyö to Poroszló. By 2:00 p.m. Liechtenstein was in possession of Poroszló. All he found there was a rear guard of a few hussar detachments, who hastily retreated when our troops approached.

Nr. 39 who, equipped with discharge papers, had found a way on 27 February to get through Tisza-Füred and Poroszló to Gyöngyös, where they reported to *Generalmajor* Parrot on the 28th.'

137 Whenever Nobili observes 'there was no option', we should consider what options there were: Windisch-Grätz could have crossed elsewhere, e.g., at Tokay, or in fact by boat anywhere, to continue his pursuit; perhaps the *Banus* could have been trusted to fight a delaying action and/or fall back on the fortress at Buda if attacked, and to hold out long enough for Windisch-Grätz to fall on the enemy's rear like hammer and anvil. All too often, Windisch-Grätz's caution seems based on a keen appreciation of his own risks and problems without sufficient thought about the enemy's own concerns.

138 We have previously noted this many times: Windisch-Grätz urging action and his subordinate demurring. Three days later, Liechtenstein shows that Wrbna's fears were groundless.

Poroszló was now held by our troops for the first time since the outbreak of war. There was no trace of the entrenchments whose existence had been reported just a few days earlier, and that it had been supposed would make attacking Poroszló so difficult. However, when he followed swiftly behind the retreating enemy toward the Theiss bridge with the H.v. Parma battalion and a few rocket launch stands, inflicting some damage, *Feldmarschall Lieutenant Fürst* Liechtenstein did establish that forcing the crossing under the eyes of an enemy army would have been quite unfeasible. As stated above, the bridge could only be approached along a narrow causeway over 6 km long, and the enemy had constructed batteries at the end of the bridge as well as on the left bank of the Theiss. Liechtenstein therefore gave up on advancing any further toward the great Theiss bridge and contented himself with barring the enemy from debouching toward Poroszló by demolishing and burning the many bridges along the causeway, as well as setting fire to the large bridge across the Erlau that interrupts the causeway between Poroszló and the Theiss. Concerning the mission he had been given of finding out whether the enemy's *débouchement* could not be obstructed by constructing fieldworks at Poroszló, he stated that because of the great extent of the line to be entrenched, and the state of the soggy and often bottomless soil, and finally the possibility of outflanking the position by using the many ferries on the Theiss, this was not feasible.[139]

After completing the demolition work described above and also sinking every boat to the bottom, so that there was no more need to worry about the enemy debouching through Poroszló in the near future, *Feldmarschall Lieutenant Fürst* Liechtenstein set his troops on the march on the 7th and rejoined *Feldmarschall Lieutenant Graf* Schlick's corps that had arrived in Jász-Berény in the meantime.

The last detachments of our troops had scarcely left the area when armed bands of 40 to 60 men came down from the nearby Mátra Mountains and made the roads unsafe. Thus on the 5th not far from Maklár five ammunition carts that were following II. Armeekorps escorted by a detachment of *grenzers* were surprised and captured. Couriers, ambulances and the like could no longer be sent out without risk. For the time being a battalion of Brigade Fiedler had to stay behind in Gyöngyös to protect those sick and wounded who could not be moved, or else they would have been exposed to the danger of being cruelly mistreated by marauding bands and taken off into captivity.[140]

What has been learned about the Hungarian army's situation during its retreat through Poroszló is briefly as follows. The rear guard deployed at Eger-Farmos on the 1st was commanded by Klapka. Supposedly when *Feldmarschall Lieutenant Graf* Wrbna approached, he had just sat down for dinner, and reassured the anxious locals with these words: 'Today they won't attack

139 This was evidently enough of a possibility to make defending the Theiss at Poroszló unfeasible for the Austrians – yet not enough to make it feasible for them to cross there themselves. When we think of Bonaparte crossing the Po in 1796 to pursue his defeated opponent Beaulieu, we wonder why Windisch-Grätz could not do the same here. It is another instance of Windisch-Grätz and his subordinates magnifying the risks to themselves and underestimating the enemy's problems. For description and strategic analysis of Bonaparte's exploits in this respect, see Murray and Pringle, *Napoleon's 1796 Italian Campaign*.

140 Whilst guarding the sick against capture was sensible, as noted above this was a relatively restrained civil war. The one incident of 'cruel mistreatment' of imperial prisoners by the Hungarians at Güns noted earlier seems to have been an isolated instance caused by particular provocation.

me anymore, and tomorrow they won't find me anymore.'[141] After Klapka left, Görgei took over the defence of Poroszló. Dembinsky had given him the solemn order to hold this place at all costs. But the conviction that it was untenable, as well as the dangerous 5 km-long defile in his rear, caused Görgei to retreat behind the Theiss during the night of 2/3 March, which given the bottomless muddy roads and the dark night was not accomplished without considerable trouble and confusion. From the latter day (the 3rd) until the 6th, the day on which *Feldmarschall Lieutenant Fürst* Liechtenstein took possession of Poroszló, there was nothing left there apart from two hussar divisions under *Oberstlieutenant* Hertelendy. When Dembinsky learned that Poroszló had been vacated he was utterly enraged. Görgei had to explain himself to parliament, and while unable to excuse disobeying orders, he sought to justify his action by pointing to the indefensibility of Poroszló and his perilous position.[142]

It only remains to mention Division Ramberg that had been in Kaschau since the 22nd. The order for a simultaneous advance on Miskolcz that was issued to this division on the 23rd, the day on which the army's offensive operation toward Gyöngyös began, did not reach *Feldmarschall Lieutenant* Ramberg until the 28th; for the officer entrusted with its delivery, *Oberlieutenant* Usz of the Palatinal hussars, took a circuitous route to Kaschau and was thus very delayed. The *Feldmarschall Lieutenant* replied on the 28th that he had decided to advance on Miskolcz next day anyway (1 March). To justify lingering so long in Kaschau he said that his albeit erroneous spy reports had spoken of the presence of not insignificant enemy forces in Torna and Gál-Szécs, so he could not advance against Miskolcz 'with enemy corps on his flanks'; and that *Feldmarschall Lieutenant* Vogel had declined to cooperate in any way that would have taken him away from the Galician border, since he had been ordered to cover the border, etc. On the 28th Ramberg still thought that Klapka and Guyon were at Szikszó with substantial combat forces. On the 1st, leaving all the baggage behind, he marched to Hidas-Némethy, on the 2nd to Forró, and on the 3rd he entered Miskolcz without having encountered a single enemy detachment anywhere. Kaschau, Eperies, Leutschau, Rosenau and Zips County remained occupied meanwhile by 19 companies of Slovakian *landsturm* [militia] under Blaudek. If *Feldmarschall Lieutenant* Ramberg could have continued his march to the south on the 23rd, or if it had been at all possible to inform him of the true state of affairs in a timely fashion, then he could have fallen on the enemy's rear during the battle of Kápolna or immediately after it.

The *Feldmarschall* learned of Division Ramberg's march toward Miskolcz just before he returned to Ofen on the 5th, on which day, as we have seen, the army was already on the march to Jász-Berény, Czegléd, etc.

With the enemy's retreat behind the Theiss and our army's concentration between Szolnok and Pesth, a new section of the conduct of the war begins, the description of which is the object of the following chapter.

141 Whether or not this quote is absolutely true, it does encapsulate the contrast between the Austrians' apprehensive caution and the more confident, decisive Hungarian leadership.

142 Failure to obey orders was by no means only an Austrian malady, and the friction between generals was far worse on the Hungarian side.

3

From the start of the army's concentration on the middle Theiss between Szolnok and Pesth until the recall of *Feldmarschall Fürst* zu Windisch-Grätz from the army high command. The period from the beginning of March to 14 April 1849

I. Armeekorps is driven out of Szolnok, 5 March 1849

The close siege of Komorn by *Feldmarschall Lieutenant* Simunich had meanwhile reached the point where it was no longer possible for the garrison to carry out patrols to any great distance. Based on the experiences of Leopoldstadt and Eszek that surrendered after a short bombardment, on 16 February the *Feldmarschall* had already asked Simunich to make a similar attempt at Komorn, to which end the necessary high-angle artillery, particularly long-range mortars, was brought up from Leopoldstadt and Wien. Its fire was to be directed above all against the magazines, the hay and wood stores, the barns for cattle and horses, and suchlike targets vulnerable to the risk of catching fire. Besides, deserters had revealed that a large proportion of the inhabitants was in favour of surrendering since they had already suffered greatly from fire and flood and did not want to put all their remaining possessions at risk.

Since the failed attempt to destroy the bridge at Czibakháza on 24 February, nothing significant had happened with I. Armeekorps that was deployed to observe the Theiss crossings there and at Szolnok.

The mood in the country's capital and its environs was extremely agitated at that time, and there was general talk of a militia mustering at Kecskemét, Kun Sz. Miklos [Kunszentmiklós, Hungary], Solt, etc., and intending to advance on Pesth. The *Banus* therefore tried to bring forward as much as possible the arrival of the second brigade (Palffy's) requested from *Feldzeugmeister Graf* Nugent, to which end he sent *Hauptmann* Kappler of the general staff to Mohacz [Mohács, Hungary] with the transport flotilla that had been put together under the command of *Major* Obermüller of the Pionnierkorps. The embarkation and transporting of the troops was effected with such energy that in the course of 1-3 March Brigade Palffy arrived in Pesth at the disposal of the *Banus* with:

2. Bataillon Ottochaner
1. Bataillon Wimpffen (four companies)
Composite Bataillon Oguliner-Szluiner (four companies)

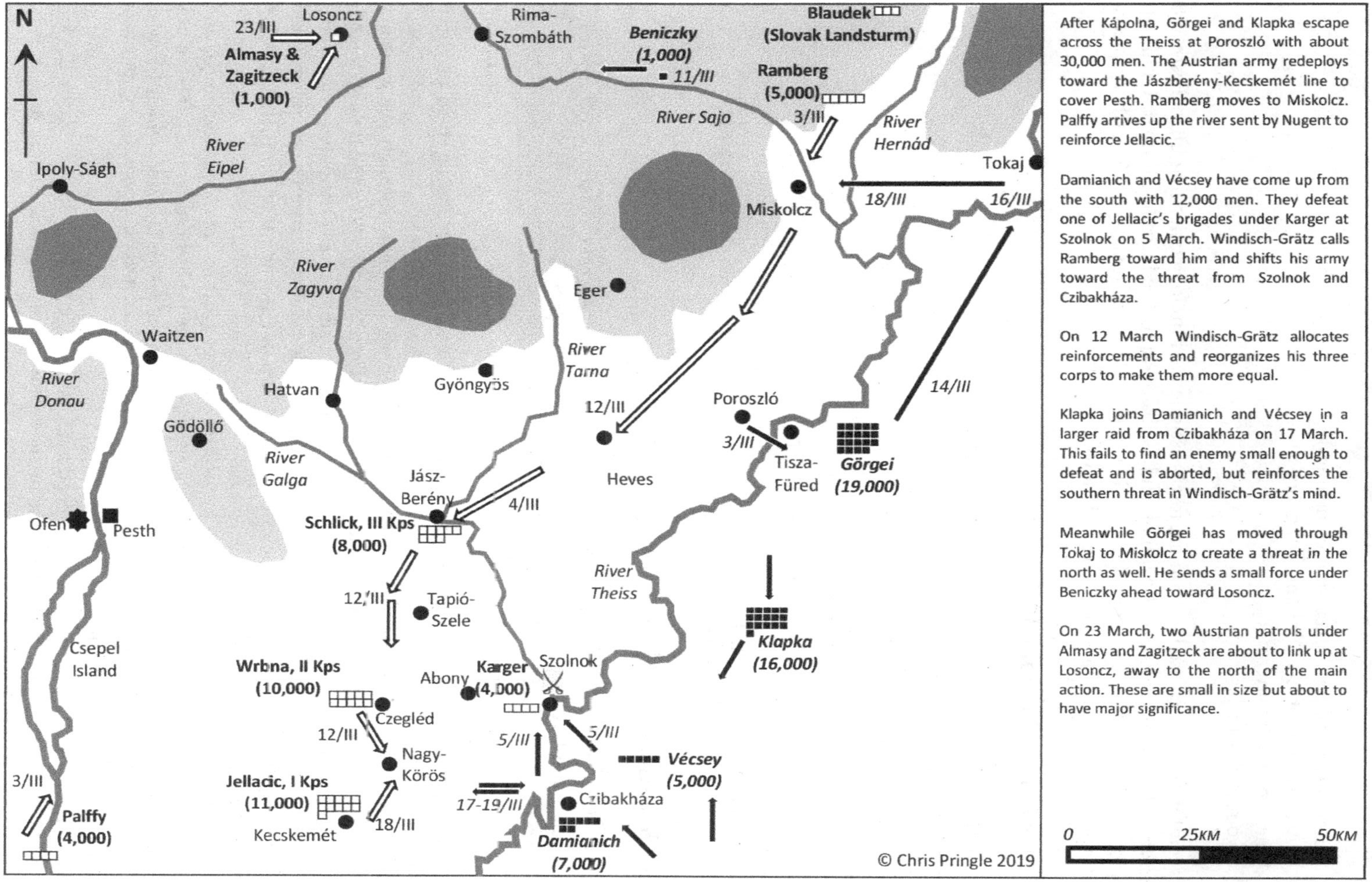

Map 5a: Fencing on the Theiss, March 1849

Composite Bataillon Ecker (four companies)
Two squadrons of E.H. Johann Dragoons
One 6-pounder battery
Two rocket launch stands.

This reinforcement increased the combat forces assigned to him for garrisoning Ofen-Pesth and observing the Theiss crossings at Szolnok and Czibakháza to five brigades: Karger, Gramont, Rastic, Palffy and Ottinger, or 14 to 15 battalions, 22 squadrons and 56 artillery pieces altogether. Two of these brigades were as follows:

Brigade Karger (in Szolnok)

3. Bataillon E.H. Karl
2. Bataillon Brooder
3. Bataillon, 2. Banal-Regiment
Two companies of 5. Jäger-Bataillon
One and a half pioneer companies
Two squadrons of Banderial-Husaren
Four squadrons of Kaiser Franz Joseph Dragoner
Kavallerie-Batterie Nr. 1
Sechspfündige Fuss-Batterie Nr. 5
Half of Zwölfpfündige Batterie Nr. 1

Brigade Ottinger (in Abany)

Six squadrons of Hardegg Cuirassiers
Five squadrons of Wallmoden Cuirassiers (the 6. Eskadron was in Nagykörös)
Kavallerie-Batterie Nr. 5
Half of Zwölfpfündige Batterie Nr. 1

The *Banus*'s other units were billeted partly in Czegléd and the surrounding area, partly in Pesth.

Through appropriate security arrangements at the Theiss crossings, through the measures taken to warn as quickly as possible if danger threatened from that direction, and finally through using the railway to transport some troops, even with the combat forces distributed as described above it was still possible to support the relatively weak detachments deployed at Szolnok and Abany in a timely manner. Nevertheless, failure of any one of the precautions the situation demanded could be disastrous.

The bridgehead at Szolnok was held by Brigade Karger with an infantry detachment and two guns. The causeway constituting the only approach to the bridgehead on the left bank was completely commanded by the fire of the batteries posted on the right bank, which likewise flanked the palisades that ran from the causeway to the river. Thus, Szolnok was sufficiently secure against a direct assault.

The point from which danger threatened was the bridge at Czibakháza, about 25 km downstream from Szolnok, which was held by the enemy. Since our failed attempt to destroy it, it had been repaired and made completely usable by wheeled traffic. It therefore seemed essential to keep this place under constant observation. During the night of 27/28 February the enemy had already levelled the breastworks protecting the approach to the Czibakháza bridge on the right bank, to make it easier to debouch from there.

At 6:00 a.m. on 3 March, *Rittmeister* Stang of the Wallmoden cuirassier detachment in Nagykörös reported 'that the rebels marched to Czibakháza from Szentes the day before, and the Theiss further downstream is now only guarded by peasants. A spy states that he heard from Damjanich himself that he intends to cross the Theiss on the 3rd.' When this was forwarded to the *Feldmarschall* at Gyöngyös on 4 March, this was appended: 'We may conclude it is fairly likely that the enemy intends to go on the offensive at Czibakháza.' It was therefore necessary to make arrangements either to counter the impending blow as forcefully as possible or, if one felt too weak for that, to evade it.

The enemy knew how to skilfully exploit the advantages that the poor vigilance and dispersal of our troops offered him. As was learned later, his strength and deployment behind the middle Theiss at the time was as follows:

8. Armee-Division (Damianich) (in Czibakháza and Szentes)

Eight infantry battalions
Two *jäger* companies
Two pioneer companies
Eight squadrons of 2. Husaren-Regiment
150 Polish lancers
20 guns

6. Armee-Division (*Graf* Karl Vecsey) (in Török Sz. Miklos)

Six infantry battalions
Six squadrons of 3. Husaren-Regiment
Two squadrons of mounted *haiduks* [Hungarian irregulars]
16 guns

These two divisions combined had approximately 10,000 infantry and 1,600 cavalry.

Damianich and Vecsey are said to have taken the decision on 28 February to carry out a surprise attack very soon on Brigade Karger in Szolnok. Damianich was to cross the Theiss at Czibakháza with his division, while Vecsey was to advance directly toward Szolnok against the bridgehead. In addition, 28. Honved-Bataillon with a division of hussars and four guns was to cross the Theiss at Csongrád and move to Kecskemét, to call up and support the militia there.

During the night of 4/5 March Damianich and his division crossed the Theiss as agreed via the Czibakháza bridge, marched halfway to Szolnok, and waited there until dawn. The river crossing and night march went undetected.

Meanwhile Vecsey had advanced along the direct route from Török-Sz. Miklos toward Szolnok as far as Puszta-Szanda [then just a farm, now the town of Szandaszőlős, Hungary], and had *Oberstlieutenant* Knesich with Infanterie-Regiment Nr. 34 cross the Theiss on punts at Vezseny between Szolnok and Czibakháza to reinforce Damianich's division.

The rebels spent the night in the open with no campfires and were glad when day broke and the renewed march warmed their half-frozen limbs again.

The cavalry patrols from Szolnok seem not to have gone any further downstream than Töszeg [Tószeg, Hungary], and must have happily convinced themselves that patrols to Czibakháza were going out direct from Abany. Be that as it may, this much is certain: that in the circumstances at that time, when an attack from the direction of the Czibakháza crossing 25-30 km away was definitely to be expected, patrols cannot have been sent out frequently enough that way from Szolnok and Abany.

Damianich formed up his troops between Várkony [Tiszavárkony, Hungary] and Töszeg, still totally undetected, and moved along the Theiss from there toward Szolnok. The right wing comprised two battalions of Infanterie-Regiment Nr. 34 with 65. Honved-Bataillon and a pioneer company. In the centre were 3. and 9. Honved-Bataillons, a battalion of the Polish Legion under Wysocky, and lastly 3. Bataillon, Infanterie-Regiment Nr. 19 and 3. Bataillon, Infanterie-Regiment Nr. 60. The left wing was formed by 2. Husaren-Regiment. The *jägers*, a company of pioneers and the Polish lancers constituted the advance guard.

Towards 6:30 a.m on the 5th, *Generalmajor* Karger's outposts reported that the enemy was approaching from Tószeg. Now the alarm was immediately sounded in Szolnok, but mustering the brigade took some time. By means of a locomotive that had been kept ready, an officer was sent to Kavallerie-Brigade Ottinger in Abany with the news of the enemy's approach and the request to hurry up in support by the shortest route.[1]

Damianich saw the locomotive head out from Szolnok but was little perturbed by this tardy reaction, since it would take at least three to four hours before Brigade Ottinger could appear on the battlefield, by when the battle should have been long decided.

Brigade Karger had deployed in the angle between the railway embankment and the Theiss. The bridgehead was held by a half-company of *jägers*, an E.H. Karl company and four guns. *Hauptmann* Ghilain was on the near side of the bridge with 7. Pionnierkompanie and half of 16. Pionnierkompanie. The railway station was occupied by four E.H. Karl companies. The right wing was formed by four squadrons of Kaiser Franz Josef dragoons and two squadrons of Banderial hussars.

Toward 8:00 a.m. the enemy opened fire, to which our artillery gave very good reply. The enemy cavalry pushed forward toward the station supported by two horse artillery batteries, whereby the designated line of retreat for the baggage train as well as for the retreat to Abany in general was under threat right from the start of the battle. After the artillery duel had carried on for a while, the enemy with his twofold superior numbers advanced in several columns to attack Szolnok. Despite fierce resistance he penetrated into the town, whose inhabitants immediately joined in the fight and fired on our troops from windows and rooftops as they fell back.

Meanwhile the retreat had continued step by step. But it soon became obvious that there could be no thought of holding out any longer, for the enemy Division Vecsey had now also

1 This is a notable innovative use of the railway as a means of raising the alarm. In fact, as far as I can establish, this conflict saw the first ever substantial military use of railways. The only possible earlier claim that I am aware of is the use of rail to transport troops to suppress the insurrection in Krakau in 1846.

stormed the weakly held bridgehead and was pressing on from there toward the bridge with four fresh battalions, closely followed by six squadrons and 16 guns. *Hauptmann* Ghilain of the Pionnierkorps was just trying to withdraw the guns that were still in the bridgehead, intending then to demolish the bridge, when the enemy took position right on the riverbank and prevented the demolition with his fire. Under an intense hail of bullets, *Pionnier Lieutenant* Munschke and his pioneer detachment could do no more than fling eleven planks from the bridge deck into the water, during which he lost a *Feldwebel* and five pioneers. With the help of the locals, the enemy very quickly made the bridge usable again, and now pressed into the town from this side as well.

There was now no chance of the detachments scattered through the town carrying out an orderly retreat. It turned into disorganised street fighting lacking any structure. Each individual body of troops had to try to fight its way out through the enemy pressing in on all sides. The retreat was necessarily forced toward the northern exit from the town, since the road to Abany was already lost to the enemy cavalry. Admittedly the dragoons had repulsed the Polish lancers with the loss of 30 men, but then they in turn were obliged to retreat northward by the ever more sweeping manoeuvres of the hussars threatening their right flank.

If the battle in Szolnok involving the locals' treachery had not already been murderous enough, the further retreat over the one bridge across the Zagyva stream caused new problems and considerable losses. Our excellent artillery tried to cover the retreat with admirable calm, but at the bridge over the deep and marshy Zagyva it ran into a throng of baggage wagons, cattle and draft horses which had been driven out of Szolnok and were trying to cross the Zagyva there. At this critical moment eight squadrons of hussars and the Polish lancers charged the four squadrons of Kaiser Franz Josef dragoons. These counter-charged the hussars with rare determination and even drove back the first divisions, but taken in flank and rear by several squadrons were finally breached and thrown back on their own infantry and guns. A fearsome melee now developed in which the dragoons summoned up the utmost courage and tried to cut their way through and get across the Zagyva. *Oberstlieutenant* Regelsberg, wounded by a lance thrust, was taken prisoner. *Rittmeisters* Saharek and Landgraf were likewise wounded and captured, *Oberlieutenants* Thomsdorf and *Baron* Maltzan wounded. Fifty-nine other ranks and 69 horses were killed or wounded, though far more by the enemy artillery fire than in the melee. Gradually, and not without great effort and serious losses, the troops were able to muster on the left bank of the river and rally again to some degree.

In the street fighting in Szolnok as well as later during the confused little action at the Zagyva there were many deeds of heroic self-sacrifice, audacious courage and noble devotion. Lost guns and ammunition caissons were retaken from the enemy by individual detachments, captured officers rescued, wounded carried to safety, and the like. Alongside the artillery the *jägers*, led by their brave *Hauptmanns* Schnorbusch and Staudner, also rendered outstanding service in covering the retreat.

The pioneers had suffered significant losses. During the fighting in Szolnok *Hauptmann* Ghilain was wounded and taken prisoner, and *Lieutenant* Thym mortally wounded at the bridge over the Zagyva. *Lieutenant* Muschke still managed to bring three pontoon wagons to safety. During the crossing of the Zagyva valiant *Lieutenant* Riegel of the E.H. Karl infantry especially distinguished himself by rescuing *Hauptmann Baron* Uechtritz of his own battalion, as well as *Oberlieutenant* Thomsdorf of the Kaiser Franz Josef dragoons, who were close to drowning.

Most of Brigade Karger had reached the left bank of the Zagyva and was continuing its retreat toward Rékas [Zagyvarékas, Hungary] when Kavallerie-Brigade Ottinger appeared on the battlefield at around midday. *Generalmajor* Karger's message 'that the enemy has crossed the Theiss at Csibakháza and Tisza-Földvár [Tiszaföldvár, Hungary], and is advancing in strong columns from Tószeg to attack Szolnok' had not reached *Generalmajor* Ottinger in Abany until 8:00 a.m. At this news he quickly mustered his brigade (six squadrons of Hardegg-Kürassiere, five squadrons of Wallmoden-Kürassiere, Kavallerie-Batterie Nr. 5, half of Zwölfpfündige Batterie Nr. 1) and instead of advancing directly to Szolnok moved in the direction of Tószeg, hoping to fall on the enemy's flank during his advance, which would have met with great success if the news had been received in good time three hours sooner. Not until Ottinger had got within about 2 km of Tószeg did he discover the enemy batteries along the Szolnok railway embankment, whereupon he quickly turned left in the direction of Szolnok. However, when he reached the gentle hill from which he had a complete view over Szolnok and the railway embankment, this was already at the point when Damianich and Vecsey combined had formed up facing Abany and the Zagyva, and indeed the thunder of the guns was gradually beginning to fall silent.[2]

Continuing his flank march, *Generalmajor* Ottinger crossed the railway embankment at a railway watchman's house about 3,000 paces above Szolnok, got onto the Abany road there, and deployed astride the road covered by his horse artillery battery.[3] His appearance caused the enemy to send a large part of his cavalry and artillery along the Abany road to confront the Kürassier-Brigade, which gave Brigade Karger breathing space to continue its retreat more easily. *Generalmajor* Ottinger could achieve nothing more for the moment with the modest means at his disposal. He therefore contented himself with this result and after sending a report to *Feldmarschall Lieutenant* Hartlieb at Czegléd, later retreated in the direction of Abany.

However, his retreat did not go entirely unchallenged. When half of his brigade was through the defile at the railway, the hussars advanced to attack, supported by the fire of a battery. The four squadrons of Hardegg cuirassiers at the tail of the column, still on this side of the defile, had just enough time to deploy, while Kavallerie-Batterie Nr. 5 moved up screened by them and then opened up a heavy fire. The cuirassiers threw themselves upon the leading squadrons of 2. Husaren-Regiment so impetuously that the hussars had to retreat behind the protection of their artillery with the loss of one staff officer, two field officers and 43 men left dead on the field.

Oberstlieutenant Stauffer, *Majors* Algyay and *Baron* Roden, *Rittmeister Graf* Montjoye and *Rittmeister* Reinle, the latter being lightly wounded, had especially distinguished themselves in this glorious charge. Our losses came to just one man and two horses killed, and eight men and four horses wounded. However, four ammunition caissons (three from Zwölfpfündige Batterie Nr. 1 and one from Kavallerie-Batterie Nr. 5) got stuck in a patch of marsh and fell into enemy hands.

When *Feldmarschall Lieutenant* Hartlieb received *Generalmajor* Ottinger's message about the enemy's advance, he set off from Czegléd with three infantry battalions, one squadron of Banderial hussars, one 12-pounder battery, one 6-pounder battery and half a rocket battery, and marched toward Törtel so as to operate against the enemy's line of retreat if *Generalmajor* Karger still held Szolnok. However, when he reached Törtel he learned of Brigade Karger's retreat. He now turned toward Abany, arriving there at 5:00 p.m., and camped alongside Kavallerie-Brigade

2 This gentle hill is presumably Szőllősi hegy on the 2nd Military Survey map, nowadays across the railway to the southwest of the Szolnok suburb of Pletykafalu.

3 The watchman's house is presumably the one marked W.H.N 19 on the 2nd Military Survey map.

Ottinger that was already there. Kavallerie-Brigade Bellegarde, which formed the vanguard of the army that was approaching from Maklár and Poroszló, had also been there since 1:00 p.m.

When the enemy's pursuit slackened off somewhat, Brigade Karger had turned west again, and part of it reached Abany late that night.

Our losses came to: 5. Jäger-Bataillon: seven men dead, 12 missing; 3. Bataillon E.H. Karl: *Hauptmann* Kappler wounded and 227 men absent either dead, wounded or missing; 3. Bataillon, 2. Banal-Regiment: ten men dead, 212 missing, altogether 222 men; 2. Bataillon Brooder: 12 men dead, 13 wounded, 81 missing; and Kaiser Franz Josef Dragoner: 97 men of *Wachtmeister* rank and below, 92 horses. No casualty returns are available for the artillery, transport or pioneer corps. Brave *Lieutenant* Bronn of the 12-pounder half-battery died a hero's death. Losses of guns and caissons were: Sechspfündige Batterie Nr. 5: one gun, five caissons; Kavallerie-Batterie Nr. 1: three guns, five caissons; and Zwölfpfündige Batterie: one gun, three caissons, as well as the ammunition reserve under *Oberlieutenant* Petit. Our overall losses, insofar as these can be known on the day after the battle, can be estimated at: 12 officers killed or wounded; 158 men of *Feldwebel* or *Wachtmeister* rank and below killed or wounded; six officers captured or missing; 375 men of *Feldwebel* or *Wachtmeister* rank and below captured or missing; 90 horses killed or wounded; and 221 horses captured or missing.

The Hungarians Avoid Being Counter-attacked at Szolnok, 6-10 March 1849

On the 5th, the same day on which this unfortunate action at Szolnok took place, the *Feldmarschall* returned to Ofen from Gyöngyös. The next day, before a detailed account of what had occurred had reached him, he sent *Oberst Graf* Zedtwitz of his headquarters staff to His Majesty the *Kaiser* in Olmütz, to present most humbly the following submission, which set forth and explained in detail how inadequate the available combat forces in Hungary were for the continued prosecution of the war. This most humble presentation, dated 6 March 1849 from Ofen, states verbatim:

> I have already had the opportunity on repeated occasions to draw Your Majesty's Supreme attention to the insufficiency of the combat forces at my disposal here. This factor prevents me from pursuing the enemy effectively when he falls back since I cannot keep an adequate reserve anywhere, as is especially necessary in such a large rebellious country, in that the hostile mood and the efforts on all sides to hinder our progress can only be suppressed by physical force. I especially feel the lack of cavalry, particularly light cavalry, of which I have an extremely small number available while they form the enemy's main force and the terrain on which my operations are taking place requires their use everywhere. The cavalry I have consists for the most part of cuirassier and dragoon regiments who have to do light cavalry duty in which their heavy horses conspicuously suffer. In addition, my cavalry regiments have lost many horses from cannon fire, and many men in melees with the hussars, which have been especially frequent lately now that the Hungarians are standing to fight more often.
>
> I must most respectfully request of Your Majesty to grant me Your supreme and extremely necessary support in this regard.
>
> The provinces are so denuded of troops of all arms, but above all of cavalry of this kind, that it is completely impossible to meet the need from there. However, there are

eight regiments of mostly light cavalry (Radetzky and Reuss hussars, König von Baiern and Boineburg dragoons, Liechtenstein and Windisch-Grätz *chevauxlegers*, and Kaiser and E.H. Karl *uhlans*) with the army in Italy, while the terrain there is so unfavourable for their employment that as is well known, not a single significant cavalry action took place in the recent campaign there.[4]

If I may permit myself, I most respectfully request of Your Majesty to place at least two light cavalry regiments of these eight at my disposal, and to summon them right away to the active army here, for which purpose I would suggest one of the two *uhlan* regiments and one of the *chevauxleger* regiments. This would leave six cavalry regiments in Italy, which should be quite enough even if hostilities should resume again, for their use there will remain the exception, whereas here the battles must usually be decided by this arm. In exchange for this reduction in combat strength in Italy of about 2,000 men, I have already sent there an equivalent number of Hungarian prisoners, increasing the bayonet strength of the army in Italy by 2,000 men, which will be of more use to it than the same number of cavalry.

I request Your Majesty's supreme decision approving this very soon.

When the *Feldmarschall* received the official report of the battle at Szolnok, with which the *Banus* also let him know that a strong enemy column was approaching from Kecskemét, the order was sent to *Feldmarschall Lieutenant Graf* Schlick and *Feldmarschall Lieutenant Graf* Wrbna to expedite their march to Czegléd.

On the 6th the *Feldmarschall* wrote to the *Banus* that as a result of the march orders issued, 15 battalions would arrive in Czegléd that day or the next (the 7th) at the latest. Together with the 13 battalions already in the area that would constitute a combined force of 28 battalions, 32 squadrons and 92 guns, though some of the battalions only had four companies and Brigade Karger had been greatly weakened by the losses it had suffered. However, Brigades Pergen and Deym would arrive in Jász-Berény on the 7th. The *Banus* was also tasked with obtaining accurate information about the enemy's strength and position, so as to wrest away from him again the temporary advantage he had gained; for it would not do to let the reverse that had been suffered go unpunished when such substantial combat forces were available. Finally, as far as the information about Kecskemét being occupied by significant enemy combat forces was concerned, a reliable informant who had left Kecskemét at 4:00 a.m. on the 6th had definitively stated that neither any militia nor a single man of the rebel army were there.

More precise details of the battle at Szolnok were received a couple of days later from *Rittmeister Graf* Wartensleben of 2. Husaren-Regiment, who had come over to our side from the rebel ranks during the battle. As a result of this information the *Feldmarschall* felt himself

4 The *Feldmarschall* is referring to the campaign which had effectively ended in August 1848 when Sardinia and Austria signed the Salasco armistice after the battle of Custoza. War broke out again in Italy when Sardinia ended the armistice on 12 March 1849, less than a week after Windisch-Grätz wrote to the *Kaiser*. Windisch-Grätz's claim about light cavalry being under-utilised in Italy is perhaps disingenuous: the light cavalry were largely distributed among the infantry at two squadrons per infantry brigade, where they would have been constantly busy scouting, liaising, covering flanks, doing picket duty, providing couriers, etc. Michael Embree, *Radetzky's Marches: The Campaigns of 1848 and 1849 in Upper Italy* (Solihull: Helion, 2011).

obliged to issue a special message on 8 March in which he noted that the surprise attack at Szolnok only came about because the necessary security measures had been neglected, enabling the enemy to cross the Theiss at Czibakháza undetected and to remain undetected next day while he advanced halfway to Szolnok. The *Feldmarschall* made his displeasure known to those concerned,[5] and reiterated his instructions about the need for meticulous performance of outpost duties and constant vigilance. At the same time the instruction was sent to *Feldmarschall Lieutenant* Ramberg to march without delay through Kápolna and Árok-Szállás to Jász-Berény and to await further orders there.

Following the battle of Szolnok the enemy had taken position in front of the town. Satisfied with the advantages he had gained, he contented himself with carrying off the supplies of salt that had been accumulated at Szolnok, from lack of which the rebels were already suffering.

The *Feldmarschall* had left it to the *Banus* to organise the positioning of the units allocated to him for the attack on Szolnok. Accordingly, the *Banus* asked that the units of his own corps should retreat from their advanced positions at Abany and Czegléd to Berczel [Ceglédbercel, Hungary], N. Irsza, Alberti [now merged together into Albertirsa, Hungary] and Pilis on the 8th, and that II. Armeekorps's formations should push forward to Czegléd and Abany instead. However, this request did not come to be implemented, for as we have said, it was the *Feldmarschall*'s intention to drive the enemy out of Szolnok and withdrawing the nearest troops from there to Pilis and Alberti would not have been in keeping with that. Instead, on the 8th he felt compelled to give *Feldmarschall Lieutenant Graf* Schlick the mission of taking the other units already approaching from Poroszló and originally designated to go to Jász-Berény – Brigades Deym, Kriegern, Fiedler and Montenuovo – and moving them up without pause to Czegléd and Tapio-Szele, for what mattered to him most was to concentrate the army to face the crossings at Szolnok and Czibakháza with the utmost urgency.

While this message was being expedited to *Feldmarschall Lieutenant Graf* Schlick at Tapio-Szele, the latter had gone off to Czegléd for a conference in response to an invitation signed by the *Banus*, *Feldmarschall Lieutenant Graf* Wrbna and *Generalmajor* Zeisberg. At 9:00 p.m. that same evening (the 8th), this collective representation was sent from Czegléd by the three corps commanders to the *Feldmarschall*:

> All reports concur that the enemy facing us is very strong, of which there is no doubt since he has moved all his combat forces up to the left bank of the Theiss and columns are also moving against our right flank on the near bank. It therefore seems urgently necessary to us that we too should concentrate our whole army at Czegléd and Alberti before we conduct any operation.
>
> We therefore request that Your Highness should issue orders to the rearmost brigades (Deym, Fiedler, Kriegern and Montenuovo) to move from Jász-Berény to Czegléd as fast as possible. It would also be desirable that *Feldmarschall Lieutenant* Ramberg should accelerate his march hither, and that the garrison of Gyöngyös and all the sick who can be moved from there should be taken to Pesth without delay.
>
> Czegléd, 8 March 1849, 9:00 p.m.

5 Without having seen the actual messages the *Feldmarschall* sent, we cannot help suspecting this took the form of some mild chiding that the recipients shrugged off. Certainly there does not seem to have been anyone removed from command or other such exemplary punishment to ram his displeasure home.

Schlick m. p.
Wrbna m. p.
Jellačić m. p.

The actions that the three corps commanders regarded as the most beneficial, and that they found themselves compelled to recommend to the *Feldmarschall* in a way that is very unusual in the army,[6] had as we have seen already been enacted by the letter sent to *Feldmarschall Lieutenant* Ramberg on the 6th, and by that to *Feldmarschall Lieutenant Graf* Schlick which did not reach him until the next day because of his journey to Czegléd for the conference. The *Feldmarschall* therefore restricted himself to informing *Feldmarschall Lieutenant Graf* Wrbna on the 9th as follows:

> In response to the representation of the 8th, I inform Your Honour that in accordance with an order issued to *Feldmarschall Lieutenant Graf* Schlick yesterday, Brigades Deym, Kriegern, Fiedler and Montenuovo had already been ordered to continue their march without interruption to Czegléd. Concerning Division Ramberg, that too is already on its way here. Similarly, orders were already issued some days ago for removal of those sick who can be moved and of the garrison from Gyöngyös.

At 10:00 p.m. on the 9th it was reported that a Jewish cigar-seller coming from Szolnok had stated that significant reinforcements under Klapka and Repasy had arrived, so that the combat forces assembled there came to 32,000 men with 80 guns. There were also strong reserves in Török Sz. Miklos and Tisza-Földvár. A pontoon bridge had been built between Tószeg and Barkanyi.

When the *Banus* brought this to the *Feldmarschall*'s attention, he added that *Feldmarschall Lieutenant* Hartlieb had been ordered to establish for certain whether there really was a pontoon bridge at Tószeg. However, on the 10th, *Generalmajor* Ottinger reported 'the enemy has completely vacated Szolnok during the night of 9/10 and burned the Theiss bridge there behind him!' By this spontaneous retreat on the part of the rebels, the opportunity passed for using the superior combat forces available on the 7th to throw them violently back across the Theiss with serious losses.

The Imperial Army Shifts Southward and Reorganises, 10-12 March 1849

Szolnok was not re-occupied for the moment, but strong reconnaissance patrols were sent out daily from Abany. The destruction of the bridge at Szolnok meant that the points at which the enemy could go on the offensive again on the middle Theiss shifted further south to Czibakháza and Csongrád. It therefore seemed appropriate to move the army in that direction, which also conformed to the views and wishes of the *Banus*. On the 10th he wrote personally to the *Feldmarschall*:

6 Wrbna and Zeisberg have previous form, of course, Wrbna having called a similar council of war, urging similar caution, less than a week earlier on 2 March before Poroszló.

As the enemy has left Szolnok and it is very possible that he intends to fall on *General* Thodorovich with his whole force, it is of the utmost importance to hold out a hand to this general without delay, which should be all the easier to do as I am reliably informed that Korps Thodorovich is partly in Theresiopel.[7]

Since every moment is precious, permit me to respectfully request that Your Highness make the following dispositions which are also in accord with the sense of the noble directions already given to me earlier.

1. That *General* Thodorovich be respectfully instructed to move by forced marches to Halas [Kiskunhalas, Hungary] by whatever route he judges best.
2. That I. Armeekorps under my own command should march without delay to Kecskemét, while Czegléd should be occupied by III. Armeekorps and Köres by II. Armeekorps.
3. That *General* Thodorovich should be instructed that he is placed under my orders with immediate effect and is to report to me without delay when he has begun his march and to attach his march plan.

This last arrangement is not only essential to gain time – which was never more precious than it is now – but will also pave the way advantageously for me to resolve matters in Serbia.[8]

If I may venture thus to convey to Your Highness my view founded on the deepest conviction, I beg you to recognise in it solely and only my boundless devotion to the cause of the Monarchy, which can only seek and find salvation now in energetic decisions and decisive action.

What the *Banus* requested here was partly granted and had partly already been suggested by the *Feldmarschall*. Thus, the order to *Generalmajor* Thodorovich to move closer to the *Banus* if possible via Theresiopel, Halas and Vad-Kert had already gone out on the 8th, and another had gone to *Feldmarschall Lieutenant Baron* Rukavina at the same time to provide Thodorovich with a detachment of regular cavalry, for this would be extremely necessary during his march across the plain between the Danube and the Theiss.

The *Feldmarschall* accordingly limited himself to giving the following reply to the *Banus* on the 10th:

To Your Excellency's letter of today I can only reply that the requests submitted by your noble self have in part been realised already, and in part are in the process of being implemented. Specifically, I have already ordered General Thodorovich respectfully to advance with all his troops through Vad-Kert toward Kecskemét, and at the same time

7 Footnote in the original says: '*At that time Generalmajor Thodorovich was in T. Kanisa [Törökkanizsa, now Novi Kneževac, Serbia]. An expedition against Theresiopel undertaken by Major Dragic on 5 March had failed, and the town was fortified and reportedly held by 10,000 rebels.'

8 'Matters in Serbia' is an ambiguous phrase. The *Banus* may mean defeating the Hungarian rebels on the Serbian front; or he may be referring in a sideways manner to the friction between the Serbs and his Croats, which as we shall see would come to open fighting between Serbian and Croatian units in Nugent's command in late March; or to political affairs in the Vojvodina (the Serbian area within the Kingdom of Hungary which had declared itself independent from Hungary in May 1848).

made him aware that Your Excellency will endeavour to establish communications with him from the latter place. As far as placing him under Your Excellency's orders is concerned, this cannot happen until after successfully linking up.

As your noble self knows, I had already suggested transferring Your Excellency's corps to Kecskemét, and Your Excellency is now desired to effect this, while at the same time I shall also instruct II. Armeekorps to march to N. Körös and *Feldmarschall Lieutenant Graf* Schlick's corps to concentrate at Czegléd.

On the 12th the corps moved into their new locations: I. Korps to Kecskemét, II. Korps to Nagy-Körös and III. Korps to Czegléd.

So as to remain constantly aware of whatever might occur on the upper Theiss while the army was concentrating southward, on the 11th *Feldmarschall Lieutenant* Ramberg was instructed to move from Jász-Berény to Heves. From there he was to send out patrols to observe the upper Theiss and in particular the crossing at Poroszló, and to bring any important occurrence to the *Feldmarschall*'s attention immediately. He was also tasked with immediately bringing up his division's baggage train that had been left behind in Kaschau with a small escort, which however could only be done safely via Leutschau.

The army had recently been joined by Brigades Dietrich and Palffy, making it necessary to revise the order of battle. The *Feldmarschall* used the moment when the army was united between Czegléd and Kecskemét for this, dissolving the Reserve-Armeekorps, and issued the following order of battle on the 12th:

I. Armeekorps

Corps Commander: *Feldmarschall Lieutenant* and *Banus Baron* Jellacic
Chief of staff: *Generalmajor* Zeisberg

Division *Feldmarschall Lieutenant* Hartlieb

Brigade *Generalmajor* Gramont

	Battalions	Squadrons	Artillery
5. Jäger-Bataillon	1		
3. Bataillon Liccaner	1		
2. Bataillon Gradiscaner	1		
Sechspfündige Fussbatterie Nr. 6			6

Brigade *Generalmajor* Rastic

	Battalions	Squadrons	Artillery
1. Bataillon Ottochaner	1		
2. Bataillon Ottochaner	1		
3. Bataillon Oguliner-Szluiner	1		
3. Bataillon, 1. Banal-Regiment	4/6		
Sechspfündige Fussbatterie Nr. 1			6

Division *Feldmarshall Lieutenant* Schulzig

Brigade *Generalmajor* Kleinberger

	Battalions	Squadrons	Artillery
3. Bataillon, 2. Banal-Regiment	1		
2. Bataillon Brooder	1		
3. Bataillon E.H. Karl	1		
Sechspfündige Fussbatterie Nr. 5			6

Brigade *Generalmajor* Dietrich

	Battalions	Squadrons	Artillery
4. Bataillon, 2. Banal-Regiment (doing duty in Ofen)	4/6		
4. Bataillon Warasdiner-Kreutzer	4/6		
Kombinirtes Bataillon, Eckher	4/6		
2. Bataillon Szluiner	4/6		
Slavonische sechspfündige Fussbatterie Nr. 1			6

Division *Generalmajor* Ottinger
Brigade *Oberst* Sedelmayer

	Battalions	Squadrons	Artillery
Wallmoden Kürassiere		6	
Hardegg Kürassiere		6	
Kavalleriebatterie Nr. 10			6

Brigade *Oberst* Sternberg

	Battalions	Squadrons	Artillery
Kaiser Franz Josef Dragoner		6	
König von Sachsen Kürassiere		2	
Banderial-Husaren		6	
Kavalleriebatterie Nr. 5			6

Korps Geschütz-Reserve
Korps *Artillerie-Kommandant Major* Peter

	Battalions	Squadrons	Artillery
Sechspfündige Fussbatterie Nr. 2			6
Kavalleriebatterie Nr. 9			6
Slavonische halbe Kavalleriebatterie Nr. 2			3
Raketenbatterie Nr. 16			6
Zwölfpfündige Batterie Nr. 1			6
Zwölfpfündige Batterie Nr. 2			6
13. Pionnierkompagnie with four bridging trains	1/6		

Strength of I. Armeekorps:
14 battalions, 26 squadrons, 69 artillery pieces, one pioneer company and four bridging trains.

II. Armeekorps

Corps Commander: *Feldmarschall Lieutenant Graf* Wrbna
Chief of staff: *Oberst* Pott

Division *Feldmarschall Lieutenant Baron* Csorich

Brigade *Generalmajor* Wyss

	Battalions	Squadrons	Artillery
2. Jäger-Bataillon	4/6		
3. Bataillon Fürstenwärther	1		
1. Bataillon Schönhals	1		
1. Landwehr-Bataillon G.H. Baden	1		
Kavalleriebatterie Nr. 2			6

Brigade *Generalmajor Fürst* Colloredo

	Battalions	Squadrons	Artillery
6. Jäger-Bataillon	4/6		
1. Bataillon E. H. Stefan	1		
2. Bataillon E. H. Stefan	1		
1. Landwehr-Bataillon Paumgarten	4/6		
Sechspfündige Fussbatterie Nr. 8			6

Division *Feldmarschall Lieutenant Fürst* Edmund Schwarzenberg

Brigade *Generalmajor* Schütte

	Battalions	Squadrons	Artillery
Grenadier-Bataillon Fischer (in Gran and Ofen)	1		
Grenadier-Bataillon Richter (in Ofen)	1		
Grenadier-Bataillon Bitermann (in Ofen)	1		
Sechspfündige Fussbatterie Nr. 12			6

Brigade *Generalmajor* Liebler
(designated garrison of Ofen-Pesth)

	Battalions	Squadrons	Artillery
Grenadier-Bataillon Schneider	1		
Grenadier-Bataillon Martini	1		
Grenadier-Bataillon Rattay	1		
4. Bataillon Hohenlohe	4/6		
Sechspfündige Fussbatterie Nr. 13			6

Brigade *Generalmajor Graf* Bellegarde

	Battalions	Squadrons	Artillery
Auersperg Kürassiere		6	
E.H. Johann Dragoner		4	
Civallart Uhlanen		5	
Kavalleriebatterie Nr. 4			6

Korps Geschütz-Reserve

Korps *Artillerie-Kommandant Major* Schmit

	Battalions	Squadrons	Artillery
Sechspfündige Fussbatterie Nr. 10			6
Sechspfündige Fussbatterie Nr. 11			6
Halbe Kavalleriebatterie Nr. 6			3
Raketenbatterie Nr. 15			6
Zwölfpfündige Batterie Nr. 3			6
Zwölfpfündige Batterie Nr. 4			6
8. Pionnierkompagnie	1/6		

Strength of II. Armeekorps:
15 battalions, 15 squadrons, 63 artillery pieces and one pioneer company.

III. Armeekorps

Corps Commander: *Feldmarschall Lieutenant Graf* Schlick
Chief of staff: *Major Baron* Gablenz

Division *Feldmarschall Lieutenant Fürst* Lobkowitz

Brigade *Generalmajor* Kriegern

	Battalions	Squadrons	Artillery
2. Jäger-Bataillon	2/6		
3. Bataillon Warasdiner-St. Georger	1		
1. Bataillon E.H. Wilhelm	1		
1. Landwehr-Bataillon H.v. Parma	1		
3. Bataillon Nugent	1		
Sechspfündige Fussbatterie Nr. 36			6

Brigade *Generalmajor Graf* Pergen

	Battalions	Squadrons	Artillery
3. Bataillon Warasdiner-Kreuzer	1		
3. Bataillon E.H. Wilhelm	1		
3. Bataillon Koudelka	1		
2. Bataillon Latour	1		
Sechspfündige Fussbatterie Nr. 34			6

Division *Feldmarschall Lieutenant Fürst* Franz Liechtenstein

Brigade *Generalmajor* Fiedler

	Battalions	Squadrons	Artillery
3. Bataillon E.H. Stefan	1		
1. Bataillon Ottochaner	1		
2. Bataillon Hartmann	1		
3. Bataillon Mazzuchelli	1		
Sechspfündige Fussbatterie Nr. 3			6

Brigade *Generalmajor* Parrot

	Battalions	Squadrons	Artillery
Prinz von Preussen Kürassiere		6	
Sunstenau Kürassiere		2	
Kaiser Chevauxlegers		4	
Kress Chevauxlegers		3	
Kavalleriebatterie Nr. 3			6

Korps Reservegeschütz
Korps *Artillerie-Kommandant Hauptmann* Groftsick

	Battalions	Squadrons	Artillery
Sechspfündige Schlick'sche Fussbatterie			6
Galizische Raketenbatterie Nr. 11			6
Galizische halbe Raketenbatterie Nr. 12			3
Zwölfpfündige Batterie Nr. 5			6
Zwölfpfündige Batterie Nr. 11			6

Strength of III. Armeekorps:
12 and two sixths battalions, 15 squadrons and 51 artillery pieces.

Geschütz-Hauptreserve

	Artillery
Sechspfündige Fussbatterie Nr. 4 (in Raab)	6
Kavalleriebatterie Nr. 1	6
Kavalleriebatterie Nr. 7 (with Division Simunich outside Komorn)	6
Kavalleriebatterie Nr. 8	6
Kavalleriebatterie Nr. 11 (with Division Simunich outside Komorn)	6
Raketenbatterie Nr. 13	6
Raketenbatterie Nr. 17	6
Raketenbatterie Nr. 23 (half of the battery in Gran)	6
Zwölfpfündige Batterie Nr. 6	6
Zwölfpfündige Batterie Nr. 7 (with Division Simunich outside Komorn)	6
Zwölfpfündige Batterie Nr. 8	6

Strength of the Geschütz-Hauptreserve:
66 artillery pieces, of which 27 detached, 39 present.

Pionnierkorps

Kommandant Major Obermüller

	Battalions	Bridging trains
6. Pionnierkompagnie (with Division Simunich)	1/6	2
7. Pionnierkompagnie	1/6	
8. Pionnierkompagnie (with II. Armeekorps)	1/6	
13. Pionnierkompagnie (with I. Armeekorps)	1/6	4
14. Pionnierkompagnie	1/6	
16. Pionnierkompagnie	1/6	5

Strength of the Pionnierkorps:
One battalion with 11 bridging trains, of which ten had transport and one did not.

Summary

	Battalions	Squadrons	Artillery	Bridging trains
I. Armeekorps	14 1/6	26	69	4
II. Armeekorps	15 1/6	16	63	
III. Armeekorps	12 2/6	19	51	
Geschütz-Hauptreserve			39	
With Division Simunich				2
With the army				9
Total	41 4/6	56	222	11[9]

The troops besieging Komorn under *Feldmarschall Lieutenant* Simunich, and Division Ramberg which numbered no more than 1,420 files fit for duty anyway, were treated as detached, therefore not included in the order of battle.[10]

Meanwhile on the lower Danube the Hungarians had made progress in organising their militia; also, riverine transport had been partly interrupted or even endangered. Already on 4 March the *Banus* had sent *Oberstlieutenant Graf* Nugent with six infantry companies, half a squadron of cavalry and two rocket launch stands on steamboats to Solt to disarm that town and disperse the militia. However, Nugent returned to Pesth on the 6th leaving the job undone because Solt was completely surrounded by water and the only approach along a narrow causeway was extremely difficult. He brought the news that there were 1,200 *honvéds* with four guns between Kalocsa and Solt, and that the militia had been called up from the whole area.

Oberst Baron Moritz Lederer had been sent by *Feldzeugmeister Graf* Nugent with two companies of 5. Bataillon of 2. Banal-Regiment, two squadrons of König von Sachsen cuirassiers and a half-battery to march through Tolna and Paks to Földvar to clear the rebels from the bank of the Danube. He sent word that the militia was organised everywhere along the left bank of the Danube. He had also learned from *Lieutenant* Knezich of Infanterie-Regiment Nr. 19 (who had come over to our side from the rebels, not without risk) that the enemy reportedly held Szegedin with 15,600 infantry, of which 10,000 were militia, and 1,000 cavalry; that there were 1,200 infantry and 120 hussars in Horgos; and finally there were 10,400 infantry, including 4,000 militia, and 848 hussars under *Oberstlieutenant* Gaal in Theresiopel, from which latter place they were patrolling as far as the bank of the Danube. On the 12th the *Feldmarschall* therefore

9 The alert reader will notice that this column does not add up. That is because Nobili has double-counted the four trains attached to I. Armeekorps as also being 'with the army'. See the order of battle for the Pionnierkorps above.

10 Nobili uses the term '*Rotte*' which generally means a file comprising a corporal and three private soldiers. Müller, *Allgemeines Verteutschungswörterbuch*, p.72. Division Ramberg consisted of Brigades Götz and Jablonowsky, which were reported earlier as comprising 'seven battalions, three squadrons, 26 guns'. Since the establishment strength of these would be about 8,000 men, then allowing for losses in combat and sickness it is plausible that 1,420 files means a combat strength of 5,680 men.

sent *Oberst Baron* Horvath with Grenadier-Bataillon Richter, 1. Bataillon Ceccopieri and half a rocket battery by steamboat and barge down the Danube to Mohacs to clear the vicinity of the riverbank of marauding rebel bands, to restore order in the towns along the river, and finally to ensure free movement on the river; but then to return to Pesth again as quickly as possible. *Feldzeugmeister Graf* Nugent was also informed of this expedition and was asked for his part to ensure the security of river transport on the Danube as far as possible by garrisoning the most important towns.

After sending off Brigades Dietrich and Palffy, only a very small combat force remained at *Feldzeugmeister Graf* Nugent's disposal; all the more so as some of his troops had been undertaking the close siege of Peterwardein led by *Oberst* Mamula of the engineer corps. However, the means for this were insufficient. The garrison of Peterwardein comprised 5,000 regular infantry and 7,000 armed peasants. Against these the active and energetic *Oberst* Mamula had scarcely 4,000 men at his command, of which only the Piret infantry battalion was properly combat-ready, the other three being 4th [i.e., *Landwehr*] battalions of *grenzers* which were not fully equipped or organised.

The garrison of Peterwardein was very accurately informed of the strength and composition of the besieging force. They stated that, 'we know very well that there are only five or six companies of German troops among the besieging units, the rest being made up of hastily conscripted peasants'.

On the 12th *Feldzeugmeister Graf* Nugent therefore felt himself obliged to ask the *Feldmarschall* at least to send back Brigade Palffy, saying that, 'with customary due compliance I have already detached two brigades from my corps as ordered, but am now so very short of troops that I can achieve absolutely nothing worthwhile'.

It was not possible for the *Feldmarschall* to grant the *Feldzeugmeister*'s urgent and certainly fully justified request. However, with the remaining modest means available to him the latter had still made such purposeful dispositions, and by constructing fieldworks had brought the siege of Peterwardein to such an effective state, that negotiations for the capitulation of the fortress had already progressed a long way. In the end these were only thwarted by a gang of the most militant, among whom the *honvéd* artillery and 2. Honved-Bataillon especially stood out.

Meanwhile, at Komorn, communications between the besieging forces had been established by construction of a pontoon bridge next to Puszta-Lovad [this was west of Komorn on the south bank of the Danube, due south of what is now Vel'ký Lel, Slovakia]. The previous fortress commandant Majthenyi had handed over command to the former imperial *Ingenieur-Oberstlieutenant* Török, quit the fortress completely, and handed himself in to the besiegers' outposts on 7 March. On the 11th, the garrison of Komorn made a sortie with three battalions, four guns and one squadron in the direction of Zsitvatö [Žitava, now part of Radvaň nad Dunajom, Slovakia], but this was soon driven back into the fortress by *Generalmajor* Veigel, who had taken over command of *Fürst* Lobkowitz's brigade when Lobkowitz was promoted to *Feldmarschall Lieutenant*.

In the meantime, *Oberst Graf* Zedtwitz had arrived at the *Feldmarschall*'s headquarters with the written expression of His Majesty the *Kaiser*'s will concerning the previously mentioned most humble report from the *Feldmarschall*. The *Fürst* [Windisch-Grätz] was instructed by this supreme edict to reach agreement with *Feldmarschall Graf* Radetzky concerning his request for aid in the form of light cavalry.[11]

Abortive Preparations for a Reconnaissance in Force across the Theiss, 14-17 March 1849

Returning to the main army's operations, we must first note that the *Feldmarschall*'s aim now was not to waste the opportunity presented by having the whole army concentrated between Czegléd and Kecskemét.

Information about the enemy's strength and movements behind the Theiss was only very vague and unreliable. In some quarters attempts were made to promote the idea that the enemy main body would now move down the Theiss.[12] The *Feldmarschall* did not share this view; he regarded it as much more likely that the enemy would turn toward the upper Theiss again and resume his operations through Gyöngyös or through Miskolcz and Losoncz. As we have seen, he had pushed Division Ramberg forward to Heves so as to hear about any such enemy moves in good time.

So as to discover the enemy's strength and position on the middle Theiss for certain and to force him to reveal his true intentions, the *Feldmarschall* took the decision to secure the crossing points and Czibakháza and Szolnok before anything else. He would then only undertake a further advance with the army on the left bank of the Theiss if he had become completely convinced that he had the enemy main body in front of him. Seeking this out and beating it was now the aim he strove for, the sole object of operations that had to be pursued. An offensive manoeuvre against Grosswardein or Debreczin, the so-called 'Seat of Magyardom', from which some sort of major result was promised, would have brought no advantage if the enemy main body was not encountered there – and this was much more likely meanwhile to have crossed to the right bank of the Theiss at Poroszló or Tokay. On the contrary, such a move could actually have resulted in the army's ruin. It would soon have been completely cut off from all communications with the territory to its rear,[13] the one and only direction from which its supplies of ammunition and other military necessities, reinforcements, etc. could arrive, if it did not keep the river crossings in its rear as well as the lines of communications between Pesth and Szolnok constantly strongly held; yet this could not be done without weakening the field army so much as to be incapable of success.

On the 14th the *Feldmarschall* issued the following orders for the planned reconnaissance across the Theiss:

> The time has now arrived to establish a foothold on the Theiss and cross that river with our army that has already concentrated between Kecskemét and Czegléd. The enemy's strength and positions on the left bank of the Theiss are not known with any certainty; this operation therefore seems all the more urgent and simple as we will thereby force him to commit to a decisive manoeuvre and reveal his true intentions,

11 In other words, the two *Feldmarschalls* were to resolve the matter between themselves like gentlemen.
12 We may suspect 'some quarters' means the *Banus*, ever sensitive about Croatia and the southern front.
13 Debreczin is 200 km from Pesth; Grosswardein over 230 km.

which will tell us the direction for our future operations. Based on this assumption, what matters principally is to keep the crossings at Szolnok and Czibakháza constantly secure, and generally to establish a base on the Theiss from which we can operate safely in future and be protected against the adverse consequences of any reverse. As the most suitable manoeuvres for the intended purpose, I see fit to order that I. Armeekorps should effect its crossing at Alpár and move downstream between the Theiss and the Harmas-Körös;[14] meanwhile, III. Armeekorps shall head toward the crossing at Czibakháza. Given that the nature of the local terrain there is so unfavourable for the attack, III. Armeekorps shall cross the river either above or below the existing bridge and establish communications with I. Armeekorps as quickly as possible. Whether the town of Szolnok should be occupied by a few battalions of III. Armeekorps or by a suitable detachment of Division Csorich, in either case suitably provided with artillery, I leave to the collective judgement of the *Herren* corps's commanders. I merely add that a sustained demonstration should also be carried out from there to pin the enemy beyond Szolnok and to divide his forces, which should be so arranged that the enemy himself does not cross to the right bank of the Theiss near Szolnok. As soon as we are on the left bank, the crossings at Czibakháza and Szolnok are to be suitably defended with entrenchments equipped with the necessary artillery. The units under command of *Feldmarschall Lieutenant Baron* Csorich are to hold in a central position to the rear between Alpár and Czibakháza and be ready to move to the left or right, or against any enemy who should advance from Csongrád or even further downstream through Felegyháza and who could threaten the crossing at Alpár.

It is furthermore my decided intention that after successfully linking up, the two Armeekorps should then only move out on the line through Török-St. Miklos and Kárdszag if they are completely convinced that they have the enemy main body in front of them. I seriously advise this observing this precaution, because whatever happens, it is important to avoid pursuing small enemy columns if the enemy's main body is perhaps heading upstream or downstream along the Theiss and daring another offensive manoeuvre on the right bank covered by a screening force. Our first task is to establish the foothold on the Theiss. Subsequent operations will depend on what the enemy does, but in any case will be successfully prepared for by securing the crossings over this river.

I can only indicate the essential features of the operation I have just sketched out, and I ask the *Herren* corps's commanders to arrange the details according to their own experienced judgement; but nevertheless to act in constant harmony in doing so, because this is the only way we can be sure of success. The operation should start immediately as soon as all the necessary preparations have been made, and I am to be notified here of the time when it is to begin. Since I recommend that the strictest secrecy about this should be maintained, I further think that the collection of the necessary means of transport from the countryside for supplying the army's needs from Szolnok across the Theiss, particularly for bread and firewood, should be carried out

14 The River Körös is a tributary that runs into the Theiss south of Alpár. Because it is a confluence of three rivers, it is also known as the Harmas-Körös – the 'triple Körös'.

> now without any fuss. The more that all precautions to this end can be speeded up, the better it will be, so that we will leave the enemy no time to decide on any manoeuvres elsewhere and to appear at any point where we are numerically inferior.
>
> Division Ramberg will remain in Heves for the time being, pushing forward suitable detachments to observe the crossing from Tisza-Füred toward Poroszló, which however shall remain constantly mobile so as not to expose themselves to being defeated by standing still. *Feldmarschall Lieutenant* Ramberg is likewise instructed to discover from reliable spies everything that the enemy is up to upstream as far as Tokaj, and to inform me of any important developments by courier immediately.

While issuing these general dispositions, the *Feldmarschall* saw fit to provide for possible transfer of command of the units designated for the impending operation to the *Banus*, and wrote to him on the 14th: 'So as to achieve the unity of high command that is so necessary in the forthcoming operation across the Theiss even if I should be prevented from being present in person, in that case I see fit for Your Excellency to take command over Division Csorich and III. Armeekorps as well.'

Since *Feldmarschall Lieutenant Graf* Schlick had seniority over the *Banus* yet was subordinated to him by the contingency order above, when the *Feldmarschall* informed Schlick of his decision he wrote: 'I cherish the firm conviction that this measure will not in the least disrupt the fine harmony and cooperation toward furthering our war aims, which is completely guaranteed for me by the character of two generals such as you and the *Banus*.' The measure subordinating Schlick to the *Banus*, which was brought about by the latter's high political position and had been established in agreement with Schlick, was resolved soon thereafter anyway by the *Banus*'s subsequent promotion to *Feldzeugmeister*.

Feldmarschall Lieutenant Graf Wrbna, part of whose corps was in Ofen-Pesth, was called to Ofen to take over command of the military district there.

The information about the enemy obtained by sending out spies was very contradictory. While *Feldmarschall Lieutenant Graf* Wrbna reported that the enemy was moving up the Theiss, *Major Baron* Gablenz had information that apart from Görgei, the enemy's main body had moved downstream toward Szegedin. On the 16th the *Feldmarschall* came into possession of the following letter that had been captured in the area of Sz. Miklos and was addressed by the rebel general Damjanich to *Oberst* Nagy-Sandor commanding at Czibakháza:

> The enemy is moving downstream; everything depends on making him think that my corps is debouching from Czibakháza. Therefore send strong detachments toward Kecskemét and Körös as if on reconnaissance, but do not expose them to any risk. Meanwhile I will head for Tisza-Füred by forced march, where I will throw a bridge across at Valk [Tiszavalk, Hungary] to facilitate crossing there and at Tisza-Füred. I need three days for this manoeuvre, if General Görgei will support me strongly. Then since the enemy has issued orders to abandon the railway, I will hurl myself through Gyöngyös and Hatvan against Waitzen and see whether I can force a crossing of the Danube. Keep the enemy occupied, Czibakháza is strong, but I commend Szentes and Szegedin to you.

> Török Sz. Miklos, 13 March 1849.
> Damjanich m. p.
> General.
> Urgent.

From the signature and official seal there was no doubt that this letter was genuine. But it remained uncertain whether it might not have been allowed to fall into our hands deliberately. As we have seen, the *Feldmarschall* had always thought it most likely that the enemy combat forces would move up to the upper Theiss, and he found one more piece of evidence for that in this captured letter. Accordingly, what mattered to him most was to find out for certain what was going on behind the Theiss, for which the necessary actions were initiated by the orders issued on the 14th. These orders remained in effect, but the *Banus* was informed about the captured letter and ordered not to move the units under *Feldmarschall Lieutenant Baron* Csorich any further [south] than N. Körös, because if the information about enemy combat forces gathering on the upper Theiss should be confirmed, these units could be needed to reinforce Division Ramberg. Furthermore, the order was rammed home again that after gaining the left bank of the Theiss, I. and III. Armeekorps were not to advance any further unless the enemy main body really was there. In that case it would still be possible for II. Armeekorps (Division Csorich and Brigade Bellegarde) also to follow after I. and III. Korps from N. Körös through Szolnok.

This order read as follows:

> I am sharing with Your Excellency a copy of a letter from the rebel *General* Damjanich that was captured on the far side of the Theiss near Török Sz. Miklos, from which your noble self will see what the enemy seems to be planning. From such things as the seal and signature there is no doubt that this item is genuine, though it remains possible that the enemy let it fall into our hands deliberately. In any case caution dictates that we prepare for all possible eventualities. I therefore request Your Excellency during the planned operation beyond the Theiss not to move II. Armeekorps's full strength (namely Division Csorich and Brigade Bellegarde) any further away, but to keep these units at N. Körös so that in the event that the operation indicated in the above letter should happen, they will be ready instantly to move north and reinforce Ramberg's weak division at Heves. But if the enemy wants to undertake this manoeuvre with any prospect of success at all, he cannot be weak there. Thus there is scarcely any need to worry that he might be in a position to execute any kind of substantial manoeuvre from his left wing as well, namely from Szegedin or Csongrád. Given these assumptions, whose accuracy it would be best to test with reliable and skilful spies that Your Excellency may wish to send out in various directions, it goes without saying that your noble self would only encounter light resistance in crossing the Theiss with I. and III. Armeekorps, and would only have a small part of the enemy combat forces in front of you. Therefore I must request again in the spirit of my dispositions of the 14th that you should only advance further to the east if you really are facing the enemy's main body.

The information about the contents of the captured letter was sent to *Feldmarschall Lieutenant* Ramberg at the same time, with the instruction to send out spies as well as patrols to find out for certain about any enemy manoeuvre on the upper Theiss, especially at Poroszló, and to report about this without delay.

In response to the orders sent to him on the 14th to cross the Theiss at Alpár, the *Banus* replied on the 16th that he and *Feldmarschall Lieutenant Graf* Schlick were of one mind about this, stating:

> As far as the crossing itself is concerned, I must pronounce myself in favour of the crossing point at Szolnok.[15] Deploying and manoeuvring troops opposite Alpár would be very difficult because of reeds and patches of marsh, while at Czibakháza the geographical situation is so totally disadvantageous for us that General Ottinger regards crossing there as extremely difficult and unsafe. A crossing at Szolnok offers the most advantages; the right bank dominates the left for a long way, and since Kardszag and Debreczin are our operational objectives for the time being, we will be 50 km closer without a fight. The 18-pounder guns deployed there will facilitate the crossing. It would be desirable if I were to receive six [artillery] pieces that could remain in position there. Since *General* Thodorovich has discharged the Serbian auxiliaries and only has seven battalions and 1,900 cavalry (the latter being newly raised and of little value), we cannot rely on much cooperation from him with our offensive operation.[16] However, I nevertheless request that Your Highness should make him aware of my advance and should ask him to make one more effort with all his resources. It would be desirable if the commanders in Transylvania and the Banat were to be informed and instructed likewise.
>
> I will endeavour to keep Your Highness as fully informed as possible about my operations.

On the 17th the *Feldmarschall* replied to the above counterproposal:

> Whilst the crossings at Alpár and Czibakháza may present those local terrain difficulties you describe; I must say that the same certainly applies to that at Szolnok. I will make this comment, though: that the crossing at Czibakháza must in any case remain heavily screened so that any enemy offensive effort from there can be vigorously opposed. But as soon as the crossing of the Theiss has been forced at Szolnok, the bridge at Czibakháza must also be secured. Furthermore, I confess to Your Excellency that it is only with some reluctance that I consent to alteration of the dispositions of the 14th; and that I can only be completely reassured about the reasons put forward by your noble self if the crossing at Szolnok, in which any deception of the enemy is out of the question and instead a simple frontal attack takes place, can give the same guarantee of success as the fairly certain prospect which the flank operation through Alpár at least seemed to offer.

15 Yet again the *Feldmarschall's* subordinates conspire to obstruct and alter his plans.

16 Not only was the Serbian auxiliaries' combat value offset by the trouble they caused (friction with the Croat troops, and rape and pillage of civilians, including against ethnic Serbian imperial subjects); there was also the issue of Serbian nationalist aspirations being a problem for imperial policy. See discussion of this in Appendix II.

During this the *Banus* had also received the message of the 16th indicating that Division Csorich and Brigade Bellegarde should not move any further down the Theiss than N. Körös.

Although the dispositions issued on the 14th had not suffered any essential alteration hereby, the *Banus* did feel he had to insist that not only Division Csorich but also Division Ramberg should be allocated to him. The *Banus* also said that if the *Feldmarschall* was only letting I. and III. Armeekorps cross the Theiss, this could be done at Szeged, where they could be joined by *Generalmajor* Thodorovich's force and then the advance could continue toward Grosswardein and Debreczin. In this operation that he (the *Banus*) regarded as extremely useful, indeed decisive, would the *Feldmarschall* still keep almost half the army at his own disposal?

Immediately after receiving this proposal the *Feldmarschall* proceeded to Czegléd, where this matter was verbally debated and dismissed.[17] However, after the end of the discussion he returned to Ofen again, handing over command of the united army facing the enemy river crossings at Szolnok and Czibakháza to the *Banus*.

The Brief Hungarian Foray from Czibakháza, 17-19 March 1849

While this precious time was spent on proposals for operations that the *Feldmarschall* regarded as digressions, the enemy himself had undertaken an offensive manoeuvre on the right bank of the Theiss from Czibakháza. Sufficient information about these operations directed toward Pesth is given in the letter found in the Hungarian files from Vetter to Görgei – the former at that point having taken over as commander-in-chief of the Hungarian army while the latter was on the upper Theiss at Tokay – as well as in a second letter to the 'brigade in Tisza-Füred'.

The first correspondence stated:

> The offensive operations aimed at taking Pesth shall be begun from here tomorrow morning (the 17th) by *General* Damjanich's and *Oberst* Klapka's corps. The *Herr General* (Görgei) is herewith requested and instructed for your part also to go on the offensive and move closer to the operational objective, and to prevent the enemy from turning toward the corps advancing from here with the whole of his force. The enemy's main body is concentrated on the line of Czegléd, N. Körös and Kecskemét. Any significant spy reports and the results of all manoeuvres are to be imparted to me in detail.
>
> Headquarters, Czibakháza, 16 March 1849.

The letter dispatched to the brigade commander in Tisza-Füred read as follows:

> The offensive operations aimed at taking Pesth shall be begun from here tomorrow morning (the 17th) by *General* Damjanich's and *Oberst* Klapka's corps.

17 This time the *Banus* evidently frustrated the *Feldmarschall* enough to provoke a personal visit. But perhaps even stronger measures were called for: the *Feldmarschall* probably could and should have taken direct control of this operation himself to ensure it was carried out to his satisfaction. His hands-off approach to leadership must have contributed to the way his subordinates felt able, and were able, to subvert his intentions repeatedly.

> The brigade commander is accordingly instructed to keep the enemy occupied by continual demonstrations through Poroszló to pin some of his forces, and to prevent the repair of the burned-down bridge over the Theiss Arm [a branch of the Tisza that has now disappeared in the reservoir that is Lake Tisza], as well as to establish communications with the advancing corps by occupying Poroszló.
>
> Furthermore, it is the brigade commander's strictest obligation to construct the planned *fleche* on the right bank to guard the Theiss bridge there.
>
> Suitable orders are to be given to the national guards posted along the river from Tisza-Füred to Tokay that any enemy attempt to build a bridge is to be opposed and its detection is to be reported diligently, quickly and accurately. The enemy's main body is concentrated on the line of Czegléd, N. Körös and Kecskemét. Any significant spy reports and the results of all manoeuvres are to be imparted to me in detail. My headquarters is in Czibakháza for the time being.
>
> Headquarters, Czibakháza, 16 March 1849.
> Vetter m. p.

Accordingly, Damjanich's and Klapka's corps (28,000 men) crossed the Theiss at Czibakháza on the 17th and 18th and advanced halfway toward N. Körös, where they made camp.

Several days' rain had made the roads very bad, and also on the morning of the 19th a thick fog had come down that greatly hampered any offensive manoeuvre. These factors, and the information that 'the *Banus* has 12,000 men more than the rebel army, and finally the consideration that in the event of an unfavourable outcome the whole army only has the bridge at Czibakháza for its retreat' caused Vetter to abandon the newly-begun offensive manoeuvre. The march back began on the 19th so that by evening the whole army had already reached the safety of the tongue of land this side of Czibakháza.

The Hungarian army's crossing of the Theiss that had taken place on the 17th remained undiscovered, as stated above. On the 18th I. Armeekorps had moved up from Kecskemét to N. Körös (17 km away) whereby the whole army (35 battalions, 52 squadrons, 156 guns) was scarcely 20 km from the rebel army's camp, without having heard any definite news about it.

On the 21st the *Feldmarschall*, who had come to learn indirectly about the enemy river crossing at Czibakháza, expressed his astonishment that such a fine opportunity to wipe out this enemy corps had been missed.[18]

The New Hungarian Plan to Debouch through Poroszló

Immediately after the Hungarian army's subsequent retreat to the left bank of the Theiss, a new plan of operations was devised in the enemy camp, according to which the whole Hungarian army would debouch at Poroszló by 26 or 27 March. The march was arranged so that the vanguard under Aulich would arrive in Poroszló on the 25th, on which day Damjanich's corps would reach Tisza-Füred, where Klapka's corps would not arrive until the 26th. Only *Oberstlieutenant* Asboth's mobile division would remain behind on the middle Theiss to cover

18 And not for the first time; and again because of his subordinates' caution and hesitation.

this march, holding the bridge at Czibakháza while national guards watched the bank of the Theiss from Szentes to Tisza-Füred. As a result of the orders Görgei had received, his VII. Korps that was supposed to join the others at Poroszló was in Miskolcz on the 18th, with its advance guard under Pöltenberg pushed forward to Harsány, from where it continued its march through Mezö-Kövesd to Kápolna, Besenyö and Poroszló.

Understandably, the *Feldmarschall*'s headquarters had heard nothing of Damjanich's and Klapka's corps' flank march toward Poroszló, covered as it was by the Theiss, but *Feldmarschall Lieutenant* Ramberg did report Görgei's approach on the 19th. This report datemarked from Heves indicated that a spy returning from Miskolcz stated:

> [T]his town and all the surrounding villages are overflowing with troops from Görgei's corps. Its strength is given as 40,000 men [Nobili notes that in reality it was only 18,000 men], a mix of line infantry and *honvéds* with 1,000 hussars and 40 guns, of which eight are 12-pounders and another eight long howitzers. As the spy was leaving Miskolcz yesterday morning (the 18th), Görgei was setting off from there straight away and taking the road to Mezö-Kövesd. At 10:00 a.m. Brigade Pöltenberg entered Abrány [Bükkábrány, Hungary].

At the end of this report, Ramberg added in his own hand: 'The spy who brought the above information is a thoroughly reliable, very judicious man who would guarantee his statements with his life.'

The following order of battle for Görgei's VII. Korps dated 18 March from Miskolc, as found later in the insurgents' files, shows that this spy report was really very accurate.

Division Gaspar

Brigade Horvath

	Battalions	Squadrons	Artillery
39. Honved-Bataillon	1		
Husaren-Regiment Nr. 9		6	
Kavallerie-Batterie Nr. 2			5

Brigade *Major* Waldberg

	Battalions	Squadrons	Artillery
1. Bataillon, Infanterie-Regiment Nr. 60	1		
Fussbatterie Nr. 4			8

Brigade *Major* Petheő

	Battalions	Squadrons	Artillery
Neograder Bataillon	1		

Pioneers	2/6		
Ujhazi-Jäger	2/6		
Pressburger Batterie			5

Division Kméti

Brigade Gergely

	Battalions	Squadrons	Artillery
10. Honved-Bataillon	1		
23. Honved-Bataillon	1		
Pioneers	1/6		
Fussbatterie Nr. 3			7

Brigade Ujvary

	Battalions	Squadrons	Artillery
45. Honved-Bataillon	1		
Ungarische Jäger	2/6		
Husaren-Regiment Nr. 10		4	
Kavallerie-Batterie Nr. 4			8

Brigade *Major* Uichtritz

	Battalions	Squadrons	Artillery
33. Honved-Bataillon	1		
2. Neusohler Bataillon	1		
Husaren-Regiment Nr. 12		2	
Kavallerie-Batterie Nr. 5			6

Division Pöltenberg

Brigade *Major* Kossuth

	Battalions	Squadrons	Artillery
1. Honved-Bataillon	1		
1. Neusohler Bataillon	1		
Husaren-Regiment Nr. 4		2	
Fussbatterie Nr. 5			7

Brigade *Oberstlieutenant* Zambely

	Battalions	Squadrons	Artillery
14. Honved-Bataillon	1		
1. Pesther Bataillon	1		
Husaren-Regiment Nr. 4		4	
Kavallerie-Batterie Nr. 1			7

Division *Oberstlieutenant* Simon

Brigade *Oberstlieutenant* Weissel

	Battalions	Squadrons	Artillery
Grenadier-Bataillon	4/6		
3. Bataillon Infanterie-Regiment Nr. 48	1		
Deutsche Legion	1/6		
Haubitz-Batterie			6

Brigade *Oberstlieutenant* Liptay

	Battalions	Squadrons	Artillery
Tiroler-Schützen	4/6		
Pioneers	1/6		
Kavallerie-Haubitz-Batterie			5
Raketen-Batterie			2

Temporarily detached:

Toward Losoncz

	Battalions	Squadrons	Artillery
15. Honved-Bataillon	3/6		
Benyczki Infanterie	2/6		
Husaren-Regiment Nr. 12		1/4	
Pressburger Batterie			2

On the Theiss, in Tisza-Füred, etc.

	Battalions	Squadrons	Artillery
13. Honved-Bataillon	1		

2. Infanterie-Regiment	1		
Pioneers	2/6		
Husaren-Regiment Nr. 9		2	
Husaren-Regiment Nr. 10		2	
Hunyady-Husaren		2	
Husaren-Regiment Nr. 9		2	

Altogether Görgei's corps comprised 19 and three sixths battalions, 26 squadrons and 68 artillery pieces, with a strength of 16,644 infantry and 2,436 cavalry.

The *Feldmarschall* Prepares to Receive the New Hungarian Attack, 19-25 March 1849

Upon receiving this information from *Feldmarschall Lieutenant* Ramberg on the 19th, the *Feldmarschall* had immediately ordered Division Csorich, Kavallerie-Brigade Bellegarde and the Artillerie-Reserve of II. Korps (eight battalions, 13 squadrons and 48 guns altogether) to Jász-Berény to stand ready to support Division Ramberg if the enemy should advance any further.

Finally, on the 20th, a second message from Ramberg not only confirmed the previous report but also talked about Klapka approaching simultaneously with 15,000 men and 20 guns, and said that these had already driven back Ramberg's outposts from Besényö to Tenk that same day. Thus, there no longer seemed any doubt that the enemy intended to advance along the Gyöngyös road with substantial combat forces.

Accordingly, on the 20th Division Ramberg, whose position in Heves was under threat, was instructed not to get involved in any serious fighting but instead to retreat through Árok-Szallas toward Hatvan with all possible speed. At the same time, Division Csorich and Kavallerie-Brigade Bellegarde were also ordered to force march to Hatvan from Jász-Berény, as was *Feldmarschall Lieutenant Graf* Schlick with III. Armeekorps from Czegléd. Meanwhile, the *Banus* received the order to move with I. Armeekorps from N. Körös to Czegléd, from where he was to keep a keen eye on the Theiss crossings at Szolnok and Czibakháza. In addition, on the 20th *Oberst Graf* Almasy of the Civallart-Uhlanen, who had been sent on a reconnaissance patrol from Neusohl to Losoncz with a squadron of *uhlans* and two companies of Paumgarten infantry, was advised to be very careful, as too was *Oberstlieutenant* Zagitzeck, who was also on the march to Losoncz with a Wimpffen battalion and two rocket launch stands from Waitzen. These two columns were supposed to meet up in Losoncz on the 24th. The former was warned with the words: 'I recommend that you exercise maximum caution during your march to Losoncz, and will only add that, should you encounter superior enemy forces, you should return to Neusohl again.' The other was told, 'to exercise maximum caution during the rest of your march toward Losoncz, and to take care not to have any mishap inflicted on you by the rebel bands marauding in that area, who are by no means weak'. Lastly, two 12-pounder batteries, one horse artillery battery and a rocket battery escorted by Grenadier-Bataillon Bitermann as well as a division of Wrbna-Chevauxlegers and a division of E.H. Johann Dragoner were directed from Pesth to reinforce the units concentrating around Hatvan.

According to the orders issued, 28 battalions, 34 squadrons and 123 artillery pieces were supposed to gather there. The fact that this place had been chosen correctly emerges from a letter from Görgei to Klapka found in the Hungarian files after the end of the war and dated 18 March from Miskolcz, which says: 'Heves is my next operational objective, the one after that being Hatvan via Árok-Szallas. I have little desire to make my troops fall back behind the Theiss yet again, since they indisputably suffered more on the march from Tisza-Füred to Tokay than on the march through the Mining Towns.'

Feldmarschall Lieutenant Ramberg marched to Árok-Szallas on the 21st and to Hatvan on the 22nd. Before his departure from Heves he reported that the enemy's manoeuvres had come to a mysterious halt. He also mentioned 'that a column composed of cavalry and infantry, whose strength could not be gauged because of the haze, has moved toward Poroszló. On the other flank, *Hauptmann* Zagitzeck who was with the outposts has learned from a spy "that Görgei has marched to Erlau with approximately 14,000 men and 47 guns. The informant saw this himself"'.

Some uncertainty about the enemy's true intentions arose from these reports and from the pause in his advance. It was possible that after learning about the approach of our columns, Görgei had abandoned his advance toward Gyöngyös and was now trying to link up with the troops under Damjanich that were still thought to be at Szolnok and Czibakháza, so as to go on the offensive toward Pesth from there. On the other hand he might perhaps just want to pin us at Gyöngyös or indeed lure us into advancing beyond that place, so as meanwhile to advance through Erlau, Petervasára and Balassa-Gyarmath to relieve Komorn.

Influenced by these considerations, on the 21st the *Feldmarschall* wrote to *Feldmarschall Lieutenant Graf* Schlick:

> It is possible, indeed likely, that the enemy is leaving some of his forces in front of us at Gyöngyös and advancing swiftly with the rest through Erlau and Balassa-Gyarmath to relieve Komorn. At least there would be a strategic logic to this manoeuvre. We must therefore not let ourselves be deceived, and it must remain our primary mission to discover Görgei's and Klapka's true strength, as well as their future intentions and manoeuvres, as soon and as accurately as possible. As preliminary preparation for this I have ordered a squadron of Wrbna Chevauxlegers to arrive in Hatvan today (the 21st) and push forward from there through Pasztó tomorrow, to investigate whether the enemy is advancing through Petervasára and into the Eipel valley and in what force. Furthermore, *Feldmarschall Lieutenant* Ramberg, who is closest to the enemy, will be able to give Your Honour the most reliable data.

Subsequently on the 22nd the following letter was sent to *Feldmarschall Lieutenant Graf* Schlick:

> From a message from *Feldmarschall Lieutenant* Ramberg on the 20th from Heves I gather that a kind of pause in the enemy's westward manoeuvres has occurred. There are two possible reasons for this. Either the enemy intends to stay passive on our front or indeed prompt us into a rash advance by a feigned withdrawal, while he throws a significant force to the right into the mountains to advance through Erlau or perhaps even through Miskolcz and Putnok to relieve Komorn; or else he thinks to deceive us at Gyöngyös, to attract our attention in that direction, and meanwhile is again moving

a considerable part of his combat forces back behind the Theiss again and quickly down its left bank to reinforce the enemy corps at Czibakháza, so as to fall on the *Banus*.

So as to remain in a suitable posture for all eventualities, I think it most advisable that Your Honour should hold the central position at Jász-Berény with the whole of III. Armeekorps for the time being, while Divisions Ramberg and Csorich together with Kavallerie-Brigade Bellegarde go to Hatvan. This will put us in a position to forcefully oppose any enemy relief attempt through the Rima and Eipel valleys by a swift manoeuvre on the interior (and therefore shortest) line to Waitzen and Ipoly-Ságh. Your Honour and III. Korps at Jász-Berény shall stand at the hub of these manoeuvres in such a way that you can turn in any direction as required, and the combat forces under your command will be able to be the decisive factor whether the enemy should attack at Szolnok or at Gyöngyös.

As it nevertheless remains of the utmost importance, especially in the present circumstances, to be constantly updated about the enemy, Your Honour is instructed to inform *Feldmarschall Lieutenant Baron* Csorich in Hatvan of everything that it is important for him to know in connection with the above, by sending out not only reliable spies but also patrols of suitable strength and composition to obtain the information required and not take your eyes off the enemy for a moment, so to speak. Division Ramberg's departure from Heves also makes it necessary to patrol diligently from Jász-Berény toward Heves and Kál. The patrols that have been ordered to be sent out from here and from Neusohl under *Oberst Graf* Almasy and *Oberstlieutenant* Zagitzeck toward Losoncz, as well as the squadron of Wrbna Chevauxlegers sent through Pasztó toward Petervására, will be of value in this respect.

It goes without saying besides that Your Honour shall have command over Divisions Csorich and Ramberg from now on, and that any orders necessary for them shall go via you.

In any case these are only such general indications as can be issued from this point of view, and they must understandably be modified by Your Honour as time and circumstances dictate, and according to the information you can glean about the enemy's movements.

Your Honour shall inform His Excellency the *Banus* of your position in Jász-Berény and of any important developments, as well as generally staying in constant communications with him.

The views expounded here partly coincided with those of *Feldmarschall Lieutenant Graf* Schlick, for on the same day on which the above edict was issued to him, he had likewise pronounced himself in favour of holding the central position at Jász-Berény. The *Feldmarschall* replied 'that it causes me particular satisfaction to know that your (Schlick's) views on the enemy's likely plans are in harmony with my own', moreover:

[T]hat it would now be most appropriate to deploy Division Ramberg to Waitzen immediately, reinforced with a squadron of Wrbna *chevauxlegers*, a division of E.H. Johann dragoons and a 12-pounder battery from the Artillerie-Hauptreserve, while deploying Division Csorich and Kavallerie-Brigade Bellegarde to Hatvan. By this troop distribution, if Görgei should move through Erlau and Petervására into the Eipel

> valley to relieve Komorn, about which we expect to be informed by the patrol sent toward Losoncz, we will remain in a position to waylay him at Ipoly-Ságh in sufficient force. Our preeminent aim now is to keep the siege of Komorn undisturbed, just as the enemy's is to strive with all his might to do the opposite, and it seems we can expect attempts to deceive us about this.[19]

Accordingly, on the 24th the reinforced Division Ramberg moved to Waitzen, and Division Csorich with Kavallerie-Brigade Bellegarde to Hatvan, while III. Armeekorps under *Feldmarschall Lieutenant Graf* Schlick stayed in the central position at Jász-Berény. I. Armeekorps had also already moved to Czegléd on the 21st, and Brigade Rastic with three cavalry squadrons had been pushed forward to Abany to observe the Theiss.

Alarming reports soon came in from there again. On the 23rd it was reported that 'various sources agree that the enemy is being reinforced opposite Szolnok and is planning a combined attack'. Later in this report it says, 'if Görgei's intention is as it was before, simply to draw away the combat forces that have been concentrated here so as to strike a blow against the units of I. Armeekorps, then Your Highness may wish to give this matter some consideration, since in such a case it would seem useful to have a division of Schlick's force march to Tapio-Szele soonest'.

With this report there was enclosed one from *Generalmajor* Rastic from Abany on the 23rd, which stated: 'It is said that the rebels are building a pontoon bridge over the Theiss at Akol-Kert (?),[20] opposite Török-Sz. Miklos, that quarters are being arranged for 12,000 men in Szolnok, that in Várkony significant numbers of troops are supposed to have moved through Czibakháza, etc.'

On the same day (the 23rd) a second report came in from the *Banus*, which said that according to spy reports the strength of the enemy troops at and behind Czibakháza and Szolnok in Török-Sz. Miklos, Mezö-Tur [Mezőtúr, Hungary] and Tisza-Földvar since the previous week came to 17 battalions and 20 squadrons. On the other hand, information had been received that Klapka and his corps were also at Török-Sz. Miklos with 70 guns.

The *Feldmarschall* gave little credence to these reports, instead consistently holding to the view that the enemy would move his combined forces to the upper region so as to rush to the aid of hard-pressed Komorn if possible. However, this time the *Banus*'s reports were given with such certainty, including partial lists of the names of the regiments and detachments comprising the enemy corps, that he shared them with *Feldmarschall Lieutenant Graf* Schlick, adding that 'although these statements do not seem very reliable to me, from Ofen I cannot judge whether you (Schlick) are in a position to agree to the *Banus*'s request according to the information

19 Thus we see both the *Feldmarschall* and Schlick uncertain about the enemy's intentions: were the Hungarians going to try a left hook from Szolnok toward Pesth, or a right hook from Poroszló toward Komorn? The position they agreed to adopt at Jász-Berény is indeed central with respect to those two possibilities, but it is also quite far forward and therefore liable to being outflanked if the Hungarians moved swiftly and with some element of surprise. The position the *Feldmarschall* subsequently fell back on at Gödöllő is much better.

20 The question mark is in the original text because it is not obvious where 'Akol-Kert' is located. The literal meaning is 'sheep-pen garden', so this may have been simply a description of a terrain feature rather than an actual place name.

you may have received about the enemy's movements. I must therefore leave it to you to take whatever precautions are required.'

The *Banus* had shared his concerns directly with Schlick, as well as his views about what future operations seemed expedient. After that the latter reported on the 23rd:

> [T]hat it is quite impossible to obtain information about the enemy from spies. A reconnaissance detachment of a half-squadron sent out under *Major* Kirchbach ran into the enemy at Heves but was unable to estimate the enemy's strength. *Feldmarschall Lieutenant Baron* Csorich has likewise been ordered to push reconnaissance detachments forward through Árok-Szállás which are to continue in the direction of Heves. However, I intend to withdraw my corps along the Szolnok-Pesth line again, to Alberti.

He attempted to justify this last manoeuvre thus:

> [I]f rainy weather should arrive as expected, it will no longer be possible to move on the black soil around Jász-Berény, while Alberti offers a good defensive position and is closer to the *Banus*'s corps. Finally, I think it best that the *Feldmarschall* should immediately resume the intended plan of sending the *Banus* and his corps to Szegedin to join the Serbs and should order that it be executed without worrying about the enemy's movements. The appearance of the *Banus* in the Serbian camp will bring great moral and practical advantages, discouraging the rebels and emboldening those sympathetic to our cause. A further consideration is that if the *Banus* were to combine with the Serbs, he would certainly not be obliged to operate through Grosswardein toward Transylvania or Debreczin. Reinforced by having linked up with them, he would instead be in a position to carry out any mission with decisive success and could equally well return to Pesth directly after linking up.

This last proposal from Schlick was based on an operation that had been suggested several times before, but which the *Feldmarschall* with his sensible view of the matter had constantly deferred.[21] This proposed operation which had been most eagerly advocated in some quarters and was now being brought up again consisted of immediately marching 40 battalions and 50 squadrons under command of the *Banus* through Kecskemét to Szegedin, crossing the Theiss there, linking up with the Serbs under *Generalmajor* Thodorovich and then advancing toward Grosswardein without a pause. Nine battalions would be left outside Komorn, six in Ofen-Pesth, and ten at Alberti as a reserve in front of Pesth. Where this reserve was to come from if the siege of Komorn was not to be abandoned completely was not exactly explained, for as can be seen from the order of battle, the field army including the Ofen-Pesth garrison numbered no more than 41 and four sixths battalions. Apart from these there was only Division Ramberg

21 This is evidence of the persistent differences of opinion between the *Feldmarschall* and his subordinates about how the campaign should be conducted. The fact that Schlick, Jellacic, Wrbna and Zeisberg were never fully committed to the *Feldmarschall*'s plans undoubtedly contributed to their frequent failure to carry out his orders promptly, or at all.

available with a mere 5,172 men, which after the departure of 40 battalions for Szegedin would only have been sufficient to constitute the proposed garrison of Ofen-Pesth.

This proposal to move the army to Szegedin at the moment when the combined Hungarian combat forces were going on the offensive through Poroszló, which would have left Pesth, Komorn, all of Upper Hungary and the lines of communications with the provinces to the rear exposed, was not approved by the *Feldmarschall*. On the 24th he replied to Schlick's letter of the 23rd:

> I fully endorse sending out wide-ranging patrols to obtain information. However, as far as the proposed deployment of III. Armeekorps at Alberti is concerned, with reference to my edict of the 23rd I cannot absolutely agree to it until we are completely sure of the enemy's strength on the upper Theiss and about his true intentions; because from the central position at Jász-Berény the whole stretch of country as far as the mountains can be fully observed, and also it enables sending troops in support toward Czegléd if necessary.

With respect to the proposed junction of the *Banus*'s corps with the Serbs under *Generalmajor* Thodorovich, he replied 'that it has certainly long been my wish to achieve a junction between the *Banus* and the Serbs, and I have not for a moment overlooked the advantages that could derive from it. However, in the present circumstances it is not feasible.'[22] At the end of this edict he added, 'should the information coming in about the enemy's position, or the state of the ground, be of such a kind as to make any troop movements around Jász-Berény quite impossible, then of course I would find myself obliged to authorise Your Honour to abandon Jász-Berény and move closer to the *Banus*'.

Meanwhile, *Feldmarschall Lieutenant Graf* Schlick had already begun his march to Alberti, without waiting for an order.[23] On the 24th he reported that:

> [I]n view of the bad weather that has arrived and taking account of a letter received from the *Banus*, I have found myself compelled to march today (the 24th) from Jász-Berény to Nagy-Kata, and tomorrow either with all four brigades to Alberti or else with just two, leaving the other two in Nagy-Kata [Nagykáta, Hungary]. There is no sign of the enemy in all the surrounding area. I must therefore assume that there is little or nothing facing me, and that the enemy may have divided his force so as to threaten Komorn with one corps, perhaps also advancing with a small force through Kápolna toward Gyöngyös; or finally to retreat across the Theiss again and then move to Nagy-Körös and Kecskemét to prevent us from moving closer to the Serbs.

22 Quite apart from the question of the feasibility of a junction with the Serbs, and of whether enough battalions actually existed to do as Schlick and the *Banus* proposed, there is the question of what the point of it would have been. The course of the campaign so far had already shown that taking even the most important cities was not in itself decisive. The critical objective had to be the destruction of the main Hungarian army. A march to the south would have moved away from that, not towards it.

23 This is bordering on insubordination. Most commanders-in-chief would not have tolerated such repeated lack of cooperation.

By abandoning Jász-Berény completely, all hope of learning anything reliable about the enemy's movements around Heves and Poroszló disappeared. It also resulted in an accumulation of troops on the Szolnok-Pesth line that was at odds with the *Feldmarschall*'s views about the suspected enemy operations. The *Feldmarschall*'s concerns were greatly increased when at the same time (on the 25th) he received news that the patrols under *Oberst Graf* Almasy and *Oberstlieutenant* Zagiteck had been attacked in Losoncz on the 24th. In his message about this, the *Oberst* said: 'I cannot gauge how strong the enemy is, but I am certain that he has more than 6,000 men.' This factor, and the pause that had apparently occurred in the enemy's advance along the Heves and Gyöngyös road, and finally a message from Schlick on the 25th that said 'this much is certain, and the reports are unanimous about it, that bodies of troops have been marching from Poroszló toward Erlau and Petervásara for the last six or seven days', necessarily further strengthened the *Feldmarschall*'s view that the enemy was advancing through the Eipel valley to relieve Komorn. Without wasting a moment, he therefore made the necessary arrangements to thwart this scheme.

Feldmarschall Lieutenant Ramberg was ordered to move immediately from Waitzen to Balassa-Gyarmath in the Eipel valley. *Feldmarschall Lieutenant Baron* Csorich was sent to Waitzen to reinforce him with six battalions, six squadrons and proportionate artillery, leaving *Generalmajor Graf* Bellegarde with two battalions and seven squadrons in Gödöllő for the time being. *Feldmarschall Lieutenant Graf* Schlick's corps was also ordered to move to Gödöllő, with the remark to Schlick 'that this marching to and fro is extremely fatiguing for the troops and could easily have been avoided if reliable information about the enemy's position, strength and intentions could have been obtained, and if you had not undertaken to march to Alberti without waiting for a definite order to do so'.

By echeloning the units in accordance with the dispositions given above – namely Division Ramberg in Balassa-Gyarmath, Division Csorich in Waitzen and Schlick's force in Gödöllő – the *Feldmarschall* was once more in a position to confront the enemy with 23 battalions, 25 squadrons and 102 artillery pieces within two or at most three days' march, whether in the Eipel valley or on the Gyöngyös road at Gödöllő.

Events on Other Fronts, 10-25 March 1849

Before we follow the development of operations in that area any further, it is necessary to mention some details that partly only became known after the end of the campaign: for example, concerning the surprise attack at Losoncz, the enemy's movements on the Theiss, and the like; and finally concerning what had occurred meanwhile with the other more distant army formations.

The patrols under *Oberst Graf* Almasy and *Oberstlieutenant* Zagitzeck had effected their link-up at Losoncz on the 24th as per their orders without any problem. At the same time, Görgei had set *Major* Benyczki to march from Miskolcz toward Losoncz with three companies of 15. Honved-Bataillon, two companies of Benyczki *jägers*,[24] 34 hussars and two guns. This

24 Benyczki was responsible for 'two *honvéd* battalions and a few thousand mobilised militiamen and national guardsmen' (Bona, *Hungarian Revolution*, p.280) but not for any specially trained *jäger* unit as far as I am aware. This reference to *jägers* may just be an honorific title for some of Benyczki's irregular volunteers.

raiding force arrived in Putnok on the 21st and Rima-Szombath on the 22nd, on which day it heard that an imperial detachment would enter Losoncz on the 23rd. Upon this news Benytzki decided to carry out a surprise attack and set off from Rima-Szombath at 8:00 p.m. in the evening of the 23rd. In Osgyan he learned that the billeting officer of the Wimpffen battalion that had been announced as arriving in Losoncz was already there, while the battalion, together with its rocket launch stands, was to meet up in Losoncz next day (the 24th) with the imperial cavalry detachment coming from Neusohl. Benytzki and his detachment stayed in Osgyan that night and exploited the snowfall the following morning to carry out his plan. He managed to reach Apátfalva [Opatová pri Lučenci, Slovakia] undetected, where he received news that the Wimpffen battalion and the cavalry had successfully arrived in Losoncz. Although this made him hesitate somewhat, nevertheless since he had not encountered any enemy patrols or outposts, he went onto the attack without delay, attacking from three sides simultaneously. The local inhabitants supported this surprise attack, firing down on the imperial troops from houses and towers as they mustered, and adding to the confusion. A few companies had meanwhile taken position at the bridge over the Tugar [Krivánsky] stream but were so bombarded with cannister by the two enemy guns that they found themselves obliged to fall back from the enemy infantry who were now advancing across the bridge with fixed bayonets. A company of the Wimpffen battalion under *Oberlieutenant* Zuccato defended itself for some time in a barracks but was cut off and captured. An *uhlan* detachment that had likewise mustered charged the enemy guns and their escort. The *Rittmeister* leading them had his horse shot from under him. Nevertheless, like the rest of the cavalry, since the infantry had already vacated the town and the rockets had also retreated out of the melee, this detachment had to get out too. Outside the town *Oberst Graf* Almasy attempted to rally again but gave up when the rebels pursued, and retreated through Ludány [Ludányhalászi, Hungary] to Balassa-Gyarmath, where he arrived during the night of 24/25. On the 26th he continued his march toward Waitzen, during which he met the advance guard of Division Ramberg moving toward him as a result of his message sent on the 25th. In this surprise attack, which cost numerous dead and wounded, one staff officer, six field officers, 170 infantrymen, 36 *uhlans* and 56 horses were captured. One flag, the regimental paychest and several officers' personal property were lost. The insurgents returned to Rima-Sombath that same night.

Infuriated that the enemy's surprise attack at Losoncz was able to succeed so completely solely because of the careless failure to take any precautions, the *Feldmarschall* made his serious displeasure known to the patrol commanders. In addition, he found himself obliged to publish a detailed army order reiterating yet again the instructions given previously concerning meticulous implementation of security measures, and making it every individual's most sacred duty to carry these out to the letter.[25]

On the 17th *Oberst Baron* Horvath, whom the *Feldmarschall* had sent to Baja with six companies on the steam warship *Schlick* and some barges to clear the bank of the Danube, reported that the rebel bands there had hastily retreated when he appeared. Because of the wicked behaviour of the town of Baja, particularly toward a Warasdiner-St. Georger company that had been posted there previously, he had decreed that it should be punished by looting it of

25 The *Feldmarschall*'s impotent inability to get his subordinates to comply with his repeated orders seems to have extended from his corps commanders right down to field officer level.

30,000 forint worth of goods. However, only 6,000 forint worth of this was raised, since on the 23rd the *Feldmarschall* summoned him to return to Pesth as quickly as possible.

On the 20th, *Oberlieutenant* Grivicics of the general staff brought news from *Generalmajor* Thodorovich commanding the Austro-Serbian forces that the floating bridge across the Theiss at Török-Kanisa [Novi Kneževac, Serbia] was complete, and the earthworks for establishing a bridgehead at Alt-Kanisa [Magyar Kanizsa, now Kanjiža, Serbia] had made considerable progress. A trusted individual was sent to Thodorovich with the request that he move through Vad-Kert [Soltvadkert, Hungary] to link up with the *Banus* who was in Kecskemét. But since that trusted individual could not prove his identity to the *Generalmajor*'s satisfaction, and the manoeuvre being proposed seemed too risky to him, he decided he should wait for more definite orders. Besides, he complained about the lack of cavalry, weapons, ammunition, kit, etc., and also portrayed the discipline and training of his troops as leaving a great deal to be desired.[26]

On the 24th *Feldzeugmeister Graf* Nugent reported from Dalya [Dálya, Croatia] that he recognised the need to reduce Peterwardein, and also to besiege Neusatz [Novi Sad, Serbia north of the Danube, Peterwardein being the part south of the river] appropriately. To that end he would request *Oberst* Moritz *Baron* Lederer, who was in Sexard [Szekszárd, Hungary] guarding the bank of the Danube, to go there by steamboat with 800 infantry and 160 cavalry.

The close siege of Komorn and the construction of batteries had already progressed so far under *Feldmarschall Lieutenant* Simunich that at 6:15 a.m. on the 20th the bombardment of the fortress by two 60-pounder and eight 30-pounder long-range mortars could begin. On average they were firing 300 bombs every 24 hours. *Feldzeugmeister Baron* Welden had attended very well to increasing the rate of fire as well as replenishment of ammunition: he initiated a request for two 60-pounder mortars with 1,000 bombs, 4,000 30-pound bombs, 1,000 shells for long howitzers, 400 roundshot for 12-pounders and 800 for 18-pounders to be brought from Wien by steamboat for the bombardment of Komorn, starting from the 23rd. He had set himself the task of reducing this fortress as soon as possible and was armed with the necessary authority for this by the *Feldmarschall*.

Although *Feldmarschall Lieutenant* Simunich drove forward the siege works with all his energy, particularly against the Danube bridgehead, the bombardment was taking a long time to have any effect. This therefore soon prompted *Feldzeugmeister Baron* Welden to appear outside Komorn in person, so as to make the arrangements he thought appropriate on the spot. When he let Simunich know he was on his way, he asked him to continue the bombardment without interruption in the meantime and also to have fascines made, since they needed to be ready for anything, even an attempt at storming the fortress. We will return later to how the reduction of Komorn progressed, and for now only add that on the 25th the *Feldmarschall* also sent his *Feldartillerie-Direktor Generalmajor* Dietrich to Simunich to assist him as much as possible.

26 This final complaint was undoubtedly justified. Kedves describes the *serviani* (Serbs who had come over from Serbia proper to fight against the Hungarians, as opposed to *rác*, ethnic Serbs living in the Kingdom of Hungary): 'They excelled more in fanaticism than in expertise. […] Some of the *serviani* viewed their activities in Hungary as an opportunity to acquire plunder; their thieving, along with their cruelty, turned the Hungarian, German, Slovak, Romanian as well as the Serb population against one another.' Gyula Kedves, 'The Serbian Insurrection in the Summer of 1848 and Military Operations in the Southern Region until the Withdrawal of the *Honvéd* Troops', in Bona, *Hungarian Revolution*, p.198.

On 11 March the extremely sad news came from Transylvania that after a tough fight Hermannstadt [Sibiu, Romania] had been evacuated. The weak garrison of Austrian and Russian troops left there by *Feldmarschall Lieutenant Baron* Puchner had repelled an initial attack by the rebel corps under Bem on the afternoon of the 10th. However, constantly renewed attacks with fresh troops exhausted the garrison, which in the end was unable to hold the city any longer against rebel columns pressing in from three sides under cover of darkness on the 11th.

The garrison retreated through the Rothenturm [Turnu Roşu, Romania] Pass into Wallachia. With that, the last hope of holding onto even just a part of Transylvania disappeared. In addition, possession of Hermannstadt allowed the rebels to send significant reinforcements to the Theiss and to give their offensive operations there a more decisive character.

On 15 March the *Feldmarschall* had asked *General der Kavallerie Baron* Hammerstein to order *Feldmarschall Lieutenant* Malkowsky, who was deployed with five battalions, two squadrons and five guns to secure the Bukowina against rebel incursions, to go onto the offensive and harmonise his operations with those of *Oberst* Urban and *Feldmarschall Lieutenant Baron* Puchner. But Hammerstein emphatically rejected this request on the basis that this could endanger the security of Galicia and the Bukowina, the same reason for which he had rejected an urgent request sent to him on the 12th to push *Feldmarschall Lieutenant* Vogel forward from Dukla through Bartfeld to Upper Hungary.

On the 25th, when the *Feldmarschall* expressed his regret that any cooperation from the troops in Galicia had been declared unfeasible for the moment, he added: 'I hope it will at least become possible later to provide this assistance which in the present situation is extremely necessary.' It cannot be denied that an advance from Dukla through Bartfeld and Eperies even with only moderately adequate combat forces, at the moment when the combined rebel army was on the point of going on the offensive from Mözö-Kövesd and Poroszló through Gyöngyös, could have created a very effective diversion. But the concerns *General der Kavallerie Baron* Hammerstein harboured for maintaining security in the provinces entrusted to him may have been too well-founded to allow him to send out any larger detachments.

Hungarian Plans and Order of Battle, 25 March 1849

At this point it would not be without interest to make some mention of the enemy's intentions, plans and movements during such an important period as that of 16 to 25 March, about which the rebel correspondence found subsequently has given us more detailed information. As already mentioned, soon after Vetter took over as commander-in-chief of the army on 8 March he adopted the existing plan for an offensive operation toward Pesth, as a result of which Damjanich and Klapka's corps had already crossed the Theiss on 17 March. However, they were brought back to the left bank again on the 19th; for a new plan of operations had been devised, according to which the combined Hungarian forces should now advance toward Pesth via Poroszló and Gyöngyös.

For the operation through Czibakháza, Görgei had been instructed to advance from his position at Mözö-Kövesd, Dormand, Besenyö, etc., through Heves, but now because of the change of plan had to call off the manoeuvre he had already begun. He was very upset about this and expressed his displeasure in a letter to Vetter dated the 22nd from Dormand with these words: 'Finally, the undersigned corps commander requests clear orders in future so as to be able to operate in harmony with the corps on the middle Theiss.' At the same time though he also

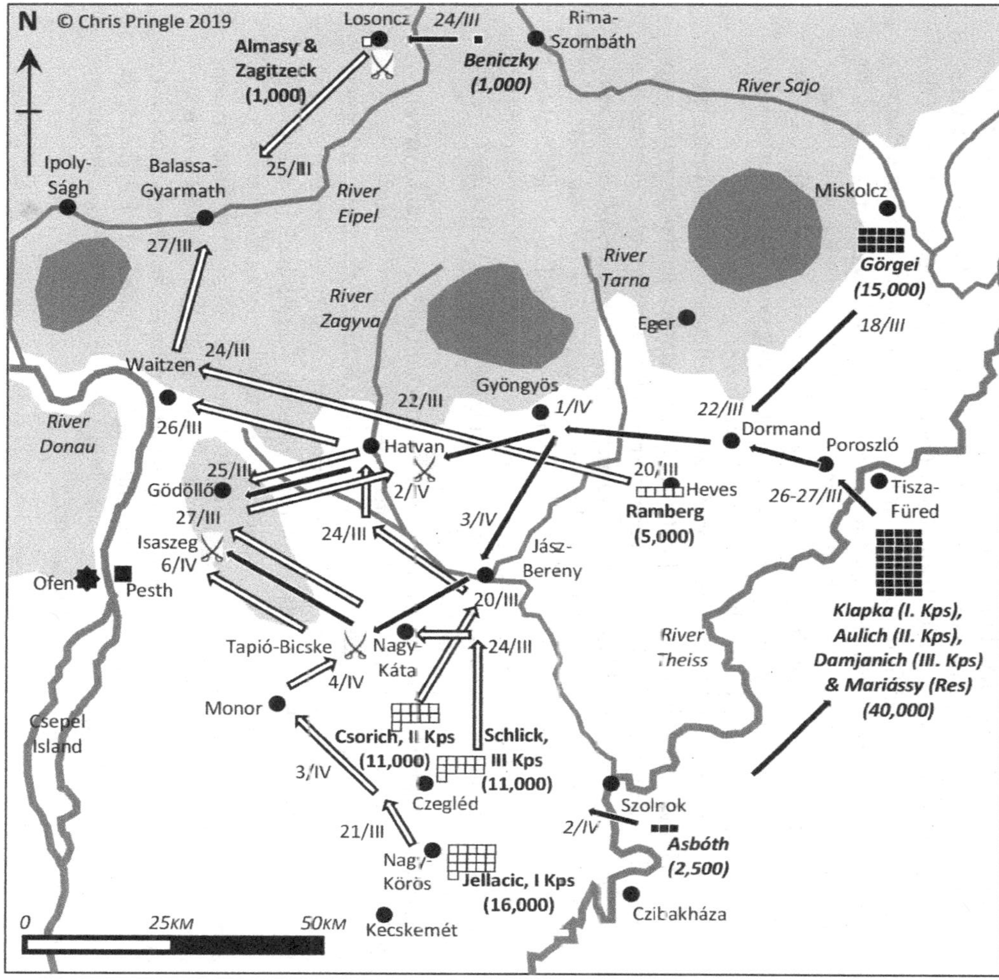

Having feinted twice through Czibakháza and drawn the Austrian army south, the Hungarian army now shifts all its weight northward. Görgei advances from Miskolcz while 40,000 men mass to cross the Theiss at Poroszló.

Concerned both about his right and his left flanks, and trying to protect both Pesth and the siege of Komorn, Windisch-Grätz leaves I Kps covering Szolnok but brings II and III Kps further north. On 24 March they are at Hatvan and Jászberény respectively, while Ramberg has been pulled back to Waitzen to cover the left.

On this day Beniczky surprises and defeats the small Austrian force at Losoncz. The embarrassed Austrian commanders inflate the enemy numbers, making Windisch-Grätz fear a serious outflanking attempt to relieve Komorn. He orders Ramberg north to Balassa-Gyarmath, sends Csorich to replace Ramberg in Waitzen, and pulls Bellegarde back to Gödöllő. Schlick diverts off to Nagy-Káta contrary to orders, but eventually reaches Gödöllő on 27 March.

On this day the main Hungarian force has crossed the Theiss at Poroszló and is moving to join Görgei, who has been waiting frustratedly for action for days. The Hungarians advance to Gyöngyös on 1 April.

Windisch-Grätz is also frustrated and anxious because he really does not know where the Hungarian thrust is aimed. He sanctions a reconnaissance in force by Schlick. A clash results at Hatvan on 2 April, after which the *Feldmarschall* wisely opts to fall back on Gödöllő.

He calls in Jellacic who has been sitting at Czegléd since 21 March. Jellacic is slow to move. On 4 April he gets caught at Tapió-Bicske: Görgei has launched a bold left hook through Jászberény with the whole Hungarian force except for Gaspár's VII. Kps, which is to make a pinning attack from Hatvan directly toward Gödöllő.

Jellacic falls back toward Windisch-Grätz and Schlick at Gödöllő, without making clear the scale of the Hungarian outflanking maneuver. The stage is set for the battle of Isaszeg.

Map 5b: Lead-up to Isaszeg, late March/early April 1849

turned to Kossuth to express his disapproval of commander-in-chief Vetter and the operations stemming from him, and to request that Kossuth remedy the matter. The answer Kossuth gave him is too interesting and the information it reveals about personalities and circumstances is too important for us not to provide a translation of it here:

> My honourable friend!
>
> I have already replied today by courier to your letter number 25 T. sent from Dormand on 22 March; since then I have received your earlier letter number 22 of 21 March.
>
> I enclose herewith *Obergeneral* Vetter's letter of 23 March, from which you *Herr General* will perceive that the main army will lose no time in cantonments, 'since today (the 23rd) the headquarters is already in Tisza-Füred, and tomorrow (the 24th) it will cross the Theiss'. Your concern on this point is therefore unfounded.
>
> I can also assure you, my honourable friend, that the operational objective still remains the same as was decided earlier: namely that you should advance along the Hatvan road, either to march directly to Pesth if we should be so fortunate as to beat the enemy soundly and cut him off from Pesth (since in that case I do not think Ofen would hold out if you could get to Pesth sooner than the beaten enemy could cross the Danube and move to Ofen from downstream); or else, if that cannot be done, that you should move to Waitzen and then operate toward Ofen from the rear together with half of the Komorn garrison. The only difference is this, that by crossing at Czibakháza we intended to beat the enemy in the Körös area and thus advance level with you – but now (if whole-hearted unity and cooperation are not lacking) you will join up with us first so as to be all the more certain of beating the enemy.
>
> The reason the Czibakháza expedition did not succeed is not down to Vetter since it was not his idea. He found the plan for it already devised when he took over the high command. The bridge at Szolnok had been burned, all the bridging equipment had been floated down to Czibakháza, and 11,000 men already sent there. When the army returned from its march to Körös without having achieved its aim because of the foul weather and the enemy's reported numerical superiority, it was Damjanich, he who had organised the debouchement from Czibakháza, who was first to say the operation should be abandoned; indeed when asked for his opinion he opposed the flank march toward Abany that Vetter wanted to carry out.
>
> And now I ask you, can we cast suspicion on Vetter for this? Or should I somehow suspect Damjanich? May God Himself protect me from the shadow of such suspicion; Damjanich is as loyal a son of this country as a man could be. The whole thing was fated, as many an operation has been, but we cannot lose confidence in anyone for that. I had my reservations about the debouchement through Tisza-Füred; in truth I only set them aside because Klapka and Aulich said Vetter's idea was completely sound, and nor did Damjanich have anything against it. I therefore beg you in God's name, my honourable friend, not to entertain any suspicions now. I myself will be present at Tisza-Füred – I with honest love of the homeland in my selfless breast, and with responsibility for the nation and the trust of the people loaded onto my weak shoulders. God wished it so, I did not seek that responsibility, and yearn to be rid of it; yet it is so – and this has some weight in the balance.

I know Vetter and his character. He is not tied to the homeland's cause by such bonds as we are; this is why he hesitated to assume command. But now that he has taken it on, he would rather let himself be hacked to pieces than take a step back or incur shame. Therefore for the good of the nation I stand by him, even though in truth I am not enamoured of him.

Our victory is certain if you now stand whole-heartedly together – but if not, then I say: my poor, poor homeland! All we need is one victory, just one. Also I would say to you about Mészáros, whom you must and will respect, that he is weak but honourable.

So, unity! Unity! While we face the foe. I will see to it that no one goes too far and risks the homeland's cause.

We shall see each other the day after tomorrow. I embrace you in true friendship. Debreczin, night of 23 March.

Your loyal friend, Kossuth[27]

The next day, Kossuth sent the following letter to Görgei:

Dear comrade!

I received your letter of 22 March from Dormand while sick in bed, and for tomorrow I must be healthy and go to the camp; for I believe we are approaching the decisive moment for our homeland's cause.

First I must talk to you about the cause, and then about feelings, and I will do so with the candour due man to man, friend to friend. Yesterday I happened to send Ludwigh to you with a letter in which I explained the causes of the failure of the Czibakháza expedition. This is the whole of the affair, no more and no less. The generals dutifully gave me their account of the reasons for the retreat, but neither Vetter nor anyone else said a word about retreating because they did not know where they were. Nobody said that. Rather, the whole business went like this: I was already at Török-Sz. Miklos, on my way back from Czibakháza, when Ludwigh arrived unexpectedly. He told us that you were in Mözö-Kövesd at that time and had sent Vetter a hussar regiment, etc. To this Vetter responded: 'I am commander-in-chief yet I only learn these important things by chance. If *Herr* Ludwigh had not unexpectedly strayed this way, to this day I would not have known one syllable about Görgei's position, nor about where the hussar regiment is; so now I have unnecessarily carried out a three-day march that I would not have needed to do if *Herr General* Görgei had kept me informed of the fact that he was sending out this regiment and of its route of march, for situations change frequently in warfare. I am commander-in-chief, I have to conduct all my operations in harmony with all the commanders in the army, yet since I became commander-in-chief I have not received even a one-line report from *General* Görgei, when mutual agreement is so

27 The original Hungarian text of these two letters from Kossuth may be found in Volume 21, Chapter 24 of Bánlaky, *A magyar nemzet*.

crucial that we cannot operate successfully without it.'[28] This is what Vetter said and not a single letter more. He did not utter a single syllable about uncertainty concerning your position having caused the wasted effort at Czibakháza (which is all that was lost there).

This is therefore how things stand; furthermore, Mészáros was only able to order you to Tokay on the 11th because at that time Vetter had not yet taken over the high command. Since then he has not interfered in military operations again, nor can he.

As far as the domain of feelings is concerned, I beg you in the name of God and the homeland: do not be overly sensitive. Don't you see, my honourable friend! When you said in your proclamation issued from Waitzen[29] that you obey no one but the war minister (Mészáros) or his deputy (Vetter), this outraged that part of Hungary that we still controlled, so that you were regarded as a rebel who wanted to play the part of a Dumourier or a Monk[30] or to instigate a military coup[31] – and people came to me, people asked questions in Parliament and sought to show by long tirades how much this episode pained them! If now, wracked with pain – for it grieved me that your declaration could give the ill-disposed the excuse to refuse to obey the government that you yourself had denounced, and then the homeland would have been lost – if I, wracked with pain, had harboured displeasure and issued a couple of decrees accordingly, what would have become of us? The enemy would already be ruling us by now, for the horrors of civil war would have torn apart the bosom of the homeland!

From this, may merciful God protect the freedom of our poor homeland from this – at least until we have finished with the enemy. The nation can quarrel with itself after that if it still has the breath to do it.

Don't you see, my dear friend! Amidst a thousand terrible mental torments, amidst thousands of miseries, through tangled webs of selfishness and intrigue, I hold the fate of the nation in my hand – and how can I keep it standing? By not allowing momentary vindictiveness to hold sway over the nation's views, and by always saying: let us just stay united, even when mistakes are made! And I gave way, where not giving way would have given rise to division; only wanting to avoid any failure that could expose the nation's weal and woe. I sought to correct small mistakes and to counteract larger ones – I tolerated – I suffered with scarcely believable patience – I did not give way to

28 This backbiting among the Hungarian commanders is striking. Furthermore, by relaying to Görgei what Vetter had said about him, Kossuth surely only exacerbated the ill-feeling rather than allaying it. Contrast the florid and emotive tone of Kossuth's letters and of Görgei's proclamations with the restrained and diplomatic exchanges between Windisch-Grätz and his lieutenants, and we see two armies of very different character: impetuous passionate revolution versus sedate courtly manners.

29 See the text of Görgei's proclamation in Chapter One.

30 Presumably Kossuth means Charles François Dumouriez, a general of the French revolutionary war who went over to the Austrians (https://www.britannica.com/biography/Charles-Francois-du-Perier-Dumouriez, accessed 30 July 2019); and General George Monck who served Cromwell but was then instrumental in the restoration of Charles II as King of England (http://bcw-project.org/biography/george-monck, accessed 30 July 2019).

31 Another example fresh in people's minds might have been Napoleon III. Although he had not come to power at the head of an army, in December 1848 he had been elected president after the revolution earlier that year, had adopted the title 'Prince-President' and habitually wore uniform as General-in-Chief of the National Guard.

momentary rage, and we have already come so far that no one believes the enemy can do anything to us.

You say: let us die for our poor forsaken country like two martyrs of pure intent! I will gladly die for my homeland, which does not do me any particular credit since I could neither live in it nor outside it, if it should be doomed to slavery. But with a serene spirit I say: right now we are not living in hopelessness, but on the eve of the liberation of our homeland – let us not die but save our homeland.

You say my honourable friend! That your army's eyes have been opened, and that it has no confidence in Vetter, Mészáros or Parliament. But I say, let us use every means according to our best understanding, with classical simplicity, without any personal ambition, for the salvation of our homeland – and let us not risk this great aim through and because of antipathies toward individuals. I recognise the faults and failings, but I also know that I have sufficient strength within me to balance out these faults, these failings, so that they cannot put at risk our nation's victory: therefore every element must be exploited, first we must win and then we can establish order. The two of us must mutually see to it that after victory, far from danger, no one should arrogate to himself such status as to endanger the nation's freedom.

Be serene about this, my honourable friend, be of good cheer. Victory and freedom above all, from whoever it comes, that goes for me too. But let us not worry about the constitutional authorities. The time will come when these will resign of their own accord and, feeling that they have achieved their mission, will hand over power over the liberated nation. But if we were to disturb them before that, civil war would break out, and would end in a wretched contract to which every treacherous, fearful, or exhausted person would accede – while by holding together all positive elements, the nation's victory is certain, and we can calmly approach that moment when passions and personal pride can be vented without harming the nation.

You ask will we see each other? Of course we will see each other, the day after tomorrow. I will also bring a bishop with me who will bless the army's weapons with the sacred light of the priesthood. We will fight, we will win – then we will deal with the rest united.

As I already wrote yesterday, a decisive victory – this is the foundation on which we can arrange everything according to God's justice and man's.

Until then there is no other rallying cry but unity, that we might win. Let any passion be pushed into the background, let wounded feelings be silent. I can tell you one thing about Vetter: he would not commit a dishonourable act at any price; of this I can assure you – and then I will be there in camp.

I embrace you in true friendship – may the God of freedom be with us. In life and in death! Your loyal friend,

Kossuth m.p.

We can discern that Kossuth was too clever not to realise that he had to support Vetter as commander-in-chief if he were not to encourage discord, jealousy and disobedience among the generals themselves, and thereby put any chance of success into question from the start.

Finally, we add here the organisation of the Hungarian army detachments that had crossed to the right bank of the Theiss at Poroszló, as issued by Vetter on 25 March. We think we hardly need mention that these details were not known until after the end of the campaign; because of the total lack of reliable information (and indeed what he did have was often quite contrary to the facts), the *Feldmarschall* was largely reduced to deliberations and assumptions as to what the enemy could reasonably do. These dispositions and army structure were as follows:

> The new changed situation the army is entering by crossing the Theiss, together with corroborating reports about the enemy's current position and intentions, makes it necessary to keep the general organisation of the Hungarian army the way it has been until now for a little longer. The main army encamped here and hereabouts today will accordingly again be divided into the army corps under *Herr Generals* Damjanich and Aulich and *Oberst* Klapka. However, to be able to achieve the absolutely necessary unity of operations, at all times *General* Görgei's corps shall form the right wing; *General* Aulich's corps shall maintain communications between this and *General* Damjanich's that constitutes the centre; and *Oberst* Klapka's corps shall form the left wing of these combat forces thus united as the main army.
>
> However, this structure also requires the formation of an Armee-Kavallerie-Division under *Oberst* Nagy-Sandor and an Artillerie-Hauptreserve under *Oberstlieutenant* Mariassy. The composition of these and of the whole army in general by individual brigades is given in the following organisation. The order of battle shall be amended according to this organisation in every respect.

II. Korps *General* Aulich

Chief of staff: *Oberstlieutenant* Meszéna
Artillery commander: *Hauptmann* Jonak

1. Brigade *Oberstlieutenant* Sekulich
1. Bataillon, Infanterie-Regiment Nr. 39
48. Honved-Bataillon
Wiener-Legion
Berégher-Kompagnie

Mobile Korps
One division of pioneers
Half a 3-pounder battery
One squadron of 6. Husaren-Regiment

2. Brigade *Major* Mihaly
25. Honved-Bataillon
26. Honved-Bataillon
61. Honved-Bataillon
6. Fussbatterie
One squadron of 6. Husaren-Regiment

Kavallerie-Brigade *Major* Mandi
Two divisions of 6. Husaren-Regiment
One and a half squadrons of 14. Husaren-Regiment
6-pounder horse artillery battery

III. Korps *General* Damjanich

Artillery commander: *Major* Wanner
Chief of staff: *Major* Cserwelyi

Division *Oberst* Wisocky (1. and 2. Brigades)

1. Brigade and advance guard *Oberst* Knezich
1. Bataillon, Infanterie-Regiment Nr. 34
3. Bataillon, Infanterie-Regiment Nr. 34
65. Honved-Bataillon
Schemnitzer-Jäger
Pressburger-Jäger
One division of pioneers
6-pounder horse artillery battery
Half a 4-pounder rocket battery
Two divisions of 1. Husaren-Regiment

2. Brigade *Major* Czillich
3. Bataillon, Infanterie-Regiment Nr. 60
Polen-Legion
42. Honved-Bataillon
6-pounder foot artillery battery

I. Korps *Oberst* Klapka

Chief of staff: *Hauptmann* Antus
Artillery commander: *Hauptmann* Karabelli

1. Brigade *Major* Schulz
17. Honved-Bataillon
19. Honved-Bataillon
3. Bataillon, Infanterie-Regiment Nr. 39
12-pounder battery

2. Brigade *Oberstlieutenant* Dipolt
6. Honved-Bataillon
26. Honved-Bataillon
52. Honved-Bataillon
6-pounder foot artillery battery

3. Brigade *Major* Driquet
28. Honved-Bataillon
44. Honved-Bataillon
47. Honved-Bataillon
One company of pioneers
6-pounder horse artillery battery
Two divisions of 1. Husaren-Regiment

Kavallerie-Division *Oberst* Nagy-Sandor

1. Brigade *Oberst* Desewffy
Five squadrons of 8. Husaren-Regiment
Three squadrons of Lehel-Husaren
6-pounder horse artillery battery

2. Brigade *Oberst* Pikéty
Four divisions of 2. Husaren-Regiment

3. Brigade *Oberst* Kassony
Three divisions of 3. Husaren-Regiment
One squadron of *uhlans*
One division of Hunyadi-Husaren
6-pounder horse artillery battery

Reserve-Division *Oberstlieutenant* Mariássy

General staff officer: *Hauptmann* Szilany

1. Brigade *Major* Zákó
34. Honved-Bataillon
43. Honved-Bataillon
3. Bataillon, Infanterie-Regiment Nr. 52

2. Brigade *Major* Buttler
54. Honved-Bataillon
60. Honved-Bataillon
Two companies of pioneers

Artillerie-Hauptreserve

6-pounder foot artillery battery, Márkó
6-pounder foot artillery battery, Mezey
6-pounder foot artillery battery, Lechner
6-pounder foot artillery battery, Lapinsky

One detachment of *hajduks* as escort[32]

Altogether 33,504 infantry, 5,698 cavalry and 120 artillery pieces.[33]

Schlick's Reconnaissance in Force: The Action at Hatvan, 2 April 1849

Let us now return to the main army's operations. In accordance with the *Feldmarschall*'s dispositions of the 25th, Division Ramberg had arrived in Balassa-Gyarmath on the 27th where it joined *Oberst* Almasy's patrol, thus numbering eight battalions, eight and a half squadrons and 34 artillery pieces. Division Csorich moved to Waitzen on the 26th, part of it arriving late in the evening. Division Lobkowitz of *Feldmarschall Lieutenant Graf* Schlick's corps was in Gödöllő on the 27th. Division Liechtenstein was in Tapio-Bicske, from where it was moved next day to Dany and Koka. These marches were extremely taxing for the troops since they had to be carried out in very bad weather and on unpaved roads.

The information that was known about the enemy was essentially the following.

First, *Feldmarschall Lieutenant* Ramberg reported that after the attack at Losoncz the enemy had retreated to Rima-Szombath:

> In the event that he should later turn toward the Mining Towns, I will follow on his heels, while *Feldmarschall Lieutenant Baron* Csorich must march to Altsohl so as to catch the enemy between two fires there. However, in order to obtain definite information about the enemy, I will move from Balassa-Gyarmath to Ludány tomorrow (the 28th), and to Losoncz the day after (29th). From there I have decided to advance to Rima-Szombath where I will cover a significant part of the upper counties, dominate Gömörer Komitat, open communications into Zips and Brisen via Tiszólcz, make any enemy operations toward the Mining Towns and Komorn impossible, threaten Gyöngyös, Erlau and Petervásara from the flank, drive Benyczki's corps out of Miskolcz again if necessary, and be able to operate from there against the rear of Görgei's corps.

The *Feldmarschall* did not approve this proposal,[34] placed Division Ramberg under the orders of *Feldmarschall Lieutenant Baron* Csorich and ordered Ramberg most specifically not to move

32 Irregular peasant infantry.

33 Footnote in the original: '*Görgei's VII. Korps with 16,644 infantry, 3,436 cavalry and 68 artillery is not included in these figures.'

34 It is worth considering whether this would indeed have been a wild goose chase, dissipating effort rather than concentrating it as the *Feldmarschall* was trying to do; or whether it might have had the result Ramberg suggested, of creating a threat against the flank and rear of an advance by Görgei. Rima-Szombath is some 70 km east-northeast across the mountains from Balassa-Gyarmath; from there to Miskolc is another 70 km southeast. This is maybe five days' march; allow a day or two halted at Rima-Szombath for rest and reconnaissance before committing to the next stage, and Ramberg might not have arrived at Miskolc until the eve of the battle of Isaszeg, 130 km to the southwest. Whether his flank threat from that distance would have deterred the Hungarian attack would have depended on the commanders. Given the Hungarians' penchant for bold manoeuvre and their relative freedom to cut loose from supply lines and operate freely, contrasted with the Austrians' constant concern for their lines of communication, we may surmise that the Austrians would have blinked first and hastily called

beyond Balassa-Gyarmath but only to send out patrols to obtain information. The Wimpffen battalion from *Oberst Graf* Almasy's patrol was ordered to join the other battalion of the regiment at Gran, and Szirmay's *Freikorps* which Ramberg had brought with him from Waitzen was sent back there.

Next, on the 27th, *Feldmarschall Lieutenant Fürst* Lobkowitz passed on a message from *Major Baron* Baselli, who was with the outposts at Bágh in front of Gödöllő and had learned from travellers that there were no enemy in Hatvan or in Gyöngyös, but that a strong enemy corps was in Kápolna, Kál and Kompólt.

Then, at 6:30 p.m. on the evening of the 28th, *Feldmarschall Lieutenant Baron* Csorich reported that he had learned from a merchant coming from Gyöngyös that, 'on the 20th Görgei marched from Mözö-Kövesd through Verpeléth to Rima-Szombath. I believe it most likely that Görgei marched from Rima-Szombath through Vámos-Falva [Mýtna, Slovakia] to Altsohl on the 25th or 26th.' On the 29th it was reported that:

> [W]aggoners coming over the mountains from Gyöngyös and Losoncz said that Guyon and Benytzky were in Losoncz with 15,000 men, and that Görgei had 15,000 men in Gyöngyös. These two corps are maintaining communications via Sz.-Jacob [now the northern part of Szurdokpüspöki, Hungary]. These reports come via the totally reliable Lecturer Weiglein and have some credibility; because they correspond with previous reports, and because by deploying like this the enemy could aim to send Guyon through the Eipel valley to Komorn if we should fall on Görgei with all our force, or in the opposite case [i.e., if the Austrians attacked Guyon] Görgei would get breathing space to advance from Gyöngyös toward Pesth.[35]

Right after *Feldmarschall Lieutenant Graf* Schlick's departure from Alberti, alarming reports were received from the *Banus* about danger threatening I. Armeekorps from Szolnok, Czibakháza and Kecskemét. On the 27th he reported that:

> [A]ll reports indicate that the enemy has occupied the left bank of the Theiss with a dense outpost screen and is patrolling it vigorously. No one is being allowed to cross over to this side from Szolnok or the surrounding area. According to several reports, Bem has arrived and the 10,000 reinforcements he has brought are already approaching. It is increasingly confirmed that Kun-Hegyes, Török-Sz. Miklos and Czibakháza are overflowing with enemy troops. This information seems to me to be of such importance that I believe I must bring it to Your Highness's noble attention.

At midday that same day (27th) the *Banus* sent the following message:

Ramberg back rather than risk him being left out on a limb, especially after Isaszeg. The *Feldmarschall* was therefore probably correct.

35 Csorich's information was badly wrong, as Görgei's raid on Losoncz had achieved its aim of attracting attention in that direction and magnifying the force there. In fact, 'in order to justify the defeat, [the Austrian commander at Losoncz] reported that he encountered a Hungarian army of several thousand soldiers – although Beniczky had hardly 1,000 at his disposal'. Bona, *Hungarian Revolution*, pp.343-344.

> The outposts have just brought in two Slovaks who left Kecskemét yesterday (the 26th). Yesterday afternoon they saw an entire enemy corps of infantry and cavalry arrive there with fife and drums playing. The enemy is said to have arrived from Czibakháza. These two men are to be believed. Enemy patrols are already roaming as far as Nagy-Körös.

The day after (the 28th) it was reported that:

> [T]he two Slovaks' statements are confirmed, insofar as according to a report from a reconnaissance patrol, the day before yesterday three battalions of infantry and a hussar regiment arrived in Kecskemét, from Alpár as well as from Czibakháza, requisitioned substantial amounts of forage [i.e., hay etc. for horses], and then withdrew again immediately. *Generalmajor* Rastic will push a strong cavalry patrol forward to the Theiss to ascertain whether a bridge really is being built at Szajol.

Finally, on 30 March *Feldmarschall Lieutenant Graf* Schlick reported from Gödöllő that:

> Hatvan and all the surrounding area are clear of enemy. Spy reports and reconnaissance reports concur that the enemy main body was still in Heves County on the evening of the 29th, mainly in Kál, Kompólt, Kápolna, Kereszend, Maklár and Szihalom, and that 80 to 84 guns have been moved up into these villages. The number of troops must be very considerable, and significantly exceeds the number facing us until now. A bridging train is also said to be with them.

About the enemy's intentions he stated that:

> [H]e will begin his advance today (the 30th), and that Görgei, with Guyon and Klapka also under his command, is to head through Pásztó for Waitzen or perhaps toward Komorn, while Skrzynecki (?) [sic] has taken over command of another corps that is concentrating in Heves and is supposed to advance from there toward Pesth depending on the state of the roads. From this it emerges that some of the enemy – namely Görgei with the better trained, more mobile elements of the rebel army – will operate through the mountains toward Waitzen and Komorn, while the less well trained part of the army stays close to the Theiss and in Heves.

With this report *Feldmarschall Lieutenant Graf* Schlick enclosed proposals to move to Gyöngyös with united force, to turn left into the mountains from there, to follow Görgei and to beat him. According to Schlick, in the prevailing favourable circumstances this could certainly have been done and would have achieved incalculable success; Ofen and Pesth could well have been threatened by other enemy formations in the interim, but this would signify little if Görgei were beaten. Command over this operation, which in Schlick's view offered the most promise of success, should be either taken over by the *Feldmarschall* himself or entrusted to the Banus.

These were the reports, the intelligence from spies, and the proposals for operations that the *Feldmarschall* received in the last days of March and on which he had to base his dispositions. Considering the certainty with which some extremely unlikely information was offered, and how conflicting were the views about what to do now, it will be conceded that the task was not an easy one.[36]

All the *Feldmarschall*'s efforts to discover anything reliable about the enemy's strength and positions remained fruitless, even though the corps and unit commanders were repeatedly asked to obtain information about the enemy by sending out strong and wide-ranging patrols. There was therefore no option but to pick out from this jumble of information that which had some likelihood, and to base appropriate dispositions on that.

We have seen that in all his instructions the *Feldmarschall* had given top priority to protecting the siege of Komorn. His worry that the enemy intended to advance via Petervásara from Gyöngyös, or even from Miskolcz, through the Eipel valley to relieve Komorn – and that to assist this operation the enemy was just trying to deceive us by demonstrations on the Hatvan-Gyöngyös road and on the middle Theiss, perhaps even to lure us into advancing in the latter direction – was fed anew by the reports and intelligence coming in now. The *Feldmarschall* therefore did not want to give up the present position at Balassa-Gyarmath, Vad-Kert, Waitzen and Gödöllő, because as already mentioned, it offered him the means to concentrate his combat forces swiftly and surely at any threatened point, whether in the Eipel valley or on the Gyöngyös road. Nothing reliable had been learned about the true strength of the Hungarian combat forces gathered behind Gyöngyös. The reports from spies mostly only referred to Görgei's corps.

Even less reliable information was known about what was facing the *Banus* on the middle Theiss. Even if little confidence was attached to the accuracy of the reports received about this, it was thought that at least one enemy corps could be assumed to be there, probably Damjanich's. So as to put an end to this uncertainty, the *Feldmarschall* decided to push *Feldmarschall Lieutenant Graf* Schlick forward along the Gyöngyös road. This seemed all the more feasible at that moment as at 1:00 p.m. on the 30th *Feldmarschall Lieutenant Baron* Csorich had reported that 'the enemy has destroyed the bridges on the road from Losoncz toward Balassa-Gyarmath', so could be assumed not to be intending to advance in that direction for the time being. Furthermore, so as to concentrate the army and not to expose the *Banus* to any reverse during this operation, his corps was to be withdrawn to Monor. The dispositions issued accordingly on 31 March ordered:

> As we lack any definite information about the enemy's strength, positions or intentions, there is no option but to undertake a large-scale reconnaissance in the direction where spy reports state that a significant part of the rebel army is deployed, and thereby to force the enemy to show his forces and perhaps even reveal his further intentions.[37]

36 Conflicting indeed: the *Banus* (who has been known to cry wolf in the past) is reporting strong and growing enemy forces facing him in the south, while Schlick is confidently asserting that the enemy aims to bypass him to the north. The *Feldmarschall* responds by splitting the difference and ordering a reconnaissance in force straight up the middle.

37 'There is no option': but perhaps there was. Space could have been traded for time; the *Feldmarschall* could have fallen back to another central position while waiting for the enemy's intentions to become clearer, whether from scouting or intelligence reports, or from small blocking forces posted on the likely axes of advance. Waitzen offers itself as a possible central position, about a day's march north of Pesth, and a day's march south of the road from Losoncz to Komorn. If the *Feldmarschall* had deployed there, he could have intervened in either direction, while also having a line of retreat directly behind him to the west should he need it.

This reconnaissance is to be carried out by III. Armeekorps. However, so as to stay in a firm mutually supporting posture, and to completely avoid any adverse event, it is necessary that I. Armeekorps should move closer and that in general our combat forces should be deployed such that they are at short intervals, namely on the line of Monor, Gödöllő, Waitzen and Vad-Kert,[38] ready for immediate concentration or mutual support at one or other of these places.

Following these general outlines, III. Armeekorps will advance to Bágh on 1 April, to Hatvan on the 2nd and to Gyöngyös on the 3rd, and by such a manoeuvre will be in a position to fully achieve the intention expressed above. I must however recommend to *Feldmarschall Lieutenant Graf* Schlick that he should not get involved in any action with superior enemy forces where the outcome is uncertain.

Should III. Korps encounter superior enemy forces it shall retreat toward Bágh with every precaution. On the other hand, I also advise against advancing any further beyond Gyöngyös, so as to remain constantly in a state to deploy III. Korps to whatever point where the enemy may appear in superior force. *Feldmarschall Lieutenant Graf* Schlick is to keep me informed daily of the results of his reconnaissance and of any news received about the enemy. *Feldmarschall Lieutenant Baron* Csorich, whose division at Waitzen forms, as it were, a deployable reserve, which must be kept ready for immediate use either at Gödöllő or for *Feldmarschall Lieutenant* Ramberg,[39] will instruct the latter *Herr Feldmarschall Lieutenant* to redouble his vigilance toward Losoncz. To cover the left flank of III. Armeekorps, *Feldmarschall Lieutenant Baron* Csorich is to send out a patrol of two *uhlan* squadrons and two cuirassier squadrons under the command of a capable officer and with a general staff officer attached, which is to move to Nagy-Berczel [Bercel, Hungary] tomorrow (1 April), to St. Jakob on the 2nd, and to Gyöngyös on the 3rd, but is also to scout on the left flank from Sz. Jakob toward Terenye [Bátonyterenye, Hungary].[40]

I. Armeekorps shall remain in its current position on 1 April, and shall send to Szolnok to bring the locomotives, wagons, supplies of salt, government monies, and other provisions to safety the same day. On 2 April the corps will move to Alberti, and to Monor on the 3rd. It would be most sensible to carry out this manoeuvre covered by a suitable rear guard which will keep the enemy in ignorance of what is happening on our side for as long as possible. Maintaining flank security and communications with III. Korps during its advance, by patrols at least, is essential. In the Monor position I. Korps will dominate the road to Szolnok and Kecskemét, cover Pesth, and be available for any possible mission further north.

At the same time *Hauptmann* Adam of the general staff, who had been entrusted with constructing some fieldworks to protect the bridge at Gran, was given the order to attend to

38 In this instance Érsekvadkért, not Soltvadkért, making the line specified by the *Feldmarschall* 80 km long. Thus, it is about two days' march from one end to the other, or a day's march to concentrate the whole force somewhere in the centre.

39 Ramberg being on the extreme left around Érsekvadkért at this point.

40 A *Feldmarschall* should not need to specify in this level of detail how his subordinates should maintain communications and screen each other's flanks.

construction of a bridge over the Gran at Kemend [Kamenín, Slovakia], for Division Ramberg could possibly be forced to retreat there.

A very favourable circumstance that the *Feldmarschall* became aware of at this time was that on the 24th His Majesty the *Kaiser* had found himself moved to order *General der Kavallerie Baron* Hammerstein, by means of a note written by his own supreme hand, to operate against Hungary with 10,000 men from Galicia immediately.

On the 27th the *Feldmarschall* expressed his deepest gratitude to His Majesty for this assistance, wishing only that this should turn out according to His supreme intention and should be in hand as quickly as the situation required. However, if Komorn were to fall soon, he would resume the offensive again without even waiting for this reinforcement. If the capture of this important fortress should not ensue within a short time but should stretch out into a long formal siege, then it would depend on the strength of the combat forces that *General der Kavallerie Baron* Hammerstein could provide whether these were sufficient to enable any further advance.

On the 27th and 31st the *Feldmarschall* told *General der Kavallerie Baron* Hammerstein about the current state of affairs and requested that he expedite his advance from Galicia to Kaschau as much as possible, for everything depended on the speed of this operation. If he was not in a position to advance immediately with the whole corps, then he should at least push a couple of battalions forward to Eperies and spread the word there that 20,000 men were following right behind them.

His Majesty the *Kaiser*'s wish to discuss some highly important matters with the *Feldmarschall* in person was the reason why at this time an invitation was brought by His Majesty's senior aide-de-camp to the *Feldmarschall* to present himself as soon as possible, and in any case within 24 hours, at the supreme court in Olmütz, and to hand over command of the army to the *Banus* ad interim.

On the 30th, immediately upon receipt of this letter, the *Feldmarschall* hastened to most humbly submit the following report to His Majesty the *Kaiser*:

> While in the process of immediately complying with the supreme command received from Your Majesty's aide-de-camp to betake myself to Olmütz, I received the news that significant enemy combat forces are approaching in the direction of Gyöngyös; consequently a clash between my army and the enemy is possible within the next few days. Your Majesty will therefore deign most graciously to excuse me if I do not abandon the army at such a moment but postpone the pleasure of presenting myself to Your Majesty in person by a few days, all the more so as the questions to be discussed may perhaps be brought closer to their solution by the events impending here. I will nevertheless make it my urgent duty to use the next suitable moment according to the state of affairs on the battlefield to proceed to Olmütz per your supreme request.[41]

41 It seems rather bold of the *Feldmarschall* to decline to comply with his monarch's instruction, however politely and deferentially he words his refusal. This could be seen as the *Feldmarschall* genuinely believing that it is unwise to hand over interim command at such a critical moment; or it could be seen as him clutching at an opportunity to improve matters before he has to explain his poor results to the *Kaiser* in person. Perhaps both motives were in play.

Feldmarschall Lieutenant Graf Schlick had begun his march from Gödöllő to Hatvan on 1 April in accordance with the *Feldmarschall*'s orders. His corps had undergone some changes to its order of battle. The three *grenzer* battalions that had been attached to it had been transferred to the *Banus*, who handed over 3. Bataillon E.H. Karl and the combined Bataillon Eckher (later Braisach) in exchange.

III. Armeekorps's order of battle was therefore the following:

Division *Feldmarschall Lieutenant Fürst* Lobkowitz[42]

Brigade *Generalmajor* Parrot
Two companies of 2. Jäger-Bataillon
3. Bataillon E.H. Karl[43]
1. Bataillon E.H. Wilhelm
1. Landwehr-Bataillon H.v. Parma
3. Bataillon Nugent
Oberstlieutenants 1. Eskadron Kaiser-Chevauxlegers
Sechspfündige Fussbatterie Nr. 36

Brigade *Oberstlieutenant* Künigl
3. Bataillon E.H. Wilhelm
3. Bataillon Koudelka
2. Bataillon Latour
Oberstlieutenants 2. Eskadron Kaiser-Chevauxlegers
Sechspfündige Fussbatterie Nr. 34

Division *Feldmarschall Lieutenant Fürst* Liechtenstein

Brigade *Generalmajor* Fiedler
3. Bataillon E.H. Stefan
Kompon. Bataillon Eckher (later Breisach), four companies
2. Bataillon Hartmann
3. Bataillon Mazzuchelli

Brigade *Oberst Graf* Montenuovo
Two squadrons Kaiser-Chevauxlegers
Six squadrons König v. Preussen Kürassiere
Two squadrons Sunstenau Kürassiere
Two squadrons Kress-Chevauxlegers
Two squadrons E.H. Johann Dragoner
Kavallerie-Batterie Nr. 3

42 Josef Franz *Fürst* Lobkowitz (1803-75).
43 The original refers to '3 Bataillone E.H. Karl' (i.e., three battalions of the regiment, rather than the third battalion), but this is surely an error.

Korps-Geschütz-Reserve

Sechspfündige Schlick-Batterie
Raketen-Batterie Nr. 11
Half of Raketen-Batterie Nr. 12

During the advance the advance guard under *Generalmajor* Parrot ran into weak hussar detachments this side of Hatvan, which however quickly withdrew. The town itself was held by a few infantry who likewise began their retreat after a short fight. *Generalmajor* Parrot had the enemy pursued for a stretch beyond Hatvan but remained in the town with the main body of the brigade while *Feldmarschall Lieutenant Graf* Schlick and the rest of the corps did not move beyond Assod [Aszód, Hungary] and Bágh. When he informed the *Feldmarschall* of this, he mentioned that the reports obtained about the enemy concurred that some of the rebel corps under Benytzky that was in the surrounding area had turned toward Miskolcz, and 'also that I think my right flank is not threatened since a patrol detached toward Jász-Berény has found that town unoccupied'.

On 2 April *Feldmarschall Lieutenant Graf* Schlick continued his advance along the Gyöngyös road. At Hort (about 10 km from Hatvan) the advance guard ran into the enemy who was himself in the process of advancing. An intense artillery duel immediately broke out. Gradually the other brigades and the artillery reserve moved up and got involved in the fighting, in which the enemy soon revealed a very significant superiority in troops and artillery. The action persisted for several hours without either side gaining ground. Finally, the enemy deployment became so extensive that Schlick saw both wings of his corps were threatened. This factor, as well as the conviction that he was dealing with a foe many times larger, so that even in the most favourable case he could not inflict a decisive defeat but was much more likely to be forced into a disadvantageous retreat himself since he had the Hatvan defile behind him, caused him to retreat to the heights in front of that town. He occupied the vineyards there with infantry and rocket launch stands, deployed some of his artillery very effectively at the edge of this curtain, and posted infantry in the town itself, so as to cover the construction of a second bridge over the Zagyva as well as the withdrawal of the cavalry and the baggage behind the river.

Although the enemy was now pressing in on Hatvan concentrically, the retreat was carried out in excellent calm and good order. *Feldmarschall Lieutenant Fürst* Franz Liechtenstein led the left wing with a judicious cool head, while *Generalmajor* Parrot's leadership of the centre deserves no less recognition. Finally, it came down to a hot rear guard action in the streets of Hatvan, especially at the bridge, which *Hauptmann Ritter* von Kalchberg defended most courageously with a company of Prohaska infantry. When every unit had crossed the Zagyva, the rear guard also crossed the bridge and demolished it despite the intense enemy artillery and small arms fire, whereby the enemy was prevented from pursuing any further and had to be content with taking possession of Hatvan. 'The orderly retreat,' says *Feldmarschall Lieutenant Graf* Schlick in his report to the *Feldmarschall* on the action at Hatvan, 'was in large part due to the determined courage and endurance with which *Hauptmann* Kalchberg and his company defended the crossing over the Zagyva.'[44]

Schlick had deployed his cavalry and artillery again on the right bank of the Zagyva behind Hatvan so as to cover his infantry's retreat to Bagh and Aszod if necessary. When darkness fell, he likewise retreated and went into quarters in Aszod. Our losses in this day's fighting came to no more than 95 men and 63 horses.[45]

The following were named among those who had especially distinguished themselves: *Feldmarschall Lieutenant Fürst* Franz Liechtenstein, *Generalmajor* Parrot, *Hauptmann* Kalchberg, *Unterlieutenant* Krasznigg, *Unterlieutenant* Ránig (these last three from the Prohaska regiment) and *Oberlieutenant* Bartelmus commanding Fussbatterie Nr. 36.

That evening, soon after arriving in Aszod, *Feldmarschall Lieutenant Graf* Schlick decided to retreat to Gödöllő at daybreak (3:00 a.m.) leaving only the Kavallerie-Brigade at Bágh and Aszod. Given the enemy's greatly superior numbers, he did not think he could hold the position at Bágh, since it could easily be outflanked. Also, his batteries had expended their ammunition.[46]

The *Feldmarschall* Concentrates around Gödöllő, 2-4 April 1849

The *Feldmarschall* first heard about the clash that had taken place between Schlick's III. Armeekorps and the enemy from *Oberstlieutenant Fürst* Lobkowitz, whom Schlick had sent to Ofen even before beginning his retreat so as to give a verbal report about the start of the fight but mainly about the significant enemy superiority.

The *Feldmarschall* had immediately realised the true state of affairs[47] and without waiting for any further reports sent an order at 10:00 p.m. on the 2nd to *Feldmarschall Lieutenant Baron* Csorich to set off with his division at 4:00 a.m. on the 3rd, and to move in a single day's march from Waitzen to Gödöllő to the increasingly necessary support of III. Armeekorps. To protect his left flank he was tasked with pushing a detachment out to K. Ujfalu [Váckisújfalu, Hungary], as well as with instructing *Feldmarschall Lieutenant* Ramberg to send a strong patrol from Vad-Kert through Romhány, Berczel and Sz. Jakob, so as to become aware in good time of any enemy manoeuvre happening further north. At the same time Grenadier-Bataillon Bitermann and the Munizions-Reserve of III. Armeekorps were also ordered to Gödöllő.

44 A fighting withdrawal across a river is a difficult and dangerous operation which Schlick evidently carried out in exemplary fashion: sensibly constructing a second bridge, making good use of covering positions and well-deployed, effective rear guards with well-chosen leaders. It is questionable, though, just how serious the Hungarian attack was: it may have been a genuine attack, but equally, it may have been part of Gáspár's mission of engaging and pinning without fully committing to the attack.

45 Bánlaky says that: 'According to the "Winterfeldzug" the Austrians lost just 95 men and 63 horses. However, Lieutenant Kocziczka who served in Schlick's corps gives its casualties as 56 men and 68 horses killed; 1 officer, 48 men and 19 horses wounded; and 85 missing, for a total of 202 men and 75 horses. The Hungarians reported 150 men lost.' Bánlaky, A magyar nemzet.

46 We have noted earlier the Army of the Danube's shortage of reserve ammunition wagons at the start of the campaign in December 1848. Perhaps that had been rectified to some degree by April, but it may still have contributed to Schlick's artillery running low here.

47 Or had he? On the 4th he orders an advance to Bágh and Aszod to oppose any Hungarian move against Waitzen (while still covering the direct approach to Pesth) but 'this reconnaissance produced no result', so on the 5th he intends to attack Hatvan 'to bring about a decisive battle' – as he still has not really worked out where the enemy is located.

An equally urgent measure was to bring I. Armeekorps closer, which was supposed to arrive in Monor on 3 April according to the orders issued on 31 March. But by 2 April this corps still had not moved! As luck would have it, on 1 April at the initiative of the supply department a letter was sent to I. Armeekorps command ordering it to bring salt out of Szolnok. The result of this instruction was that right away a detour was added to the coordinated march dispositions issued the day before. Learning of this, the *Feldmarschall* expressed his regret about it and ordered that serious efforts should be made so that on the 3rd I. Armeekorps should march back from Czegléd and Abany toward Monor at least far enough that it could quickly move to support III. Korps if necessary. All these arrangements had already been made at 10:00 p.m. on the 2nd before *Feldmarschall Lieutenant Graf* Schlick's detailed written report about the outcome of the action at Hatvan and his retreat to Gödöllő arrived at 5:00 a.m. on the 3rd.

What needed to be done as a result of this had already been done by summoning Division Csorich to Gödöllő and ordering I. Armeekorps to speed up its march as much as possible. Nevertheless, on the 3rd the order was now sent to the latter to march to Koka and Dany, where it was to stand ready to harass the enemy's left flank and to support III. Armeekorps if necessary. Just one weak brigade was to be deployed to Monor to keep an eye on the Szolnok road and to discover any subsequent enemy advance from that direction in good time. At the end of this letter the *Feldmarschall* added in his own hand: 'I urge Your Excellency to speed up your march as much as possible and to continue it without interruption so as to reach the points noted above (Koka and Dany) soon.'

On the 3rd *Feldmarschall Lieutenant Graf* Schlick was informed of all the arrangements that had been made and was told this:

> With the reinforcement coming to Your Honour in the form of the whole of Division Csorich, I hope that you may be in a position to drive the enemy back again and at least to regain the position at Bágh, which remains the most suitable place to oppose any manoeuvre toward Waitzen as this cannot easily be prevented from Gödöllő. It is especially important that we should avoid the inevitable disadvantage that would result from an enemy operation of that kind undertaken toward Waitzen in force; for it is not impossible that the enemy will engage and pin Your Honour frontally while sending a strong detachment toward Waitzen, which is why I must draw this matter to Your Honour's particular attention. For if a strong enemy column penetrates between III. Korps and *Feldmarschall Lieutenant* Ramberg and reaches Waitzen, our main aim of protecting the siege of Komorn will be endangered to a high degree.[48]

On the afternoon of the 3rd the *Feldmarschall* betook himself to Gödöllő to take over the direction of operations there. Before his departure he had charged the Ofen military district command with holding ready Grenadier-Bataillon Richter, 1. Bataillon Ceccopieri and the

48 It is curious that the *Feldmarschall* who is so sensitive about threats to his own line of communications does not imagine the enemy might feel the same. It is hard to believe that if the positions were reversed, the *Feldmarschall* would have conceived of marching through a gap between two enemy corps to relieve a distant fortress when the enemy could surely close the gap behind him before he reached it, yet he regards this as a serious option for his adversary. Again he is underestimating the enemy's problems and exaggerating his own.

Warasdiner-Kreutzer battalion from the Ofen-Pesth garrison to be able to move out as soon as ordered, after which the garrison under *Generalmajor* Liebler would comprise no more than three and two sixths battalions. *Generalmajor* Schütte was ordered to Gödöllő to be employed according to the situation.

Feldmarschall Lieutenant Baron Csorich arrived in Gödöllő promptly on the 3rd with his division and Kavallerie-Brigade Kisslinger (Bellegarde), but by contrast I. Armeekorps got no further than Tapio-Bicske with three brigades, while two (Rastic and Sternberg) only reached Alberti. When the *Banus* informed the *Feldmarschall* of this, he added, 'I thought I should have Brigades Rastic and Sternberg follow a day's march behind, so as not to encourage the enemy to follow me by retreating too quickly.'[49]

On the 4th the *Feldmarschall* informed the *Banus* of what he had done to concentrate units at Gödöllő, and added:

> As the strength of the enemy facing me is reportedly very considerable, and as he is also occupying Heves and the surrounding area there, and furthermore as most information indicates that the enemy intends to advance in superior force on Pesth, it appears to be of the utmost importance to maintain good observation of the roads leading to Pesth from Árok-Szallas and Jász-Berény, as well as the Zagyva crossing at Fenszaru [Jászfényszaru, Hungary]. For this Your Excellency's position at Dany and Koka remains very appropriate, from where the necessary patrols must be sent out to discover the enemy's approach in good time.

The information that had come in meanwhile about the enemy's movements was limited to the following:

First, *Feldmarschall Lieutenant Graf* Schlick reported that 'the enemy has occupied Hatvan, and the rest of Görgei's corps is encamped next to the town. I believe the enemy must likewise have used up most of his ammunition in yesterday's action, and therefore cannot advance until he has replaced it.'

Next, news came in from *Oberstlieutenant Baron* Minutillo, whom *Feldmarschall Lieutenant Baron* Csorich had sent out with a patrol of four squadrons and an infantry battalion from Waitzen through Berczel toward St. Jakob, that he had encountered six hussar squadrons and a *honvéd* battalion with artillery between Buják and Csécse, and had also detected infantry detachments further back at the edge of a forest. In the circumstances he had deemed it appropriate to remain in Berczel for the time being. According to statements from the notary and the priest in Buják, there were 5,000-6,000 men in that area and a corps at Losoncz as well.

Also, *Rittmeister* Brudermann, whom *Feldmarschall Lieutenant* Ramberg had sent out with a patrol of one squadron from Vad-Kert toward Gyöngyös, had run into enemy outposts at Surdok-Püspöki. He had learned from a former imperial officer that there were six hussar squadrons, three infantry battalions and a 6-pounder battery in Páta, 7,000 men in Hatvan and 8,000 in Gyöngyös. He reported, 'Klapka and Guyon are said to be in Losoncz and Rima-Szombath.'

49 The *Banus* has had repeated urgent orders to move north, he has already been delayed once, his usual response to any enemy threat is to exaggerate it and request reinforcements, yet here he is dragging his feet and exposing part of his force to attack. This peculiar rationale therefore sounds like a poor excuse for his failure to get his troops to march as far and as fast as they should have.

On the 3rd Ramberg had pushed forward an infantry battalion with two squadrons and three rocket launch stands from Vad-Kert to Berczel to observe the road from Gyöngyös.

Finally, a report dated 2 April came in from the local command at Schemnitz that mentioned a 15,000-strong corps at Rima-Szombath as well as the militia being very actively organised in Neograd [Nógrád, Hungary] and Gömör counties. This was all that had been learned about the enemy in the course of the 2nd and 3rd.

Immediately following his arrival in Gödöllő the *Feldmarschall* had decided to advance next day (the 4th) with the units gathered there to the position at Bágh and Aszod, and to push on from there toward Hatvan according to the situation. The troops therefore set off at 8:00 a.m. on the 4th. III. Armeekorps deployed in and forward of Bágh, Division Csorich at Aszod, while the *Feldmarschall* advanced with the cavalry to reconnoitre further on toward Hatvan. Hereupon enemy detachments were encountered – probably advancing from Hatvan with similar intention – that were gradually reinforced to 8,000-10,000 men, but after a few cannon shots they retreated again to the left bank of the Zagyva behind Hatvan. As darkness fell, our cavalry also returned to the main body's position, leaving outposts behind. This reconnaissance produced no result. No prisoners were taken, and the ground on the left bank of the Zagyva where the enemy had his actual position is so covered by vineyards and hills that absolutely no overview of it could be had.

To finally bring about a decisive battle, after returning to Aszod the *Feldmarschall* ordered a general advance for the next day (the 5th) to attack the position at Hatvan, in which I. Armeekorps was also to participate. Therefore at 10:00 p.m. on the 4th the following letter was sent to the *Banus*:

> It is my intention to attack the enemy at Hatvan tomorrow (the 5th) from Bágh and Aszod. However, since I suspect that the forces he revealed today (the 4th) may only be a small part of his total force, a frontal attack is fraught with difficulty because of the nature of the terrain and the defile in front of Hatvan. Taking that into account I must therefore desire that Your Excellency should simultaneously advance from your position toward Fenszaru, cross the Zagyva there, and press into the enemy's flank and rear.[50] Given the nature of the terrain, cavalry would be most suitable for this, but strong infantry detachments with appropriate artillery should also be attached to them, since I assume that the enemy will have occupied the crossing at Fenszaru.
>
> A close eye should also be kept on the road from Jász-Berény, because it is not beyond the bounds of possibility that an enemy column could advance along it toward Pesth. If contrary to expectations Your Excellency should receive completely reliable information about an enemy column approaching from Szolnok or Czibakháza and this has already advanced as far as Alberti, Your Excellency ought certainly to turn your attention in that direction. I will move out from the position at Bágh and Aszod at 08:30 a.m., so Your Excellency should set the time for your own march accordingly so

50 This shows how wrong the *Feldmarschall* was about the enemy's position. Far from threatening the enemy's flank and rear, this move would have ensured the *Banus* was utterly outflanked by the Hungarian advance via Jász-Berény. At least the *Feldmarschall* notes that this risk is 'not beyond the bounds of possibility'.

as to accomplish your crossing at Fenszaru in good time. I request that Your Excellency should give my orderly officer a definite answer to bring back to me.

This edict had not yet been sent out when the *Feldmarschall* received the following two reports from the *Banus*:

My rearguard, Brigade Rastic, has been under enemy attack for more than an hour. It seems that it has been separated from Kavallerie-Brigade Sternberg, which is closer to me. Heavy cannon fire can be heard from the area of Tapio-Bicske.[51] I therefore find myself obliged to halt the corps here and at Koka to await further messages and events.

Szecsö [Tapiószecső, Hungary], 4 April 1849, 2:00 p.m.

Immediately afterwards:

I am staying here in the position between Szecsö and Koka to receive Brigades Rastic and Sternberg. The former has been through a tough fight and taken several guns from the enemy, four of which have already been sent on to me. The two Ottochaner battalions took these and have displayed great courage; the Banderial hussars also charged the enemy victoriously, but brave *Major Baron* Riedesel and *Rittmeister* Gyurkovic have fallen. I am under strong enemy threat from the south. I request your orders as to what to do next.

Szecsö, 4 April 1849, 4:00 p.m.

Whilst these reports contained none of the more detailed information that could have been given about the enemy's strength, direction of march and intentions, still they had to put in question whether I. Armeekorps would be in a position to cooperate with the planned attack on Hatvan.

When the *Feldmarschall* expressed this concern in connection with his edict above, he indicated 'that it might perhaps be possible for you [the *Banus*] to pursue the enemy, who has been repulsed by Brigades Rastic and Sternberg with great sacrifice, with a suitable portion of your corps'. Finally, he once again indicated the need for the *Banus* to reply immediately and share his views by giving them to the returning courier.[52] The reply from the *Banus* arrived the next day (the 5th) at 9:30 a.m., and went as follows:

Since Your Highness regards my mission to cross the Zagyva at Fenszaru and operate in force against the enemy's flank and rear as decisive, my corps will set off without delay to fulfil your noble order. I am therefore not in a position to exert a direct influence

51 The action at Tapio-Bicske is described in full in the section on 'Hungarian forces and movements leading up to the battle of Isaszeg, 25 March to 6 April'.

52 The *Banus*'s sketchy report evidently misled the *Feldmarschall* into thinking the Hungarians had been emphatically repulsed, when in fact Brigades Rastic and Sternberg had done well simply to escape and avoid being crushed by superior numbers.

on covering Pesth. Yesterday morning the enemy was in Nagy-Kata in force. *General* Rastic states that he was facing 10,000 men yesterday (the 4th). The enemy had already abandoned all pursuit by nightfall. His outposts are 8 km from here, toward Tapio-Bicske. It has so far been impossible for me to discover what direction of march his columns are taking or have taken overnight.

The *Feldmarschall's* Reconnaissance toward Hatvan and the Deployment at Gödöllő, 5 April 1849

This report was really not the kind to reassure the *Feldmarschall* that he could rely on I. Armeekorps participating undisturbed in the attack on the Hatvan position. Apart from the fact that the *Banus* was protesting that it was unreasonable to demand that he should protect Pesth, and was not able to provide anything reliable about the enemy's movements, his march from Szecsö to Fenszaru now seemed extremely risky since the strong enemy column that had attacked Brigade Rastic at Tapio-Bicske and whose outposts had been pushed forward toward Szecsö only needed to advance in this direction in order to take I. Armeekorps in rear while it was marching to Fenszaru. These considerations caused the *Feldmarschall* not only to call off I. Armeekorps's dangerous march immediately, but also to limit the planned attack on Hatvan to a mere reconnaissance.[53] The relevant order to the *Banus* also contained the instruction that:

> [T]he protection of Pesth against any enemy move from Jász-Berény or Czegléd is now again your [the *Banus*'s] mission, and you should adopt a suitable deployment for this purpose. I [the *Feldmarschall* himself] will move in this direction in the event that I should receive reports that the enemy has moved from Hatvan to there. The need to protect Pesth seems to me all the more essential since reports show that the enemy crossed the Theiss at Szolnok and Czibakháza on the 3rd.[54]

The latter reports he mentions came from *Feldmarschall Lieutenant Graf* Wrbna who had been left in Ofen as military district commander. The concluding part of this order contained the request to make every effort to obtain definite information about the enemy's movements, and to make the *Feldmarschall* aware of any such without delay.

During the reconnaissance led in person by the *Feldmarschall*, an exceptionally glorious cavalry action took place this side of Hatvan. *Feldmarschall Lieutenant Fürst* Franz Liechtenstein with two squadrons of Civallart-Uhlanen, two squadrons of Kress-Chevauxlegers and two rocket stands had driven the enemy's forward elements back into the Hatvan position when six squadrons of hussars debouched from the town onto the right bank of the Zagyva and advanced to the attack. The *chevauxlegers* and *uhlans* hurled themselves so skilfully and impetuously against the front and flank of the charging hussars that these were completely defeated and

53 At last the *Feldmarschall* is getting the picture.

54 In fact all the major Hungarian formations in the area (I., II., III. and VII. Armeekorps) were nowhere near Szolnok or Czibakháza but had concentrated east of Gyöngyös by the end of March. The crossing reported by Wrbna was presumably the diversion by *Oberstlieutenant* Asboth's detachment at Török-St.-Miklos, which was ordered on 3 April to cross the Theiss immediately, destroy the Szolnok railway and inflict as much damage as possible (see the section on 'The Retreat to Pesth, 7 April 1849').

most vigorously pursued. The Zagyva bridge that the hussars had to escape across caused a huge jam which the pursuing *uhlans* with their lances and the skilful *chevauxlegers* with their sharp-pointed swords exploited so splendidly that 53 hussars were left dead on the field, while two officers, 17 men and many horses were captured.

The official report names the following as distinguishing themselves in this cavalry action: *Oberst Graf* Montenuovo, *Rittmeister* Kugstatscher, *Oberlieutenants Graf* Waldek and Pulz of the Kress-Chevauxlegers, *Rittmeisters Baron* Wimmer and Ivichich and *Lieutenant* Kadisch of the Civallart-Uhlanen, and army *Rittmeister Graf* Török.[55]

After this action the troops returned to their bivouacs at Bágh and Aszod again without being pursued by the enemy. The *Feldmarschall* also went to his headquarters in Aszod. During this reconnaissance he had become convinced by what he had seen himself as well as from prisoner statements that the enemy main body was no longer behind Hatvan. But as for where it might have moved to, nothing definite was known, so he was reduced to mere conjecture about the enemy's likely movements and intentions. These could be directed either toward driving the *Feldmarschall* away from Pesth entirely by advancing through Jász-Berény, or else just to engaging him and pinning him on his front and right flank while at the same time sending a strong column to Waitzen or even further upstream to relieve Komorn.

The position of II. and III. Armeekorps concentrated at Bágh and Aszod under the *Feldmarschall*'s direct command, in conjunction with I. Armeekorps deployed at Dany and Koka, was perfectly suited for covering both Pesth and Waitzen against an enemy advance directly from Hatvan; but from the moment when the enemy advanced in significant force through Jász-Berény, Nagy-Kata and Tapio-Bicske, as it emerged he had done from the action at the latter place and from the *Banus*'s messages of the 5th, it seemed too far forward to protect Pesth and too dangerous.

This consideration caused the *Feldmarschall* to have the army withdraw to the position at Gödöllő without further delay, and without waiting for the enemy to gain any more ground on either of his flanks. How wise this decision was will become sufficiently clear from the enemy's plans and manoeuvres, about which of course no information was known until after the end of the war.[56]

The position at Gödöllő is exceptionally favourable for the defence. Formed by a fairly steep range of wooded hills, it is all the more suitable for stubborn resistance as it is only crossed by a single road fit for wheeled transport. The enemy's superiority in cavalry and artillery was therefore more than offset by the nature of the terrain. It was also much closer to the *Banus*'s corps, which had meanwhile moved to Isaszeg, together with which any enemy operation toward Pesth could be opposed in good time, whether it should come through Gödöllő or further south. On the other hand Waitzen was left exposed, for after abandoning Aszod and Bágh it was possible for the enemy to move swiftly through the Galga valley to gain Waitzen and thereby the road to Komorn before he could be prevented from doing so. Consequently, the *Feldmarschall* deemed it appropriate only to pull back III. Armeekorps into the naturally favoured advantageous defensive position at Gödöllő, and to send Division Csorich through the

55 Miklós Török (1812-84) was a former imperial officer who became a major in the new Hungarian national guard in June 1848. He took part in the fighting against the imperial forces invading from Galicia in December 1848, but in January 1849 went over to the imperial side. Bona, *Tábornokok*.

56 A wise decision indeed.

Galga valley from Aszod to Waitzen instead, where in combination with Division Ramberg it would be in a position to thwart any operation toward Komorn, even if that should be attempted through the Eipel valley, which must still be assumed to be a possibility.

This measure will be obvious to anyone who grasps the full significance of the importance of covering Komorn, and who knows that in a country like Hungary, especially in springtime when the roads become quite unusable after a little rain, the effectiveness of flanking positions like for example that of Gödöllő with respect to the road from Aszod to Waitzen through the Galga valley cannot absolutely be relied on; for one runs the risk of being unable to overtake the enemy once he has gained a head start.

The order to vacate the position at Aszod and Bágh was issued at midnight on the 5th. *Feldmarschall Lieutenant Graf* Schlick was ordered to:

> [D]epart for Gödöllő at 6:00 a.m. on the 6th with your corps as well as Grenadier-Bataillon Bitermann, six squadrons of Auersperg cuirassiers, the Artillerie-Reserve and the bridging trains, and to take position there. The cooks, forage parties and baggage trains are to set off for Gödöllő at 4:00 a.m., to prepare rations and obtain the necessary forage, so that the troops will be in a position to be able to continue the march if necessary. A rear guard of cavalry and a half-battery of horse artillery is to be left behind to protect the march.

The order was sent to *Feldmarschall Lieutenant Baron* Csorich to:

> [S]et off from Aszod at 6:00 a.m. with your infantry division, five squadrons of Civallart-Uhlanen, two squadrons of E.H. Johann Dragoner and the Artillerie-Reserve of II. Armeekorps and to move to Waitzen in a single day's march. There you should remain in readiness to move immediately according to whether the enemy turns toward Pesth or Komorn. Division Ramberg is assigned to you.

Finally, the following edict was sent to the *Banus*:

> From the information that has come to me from patrols, spies and prisoners, I am convinced that the enemy is not concentrated directly behind Hatvan in such significant strength as it seemed initially, but rather that his troops are deployed in several other places to the side and rear. In attacking Hatvan and beyond I would most likely only encounter a smaller portion of the enemy combat forces, while his main body perhaps turns in another direction toward Pesth or Waitzen and I in any case would have moved too far away from Pesth, which I do not on any account wish to expose. Since Your Excellency has reported to me besides that significant enemy combat forces are to the south in front of Szecsö, I find myself moved to transfer III. Armeekorps tomorrow morning from the position at Bágh and Aszod to Gödöllő, and Division Csorich to Waitzen. In this deployment I will be in a position to rush forces quickly to any point, be it to cover Pesth on the one side or Komorn on the other. However, I must request Your Excellency also to choose a position for your corps that makes it possible to effect a junction of I. and III. Armeekorps at any point where it may be required, so as to achieve the main aim, namely covering Pesth, with complete certainty. I urge Your

> Excellency to let me know of the position you select for this purpose all the more swiftly and surely as I have received no report from you since this morning, and I remain in ignorance of whether the order sent to you by means of two orderlies in succession concerning the calling-off of your advance through Fenszaru has actually reached you.

At 6:00 a.m. on the 6th the troops moved out of the position at Aszod and Bágh as ordered. By 10:30 a.m., III. Armeekorps had already occupied the Gödöllő position. Soon after that a note written in pencil by the *Banus* at 5:00 p.m. on the 5th arrived which said, 'I am marching immediately through Zsambok to Dany, and tomorrow (the 6th) to Isaszeg. Enemy columns south of me are marching toward Pesth.' This was all that had been learned from I. Armeekorps in the course of 24 hours about the enemy's movements and about the enemy forces facing it.

At 12:15 p.m. on the 6th the *Feldmarschall* replied from Gödöllő:

> I have just received Your Excellency's pencilled note of the 5th which reassures me that my order to your noble self yesterday arrived in good time, and completely relieves the concern that I had necessarily harboured for a moment for Your Excellency's corps, all the more so as no news had arrived from Your Excellency for 24 hours. Now that Your Excellency tells me that enemy columns south of you are heading toward Pesth, I desire that your noble self should obtain as full information as possible about their actual strength and direction of march. In the course of this I ask that Your Excellency should not hesitate to attack them if that should offer the prospect of a notable success. This is all the more the case since as soon as I receive word from Your Excellency about the arrangements you have made, I am in a position to set off by 2:00 p.m. with the whole of III. Armeekorps, or part of it according to the situation, to the support of your noble self in whichever direction Your Excellency should designate as the right one. Thus, I request Your Excellency to keep me appropriately informed immediately about everything that your noble self proposes to arrange in this respect. There is no time to lose, as although the enemy was still at Hatvan this morning he could quite possibly have advanced, and I repeat once more, you may rest assured of the most powerful support from my side. The destruction of any one enemy column, even of modest size, could deliver an important result in the present situation. Understandably it is also of particular importance to me to know exactly where Brigade Mihic is at this moment, which was detached to Monor, and what enemy it finds itself facing. Finally, I request Your Excellency to make enquiries as to the state of the roads from Isaszeg directly to Czinkota, Keresztur, Vecses and Mende, because these are the lines on which we could be in a position to move around Pesth. This is likewise to be reported to me.
>
> At this point I am not worried that any enemy column might be moving toward Pesth from Kecskemét, because mail from there was still arriving in Ofen yesterday.

About an hour after the above letter had gone off to its destination, a report arrived from the *Banus* in which he informed the *Feldmarschall* that he had set off from Dany that day (the 6th) at 6:00 a.m., reached Isaszeg at 11:00 a.m., and set up camp there. During the march he had been followed at some distance by one enemy infantry battalion, a battery and three divisions of hussars.

> I can now easily link up with III. Armeekorps, and await further orders; for my troops are too fatigued to march any further anyway. Constant enemy troop movements have been observed south of my direction of march – about four columns, whose strength could not be estimated because they were too far away.
>
> As far as where to move next is concerned [the report concluded], perhaps Your Highness might consider it appropriate to order further operations to be carried out by I. and III. Armeekorps combined.

The Battle of Isaszeg, 6 April 1849

After the units of III. Armeekorps had arrived in the camp at Gödöllő they hurriedly prepared to eat. Thousands of wagons of provisions had come from Pesth and been driven every which way onto the town square and the limited area of valley bottom in front of the Grasalkovich Palace [Gödöllői Királyi Kastély, now the Royal Palace of Gödöllő], but the tired troops had not yet been issued their rations. They did not get around to this anyway, since at 1:00 p.m. word arrived that enemy detachments were approaching from Bágh. Division Lobkowitz therefore had to move immediately into its battle position forward of Gödöllő. But soon after this the thunder of guns came from the south, leaving no doubt that the *Banus* was under serious attack.

At the first cannon shots the *Feldmarschall* had got ready to rush to the battlefield. Division Liechtenstein, which was following Division Lobkowitz, was directed to the range of hills that lies between Gödöllő and Isaszeg and forms part of the large game park there. The *Feldmarschall* had immediately recognised that it was most likely that only a strong demonstration was to be expected from the direction of Bágh, which Division Lobkowitz would be strong enough to oppose, while the main attack might be directed against I. Armeekorps.

Where one emerges into the open from the game park right above Gödöllő, there is a large vineyard in the direction of Isaszeg. On its left the vineyard joins the St. Kiralyer-Wald [Szent Király Erdö, 'Saint King's Wood' – the Saint King being St Stephen], which extends a long way from there toward Valkó and the farm at St. Lászlo [Valkószentlászló, Hungary]. On its right the Rakos stream coming down from Gödöllő flows through a marshy valley and can only be crossed in a few places, in particular at Isaszeg and at a mill about 3 km upstream from there.

When the *Feldmarschall* and Division Liechtenstein reached the vineyard, Isaszeg was already in flames and the *Banus* had occupied his second position behind the Rakos.[57] From the southern end of the vineyard a clear view could be had across the actual battlefield and it was immediately obvious that the enemy had brought significant forces into action. He had already moved down from the hills into the totally open valley of the Rakos, and was just about to renew his attack on I. Armeekorps when the head of Division Liechtenstein burst forth from the edge of the vineyard full onto the enemy's right flank.

57 It is surprising that Nobili does not describe what had happened in the *Banus*'s first position. According to Bánlaky (*A magyar nemzet*), Brigades Rastic and Gramont were deployed along the southeast and eastern edges of the King's Wood as a screen or rear guard. They were driven out by Klapka's corps. To help Rastic and Gramont to withdraw through Isaszeg across the Rakos, the *Banus* sent forward two brigades of Schulzig's division. These caused Zako's brigade to fall back in disorder and confusion, and Bobics's brigade was caught up in infectious rout. These two fragile Hungarian formations had embarrassed themselves similarly at Tapio-Bicske, and subsequently were to do so again at Nagy-Sallo.

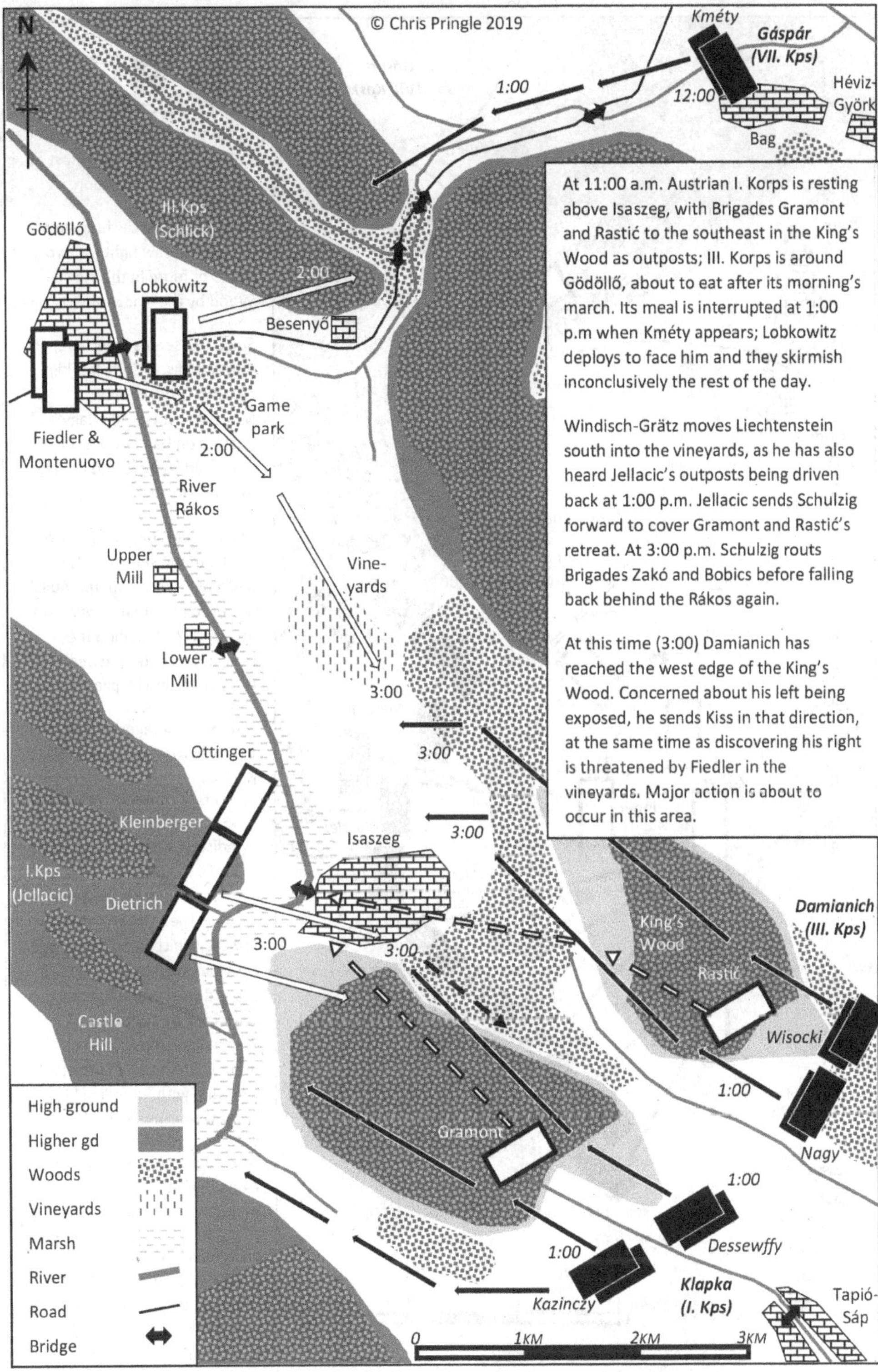

Map 6a: The battle of Isaszeg, 6 April 1849 – opening moves

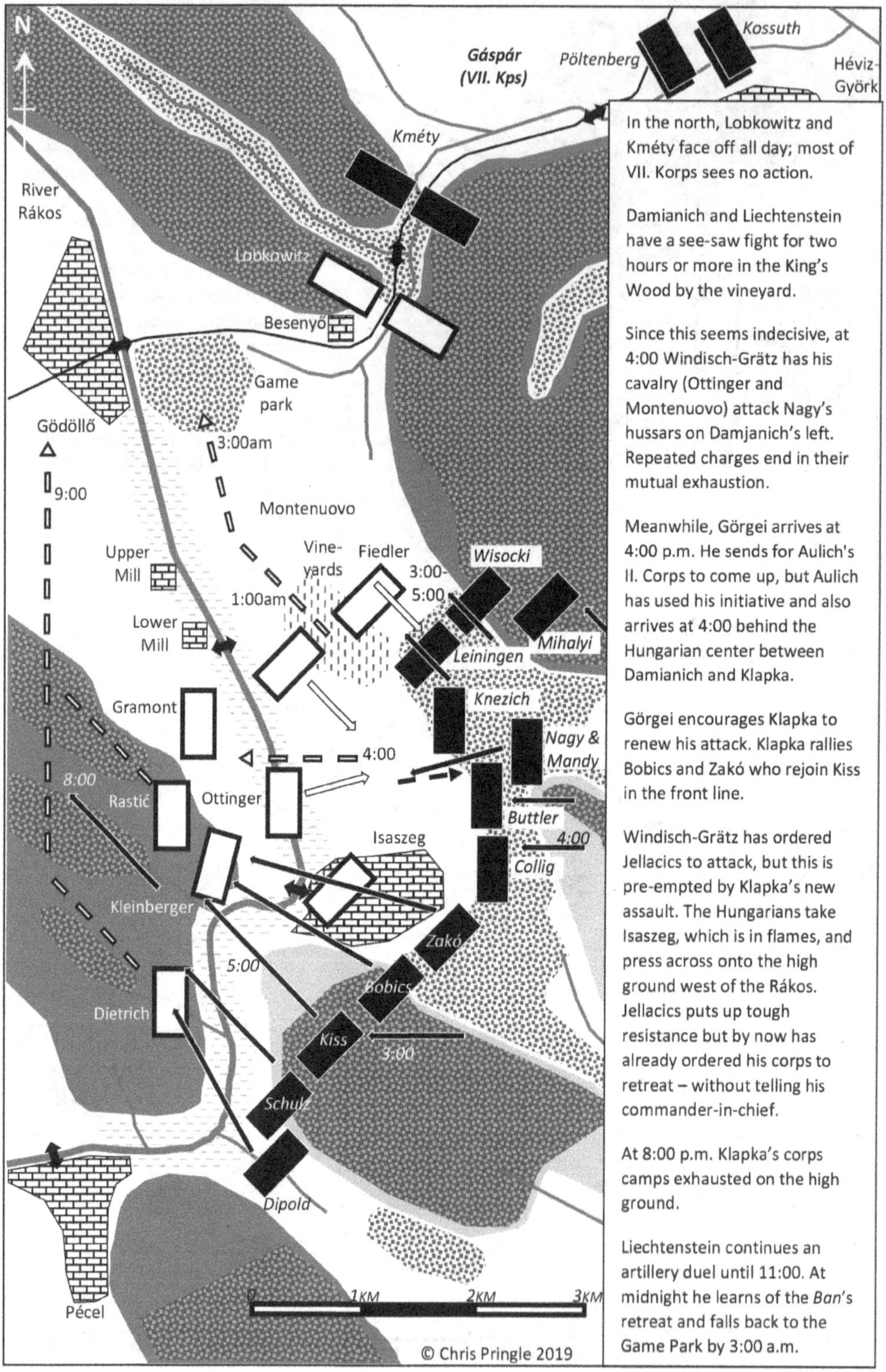

Map 6b: The battle of Isaszeg, 6 April 1849 – second phase

The *Feldmarschall* deployed a 12-pounder battery on a dominant point that completely flanked the enemy columns, and also a rocket battery close by in the vineyard, suitably protected by some detachments of Brigade Fiedler while the rest of the brigade pushed in succession into the nearby wood. Behind the 12-pounder battery, hidden by the wood, stood *Oberst Graf* Montenuovo with three squadrons of Kress Chevauxlegers and one of Auersperg Kürassiere. *Oberst* Kisslinger had already been detached earlier to the more favourable ground for cavalry along the Rakos to support I. Armeekorps directly with two squadrons of his regiment (Auersperg Kürassiere) and the Kürassier-Regiment Prinz von Preussen and Raketen-Batterie Nr. 11.

The aforementioned 12-pounder battery opened fire with such effect that right after its first salvo the advancing enemy columns began to waver. Before long they hastily sought to fall back onto the hills to their rear from which they had come down to attack the *Banus*'s position. This they managed to do, but not without significant losses.

The enemy now realised just too late the importance of the wood on his right flank that he had not occupied in sufficient force.[58] He sent strong detachments there who got into a very intense and murderous fight with the units of Brigade Fiedler that had been deployed in that direction.

The Hartmann battalion led by brave *Major Baron* Piattoli had been first to push into the wood. It had already made the enemy detachment posted there give way when it was driven back again by the arrival of enemy reinforcements, at which point *Major Baron* Piattoli and *Lieutenant* Hahn died a hero's death.

The forest fight was carried on without a pause, with equal ferocity and fluctuating fortunes, by 3. Bataillon Mazzuchelli and the combined Bataillon Braisach (Ecker) that had rushed up meanwhile and that were soon followed by 3. Bataillon E.H. Stefan; for the enemy constantly deployed new battalions into the wood, and generally strained every effort to claim possession of it. Then at the right moment the *Feldmarschall* ordered 5. Jäger-Bataillon, which the *Banus* had deployed at the mill above Isaszeg to cover his left flank but which had become redundant there because of the arrival and involvement of the units of III. Armeekorps, to support those fighting in the wood.

This battalion now charged forward. All the rest followed its example with the same determination so that the enemy, driven back at every point, had to abandon possession of the wood entirely to our troops.

During the fight in the wood, and while the batteries brought up one by one in front of the vineyard to support the 12-pounder battery had continued firing without pause, albeit also suffering some losses from the numerous enemy guns posted on the heights, a lull had developed in the centre of I. Armeekorps's position. But on the wooded hills forming the right wing of the position the fighting became increasingly fierce, and the battalions deployed there were having to make extreme efforts just to hold on.

58 Bánlaky says Damjanich, commanding III. Corps on the Hungarian right, had assumed Gaspar's VII. Corps would be pressing forward there. It is also Görgei's turn to be criticised for not being close enough to the action. While Windisch-Grätz was right at the forefront on this occasion, Görgei did not arrive on the battlefield until 4:00 p.m., and although in his orders he had said his headquarters would be in Dany, in fact he set up in Koka but without telling his corps commanders. Thus, reports about the battle did not reach him until 3:00 p.m. The Hungarian attacking efforts may have missed his overall guiding hand, as they would do again at the battle of Pered in June 1849. Bánlaky, *A magyar nemzet*.

The *Feldmarschall* desired that I. Armeekorps should advance again against the enemy centre, specifically the cavalry under *Generalmajor* Ottinger, to whom he sent a direct request to do so. *Oberst* Kisslinger was to join Brigade Ottinger with his eight squadrons and Raketen-Batterie Nr. 11, while *Oberst Graf* Montenuovo was to contribute to the larger goal with a flank attack from his concealed position at the edge of the wood.

Generalmajor Ottinger was supposed to debouch with his cavalry at Isaszeg, but the fact that the village was in flames while the bridge across the Rakos was very effectively raked by the enemy batteries caused him to seek a crossing further upstream. He had indeed actually identified one, and the larger part of his brigade had already crossed the Rakos, when he was received by the enemy batteries that had moved up onto the heights in the meantime with such murderous successive salvoes of cannister fire that the attack had to be abandoned to avoid suffering excessive losses. Raketen-Batterie Nr. 11 under *Oberlieutenant* Angerer had meanwhile moved up to within 800 paces of the enemy batteries and had opened up a very effective fire on them, in which it benefited from the fact that the enemy batteries deployed on the heights mostly overshot it. But suddenly four divisions of hussars formed up in echelon dashed forward in a charge. They galloped down from the heights and forced the rocket battery to retreat toward the Rakos. The leading hussar detachments had just reached the plain and were very close to the battery when *Oberst Graf* Montenuovo led his squadrons from inside the edge of the wood with lightning speed into the flank and rear of the last echelon of the hussars and caused such consternation that scarcely had the right wing of that echelon been beaten than all the rest raced back in wild flight. A fresh division approached later but this too was defeated by the brave Kress-Chevauxlegers, after which the two sides' cavalry just stood staring at each other, their horses utterly exhausted by the deep sandy soil.

After this cavalry attack, and after all the enemy's efforts to gain control of the wood had been bloodily repulsed as already described, the enemy completely gave up any further offensive manoeuvres.[59]

Just before dusk, the *Feldmarschall* was still next to some scattered harvesting baskets[60] in front of the large vineyard when one of the *Banus*'s aides-de-camp (*Major* Schweiger) arrived and asked for orders for what I. Armeekorps should do. The *Feldmarschall* replied with the words: 'Tell His Excellency he may deploy outposts in his present position and have his cavalry pursue the enemy, after which he can link up with III. Armeekorps later.'

59 According to Bánlaky, this is untrue. Görgei's arrival had galvanised a renewed assault, which Nobili's account glosses over. Klapka's and Aulich's corps had taken Isaszeg, crossed the Rakos, and driven back the *Banus*'s right wing. This caused the *Banus* to retreat toward Gödöllő, but without informing the *Feldmarschall* until he actually arrived there at 9:00 p.m. Meanwhile at 8:00 p.m. the Hungarian chief of staff, Bayer, realising the situation, had ordered Klapka to advance to Kerepes, which would have placed him astride the Austrian line of retreat. Klapka ignored this order because of his troops' fatigue. He was later criticised by Bayer for this serious omission. Bánlaky, *A magyar nemzet*.

60 The original text says '*Fähren*'. Normally this means 'ferries'; in archaic language it could be any kind of vessel, not just in water; it could even be anything that helps transport such as a path (a 'thoroughfare'). In the present case it is not clear whether the isolated or scattered objects around the *Feldmarschall* were punts off the Rakos, or containers for collecting grapes, or caissons or limbers from the batteries that had been deployed there. I have opted for the grape baskets.

During the battle at Isaszeg Division Lobkowitz had held its position forward of Gödöllő against the enemy detachments advancing from Bágh without any great effort, for at this point the enemy only moved forward very cautiously despite his superior numbers.

The losses in the encounter at Isaszeg cannot be fully assessed from the files.[61] Only those of Division Liechtenstein are recorded as follows: Killed: *Major* Piattoli and *Lieutenant* Hahn of the Hartmann infantry, *Lieutenant* Boschina of E.H. Stefan, and 61 men; Wounded: *Hauptmann* Lanko, *Oberlieutenant* de Begg and *Lieutenant* Mager of the Hartmann infantry, *Oberlieutenants* Grubishich and Prevôt of the E.H. Stefan infantry, *Rittmeister* Hoffmann of the Prinz von Preussen Kürassiere, and 78 men; Captured and wounded: *Oberarzt Dr.* Sauernik of the Prinz von Preussen Kürassiere.

In his after-action report, *Feldmarschall Lieutenant Graf* Schlick named the following as having distinguished themselves: *Feldmarschall Lieutenant Fürst* Franz Liechtenstein; *Generalmajor* Fiedler; *Major Baron* Gablenz of the general staff; *Oberst Graf* Montenuovo and *Major* Alberti of the Kress-Chevauxlegers; *Hauptmann Baron* Brandenstein of the Geppert infantry and *Oberlieutenant* Vincenti of the Grossherzog von Baden infantry, both attached to the general staff; *Rittmeister Graf* Soltik of the Grossfürst Alexander-Husaren; *Major* Piattoli, *Oberlieutenants* Pokorny and de Begg, and *Lieutenants* Gugenmós and Makowsky of 2. Bataillon Hartmann; *Lieutenant* Szulkiewicz of 3. Bataillon E.H. Stefan; *Lieutenant* Hesky of 3. Bataillon Mazzuchelli; *Major* Braisach, *Hauptmann* Gaver, *Oberlieutenants* Stradiot and Maina and *Lieutenant* Bernhardt of the Hess infantry; *Lieutenant* Krassnigg of the Prohaska infantry; *Lieutenant Baron* Deken of the Kress-Chevauxlegers; *Oberlieutenant* Hauk of the artillery; *Regimentsarzt Dr.* Neuhold of the E.H. Wilhelm infantry; and *Regimentsarzt Drs* Klein and Nar of the Auersperg Kürasssiere.

Toward 9:00 p.m. the *Feldmarschall* returned from the battlefield to his headquarters in Gödöllő again. Soon after that the *Banus* arrived there too, reporting that 'I. Armeekorps cannot spend the night in its disadvantageous position, and will arrive in Gödöllő immediately'. Thus no outposts had been deployed, nor had the cavalry carried out any pursuit. Only *Oberst Baron* Horvath, attracted by the thunder of the guns at Isaszeg, had joined up with Brigade Mihic (which had been detached to observe the Szolnok road) on the afternoon of the 6th, advanced toward Sáp, driven back the enemy detachments deployed there and taken prisoners in the enemy's rear.

There was not much doubt about what the *Feldmarschall* had to do. Now that I. Armeekorps had marched to Gödöllő, that immediately ruled out any thought of holding this position; for the enemy could now march unhindered to Pesth by the more direct route, namely through Isaszeg.

The Retreat to Pesth, 7 April 1849

Two roads were open for the retreat that had become unavoidable – that to Pesth, and that to Waitzen. By choosing the first route, Pesth would be covered, where – quite apart from its political significance – there were all the accumulated stores of rations and ammunition, and

61 Bánlaky gives Hungarian losses as 800-1,000 men, about 3% of those engaged, and says various sources give Austrian losses as between 600 and 1,500. Bánlaky, *A magyar nemzet*.

more than 5,000 sick and wounded in the hospitals. Retreating to Waitzen would sacrifice Pesth but would thwart any move the enemy might intend to relieve Komorn, and after bringing up reinforcements the *Feldmarschall* would also remain in a position to go on the offensive again toward Pesth or into the rear of the enemy army. But securing rations in Waitzen would be absolutely impossible for the first 24 hours. On the evening of the battle at Isaszeg the troops had not a single piece of bread left, the horses not one more feed of oats; for at the first cannon shots, before the rations had even been doled out, the supply trains had hastily headed back from Gödöllő to Pesth! This factor alone would have been enough to decide in favour of retreating to Pesth. But there were still other reasons for doing so. In the course of the battle of Isaszeg the *Feldmarschall* had become convinced that Pesth was the objective the enemy strove to reach and to drive his own army away from. At least so it seemed to emerge from the superior numbers the enemy had thrown against the right wing of his position at Isaszeg, and from the hesitant mere pinning attack against the left wing at Gödöllő. Thus what mattered to the *Feldmarschall* above all was to thwart this aim of the enemy's, which seemed all the more feasible as from Pesth the army would still always be in a position to use shorter interior lines to move through Gran to oppose any operation the enemy might direct at the relief of Komorn later. Assuming that the direct route from Waitzen to Komorn, namely that in the defile along the Danube through Verőcze and Szobb [Szob, Hungary] was denied to the enemy, which could be achieved with a modest force because of the local terrain, the enemy would therefore be reduced to taking the detour through Rétság and Ipoly-Ságh.

Accordingly, since in any case the army was not strong enough to cover both Pesth and Waitzen, the *Feldmarschall* decided to concentrate the army in front of Pesth, but to leave a flanking detachment in Waitzen with instructions to retreat along the Danube behind the Gran and burn all the bridges behind it if superior enemy forces approached. This should be sufficient to deny the enemy the room to advance directly and in force through the road defile formed by the Danube and the steep mountain slopes.

The dispositions for the march back to Pesth were issued during the night of 6/7 April. To execute the march with both corps in a single column would have been extremely time-consuming and dangerous but identifying a route for a second column through this wooded, hilly, exceptionally broken terrain was not that easy. It came as if in answer to a prayer, then, that *Rittmeister Graf* Török,[62] who was completely familiar with the area, knew a road running parallel with the highway; so he was given the task of leading I. Armeekorps along that road, while the highway was allocated to III. Armeekorps. The latter corps was to leave a strong rear guard forward of Gödöllő to cover the retreat. At the same time the order was sent to *Feldmarschall Lieutenant Baron* Csorich to set off with his division from Waitzen without delay so as to join up with the army via Dunakeszy and Kerepes, while *Feldmarschall Lieutenant* Ramberg was ordered to march to Waitzen. Finally, the request was sent to *Feldmarschall Lieutenant Graf* Wrbna back in Ofen to arrange for feeding the troops that were on their way there, with the words:

> The men and the horses are very severely drained because it has been impossible to get the necessary rations to the unanticipated places where they were needed during their

62 Remember this is the Hungarian officer who defected back to the imperial side in January 1849.

> many marches and manoeuvres. I therefore urge Your Honour at least to ensure that all necessary supplies of bread, forage, wine and beef cattle be held ready to be issued to them quickly.

The night of 6/7 April passed quietly, though the enemy had pushed his outposts forward to Isaszeg when he noticed I. Armeekorps's departure.

On the 7th the retreat began in accordance with the dispositions issued, in good order and without being disturbed by the enemy in the slightest. The army was completely through the defile in the woods behind Gödöllő and had already reached the open high ground between Kerepes and Czinkota when the enemy advance guard appeared at the edge of the wood by Kerepes but retreated again after a few cannon shots.

For a moment the *Feldmarschall* considered taking position on the defensible heights this side of Czinkota. However, the enemy was not following in force along the highway, the position in question lacked any points of support for the wings, and the enemy main body could be advancing from Isaszeg directly through Keresztur toward Pesth and could thereby outflank the right wing of the position at Czinkota, where there were actually no enemy columns visible. The retreat therefore continued to behind the Rakos, where the army arrived toward 2:00 p.m. and adopted the following positions: I. Armeekorps astride the Üllö road, occupying the Steinbrucher vineyards [now Óhegy, District X, Budapest, Hungary]; III. Armeekorps astride the Kerepes road; and finally, II. Armeekorps (Division Csorich), which had joined up with the army at Czinkota, in reserve forward of the Pesth-Steinbrucher line.

Brigade Mihic that had been detached on the Szolnok road had likewise rejoined the army, as had the troops under *Oberst Baron* Horvath, so that apart from Division Ramberg that had stayed deployed in Waitzen, all the combat forces were concentrated in front of Pesth.

By the above deployment, in which the troops found a secure campsite behind the marshy Rakos that could only be crossed in a few places, Pesth was completely protected. It also made it possible to take care of rations and of the army's other needs, both immediate and long term. Finally, in the event that the enemy should turn upstream toward Komorn, it allowed the possibility of moving through Gran to protect the siege corps.

Feldmarschall Lieutenant Graf Wrbna had made the necessary preparations for issuing rations, so that the exhausted troops, of whom many had not eaten properly or at all for 48 hours, were given what they needed soon after they arrived in camp. Ammunition replenishment was likewise attended to without delay.

The *Feldmarschall* had transferred his headquarters to Pesth in a small inn on the Kerepes road so as to be closer to the troops, and to be able to make the necessary dispositions without losing any time in the event of an enemy attack.

Hungarian Forces and Movements Leading Up to the Battle of Isaszeg, 25 March to 6 April 1849

Before we follow the course of events here any further, we should mention what has become known since the end of the war about the enemy's combat forces and movements, as well as what had happened meanwhile with the other army formations, particularly in front of Komorn.

Toward the end of March the Hungarian combat forces were organised in eight army corps comprising:

69 *honvéd* battalions
One grenadier battalion
20 fusilier battalions[63]
Eight *szekler* battalions[64]
Four *jäger* battalions
Three pioneer battalions
One German Legion
One Italian Legion
Two Polish Legion battalions
15 hussar regiments, of which five (Hunyady, Lehel, Matyas, Bocskay, Frangipani) were newly-raised
Four squadrons of Polish lancers
46 batteries, each of eight guns

Thus altogether 107 battalions, 124 squadrons, 368 artillery, whose strength came to at least 123,000 infantry and 11,000-12,000 hussars.

These combat forces were easily increased by half again by the militia that was partly already organised, partly newly levied by Kossuth. While this poorly armed rabble with its bare minimum of training or indeed none at all was not fit to provide any serious support to field operations, it served to provide garrisons, watch the line of the Theiss, guard convoys and the like, which left all the regular troops fully available.[65]

Of the eight army corps, I., II., III. and VII. (Klapka, Aulich, Damjanich and Görgei) were on the Theiss; IV. (Perczel) in the Banat; V. (Vecsey) on the Maros; VI. (Bem) in Transylvania; and part of VIII. (Guyon) in Komorn.

We have seen that after the abortive attempt of 19 March to advance toward Pesth via Czibakháza, the decision was taken in the enemy camp to go on the offensive through Poroszló with concentrated force.

On 25 and 26 March – thus right at the time when *Feldmarschall Lieutenant Graf* Schlick's corps was marching from Jasz-Berény to Alberti, and reports were coming in about enemy combat forces massing opposite Szolnok, and the renewed request had been made to let the *Banus* move to Szegedin – the enemy's I., II., III. and VII. corps had joined up on the right bank of the Theiss at Poroszló. The strength of these four corps came to 50,148 infantry, 8,134 cavalry and 188 artillery pieces. Of these, 16,644 infantry, 2,436 cavalry and 68 artillery belonged to

63 These were the former imperial regular infantry battalions that recognised the Hungarian government's authority in December 1848.

64 The core of these was four former imperial *Szekler Grenzer* battalions that recognised the Hungarian government's authority in December 1848, *szeklers* being ethnic Hungarians in Transylvania.

65 Militia of this kind, armed mostly with scythes or pikes, had formed a large proportion of the Hungarian army that pursued Jellacic into Austria in October 1848. Their infectious rout contributed to the Hungarian defeat at the battle of Schwechat. It is not until toward the end of the war, when the Hungarians are facing both the Austrian and Russian armies and desperate for manpower, that large contingents of such troops are seen on the battlefield again. At the battle of Szőreg, Dembinski manages to avoid getting them involved in combat, but at the final battle of Temesvár it is again a corps of untrained scythe-armed troops that sparks the Hungarian rout.

VII. Korps (Görgei), and the remaining 33,504 infantry, 5,698 cavalry and 120 artillery to the other three corps.

Meanwhile, Vetter had fallen seriously ill, so command of the Theiss-Armee was subsequently transferred to Görgei, while Klapka took the lead in planning operations.

On 30 March, the enemy corps positions were:

I. Armeekorps in Dormánd
II. Armeekorps in Bod
III. Armeekorps in Kápolna
VII. Armeekorps already in Halmaj, 10 km from Gyöngyös.

On 31 March they were:

I. Armeekorps in Kápolna
II. Armeekorps stayed in Bod
III. Armeekorps in Halmaj
VII. Armeekorps in Gyöngyös, with its advance guard in Hort.

It was on this day that the *Feldmarschall* sent the order to *Feldmarschall Lieutenant Graf* Schlick to advance along the Gyöngyös road to undertake a major reconnaissance. All that had been learned of the enemy's movements was a report that Görgei was at Kerecsend and Maklar on the 24th.

On 1 April:

I. Armeekorps was in Deth [presumably Detk]
II. Armeekorps in Halmaj
III. Armeekorps in Gyöngyös
VII. Armeekorps in Gyöngyös and Hort, with its advance guard at Hatvan.
On 2 April:

I. Armeekorps was in Árok-Szállás
II. Armeekorps in Vámos-Györk
III. Armeekorps in Árok-Szállás and Csany
VII. Armeekorps in Gyöngyös, Hort and Hatvan.

As we know, on 1 April, *Feldmarschall Lieutenant Graf* Schlick had driven the enemy advance guard out of Hatvan. On that evening Klapka sent the following letter from Árok-Szállás to Görgei:

> If the enemy should advance further along the Gyöngyös road tomorrow (the 2nd), my view is that our army's position by then will be a good one in which to meet him. If his advance today was merely a reconnaissance, we have no time to lose; in that case it is my view that we should not take a rest day (since it is already fairly certain that he is concentrated behind the Galga, albeit on a fairly broad front) but instead should make a forced march, and if necessary a night march, to fall on him on the 4th. Tomorrow

> I will endeavour to get the necessary scouting reports about Árok-Szállás and Jasz-Berény and share these with you, which will then help us to decide what to do. I am with the main body eagerly awaiting you. Your presence is vital. I want to be in Jasz-Berény as soon as possible. If the enemy is indeed ensconced there, we have one more job to get out of the way – the bridge at Szolnok must be repaired at all costs, so I ask you to order a suitable officer to go there tomorrow to do this. I am sure that you will fully agree with my views, and that you will not blame me for expressing them.

On 2 April *Feldmarschall Lieutenant Graf* Schlick continued his march through Hatvan toward Gyöngyös, where he had the fight described above with the enemy's VII. Armeekorps and also some units of II. Armeekorps, after which he began his retreat back to Gödöllő. If instead of putting up strong resistance against Schlick, the enemy had feigned a retreat to lure him into advancing further toward Gyöngyös, his corps could have got into an extremely worrying situation, since the enemy's I. and III. Korps would have been on his flank.[66] Marching these two enemy corps to Árok-Szállás accomplished the first preparatory move for the planned sweeping strategic outflanking of the right wing of the *Feldmarschall*'s army.

The Hungarian camp's view of Schlick's advance, and of how much the enemy expected to be attacked anew on the following day (the 3rd), is shown clearly by Klapka's letter of the 2nd to Görgei:

> From the enemy's manoeuvre today it may be concluded that he might attack tomorrow in greater strength. If I. and III. Armeekorps make their flank marches to Jasz-Berény simultaneously with II. Reservekorps's, it could easily happen that the enemy could oblige VII. Armeekorps to fall back by throwing his whole force against it. To be on the safe side, the undersigned (I. Korps) and General Damjanich (III. Korps) have decided to remain in their present positions until midday tomorrow, all the more so as Brigades Leiningen and Wyszocki are absent, having been detached to the vicinity of Hatvan.
>
> If the enemy has not attacked by midday, all units will march from here toward Jasz-Berény so that 30,000 men will have crossed the Zagyva by the morning of the 4th.
>
> To mask our manoeuvre, I would ask that VII. Armeekorps (Gaspar)[67] be ordered to demonstrate beyond Hatvan, and the *Herr General* to be so gracious as to order Brigades Leiningen and Wyszocky to Csany, where they will then receive the necessary instructions from III. Armeekorps (Damjanich) concerning the flank march they are to perform. I hereby submit my provisional orders to the army high command. In the event that no further orders should arrive from headquarters in Gyöngyös by 3:00 a.m. tomorrow, the corps should hold firm. However, they are to be in readiness to be able to march at the first signal. I await approval of the arrangements I have made for now,

66 This is debatable. The strong Hungarian resistance surely contributed to the *Feldmarschall* thinking the main enemy army was still in front of him, whereas a feigned retreat could well have made him suspect he was being outflanked by the main body.

67 Footnote in the original: '*When Görgei was named army commander, Gaspar was designated commander of VII. Armeekorps, while *Major* Kossuth took over his division.'

> or else orders to the contrary. If the enemy attacks the Hatvan position tomorrow in full force, III. Armeekorps (Damjanich) will advance to take the enemy in flank, but I. Armeekorps (Klapka) will stay halted in front of Árok-Szállás and await further orders.

We follow this letter with a second from Árok-Szállás at 11:30 a.m. the same day, in which Klapka's intentions and proposals are developed in still more detail:

> At the present time Jasz-Berény is not held by the enemy, and according to reports coming in, Fenszaru is also clear of enemy. This is favourable for us but must be exploited straight away. In any case I shall send a brigade to Jasz-Berény this afternoon to facilitate our crossing of the Zagyva. It will be of the utmost importance to set off from here this evening so as to be able to cross the Zagyva with all our force by tomorrow morning. It is true that our pioneers are not very good, and that in the enemy's view it is therefore unfeasible for us to cross the Zagyva, but we have moonlight and this will favour our march.
>
> My idea is the following: if I set off from here at 5:00 p.m. with my whole corps, I am in a position to get to Jasz-Berény by 5:00 a.m. tomorrow morning without wearing out my men, since they would have to camp here anyway. By 5:00 p.m. they will have eaten and be fit to march again, for today they have not even covered 15 km. Jasz-Berény is also only 15 km from here. *General* Damjanich should be ordered to set off at such a time as to reach the bridge at Jasz-Berény at 5:00 a.m. tomorrow; thus he should not march until after midnight. In this way 23,000 men will have made the crossing by 11:00 a.m. tomorrow. If *General* Aulich (II. Korps) gets to the bridge at 8:00 a.m., he can cross the Zagyva unimpeded. Now it would be pointless to detach him to Jákóhalma [Jászjákóhalma, Hungary]. Since the enemy has left his right flank exposed and allowed us to reach Jasz-Berény unhindered, Aulich can follow right behind in reserve. As soon as we have all successfully crossed the Zagyva, part of VII. Armeekorps should turn toward Fenszaru, and this would complete the flanking manoeuvre.
>
> If you approve my proposal and give me permission to begin my march, please be so good as to give the orders to *Generals* Damjanich and Aulich as well, but it would be best if you were to transfer your headquarters to here at Árok-Szállás today. I beg you, dear Görgei, to exploit the opportunity the enemy is offering us; but actually I should not be begging you, since I am sure that you yourself will know to seize this moment; it is only my own impatience that causes me to share my views with you.

Görgei replied from Gyöngyös at 9:30 p.m. on the 2nd in the following way:

> Based on your messages today, your proposal is approved and its implementation ordered; all the more so as according to statements from all our spies sent to Balassa-Gyarmath, the enemy brigades that were detached there have already left to rejoin the main body of the army.
>
> *Herr General* Damjanich's corps and *Herr Oberstlieutenant* Mariassy's reserve division have accordingly already received the order to move out immediately for

> Jasz-Berény. The orders could not be issued sooner because of the delayed arrival of your letter written at 11:30 a.m., which only reached army headquarters at 8:30 p.m.

On 3 April VII. Armeekorps remained at Hatvan, I. and III. moved to Nagy-Káta and Jasz-Berény, and II. marched to Jákóhalma. *Oberstlieutenant* Asboth, deployed in Török-St.-Miklos was ordered to cross the Theiss immediately with his regular troops, to destroy the Szolnok railway and to inflict as much damage as possible on the Austrian army.[68]

As we know, on this day (the 3rd) the *Feldmarschall* had arrived in Gödöllő, and – although he knew nothing of all these enemy manoeuvres – had had Division Csorich move to Gödöllő to reinforce *Feldmarschall Lieutenant Graf* Schlick's corps, while the *Banus*'s corps, whose departure from Czegléd had been delayed, was instructed to force march toward Koka and Dany.

On 4 April the enemy VII. Korps demonstrated from Hatvan toward Bágh. Meanwhile the enemy I., II. and III. Korps continued their turning manoeuvre: I. Korps moved through Nagy-Káta to Tapio-Bicske, III. Korps to Nagy-Káta, and II. Korps to Farmas in reserve.

On this day the *Feldmarschall* had advanced from Gödöllő to Bágh and Aszod with III. Armeekorps and elements of II. Armeekorps (Division Csorich and Kavallerie-Brigade Kisslinger), pushed on from there toward Hatvan, and driven the advancing enemy detachments back into the Hatvan position. I. Armeekorps was instructed to maintain good observation of the roads leading from Árok-Szállás and Jasz-Berény toward Pesth, as well as the crossing of the Zagyva at Fenszaru, and finally to send out patrols to discover any approaching enemy in good time.

On the evening of the 4th the *Feldmarschall* had requested that the *Banus* participate in the planned attack on Hatvan on the 5th by advancing through Fenszaru. But then, as we have seen, word came just in time that Brigades Rastic and Sternberg bringing up the rear of I. Armeekorps had been through a 'tough fight' at Tapio-Bicske, and that the *Banus* was 'under serious threat from enemy to my south'. This was the first time that the *Feldmarschall* had any indication of the presence of enemy combat forces in that area, thanks to Brigade Rastic's quite accidental clash with the enemy. The action that took place here therefore acquires special significance, and consequently deserves more detailed description for that reason as well as for the bravery the troops displayed on this occasion.

Brigade Rastic (1. and 2. Bataillon Ottochaner, 3. Bataillon Oguliner-Szluiner, 3. Bataillon 1. Banal-Regiment, sechspfündige Batterie Nr. 1) and Brigade Sternberg (six squadrons of Kaiser Franz Josef Kürassiere, two squadrons of König von Sachsen Kürassiere, six squadrons of Banderial-Husaren, Kavallerie-Batterie Nr. 5) reached Tapio-Bicske toward 10:00 a.m. on the 4th after carrying out their extremely arduous march from Abany with hardly a pause. Arriving on the hills this side of the village, they could still see I. Armeekorps's baggage train that had left Tapio-Bicske barely an hour earlier.

Since the troops had marched all night, *Generalmajor* Rastic decided to let them rest for an hour outside the village, but then to continue the march again. The cavalry under *Oberst Graf* Sternberg had scouted the area to the right barely as far as the main Tapio stream [the Felső-Tápió] and since they found no cause for concern, they continued their march until they came to

68 This diversion by Asboth was evidently effective in deceiving the Austrians.

an open area suitable for foddering their horses, where they likewise halted. Only the Banderial hussars stayed back with Brigade Rastic.

After an hour and a quarter's rest the latter brigade prepared to continue its march. But scarcely had the troops formed up to do so than the enemy approached quite unexpectedly in strong detachments accompanied by artillery. This was the enemy I. Armeekorps under Klapka coming through Nagy-Káta. It proceeded to attack Brigade Rastic on three sides, partly from the rear.

Generalmajor Rastic quickly sent the Banderial hussars to confront the enemy cavalry. But they were defeated and the brave and widely respected *Major Baron* Riedesel and *Rittmeister* Gyurkowic died nobly.[69]

Meanwhile the enemy had posted his batteries on the heights and these opened up an intense fire. It was necessary at least for the one battery present to oppose him as well as it could, to which end this was sent with the Oguliner-Szluiner battalion to a hill about 1,000 paces to the left of Tapio-Bicske.

During this, strong enemy columns had approached very close and threatened to cut off the detached battalion. This was a critical moment. *Generalmajor* Rastic now ordered both the Ottochaner battalions to perform a bayonet charge. This was carried out so impetuously that the much more numerous enemy was broken and put to flight. A cavalry detachment that tried to stop the pursuit was attacked with the bayonet by a swarm of skirmishers and driven back. Certainly a rare example in the history of war![70] The enemy tried to rally again sheltering under the fire of his battery, but there too the brave Ottochaners charged him with the bayonet, flung him down off the hills to beyond the Tapio marsh, captured ten guns and four ammunition caissons and took two officers and 123 men prisoner, not counting those wounded who had had to be left behind in the village of Tapio-Bicske.

This success re-established communications with the units detached to the left, which had likewise gained ground. Now Kavallerie-Brigade Sternberg also arrived on the battlefield. The ground was very unfavourable for the cavalry, partly ankle-deep soft sand, partly marsh. Yet their appearance had an advantageous effect, all the more since the horse artillery battery, protected by a division of Hardegg cuirassiers, was able to cross the Tapio and to open up a very effective fire against the enemy.

It must have been about 1:30 p.m. when the enemy III. Armeekorps under Damjanich arrived at Tapio-Bicske and linked up with the enemy I. Korps.

Generalmajor Rastic's thoughts now had to turn to retreat, which he began in good order after his brave troops had bloodily repulsed one more attempted attack on Tapio-Bicske by the 3. and 19. Honved-Bataillons, 3. Bataillon Infanterie-Regiment Nr. 39 and the Polish Legion.[71] The

69 This cavalry action was preceded by a duel between the two opposing cavalry commanders, *Major Baron* Riedesel and *Major* Alajos Sebő, in which Sebő was victorious.

70 Rare indeed for cavalry to be driven off by charging skirmishers in this period, though it is not clear how large a 'detachment' this was.

71 Whilst not disguising the rout of Brigades Dipold and Bobics, Hungarian historiography shows the subsequent Hungarian attack in a more positive light. In particular, there is a famous episode where 3. and 9. (not 19.) Honved-Bataillons vied to be first to assault across the bridge over the Tapio, which was resolved by the commander of the 3rd seizing the flag of the 9th and leading them both in a successful charge. The old wooden bridge is still there, with a monument nearby. Bánlaky, *A magyar nemzet*.

enemy only followed very cautiously, contenting himself mainly with bringing his numerous batteries into action. The action was broken off completely toward 5:00 p.m., and by 8:00 p.m. the two brigades had rejoined the *Banus*'s corps that had halted in Szecsö.

Taking into account that Brigade Rastic had no more than 743 files,[72] that it had to deal with one enemy corps initially and then two by the end, that the troops had been marching for a full 24 hours with little rest and without a cooked meal, yet took ten guns from the enemy who did not manage to achieve any successes of his own to boast about, it must be acknowledged that this was one of the most glorious and notable of actions. However, for lack of horse teams only four of the captured guns could be dragged away across the deep sandy soil, mostly pulled by prisoners. The other six had to be spiked and left behind.

Görgei's dispositions for 5 April were the following:

> VII. Armeekorps shall stay in Hatvan and draw in Division Kméty to it, occupy Fenszaru with one battalion, and keep an outpost in Ecséd.
>
> I. Armeekorps shall move from Tapio-Bicske to Suly at 6:00 a.m.
>
> After I. Korps has left, III. Armeekorps shall move from Tapio-Bicske to Szecsö.
>
> II. (Reserve) Korps shall set off for Toth-Almás at 6:00 a.m. sharp.
>
> The Haupt-Munitionsreserve shall move to Jasz-Berény.
>
> If the battle should turn out unfavourably, VII. Korps shall retreat to Gyöngyös, I., II. and III. Korps to Jasz-Berény.

The *Feldmarschall* knew nothing of these manoeuvres. On the 5th the *Banus* had reported: '[I]n order to comply with the request issued to me to participate in the (possible) attack on Hatvan, I will move immediately to Fenszaru, but then I can no longer exert any influence on the protection of Pesth. *Generalmajor* Rastic asserts that the enemy in Nagy-Káta yesterday morning was 10,000 strong.' This last statement sufficed to convince the *Feldmarschall* that advancing to Hatvan would be risky, and especially for the *Banus* if he advanced toward Fenszaru. He therefore immediately sent an order to the latter to call off his march to Fenszaru and to adopt a position further to the rear in which he could cover Pesth against any enemy advance from Jasz-Berény.

How appropriate this instruction was only becomes completely clear now that we know that three enemy corps were manoeuvring against the *Banus*'s flank and rear, specifically toward Suly, Szecsö and Tot-Almás [Tóalmás, Hungary]. The *Feldmarschall*'s decision to march back to Gödöllő must be regarded as equally well judged. If he had known of the enemy's manoeuvres against his right flank and their actual strength, then he certainly would not have detached Division Csorich to Waitzen, which as we have seen was caused simply and solely by his concern about being outflanked on his left. But given the uncertainty about the enemy's intentions, the fact that the *Feldmarschall* regarded an outflanking on his left as more likely could well seem justified in the situation described, since strategically this operation had much in its favour – it could lead the enemy to the relief of Komorn and thereby indirectly to the occupation of Pesth.

72 The original refers to 'files' ('*Rotten*'). Assuming a *Rotte* is four men, that means Brigade Rastic had 2,972 men.

Görgei, who wrongly thought the *Feldmarschall* was still on the Galga at Aszod and Bágh, gave the following instructions for 6 April:

> VII. Korps shall advance toward Aszod on the Galga and attack Bágh. This must be taken at all costs, preferably from the Tura side [i.e., the southeast, on the west bank of the Galga]. The other corps shall continue their offensive thus:
>
> I. Korps shall move to Suly [Tápiósüly, now part of Sülysáp, Hungary] and along the mountain ridge to Isaszeg, while detaching its left wing brigade to Peczel [Pécel, Hungary]. III. Korps shall move through Koka, the St. Kiralyer-Wald and the manor farm, with the most rigorous precautions, to Isaszeg, and shall have detachments occupy the St. Kiraly and St. Lásló farms.[73] II. Armeekorps shall move from Tot-Almás to Dany and put a strong detachment in Zsámbók.
>
> I., II. and III. Korps are to set off at 5:00 a.m. sharp.
>
> The corps shall maintain as close communications as possible for mutual information and support. The army headquarters shall move from Suly to Tot-Almás.
>
> Boldly ever onward.

The *Banus*'s corps marched back to Dany on the 5th, left there at 6:00 a.m. on the 6th, and reached Isaszeg at 11:00 a.m. where it made camp. The report about this that arrived in Gödöllő at 1:00 p.m. on the 6th included the note that 'during the march four enemy columns have been continuously visible to the south, whose strength however could not be estimated because of their great distance away'. Half an hour later the first cannon shots sounded the prelude to the battle of Isaszeg, which we have already described, but we will now add what has become known since about the enemy's manoeuvres.

On the 6th the enemy's VII. Armeekorps under Gaspar's command had begun advancing from Hatvan very cautiously to attack the *Feldmarschall* in the position at Bágh that he had already left early that morning. Gaspar had left Brigade Weissel in Hatvan to guard his rear and advanced against Bágh with three divisions. Division Kméty formed the vanguard, followed by Division Pöltenberg and then by Division Kossuth. Brigade Zambely covered the right flank. On arriving at the point where the road to Héviz turns off, Division Kméty went that way, while Division Kossuth moved to Tura summoning the detachment from Fenszaru to join it.

Thus, only Division Pöltenberg marched along the highway. On its way to Bagh it ran into the weak imperial rear guard comprised only of cavalry. After this had fallen back and the position at Bágh was found to be abandoned, the corps concentrated again at Bágh, with the exception of Division Kméty which was pushed forward to the exit from the Gödöllő defile.

III. Armeekorps (Damjanich) had meanwhile advanced through Koka – with Division Knezich bypassing the village – toward Isaszeg, and run into the *Banus*'s rear guard formed by Brigade Rastic, while I. Armeekorps (Klapka) advanced through Suly and II. (Aulich) through Dany. These three corps must have numbered 30,000-35,000 men with more than 100 artillery. Arriving in the area of Isaszeg, they gradually brought eight to ten batteries into action. Klapka

73 The St. Kiraly farm is now the village of Szentkirály, 4 km southeast of Isaszeg. I cannot identify a St. Lásló farm; the only other candidate farm in the area is the one shown on Bánlaky's map as 'Sz. Gy[örgy] major'. It may be that this is the place Görgei meant but he used a wrong or alternative name for it. Bánlaky, *A magyar nemzet*.

pressed into the right flank of the *Banus*'s camp and Damjanich against the front, while Aulich stayed back at Dany, since he did not think his right flank toward Tura was yet sufficiently secure.

The 28. and 44. Honved-Bataillons at the head of Klapka's corps were initially thrown back with serious losses by a division of König von Sachsen and a wing of Hardegg cuirassiers. But soon after that Brigade Schulz penetrated further and further into the right flank, covered by the woods, and since Damjanich was also advancing frontally at the same time in greatly superior numbers, the *Banus* retreated onto the heights behind the Rakos, sustaining the action with artillery.

This was the moment when Brigade Fiedler from *Feldmarschall Lieutenant Graf* Schlick's corps burst out of the Kiralyer-Wald into Damjanich's right flank and, together with Kavallerie-Brigade Montenuovo, forced him to retreat. Damjanich – thinking the *Feldmarschall* was still in the position at Bágh where he had been the day before – must have paid too little attention to the wood on his right flank. Now Aulich's corps was brought up from Dany but had no better success in gaining control of the Kiralyer-Wald. Likewise, on the extreme left wing Klapka had attempted a sustained attack with 28., 44. and 47. Honved-Bataillons, which produced no result.

Gaspar's VII. Korps had meanwhile limited itself to inconsequential demonstrations against Gödöllő.

We observe that the enemy was not able to make full use of his very substantial numerical superiority (he had at least 50,000 men and 188 artillery, while the *Feldmarschall* had barely 23,000 men and 173 artillery with which to oppose him). Strictly speaking, only Klapka's and Damjanich's corps took part in the battle of Isaszeg. Aulich arrived too late and Gaspar did nothing at all, which can be ascribed to the *Feldmarschall*'s withdrawal from Bágh to Gödöllő not being foreseen in the enemy's dispositions for the attack.[74]

As soon as he learned of the *Banus*'s departure from Isaszeg to Gödöllő on the evening of the 6th, Görgei ordered a concentric attack on the latter place next day (7 April), hoping to find the *Feldmarschall* still there and to drive him away from Pesth. His dispositions were:

> VII. Armeekorps shall move from Aszod and Bágh upon Gödöllő.
> I. and III. Korps shall move from Isaszeg to Gödöllő and Kerepes.
> II. Korps shall move along the St.-Kiralyer-Wald to Gödöllő.
> The left wing brigade of I. Korps shall move from Peczel to Kerepes.

74 Nobili does not give us a proper summary of the battle of Isaszeg anywhere. It deserves one. By their audacious manoeuvres, the Hungarians achieved a high degree of strategic deception and operational surprise. Windisch-Grätz was completely in the dark as to Hungarian intentions up until the last moment, as witness his repeated forays up the central road toward Hatvan. Even after the *Banus* is attacked at Tapio-Bicske the *Feldmarschall* is still proposing to attack in a direction that would expose his own flank. Just in time, his innate caution saves him and he falls back to Gödöllő. In the battle itself, he does well in shifting troops south, away from Gaspar's inadequate pinning effort, and stymies the first Hungarian attack on Isaszeg. However, the arrival of Aulich's corps (on Aulich's own initiative) and Görgei on the field revives the Hungarians who force their way across the Rakos and drive the *Banus* away, turning the Austrian right flank, which the *Feldmarschall* does not realise until later. He is fortunate that the Hungarians are too exhausted to exploit this and cut his exposed line of retreat to Pesth at Kerepes. He therefore manages to escape a renewed concentric Hungarian attack the next day. Nevertheless, while losses in men were roughly equal or slightly in favour of the imperials, it was a Hungarian victory in that Windisch-Grätz's army was forced to fall back on Pesth, thus opening the way for another bold Hungarian flank march to relieve Komorn.

The detachments of VII. and II. Korps shall move from Zsambók to Dany, and from Fenszaru to Zsambók.
The army headquarters shall move from Tót-Almas to Dany.

The time for the march to begin is 5:00 a.m. sharp. The attack is to be carried out by all the corps simultaneously. For this VII. Korps will form the right wing, III. the centre, I. the left wing and II. Korps the reserve. They will deploy in three lines with the cavalry in the third line, except for those detachments tasked with covering the flanks of the first and second lines. *Oberst* Nagy-Sandor will be in overall command of all the cavalry.

If the battle should turn out unfavourably, VII. Korps will retreat to Aszod, III. Korps to Szecsö, I. Korps to Suly, II. Korps to Tót-Almás, and the headquarters to Nagy-Káta.

Such were Görgei's dispositions for the battle he hoped to have with the *Feldmarschall* in the Gödöllő defiles. However, although the hour for the start of the march was set so early, the advance must have proceeded very slowly and cautiously since the enemy did not reach Gödöllő until toward 11:00 a.m., by which time the *Feldmarschall* was already far beyond Kerepes, and also Division Csorich had been brought up from Waitzen and had arrived in the vicinity.

The four enemy corps set up camp at Gödöllő and limited themselves to pushing forward an advance guard to Kerepes and a brigade of VII. Armeekorps to observe the road from Waitzen.

The Siege of Komorn Progresses, Reinforcements Arrive and Events on the Southern Front, 29 March to 10 April 1849

Let us now provide a synopsis of the events that had transpired since the end of March in other parts of the extensive theatre of operations. In front of Komorn the siege works and the bombardment had pressed ahead most industriously. On 29 March *Feldmarschall Lieutenant* Simunich was ordered by *Feldzeugmeister Baron* Welden to undertake a major assault on Komorn on the 31st. The *Feldzeugmeister* himself had arrived in Acs from Wien with an escort of 100 *seressaners* and 200 Ottochaners.[75] Consideration of the difficulty of this operation once he had a fuller understanding of the situation caused the *Feldzeugmeister* to call it off. A feint attack was ordered for the 31st instead, to be carried out by Brigade Veigel against the Waag bridgehead [on the east bank of the Waag where it flows into the Danube], and by Brigade Sossay against the Palatinal Line and the Apati-Insel [a large island in the Waag just north of Komorn, now the Apálsky Ostrov Nature Reserve]. The intention was to ascertain whether the Komorn garrison had a sufficient number of artillerymen available to man all its guns at the same time along its very extensive defensive works. The conclusion was that the guns were indeed manned everywhere, and very well served. Brigade Veigel lost eight men dead, 23 wounded and seven horses killed; Brigade Sossay suffered the loss of one man dead, three wounded and three horses killed. On 1 April the *Feldzeugmeister* returned to Wien again.

75 *Seressaners* were Croatian paramilitary gendarmerie. Every *grenzer* battalion had a detachment of *seressaners*.

Feldmarschall Lieutenant Simunich concentrated his attack mainly on the Danube bridgehead, against which 36 artillery pieces of the largest calibre had been brought into action since 4 April, while the bombardment of the city continued unabated.

On the 4th it was learned from deserters that the inhabitants of Komorn were urging surrender and keeping white flags ready, that there was a serious shortage of meat, etc.; but on the other hand two enemy artillerymen in peasant clothes had managed to sneak through the marshes between the Waag and the Neutra into the fortress and spread the news that Görgei was approaching with a substantial relief force.

Toward mid-April the work of destroying the Danube bridgehead had progressed so far that it was hoped this could imminently be taken by storm. Likewise, the bombardment of the fortress was so effective that the enemy *Artillerie-Direktor* Mack gave up hope of holding out any longer. The prospect of relief was also beginning to fade away, since the news mentioned above that Görgei was near had still not been confirmed, so was taken to be an empty rumor. All these factors justified the expectation that Komorn would soon fall.

The forces at *Feldmarschall Lieutenant* Simunich's disposal toward the end of March were organised into three brigades: Lederer, Sossay and Veigel. They comprised 13 and four sixths battalions, eight squadrons and 42 field guns, from which, however, four sixths of a battalion had been detached. Since the assignments of battalions and squadrons to the brigades were subject to frequent changes, we limit ourselves here to listing the units:

	Battalions
3. Bataillon Welden (Hochenegg)	1
3. Bataillon Hess	1
1. Landwehr-Bataillon Hess	2/6
1. Landwehr-Bataillon Khevenhüller	1
2. Landwehr-Bataillon Khevenhüller	1
1. Landwehr-Bataillon Grossfürst Konstantin	1
1. Landwehr-Bataillon Kaiser	1
1. Landwehr-Bataillon E.H. Wilhelm	1
2. Bataillon Ceccopieri	1
1. Bataillon Hartmann	1
3. Bataillon Haynau	1
4. Bataillon Szluiner	1
12. Jäger-Bataillon	2/6
1. Landwehr-Bataillon Nugent	1
3. Bataillon E.H. Ludwig	1
Six squadrons Ficquelmont-Dragoner	
Two squadrons E.H. Karl-Chevauxlegers	

With a total strength of 11,256 infantry, 1,121 cavalry and 1,756 engineers and artillerymen.[76]

Incidentally, the fact that the work of the besieging force was well managed emerges from the following letter written by Kossuth to Görgei from Erlau on 1 April 1849:

> I am greatly concerned to have learned that neither Guyon nor any other of the officers sent to Komorn with money four or five weeks ago has been able to get in there. For my part I call this major ineptitude; for even if Komorn is so tightly besieged that even one lone man cannot sneak in, it is inconceivable that the garrison could never make a sortie and break through the cordon at some point. The job of the officers sent there would therefore be this: to stay in a nearby village observing the situation, and then promptly use the moment of a sortie to quickly get the money into the fortress per their orders.
>
> But these gentlemen do not do this, they just try the road; when that doesn't work, then instead of going as close as possible to wait for a favourable opportunity, one of them goes to Erlau, another to Szabadka, and the third God knows where, and they wait for roast pigeons to fly into their gobs. So Komorn starves. I would be less concerned if the present fortress commander had any initiative since he could levy a compulsory loan from the city for a couple of months. But he is clueless.[77]

Feldzeugmeister Baron Welden's activity was not limited to urging an assault on Komorn. At the beginning of April he had seen to it besides that considerable reinforcements were sent to the army in Hungary. In a memo he submitted to on high at the end of March, he also expounded his views on the conduct of future military operations in Hungary.[78] As the first step toward reinforcing the army in Hungary, Welden had sent *Oberstlieutenant Graf* Crenneville to Neuhäusel with a mobile column. Soon after this the following three brigades were mobilised, for which units were brought from Bohemia, Moravia, Austria and Styria:

Brigade *Generalmajor* Herzinger
3. Bataillon Paumgarten
1. Landwehr-Bataillon Khevenhüller
4. Bataillon Oguliner
Two squadrons of Wrbna-Chevauxlegers
Sechspfündige Batterie Nr. 18

76 Of Simunich's 13 and four sixths battalions (82 companies), only 14 companies – a sixth – are fully trained 1st or 2nd battalions, the great majority being either the poorer quality 3rd or 4th battalions or – in the case of almost half of his battalions – *landwehr.*

77 Interesting that the city seems to starve, not so much because there is no food to be had, but because the commander does not have money with which to pay for it. Perhaps this tells us something about the revolutionary regime's respect for bourgeois values concerning property, commerce, and law. In any case, we cannot help but enjoy Kossuth's acerbic and exasperated tone.

78 Whether intentionally or not, submitting his views in this way may have served as his application to take over the *Feldmarschall*'s job, which of course he did in April 1849.

Brigade *Oberst* Teuchert
1. Bataillon Mazzuchelli
2. Bataillon Mazzuchelli
Grenadier-Bataillon Hora
Two squadrons of Kaiser Ferdinand-Kürassiere
Sechspfündige Batterie Nr. 20

Brigade *Generalmajor* Theissing
4. Bataillon Ottochaner
1. Landwehr-Bataillon E.H. Stefan
2. Bataillon E.H. Ferdinand d'Este
Two squadrons Civallart-Uhlanen
Sechspfündige Batterie Nr. 19

Altogether: nine battalions, six squadrons and 18 guns.[79]

On 5 and 7 April the *Feldzeugmeister* sent a report to the *Feldmarschall* about this attached to the order of battle in question and wrote: 'I do not know if I am doing the right thing, but all my aims and endeavours are geared toward rustling up reinforcements for Hungary. If anything I have done should not be entirely as you would wish it, I crave Your Highness's pardon and hope that you will not misjudge the eager zeal which alone guides me in this matter.' The *Feldmarschall* replied to this on 10 April:

> I have received Your Excellency's report of the 7th and feel myself bound to express my repeated most obliged thanks to your noble self for your many efforts to support the army operating in Hungary and thus for the good of our supreme service [to His Majesty]; for being reinforced by these three brigades from Wien puts me in a position to meet all eventualities with increased strength. These reinforcements are extremely important to me, particularly if they should be pushed forward at maximum speed, as Your Excellency is accustomed to do and which is doubly necessary at the present moment; since, as your noble self knows, the army is in such a position that it is only by the utmost exertions that it can fulfil the highly important mission it has been given.
>
> It is with genuine pleasure that I see from Your Excellency's report that about 10,000 men will have been deployed between the Gran and Pressburg toward the 15th of this month; nevertheless I urge that your noble self should instruct the more rearward units to join the *Herr Feldmarschall Lieutenant* Simunich as quickly as possible, from whom they will receive further instructions.
>
> My overall intention is to combine the three brigades from Wien with Brigade Veigel and Division Ramberg into one considerable corps. I will thereby remain master of all events, able to emphatically block any attempt the enemy might make to relieve Komorn, and indeed to clear the rebels out of the upper counties in the mountains for good and arrive on the Theiss with superior numbers as soon as the

79 Of which just three are properly trained 1st or 2nd battalions.

> corps advancing from Galicia should have arrived via Eperies and Kaschau. With everything Your Excellency has arranged, you need have absolutely no worries about having misinterpreted my intentions, and in this respect I desire that you should be soothed by my sincere assurance that your noble self's well-known good judgement and the eager zeal that you are accustomed to bring to all the arrangements you make are the fullest guarantee that I will be in complete agreement every time.[80]

Command over the three brigades that were on their way, which were to be joined by Division Ramberg and Brigade Veigel from the siege corps outside Komorn as noted above, was to be given to *Feldmarschall Lieutenant* Wohlgemuth, whose arrival from Italy was expected at any moment.[81]

On the 9th Brigade Herzinger was already in Neuhäusel. But at this time Brigade Teuchert had not yet crossed the Waag; Brigade Theissing was still further back. So as to get these brigades to the Gran without losing any time, *Feldmarschall Lieutenant* Simunich was instructed that as they each arrived he should send them immediately to Keménd and Köbelkut, while directing Brigade Veigel from Kurtakeszi [Krátke Kesy, Slovakia] to Parkany and Gran; and generally to keep an eye on these units' movements, since their task was so closely connected with covering Komorn.

At the *Feldmarschall*'s request, *General der Kavallerie Baron* Hammerstein had already pushed the advance guard of the corps designated to march into Hungary across the border toward Eperies on 8 April, and had it announce that quarters were needed for 20,000 men. The corps itself was to concentrate at Dukla on 18 April, and then to begin operations without delay. *Feldmarschall Lieutenant* Vogel was named as its commander. The order of battle was:

Brigade *Generalmajor* Benedek[82]

	Battalions	Squadrons	Artillery
Palombini Infanterie	2		
Herzog von Parma	1		
E.H. Karl Ludwig Chevauxlegers		2	
6-pounder battery			6

80 This exchange between Welden and the *Feldmarschall* is a fine example of Austrian courtly manners.

81 Ludwig *Freiherr* Wohlgemuth (1788-1851) served with distinction as a brigade commander in Italy in 1848, thereby earning his appointment to command a corps in Hungary in April 1849. He fought at the battle of Pered and the second and third battles of Komorn. He was then appointed governor of Transylvania but fell terminally ill soon after. *BLKÖ*, Vol.57, pp.238-241.

82 Ludwig von Benedek (1804-1881) served with distinction as a brigade commander in Italy in 1848. In the battle of Szőreg in August 1849 he was wounded while gallantly leading his brigade in the assault. He would go on to be one of the more successful Austrian corps commanders in the Italian war of 1859, but as commander-in-chief in the Austro-Prussian War of 1866 he was beaten at Königgrätz and was made the scapegoat for Austria's defeat. *BLKÖ*, Vol.1, pp.265-267.

Brigade *Generalmajor* Barco

	Battalions	Squadrons	Artillery
Deutschmeister Infanterie	2		
Hartmann Infanterie	1		
Kaiser-Chevauxlegers		2	
6-pounder battery			6

Brigade *Generalmajor* Ludwig

	Battalions	Squadrons	Artillery
Welden Infanterie	1		
Haynau	1		
E. H. Wilhelm	1		
Bianchi	1		
Trenk Grenadiere	1		
Sunstenau-Kürassiere		2	
Kaiser-Chevauxlegers		2	
6-pounder battery			6
6-pounder horse artillery battery			6

Altogether: 11 battalions, eight squadrons and 24 guns.

This corps was originally meant to advance through Kaschau and Miskolc. However, recent events made it necessary to give it a different direction of march. On 10 April the *Feldmarschall* therefore informed *General der Kavallerie Baron* Hammerstein that in view of the recent change in the situation on the Theiss, and given the enemy's significant numerical superiority and the fact that the local inhabitants predominantly sympathised with the enemy, he (the *Feldmarschall*) had to deploy his main forces in front of Pesth so as thereby not only to cover the country's capital but also to be in readiness to defend powerfully against any enemy attempt to relieve Komorn. In these circumstances the *Feldmarschall* felt that to achieve the fastest possible concentration of his combat forces that was necessary for striking a decisive blow, it was most appropriate that the Galician corps should direct its march from Eperies or Kaschau to Rima-Szombath, while he himself would be in a position to link up with this corps most easily from Waitzen.

On 1 April *Feldzeugmeister Graf* Nugent reported that the inadequate training of the imperial Syrmian units at Zombor [Sombor, Serbia], as well as the discord escalating to open conflict between the Syrmian Provinzial-Bataillonen[83] and the Serbians, had caused him to abandon the very extensive and incomplete entrenchments at Zombor. He was also prompted to do so by the fact that the enemy in that area had been reinforced considerably, and an attack was expected at any moment which he was not in a position to withstand with his present insufficient means. He

83 I.e., Croatian troops. Syrmia is the plain between the Danube and the Sava, nowadays in Serbia and Croatia.

was going to send the troops from there to help *Oberst* Mamula with the siege of Peterwardein. On 29 March the garrison of that fortress had made a sortie which however was forcefully repelled and in which the enemy lost 150 dead and 200 wounded. On the 27th Perczel and Kasimir Batyany had arrived in Neusatz with a *honvéd* division, a division of Husaren-Regiment Nr. 3 and a horse artillery battery, where they were received with great enthusiasm. Free passage to leave the fortress had been offered to those former imperial officers in the Peterwardein garrison who no longer wished to serve in the Hungarian army. Many staff and field officers had taken advantage of this permission, including the former fortress commandant, *Feldmarschall Lieutenant* Blagoevich.

On the 4th the *Feldzeugmeister* reported that the St. Tomas [Srbobran, Serbia] entrenchments had been vacated. This place could not be adequately held either for lack of troops. The weak garrison had to retreat as the result of an attack by 6,000-7,000 insurgents under Perczel. *Feldzeugmeister Graf* Nugent had already asked repeatedly for reinforcements, even if it be only a couple of battalions, to stiffen his newly organised units. Much as the *Feldmarschall* regarded this wish as justified, the events that had occurred made it impossible for him to send even such a small detachment, so he was unable to meet this request.

The total number of troops under *Feldzeugmeister Graf* Nugent's command on 9 April was 6,987 infantry, 581 cavalry and 36 artillery. Of these, 2,165 men were fully armed and equipped, 953 were well armed but only partly equipped, while 3,869 men lacked everything and were of little use.[84] The cavalry were well mounted, but only 21 of the guns had horse teams. The organisation of these troops was as follows:

Under *Oberst* Mamula before Peterwardein:
3. Bataillon Piret
2. Bataillon E.H. Ferdinand d'Este
4. Bataillon St. Georger
4. Bataillon 1. Banal-Regiment
4. Bataillon Brooder
4. Bataillon Gradiskaner
29 guns

Under *Oberst Baron* Moritz Lederer on the lower Danube:
Four companies of *seressaners*
Four squadrons of König von Sachsen-Kürassiere
Two squadrons of E.H. Johann-Dragoner
Six guns

In reserve under *Major* Plattner:
Two companies of Piret infantry
One company of 4. Bataillon 2. Banal-Regiment
A detachment of 9. Jäger-Bataillon

84 Just as the Hungarian army found itself forced to resort to levying poorly armed militia, so too did the imperial forces.

A detachment of Windischgrätz-Chevauxlegers
One gun

This was all that remained at *Feldzeugmeister Graf* Nugent's disposal. With this, by his good judgement and tireless activity he not only held the garrison of the fortress of Peterwardein constantly in check but also secured and dominated the area of the lower Danube, thereby making it safe for river transport and enabling all the steamboats and considerable supplies of war *matériel* to be recovered later.

Finally, on 10 April after the fall of St. Tomas, *Generalmajor* Thodorovich had retreated to Mokrin with the Serbian troops, so as to be in a position to defend against any enemy attempt to cross the Theiss.

Screening Pesth, 8-11 January 1849, and the Action at Waitzen on 10 January 1849

Let us now return to the operations of the army concentrated in front of Pesth. It must be remembered above all that the *Feldmarschall* understandably knew nothing of the true strength of the enemy facing him, nor of his position – in short, any of the details that we have provided from the Hungarian files. All that had become clear in the course of the battle of Isaszeg was that he had to deal with a far more numerous enemy.[85]

On the 8th, the day before arriving outside Pesth, the *Feldmarschall* wanted to conduct a reconnaissance to force the enemy to reveal his positions. However, this was not carried out because of objections about the exhausted state of the troops.[86]

On the 9th activity was limited to sending out wide-ranging patrols, but the order was issued for a sustained reconnaissance, possibly resulting in a serious fight, to be carried out on the next day (the 10th). The order for the operation included this at the end:

> Should the reconnaissance to be carried out reveal that the enemy's main body is no longer in front of us, it may be assumed with reasonable certainty that a considerable portion of the rebels has probably moved away in the direction of Waitzen to relieve Komorn. This is all the more likely as reports have come in that enemy columns have moved through Fót and Palota [Rákospalota, now District XV, Budapest, Hungary]

85 In fact, the opposing forces were fairly equal. Bánlaky says the Hungarian army at Isaszeg numbered 48,000 men, against which the Austrian I. and III. Korps fielded 27,000, so it is true that the *Feldmarschall* was outnumbered on the Isaszeg battlefield; however, with II. Korps and the other elements that were not at Isaszeg, the Austrian army operating around Pesth likewise had 48,000-50,000 men. Bánlaky, *A magyar nemzet*.

86 Given their track record, we may guess that these objections came from the *Feldmarschall*'s two senior subordinates: Schlick and the *Banus*. (In the circumstances, their objections may have been well-founded, of course.) On the occasion of this latest attempt at reconnaissance, it may be pertinent to mention what Clausewitz said of the *Feldmarschall*'s illustrious predecessor, Archduke Charles, when he similarly ordered a reconnaissance after the battle of Stockach in 1799: 'This is an age-old favourite practice of the Austrians whenever they lack the spirit of enterprise and begin to feel embarrassed about it. Daun was always ordering general reconnaissance, and later on we see Schwarzenberg carry this bashful gesture to the point of ridiculousness.' Murray and Pringle, *The 1799 Campaign in Switzerland*, Section 13.

toward Dunakeszi today. In that event I will send II. Armeekorps (Division Csorich and its attached cavalry and artillery) to march to Gran.

This and the order issued to Division Ramberg to retreat from Waitzen along the Danube through Szalka [Salka, Slovakia] and Kéménd behind the Gran if attacked by superior force expressed the first preparations for covering the siege of Komorn, the first notion of possibly concentrating considerable combat forces on the Gran.

At 7:00 a.m. on the 10th the units of I. and III. Armeekorps set out on their reconnaissance, while II. Armeekorps was held in readiness in the camp outside Pesth. I. Armeekorps took the road toward Czinkota with Brigade Ottinger in the lead, while III. Armeekorps crossed the Rákos further down at the Tarczál mill and moved further left toward Palota.

After a while both corps advanced guards ran into the enemy, who was himself apparently in the act of advancing on a reconnaissance in force.[87] A lively cannonade immediately developed in which the enemy brought five or six batteries into action. But since the enemy columns stayed a long distance away, mostly concealed by hills and vineyards, it was not possible to get a good view of them. Because of the additional fact that it had rained heavily all day and the roads were a sea of mud, the *Feldmarschall* gradually withdrew the troops back into camp without the enemy advancing any further from his concealed position.

On the 11th it was reported from several sources that the enemy was preparing to effect a crossing of the Danube at Dunakeszi. Our observation post had already been dislodged from Sz. Endré Island. News also came in that enemy detachments had already crossed the Danube at Földvár and were urging the people to take up arms everywhere. *Oberst Baron* Horvath was therefore ordered without delay to Sz. Endré with two battalions, two squadrons and half of Kavallerie-Batterie Nr. 6 to observe the Danube between Pesth and Waitzen; while *Rittmeister Baron* Eschrich was detached downstream with one squadron and two rocket launch stands.

Toward 2:00 p.m. on the 11th the enemy advanced along the whole front on a sustained reconnaissance, whereupon the whole camp on the Rakos stood to. In the direction of Palota and Czinkota this was limited to a cannonade, but a strong column advanced from Keresztur to the Steinbrucher vineyards that were held by the *grenzers*, and had indeed gained some ground when *Generalmajor* Ottinger and his cuirassier brigade rushed up from Pesth racecourse and put the enemy to flight with very considerable losses. By 5:30 p.m. the enemy had retreated back to his original position at all points.

On the 12th the *Feldmarschall* received the report about the action fought at Waitzen on the 10th by Division Ramberg and the consequent evacuation of that town. There had already been rumours circulating about this the day before, but as stated, the official message did not arrive until the 12th.

At this point this division comprised:

1. Bataillon H.v. Nassau
2. Bataillon H.v. Nassau
3. Bataillon H.v. Nassau

87 Actually, this Hungarian move and that on the 11th were not reconnaissances but demonstrations to pin the imperial forces and mask the main body's move toward Komorn, which they successfully did. See the section 'Hungarian Dispositions, 7-18 April 1849' below.

1. Landwehr-Bataillon H.v. Nassau
1. Bataillon Palombini
3. Bataillon Bianchi
12. Jäger-Bataillon
Two and a half squadrons E.H. Karl-Chevauxlegers
Two squadrons Wrbna-Chevauxlegers
Two squadrons E.H. Johann-Dragoner
One squadron Kress-Chevauxlegers
One pioneer company
One 6-pounder foot artillery battery
Half a horse artillery battery
One and a half rocket batteries
One 12-pounder battery

Altogether seven battalions, seven and a half squadrons and 27 artillery.

Command of these had been transferred to *Generalmajor* Götz several days earlier since *Feldmarschall Lieutenant* Ramberg had fallen seriously ill and had to be taken to Ofen.

At 8:00 a.m. on the 10th *Generalmajor* Götz had confirmed to the *Feldmarschall* that he had correctly received the order instructing him to redouble his security measures, to send his baggage and his sick and the like back to Gran immediately, and to retreat on the road along the Danube through Szalka and Kéménd behind the Gran if attacked by superior force. At the same time he reported that to protect his retreat better he had occupied Nagy-Maros [Nagymaros, Hungary], and he drew the *Feldmarschall*'s attention to Sz. Endré Island where the enemy seemed to be planning a crossing of the Danube.

One and a half hours after this report was sent, the enemy advanced to attack Waitzen. *Generalmajor* Götz cannot have thought this was a serious enemy operation, for otherwise – mindful of the instruction he had been given – he would have formed up immediately on the advantageous heights right behind Waitzen. These cover the entrance to the road designated for his retreat that runs through the defile between the Danube on one side and steep slopes on the other.[88] Instead, his troops and artillery were gradually committed against the enemy outside Waitzen. But the enemy soon deployed such superior force, particularly in artillery, that *Generalmajor* Götz recognised that it was necessary to order the retreat. To that end he sent *Generalmajor Fürst* Felix Jablonowsky back to Waitzen charged with preparing to evacuate the town, while he himself stayed behind with the units still engaged in the action.

Generalmajor Fürst Jablonowsky took the troops and artillery that were still in the town and deployed them on the heights outside it, placing one 12-pounder battery, one 6-pounder battery and a rocket battery there so that they completely commanded the exit from the town. He detached *Oberst* Strastil with four companies of Nassau *landwehr* and a Palombini company to cover his left flank (the right being completely protected by the Danube). In this very suitably chosen position, Jablonowsky received the troops that were falling back step by step. The Bianchi battalion and 12. Jäger-Bataillon were the last, contesting the enemy's entry into the town led by

88 Perhaps Götz was deceived by the Hungarian feint toward Sz. Endré Island and did not think the Hungarian main effort would be directed through Waitzen and therefore at him.

Generalmajor Götz in person. Then right at the moment when this position could also be vacated without detriment to the other units, the gallant general was struck by a bullet in the middle of his forehead. He slumped from his horse and soldiers of the E.H Ferdinand d'Este regiment carried him to the nearby reformatory, where he expired shortly after.

These battalions suffered heavy losses as they retreated through the town because many of the inhabitants also joined in the fight.

At this very difficult moment after the death of *Generalmajor* Götz, command of the division devolved to *Generalmajor Fürst* Jablonowsky. He collected all the troops into his very suitably chosen position and had his artillery open up such effective fire on the pursuing enemy that they soon had to give up completely on debouching from the town and indeed on any further attack.

After dismounting three enemy guns and silencing the rest, *Generalmajor Fürst* Jablonowsky began retreating gradually up the road along the Danube. At Veröcze his rear guard took position again, while the main body continued its march and arrived at Szalka on the right bank of the Eipel at 12:30 a.m. at night. After the rear guard had also arrived there the bridge over the Eipel was burned. The next day (the 11th) the retreat continued through Kemënd behind the Gran.

Oberst Strastil and his five companies had diverged from the designated direction of retreat. He had retreated through Kospollag [Kóspallag, Hungary], Maria-Nostra [Márianosztra, Hungary], Tölgys [Ipolytölgyes, Hungary] and Ganod [presumably the farm north of Ipolytölgyes shown on the 2nd Military Survey map as Puszta Ganád] and did not rejoin the division at Kemënd until the 12th.

The losses in the action at Waitzen that lasted from 9:30 a.m. until 3:00 p.m. were significant. According to *Generalmajor Fürst* Jablonowsky's report of 12 April from Kemënd they included: dead: *Generalmajor* Götz, *Hauptmann* von Brandenstein and *Oberlieutenant Baron* Marenbolz of 12. Jäger-Bataillon and 56 men of *Feldwebel* rank and below; wounded: nine officers and 60 men; and missing: 215 men. In addition, 23 horses were killed, nine wounded and ten missing. One howitzer was dismounted and thereby temporarily put out of action. The enemy's reports falsely claimed to have taken three guns and an entire bridging train.

The troops had fought against an enemy many times stronger than they with rare courage and endurance. *Oberlieutenants* Jüngling and Fiala of the artillery had especially distinguished themselves.[89]

The *Feldmarschall's* Last Plans are Thwarted by His Subordinates and He is Removed from Command, 12-15 January 1849

The battle at Waitzen, and the reports from *Oberst* Hofmann of the quartermaster-general staff whom the *Feldmarschall* had posted in the Ofen observatory on the Blocksberg to observe the enemy's movements and who saw enemy columns moving in the direction of Waitzen on the 11th and 12th, led the *Feldmarschall* to suspect that the enemy intended to continue his operation from there in force to relieve Komorn. The *Feldmarschall* recognised clearly that the combat forces at his disposal were not sufficient both to cover Pesth against all eventualities and

89 Hermann notes that this was the Hungarian III. Corps's third victory within a week, while in their first action for several months Götz's men suffered a defeat, with contrasting effects on the morale of the two sides. But the battle's major result was indeed to alert the *Feldmarschall* to the Hungarian move toward Komorn. Hermann, *Az 1848–1849-es.*

to prevent the relief of Komorn, if it were the case that the enemy was determined to achieve that. He did not hesitate for a moment over which of these two places should be held and which left exposed. For all the certainly undeniable military and political significance of Pesth, protecting the siege of Komorn – which was expected to fall any day now – was strategically more important, if only because the relief of Komorn would necessarily have to result in the evacuation of Pesth as well. Therefore, as soon as the *Feldmarschall* was convinced that the enemy's main body was no longer in front of him but had moved upriver, he took the decision to abandon the position outside Pesth and move his troops to Ofen on the right bank. However, he planned to send a considerable force from there through Gran back onto the left bank, so as to join the six brigades already there (Division Jablonowsky and Brigades Herzinger, Veigel, Teuchert and Theissing) and waylay the enemy on the road to Komorn.

I. Armeekorps was provisionally tasked with staying behind in Ofen and holding the right bank of the Danube; II. and III. Korps, though, were to move through Gran to the left bank of the Danube (the former leaving four battalions behind to garrison Buda Castle). This would have united 41 and two sixths battalions, 44 squadrons and 162 artillery behind the Gran – a force that would not only have sufficed to frustrate any attempt to relieve Komorn, but also have been very suitable for resuming the offensive again from there with the prospect of success.

The correctness of the views on which this operation was based can now hardly be denied. But at the time when it needed to be put into effect, things were quite different! The *Feldmarschall* summoned the two corps commanders – the *Banus* and *Feldmarschall Lieutenant Graf* Schlick – as well as their chiefs of staff, *Generalmajor* Zeisberg and *Major Baron* Gablenz, to inform them of his decision and to explain his reasons for it in more detail. None of them wanted to agree to possibly abandoning Pesth. On the one side it was asserted that 'we might not meet the enemy on the Gran at all, since if he learns that we have appeared there in superior force, he will avoid any clash just as he usually has done previously. Thus it could happen that we lose Pesth without obtaining any advantage elsewhere.' On the other side, in direct contrast to the *Feldmarschall*'s views, the operation against Szeged was suggested again, this time in more definite official form. The proposal was presented to the *Feldmarschall* on the 12th in this letter summarising it:

> The *Banus* should immediately go on the offensive with 35 battalions, 44 squadrons and 150 artillery ('Süd-Armee' [Army of the South]) through Kecskemét and Theresiopel, cross the Theiss at Szegedin or Klein-Kanischa [presumably Török-Kanisa, now Novi Kneževac, Serbia] and then, reinforced by the Serbs, etc., advance toward Debreczin and Grosswardein. Meanwhile ten battalions and six squadrons should stay outside Komorn; six battalions and six squadrons should garrison Ofen-Pesth; and the rest should remain in the field as the Nord-Armee [Army of the North], initially only on the defensive, to cover Pesth and Komorn.[90] [If the rebels should accept battle at Debreczin, this so-called 'Nord-Armee' was] to advance toward Debreczin by forced

90 In the original text, Nobili interpolates the following here: '(In the memo in question, this "rest" was given as 30 battalions and 24 squadrons, in which however the 11 battalions awaited from Galicia were obviously included. But since these did not concentrate at Dukla until 18 April, the true strength available for the moment to the so-called "Nord-Armee" came to no more than 19 battalions and 20 squadrons.)'

> march through Szolnok and Kardszag, while if the enemy were to avoid any encounter by retreating, it would move to Miskolcz, etc.[91]

The *Feldmarschall* did not approve of this proposed operation since he did not find it acceptable to detach half of the army to Szegedin at the moment when the combined enemy army was in front of him and in all probability about to move upriver to relieve Komorn. He therefore held to his view but agreed not to abandon the position in front of Pesth and concentrate the army behind the Gran until he was certain that the enemy's main body really had moved upriver, and also that it had progressed so far in that direction that it could no longer turn round and give up on the Komorn operation without accepting battle.

That certainty could only be established by a powerful reconnaissance.[92] The plan also required careful observation of the line of the Gran between Kálna [Kalná nad Hronom, Slovakia] and Párkány, and in addition that all the troops present in that area or approaching it should be concentrated without delay at a point where it remained possible to reinforce them quickly and adequately if necessary, whatever the situation. Both of these were duly arranged. A reconnaissance toward Czinkota and Keresztur was ordered for the 13th, and *Generalmajor Fürst* Jablonowsky was given the order not to get himself tied down in any cordon-type deployment along the Gran but just to observe the line of the river as far as Kálna with patrols and raiding parties. He was to stay in Keménd with his division, while at the same time Brigades Herzinger, Veigel, Teuchert and Theissing were instructed to go to Gran, Párkány and Köbelkut. This concentrated position would secure Gran and thus also the line communications of the army deployed just one day's march away in front of Pesth, and thus the *Feldmarschall* would be in a position to oppose the enemy in force, whether he should advance to relieve Komorn either from Waitzen along the Danube or by a detour through Ipoly-Ságh.

At 9:00 p.m. on the 12th *Feldmarschall Lieutenant* Wohlgemuth – who was to take command of the troops deployed on the Gran – was notified accordingly, and this was attached to the end of the instruction: 'Should Your Honour obtain completely reliable information that the enemy is advancing in such disproportionate strength that there is no way you can withstand him, inform me of this immediately so that I can send you the necessary assistance.'

The reconnaissance carried out on the 13th produced no significant result. According to the plan, I. and III. Armeekorps were to be used for this, but as a result of objections raised against it,[93] each corps only pushed forward eight squadrons and two batteries. The enemy therefore remained hidden in his position behind the Czinkota heights, contenting himself with

91 This is interesting on two counts. One is that, after the defeat at Isaszeg, Schlick and the *Banus* should both be so disillusioned with the *Feldmarschall*'s leadership as to formally propose an alternative plan to his. The other is the plan itself. As discussed earlier, when the capture of Ofen-Pesth failed to end the war, the *Feldmarschall* realised only destruction of the enemy's combat power would suffice. However, his subordinates' proposal still seeks victory in taking locations, actively avoids the enemy's main body, and seems to make no mention of any objective other than 'advance toward Debreczin and Grosswardein'.

92 If in doubt – reconnoitre! Yet this was not the only option. If the *Feldmarschall* had imposed his will and moved decisively and immediately through Gran to cut Görgei off, things might have turned out better for the Austrians.

93 We have now seen such objections to the *Feldmarschall*'s plans raised many times. He has lost his grip on his army.

bringing his batteries into action at advantageous points. After a pointless cannonade in which we lost some men and several horses without having identified the enemy's actual position, the reconnaissance detachments returned to camp again. However, this much had emerged: that the enemy could not be as strong there as he had been earlier. Also, it seemed certain that the outpost report that had come in the day before, according to which 'an enemy corps of 12,000 men is supposed to have marched to Czinkota', was inaccurate.

A report came in from *Oberst Baron* Horvath at St. Endre dated 7:00 p.m. on the 12th which said: '[T]he rebel camp can clearly be seen west of Waitzen. His apparent strength may be some 12,000–15,000 men. A *Kadet* from the H.v. Nassau infantry who has returned from captivity in Waitzen and who accompanies the bearer of this message, *Lieutenant* Lerch of the E.H. Wilhelm infantry, to Ofen states that Görgei, Klapka and Damjanich were all there together.'

The long foreseen enemy operation to relieve Komorn therefore appeared to be approaching realisation, so the arrangements that had been decided upon to frustrate it had to be put into effect straight away. As the first step toward this, all the bridging trains were moved to Dorog on the 13th. There they stood ready to throw a second bridge across the Danube at Gran if necessary, or to be used on the River Gran. The *Armee-Intendant* [commissariat officer], *Major* Kovacsevich, was instructed to divert food supplies to that area and to ensure that 35,000 men and 8,000 horses were provided for. Furthermore, in order to strike one more blow against the weak enemy detachments deployed in front of Pesth immediately before the reinforcements for the Gran departed, the *Feldmarschall* ordered a general attack on them for the next day (the 14th). The dispositions for this began with the words: 'As the majority of the enemy combat forces have moved toward Waitzen, and thus the enemy will only have a very small force deployed on our front, I feel compelled to order a general attack tomorrow (the 14th). This will be undertaken by I. and III. Armeekorps, and must be done in such a way that the troops leave camp at 3:00 a.m. III. Armeekorps will head for Czinkota, while I. Armeekorps moves toward Keresztur [Rákoskeresztur, now in District XVII, Budapest], etc.'

It was left to the two corps commanders to work out the detailed arrangements for this together. However, at 11:30 p.m. these two reported that as a result of reliable information that the defile at Keresztur was so strongly held by the enemy that forcing it would be subject to great difficulties, they had therefore to advise against the operation.[94]

Two hours later, that is at 1:30 a.m. during the night of 13/14 April 1849, His Majesty the *Kaiser*'s aide-de-camp *Major Graf* Wrbna presented the *Feldmarschall* with a note written in His Majesty's supreme hand containing his recall from the army. The *Feldmarschall* complied with this supreme order with the same unshakeable calm and devotion he had exercised at so many various important moments in his life. He left Ofen during the night of 14/15 April and betook himself to the imperial court at Olmütz.

As the newly designated commander-in-chief, *Feldzeugmeister Baron* Welden, had not yet arrived, the *Banus* took over interim command of the army and *Generalmajor* Zeisberg the general staff matters.

Shortly before the *Feldmarschall*'s departure, a report had arrived from Gran dated 12:30 p.m. on the 14th from *Hauptmann* Adam of the general staff, whom the *Feldmarschall* had sent specifically to observe the line of the Gran and to obtain spy reports from that area, and

94 The second time in two days that they obstructed the *Feldmarschall*'s plans.

who diligently carried out this important mission. This report said that: '[A]t midday on the 13th two or three enemy brigades were in Ipoly-Ságh, while a fourth brigade under Görgei had remained behind in Waitzen but was going to follow the others. These are all definitely moving into the mountains so as to go via Léva and cross the Gran at Kálna. Corroborating information about this has come in both from a trusted informer and from an enemy deserter.' At this the *Feldmarschall* immediately ordered what could be ordered, in that during the night of 14/15 April [the original text says 'the night of the 14th to the 16th'] he wrote to *Feldmarschall Lieutenant* Wohlgemuth:

> Reliable information has reached me that the enemy's main body, or at least a strong column from it, has turned toward Ipoly-Ságh. He presumably intends to advance from there through Kálna toward Komorn. Your Honour should therefore turn your full attention in that direction and take appropriate action with the very considerable combat forces at your disposal to prevent such an operation;[95] or if this enemy column should take a different direction, to follow close on its heels.

This was *Feldmarschall Fürst* zu Windisch-Grätz's last order. It was appropriate for the situation at the time, and if followed it would certainly have been enough to prevent the enemy building his bridge at Kálna across the River Gran – whose waters at that time were very high and which constituted a significant military obstacle – long enough for the necessary reinforcements to accrue, whose urgency was further emphasised by the reports that came in during the course of the 15th. Finally, in the worst case it still remained possible to unite sufficient force at Nagy-Sarló or even at Perbete [Pribeta, Slovakia], the latter place being the furthest point that the most distant corps (namely the one at Ofen-Pesth) could reach via Gran in two days' march if necessary. But it was not to be! Scarcely had the *Feldmarschall* left Ofen than his last order was cancelled by a change of plan. This instruction was issued during the night of 14/15 April to the troops deployed on the Gran: '[R]etreat immediately to the right bank of the Danube. Only one brigade shall remain in Párkány to cover the bridge over the Danube at Gran.'

Feldmarschall Lieutenant Wohlgemuth had still not yet arrived. This order reached the hands of the troops' interim commander, *Generalmajor* Herzinger, right when he was on the point of following the *Feldmarschall*'s order, all the more readily since he himself recognised the danger threatening at Kálna as well as the need to prevent or at least hinder the enemy crossing there, and had reported about that. However, the change of orders that arrived later forced him against his better judgement to call off the march that he had already begun, and to retreat with all his troops to Keménd and Gran!

Generalmajor Herzinger's situation and that of the brigades deployed on the Gran in general was a very awkward one, for contradictory orders and instructions were reaching them from Wien, Ofen and Pesth all at the same time.

95 Footnote in the original: '*These comprised 19 and two sixths battalions, 18 squadrons and 57 artillery, thus:
Division Jablonowsky (Ramberg): seven battalions, eight squadrons, 27 guns; Brigade Herzinger: three battalions, two squadrons, six guns; Brigade Teuchert: three battalions, two squadrons, six guns; Brigade Veigel: three and two sixths battalions, four squadrons, 12 guns; Brigade Theissing: three battalions, two squadrons, six guns.'

Hungarian Dispositions, 7-18 April 1849

Finally, it only remains for us to describe the enemy's dispositions since 7 April – the day he reached Gödöllő. The following orders were given for the 8th:

> VII. Armeekorps shall march to Fót and send a detachment to Dunakeszi to destroy the railway. III. Korps shall move to Magyaród, II. Korps to Isaszeg, I. Korps stays in Kerepes.
>
> Asboth's mobile division (four companies of 49. Honved-Bataillon with 611 men; 63. Honved-Bataillon, 813 men; Pressburger-Jäger, 130 men; pioneers, 160 men; two squadrons Bocskay hussars, 300 men; altogether 1,714 infantry, 430 cavalry and some 3-pounder guns) shall stay in Monor and Gyömrö.
>
> The ammunition reserve shall move from St. Márton-Káta [Szentmártonkáta, Hungary] to Dány. Army headquarters shall stay in Gödöllő, as shall a cavalry division from VII. Armeekorps, which shall also occupy Szada and maintain communications with Fót. All arms of service will replenish their ammunition today (the 8th).
>
> The cavalry picket at Dunakeszi shall deploy its outposts toward Pesth and Waitzen and secure the right flank of the army toward Csomád and Szada.
>
> VII. Armeekorps shall arrange for the bridging train to be brought from Hatvan to Aszod today.

And for 9 April:

> I. Armeekorps shall march from Kerepes to Csomád, deploy outposts toward Waitzen, and maintain communications with VII. Armeekorps on its left and III. Armeekorps on its right.
>
> VII. Armeekorps shall remain in Fót; III. Armeekorps shall move from Magyaród [Mogyoród, Hungary] to Veresegyháza, keep outposts toward Waitzen, maintain communications with I. Korps on its left, and occupy the village of Mácsa [Galgamácsa, Hungary] as a point of support for its right wing.
>
> In the event of a reverse, the line of retreat shall be toward Gödöllő.
>
> II. Korps shall move from Isaszeg to Czinkota, send a detachment to Czömör, maintain communications with VII. Korps in Fót and keep a chain of outposts from Czömör through Czinkota to Csaba and Péczel.
>
> The mobile Division Asboth shall move to Üllő.
>
> Army headquarters shall remain in Gödöllő.

For 10 April:

> VII. Armeekorps shall demonstrate toward and as far as Palota, shall be prepared to engage the enemy, and in any case shall bivouac at Dunakeszi at 5:00 p.m., maintaining outposts only toward Pesth if Waitzen shall have fallen into our hands.
>
> In that case the line of retreat shall be toward Waitzen, otherwise toward Gödöllő.
>
> The brigade in Fót shall stay detached and shall be kept in communications with II. Armeekorps by the detachment in Magyaród.

> II. Armeekorps shall remain ready for battle until 4:00 p.m., when it shall go into camp at Kerepes facing Pesth, and shall send detachments to Magyaród and Péczel, thereby staying in communications with VII. Armeekorps on its right and Asboth's column on its left; the outpost chain shall run through Nagy-Tarcsa [Nagytarcsa, Hungary] and Csaba toward Ecser. Line of retreat: toward Gödöllő.
>
> III. Armeekorps shall set off at 6:00 a.m. sharp from Bercsegyháza via Szöd [Sződ, Hungary] toward Waitzen, attack there, try to make it impossible for the enemy to retreat toward Neograd, and push him toward Balassa-Gyarmath. It shall then set up camp beyond Waitzen. Line of retreat: Bercsegyháza and Gödöllő.
>
> I. Armeekorps shall move at 7:30 a.m. to Csomád, following III. Armeekorps in the direction given above.
>
> Asboth shall remain in Üllő and his outposts shall link up with those of II. Armeekorps at Ecser.
>
> The ammunition reserve shall remain in Gödöllő with an escort from II. Armeekorps.
>
> Should Waitzen be taken, army headquarters shall move to there, otherwise it shall remain in Gödöllő.

Thus, Division Ramberg in Waitzen had to contend with the enemy's I. and III. Armeekorps. I. Armeekorps under Klapka had ten battalions, 16 squadrons and 30 guns. At this point, III. Armeekorps comprised:

Division Knecic

Brigade Kiss
1. Bataillon, Infanterie-Regiment Nr. 34
3. Bataillon, Infanterie-Regiment Nr. 34
9. Honved-Bataillon
Half a battery

Brigade Kökenycsi
65. Honved-Bataillon
3. Bataillon, Infanterie-Regiment Nr. 52
Two companies of *jägers*
Two companies of pioneers with four bridging trains
Half a rocket battery

Division Wisocky

Brigade Czillich
Polish Legion
42. Honved-Bataillon
3. Bataillon, Infanterie-Regiment Nr. 60
Half a battery

Brigade Leiningen
3. Bataillon, Infanterie-Regiment Nr. 19
3. Honved-Bataillon
Eight guns

Brigade Kaszony
Two squadrons of lancers
3. Husaren-Regiment
Eight guns

***Oberst* Pikéti**
2. Husaren-Regiment
Hajduk detachment

Klapka's I. Armeekorps numbered ten battalions, 16 squadrons and 30 artillery pieces. Thus, the enemy had at least three times as many troops as *Generalmajor* Götz, yet the battle lasted a full seven hours, and the enemy still did not manage to drive Götz's force away toward Balassa-Gyarmath as he intended!

The enemy detachments encountered on this day by the *Banus*'s corps and that of *Feldmarschall Lieutenant Graf* Schlick as they pushed forward from Pesth belonged to the enemy's II. and VII. Armeekorps (Aulich and Gaspar) and were supposed to screen the manoeuvre toward Waitzen.

On 11 April VII. Armeekorps advanced beyond Palota just as on the previous day. Toward 2:00 p.m. a cannonade developed that lasted until 4:30 p.m. At the same time three battalions, eight squadrons and four batteries from the enemy's II. Armeekorps had advanced from Keresztur toward the Steinbruch [quarry], while *Oberst* Asboth and his column swung still further to the left. These were the detachments that *Generalmajor* Ottinger drove back with significant losses. On 12 April VII. Armeekorps followed the other corps to Waitzen. With this manoeuvre the enemy main body began its operation to relieve Komorn.

From this day on, only Aulich's II. Armeekorps and the column under Asboth remained in front of Pesth, the former at Czinkota, the latter at Keresztur. The combined strength of these two formations did not exceed 12,000 men.

The cannonade that was opened up along the whole line the previous day was probably intended to make the *Feldmarschall* think that the whole army was still in front of him, and thereby to mask for as long as possible the march through Waitzen toward Komorn that had already been decided on and that was begun immediately after.

On 13 April: (we do not know what manoeuvres took place on this day.)

On 14 April:

> VII. Armeekorps. Division Kméty shall remain as garrison in Waitzen and post outposts toward Dunakeszi. The rest of the corps shall move to Retság.
>
> I. Armeekorps to Oroszi.
>
> III. Armeekorps to Ipoly-Ságh.
>
> II. Armeekorps (Aulich) shall remain in Czinkota and Keresztur.

Asboth forward of Vecses.[96]

This was the position of the enemy army on 14 April, the day on which the *Feldmarschall* relinquished command of the army.

We do not know the enemy's dispositions for the 15th, 16th and 17th. All that we do know is that the enemy army did not complete its crossing of the Gran at Kálna until the 18th. The water was high and fast-flowing, making bridge construction difficult. The fact that there was no attempt to oppose it meant that the bridge construction could be started from both banks at once which made it fundamentally quicker and easier.

Concluding Remarks

This is not the place to describe the events that took place after 14 April. However, we believe we have shown that the subsequent relief of Komorn eight days later and the army's consequently unavoidable retreat to Raab and Pressburg cannot be regarded as the result of the *Feldmarschall*'s orders. As we have seen, he had ordered a general attack on the enemy formations in front of Pesth on the 14th, and if this had not been left undone it really would have established for certain that the enemy's main body was no longer in front of him. The fact that the *Feldmarschall* did not simply sit inactive in front of Pesth with the whole army for eight full days can be inferred unmistakeably from his repeatedly expressed views of the state of affairs as well as from his energetic orders based on these.[97]

We do not wish to get involved in drawing any conclusions about what might have happened if the enemy's relief of Komorn had not succeeded. This much is certain and acknowledged by the enemy himself: without the help that reached it, the fortress of Komorn could not have held out for more than another eight days. Quite apart from the major strategic importance of this base and the fact that the fall of Komorn would have opened up river traffic along the Danube, its fall would also have made the siege force of 13 battalions, eight squadrons and 42 field guns available to be used for other purposes. If we add to this the three newly arrived brigades with their nine battalions, six squadrons and 18 guns, and finally *Feldmarschall Lieutenant* Vogel's corps invading from Galicia with 11 battalions, eight squadrons and 24 guns, it follows that in the second half of April the army could have resumed offensive operations again augmented by 33 battalions, 22 squadrons and 84 guns, mostly fresh troops, thus with a total strength of 81 battalions, 84 squadrons and 333 guns!

96 Footnote in the original: "*Asboth reported to Aulich on the 14th: "In the enemy council of war held the day before yesterday (12th), Schlick and Jellachich are supposed to have proposed a general retreat to Raab, since otherwise the army would be lost; yet Windisch-Grätz insisted on defending Pesth to the utmost?"' This is curious as it seems at odds with Nobili's assertion mentioned above that on 12 January 'none of them [the Banus, Schlick, Zeisberg and Gablenz] wanted to agree to possibly abandoning Pesth' and that it was the *Feldmarschall* who advocated doing so.

97 However, Hermann points out something which Nobili omits: the Hungarians were fortunate that after the battle of Isaszeg, the *Feldmarschall* ordered Csorich's division to move from Vác to Ofen-Pesth, leaving Götz's (formerly Ramberg's) division in Vác to face overwhelming Hungarian forces alone. Earlier on in this section, Nobili has told us that the *Feldmarschall* correctly decided that Komorn was of more strategic significance than Pesth. If that was so, then why did he concentrate forces in front of Pesth and leave the road to Komorn via Vác so exposed? Hermann, *Az 1848–1849-es.*

With this concise reflection resting on simple facts and figures we conclude our description of the winter campaign in Hungary, except that we feel we ought just to append the *Feldmarschall*'s farewell message to the brave army he had commanded, and his proclamations to Hungary.

The *Feldmarschall's* Farewell Messages

Army Order

Olmütz, 24 April 1849
It has pleased His Majesty the *Kaiser* to recall me from command of the army in Hungary and to entrust the same to the *Herr Feldzeugmeister Baron* Welden.

While it would remain a heavy sacrifice for me at any time to leave a body of men with whom I have spent such a long time and so many years of my life, I cannot deny that it is doubly difficult for me to leave you at this moment when after so much exertion and proof of your devotion to your Monarch and to His legitimate cause, you have the prospect – with substantial reinforcements imminent – of glorious days ahead as reward for what you have already achieved.

All the qualities you have displayed in this arduous campaign, the evident devotion and trust you have given me – these will remain a precious memory to me.

This army has done a great service to the world; under my leadership it has accomplished so much to preserve the social structure, to restore law and order, that these deeds alone are sufficient to earn it a place in history beyond compare. It has been a privilege for me, and I shall remain forever proud, to have led you through this period of calamity and to have found in you a spirit that transcends the corruption of these times.

My best wishes, my warmest sympathy shall follow you everywhere, and if I can indeed only deeply regret that I can no longer witness the deeds that now lie before you, I cherish the firm confidence that all those expectations that I myself had of you will still be met under the wise leadership that now joins you.

I thank you once again for all that you have achieved under me, from beginning to end, and I will retain my warm attachment to you for all time.

Alfred *Fürst* zu Windisch-Grätz m.p.
Feldmarschall

To the people of Hungary!

It has pleased His Majesty the *Kaiser* to transfer the authority entrusted to me over the Kingdom of Hungary to the *Herr Feldzeugmeister Freiherr* von Welden.

A period of disaster, the result of the criminal subversions of the revolutionary party, has broken out across the country and has overwhelmed it with hardships that will perhaps still be felt for generations to come. Passing events that seem to nourish the hopes of this party can only increase the misery and distress that already spread across the land, as well as leading finally to the total dissolution of social order.

As I leave the country, I turn once more to the right-minded and enlightened to ask them not only from duty and conscience but for their own sake to support the government, to intervene firmly and to exert their influence on their misguided fellow citizens to put an end to this unfortunate state of affairs.

Even the criminal party itself cannot have any illusion that it will succeed; the government will find the means to defeat it and to conquer the country. But the longer this takes, the greater the effort needed, and the more profoundly the country's peace will be shattered and its welfare jeopardised.

I therefore call on you for the last time at the moment when I relinquish my role as His Majesty's representative, on a nation otherwise so pervaded by noble sentiments, to pluck up courage to make every effort to put an end to the present and potentially even greater disaster.

I thank all the officials of every rank whom I found myself caused to have put into effect my authority for the assistance they have rendered me, and for the proof they have given me of their honesty and decency. My intentions and proposals for this Kingdom, as I humbly submitted them to His Majesty according to my convictions, had as their only purpose to promote the wellbeing of this country and its profound association with the monarchy; if implemented and applied appropriately, they will bear the most beneficial fruit.

May Divine Providence grant you Hungarians its aid to reach this goal soon. Even though my presence among you was only of short duration, my profound sympathy for this country and my concern for all its honest citizens will never fade.

Olmütz, 22 April 1849
Alfred *Fürst* zu Windisch-Grätz m.p.
Feldmarschall

Epilogue

Events on the Main Front from 15 April to the Beginning of May 1849

Nobili's account essentially ends with Windisch-Grätz's departure on the night of 14/15 April. All he tells us about events after that is that the *Feldmarschall*'s orders for what was to happen next were countermanded, and that things could have turned out much better if they had been implemented. This leaves an important gap between Nobili's history of the Winter Campaign and Ramming's history of the Summer Campaign. This brief epilogue is designed to fill that gap.

The Galician Corps's operations

Hammerstein had been ordered by the *Kaiser* to form another new corps in Galicia to support Windisch-Grätz. This was commanded by *Feldmarschall Lieutenant* Vogel and comprised Brigades Benedek, Barco and Ludwig, with the following units:

Brigade *Generalmajor* Benedek
One battalion Palombini-Infanterie
One battalion Parma-Infanterie
Two squadrons of E.H. Karl Ludwig-Chevauxlegers
One 6-pounder battery (six guns)

Brigade *Generalmajor* Barco
Two battalions Deutschmeister-Infanterie
One battalion Hartmann-Infanterie
Two squadrons of Kaiser-Chevauxlegers
One 6-pounder battery (six guns)

Brigade *Generalmajor* Ludwig
One battalion Welden-Infanterie
One battalion Haynau-Infanterie
One battalion E.H. Wilhelm-Infanterie
One battalion Bianchi-Infanterie
Trenk Grenadier-Bataillon
Two squadrons of Sunstenau-Kürassiere

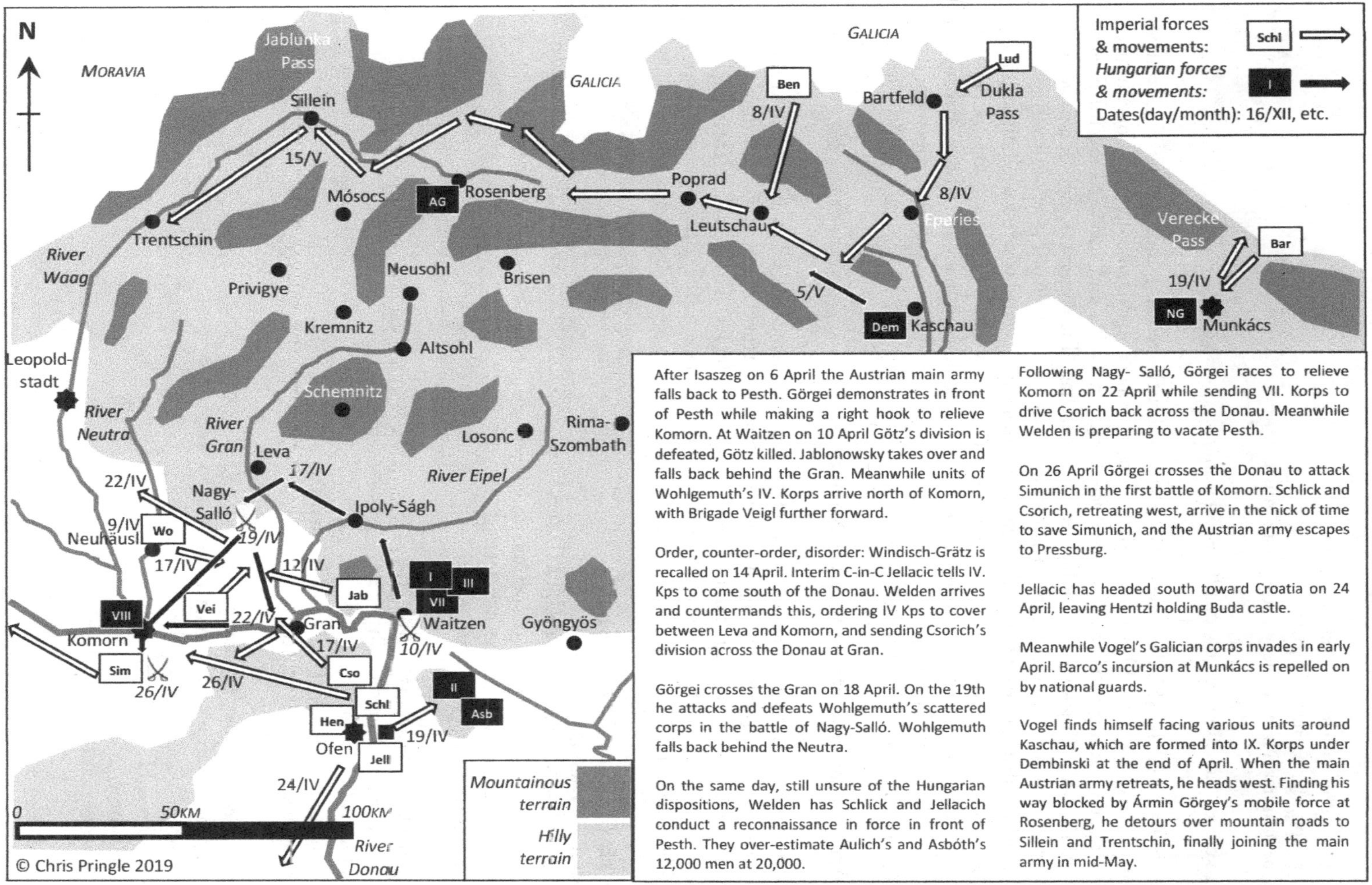

Map 7: Epilogue, April 1849

Two squadrons of Kaiser-Chevauxlegers
One 6-pounder battery (six guns)
One 6-pounder horse artillery battery (six guns)

Total: eleven battalions, eight squadrons, 24 guns.

Brigade Barco operated independently on the left, briefly invading through the Verecke Pass toward Munkács around 19 April, but then being repelled and driven out again. Vogel himself with Brigade Ludwig had already crossed the border at Dukla and advanced toward Eperies on 8 April, while Brigade Benedek headed for Leutschau. The corps was supposed to advance through Kaschau to Miskolcz. After the battle of Isaszeg, on 10 April it was ordered to move to Rima-Szombath instead; but then when the main army retreated west (as we shall see), it too changed direction again, moved to Poprad, and then away across the Waag to make contact with the main army without getting involved in any serious military operations. Because of guerrilla attacks and having to detour to avoid Hungarian positions obstructing its path, it did not rejoin the main army until mid-May.

IV. Armeekorps concentrates to screen Komorn

Shortly before Windisch-Grätz's departure, a new IV. Armeekorps had been created under *Feldmarschall Lieutenant* Wohlgemuth. This was formed from the three brigades of reinforcements from Bohemia, Moravia, Austria and Styria under Herzinger, Teuchert and Theissing, plus Jablonowsky's division (formerly Götz's) retreating from Waitzen. The reinforcements comprised the following units:

Brigade *Generalmajor* Herzinger
3. Bataillon Paumgarten
1. Landwehr-Bataillon Khevenhüller
4. Kompagnie, Oguliner Grenz-Regiment
Two squadrons of Wrbna-Chevauxlegers
Nr. 18 sechspfündige Fussbatterie

Brigade *Oberst* Teuchert
1. & 2. Bataillons Mazzuchelli
Hora Grenadier-Bataillon
Two squadrons of Kaiser Ferdinand-Kürassiere
Nr. 20 sechspfündige Fussbatterie

Brigade *Generalmajor* Theissing
4. Kompagnie, Ottochaner Grenz-Regiment
1. Landwehr-Bataillon E.H. Stephan
2. Bataillon E.H. Ferdinand d'Este
Two squadrons of Civallart-Uhlanen
Nr. 19 sechspfündige Fussbatterie

Total: nine battalions, six squadrons and 18 guns; 10,000 men altogether, including 900 cavalry. Thus, with Jablonowsky's division, IV. Korps was about 16,000 strong. As Nobili indicates, Windisch-Grätz had directed it to muster along the Gran river to cover the siege of Komorn.

Jellačić as temporary commander-in-chief had countermanded the *Feldmarschall*'s sensible orders to IV. Korps and ordered Wohlgemuth instead to move south to cross the Donau. On 16 April, Welden reversed this, but instead of ordering IV. Korps to defend the river line, simply told Wohlgemuth to bar the road from Léva to Komorn.

The Battle of Nagy-Salló, 19 April 1849

On the 18 April the Hungarians crossed the Gran before pushing south, resulting in the battle of Nagy-Salló on the 19th. Battle began at dawn when Brigade Strasdil pushed a Hungarian ration party out of Nagy-Salló. Klapka and Damjanics responded rapidly and recaptured the village and repelled a renewed assault by the whole of Jablonowsky's division. A new threat then appeared on their flank in the form of Herzinger, who had marched to the sound of the guns. Dessewffy's men, who had embarrassed themselves at Tápió-Bicske and at Isaszeg, were again driven back. Klapka brought up reinforcements and restored the situation.

At this point Wohlgemuth decided the odds were too great and prepared to retreat towards Komorn. However, his right flank was now attacked by the Hungarian VII. Korps. In order to avoid being trapped, Wohlgemuth changed direction and retreated northwest behind the Neutra river and then beyond the Waag, leaving the Hungarians free to march to the relief of Komorn. In this clash between about 25,000 Hungarians and 20,000 imperial troops, Hungarian losses were 600-700 men against Austrian losses estimated between 800 and 2,000.

The Hungarian 1. and 2. Korps forced march to arrive outside Komorn on 22 April and obliged Simunich's siege force to withdraw to the right bank of the Donau, ending the blockade of the fortress. 7. Korps meanwhile drove Division Csorich back from Kéménd to Gran.

On 19 April – the day of the battle at Nagy-Salló – Welden conducted yet another classic Austrian reconnaissance in force from Pesth with his 1. and 3. Korps. Jellacic reported 20,000 enemy in front of him, when in fact there were only 12,000. This plus the news of the defeat at Nagy-Salló decided Welden to abandon Pesth and withdraw to the west to concentrate his forces at Pressburg, collecting the siege force from Komorn along the way. Jellacic's 1. Korps was left in Pesth to cover the retreat initially, after which it was finally to conform to the *Banus*'s wish and move south to its home territory of Slavonia. On 24 April 1. Korps marched south, leaving a garrison of 5,000 men in the Ofen fortress under *Generalmajor* Hentzi.

The First Battle of Komorn, 26 April 1849

After relieving Komorn, the Hungarian army had been delayed for several days by the need to build a new pontoon bridge across the Donau. Once this was done, Görgei stealthily moved his force across the river during the night. In a brilliant night attack, five Hungarian brigades mustered by the Star Fort and attacked with cold steel only, carrying the Austrian works by storm. Simunich's small besieging force fell back divided, some moving west, some southeast. As day broke, while more Hungarians crossed the Danube, Schlick's 3. Korps joined part of 2. Korps in the Austrian centre. Although his orders were to retreat west, Schlick realised the best way to secure the retreat was to attack, and ordered a general advance. The battle ebbed and flowed, but at some 30,000 men each, the two sides were too evenly matched for either to prevail. Had the Hungarian 7. Korps arrived as ordered, it might have turned the battle, but bad roads made this impossible. The Austrians were thus able to retreat to Raab with their siege guns, but were obliged to abandon many wagons laden with supplies, ammunition and engineer stores. They lost over 2,000 men, the Hungarians about half as many.

While Welden's army retreated to Pressburg and reorganised, the victorious Hungarians then marched south to besiege the garrison in Ofen. Thus, shortly after Windisch-Grätz's departure his Winter Campaign had culminated in the virtual expulsion of all Austrian field forces from Hungary.

Appendix I

The Transylvanian Front

Nobili's account focuses on the operations of those forces under *Feldmarschall Fürst* Windisch-Grätz's control in the main theatre of operations. It touches only tangentially and occasionally on events in the two secondary theatres, Transylvania and the southern front. For completeness, these are therefore covered briefly in two Appendices. This first Appendix deals with Transylvania.

Transylvania was an ethnically mixed province inhabited by about 1,000,000 Vlachs (Romanians), 400,000 *Szeklers*, 300,000 other Hungarians, 200,000 Saxons (ethnic Germans) and 50,000 miscellaneous others. There was a particular concentration of *Szeklers* – ethnic Hungarians – in the Székelyföld, five districts in the south eastern corner of Transylvania. A class divide reinforced this ethnic and linguistic divide, as landowners were predominantly Hungarian, while the peasantry were mostly Romanian.

Events in Transylvania during the Winter Campaign fall into four phases:

1. In October/November 1848, a Romanian uprising helps imperial forces to drive the newly-created Hungarian army out of Transylvania.
2. In December, the dynamic Polish general Bem takes charge and expels the Austrians from northern Transylvania, but they suppress the Szeklers.
3. In January 1849, Bem follows up his success by marching south against the Austrian base at Hermannstadt. Puchner invites the Russians in and with their help is able to force Bem to fall back down the Maros River; but while the Austrians are distracted, the Szekler army rises again.
4. In February-March 1849, reinforced from the force besieging Arad, Bem can attack again. With astonishing speed and decisive violence, he repeatedly outmanoeuvres the Austrians, defeats a new Austrian incursion in the north, seizes Hermannstadt by coup de main, and expels the Austrians and their Russian allies to Wallachia.

These complex and frequently dramatic operations merit a whole book in their own right. There is not space here to describe them in full; still, let us examine these four phases in a little more detail.

October-November 1848

When the Hungarian revolution began and the Hungarian government tried to enforce its new conscription law in mid-October 1848, the Vlachs and Saxons rebelled. Rebels coalesced around small imperial loyalist units under *Oberst* Karl Urban near Bistritz, and *Generalmajor* Josef Riebel in western Transylvania, while thousands more rose up in the Ore Mountains [Munţii Metaliferi, Romania]; the main imperial force in Transylvania, about 7,000 men under *Feldmarschall Lieutenant* Puchner (the military governor of Transylvania), was at the important base of Hermannstadt in the very south of the province. On Puchner's order, the imperials began trying to disarm the Hungarian national guards. This resulted in some massacres of Hungarian civilians, followed by Hungarian retaliation.

The Hungarians responded to this uprising and its accompanying massacres. The Szeklers swiftly raised a force of about 8,000 in the Szeklerföld. They and about 5,000 regular troops under Baldacci, based in Klausenburg, achieved a number of initial successes against Urban and the Vlachs in central Transylvania between Neumarkt [Marosvásárhely in Hungarian; now Târgu Mureş, Romania], Klausenburg and Weissenburg in late October.[1] Gaál also pushed up the Maros with 6,000 men, confronting Riebel who was descending to try to relieve Arad.[2] Gaál forced Riebel to fall back into the mountains onto the support of Avram Iancu's Vlachs. Gaál then returned to besiege Arad.

At the start of November, Puchner therefore sent Brigade Gedeon from Hermannstadt to help Urban. The Szeklers had lost some of their discipline after their victory over Urban and were defeated at Neumarkt on 5 November. Most of their army disintegrated and went home.

In mid-November, Puchner was then able to have Gedeon and Urban converge on Klausenburg from the east. They were joined by Wardener's 3,000 men approaching from Bistritz, having entered Transylvania from the Bukowina, and by Kalliany directly from Hermannstadt in the south. Baldacci advanced to face Urban, put up brief resistance but had to flee through the Csucsa Pass [Ciucea, Romania].

A few days later, a new Hungarian column of 5,000 mostly national guards under *Major* Miklós Katona pressed up the Szamos from Szatmár [Satu Mare, Romania] into northern Transylvania. Puchner sent Urban to face this threat. Urban defeated Katona at Deesch [Dej, Romania] on 25 November.

1 Baron Emánuel Baldacci (1807-52) was made colonel of the 51. Karl Ferdinand-Infanterie in Klausenburg in March 1848. In May 1848 he chaired the body establishing the new National Guard and also helped establish the first *honvéd* battalions. Appointed general in October, his combat record against Urban in November was so inglorious that he was arrested for investigation. He was held in Pesth where he fell into imperial hands in January 1849. He retired, then after the war was stripped of his rank and sentenced to two years in prison. He was pardoned in 1852 but died shortly after. Bona, *Tábornokok*.

2 Miklós Gaál (1799-1854) was a lieutenant colonel in the imperial engineers. He resigned in September 1848 to join the new Hungarian army. After operating with Perczel in the southwest of Hungary, he commanded the siege of Arad. When this was interrupted by an imperial foray from Temesvár, he was held responsible and removed from command. Instead, he was put in charge of planning fortifications. The course of the war made his work irrelevant, and in July 1849 he retired. After the war he turned himself in. He was sentenced to death, but this was commuted to 20 years' imprisonment. He died in the Pesth prison hospital. Bona, *Tábornokok*.

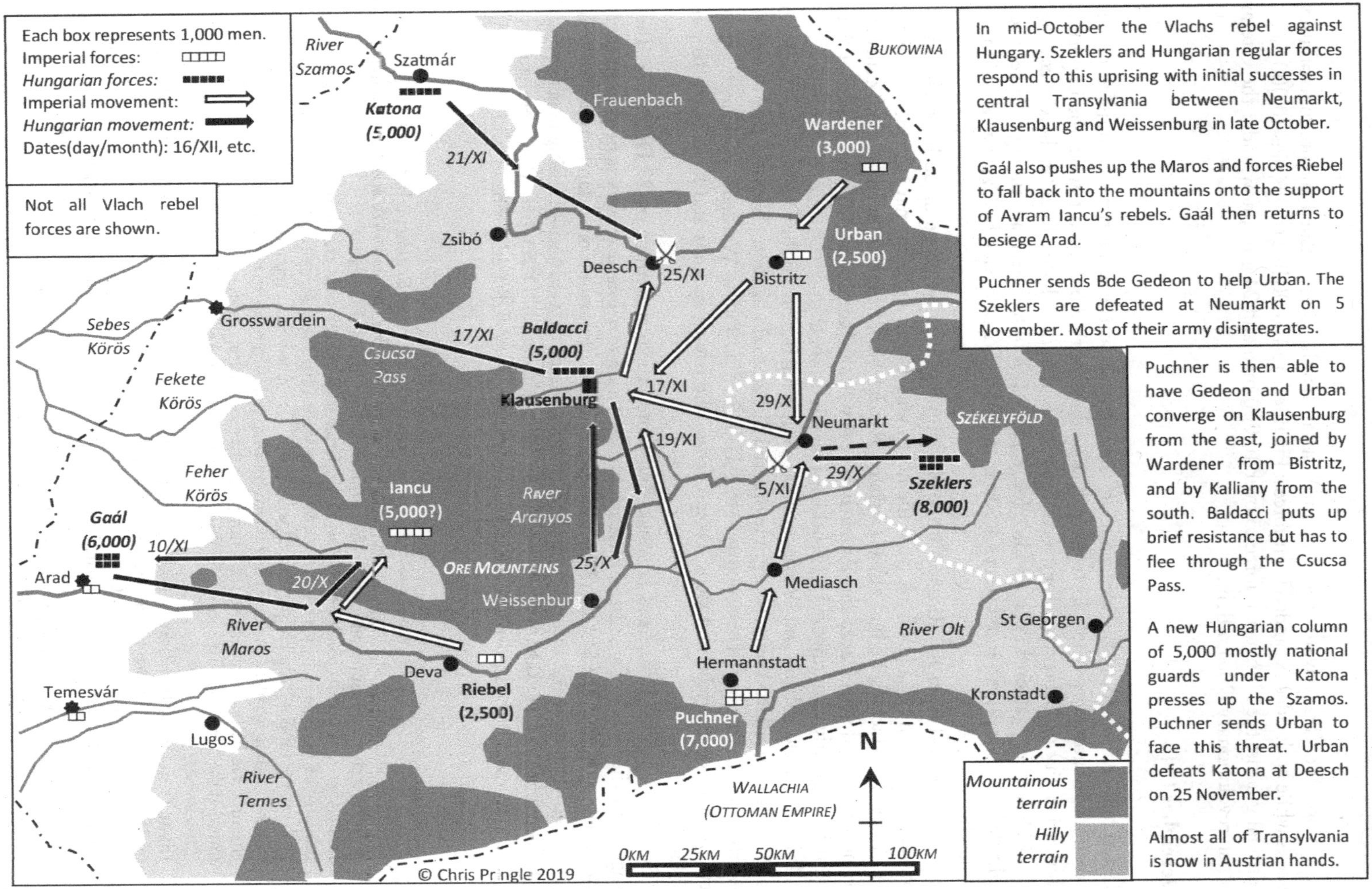

Map 8a: Transylvania, October-November 1848

Almost all of Transylvania was now in Austrian hands. There ensued an interlude of a few weeks while both sides expanded their forces: Puchner's to 16,000 line troops plus 10,000 Saxon national guards; the Hungarian force to over 10,000 men and 24 guns, now under the veteran Polish revolutionary *General* Bem.

December 1848

Rested and reinforced, both sides went on the offensive at the same time in mid-December. Urban and Wardener pushed down from Klausenburg with 3,500 men toward the important Hungarian city of Debreczin. They were repulsed by Riczkó's larger force at the Csucsa Pass on 19 December.[3] Jablonski's small force (only about 1,000) had been advancing to cover their right flank. Jablonski ran into Czetz's 4,500 men and was driven back by Czetz at Zsibó on 20 December.[4]

Bem's plan had been for Riczkó's to be the pinning force while he made his main attack toward Klausenburg in a left hook from the north with Czetz and Zsurmay.[5] At the time when the Austrians attacked, he had already briefed Riczkó before moving north to join Zsurmay. He now advanced with Czetz and Zsurmay – nearly 10,000 combined – and won another fight against the greatly outnumbered Jablonski at Deesch on the 23rd.

This threatened Urban's and Wardener's rear as they fell back from the Csucsa Pass. Wardener hastily retired south to Weissenburg. He ordered Urban to do likewise, but Bem had moved so swiftly that he occupied Klausenburg before Urban could follow Wardener. Urban therefore actually had to dodge behind Bem, escape across the Meleg Szamos and head north to join Jablonski.

Bem then pursued Urban and Jablonski and routed them at Bethlen on 29 December. They fought a further series of small and increasingly desperate rear-guard actions as he chased them out of Transylvania. The last of these took place in the Bukowina on 5 January before Bem returned to Transylvania. By this time the battered Austrians were almost falling apart.

In the Székelyföld, skirmishing had gone on all through December. Puchner had sent Gedeon to reinforce Heydte's patrol force. Together, they defeated Dobay's and Sombory's

3 Károly Riczkó (1816-49) was a lieutenant in the 9th Miklós Hussar Regiment. In spring 1848 he took part in establishing and recruiting the new National Guard. He was killed in action at Királynémeti fighting against the imperial invasion from the Bukovina. Bona, *Tábornokok*.

4 János Czecz (Czetz) (1822-1904) was an imperial staff officer who transferred to the Hungarian ministry of defence in July 1848. In October he went into the field as Baldacci's chief of staff, then took over from Baldacci. He performed well in the Transylvanian campaign but his war was ended by a serious riding accident in May 1849. He went into exile after the war and was sentenced to death in absentia. He helped to organise the Hungarian Legion in Italy. Later he emigrated to Argentina and founded the Mapping Institute of the Buenos Aires Military Academy. He died in Buenos Aires. Bona, *Tábornokok*.

5 Lipót Zsurmay (1816-67) was a Polish noble who had been exiled to Hungary after the Polish uprising of 1830-31 and became an imperial lieutenant in the 10th Hussars. In October 1848 he led two squadrons of his regiment from Galicia to join the Hungarian forces. He served in the Transylvanian campaign and also fought at the battle of Temesvár. After the war he briefly performed compulsory service in the imperial army again until pardoned under a general amnesty. He emigrated in 1853 and served as a colonel in the Hungarian Legion in Italy in 1860 and then in the Italian army before returning to Pesth after the 1867 Compromise. Bona, *Tábornokok*.

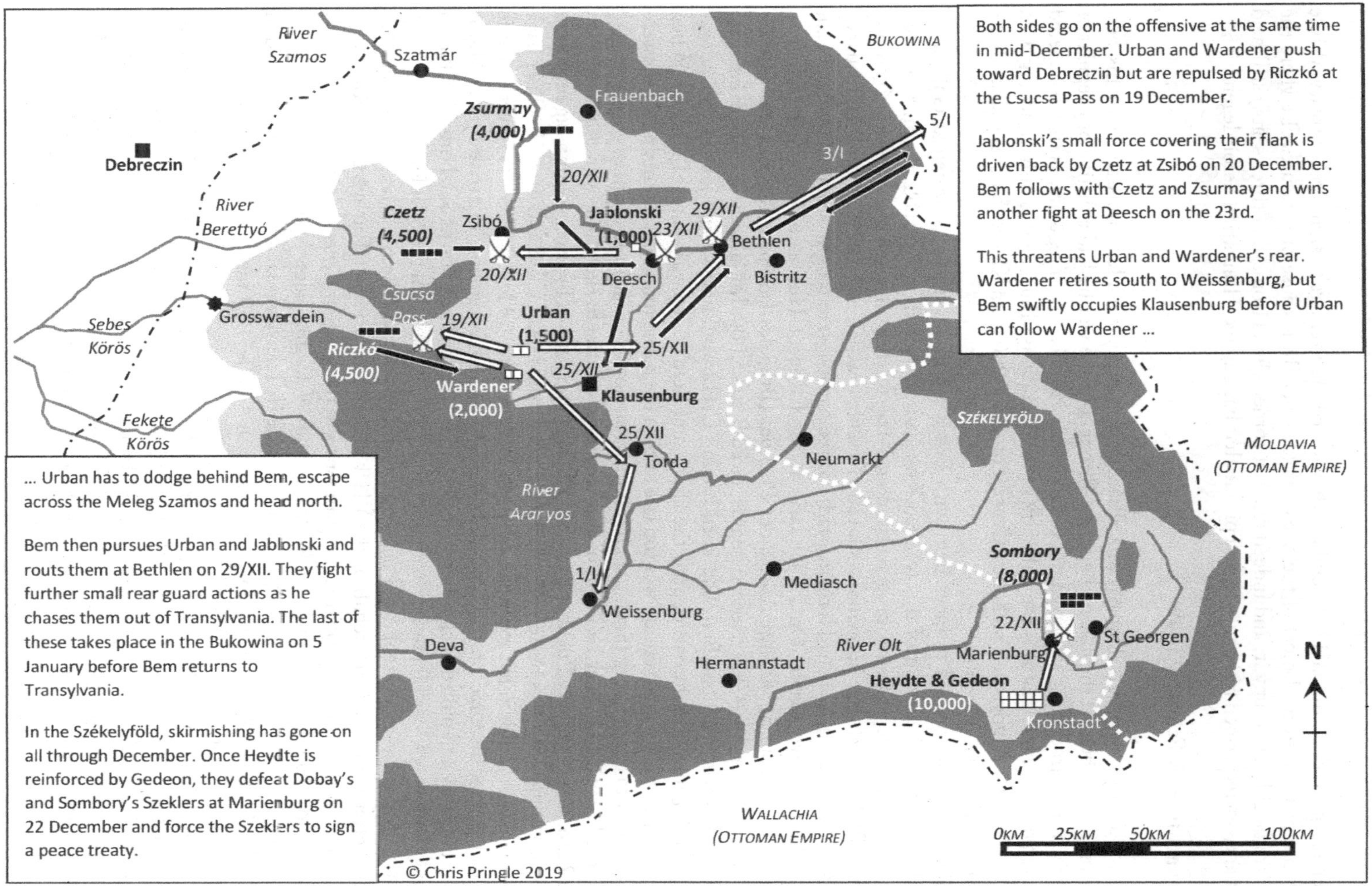

Map 8b: Transylvania, December 1848 to early January 1849

Szeklers at Marienburg on 22 December. They forced the Szeklers to sign a peace treaty. While this nominally disarmed most of the Székelyföld, crucially, because of pressures elsewhere the Austrians did not occupy it; and indeed one last corner, the Háromszék ('three seats') still held out and offered armed resistance in an episode that has entered Hungarian heroic legend.

January to early February 1849

Having cleared northern Transylvania, Bem now marched on Hermannstadt with his best troops, leaving behind the national guards. Throughout the war he had a dislike of irregular or poorly trained troops and preferred not to mix them with his core of regulars, as they hampered the rapid manoeuvre that was the hallmark of his operations. Thus, he was only attacking with about 6,000 men altogether, including Czetz's force of 2,000 from Klausenburg as well as Bem's own column of 4,000-5,000.

Puchner came forward to meet Bem with Brigade Kalliany and was beaten at Gallendorf on 17 January. When word of this reached Kronstadt, it caused considerable alarm. Schurtter, commanding there, actually briefly abandoned the fortress and retreated toward Törcsvár [Bran, Romania – better known nowadays as Dracula's castle], not returning until 26 January.

Bem pursued Puchner to Hermannstadt. Three battles were fought around Hermannstadt over the next two weeks. On 21 January, at the battle of Hermannstadt (Nagyszeben in Hungarian), about 5,000 imperials under Puchner (Brigades Losenau, Kalliany and Riebel) supported by perhaps 4,000 national guards, faced Bem's 5,000. Initial attacks by Bem bounced off the Austrian redoubts. Bem had been hoping Czetz would arrive and join in, but he was delayed. Puchner therefore went onto the attack and Bem's force was sent reeling back. When Czetz appeared, his intervention was too late to turn the battle round, and Bem and Czetz were driven back to Stolzenburg (Szelindek in Hungarian; now Slimnic in Romania).

On 19 January Puchner had summoned Gedeon from the Székelyföld, who joined him on the 22nd. On 24 January Puchner launched an enveloping attack by three columns against Bem at Stolzenburg. This was beaten off; the Hungarians counter-attacked and drove Puchner back to Hermannstadt. Bem felt too weak to storm Hermannstadt. He left Czetz to screen it while he sent part of his force west to help clear the way for reinforcements to arrive up the Maros from Hungary and pulled back others to create an entrenched position at Salzburg (Vizakna in Hungarian; now Ocna Sibiului in Romania) and wait for help from the Szeklers.

After his defeat at Stolzenburg, Puchner did not feel confident he could beat Bem alone. He sent a letter – nominally on behalf of the Vlach and Saxon people of Transylvania, rather than an official request from the Austrian government – to the Russian *General der Infanterie* Lüders, whose corps had been stationed in Moldavia and Wallachia since March 1848 to suppress revolutionary activity there, asking him to intervene in Transylvania. The Russians marched in accordingly: *General* Engelhardt to Kronstadt with 4,000-5,000 men, and *Oberst* Skarjatin to Hermannstadt with 2,000.

This emboldened Puchner to attack Bem at Salzburg on 4 February with 8,000 troops supported by a large contingent of Vlachs. This was too much for Bem's small weary force. Despite ferocious defence and counterattack, Bem was forced to retreat, losing almost all his artillery. His army was split, part retreating to Mediasch, while he himself escaped west to Déva with a much diminished force of just 1,500 men, pursued by Puchner and harassed by Vlachs.

Having cleared northern Transylvania, Bem now marches on Hermannstadt with his best troops, leaving behind the national guards. Puchner comes to meet him with Bde Kalliany and is beaten at Gallendorf on 17 January. This causes such alarm that Schurtter briefly abandons Kronstadt.

Bem pursues Puchner to Hermannstadt. Bem is joined by Czetz, and Gedeon soon joins Puchner. Three battles are fought around Hermannstadt on 21 and 24 January (Stolzenburg) and 4 February (Salzburg). Bem withstands the initial assaults, waiting for help from the Szeklers, but then Puchner is reinforced by Skaryatin's Russian force from Wallachia.

This is too much for Bem's small weary force. Bem is forced to retreat. Much diminished, pursued by Puchner and harassed by Vlachs, he escapes west to Deva.

However, there he links up with Hrabowsky and prepares to return to the fray. Meanwhile the embers of the Szekler resistance have blazed up again and on 2 February a Szekler attack on Kronstadt is repulsed.

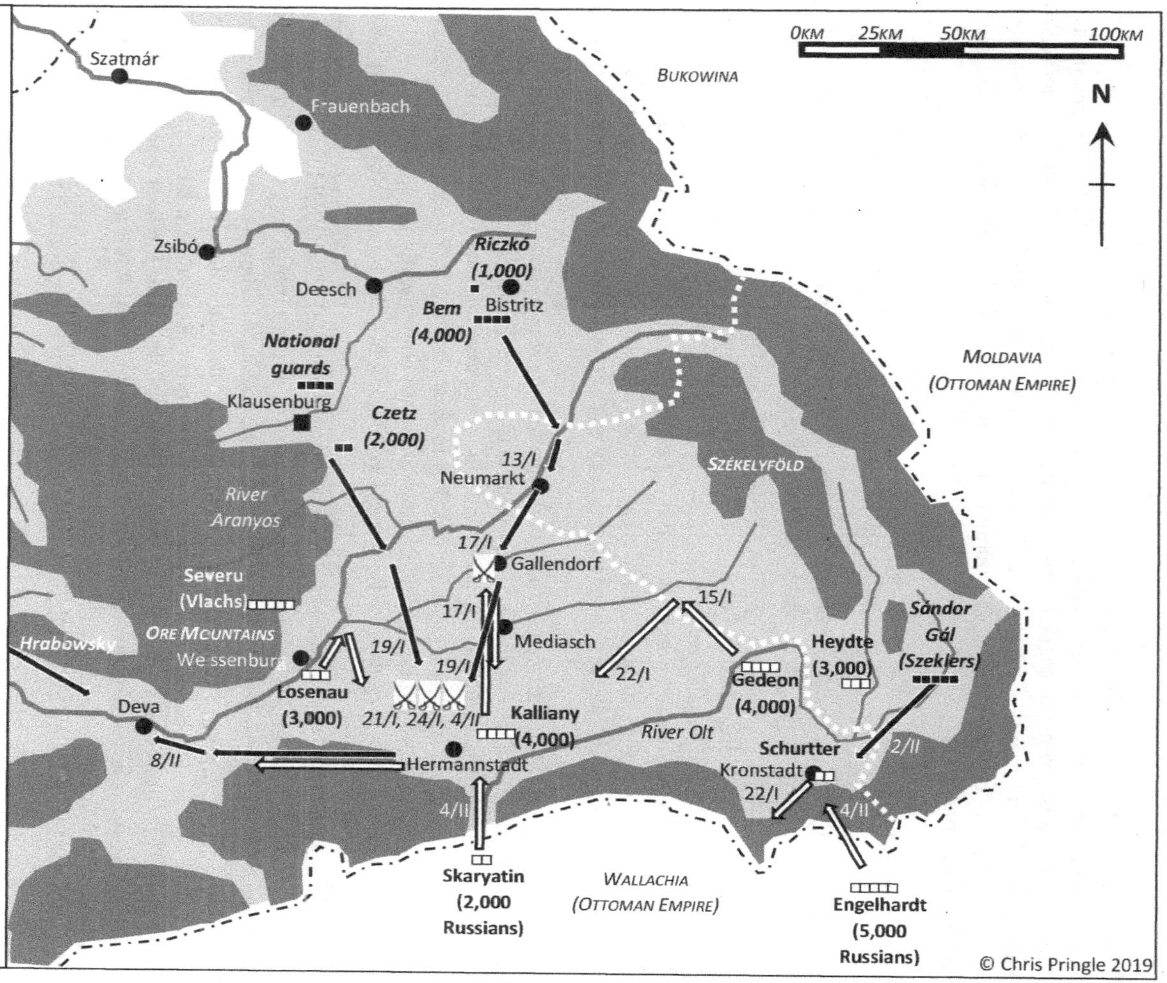

Map 8c: Transylvania, January to early February 1849

However, at Déva Bem met Hrabowsky's division coming up from Arad.[6] Thus reinforced, the indomitable Pole prepared to return to the fray. Meanwhile the embers of the Szekler resistance had blazed up again from the spark in the Háromszék. A force of about 5,000 Szeklers had formed under the command of Sándor Gál and advanced on Kronstadt.[7] While it was repulsed on 2 February, this renewed threat to Puchner's rear would cause him problems in the next phase of the campaign.

February and March 1849

Bem now had 8,000 men, about the same as Puchner's pursuing force, not counting the Vlachs in the mountains surrounding Bem. On 9 February, Puchner ordered an attack which resulted in the desperate battle at Piski. This was an intense and see-saw struggle in which Bem's determination won out: his final assault of the day with exhausted troops was enough to make the equally exhausted imperials give way.

Puchner fell back to cover Hermannstadt and detached a brigade to hold Weissenburg. Bem out- manoeuvred him by dashing past to Mediasch to meet Zsurmay, who was chasing Heydte out of the Székelyföld. To avoid being trapped between them, Heydte had to escape toward Hermannstadt.

At this point Bem learned that Urban had invaded northern Transylvania again. With Malkowsky's division following in support, Urban had driven Riczkó's small force back from Bistritz. Bem left Czetz at Mediasch with half his army and took half the army north on another of his lightning marches, covering 150 km in four days. On 23 February he defeated Urban at Borgo, who was therefore obliged to retreat out of Transylvania yet again.

On 28 February – over a week after Bem had left Mediasch – Puchner finally realised how weak Czetz was and ventured out to attack him with 9,000 men. However, by then Bem was already on his way back: Bem's rapid marching brought him to the battlefield just in time to prevent Puchner's attack of 3 March routing Czetz. Instead, the Hungarians were forced back to Schässburg. Puchner tried to outflank Bem from the south, but Bem sidestepped him once more. In an audacious move, he raced for Hermannstadt, defeated the Russians and actually took the place on 11 March, forcing Skaryatin out through the Rothenturm Pass.

The loss of this important base dismayed the imperials. The ailing Puchner handed over to Kalliany, who led his force east toward Kronstadt, pursued by Bem. After losing a small action at Zeiden on 18 March, the allies withdrew to Wallachia.

In the southwest, Leiningen's small imperial force had advanced from Arad to seal the Maros valley, while Vlach rebels still roamed the Ore Mountains. Apart from here, though, the whole of Transylvania was once again under Hungarian control.

6 György Hrabovsky (Hrabowsky) (1802-69) was a captain in the 1st Hussars in June 1848 fighting the Serbian insurrection. Bona, *Tábornokok*.

7 Sándor Gál (1817-66) was a Grenzer captain in 1848. He left imperial service to serve the Batthyány government in April 1848 and was sent to Transylvania by Klapka to assess mobilization of the Szekler border guards. He played a major role in raising some 25,000 Szekler troops during the campaign. At the end of the war he went into exile. He served in Garibaldi's Hungarian Legion in 1860. He died in Italy. Bona, *Tábornokok*.

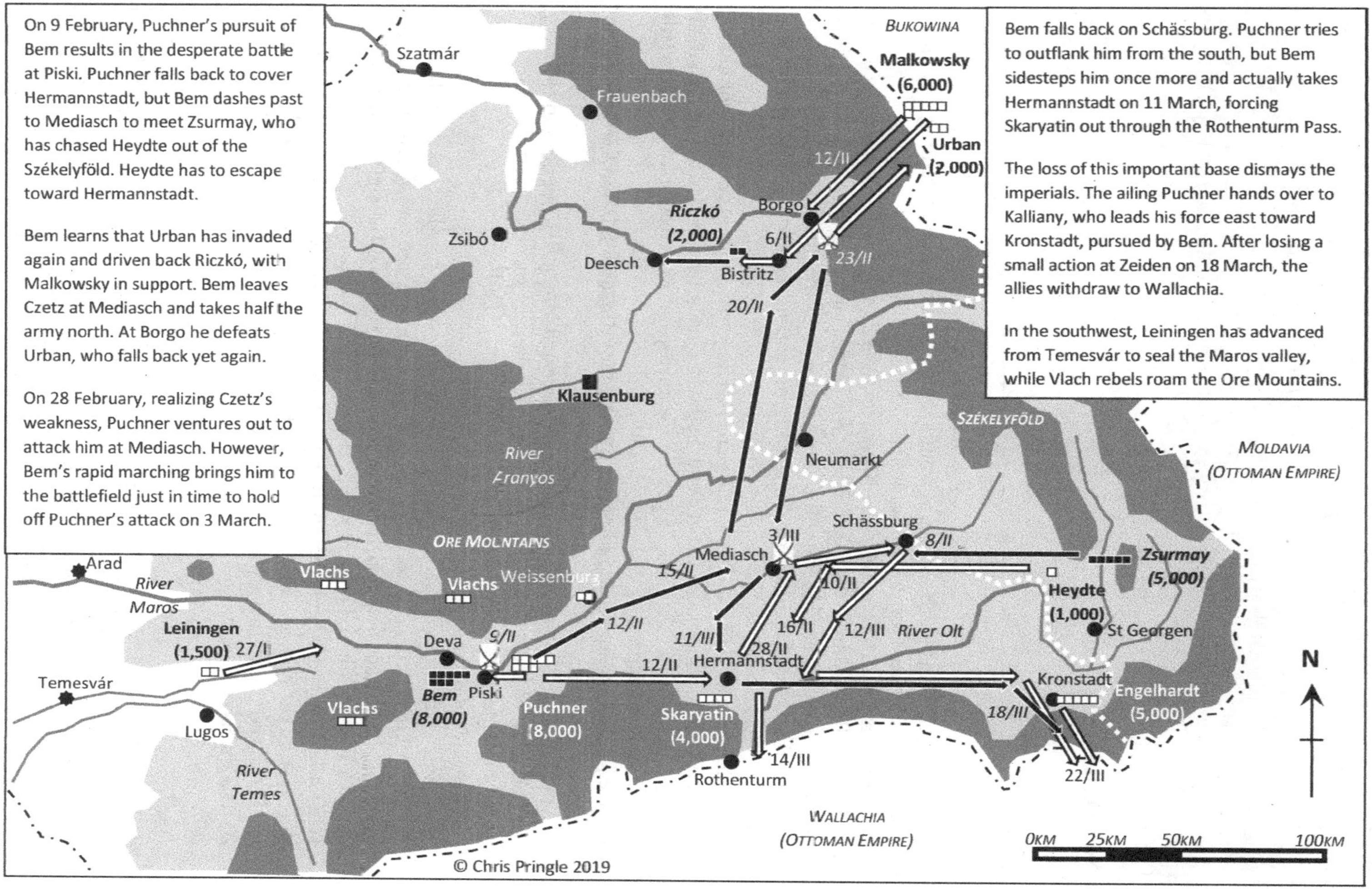

Map 8d: Transylvania, February and March 1849

Appendix II

The Southern Front

Nobili's references to events on the southern front are as intermittent and patchy as they are to Transylvania, hence the need for this Appendix.[1]

The southern front broadly comprised the Bácska and the Banat. The Bácska was essentially the then county of Bács-Bodrog, the area between the Donau and the Theiss, with its northern boundary almost as far up as Szegedin. The Banat lies east of the Theiss, similarly bounded to the south by the Donau, to the north by the Maros, and to the east by Transylvania and Wallachia.

The population of the Bácska was about 50 percent Hungarian, the rest evenly split among *Donauschwaben* (ethnic Germans), Croats and Serbs. Conversely, the Banat was about 40 percent Romanian (mostly in the east), 25 percent Germans, and 15 percent each Serbs (mostly in the west) and Hungarians.[2]

Events here just before, during and just after the Winter Campaign fall into four phases:

1. In late November 1848 to early January 1849, repeated Hungarian attempts to clear the Serbs out of their fortified camps enjoy only limited success. The Serbs hang on in the Banat and remain encamped in force along the Franzenskanal (Ferenc-csatorna) in the Bácska.
2. Mid-January to mid-February, after the Hungarian army is called north to face Windisch-Grätz, the Austro-Serbs go on the offensive up the Theiss against Szegedin, and from Temesvár toward Arad. All three prongs of their attack are blunted. Essegg falls and Nugent moves to besiege Peterwardein.
3. After a lull, in mid-March the Hungarians attack. Mór Perczel smashes through the Serbs on the Franzenskanal and relieves Peterwardein. Then he repeatedly routs the Serbs west of the Theiss who seek refuge on the Titel Plateau. By mid-April the Bácska is almost cleared.

1 For a full account of the war on the southern front, seeÖdön Olchváry, *A magyar függetlenségi harc 1848-1849-ben a Délvidéken* (Zenta: Vajdasági Magyar Művelődési Intezét – Forum Könyvkiadó, 2009).

2 For population data for the whole of the Carpathian Basin from 1495 onward, including maps showing which ethnic group was in the majority in which area in 1784 and 1880. See Hungarian Academy of Sciences, 'Series of ethnic maps of the Carpatho-Pannonian area (1997-2005)'.

4. In mid-April the Hungarian government tries to finish things in the south before the Russians arrive in the north. Perczel drives Todorovich all the way from Szegedin back across the Donau, while Bem's flank attack makes Malkowsky's force invading from Wallachia turn back as well. By mid-May the re-conquest of the south is all but complete.

Each phase is described more fully below.

Late November 1848 to early January 1849: The Hungarians Fail to Drive Out the Serbs

As briefly mentioned in the Prologue at the start of this volume, peace talks between the Serbs and the Hungarians broke down in November 1848. The Hungarians had some 40,000 men: 15,000 in the Bácska under *General* Sándor Bakonyi[3] (then *Oberstlieutenant* Sándor Esterházy from December), 22,000 in the Banat under *General Lieutenant* Ernő Kiss, and *General Lieutenant* Imre Blagojevich's garrison in and around Peterwardein.[4] These were facing some 38,000 Austro-Serbs: 13,000 Serbs in the camps in the Banat; another 10,000 Serbs under *Oberst* Stevan Suplikac in the Bácska;[5] 6,000 more on the right bank of the Donau; these and the small garrison of Arad all answering to *Feldmarschall Lieutenant Baron* Rukavina and his garrison of 5,000 in Temesvár.

In Kiss's absence, *General* Antal Vetter decided on a general offensive in the Banat and launched three widely separated attacks, all on 30 November. Only that at Ördöghídja ('Devil's Bridge') succeeded. A supporting attack in the Bácska had little effect.

Kiss returned and decided to concentrate 10,000 men for one decisive attack on Tomasevac. This was repulsed on 4 December.

In a repeat attempt on 12 December, *Oberst* János Damjanich took the camp at Alibunar, then repulsed a Serb attack at Jarkovac on 14 December, after which the Serbs vacated Tomasevac. Instead of pursuing to complete their rout, Kiss returned to invest Temesvár.

This was because the sieges of Arad and Temesvár had not proceeded as the Hungarians hoped. In October *Major* János Máriássy, besieging Arad, had been obliged to send *Oberst* Miklós Gaál up the Maros with several thousand men, first to suppress Vlach uprisings, and then to chase *Major* Joseph Riebel's imperial force into the Transylvanian mountains. On 10 November Gaál returned to Arad, where an imperial relief force from Temesvár arrived,

3 Baron Sándor Bakonyi (1805-51) was made colonel of the 2. Kaiser Alexander-Infanterie in April 1848. He led his regiment against the Serbian insurgency in July, was promoted to general in October, and given command of the Bácska corps in November. In December he requested extended leave and handed himself in to the imperial forces in Pesth in January 1849. In April he was briefly arrested by the Hungarians but then released. After the war he was stripped of his rank. Bona, *Tábornokok.*

4 Baron Imre Blagoevich (1784-1850) was a lieutenant general appointed in command of imperial forces in Slavonia in July 1848. In October he recognized the authority of the Hungarian ministry of defence and flew the Hungarian flag over Peterwardein. In January 1849 he went on sick leave and urged that Peterwardein capitulate to the imperial forces. Perczel expelled him from the fortress and he turned himself in to the imperials. After the war he was to be brought to trial but died in custody. Bona, *Tábornokok.*

5 Stevan Šupljikac (Stephan Suplikac or Šuplikać) (1786-1848) was a former imperial Grenzer officer who was elected as the first voivode (prince or duke) of the Serbian Vojvodina. *BLKÖ.*

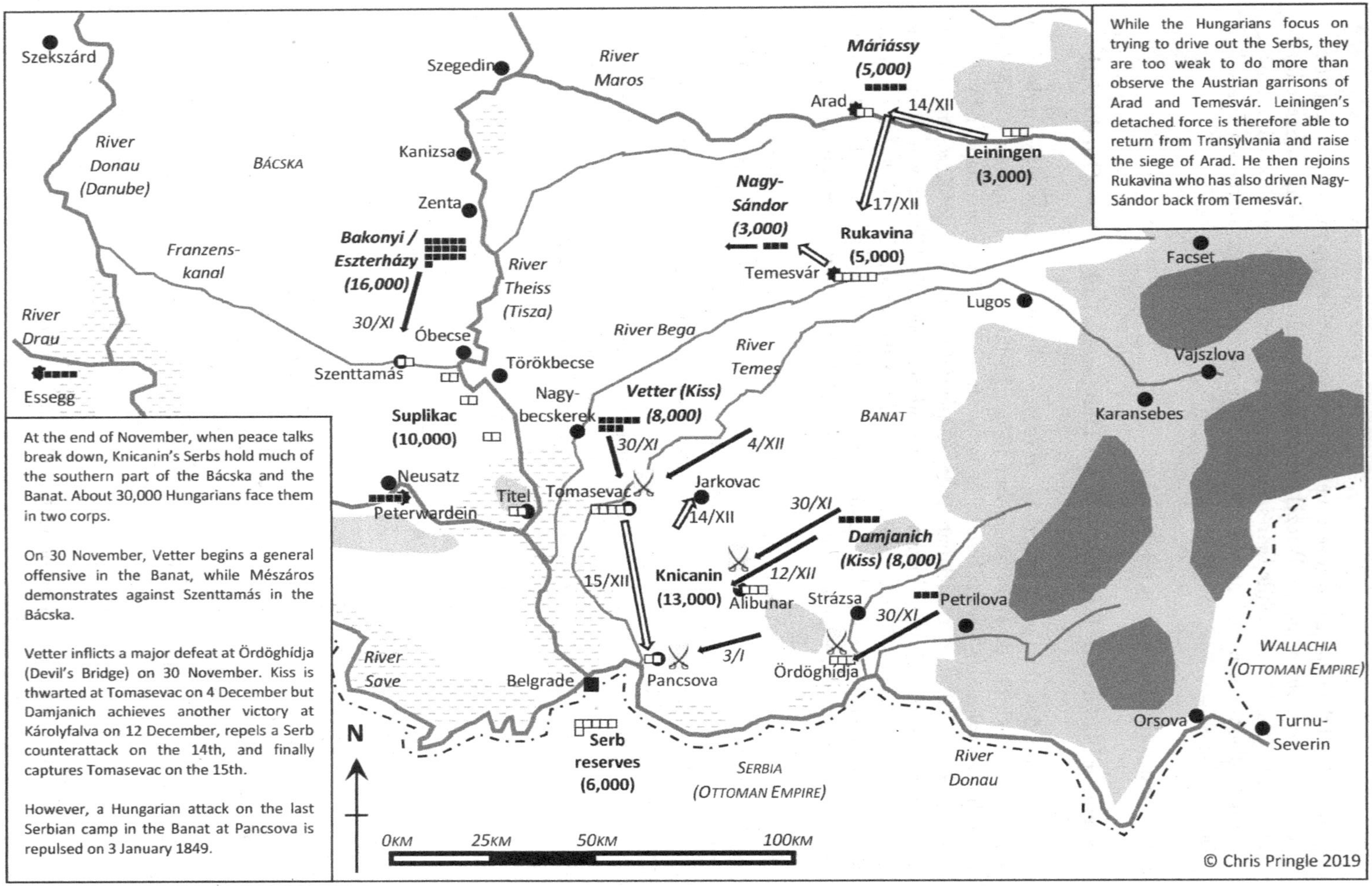

Map 9a: The southern front, late November 1848 to early January 1849: The Hungarians fail to drive out the Serbs

interrupted the siege and re-provisioned the fortress. The fortress was invested again on 17 November and the siege proper resumed at the end of November. An attempt at storming it failed on the night of 3/4 December.

General Christian zu Leiningen-Westerburg (not to be confused with his nephew Karl zu Leiningen-Westerburg, who fought heroically on the Hungarian side and was executed at Arad on 6 October 1849) returned from Transylvania, again interrupted the siege and broke through to Arad with a plentiful quantity of food on 14 December.[6] He then returned to Temesvár on 17 December.

While this was going on outside Arad, Rukavina also forced *Oberstlieutenant* Nagy-Sándor's small corps observing Temesvár to fall back.[7]

Kiss made one last effort to defeat the Serbians. On 29 December he gathered his army at Zichyfalva and marched on Pancsova in three columns, attacking it on 3 January. Behind strong fortifications, *Oberst* Stevan Petrović Knicanin withstood the attack and repulsed it with bloody loss.[8] On 5 January Kiss was replaced by Damjanich.

Mid-January to mid-February: Todorovich's Offensive Up the Theiss is Thwarted at Szegedin

On 16 January the Hungarian government decided it needed to move its southern armies north to oppose Windisch-Grätz, so the Hungarian populace was abandoned to the enemy's revenge. Consequently, many refugees fled north from the southern Banat. As many as 60,000 people lost their homes.

On 20 January the first Hungarian units departed from Nagy-Becskerek, and within a few days Damjanich's whole army had moved to Ó-Arad.

The Army of the Bácska had also been ordered northward. Eszterházy objected and was replaced by *General* Károly Vécsey, who set off for Szeged on 20 January with 6,000 men, and from there to Szentes, then to Szolnok. He was followed by Damjanich from Arad, who also sent István Hrabowsky's division of 5,000-6,000 men to Transylvania to help *General* Józef Bem. Vécsey and Damjanich's forces were combined to form III. Korps.

This only left about 4,000 national guards around Peterwardein, Neusatz and Futak under *Oberstlieutenant* Miklós Bezerédy; *General* Antal Csuha in Peterwardein itself with perhaps

6 Christian Franz Seraphin Vincenz Graf Leiningen-Westerburg (1812-56). *BLKÖ*.

7 Georg Freiherr Rukavina von Vidovgrad (1777-1849) served with distinction as a field officer in the Austrian army during the Napoleonic Wars. In 1835 he put an end to raids by the neighbouring Bosnians when he defeated 12,000 of them at Gross-Kladus. In October 1848 as commandant of the fortress of Temesvár his decision to declare for the Kaiser was crucial, and it was his leadership that enabled the fortress to survive the epic siege. He died shortly after the fortress was relieved. *BLKÖ*.

8 Stevan Petrović Knicanin (1807-55) was a functionary in the Principality of Serbia within the Ottoman Empire. When Prince Aľeksandar responded to the request from the Serbs in Hungary for aid in May 1848, Knicanin was chosen to command the volunteers.

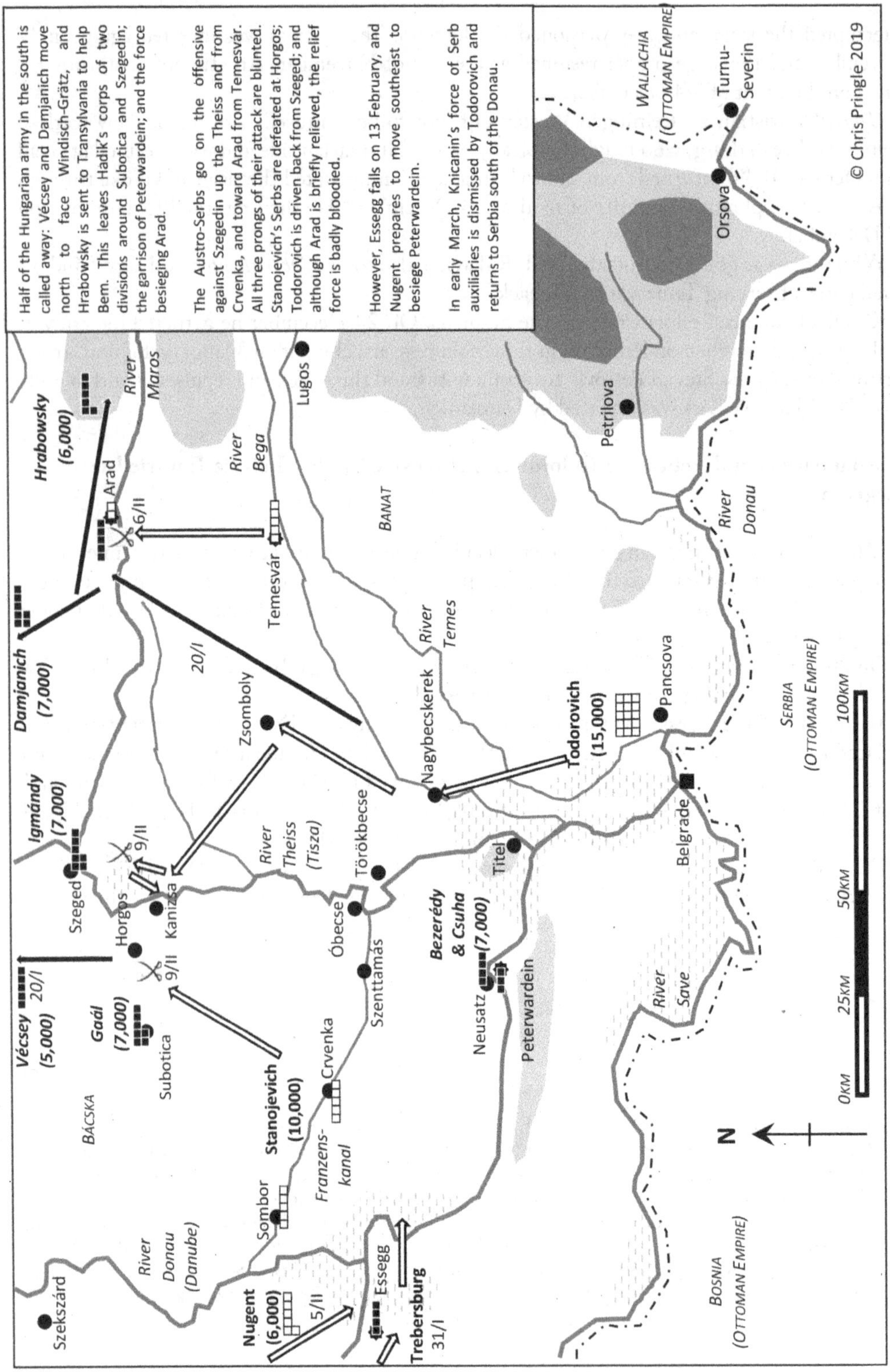

Map 9b: The southern front, mid-January to mid-February 1849: Todorovich's offensive up the Theiss

3,000 *honvéds*;[9] and *Oberst Graf* Gusztáv Hadik with a couple of battalions around Szegedin.[10] *Oberst* Miklós Gaál continued to besiege Arad, while *Oberst* Friedrich Eder von Eichenhain was besieged in Essegg with about 4,500 men.[11] Thus most of the southern part of the Bácska and the Banat was abandoned to Austro-Serb control. However, between the end of January and mid-February, VI. Korps had grown from 3,500 troops and a few thousand national guards to 5,000 regulars and 9,000 national guards. Hadik divided it into Division Gaál (to cover Szabadka) and Division Igmándy (holding Szegedin, Szőreg and Makó).

The Serbs were establishing their Vojvodina (the Serbian Voyvodate; in Hungarian, the Vajdaság) to make their political ambitions reality. Their organised forces in the Bácska under *Major* Stanojevich held the line of the Franzenskanal, with their main forces in Zombor and Cservenka. *Oberst* Todorovich had been appointed a *voivode*. At the start of February, he advanced to Zsomboly [Jimbolia, Romania], extending his right to link up with Temesvár and his left to Nagy-Kikinda. Temesvár and Arad were still held by the Austrians.

The Austro-Serbian plan repeated the mistake Vetter had made – attacking in three directions at once. Stanojevich on the left and Todorovich in the centre were to advance separated by the Theiss and converge on Szegedin. On the right, a force from Temesvár together with Serbs and Vlachs was to relieve Arad and advance on Grosswardein. Meanwhile, Nugent was to besiege and take Essegg and Peterwardein.

On 6 February the force from Temesvár arrived outside Arad. The Austro-Serbs became distracted by looting instead of fighting, whereupon they were attacked by the Hungarians and hundreds killed. This force fell back to Temesvár, but not before replenishing Arad's food supplies again.

On 9 February, Todorovich's vanguard reached Szőreg. Hadik crossed the frozen Theiss, attacked Todorovich at Szőreg on 12 February, defeated him and drove him back to Török-Kanizsa. The Serb left advancing on Szegedin was likewise repulsed at Horgos by *Oberstlieutenant* Lajos Bene.

The Serbs and the Austrians now fell out over Serbian nationalist aspirations. In early March, Knicanin took his 12,000-man Serb army home to Serbia. This is the episode Nobili referred to

9 Antal Csuha (1794-1867) was an imperial major commanding a battalion of 39. Don Miguel-Infanterie in Peterwardein in 1848. He organised the Szeged National Guard and fought against the Serbian insurrection. In November he was offered command of the army in Transylvania but declined because of illness. When the imperials besieged Peterwardein, after an initial defence he was prepared to capitulate and in March 1849 he signed a surrender document but was prevented from doing so by his own men. Perczel dismissed him from command, and in May 1849 he retired. After the war he was stripped of his rank and pension. Bona, *Tábornokok*.

10 Ágoston (Gustav) Hadik (1801-96) was an imperial lieutenantcolonel who had retired in 1844. In June 1848 he became a lieutenant colonel in the new Hungarian National Guard and served against the Serbian insurrection on what became the southern front. In March 1849 he fell ill with typhoid. When he recovered in May he commanded a division of the reserve corps forming at Szeged but fell ill again in July. After the war he was sentenced to death, commuted to imprisonment, and amnestied in 1851. Bona, *Tábornokok*.

11 Friedrich Eder von Eichenhain (1782-1850) was an imperial brigadier in Szeged in 1848. In June he fought against the Serbian insurrection until appointed commander of the fortress of Eszek in October. Because his garrison was mostly inexperienced national guards, and because there seemed no prospect of relief, Eder capitulated relatively swiftly. Despite this, after the war he was stripped of his rank. Bona, *Tábornokok*.

as Nugent dismissing Serb auxiliaries. In his *Szabadságharc hadtörténete*, Hermann says that on 9 March 1849, at the demand of the Austrian government and under pressure from the Ottoman government, Garasanin, the Serbian foreign minister ordered the return of the *serviani* (the volunteers from Serbia). Hermann writes that only some of them returned to Serbia.[12]

As for Nugent: on 10 January he was at Nagy-Kanizsa when Windisch-Grätz asked him to send Brigade Dietrich north. Then he heard that a certain Nemegy's band of freedom fighters was at Fünfkirchen threatening *Generalmajor* Johann Schneckel von Trebersburg's siege of Essegg.[13] Nugent called back *Feldmarschall Lieutenant* Anton Dietrich and moved to Fünfkirchen with 7,000 men. Meanwhile, on 31 January, Trebersburg seized the outskirts of Essegg. Nemegy fell back from Nugent across the Donau to link up with Hadik; Nugent then headed for Essegg. On 13 February, Essegg surrendered. After this, Nugent sent first Brigade Dietrich, then Brigade Pálffy north to help Windisch-Grätz, while he himself moved on to besiege Peterwardein.

Mid-March to mid-April 1849: Perczel Clears the Bácska

Apart from various small skirmishes around Peterwardein, there was a general pause from mid-February to mid-March as Knicanin's Serbs left and both sides replenished and reinforced. The only action of any size was on 4 March when a force of 4,000 Serbs from Zombor was rebuffed at Subotica. Gaál pursued them to Bajmok with 3,000 men, attacked them in their camp and routed them.

After Essegg fell, the Hungarian government decided it was crucial to relieve Peterwardein, its only remaining stronghold on the southern border. Perczel's IV. Korps was given this mission. His plan was: first, to retake the camps the Serbs had reoccupied at Szent-Iván, Szőreg, Deszk and Kis-Zombor; then, to attack from Szegedin to Ó-Kanizsa, and from Subotica to Zenta, and drive the Serbs across the Theiss. After this three-pronged operation, he intended to unite his forces at Csantavér to break through the Serb line on the Franzenskanal at Hegyes and Szeghegy, and to exploit through Ó-Kér to relieve Peterwardein.

Accordingly, on 22 March IV. Korps advanced all along the line. Perczel himself took on the 5,000 Serbs in Szőreg; *Oberstlieutenant* Henryk Forget Chevalier de Barst faced half as many at Szent-Iván.[14] On the same day, national guards crossed the Maros from Makó and took Kis-Zombor. Thus, Perczel's first phase was achieved by 23 March. On 24 March he

12 Róbert Hermann, *A szabadságharc hadtörténete* (Budapest: Korona Kiadó, 2001), p.264.

13 Bódog Nemegyei (1826-1904) was an engineer lieutenant in the Komorn fortress in July 1848. By December he was a major and was tasked with raising a force in Transdanubia. In January 1849 he and his 2,500 men were charged with relieving Eszek. He failed to do this, moving north away from the fortress rather than toward, and was therefore put under investigation. He was acquitted in May and continued as chief of staff, first of IX. Korps and then of the army on the middle Theiss. After the battle of Temesvár he escaped, first to the Ottoman Empire, and then in 1851 to the United States where he lived for the rest of his life. Bona, *Tábornokok*.

14 Henryk Forget Chevalier de Barst (1818-?) was a former imperial lieutenant from a Polish family of French origin. He came to Hungary in the summer of 1848 volunteering to fight the Serbian insurgents. He served on the southern front throughout, being seriously wounded at Titel in April 1849, after which he served as chief of staff and then as a brigadier in the reserve corps formed at Szeged. He surrendered at Világos, was sentenced to death, commuted to imprisonment, and then amnestied in 1850. Bona, *Tábornokok*.

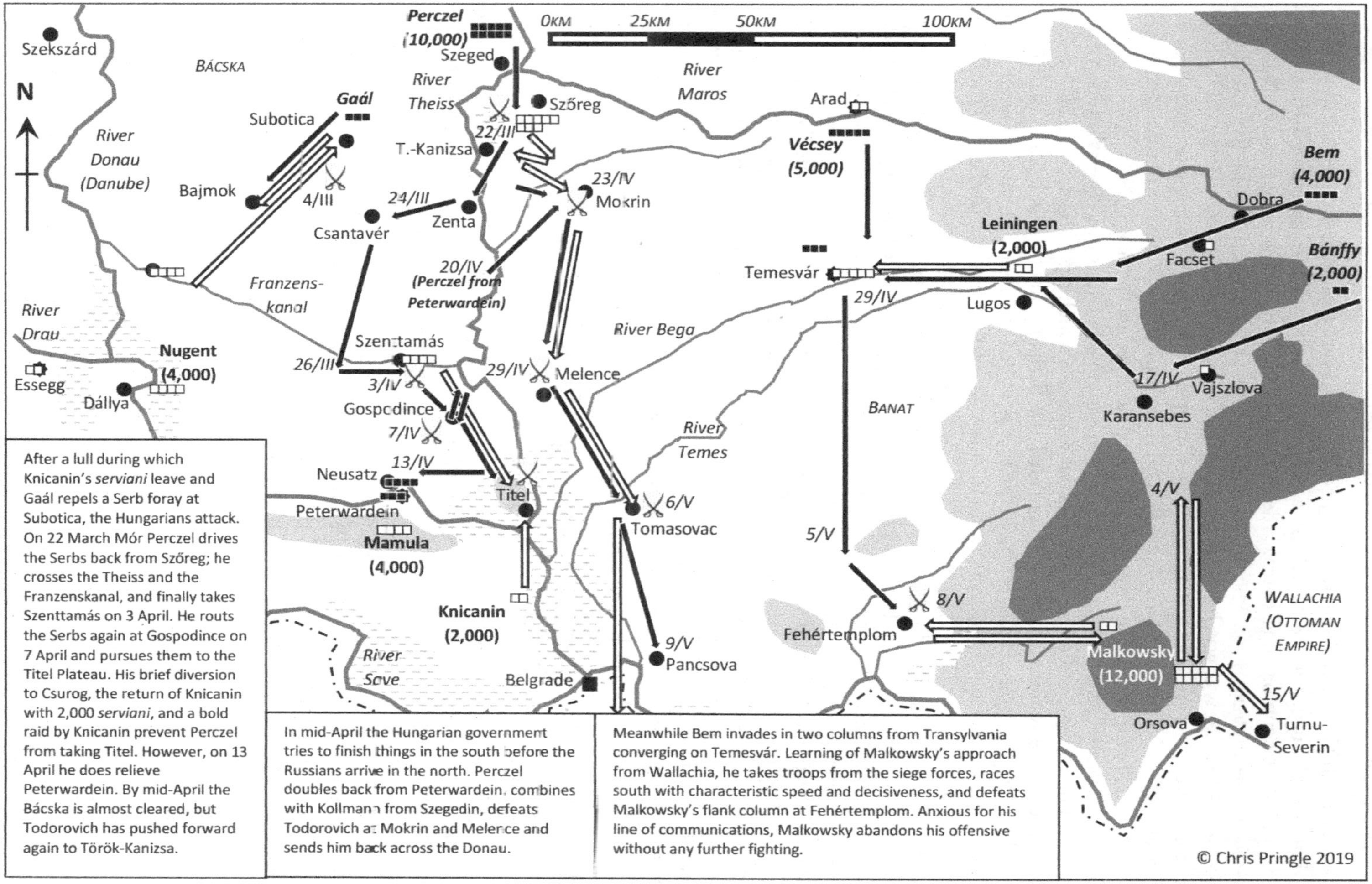

Map 9c: The southern front, March to mid-May 1849: clearing the Bácska and the Banat

concentrated 7,000 men at Csantavér, advanced to the Franzenskanal, and broke through on 26 March as planned. On 27 March he advanced to Kis-Kér. Here he learned that strong enemy forces were approaching Peterwardein from behind him. These were some of Nugent's 8,500 men. *Oberst* Lazarus von Mamula was already outside Peterwardein with five battalions; *Obert* Moritz Lederer was watching the lower Donau between Mohács and Szekszárd with six squadrons and some *seressaners*; Nugent himself was with *Major* Plattner's four battalions in reserve at Dállya. Nugent tried to cut off Perczel from behind, but Perczel still managed to get through triumphantly to relieve Peterwardein, then returned to Verbász.

On 3 April Perczel attacked the 4,000 Serbs at Szenttamás in two converging columns, routed them, and finally destroyed the camp and its fortifications, which the Hungarians had besieged three times before without success. He pursued the Serbs to among the Römerschanzen at Gospodinci (Boldogasszonyfalva).[15] On 7 April he assaulted and routed them again here. They fled to the Titel plateau, a distinctive terrain feature at the junction of the Donau and the Tisza, surrounded by marshes and only accessible in a few very defensible places.

After the battle at Gospodinci, Perczel should have advanced against Titel immediately as the last Serb stronghold in the Bácska. Had he done so he could have taken it cheaply. Instead he turned north to make sure his rear was secure first, even though there was no threat there, before coming back toward Titel.

Perczel had 6,000-8,000 men in four brigades. Knicanin had now returned from Serbia bringing 2,000 men with him, so had about 8,000 and 30 guns on the plateau. On the night of 12 April, as Perczel was preparing to attack next morning, Knicanin launched a surprise attack from his entrenchments. This was beaten off but persuaded Perczel that he was too weak to attack Knicanin, so on 13 April he withdrew beyond Sz.-Ivan and then to Neusatz, where he rested his army for three days. There he received an order from the government to cooperate with Bem in retaking the Banat.

Mid-April to mid-May: Perczel and Bem Clear the Banat

Perczel's and Bem's brilliant successes in the Bácska and Transylvania, and the threat of the impending Russian intervention, persuaded the Hungarian government to try to break the enemy in the Bácska and the Banat as soon as possible and then mass all its armies on the Donau to face the Austro-Russian threat further north. The plan was that having secured the Transylvanian border passes and invested Weissenburg, Bem was to push into the Banat, drive back that part of the Temesvár garrison that had pushed toward Translvania, and join up with Vécsey to invest Temesvár. Meanwhile Perczel was to cross to the left bank of the Theiss, secure the southwestern part of the Banat, and then take the Titel Plateau.

Perczel called *Oberst* Josef Kollmann into action from Szegedin.[16] On 15 April Kollmann's four battalions drove Todorovich and his Serbs out of Török-Kanizsa and back toward

15 The Römerschanzen were extensive ancient Roman earthworks northeast of Neusatz.

16 Josef Kollmann (Kohlmann) (1808-89) was a captain in the 52. Franz Karl-Infanterie fighting the Serbian insurrection in the summer of 1848. He became chief of staff under Móga and was promoted to colonel, but in December he asked to be relieved, moving to Szeged where he got married in January 1849. In March he was back on active service as chief of staff of Perczel's IV. Korps, then a brigadier, then commanding forces in the Banat. At the end of the war, he was condemned to death in absentia

Nagybecskerek. Perczel re-crossed the Theiss, linked up with Kollmann, and on 23 April defeated the Serbs again at Mokrin. 29 April was a day of major battle with Todorovich's 10,000 men near Melence. The Serbs lost and fell back. On 6 May, Perczel attacked the demoralised Serbs yet again at Tomasovac. These now fled all the way across the Danube; Perczel pursued and took Pancova on 10 May. Only the Titel Plateau remained to be taken.

As for Bem: in mid-April he had collected eight battalions in two divisions (Bánffy and Pereczy) at Déva. The former was to move via Dobra and Facset, and the latter via Hátszeg and Vaskapu, into the Temes valley. Facing them, Leiningen held Lugos with four imperial battalions; he had a strong detachment at Facset, and two battalions at Voislova. Bem ordered the investment of Weissenburg, then on 15 April sent off *Oberst* Mihály Pereczy, who reached Karansebes on 17 April without a fight. Here he learned that *General* Ignaz Dammwalden von Malkowsky was marching to invade the Banat from Wallachia via Orsova with 14,000 men (these actually crossed the border between 22-25 April). Bem marched to Lugos, which Leiningen's 1,500 men vacated ahead of him. Bánffy's 2,000 arrived at Lugos as well. Bem tried to get Vécsey to move from Arad in time to cut off Leiningen, but Leiningen escaped to Temesvár. On 29 April, Bem camped at Freydorf, south of Temesvár. Learning that Malkowsky was now heading up the Cserna valley with 12,000 men, Bem left 3,000 at Temesvár and took the rest to stop Malkowsky joining up with Todorovich. He sent a detachment under *Oberstlieutenant* Károlyi ahead to hold Oravica and Fehértemplom.[17]

On 4 May Malkowsky was strung out along the Karansebes road between Slatina and Mehádia. He was planning to link up with the garrisons of Temesvár and Arad via Karansebes and Lugos with his main body, and to send a small column to establish communications with Todorovich via Karansebes and Német-Bogsán. But when he learned that Todorovich had been driven back to Nagy-Becskerek, he decided to send it through Fehértemplom instead. This small detachment was attacked by *Oberstlieutenant* Miksa Károlyi on 8 May, and then pursued by Bem when he arrived as well on 10 May.

Malkowsky, worried about this threat to his flank and rear, abandoned any further advance and on 15 May withdrew from the Banat back into Wallachia, where he stayed for 40 days. There were still 9,000 imperials remaining in Temesvár, and 1,500 in Arad, facing only 3,000 besiegers until Vécsey returned from Bem with 4,000. Apart from these fortresses and the Titel Plateau – which would play an important part in the Summer Campaign – the Hungarians had now reconquered the whole of southern Hungary as well as the rest of the country.

as he had escaped to the Ottoman Empire. There he joined the Ottoman army and took part in the defence of Kars during the Crimean War. When he died he held the rank of general. Bona, *Tábornokok.*

17 Miksa Károlyi (1816-90) was a captain in the 6th Württemberg Hussars fighting the Serbian insurrection in summer 1848. In February 1849 he moved from the Banat to the Transylvanian theatre. He was with one of the last contingents to surrender, Kazinczy's column, which laid down its arms at Zsibó on 25 August 1849. Bona, *Tábornokok.*

Appendix III

Notes on Orders of Battle

Orders of battle appear scattered through the text. This list is provided to make it easier for the reader to find these important data. Note that these orders of battle were subseqently subject to many small changes (attachments and detachments) which can only be discovered by thorough reading of the text. Formations are listed in chronological order and are all Austrian unless noted otherwise.

Bibliography

The best history of the conflict available in English is Gábor Bona, *The Hungarian Revolution and the War of Independence, 1848-1849*. The best modern work is Róbert Hermann, *A szabadságharc hadtörténete*. The most comprehensive and detailed is József Bánlaky's magisterial and encyclopaedic *A magyar nemzet hadtörténelme*. I have drawn mainly on these three works, especially Bánlaky, for the editorial annotations and appendices in this volume.

Published Sources

Allen, William & Muratoff, Paul, *Caucasian Battlefields: A History of the Wars on the Turco-Caucasian Border, 1828-1921* (Cambridge: Cambridge University Press, 2011).

Ascoli, David, *A Day of Battle* (Edinburgh: Birlinn, 2001).

Bach, Maximilian, *Geschichte der wiener Revolution im Jahre 1848* (Vienna: Ignaz Brand 1898).

Bánlaky, József, *A magyar nemzet hadtörténelme* (Budapest: Grill Károly, 1928-1942) available online at <http://mek.oszk.hu/09400/09477/html>

Bátori-Schulcz, Bódog, *Emlékiratai 1848/9-ki szabadságharczból* (Pest: Vódiáner, 1870).

Bencze, László, 'The Military System of the Habsburg Empire and the Hungarian Units of the Army on the Eve of the Revolution', in Bona, *Hungarian Revolution.*

Bona, Gábor (ed.), *The Hungarian Revolution and the War of Independence, 1848-1849* (New York: Columbia University Press, 1999).

Bona, Gábor, 'Armed Forces of the Hungarian War of Independence', in Bona, *Hungarian Revolution*, pp.73–112.

Bona, Gábor, *Tábornokok* és *törzstisztek az 1848/1849.* évi *szabadságharcban* (Budapest: Heraldika, 2000) available online at <https://www.arcanum.hu/hu/online-kiadvanyok/Bona-bona-tabornokok-torzstisztek-1/tabornokok-es-torzstisztek-az-184849-evi-szabadsagharcban-23DD/>

Chastain, James (ed.) *Encyclopedia of 1848 Revolutions* available online at <https://www.ohio.edu/chastain/index.htm>

Csikány, Tamás, *A Szabadságharc Hadművészete, 1848-1849* (Budapest: Zrínyi, 2015).

Csikány, Tamás, 'Logistics of the Honvéd Army', in Bona, *Hungarian Revolution*, pp.113-144.

Embree, Michael, *Radetzky's Marches: The Campaigns of 1848 and 1849 in Upper Italy* (Solihull: Helion, 2011).

Encyclopaedia Britannica, 1911 edition available online at <https://en.wikisource.org/wiki/1911_Encyclop%C3%A6dia_Britannica/>

Gárdonyi, Albert, *A Krisztinaváros településtörténete* available online at <https://library.hungaricana.hu/hu/view/ORSZ_BPTM_TBM_03/?pg=58&layout=s&query=V%C3%A9rm ez%C5%91%20>

Görgey, Arthur, *My Life and Acts in Hungary in the Years 1848 and 1849* (New York: Harper & Brothers, 1852).

Hermann, Róbert, *A szabadságharc hadtörténete* (Budapest: Korona Kiadó, 2001).

Hermann, Róbert, *Az 1848-1849-es szabadságharc nagy csatái* (Budapest: Zrínyi, 2004).

Hermann, Róbert, 'A pákozdi csata, 1848. szeptember 29.', *Hadtörténelmi közlemények*, Vol. 127, No. 2 (2014), pp.353-394.

History of the University of Miskolc available online <http://www.uni-miskolc.hu/history>

Hungarian Academy of Sciences, 'Series of ethnic maps of the Carpatho-Pannonian area (1997-2005)' available online at <http://www.mtafki.hu/konyvtar/kiadv/etnika/>

Kedves, Gyula, 'The Serbian Insurrection in the Summer of 1848 and Military Operations in the Southern Region until the Withdrawal of the *Honvéd* Troops', in Bona, *Hungarian Revolution*, pp.187-231.

Kinglake, Arthur, *The Patriot and the Hero: General Guyon on the Battle Fields of Hungary and Asia* (London: Hamilton, Adams & Co., 1856).

Magyar Életrajzi *Lexikon 1000-1990* available online at <http://mek.niif.hu/00300/00355/html/ABC09732/10648.htm>

Mahan, Dennis Hart, *An Elementary Course of Military Engineering, Part I: Comprising Field Fortification, Military Mining and Siege Operations* (New York: John Wiley & Son, 1867).

Monostori Erőd Komárom: az erődrendszer története [*Monostor Fort, Komárom: The History of the Fortification System*] available online at <http://www.erod.hu/erodrendszer/az-erodrendszer-toertenete>

Müller, Karl Christian, *Allgemeines Verteutschungswörterbuch der Kriegssprache* (Leipzig: Bruder und Hofmann, 1814) available online at <https://books.google.de/books?hl=de&id=B-BIAAAAcAAJ&q=doppelhaken#v=snippet&q=doppelhaken&f=false>

Murray, Nicholas and Pringle, Christopher (ed. and transl.), *Carl von Clausewitz, Napoleon's 1796 Italian Campaign* (Lawrence, KS: University Press of Kansas, 2018).

Murray, Nicholas and Pringle, Christopher (ed. and transl.), *Carl von Clausewitz, Napoleon Absent, Coalition Ascendant: The 1799 Campaign in Switzerland, Vol.1* (Lawrence KS: University Press of Kansas, forthcoming 2020).

Olchváry, Ödön, *A magyar függetlenségi harc 1848-1849-ben a Délvidéken* (Zenta: 2009, Vajdasági Magyar Művelődési Intezét – Forum Könyvkiadó).

Österreichisches *Biographisches Lexikon, 1815-1950* available online at <https://www.biographien.ac.at/oebl/>

Pasley, Sir Charles, *A Course of Elementary Fortification*, 2nd edn (London: John Murray, 1822).

Pražák, Albert, 'Czechs and Slovaks in the Revolution of 1848', *Slavonic Review*, Vol. 5, No. 15 (1927), pp.565-579.

Rapant, Daniel, 'Slovak Politics in 1848-1849', *Slavonic and East European Review*, Vol. 27, No. 68 (1948), pp.67-90.

Rapant, Daniel, 'Slovak Politics in 1848: Part II', *Slavonic and East European Review*, Vol. 27, No. 69 (1949), pp.381-403.

Szinnyei, József, *Magyar írók élete és munkái* (Budapest: Hornyánszky, 1891-1914) available online at <http://mek.oszk.hu/03600/03630/html/sz/sz26330.htm>

Skvarna, Dusan, 'Bedich Bloudek', in Chastain, *Encyclopedia of 1848 Revolutions* available online at <https://www.ohio.edu/chastain/ac/bloudek.htm>

Smith, Brian G., 'Ban Josip Jellacic', in Chastain, *Encyclopedia of 1848 Revolutions* available online at <https://www.ohio.edu/chastain/ip/jellacic.htm>

Smola, Joseph Freiherr von, *Handbuch* für *k.k.* österreichische *Artillerie-Offiziere* (Vienna: Fr. Beck'schen Universitäts-Buchhandlung, 1839) available online at <https://archive.org/stream/bub_gb_vrNTAAAAcAAJ/bub_gb_vrNTAAAAcAAJ_djvu.txt>

'A Franz I: a czászári-királyi szabadalmazott első dunagőzhajózási társaság első hajója', *SRY Modell* (2004) available online at <http://sry.atw.hu/franz.htm>

Symonds, Craig L., *A Battlefield Atlas of the American Revolution* (El Dorado Hills, CA: Savas Beattie, 2018).

UK Ministry of Defence, *Joint Doctrine Publication (JDP) 0-01: UK Defence Doctrine*, 5th edn (London: Ministry of Defence, 2014).

Vernon, Simon François Baron Gay de (transl. John O'Connor), *A Treatise on the Science of War and Fortification* (New York: J. Seymour, 1817).

Wurzbach, Constant von, *Biographisches Lexikon des Kaisertüms* Österreich (Vienna: K.K. Hof & Staatsdrückerei, 1856-1891 available online at <http://www.literature.at/viewer.alo?objid=12543&viewmode=fullscreen&scale=5&rotate>

Zeinar, Hubert, *Geschichte des* österreichischen *Generalstabes* (Vienna: Böhlau Verlag, 2006).

Personal Correspondence

Hermann, Róbert. Personal communication, via Dr Szilárd Szilágyi, 6 March 2019.

Szilágyi, Szilárd. 'Re: Siege of Buda', email, correspondence, 18 December 2018.

Index

This index only covers those individuals or locations that played a significant role in the campaign. Division commanders and above are included; more junior officers only if they are of particular interest. Places are indexed using the old form as it appears in Nobili's text. Their modern names can be found in the Table of Place Names at the front of the book.

The period 1815-1914 is sometimes called the long century of peace. It was in reality very far from that. It was a century of civil wars, popular uprisings, and struggles for Independence. An era of colonial expansion, wars of Empire, and colonial campaigning, much of which was unconventional in nature. It was also an age of major conventional wars, in Europe that would see the Crimea campaign and the wars of German unification. Such conflicts, along with the American Civil War, foreshadowed the total war of the 20th century.

It was also a period of great technological advancement, which in time impacted the military and warfare in general. Steam power, electricity, the telegraph, the radio, the railway, all became tools of war. The century was one of dramatic change. Tactics altered, sometimes slowly, to meet the challenges of the new technology. The dramatic change in the technology of war in this period is reflected in the new title of this series: From Musket to Maxim.

The new title better reflects the fact that the series covers all nations and all conflict of the period between 1815-1914. Already the series has commissioned books that deal with matters outside the British experience. This is something that the series will endeavour to do more of in the future. At the same time there still remains an important place for the study of the British military during this period. It is one of fascination, with campaigns that capture the imagination, in which Britain although the world's predominant power, continues to field a relatively small army.

The aim of the series is to throw the spotlight on the conflicts of that century, which can often get overlooked, sandwiched as they are between two major conflicts, the French/Revolutionary/Napoleonic Wars and the First World War. The series will produced a variety of books and styles. Some will look simply at campaigns or battles. Others will concentrate on particular aspects of a war or campaign. There will also be books that look at wider concepts of warfare during this era. It is the intention that this series will present a platform for historians to present their work on an important but often overlooked century of warfare.

Submissions

The publishers would be pleased to receive submissions for this series. Please contact series editor Dr Christopher Brice via email (christopherbrice@helion.co.uk), or in writing to Helion & Company Limited, Unit 8, Amherst Business Centre, Budbrooke Road, Warwick, Warwickshire, CV34 5WE.

Books in this series:

1. *The Battle of Majuba Hill: The Transvaal Campaign 1880-1881* John Laband (ISBN 978-1-911512-38-7)*
2. *For Queen and Company: Vignettes of the Irish Soldier in the Indian Mutiny* David Truesdale (ISBN 978-1-911512-79-0)*
3. *The Furthest Garrison: Imperial Regiments in New Zealand 1840-1870* Adam Davis (ISBN 978-1-911628-29-3)*
4. *Victory over Disease: Resolving The Medical Crisis In The Crimean War, 1854-1856* Michael Hinton (ISBN 978-1-911628-31-6)*
5. *Journey Through the Wilderness: Garnet Wolseley's Canadian Red River Expedition of 1870* Paul McNicholls (ISBN 978-1-911628-30-9)*
6. *Kitchener: The Man Not the Myth* Anne Samson (ISBN 978-1-912866-45-8)
7. *The British and the Sikhs: Discovery, Warfare and Friendship (c.1700–1900)* Gurinder Singh Mann (ISBN 978-1-911628-24-8)*
8. *Bazaine 1870: Scapegoat for a Nation* Quintin Barry (ISBN 978-1-913336-08-0)
9. *Redcoats in the Classroom: The British Army's School for Soldiers and Their Children During the 19th Century* Howard R. Clarke (ISBN 978-1-912866-47-2)
10. *The Rescue They Called A Raid: The Jameson Raid 1895-96* David Snape (ISBN 978-1-913118-77-8)*
11. *Hungary 1848: The Winter Campaign* Johann Nobili (ISBN 978-1-913118-78-5)

* Denotes books are paperback 248mm × 180mm.